500 FABULOUS CAKES AND BAKES

500 FABULOUS CAKES AND BAKES

HH
HERMES HOUSE

This paperback edition published by Hermes House
an imprint of
Anness Publishing Limited
Hermes House
88-89 Blackfriars Road
London SE1 8HA

A CIP catalogue record for this book is available from the British Library

ISBN 1 84309 016 3

Publisher: Joanna Lorenz
Managing Editor: Linda Fraser
Designer: Siân Keogh
Photographers: Karl Adamson, Edward Allwright, David Armstrong, Steve Baxter, James Duncan, John Freeman, Michelle Garrett, Amanda Heywood, Tim Hill, Don Last, Michael Michaels
Recipes: Alex Barker, Carole Clements, Roz Denny, Christine France, Shirley Gill, Patricia Lousada, Norma MacMillan, Sue Maggs, Janice Murfitt, Annie Nichols, Louise Pickford, Katherine Richmond, Hilaire Walden Steven Wheeler, Elizabeth Wolf-Cohen
Food for Photography: Carla Capalbo, Carole Handslip, Wendy Lee, Sarah Maxwell, Angela Nilsen, Jane Stevenson, Liz Trigg and Elizabeth Wolf-Cohen
Stylists: Madeleine Brehaut, Maria Kelly, Blake Minton, Kirsty Rawlings, Fiona Tillett

Printed and bound in Hong Kong

10 9 8 7 6 5 4 3 2 1

MEASUREMENTS:
Measurements have been provided in the following order: metric, imperial and American cups. Do not mix units of measurement within each recipe.
Size 3 (medium) eggs should be used unless otherwise stated.

Contents

Introduction

Baking is one of the most satisfying of all the culinary arts. It fills the house with the most wonderful aroma, gives ample reward for minimal effort and always meets with approval, especially from younger members of the family. Bake a batch of brownies, a fresh fruit pie, a crusty loaf of bread or a luxurious gâteau, and watch your rating rise!

This bonanza collection - five hundred of the finest recipes - is all you need to earn your champion baker's badge. It ranges from simple treats like drop scones and basic biscuits to elaborate cakes for special celebrations. Each recipe carries a full colour illustration of the finished bake, and the step-by-step instructions are so simple and straightforward that even a novice will find them easy to follow.

In fact, novice cooks often make the best bakers, preheating the oven in plenty of time, taking care to measure ingredients accurately and following recipe methods to the letter. All these elements are important in baking, which demands more precision than many other types of cooking. With a soup or stew you can happily sling in extra ingredients or cheat a little when it comes to exact quantities, but the balance of ingredients, the temperature and the timing are all very important when you are baking a cake or pastry. It is worth reading the chosen recipe carefully before you begin, doing any advance preparation such as browning almonds or softening butter, then setting out the ingredients in the style of the TV cook.

Advice on lining tins is given in individual recipes. Greaseproof paper is the traditional lining material, but non-stick baking paper is even easier to use and gives excellent results. To base-line

a tin, place it on the paper and draw around the outside edge, then cut out the shape. Grease the base of the tin with a dab of oil or butter to hold the paper in place, then fit it in the tin. Grease the paper (if using greaseproof) and the sides of the tin.

Whether or not to grease tins used for pastry is a matter of choice. If the pastry is high in fat, such as shortcrust, flaky or puff, it is not usually necessary; however, spills from fillings may stick. When in doubt, grease the tins lightly.

If you are a novice baker, start with some of the simpler recipes, such as Chocolate-chip Cookies, Chive and Potato Scones or a Quick-mix Sponge. Try some of the delectable breads, from a traditional Plaited Loaf to the contemporary Saffron Focaccia.

You'll find every occasion amply catered for, from Valentine's Day through to a wedding. There are cakes for christenings, anniversaries and every possible birthday, from novelty teddies to telephones - including a mobile! For the family, the collection includes wonderful ways of keeping the cake tin and biscuit barrel brimming with healthy snacks, including a selection for those with dietary restrictions. With vegans in view, there's a special chocolate gâteau and a Dundee cake, and an entire chapter is devoted to low-fat cakes and bakes.

In *500 Fabulous Cakes and Bakes* there's a sweet or savoury treat for every moment of the day, from breakfast Blueberry Muffins to a late-night slice of Pecan Tart. Tempted to embark on an immediate baking session? Go right ahead. Baking is a wonderfully therapeutic occupation - with sheer indulgence as the reward!

Farmhouse Biscuits

Delightfully wholesome, these farmhouse biscuits are ideal to serve with morning coffee.

Makes 18

115g/4oz/½ cup butter or margarine, at room temperature
90g/3½oz/7 tbsp light brown sugar
65g/2½oz/5 tbsp crunchy peanut butter
1 egg
50g/2oz/½ cup plain flour
2.5ml/½ tsp baking powder
2.5ml/½ tsp ground cinnamon
1.5ml/¼ tsp salt
175g/6oz/1½ cups muesli
50g/2oz/½ cup raisins
50g/2oz/½ cup chopped walnuts

1 Preheat the oven to 180°C/350°F/Gas 4. Grease a baking sheet.

2 Cream the butter or margarine and sugar until light and fluffy. Beat in the peanut butter and then beat in the egg.

3 Sift the flour, baking powder, cinnamon and salt over the peanut butter mixture and stir to blend. Stir in the muesli, raisins and walnuts. Taste the mixture to see if it needs more sugar, as the sugar content of muesli varies.

4 Drop rounded tablespoonfuls of the mixture on to the prepared baking sheet about 2.5cm/1in apart. Press gently with the back of a spoon to spread each mound into a circle.

5 Bake until lightly coloured, about 15 minutes. With a palette knife, transfer to a wire rack to cool. Store in an airtight container.

Crunchy Oatmeal Biscuits

For nutty oatmeal biscuits, substitute an equal quantity of chopped walnuts or pecan nuts for the cereal.

Makes 14

175g/6oz/¾ cup butter or margarine, at room temperature
175g/6oz/¾ cup caster sugar
1 egg yolk
175g/6oz/1½ cups plain flour
5ml/1 tsp bicarbonate of soda
2.5ml/½ tsp salt
50g/2oz/⅔ cup rolled oats
50g/2oz/⅔ cup small crunchy nugget cereal

1 Cream the butter or margarine and sugar together until light and fluffy. Mix in the egg yolk.

2 Sift over the flour, bicarbonate of soda and salt, then stir into the butter mixture. Add the oats and cereal and stir to blend. Chill for at least 20 minutes.

3 Preheat the oven to 190°C/375°F/Gas 5. Grease a baking sheet.

4 Roll the mixture into balls. Place them on the baking sheet and flatten with the base of a floured glass.

5 Bake until golden, about 10–12 minutes. Then with a palette knife, transfer to a wire rack to cool. Store in an airtight container.

Apricot Yogurt Cookies

These cookies do not keep well, so it is best to eat them within two days, or to freeze them.

Makes 16

175g/6oz/1½ cups plain flour
5ml/1 tsp baking powder
5ml/1 tsp ground cinnamon
75g/3oz/scant 1 cup rolled oats
75g/3oz/½ cup light muscovado sugar
115g/4oz/½ cup chopped ready-to-eat dried apricots
15ml/1 tbsp flaked hazelnuts or almonds
150g/5oz/scant ⅔ cup natural yogurt
45ml/3 tbsp sunflower oil
demerara sugar, to sprinkle

1 Preheat the oven to 190°C/375°F/Gas 5. Lightly oil a large baking sheet.

2 Sift together the flour, baking powder and cinnamon. Stir in the oats, sugar, apricots and nuts.

3 Beat together the yogurt and oil, then stir evenly into the mixture to make a firm dough. If necessary, add a little more yogurt.

4 Use your hands to roll the mixture into about 16 small balls, place on the baking sheet and flatten with a fork.

5 Sprinkle with demerara sugar. Bake for 15–20 minutes, or until firm and golden brown. Transfer to a wire rack to cool. Store in an airtight container.

Oat and Apricot Clusters

You can change the ingredients according to what's in your cupboard – try peanuts, pecan nuts, raisins or dates.

Makes 12

50g/2oz/4 tbsp butter or margarine
50g/2oz/4 tbsp clear honey
50g/2oz/½ cup medium oatmeal
50g/2oz/¼ cup chopped ready-to-eat dried apricots
15ml/1 tbsp banana chips
15ml/1 tbsp dried coconut shreds
50–75g/2–3oz/ 2–3 cups cornflakes or crispy cereal

1 Place the butter or margarine and honey in a small pan and warm over a low heat, stirring until well blended.

2 Add the oatmeal, apricots, banana chips, coconut and cornflakes or crispy cereal and mix well.

3 Spoon the mixture into 12 paper cases, piling it up roughly. Transfer to a baking sheet and chill until set and firm.

Oaty Coconut Biscuits

The coconut gives these biscuits both a wonderful texture and a great taste.

Makes 48

175g/6oz/2 cups quick-cooking oats
75g/3oz/1½ cups desiccated coconut
225g/8oz/1 cup butter
115g/4oz/½ cup caster sugar
50g/2oz/¼ cup dark brown sugar
2 eggs
60ml/4 tbsp milk
7.5ml/1½ tsp vanilla essence
115g/4oz/1 cup plain flour, sifted
2.5ml/½ tsp bicarbonate of soda
2.5ml/½ tsp salt
5ml/1 tsp ground cinnamon

1 Preheat the oven to 200°C/400°F/Gas 6. Spread the oats and coconut on a baking sheet. Bake for 8–10 minutes.

2 Cream the butter and sugars. Beat in the eggs, milk and vanilla. Fold in the dry ingredients. Add the oats and coconut. Drop spoonfuls of mixture on two greased baking sheets. Bake for 8–10 minutes. Cool on a wire rack.

Crunchy Jumbles

For even crunchier biscuits, add 50g/2oz/½ cup walnuts, coarsely chopped, with the cereal and chocolate chips.

Makes 36

115g/4oz/½ cup butter or margarine, at room temperature
225g/8oz/1 cup caster sugar
1 egg
5ml/1 tsp vanilla essence
150g/5oz/1¼ cups plain flour, sifted
2.5ml/½ tsp bicarbonate of soda
1.5ml/¼ tsp salt
50g/2oz/2¼ cups crisped rice cereal
175g/6oz/1 cup chocolate chips

1 Preheat the oven to 180°C/350°F/Gas 4. Grease two baking sheets. Cream the butter or margarine and sugar until fluffy. Add the egg and vanilla essence. Add the flour and bicarbonate of soda and the salt and fold in.

2 Add the cereal and chocolate chips and mix thoroughly. Drop spoonfuls 5cm/2in apart onto baking sheets and bake for 10–12 minutes. Transfer to a wire rack to cool.

Cinnamon-coated Cookies

Walnut cookies are rolled in a cinnamon and sugar mixture to give a delicate spicy flavour.

Makes 30

Preheat the oven to 190°C/375°F/Gas 5. Grease two baking sheets. Cream 115g/4oz/½ cup butter, 225g/8oz/1 cup sugar and 5ml/1 tsp vanilla essence. Beat in 2 eggs and 50ml/2fl oz/¼ cup milk. Sift over 350g/12oz/3 cups plain flour and 5ml/1 tsp bicarbonate of soda. Stir in 50g/2oz/½ cup chopped walnuts. Chill for 15 minutes then roll into balls. Roll the balls in a sugar and cinnamon mixture. Bake for 10 minutes, then cool on a wire rack.

Ginger Biscuits

So much tastier than shop-bought varieties, these ginger biscuits will disappear quickly, so make a large batch!

Makes 60

275g/10oz/2½ cups plain flour
5ml/1 tsp bicarbonate of soda
7.5ml/1½ tsp ground ginger
1.5ml/¼ tsp ground cinnamon
1.5ml/¼ tsp ground cloves
115g/4oz/½ cup butter or margarine, at room temperature
350g/12oz/1¾ cups caster sugar
1 egg, beaten
60ml/4 tbsp treacle
5ml/1 tsp fresh lemon juice

1 Preheat the oven to 160°C/325°F/Gas 3. Lightly grease three to four baking sheets.

2 Sift the flour, bicarbonate of soda and spices into a small bowl. Set aside.

3 Cream the butter or margarine and two-thirds of the sugar together. Stir in the egg, treacle and lemon juice. Add the flour mixture and mix in thoroughly with a wooden spoon to make a soft dough.

4 Shape the dough into 2cm/¾ in balls. Roll the balls in the remaining sugar and place about 5cm/2in apart on the baking sheets.

5 Bake until the biscuits are just firm to the touch, about 12 minutes. With a palette knife, transfer the biscuits to a wire rack and leave to cool.

Cream Cheese Spirals

These biscuits look so impressive and melt in the mouth, yet they are surprisingly easy to make.

Makes 32

225g/8oz/1 cup butter, at room temperature
225g/8oz/1 cup cream cheese
10ml/2 tsp caster sugar
225g/8oz/2 cups plain flour
1 egg white, beaten with 15ml/1 tbsp water, for glazing
caster sugar, for sprinkling

For the filling

115g/4oz/1 cup finely chopped walnuts
115g/4oz/¾ cup light brown sugar
5ml/1 tsp ground cinnamon

1 Cream the butter, cream cheese and sugar until soft. Sift over the flour and mix until combined. Gather into a ball and divide in half. Flatten each half, wrap in greaseproof paper and chill for 30 minutes. Meanwhile, mix all the filling ingredients together and set aside.

2 Preheat the oven to 190°C/375°F/Gas 5. Grease two baking sheets. Working with one half of the dough at a time, roll out thinly into a 28cm/11in circle. Using a dinner plate as a guide, trim the edges with a knife.

3 Brush the surface with the egg white glaze, and then sprinkle evenly with half the filling.

4 Cut the circle into 16 segments. Starting from the base of the triangles, roll up to form spirals.

5 Place on the baking sheets and brush with the remaining glaze. Sprinkle with caster sugar. Bake until golden, about 15–20 minutes. Cool on a wire rack.

Italian Almond Biscotti

Serve biscotti after a meal, for dunking in sweet white wine, such as an Italian Vin Santo or a French Muscat.

Makes 48

200g/7oz/1¾ cups whole unblanched almonds
215g/7½ oz/scant 2 cups plain flour
90g/3½ oz/½ cup sugar
pinch of salt
pinch of saffron powder
2.5ml/½ tsp bicarbonate of soda
2 eggs
1 egg white, lightly beaten

1 Preheat the oven to 190°C/375°F/Gas 5. Grease and flour two baking sheets.

2 Spread the almonds on an ungreased baking sheet and bake until lightly browned, about 15 minutes. When cool, grind 50g/2oz/½ cup of the almonds in a food processor, blender, or coffee grinder until pulverized. Coarsely chop the remaining almonds in two or three pieces each. Set aside.

3 Combine the flour, sugar, salt, saffron powder, bicarbonate of soda and ground almonds in a bowl and mix to blend. Make a well in the centre and add the eggs. Stir to form a rough dough. Transfer to a floured surface and knead until well blended. Knead in the chopped almonds.

4 Divide the dough into three equal parts. Roll into logs about 2.5cm/1in diameter. Place on one of the prepared sheets, brush with the egg white and bake for 20 minutes. Remove from the oven. Lower the oven temperature to 140°C/275°F/Gas 1.

5 With a very sharp knife, cut into each log at an angle making 1cm/½ in slices. Return the slices on the baking sheets to the oven and bake for 25 minutes. Transfer to a wire rack to cool.

Orange Biscuits

These classic citrus-flavoured biscuits are ideal for a tasty treat at any time of the day.

Makes 30

115g/4oz/½ cup butter, at room temperature
200g/7oz/1 cup sugar
2 egg yolks
15ml/1 tbsp fresh orange juice
grated rind of 1 large orange
200g/7oz/1¾ cups plain flour
15ml/1 tbsp cornflour
2.5ml/½ tsp salt
5ml/1 tsp baking powder

1 Cream the butter and sugar until light and fluffy. Add the yolks, orange juice and rind, and continue beating to blend.

2 In another bowl, sift together the flour, cornflour, salt and baking powder. Add to the butter mixture and stir until it forms a dough. Wrap the dough in greaseproof paper and chill for 2 hours.

3 Preheat the oven to 190°C/375°F/Gas 5. Grease two baking sheets. Roll spoonfuls of the dough into balls and place 2.5–5cm/1–2in apart on the baking sheets.

4 Press down with a fork to flatten. Bake until golden brown, about 8–10 minutes. Using a palette knife, transfer to a wire rack to cool.

Raspberry Sandwich Biscuits

These biscuits may be stored in an airtight container with sheets of greaseproof paper between the layers.

Makes 32

175g/6oz/1 cup blanched almonds
175g/6oz/1½ cups plain flour
175g/6oz/¾ cup butter, at room temperature
115g/4oz/½ cup caster sugar
grated rind of 1 lemon
5ml/1 tsp vanilla essence
1 egg white
1.5ml/¼ tsp salt
25g/1oz/¼ cup flaked almonds
250ml/8fl oz/1 cup raspberry jam
15ml/1 tbsp fresh lemon juice

1 Process the blanched almonds and 45ml/3 tbsp flour in a food processor or blender until finely ground. Cream the butter and sugar together until light and fluffy. Stir in the lemon rind and vanilla. Add the ground almonds and remaining flour and mix well. Gather into a ball, wrap in greaseproof paper, and chill for 1 hour.

2 Preheat the oven to 160°C/325°F/Gas 3. Line two baking sheets wih greaseproof paper. Divide the biscuit mixture into four equal parts. Working with one section at a time, roll out to a thickness of 3mm/⅛ in on a lightly floured surface. With a 6cm/2½in fluted pastry cutter, stamp out circles. Using a 2cm/¾in piping nozzle or pastry cutter, stamp out the centres from half the circles. Place the rings and circles 2.5cm/1in apart on the baking sheets.

3 Whisk the egg white with the salt until just frothy. Chop the flaked almonds. Brush the biscuit rings with the egg white, then sprinkle over the almonds. Bake until lightly browned, about 12–15 minutes. Cool for a few minutes on the baking sheets then transfer to a wire rack.

4 In a saucepan, melt the jam with the lemon juice until it comes to a simmer. Brush the jam over the biscuit circles and sandwich together with the rings.

Christmas Cookies

Decorate these delicious cookies with festive decorations or make them at any time of year.

Makes 30

175g/6oz/¾ cup unsalted butter, at room temperature
285g/10oz/1½ cups caster sugar
1 egg
1 egg yolk
5ml/1 tsp vanilla essence
grated rind of 1 lemon
1.5ml/¼ tsp salt
285g/10oz/2½ cups plain flour

For decorating (optional)
coloured icing and small decorations

1 Preheat the oven to 180°C/350°F/Gas 4. With an electric mixer, cream the butter until soft. Add the sugar gradually and continue beating until light and fluffy. Using a wooden spoon, slowly mix in the whole egg and the egg yolk. Add the vanilla essence, lemon rind and salt. Stir to mix well. Add the flour and stir until blended. Gather the mixture into a ball, wrap in greaseproof paper, and chill for 30 minutes.

2 On a floured surface, roll out the mixture about 3mm/⅛in thick. Stamp out shapes or rounds with biscuit cutters. Bake until lightly coloured, about 8 minutes. Transfer to a wire rack and leave to cool completely before icing and decorating, if wished.

Apricot Specials

Try other dried fruit, such as peaches or prunes, to vary the flavour of these special bars.

Makes 12

90g/3½oz/generous ½ cup light brown sugar
75g/3oz/¾ cup plain flour
75g/3oz/6 tbsp cold unsalted butter, cut in pieces

For the topping

150g/5oz/generous ½ cup dried apricots
250ml/8fl oz/1 cup water
grated rind of 1 lemon
65g/2½oz/generous ¼ cup caster sugar
10ml/2 tsp cornflour
50g/2oz/½ cup chopped walnuts

1 Preheat the oven to 180°C/350°F/Gas 4. In a mixing bowl, combine the brown sugar and flour. With a pastry blender, cut in the butter until the mixture resembles coarse breadcrumbs.

2 Transfer to a 20cm/8in square baking tin and press level. Bake for 15 minutes. Remove from the oven but leave the oven on.

3 Meanwhile, for the topping, combine the apricots and water in a saucepan and simmer until soft; about 10 minutes. Strain the liquid and reserve. Chop the apricots.

4 Return the apricots to the saucepan and add the lemon rind, caster sugar, cornflour and 60ml/4 tbsp of the soaking liquid. Cook for 1 minute.

5 Cool slightly before spreading the topping over the base. Sprinkle over the walnuts and bake for 20 minutes more. Cool in the tin before cutting into bars.

Brandy Snaps

You could serve these brandy snaps without the cream filling to eat with rich vanilla ice cream.

Makes 18

50g/2oz/4 tbsp butter, at room temperature
150g/5oz/generous ½ cup caster sugar
20ml/1 rounded tbsp golden syrup
40g/1½oz/⅓ cup plain flour
2.5ml/½ tsp ground ginger

For the filling

250ml/8fl oz/1 cup whipping cream
30ml/2 tbsp brandy

1 Cream together the butter and sugar until light and fluffy, then beat in the golden syrup. Sift over the flour and ginger and mix together. Transfer the mixture to a work surface and knead until smooth. Cover and chill for 30 minutes.

2 Preheat the oven to 190°C/375°F/Gas 5. Grease a baking sheet. Working in batches of four, shape the mixture into walnut-size balls. Place well apart on the baking sheet and flatten slightly. Bake until golden and bubbling, about 10 minutes.

3 Remove from the oven and leave to cool for a few moments. Working quickly, slide a palette knife under each one, turn over, and wrap around the handle of a wooden spoon (have four spoons ready). If they firm up too quickly, reheat for a few seconds to soften. When firm, slide the brandy snaps off and place on a wire rack to cool.

4 When all the brandy snaps are cool, prepare the filling. Whip the cream and brandy until soft peaks form. Pipe into each end of the brandy snaps just before serving.

Chocolate Pretzels

Pretzels come in many flavours – here is a chocolate version to bake and enjoy.

Makes 28

150g/5oz/1¼ cups plain flour
1.5ml/¼ tsp salt
20g/¾ oz/6 tbsp unsweetened cocoa powder
115g/4oz/½ cup butter, at room temperature
130g/4½oz/scant ⅔ cup sugar
1 egg
1 egg white, lightly beaten, for glazing
sugar crystals, for sprinkling

1 Sift together the flour, salt and cocoa powder. Set aside. Lightly grease two baking sheets. Cream the butter until light. Add the sugar and continue beating until light and fluffy. Beat in the egg. Add the dry ingredients and stir to blend. Gather the dough into a ball, wrap in clear film and chill for 1 hour.

2 Roll the dough into 28 small balls. Chill the balls until needed. Preheat the oven to 190°C/375°F/Gas 5. Roll each ball into a rope about 25cm/10in long. With each rope, form a loop with the two ends facing you. Twist the ends and fold back on to the circle, pressing in to make a pretzel shape. Place on the baking sheets.

3 Brush the pretzels with the egg white. Sprinkle sugar crystals over the tops and bake in the oven until firm, about 10–12 minutes. Transfer to a wire rack to cool.

Ginger Cookies

If your children enjoy cooking with you, mixing and rolling the dough, or cutting out different shapes, this is the ideal recipe to let them practise on.

Makes 16

115g/4oz/8 tbsp soft brown sugar
115g/4oz/½ cup soft margarine
pinch of salt
few drops vanilla essence
175g/6oz/1½ cup wholemeal flour
15g/½oz/1 tbsp cocoa, sifted
10ml/2 tsp ground ginger
a little milk
glacé icing and glacé cherries, to decorate

1 Preheat the oven to 190°C/375°F/Gas 5. Cream the sugar, margarine, salt and vanilla essence together until very soft and light.

2 Work in the flour, cocoa and ginger, adding a little milk, if necessary, to bind the mixture. Knead lightly on a floured surface until smooth.

3 Roll out the dough on a lightly floured surface to about 5mm/1¼in thick. Stamp out shapes using biscuit cutters and place on baking sheets.

4 Bake the cookies for 10–15 minutes, leave to cool on the baking sheets until firm, then transfer to a wire rack to cool completely. Decorate with the glacé icing and glacé cherries.

Chocolate Macaroons

Roll one side of the macaroons in chopped nuts and bake nut-side up for a crunchier variation.

Makes 24

50g/2oz plain chocolate, melted
175g/6oz/1½ cups blanched almonds
225g/8oz/1 cup caster sugar
3 egg whites
2.5ml/½ tsp vanilla essence
1.5ml/¼ tsp almond essence
icing sugar, for dusting

1 Preheat the oven to 160°C/325°F/Gas 3. Line two baking sheets with greaseproof paper then grease. Grind the almonds in a food processor or blender. Transfer to a bowl, then blend in the sugar, egg whites, vanilla and almond essence. Stir in the chocolate. The mixture should just hold its shape; if too soft, chill for 15 minutes.

2 Shape the mixture into walnut-size balls. Place on the baking sheets and flatten slightly. Brush with a little water; dust with icing sugar. Bake until just firm, 10–12 minutes. With a palette knife, transfer to a wire rack to cool.

Chocolate-orange Sponge Drops

Light and crispy, with a marmalade filling, these sponge drops are truly decadent.

Makes 14–15

2 eggs
50g/2oz/¼ cup caster sugar
2.5ml/½ tsp grated orange rind
50g/2oz/½ cup plain flour
60ml/4 tbsp fine shred orange marmalade
40g/1½oz plain chocolate, cut into small pieces

1 Preheat the oven to 200°C/400°F/Gas 6. Line three baking sheets with baking paper. Put the eggs and sugar in a bowl over a pan of simmering water. Whisk until thick and pale. Remove from the pan and whisk until cool. Whisk in the orange rind. Sift the flour over and fold it in gently.

2 Put 28–30 dessertspoonfuls of the mixture on the baking sheets. Bake for 8 minutes, until golden. Cool slightly, then transfer to a wire rack. Sandwich pairs together with marmalade. Melt the chocolate and drizzle over the drops.

Coconut Macaroons

Have a change from after-dinner mints, and serve these delicious coconut macaroons with coffee instead.

Makes 24

Preheat the oven to 180°C/350°F/Gas 4. Grease two baking sheets. Sift 40g/1½ oz/⅓ cup plain flour and 1.5ml/1¼ tsp salt into a bowl, then stir in 225g/8oz/4 cups desiccated coconut. Pour in 170ml/5½fl oz/scant ¾ cup sweetened condensed milk. Add 5ml/1 tsp vanilla essence; stir from the centre to a thick mixture. Drop tablespoonfuls of the mixture 2.5cm/1in apart on the baking sheets. Bake until golden brown, about 20 minutes. Cool on a wire rack.

Peanut Butter Biscuits

For added crunchiness, stir in 75g/3oz/½ cup peanuts, coarsely chopped, with the peanut butter.

Makes 24

150g/5oz/1¼ cups plain flour
2.5ml/½ tsp bicarbonate of soda
2.5ml/½ tsp salt
115g/4oz/½ cup butter, at room temperature
170g/5¾ oz/scant 1 cup light brown sugar
1 egg
5ml/1 tsp vanilla essence
260g/9½oz/scant 1¼ cups crunchy peanut butter

1 Sift together the flour, bicarbonate of soda and salt and set aside. In another bowl, cream the butter and sugar together until light and fluffy.

2 In a third bowl, mix the egg and vanilla, then gradually beat into the butter mixture. Stir in the peanut butter and the chopped peanuts, if using, and blend thoroughly. Stir in the dry ingredients. Chill for 30 minutes, or until firm.

3 Preheat the oven to 180°C/350°F/Gas 4. Grease two baking sheets. Spoon out rounded teaspoonfuls of the dough and roll into balls.

4 Place the balls on the baking sheets and press flat with a fork into circles about 6cm/2½in in diameter, making a criss-cross pattern. Bake in the oven until lightly coloured, about 12–15 minutes. Transfer to a wire rack to cool.

Chocolate-chip Cookies

A perennial favourite with all the family, these cookies contain walnuts as well as chocolate chips.

Makes 24

115g/4oz/½ cup butter or margarine, at room temperature
45g/1¾ oz/scant ¼ cup caster sugar
100g/3¾ oz/generous ½ cup dark brown sugar
1 egg
2.5ml/½ tsp vanilla essence
175g/6oz/1½ cups plain flour
2.5ml/½ tsp bicarbonate of soda
1.5ml/¼ tsp salt
175g/6oz/1 cup chocolate chips
50g/2oz/½ cup walnuts, chopped

1 Preheat the oven to 180°C/350°F/Gas 4. Lightly grease two large baking sheets. With an electric mixer, cream the butter or margarine and both the sugars together until light and fluffy.

2 In another bowl, mix the egg and the vanilla essence, then gradually beat into the butter mixture. Sift over the flour, bicarbonate of soda and salt and stir. Add the chocolate chips and walnuts, and mix to combine well.

4 Place heaped teaspoonfuls of the dough 5cm/2in apart on the baking sheets. Bake in the oven until lightly coloured, about 10–15 minutes. Transfer to a wire rack to cool.

Almond Tile Biscuits

These biscuits are named after the French roof tiles they so closely resemble.

Makes about 24

65g/2½oz/scant ½ cup whole blanched almonds, lightly toasted
65g/2½oz/⅓ cup caster sugar
40g/1½oz/3 tbsp unsalted butter, softened
2 egg whites
2.5ml/½ tsp almond essence
40g/1½oz/⅓ cup plain flour, sifted
50g/2oz/½ cup flaked almonds

1 Preheat the oven to 200°C/400°F/Gas 6. Grease well two baking sheets. Place the almonds and 30ml/2 tbsp of the sugar in a blender or food processor and process until finely ground, but not pasty.

2 Beat the butter until creamy, add the remaining sugar and beat until light and fluffy. Gradually beat in the egg whites until the mixture is well blended, then beat in the almond essence. Sift the flour over the butter mixture and fold in, then fold in the almond mixture.

3 Drop tablespoonfuls of the mixture on to the baking sheets 15cm/6in apart. With the back of a wet spoon, spread each mound into a paper-thin 7.5cm/3in circle. Sprinkle with the flaked almonds.

4 Bake the biscuits, one sheet at a time, for 5–6 minutes until the edges are golden and the centres still pale. Remove the baking sheet to a wire rack and, working quickly, use a palette knife to loosen the edges of a biscuit. Lift the biscuit on the palette knife and place over a rolling pin, then press down the sides of the biscuit to curve it. Repeat with the remaining biscuits, and leave to cool.

Brittany Butter Biscuits

These little biscuits are similar to shortbread, but richer in taste and texture.

Makes 18–20

6 egg yolks, lightly beaten
15ml/1 tbsp milk
250g/9oz/2 cups plain flour
175g/6oz/generous ¾ cup caster sugar
200g/7oz/scant 1 cup lightly salted butter at room temperature, cut into small pieces

1 Preheat the oven to 180°C/350°F/Gas 4. Lightly butter a large baking sheet. Mix 15ml/1 tbsp of the egg yolks with the milk for a glaze. Set aside.

2 Sift the flour into a large bowl and make a central well. Add the egg yolks, sugar and butter and, using your fingertips, work them together until smooth and creamy. Gradually blend in the flour to form a smooth but slightly sticky dough.

3 Using floured hands, pat out the dough to 8mm/⅓in thick and cut out circles using a 7.5cm/3in biscuit cutter. Transfer the circles to the baking sheet, brush with egg glaze, then score to create a lattice pattern.

4 Bake for 12–15 minutes until golden. Cool in the tin on a wire rack for 15 minutes, then transfer to the wire rack to cool completely.

Ginger Florentines

These colourful, chewy biscuits are delicious served with vanilla or other flavoured ice cream.

Makes 30

50g/2oz/4 tbsp butter
115g/4oz/½ cup caster sugar
50g/2oz/¼ cup mixed glacé cherries, chopped
25g/1oz/generous 1 tbsp candied orange peel, chopped
50g/2oz/½ cup flaked almonds
50g/2oz/½ cup chopped walnuts
25g/1oz/1 tbsp glacé ginger, chopped
30ml/2 tbsp plain flour
2.5ml/½ tsp ground ginger

To finish

50g/2oz plain chocolate, melted
50g/2oz white chocolate, melted

1 Preheat the oven to 180°C/350°F/Gas 4. Beat the butter and sugar together until light and fluffy. Thoroughly mix in all the remaining ingredients, except the melted plain and white chocolate.

2 Line some baking sheets with non-stick baking paper. Put four small spoonfuls of the mixture on to each sheet, spacing them well apart to allow for spreading. Flatten the biscuits and bake for 5 minutes.

3 Remove the biscuits from the oven and flatten with a wet fork, shaping them into neat rounds. Return to the oven for about 3–4 minutes, until they are golden brown. Work in batches if necessary.

4 Let them cool on the baking sheets for 2 minutes to firm up, and then transfer them to a wire rack. When they are cold and firm, spread plain chocolate on the undersides of half the biscuits and white chocolate on the undersides of the rest.

Christmas Biscuits

These are great fun for children to make as presents, and any shape of biscuit cutter can be used.

Makes about 12

75g/3oz/6 tbsp butter
50g/2oz/generous ½ cup icing sugar
finely grated rind of 1 small lemon
1 egg yolk
175g/6oz/1½ cups plain flour
pinch of salt

To decorate

2 egg yolks
red and green edible food colouring

1 Beat the butter, sugar and lemon rind together until pale and fluffy. Beat in the egg yolk, and then sift in the flour and the salt. Knead together to form a smooth dough. Wrap and chill for 30 minutes.

2 Preheat the oven to 190°C/375°F/Gas 5. On a lightly floured surface, roll out the dough to 3mm/⅛in thick. Using a 6cm/2½in fluted cutter, stamp out as many biscuits as you can, with the cutter dipped in flour to prevent it from sticking to the dough.

3 Transfer the biscuits on to lightly greased baking sheets. Mark the tops lightly with a 2.5cm/1in holly leaf cutter and use a 5mm/¼in plain piping nozzle for the berries. Chill for 10 minutes, until firm.

4 Meanwhile, put each egg yolk into a small cup. Mix red food colouring into one and green food colouring into the other. Using a small, clean paintbrush, carefully paint the colours on to the biscuits. Bake for 10–12 minutes, or until they begin to colour around the edges. Let them cool slightly on the baking sheets, then transfer to a wire rack.

Traditional Sugar Biscuits

These lovely old-fashioned biscuits would be ideal to serve at an elegant tea party.

Makes 36

350g/12oz/3 cups plain flour
5ml/1 tsp bicarbonate of soda
10ml/2 tsp baking powder
1.5ml/¼ tsp grated nutmeg
115g/4oz/½ cup butter or margarine, at room temperature
225g/8oz/generous 1 cup caster sugar
2.5ml/½ tsp vanilla essence
1 egg
120ml/4fl oz/½ cup milk
coloured or demerara sugar, for sprinkling

1 Sift the flour, bicarbonate of soda, baking powder and nutmeg into a small bowl. Set aside. Cream the butter or margarine, caster sugar and vanilla essence together until the mixture is light and fluffy. Add the egg and beat to mix well.

2 Add the flour mixture alternately with the milk, stirring with a wooden spoon to make a soft dough. Wrap the dough in clear film and chill for 30 minutes.

3 Preheat the oven to 180°C/350°F/Gas 4. Roll out the dough on a lightly floured surface to a 3mm/⅛in thickness. Cut into circles with a biscuit cutter.

4 Transfer the biscuits to ungreased baking sheets. Sprinkle each one with sugar. Bake until golden, 10–12 minutes. With a palette knife, transfer the biscuits to a wire rack to cool.

Spicy Pepper Biscuits

Despite the warm, complex flavour added by the spices, these light biscuits are simple to make.

Makes 48

200g/7oz/¾ cup plain flour
50g/2oz/¼ cup cornflour
10ml/2 tsp baking powder
2.5ml/½ tsp ground cardamom
2.5ml/½ tsp ground cinnamon
2.5ml/½ tsp grated nutmeg
2.5ml/½ tsp ground ginger
2.5ml/½ tsp ground allspice
2.5ml/½ tsp salt
2.5ml/½ tsp freshly ground black pepper
225g/8oz butter or margarine, at room temperature
90g/3½ oz/½ cup light brown sugar
2.5ml/½ tsp vanilla essence
5ml/1 tsp finely grated lemon rind
50ml/2fl oz/¼ cups whipping cream
75g/3oz/¾ cup finely ground almonds
50ml/2 tbsp icing sugar

1 Preheat the oven to 180°C/350°F/Gas 4 . Sift the flour, cornflour, baking powder, spices, salt and pepper into a bowl.

2 Cream the butter or margarine and brown sugar until light and fluffy. Beat in the vanilla essence and lemon rind.

3 With the mixer on low speed, add the flour mixture alternately with the cream, beginning and ending with flour. Stir in the ground almonds.

4 Shape the dough into 2cm/¾in balls. Place them on ungreased baking sheets about 2.5cm/1in apart. Bake until golden brown underneath, about 15–20 minutes.

5 Leave to cool on the baking sheets for about 1 minute before transferring to a wire rack to cool completely. Before serving, sprinkle lightly with icing sugar.

Sultana Cornmeal Biscuits

These little yellow biscuits come from the Veneto region of Italy, and Marsala wine enhances their regional appeal.

Makes about 48

65g/2½oz/½ cup sultanas
50g/2oz/½ cup finely ground yellow cornmeal
175g/6oz/1½ cups plain flour
7.5ml/1½ tsp baking powder
pinch of salt
225g/8oz/1 cup butter
200g/7oz/1 cup granulated sugar
2 eggs
15ml/1 tbsp Marsala or 5ml/1 tsp vanilla essence

1 Soak the sultanas in a small bowl of warm water for 15 minutes. Drain. Preheat the oven to 180°C/350°F/Gas 4. Sift the cornmeal and flour, the baking powder and the salt together into a bowl.

2 Cream the butter and sugar together until light and fluffy. Beat in the eggs, one at a time. Beat in the Marsala or vanilla essence. Add the dry ingredients to the batter, beating until well blended. Stir in the sultanas.

3 Drop heaped teaspoonfuls of batter on to a greased baking sheet in rows about 2in apart. Bake for 7–8 minutes, or until the biscuits are golden brown at the edges. Remove to a wire rack to cool.

Mexican Cinnamon Biscuits

***Pastelitos* are traditional sweet shortbreads at weddings in Mexico, dusted in icing sugar to match the bride's dress.**

Makes 20

115g/4oz/½ cup butter
25g/1oz/2 tbsp caster sugar
115g/4oz/1 cup plain flour
50g/2oz/¼ cup cornflour
1.5ml/¼ tsp ground cinnamon
30ml/2 tbsp chopped mixed nuts
25g/1oz/¼ cup icing sugar, sifted

1 Preheat the oven to 160°C/325°F/Gas 3. Lightly grease a baking sheet. Place the butter and sugar in a bowl and beat until pale and creamy.

2 Sift in the plain flour, cornflour and cinnamon and gradually work in with a wooden spoon until the mixture comes together. Knead lightly until completely smooth.

3 Take tablespoonfuls of the mixture, roll into 20 small balls and arrange on the baking sheet. Press a few chopped nuts into the top of each one and then flatten slightly.

4 Bake the biscuits for about 30–35 minutes, until pale golden. Remove from the oven and, while they are still warm, toss them in the sifted icing sugar. Leave the biscuits to cool on a wire rack before serving.

Toasted Oat Meringues

Meringues needn't be plain. Try these oaty ones for a lovely crunchy change.

Makes 12

50g/2oz/generous 1/2 cup rolled oats
2 egg whites
1.5ml/1/4 tsp salt
7.5ml/1 1/2 tsp cornflour
175g/6oz/3/4 cup caster sugar

1 Preheat the oven to 140°C/275°F/Gas 1. Spread the oats on a baking sheet and toast in the oven until golden, for about 10 minutes. Lower the heat to 120°C/250°F/Gas ½. Grease and flour a baking sheet.

2 Beat the egg whites and salt until they start to form soft peaks. Sift over the cornflour and continue beating until the whites hold stiff peaks. Add half the sugar; whisk until glossy. Add the remaining sugar and fold in, then fold in the oats.

3 Place tablespoonsfuls of the mixture on to the baking sheet and bake for 2 hours, then turn off the oven. Turn over the meringues, and leave in the oven until cool.

Meringues

Make these classic meringues as large or small as you like. Serve as a tea-time treat or as an elegant dessert.

Makes about 24

4 egg whites
1.5ml/1/4 tsp salt
275g/10oz/1 1/4 cups caster sugar
2.5ml/1/2 tsp vanilla or almond essence (optional)
250ml/8fl oz/1 cup whipping cream

1 Preheat the oven to 110°C/225°F/Gas ¼. Grease and flour two large baking sheets. Beat the egg whites and salt in a metal bowl. When they start to form soft peaks, add half the sugar and continue beating until the mixture holds stiff peaks.

2 With a large metal spoon, fold in the remaining sugar and vanilla or almond essence, if using. Pipe or spoon the meringue mixture on to the baking sheets. Bake for 2 hours, turn off the oven. Loosen the meringues, invert, and set in another place on the sheets to prevent sticking. Leave in the oven until cool. Whip the cream and use to fill the meringues.

Chewy Chocolate Biscuits

If you have a weakness for chocolate, add 75g/3oz/1/2 cup chocolate chips to the mixture with the nuts.

Makes 18

Preheat the oven to 180°C/350°F/Gas 4. Line two baking sheets with greaseproof paper and grease. Using an electric mixer, beat 4 egg whites until frothy. Sift over 275g/10oz/2 cups icing sugar and 5ml/1 tsp coffee. Add 15ml/1 tbsp water, beat on low speed to blend, then on high until thick. Fold in 115g/4oz/1 cup chopped walnuts. Place generous spoonfuls of the mixture 2.5cm/1in apart on the sheets. Bake for 12–15 minutes. Transfer to a wire rack to cool.

Lavender Cookies

Instead of lavender you can use other flavourings, such as cinnamon, lemon, orange or mint.

Makes about 30

150g/5oz/⅔ cup butter
115g/4oz/½ cup granulated sugar
1 egg, beaten
15ml/1 tbsp dried lavender flowers
175g/6oz/1½ cups self-raising flour
leaves and flowers, to decorate

1 Preheat the oven to 180°C/350°F/Gas 4. Grease two baking sheets. Cream the butter and sugar together, then stir in the egg. Mix in the lavender flowers and the flour.

2 Drop spoonfuls of the mixture on to the baking sheets. Bake for about 15–20 minutes, until the biscuits are golden. Serve with some fresh leaves and flowers to decorate.

Chocolate Amaretti

As an alternative decoration, lightly press a few coffee sugar crystals on top of each cookie before baking.

Makes 24

150g/5oz/scant 1 cup blanched, toasted whole almonds
115g/4oz/½ cup caster sugar
15ml/1 tbsp unsweetened cocoa powder
30ml/2 tbsp icing sugar
2 egg whites
pinch of cream of tartar
5ml/1 tsp almond essence
flaked almonds, to decorate

1 Preheat the oven to 160°C/325°F/Gas 3. Line a large baking sheet with non-stick baking paper or foil. In a food processor fitted with a metal blade, process the toasted almonds with half the sugar until they are finely ground but not oily. Transfer to a bowl and sift in the cocoa and icing sugar; stir to blend. Set aside.

2 Beat the egg whites and cream of tartar until stiff peaks form. Sprinkle in the remaining sugar 15ml/1 tbsp at a time, beating well after each addition, and continue beating until the whites are glossy and stiff. Beat in the almond essence.

3 Sprinkle over the almond mixture and gently fold into the egg whites until just blended. Spoon the mixture into a large piping bag fitted with a plain 1cm/½in nozzle. Pipe 4cm/1½in rounds, 2.5cm/1in apart, on the baking sheet. Press a flaked almond into the centre of each.

4 Bake the cookies for 12–15 minutes or until they appear crisp. Remove the baking sheet to a wire rack to cool for 10 minutes. With a metal palette knife, remove the cookies to the wire rack to cool completely.

Melting Moments

These biscuits are very crisp and light – and they really do melt in your mouth.

Makes 16–20

40g/1½oz/3 tbsp butter or margarine
65g/2½oz/5 tbsp lard
75g/3oz/scant ½ cup caster sugar
½ egg, beaten
a few drops of vanilla or almond essence
150g/5oz/1¼ cups self-raising flour
rolled oats, for coating
4–5 glacé cherries, quartered, to decorate

1 Preheat the oven to 180°C/350°F/Gas 4. Beat together the butter or margarine, lard and sugar, then gradually beat in the egg and vanilla or almond essence.

2 Stir the flour into the beaten mixture, with floured hands, then roll into 16–20 small balls. Spread the rolled oats on a sheet of greaseproof paper and toss the balls in them to coat evenly.

3 Place the balls, spaced slightly apart, on two baking sheets, place a piece of cherry on top of each and bake for about 15–20 minutes, until lightly browned. Allow the biscuits to cool on the sheets for 5 minutes before transferring to a wire rack to cool completely.

Easter Biscuits

This is a seasonal recipe, but these biscuits can be enjoyed at any time of the year.

Makes 16–18

115g/4oz/½ cup butter or margarine
75g/3oz/scant ½ cup caster sugar, plus extra for sprinkling
1 egg, separated
200g/7oz/1¾ cups plain flour
2.5ml/½ tsp mixed spice
2.5ml/½ tsp ground cinnamon
50g/2oz/4 tbsp currants
15ml/1 tbsp chopped mixed peel
15–30ml/1–2 tbsp milk

1 Preheat the oven to 200°C/400°F/Gas 6. Lightly grease two baking sheets. Cream together the butter or margarine and sugar until light and fluffy, then beat in the egg yolk.

2 Sift the flour and spices over the egg mixture, then fold in with the currants and peel, adding sufficient milk to make a fairly soft dough.

3 Turn the dough on to a floured surface, knead lightly until just smooth, then roll out using a floured rolling pin, to about a 5mm/¼in thickness. Cut the dough into circles using a 5cm/2in fluted biscuit cutter. Transfer the circles to the baking sheets and bake for 10 minutes.

4 Beat the egg white, then brush over the biscuits. Sprinkle with caster sugar and return to the oven for a further 10 minutes, until golden. Transfer to a wire rack to cool.

Shortbread

Once you have tasted this shortbread, you'll never buy a packet from a shop again.

Makes 8

150g/5oz/generous ½ cup unsalted butter, at room temperature
115g/4oz/½ cup caster sugar
150g/5oz/1¼ cups plain flour
65g/2½ oz/½ cup rice flour
1.5ml/¼ tsp baking powder
1.5ml/¼ tsp salt

1 Preheat the oven to 160°C/325°F/Gas 3. Lightly grease a 20cm/8in shallow round cake tin. Cream the butter and sugar together until light and fluffy. Sift over the flours, baking powder and salt, and mix well.

2 Press the mixture neatly into the prepared tin, smoothing the surface with the back of a spoon. Prick all over with a fork, then score into eight equal wedges.

3 Bake until golden, about 40–45 minutes. Leave in the tin until cool enough to handle, then unmould and recut the wedges while still hot. Store in an airtight container.

Flapjacks

For a spicier version, add 5ml/1 tsp ground ginger to the melted butter.

Makes 8

50g/2oz/¼ cup butter
20ml/1 rounded tbsp golden syrup
65g/2½ oz/scant ½ cup dark brown sugar
115g/4oz/generous 1 cup quick-cooking oats
1.5ml/¼ tsp salt

1 Preheat the oven to 180°C/350°F/Gas 4. Line and grease a 20cm/8in shallow round cake tin. Place the butter, golden syrup and sugar in a pan over a low heat. Cook, stirring, until melted and combined.

2 Remove from the heat and add the oats and salt. Stir the mixture to blend. Spoon the mixture into the prepared tin and smooth the surface. Place in the centre of the oven and bake until golden brown, 20–25 minutes. Leave in the tin until cool enough to handle, then unmould and cut into wedges while still hot. Store in an airtight container.

Chocolate Delights

This method of making biscuits ensures they are all of a uniform size.

Makes 50

25g/1oz plain chocolate
25g/1oz bitter cooking chocolate
225g/8oz/2 cups plain flour
2.5ml/½ tsp salt
225g/8oz/1 cup unsalted butter, at room temperature
225g/8oz/generous 1 cup caster sugar
2 eggs
5ml/1 tsp vanilla essence
115g/4oz/1 cup finely chopped walnuts

1 Melt the chocolate in the top of a double boiler, or in a heatproof bowl set over a pan of gently simmering water. Set aside. In a bowl, sift together the flour and salt. Set aside.

2 Cream the butter until soft. Add the sugar and continue beating until the mixture is light and fluffy. Mix the eggs and vanilla essence, then gradually stir into the butter mixture. Stir in the chocolate, then the flour. Finally, stir in the nuts.

3 Divide the mixture into four equal parts, and roll each into a 5cm/2in diameter log. Wrap tightly in foil and chill or freeze until firm.

4 Preheat the oven to 190°C/375°F/Gas 5. Grease two baking sheets. With a sharp knife, cut the logs into 5mm/¼in slices. Place the circles on the baking sheets and bake until lightly coloured, about 10 minutes. Using a palette knife, transfer to a wire rack to cool.

Cinnamon Treats

Place these biscuits in a heart-shaped basket, as here, and serve them up with love.

Makes 50

250g/9oz/generous 2 cups plain flour
2.5ml/½ tsp salt
10ml/2 tsp ground cinnamon
225g/8oz/1 cup unsalted butter, at room temperature
225g/8oz/generous 1 cup caster sugar
2 eggs
5ml/1 tsp vanilla essence

1 Sift together the flour, salt and cinnamon together into a bowl. Set aside.

2 Cream the butter until soft. Add the sugar and continue beating until the mixture is light and fluffy. Beat the eggs and vanilla essence together, then gradually stir into the butter mixture. Stir in the dry ingredients.

3 Divide the mixture into four equal parts, then roll each into a 5cm/2in diameter log. Wrap tightly in foil and chill or freeze until firm.

4 Preheat the oven to 190°C/375°F/Gas 5. Grease two baking sheets. With a sharp knife, cut the logs into 5mm/¼in slices. Place the rounds on the baking sheets and bake until lightly coloured, about 10 minutes. Using a palette knife, transfer to a wire rack to cool.

Chunky Chocolate Drops

Do not allow these cookies to cool completely on the baking sheet or they will break when you try to lift them.

Makes 18

175g/6oz plain chocolate
115g/4oz/½ cup unsalted butter
2 eggs
90g/3½oz/½ cup granulated sugar
50g/2oz/¼ cup (packed) light brown sugar
40g/1½oz/⅓ cup plain flour
25g/1oz/¼ cup unsweetened cocoa powder
5ml/1 tsp baking powder
10ml/2 tsp vanilla essence
pinch of salt
115g/4oz/1 cup pecan nuts, toasted and coarsely chopped
175g/6oz/1 cup plain chocolate chips
115g/4oz fine quality white chocolate, chopped into 5mm/¼in pieces
115g/4oz fine quality milk chocolate, chopped into 5mm/¼in pieces

1 Preheat the oven to 160°C/325°F/Gas 3. Grease two large baking sheets. In a medium saucepan over a low heat, melt the plain chocolate and butter until smooth, stirring frequently. Remove from the heat to cool slightly.

2 Beat the eggs and sugars for 2–3 minutes until pale and creamy. Gradually beat in the melted chocolate mixture. Beat in the flour, cocoa, baking powder, vanilla and salt, just to blend. Add the nuts, chocolate chips and chocolate pieces.

3 Drop 4–6 heaped tablespoonfuls of the mixture on to each baking sheet 10cm/4in apart and flatten each to a round about 7.5cm/3in. Bake for 8–10 minutes until the tops are shiny and cracked and the edges look crisp.

4 Remove the baking sheets to a wire rack to cool for about 2 minutes, until the cookies are just set, then remove them to the wire rack to cool completely. Continue to bake in batches.

Chocolate Crackle-tops

These cookies are best eaten on the day they are baked, as they dry slightly on storage.

Makes 38

200g/7oz plain chocolate, chopped
90g/3½oz/7 tbsp unsalted butter
115g/4oz/½ cup caster sugar
3 eggs
5ml/1 tsp vanilla essence
215g/7½oz/scant 2 cups plain flour
25g/1oz/¼ cup unsweetened cocoa powder
2.5ml/½ tsp baking powder
pinch of salt
175g/6oz/1½ cups icing sugar, for coating

1 Heat the chocolate and butter over a low heat until smooth, stirring frequently. Remove from the heat. Stir in the sugar, and continue stirring until dissolved. Add the eggs, one at a time, beating well after each addition; stir in the vanilla. In a separate bowl, sift together the flour, cocoa, baking powder and salt. Gradually stir into the chocolate mixture until just blended. Cover and chill for at least 1 hour.

2 Preheat the oven to 160°C/325°F/Gas 3. Grease two or three large baking sheets. Place the icing sugar in a small, deep bowl. Using a teaspoon, scoop the dough into small balls and roll in your hands into 4cm/1½in balls.

3 Drop the balls, one at a time, into the icing sugar and roll until heavily coated. Remove each ball with a slotted spoon and tap against the bowl to remove any excess sugar. Place on the baking sheets 4cm/1½in apart.

4 Bake the cookies for 10–15 minutes or until the tops feel slightly firm when touched with your fingertip. Remove the baking sheets to a wire rack for 2–3 minutes, then with a palette knife remove the cookies to the wire rack to cool.

Chocolate-chip Oat Biscuits

Oat biscuits are given a delicious lift by the inclusion of chocolate chips. Try caramel chips for a change, if you like.

Makes 60

115g/4oz/1 cup plain flour
2.5ml/½ tsp bicarbonate of soda
1.5ml/¼ tsp baking powder
1.5ml/¼ tsp salt
115g/4oz/½ cup butter or margarine, at room temperature
115g/4oz/generous ½ cup caster sugar
90g/3½oz/generous ½ cup light brown sugar
1 egg
2.5ml/½ tsp vanilla essence
75g/3oz/scant ½ cup rolled oats
175g/6oz/1 cup plain chocolate chips

1 Preheat the oven to 180°C/350°F/Gas 4. Grease three or four baking sheets. Sift the flour, bicarbonate of soda, baking powder and salt into a mixing bowl. Set aside.

2 With an electric mixer, cream the butter or margarine and the sugars together. Add the egg and vanilla, and beat until light and fluffy. Add the flour mixture and beat on low speed until thoroughly blended. Stir in the rolled oats and plain chocolate chips, mixing well with a wooden spoon. The dough should be crumbly.

3 Drop heaped teaspoonfuls on to the baking sheets, about 2.5cm/1in apart. Bake until just firm around the edges but still soft in the centres, about 15 minutes. With a palette knife, transfer the biscuits to a wire rack to cool.

Chocolate and Coconut Slices

These tasty family favourites are easier to slice if they are allowed to cool overnight.

Makes 24

175g/6oz/2 cups crushed digestive biscuits
50g/2oz/¼ cup caster sugar
pinch of salt
115g/4oz/½ cup butter or margarine, melted
75g/3oz/1½ cups desiccated coconut
250g/9oz plain chocolate chips
250ml/8fl oz/1 cup sweetened condensed milk
115g/4oz/1 cup chopped walnuts

1 Preheat the oven to 180°C/350°F/Gas 4. In a bowl, combine the crushed biscuits, sugar, salt and butter or margarine. Press the mixture evenly over the base of an ungreased 33 x 23cm/13 x 9in baking dish.

2 Sprinkle the coconut over the biscuit base, then scatter over the chocolate chips. Pour the condensed milk evenly over the chocolate. Sprinkle the walnuts on top. Bake in the oven for 30 minutes. Unmould on to a wire rack and leave to cool.

Nut Lace Wafers

To create a different taste, add some finely grated orange peel to these delicate biscuits.

Makes 18

65g/2½oz/scant ½ cup blanched almonds
50g/2oz/¼ cup butter
40g/1½oz/⅓ cup plain flour
90g/3½oz/½ cup caster sugar
30ml/2 tbsp double cream
2.5ml/½ tsp vanilla essence

1 Preheat the oven to 190°C/375°F/Gas 5. Lightly grease two baking sheets.

2 With a sharp knife, chop the almonds as finely as possible. Alternatively, use a food processor or blender to chop the nuts very finely.

3 Melt the butter in a saucepan over a low heat. Remove from the heat and stir in the remaining ingredients and the finely chopped almonds.

4 Drop teaspoonfuls 6cm/2½in apart on the prepared sheets. Bake until golden, about 5 minutes. Cool on the baking sheets briefly, just until the wafers are stiff enough to remove. With a palette knife, transfer to a wire rack to cool.

Oatmeal Lace Rounds

These rich, nutty biscuits are very quick and simple to make and will be enjoyed by everyone.

Makes 36

165g/5½oz/⅔ cup butter or margarine
130g/4½oz/1¼ cups quick-cooking porridge oats
170g/5¾oz/¾ cup dark brown sugar
155g/5¼oz/⅔ cup caster sugar
40g/1½oz/⅓ cup plain flour
1.5ml/¼ tsp salt
1 egg, lightly beaten
5ml/1 tsp vanilla essence
65g/2½oz/generous ½ cup pecan nuts or walnuts, finely chopped

1 Preheat the oven to 180°C/350°F/Gas 4. Lightly grease two baking sheets.

2 Melt the butter or margarine in a saucepan over a low heat. Set aside. In a mixing bowl, combine the oats, brown sugar, caster sugar, flour and salt. Make a well in the centre and add the butter or margarine, egg and vanilla. Mix until blended, then stir in the chopped nuts.

3 Drop rounded teaspoonfuls of the mixture about 5cm/2in apart on the prepared baking sheets. Bake in the oven until lightly browned on the edges and bubbling all over, about 5–8 minutes. Cool on the baking sheets for 2 minutes, then transfer to a wire rack to cool completely.

Nutty Chocolate Squares

These delicious squares are incredibly rich, so cut them smaller if you wish.

Makes 16

2 eggs
10ml/2 tsp vanilla essence
1.5ml/¼ tsp salt
175g/6oz/1½ cups pecan nuts, coarsely chopped
50g/2oz/½ cup plain flour
50g/2oz/¼ cup caster sugar
120ml/4fl oz/½ cup golden syrup
75g/3oz plain chocolate, finely chopped
40g/1½oz/3 tbsp butter
16 pecan nut halves, to decorate

1 Preheat the oven to 160°C/325°F/Gas 3. Line the base and sides of a 20cm/8in square baking tin with greaseproof paper and lightly grease the paper.

2 Whisk together the eggs, vanilla and salt. In another bowl, mix together the chopped pecan nuts and flour. Set both aside until needed.

3 In a saucepan, bring the sugar and golden syrup to the boil. Remove from the heat, stir in the chocolate and butter, and blend thoroughly with a wooden spoon. Mix in the beaten egg mixture, then fold in the pecan nut mixture.

4 Pour the mixture into the baking tin and bake until set, about 35 minutes. Cool in the tin for 10 minutes before unmoulding. Cut into 5cm/2in squares and press pecan nut halves into the tops while warm. Cool on a wire rack.

Raisin Brownies

Cover these brownies with a light chocolate frosting for a truly decadent treat, if you wish.

Makes 16

115g/4oz/½ cup butter or margarine
50g/2oz/½ cup cocoa powder
2 eggs
225g/8oz/generous 1 cup caster sugar
5ml/1 tsp vanilla essence
40g/1½oz/⅓ cup plain flour
75g/3oz/¾ cup chopped walnuts
75g/3oz/generous ½ cup raisins

1 Preheat the oven to 180°C/350°F/Gas 4. Line the base and sides of a 20cm/8in square baking tin with greaseproof paper and grease the paper.

2 Gently melt the butter or margarine in a small saucepan. Remove from the heat and stir in the cocoa powder. With an electric mixer, beat the eggs, sugar and vanilla together until light. Add the cocoa mixture and stir to blend.

3 Sift the flour over the cocoa mixture and gently fold in. Add the walnuts and raisins and scrape the mixture into the prepared baking tin.

4 Bake in the centre of the oven for 30 minutes. Leave in the tin to cool before cutting into 5cm/2in squares and removing. The brownies should be soft and moist.

Chocolate-chip Brownies

A double dose of chocolate is incorporated into these melt-in-the-mouth brownies.

Makes 24

115g/4oz plain chocolate
115g/4oz/½ cup butter
3 eggs
200g/7oz/1 cup sugar
2.5ml/½ tsp vanilla essence
pinch of salt
150g/5oz/1¼ cups plain flour
175g/6oz/1 cup chocolate chips

1 Preheat the oven to 180°C/350°F/Gas 4. Then line a 33 x 23cm/13 x 9in baking tin with greaseproof paper and grease the paper.

2 Melt the chocolate and butter together in the top of a double boiler, or in a heatproof bowl set over a pan of gently simmering water.

3 Beat together the eggs, sugar, vanilla and salt. Stir in the chocolate mixture. Sift over the flour and fold in. Add the chocolate chips.

4 Pour the mixture into the baking tin and spread evenly. Bake until just set, about 30 minutes. The brownies should be slightly moist inside. Leave to cool in the tin.

5 To turn out, run a knife all around the edge and invert on to a baking sheet. Remove the paper. Place another sheet on top and invert again. Cut into bars for serving.

Marbled Brownies

Flavoursome and impressive in appearance, these fancy brownies are also great fun to make.

Makes 24

225g/8oz plain chocolate
75g/3oz/⅓ cup butter
4 eggs
300g/11oz/1½ cups sugar
150g/5oz/1¼ cups plain flour
2.5ml/½ tsp salt
5ml/1 tsp baking powder
10ml/2 tsp vanilla essence
115g/4oz/1 cup walnuts, chopped

For the plain mixture
50g/2oz/4 tbsp butter, at room temperature
175g/6oz/¾ cup cream cheese
90g/3½ oz/1½ cups sugar
2 eggs
25g/1oz/4 tbsp plain flour
5ml/1 tsp vanilla essence

1 Preheat the oven to 180°C/350°F/Gas 4 . Then line a 33 x 23cm/13 x 9in baking tin with greaseproof paper and grease.

2 Melt the chocolate and butter over a very low heat, stirring. Set aside to cool. Meanwhile, beat the eggs until light and fluffy. Gradually beat in the sugar. Sift over the flour, salt and baking powder and fold to combine.

3 Stir in the cooled chocolate mixture. Add the vanilla and walnuts. Measure and set aside 475ml/16fl oz/2 cups of the chocolate mixture. For the plain mixture, cream the butter and cream with an electric mixer. Add the sugar and continue beating until blended. Beat in the eggs, flour and vanilla.

4 Spread the unmeasured chocolate mixture in the tin. Pour over the plain mixture. Drop spoonfuls of the reserved chocolate mixture on top.

5 With a palette knife, swirl the mixtures to marble. Do not blend completely. Bake until just set, 35–40 minutes. Turn out when cool and cut into squares for serving.

Oatmeal and Date Brownies

These brownies are marvellous as a break-time treat. The secret of chewy, moist brownies is not to overcook them.

Makes 16

150g/5oz plain chocolate
50g/2oz/4 tbsp butter
75g/3oz/scant 1 cup quick-cooking porridge oats
25g/1oz/3 tbsp wheatgerm
25g/1oz/⅓ cup milk powder
2.5ml/½ tsp baking powder
2.5ml/½ tsp salt
50g/2oz/½ cup chopped walnuts
50g/2oz/⅓ cup dates, chopped
50g/2oz/¼ cup molasses sugar
5ml/1 tsp vanilla essence
2 eggs, beaten

1 Break the chocolate into a heatproof bowl and add the butter. Place over a pan of simmering water and stir until completely melted.

2 Cool the chocolate, stirring occasionally. Preheat the oven to 180°C/350°F/Gas 4. Grease and line a 20cm/8in square cake tin.

3 Combine all the dry ingredients together in a bowl, then beat in the melted chocolate, vanilla and eggs. Pour the mixture into the cake tin, level the surface and bake in the oven for 20–25 minutes until firm around the edges yet still soft in the centre.

4 Cool the brownies in the tin, then chill in the fridge. When they are more solid, turn them out of the tin and cut into 16 squares.

Banana Chocolate Brownies

Nuts traditionally give brownies their chewy texture. Here oat bran is used instead, creating a wonderful alternative.

Makes 9

75ml/5 tbsp cocoa powder
15ml/1 tbsp caster sugar
75ml/5 tbsp milk
3 large bananas, mashed
215g/7½oz/1 cup soft light brown sugar
5ml/1 tsp vanilla essence
5 egg whites
75g/3oz/¾ cup self-raising flour
75g/3oz/⅔ cup oat bran
icing sugar, for dusting

1 Preheat the oven to 180°C/350°F/Gas 4. Line a 20cm/8in square cake tin with non-stick baking paper.

2 Blend the cocoa and caster sugar with the milk. Add the bananas, soft brown sugar and vanilla essence. Lightly beat the egg whites with a fork. Add the chocolate mixture and continue to beat well. Sift the flour over the mixture and fold in with the oat bran. Pour into the prepared tin.

3 Cook in the oven for 40 minutes, or until firm. Cool in the tin for 10 minutes, then turn out on to a wire rack. Cut into squares and lightly dust with icing sugar before serving.

White Chocolate Brownies

If you wish, hazelnuts can be substituted for the macadamia nuts in the topping.

Serves 12

150g/5oz/1 cup plain flour
2.5ml/½ tsp baking powder
pinch of salt
175g/6oz fine quality white chocolate, chopped
90g/3½ oz/½ cup caster sugar
115g/4oz/½ cup unsalted butter, cut into pieces
2 eggs, lightly beaten
5ml/1 tsp vanilla essence
175g/6oz semi-sweet chocolate chips

For the topping

200g/7oz milk chocolate, chopped
215g/7½ oz/1 cup unsalted macadamia nuts, chopped

1 Preheat the oven to 180°C/350°F/Gas 4. Grease a 23cm/9in springform tin. Sift together the flour, baking powder and salt, and set aside.

2 In a medium saucepan over a moderate heat, melt the white chocolate, sugar and butter until smooth, stirring frequently. Cool slightly, then beat in the eggs and vanilla. Stir in the chocolate chips. Spread evenly in the prepared tin, smoothing the top.

3 Bake for 20–25 minutes until a toothpick inserted 5cm/2in from the side of the tin comes out clean. Remove from the oven to a heatproof surface, sprinkle chopped milk chocolate over the surface (avoid touching the side of tin) and return to oven for 1 minute.

4 Remove from the oven and, using the back of a spoon, gently spread out the softened chocolate. Sprinkle with the macadamia nuts and gently press into the chocolate. Cool on a wire rack for 30 minutes; chill for 1 hour. Run a sharp knife around the side of the tin to loosen; then unclip and remove. Cut into thin wedges to serve.

Maple-Pecan Nut Brownies

This recipe provides a delicious adaptation of the classic American chocolate brownie.

Makes 12

115g/4oz/½ cup butter, melted
75g/3oz/½ cup light soft brown sugar
90ml/6 tbsp maple syrup
2 eggs
115g/4oz/1 cup self-raising flour
75g/3oz/¾ cup pecan nuts, chopped
115g/4oz/⅔ cup plain chocolate chips
50g/2oz/¼ cup unsalted butter
12 pecan nut halves, to decorate

1 Preheat the oven to 180°C/350°F/Gas 4. Line and grease a 25 x 18cm/10 x 7in cake tin.

2 Beat together the melted butter, sugar, 60ml/4 tbsp of the maple syrup, eggs and flour for 1 minute, or until smooth. Stir in the nuts and transfer to the cake tin. Smooth the surface and bake for 30 minutes, until risen and firm to the touch. Cool in the tin for 10 minutes, then transfer to a wire rack to cool completely.

3 Melt the chocolate chips, butter and remaining syrup over a low heat. Cool slightly, then spread over the cake. Press in the pecan nut halves, leave to set for about 5 minutes, then cut into bars.

American Chocolate Fudge Brownies

This is the classic American recipe, but omit the frosting if you find it too rich.

Makes 12

175g/6oz/¾ cup butter
40g/1½oz/6 tbsp cocoa powder
2 eggs, lightly beaten
175g/6oz/1 cup soft light brown sugar
2.5ml/½ tsp vanilla essence
115g/4oz/1 cup chopped pecan nuts
50g/2oz/½ cup self-raising flour

For the frosting

115g/4oz plain chocolate
25g/1oz/2 tbsp butter
15ml/1 tbsp soured cream

1 Preheat the oven to 180°C/350°F/Gas 4. Grease then line a 20cm/8in square shallow cake tin with greaseproof paper. Melt the butter in a pan and stir in the cocoa powder. Set aside to cool.

2 Beat together the eggs, sugar and vanilla essence in a bowl, then stir in the cooled cocoa mixture with the nuts. Sift over the flour and fold into the mixture with a metal spoon.

3 Pour the mixture into the cake tin and bake in the oven for 30–35 minutes, until risen. Remove from the oven (the mixture will still be quite soft and wet, but it cooks further while cooling) and leave to cool in the tin.

4 To make the frosting, melt the chocolate and butter together in a pan and remove from the heat. Beat in the soured cream until smooth and glossy. Leave to cool slightly, and then spread over the top of the brownies. When set, cut into 12 pieces.

Fudge-glazed Chocolate Brownies

These brownies are just about irresistible, so hide them from friends – or make lots!

Makes 16

250g/9oz bittersweet chocolate, chopped
25g/1oz unsweetened chocolate, chopped
115g/4oz/½ cup unsalted butter, cut into pieces
90g/3½ oz/½ cup light brown sugar
50g/2oz/¼ cup granulated sugar
2 eggs
15ml/1 tbsp vanilla essence
65g/2½ oz/½ cup plain flour
115g/4oz/1 cup pecans or walnuts, toasted and chopped
150g/5oz white chocolate, chopped
pecan halves, to decorate (optional)

Fudgy Chocolate Glaze

175g/6oz bittersweet chocolate, chopped
50g/2oz/4 tbsp unsalted butter, cut into pieces
30ml/2 tbsp corn or golden syrup
10ml/2 tsp vanilla essence
5ml/1 tsp instant coffee

1 Preheat oven to 180°C/350°F/Gas 4. Line a 20cm/8in square baking tin with foil then grease the foil.

2 In a saucepan over a low heat, melt the dark chocolates and butter. Off the heat, add the sugars and stir for 2 minutes. Beat in the eggs and vanilla; blend in the flour. Stir in the nuts and white chocolate. Pour into the tin. Bake for 20–25 minutes. Cool in the tin for 30 minutes then lift, using the foil, on to a wire rack to cool for 2 hours.

3 For the glaze, melt all the ingredients in a pan until smooth, stirring. Chill for 1 hour then spread over the brownies. Chill until set then cut into squares.

Chocolate Raspberry Macaroon Bars

Any seedless preserve, such as strawberry or apricot, can be substituted for the raspberry in this recipe.

Makes 16–18

115g/4oz/½ cup unsalted butter, softened
50g/2oz/½ cup icing sugar
25g/1oz/¼ cup unsweetened cocoa powder
pinch of salt
5ml/1 tsp almond essence
120g/4oz/1¼ cups plain flour

For the topping

150g/5oz/½ cup seedless raspberry preserve
15ml/1 tbsp raspberry flavour liqueur
175g/6oz/1 cup milk chocolate chips
175g/6oz/1½ cups finely ground almonds
4 egg whites
pinch of salt
200g/7oz/1 cup caster sugar
2.5ml/½ tsp almond essence
50g/2oz/½ cup flaked almonds

1 Preheat the oven to 160°C/325°F/Gas 3. Then line a 23 x 33cm/9 x 13in baking tin with foil and grease. Beat together the butter, sugar, cocoa and salt until blended. Beat in the almond essence and flour to make a crumbly dough.

2 Turn the dough into the tin and smooth the surface. Prick with a fork. Bake for 20 minutes until just set. Remove from the oven and increase the temperature to 190°C/375°F/Gas 5. Combine the raspberry preserve and liqueur. Spread over the cooked crust, then sprinkle with the chocolate chips.

3 In a food processor fitted with a metal blade, process the almonds, egg whites, salt, sugar and almond essence. Pour over the jam layer, spreading evenly. Sprinkle with almonds.

4 Bake for 20–25 minutes until the top is golden and puffed. Cool in the tin for 20 minutes. Carefully remove from the tin and cool completely. Peel off the foil and cut into bars.

Chewy Fruit Muesli Slice

The apricots give these slices a wonderful chewy texture and the apple keeps them moist.

Makes 8

75g/3oz/scant ½ cup ready-to-eat dried apricots, chopped
1 eating apple, cored and grated
150g/5oz/1¼ cups Swiss-style muesli
150ml/¼ pint/⅔ cup apple juice
15g/½oz/1 tbsp sunflower margarine

1 Preheat the oven to 190°C/375°F/Gas 5. Place all the ingredients in a large bowl and mix well.

2 Press the mixture into a 20cm/8in round non-stick sandwich tin and bake for 35–40 minutes, or until lightly browned and firm. Mark the muesli slice into wedges and leave to cool in the tin.

Blueberry Streusel Slice

If you are short of time, use ready-made pastry for this delightful streusel.

Makes 30

225g/8oz shortcrust pastry
50g/2oz/½ cup plain flour
1.5ml/¼ tsp baking powder
40g/1½oz/3 tbsp butter or margarine
25g/1oz/2 tbsp fresh white breadcrumbs
50g/2oz/⅓ cup soft light brown sugar
1.5ml/¼ tsp salt
50g/2oz/4 tbsp flaked or chopped almonds
30ml/4 tbsp blackberry or bramble jelly
115g/4oz/1 cup blueberries, fresh or frozen

1 Preheat the oven to 180°C/350°F/Gas 4. Roll out the pastry on a lightly floured surface and line an 18 x 28cm/ 7 x 11in Swiss roll tin. Prick the base evenly with a fork.

2 Rub together the plain flour, baking powder, butter or margarine, breadcrumbs, sugar and salt until really crumbly, then mix in the almonds.

3 Spread the pastry with the jelly, sprinkle with the blueberries, then cover evenly with the streusel topping, pressing down lightly. Bake for 30–40 minutes, reducing the temperature after 20 minutes to 160°C/325°F/Gas 3.

4 Remove from the oven when golden on the top and the pastry is cooked through. Cut into slices while still hot, then allow to cool.

Sticky Date and Apple Bars

If possible allow this mixture to mature for 1–2 days before cutting – it will get stickier and even more delicious!

Makes 16

115g/4oz/½ cup margarine
50g/2oz/⅓ cup soft dark brown sugar
50g/2oz/4 tbsp golden syrup
115g/4oz/¾ cup chopped dates
115g/4oz/generous 1 cup rolled oats
115g/4oz/1 cup wholemeal self-raising flour
225g/8oz/2 eating apples, peeled, cored and grated
5–10ml/1–2 tsp lemon juice
20–25 walnut halves

1 Preheat the oven to 190°C/375°F/Gas 5. Then line an 18–20cm/7–8in square or rectangular loose-based cake tin. In a large pan, heat the margarine, sugar, syrup and dates, stirring until the dates soften completely.

2 Gradually work in the oats, flour, apples and lemon juice until well mixed. Spoon into the tin and spread out evenly. Top with the walnut halves.

3 Bake for 30 minutes, then reduce the temperature to 160°C/325°F/Gas 3 and bake for 10–20 minutes more, until firm to the touch and golden. Cut into squares or bars while still warm, or wrap in foil when nearly cold and keep for 1–2 days before eating.

Figgy Bars

Make sure you have napkins handy when you serve these deliciously sticky bars.

Makes 48

350g/12oz/1½ cups dried figs
3 eggs
175g/6oz/¾ cup caster sugar
75g/3oz/¾ cup plain flour
5ml/1 tsp baking powder
2.5ml/½ tsp ground cinnamon
1.5ml/¼ tsp ground cloves
1.5ml/¼ tsp grated nutmeg
1.5ml/¼ tsp salt
75g/3oz/¾ cup finely chopped walnuts
30ml/2 tbsp brandy or cognac
icing sugar, for dusting

1 Preheat the oven to 160°C/325°F/Gas 3. Then line a 30 x 20 x 3cm/12 x 8 x 1½in baking tin with greaseproof paper and grease the paper.

2 With a sharp knife, chop the figs roughly. Set aside. In a bowl, whisk the eggs and sugar until well blended. In another bowl, sift together the dry ingredients, then fold into the egg mixture in several batches.

3 Scrape the mixture into the baking tin and bake until the top is firm and brown, about 35–40 minutes. It should still be soft underneath.

4 Leave to cool in the tin for 5 minutes, then unmould and transfer to a sheet of greaseproof paper lightly sprinkled with icing sugar. Cut into bars.

Lemon Bars

A surprising amount of lemon juice goes into these bars, but you will appreciate why when you taste them.

Makes 36

50g/2oz/½ cup icing sugar
175g/6oz/1½ cups plain flour
2.5ml/½ tsp salt
175g/6oz/¾ cup butter, cut in small pieces

For the topping

4 eggs
350g/12oz/1½ cups caster sugar
grated rind of 1 lemon
120ml/4fl oz/½ cup fresh lemon juice
175ml/6fl oz/¾ cup whipping cream
icing sugar, for dusting

1 Preheat the oven to 160°C/325°F/Gas 3. Grease a 33 x 23cm/13 x 9in baking tin.

2 Sift the sugar, flour and salt into a bowl. With a pastry blender, cut in the butter until the mixture resembles coarse breadcrumbs. Press the mixture into the base of the tin. Bake until golden brown, about 20 minutes.

3 Meanwhile, for the topping, whisk the eggs and sugar together until blended. Add the lemon rind and juice, and mix well.

4 Lightly whip the cream and fold into the egg mixture. Pour over the still warm base, return to the oven, and bake until set, about 40 minutes. Cool completely before cutting into bars. Dust with icing sugar.

Spiced Raisin Bars

If you like raisins, these gloriously spicy bars are for you. Omit the walnuts if you prefer.

Makes 30

100g/3¾ oz/scant 1 cup plain flour
7.5ml/1½ tsp baking powder
5ml/1 tsp ground cinnamon
2.5ml/½ tsp grated nutmeg
1.5ml/¼ tsp ground cloves
1.5ml/¼ tsp mixed spice
215g/7½oz/1½ cups raisins
115g/4oz/½ cup butter or margarine, at room temperature
90g/3½oz/½ cup sugar
2 eggs
170g/5¾ oz/scant ½ cup black treacle
50g/2oz/½ cup walnuts, chopped

1 Preheat the oven to 180°C/350°F/Gas 4. Then line a 33 x 23cm/13 x 9in baking tin with greaseproof paper and grease the paper.

2 Sift together the flour, baking powder and spices. Place the raisins in another bowl and toss with a few tablespoons of the flour mixture.

3 With an electric mixer, cream the butter or margarine and sugar together until light and fluffy. Beat in the eggs, one at a time, then the black treacle. Stir in the flour mixture, raisins and walnuts.

4 Spread evenly in the baking tin. Bake until just set, about 15–18 minutes. Cool in the tin before cutting into bars.

Toffee Meringue Bars

Two delicious layers complement each other beautifully in these easy-to-make bars.

Makes 12

50g/2oz/4 tbsp butter
215g/7½oz/scant 1¼ cups dark brown sugar
1 egg
2.5ml/½ tsp vanilla essence
65g/2½oz/9 tbsp plain flour
2.5ml/½ tsp salt
1.5ml/¼ tsp grated nutmeg

For the topping

1 egg white
1.5ml/¼ tsp salt
15ml/1 tbsp golden syrup
90g/3½oz/½ cup caster sugar
50g/2oz/½ cup walnuts, finely chopped

1 Combine the butter and brown sugar in a saucepan and heat until bubbling. Set aside to cool.

2 Preheat the oven to 180°C/350°F/Gas 4. Line the base and sides of a 20cm/8in square cake tin with greaseproof paper and grease the paper.

3 Beat the egg and vanilla into the cooled sugar mixture. Sift over the flour, salt and nutmeg and fold in. Spread in the base of the cake tin.

4 For the topping, beat the egg white with the salt until it holds soft peaks. Beat in the golden syrup, then the sugar, and continue beating until the mixture holds stiff peaks. Fold in the nuts and spread on top. Bake for 30 minutes. Cut into bars when completely cool.

Chocolate Walnut Bars

These double-decker bars should be stored in the fridge in an airtight container.

Makes 24

50g/2oz/²/₃ cup walnuts
55g/2¼oz/generous ¼ cup caster sugar
100g/3¾ oz/scant 1 cup plain flour, sifted
90g/3½ oz/6 tbsp cold unsalted butter, cut into pieces

For the topping

25g/1oz/2 tbsp unsalted butter
90ml/6 tbsp water
25g/1oz/¼ cup unsweetened cocoa powder
90g/3½oz/½ cup caster sugar
5ml/1 tsp vanilla essence
1.5ml/¼ tsp salt
2 eggs
icing sugar, for dusting

1 Preheat the oven to 180°C/350°F/Gas 4. Grease the base and sides of a 20cm/8in square baking tin.

2 Grind the walnuts with a few tablespoons of the sugar in a food processor or blender. In a bowl, combine the ground walnuts, remaining sugar and flour. Rub in the butter until the mixture resembles coarse breadcrumbs. Alternatively, use a food processor. Pat the walnut mixture evenly into the base of the baking tin. Bake for 25 minutes.

3 Meanwhile, for the topping, melt the butter with the water. Whisk in the cocoa powder and sugar. Remove from the heat, stir in the vanilla essence and salt, then cool for 5 minutes. Whisk in the eggs until blended. Pour the topping over the baked crust.

4 Return to the oven and bake until set, about 20 minutes. Set the tin on a wire rack to cool, then cut into bars and dust with icing sugar.

Hazelnut Squares

These crunchy, nutty squares are made in a single bowl. What could be simpler?

Makes 9

50g/2oz plain chocolate
65g/2½oz/5 tbsp butter or margarine
225g/8oz/generous 1 cup caster sugar
50g/2oz/½ cup plain flour
2.5ml/½ tsp baking powder
2 eggs, beaten
2.5ml/½ tsp vanilla essence
115g/4oz/1 cup skinned hazelnuts, roughly chopped

1 Preheat the oven to 180°C/350°F/Gas 4. Grease a 20cm/8in square baking tin.

2 In a heatproof bowl set over a pan of barely simmering water, melt the chocolate and butter or margarine. Remove the bowl from the heat.

3 Add the sugar, flour, baking powder, eggs, vanilla and half of the hazelnuts to the melted mixture and stir well with a wooden spoon.

4 Pour the mixture into the prepared tin. Bake in the oven for 10 minutes, then sprinkle the reserved hazelnuts over the top. Return to the oven and continue baking until firm to the touch, about 25 minutes.

5 Cool in the tin, set on a wire rack for 10 minutes, then unmould on to the rack and cool completely. Cut into squares before serving.

Fruity Tea bread

Serve this bread thinly sliced, toasted or plain, with butter or cream cheese and jam.

Makes one 23 x 13cm/9 x 5in loaf

225g/8oz/2 cups plain flour
115g/4oz/generous ½ cup caster sugar
15ml/1 tbsp baking powder
2.5ml/½ tsp salt
grated rind of 1 large orange
160ml/5½fl oz/generous ⅔ cup fresh orange juice
2 eggs, lightly beaten
75g/3oz/6 tbsp butter or margarine, melted
115g/4oz/1 cup fresh cranberries or bilberries
50g/2oz/½ cup chopped walnuts

1 Preheat the oven to 180°C/350°F/Gas 4. Then line a 23 x 13cm/9 x 5in loaf tin with greaseproof paper and grease the paper.

2 Sift the flour, sugar, baking powder and salt into a mixing bowl. Then stir in the orange rind. Make a well in the centre and add the fresh orange juice, eggs and melted butter or margarine. Stir from the centre until the ingredients are blended; do not overmix. Add the berries and walnuts and stir until blended.

3 Transfer the mixture to the prepared tin and bake until a skewer inserted in the centre of the loaf comes out clean, about 45–50 minutes. Leave to cool in the tin for 10 minutes before transferring to a wire rack to cool completely.

Date and Pecan Loaf

Walnuts may be used instead of pecan nuts to make this luxurious tea bread.

Makes one 23 x 13cm/9 x 5in loaf

175g/6oz/1 cup chopped stoned dates
175ml/6fl oz/¾ cup boiling water
50g/2oz/4 tbsp unsalted butter, at room temperature
50g/2oz/⅓ cup dark brown sugar
50g/2oz/¼ cup caster sugar
1 egg, at room temperature
30ml/2 tbsp brandy
165g/5½oz/generous ¼ cup plain flour
10ml/2 tsp baking powder
2.5ml/½ tsp salt
4ml/¾ tsp freshly grated nutmeg
75g/3oz/¾ cup coarsely chopped pecan nuts

1 Place the dates in a bowl and pour over the boiling water. Set aside to cool. Preheat the oven to 180°C/350°F/Gas 4. Line a 23 x 13cm/9 x 5in loaf tin with greaseproof paper and then grease the paper.

2 With an electric mixer, cream the butter and sugars until light and fluffy. Beat in the egg and brandy, then set aside.

3 Sift the flour, baking powder, salt and nutmeg together, at least three times. Fold the dry ingredients into the sugar mixture in three batches, alternating with the dates and water. Fold in the nuts.

4 Pour the mixture into the prepared tin and bake until a skewer inserted in the centre comes out clean, about 45–50 minutes. Leave the loaf to cool in the tin for 10 minutes before transferring to a wire rack to cool completely.

Wholemeal Banana Nut Loaf

A hearty and filling loaf, this would be ideal as a winter tea-time treat.

Makes one 23 x 13cm/9 x 5in loaf

115g/4oz/½ cup butter, at room temperature
115g/4oz/generous ½ cup caster sugar
2 eggs, at room temperature
115g/4oz/1 cup plain flour
5ml/1 tsp bicarbonate of soda
1.5ml/¼ tsp salt
5ml/1 tsp ground cinnamon
50g/2oz/½ cup wholemeal flour
3 large ripe bananas
5ml/1 tsp vanilla essence
50g/2oz/½ cup chopped walnuts

1 Preheat the oven to 180°C/350°F/Gas 4. Line the base and sides of a 23 x 13cm/9 x 5in loaf tin with greaseproof paper and grease the paper.

2 With an electric mixer, cream the butter and sugar together until light and fluffy. Add the eggs, one at a time, beating well after each addition.

3 Sift the plain flour, bicarbonate of soda, salt and cinnamon over the butter mixture and stir to blend. Then stir in the wholemeal flour.

4 With a fork, mash the bananas to a purée, then stir into the mixture. Stir in the vanilla and nuts.

5 Pour the mixture into the prepared tin and spread level. Bake until a skewer inserted in the centre comes out clean, about 50–60 minutes. Leave to stand for 10 minutes before transferring to a wire rack to cool completely.

Apricot Nut Loaf

Apricots, raisins and walnuts combine to make a lovely light tea bread.

Makes one 23 x 13cm/9 x 5in loaf

115g/4oz/½ cup dried apricots
1 large orange
75g/3oz/generous ½ cup raisins
150g/5oz/⅔ cup caster sugar
85ml/5½ tbsp/⅓ cup oil
2 eggs, lightly beaten
250g/9oz/generous 2 cups plain flour
10ml/2 tsp baking powder
2.5ml/½ tsp salt
5ml/1 tsp bicarbonate of soda
50g/2oz/½ cup chopped walnuts

1 Place the apricots in a bowl, cover with lukewarm water and leave to stand for 30 minutes. Preheat the oven to 180°C/350°F/Gas 4. Line a 23 x 13cm/9 x 5in loaf tin with greaseproof paper and grease the paper.

2 With a vegetable peeler, remove the orange rind, leaving the pith. Chop the strips finely.

3 Drain the apricots and chop coarsely. Place in a bowl with the orange rind and raisins. Squeeze the peeled orange. Measure the juice and add enough hot water to obtain 175ml/6fl oz/¾ cup liquid. Add the orange juice mixture to the apricot mixture. Stir in the sugar, oil and eggs. Set aside.

4 In another bowl, sift together the flour, baking powder, salt and bicarbonate of soda. Fold the flour mixture into the apricot mixture in three batches, then stir in the walnuts.

5 Spoon the mixture into the prepared tin and bake until a skewer inserted in the centre of the loaf comes out clean, about 55–60 minutes. If the loaf browns too quickly, protect the top with a sheet of foil. Cool in the tin for 10 minutes, then transfer to a wire rack to cool completely.

Bilberry Tea bread

A lovely crumbly topping makes this tea bread extra special.

Makes 8 pieces

50g/2oz/4tbsp butter or margarine, at room temperature
175g/6oz/¾ cup caster sugar
1 egg, at room temperature
120ml/4fl oz/½ cup milk
225g/8oz/2 cups plain flour
10ml/2 tsp baking powder
2.5ml/½ tsp salt
275g/10oz/¾ cup fresh bilberries, or blueberries

For the topping

115g/4oz/½ cup sugar
40g/1½oz/⅓ cup plain flour
2.5ml/½ tsp ground cinnamon
50g/2oz/4 tbsp butter, cut into pieces

1 Preheat the oven to 190°C/375°F/Gas 5. Grease a 23cm/9in baking dish.

2 With an electric mixer, cream the butter or margarine with the sugar until light and fluffy. Add the egg, beat to combine, then mix in the milk until well blended.

3 Sift over the flour, baking powder and salt and stir just enough to blend the ingredients. Add the berries and stir. Transfer to the baking dish.

4 For the topping, place the sugar, flour, cinnamon and butter in a mixing bowl. Cut in with a pastry blender until the mixture resembles coarse breadcrumbs. Sprinkle the topping over the mixture in the baking dish. Bake until a skewer inserted in the centre comes out clean, about 45 minutes. Serve warm or cold.

Dried Fruit Loaf

Use any combination of dried fruit you like in this delicious tea bread.

Makes one 23 x 13cm/9 x 5in loaf

450g/1lb/2¾ cups mixed dried fruit, such as currants, raisins, chopped dried apricots and dried cherries
300ml/½ pint/1¼ cups cold strong tea
200g/7oz/generous 1 cup dark brown sugar
grated rind and juice of 1 small orange
grated rind and juice of 1 lemon
1 egg, lightly beaten
200g/7oz/1¾ cups plain flour
15ml/1 tbsp baking powder
1.5ml/¼ tsp salt

1 In a bowl, mix the dried fruit with the cold tea and leave to soak overnight.

2 Preheat the oven to 180°C/350°F/Gas 4. Line the base and sides of a 23 x 13cm/9 x 5in loaf tin with greaseproof paper and grease the paper.

3 Strain the fruit, reserving the liquid. In a bowl, combine the sugar, orange and lemon rind, and fruit. Pour the orange and lemon juice into a measuring jug; if the quantity is less than 250ml/8fl oz/1 cup, then top up with the soaking liquid. Stir the citrus juices and egg into the dried fruit mixture.

4 Sift the flour, baking powder and salt together into another bowl. Stir into the fruit mixture until blended.

5 Transfer to the tin and bake until a skewer inserted in the centre comes out clean; about 1¼ hours. Leave in the tin for 10 minutes before unmoulding.

Corn Bread

Serve this bread as an accompaniment to a meal, with soup, or take it on a picnic.

Makes one 23 x 13cm/9 x 5in loaf

115g/4oz/1 cup plain flour
65g/2½oz/generous ¼ cup caster sugar
5ml/1 tsp salt
15ml/1 tbsp baking powder
175g/6oz/scant 1½ cups cornmeal or polenta
350ml/12fl oz/1½ cups milk
2 eggs
75g/3oz/6 tbsp butter, melted
115g/4oz/½ cup margarine, melted

1 Preheat the oven to 200°C/400°F/Gas 6. Then line a 23 x 13cm/9 x 5in loaf tin with greaseproof paper and grease the paper.

2 Sift the flour, sugar, salt and baking powder into a mixing bowl. Add the cornmeal or polenta and stir to blend. Make a well in the centre. Whisk together the milk, eggs, melted butter and margarine. Pour the mixture into the well. Stir until just blended; do not overmix.

3 Pour into the tin and bake until a skewer inserted in the centre comes out clean, about 45 minutes. Serve hot or at room temperature.

Spicy Sweetcorn Bread

An interesting variation on basic corn bread; adjust the number of chillies used according to taste.

Makes 9 squares

3–4 whole canned chillies, drained
2 eggs
475ml/16fl oz/2 cups buttermilk
50g/2oz/4 tbsp butter, melted
50g/2oz/½ cup plain flour
5ml/1 tsp bicarbonate of soda
10ml/2 tsp salt
175g/6oz/scant 1½ cups cornmeal or polenta
350g/12oz/2 cups canned sweetcorn or frozen sweetcorn, thawed

1 Preheat the oven to 200°C/400°F/Gas 6. Line the base and sides of a 23cm/9in square cake tin with greaseproof paper and lightly grease the paper.

2 With a sharp knife, finely chop the canned chillies and set aside until needed.

3 In a large bowl, whisk the eggs until frothy, then whisk in the buttermilk. Add the melted butter.

4 Sift the flour, bicarbonate of soda and salt together into another large bowl. Fold into the buttermilk mixture in three batches, then fold in the cornmeal or polenta in three batches. Finally, fold in the chillies and sweetcorn.

5 Pour the mixture into the tin and bake until a skewer inserted in the centre comes out clean; about 25–30 minutes. Leave in the tin for 2–3 minutes before unmoulding. Cut into squares and serve warm.

Sweet Sesame Loaf

Lemon and sesame seeds make a great partnership in this light tea bread.

Makes one 23 x 13cm/9 x 5in loaf

75g/3oz/6 tbsp sesame seeds
275g/10oz/2½ cups plain flour
12.5ml/2½ tsp baking powder
5ml/1 tsp salt
50g/2oz/4 tbsp butter or margarine, at room temperature
130g/4½oz/scant ⅔ cup sugar
2 eggs, at room temperature
grated rind of 1 lemon
350ml/12fl oz/1½ cups milk

1 Preheat the oven to 180°C/350°F/Gas 4. Carefully line a 23 x 13cm/9 x 5in loaf tin with greaseproof paper and then grease the paper.

2 Reserve 25g/1oz/2 tbsp of the sesame seeds. Spread the rest on a baking sheet and bake in the oven until lightly toasted, about 10 minutes.

3 Sift the flour, baking powder and salt into a bowl. Stir in the toasted sesame seeds and set aside.

4 Cream the butter or margarine and sugar together until light and fluffy. Beat in the eggs, then stir in the lemon rind and milk. Pour the milk mixture over the dry ingredients and fold in with a large metal spoon until just blended.

5 Pour into the tin and sprinkle over the reserved sesame seeds. Bake until a skewer inserted in the centre comes out clean, about 1 hour. Cool in the tin for 10 minutes. Turn out on to a wire rack to cool completely.

Cardamom and Saffron Tea Loaf

An aromatic sweet bread ideal for afternoon tea, or lightly toasted for breakfast.

Makes one 900g/2lb loaf

generous pinch of saffron strands
750ml/1¼ pints/3 cups lukewarm milk
25g/1oz/2 tbsp butter
1kg/2¼ lb/8 cups strong plain flour
2 sachets easy-blend dried yeast
40g/1½ oz/3 tbsp caster sugar
6 cardamom pods, split open and seeds extracted
115g/4oz/scant ¾ cup raisins
30ml/2 tbsp clear honey
1 egg, beaten

1 Crush the saffron straight into a cup containing a little of the warm milk and leave to infuse for 5 minutes. Rub the butter into the flour, then mix in the yeast, sugar, cardamom seeds and raisins.

2 Beat the remaining milk with the honey and egg, then mix this into the flour, along with the saffron milk and strands, to form a firm dough. Turn out the dough and knead it on a lightly floured surface for 5 minutes.

3 Return the dough to the mixing bowl, cover with oiled clear film and leave in a warm place until doubled in size.

4 Preheat the oven to 200°C/400°F/Gas 6. Grease a 900g/2lb loaf tin. Turn the dough out on to a floured surface, punch down, knead for 3 minutes, then shape into a fat roll and fit into the tin. Cover with a sheet of lightly oiled clear film and stand in a warm place until the dough begins to rise again.

5 Bake the loaf for 25 minutes until golden brown and firm on top. Turn out on to a wire rack and as it cools brush the top with clear honey.

Courgette Tea bread

Like carrots, courgettes are a vegetable that work well in baking, adding moistness and lightness to the bread.

Makes one 23 x 13cm/9 x 5in loaf

50g/2oz/4 tbsp butter
3 eggs
250ml/8fl oz/1 cup vegetable oil
285g/10 1/2 oz/1 1/2 cups sugar
2 unpeeled courgettes, grated
275g/10oz/2 1/2 cups plain flour
10ml/2 tsp bicarbonate of soda
5ml/1 tsp baking powder
5ml/1 tsp salt
5ml/1 tsp ground cinnamon
5ml/1 tsp grated nutmeg
1.5ml/ 1/4 tsp ground cloves
115g/4oz/1 cup chopped walnuts

1 Preheat the oven to 180°C/350°F/Gas 4. Line the base and sides of a 23 x 13cm/9 x 5in loaf tin with greaseproof paper and grease the paper.

2 In a saucepan, melt the butter over a low heat. Set aside until needed.

3 With an electric mixer, beat the eggs and oil together until thick. Beat in the sugar, then stir in the melted butter and the courgettes. Set aside.

4 In another bowl, sift all the dry ingredients together three times. Carefully fold into the courgette mixture. Fold in the chopped walnuts.

5 Pour into the tin and bake until a skewer inserted in the centre comes out clean, about 60–70 minutes. Leave to stand for 10 minutes before turning out on to a wire rack to cool.

Mango Tea bread

A delicious tea bread with an exotic slant – baked with juicy ripe mango.

Makes two 23 x 13cm/9 x 5in loaves

275g/10oz/2 1/2 cups plain flour
10ml/2 tsp bicarbonate of soda
10ml/2 tsp ground cinnamon
2.5ml/ 1/2 tsp salt
115g/4oz/ 1/2 cup margarine, at room temperature
3 eggs, at room temperature
285g/10 1/2 oz/1 1/2 cups sugar
120ml/4fl oz/ 1/2 cup vegetable oil
1 large ripe mango, peeled and chopped
85g/3 1/4 oz/generous 1 1/2 cups desiccated coconut
65g/2 1/2 oz/ 1/2 cup raisins

1 Preheat the oven to 180°C/350°F/Gas 4. Line the base and sides of two 23 x 13cm/9 x 5in loaf tins with greaseproof paper and grease the paper.

2 Sift together the flour, bicarbonate of soda, cinnamon and salt. Set aside until needed.

3 Cream the margarine until soft. Beat in the eggs and sugar until light and fluffy. Beat in the oil.

4 Fold the dry ingredients into the creamed ingredients in three batches, then fold in the mango, two-thirds of the coconut and the raisins.

5 Spoon the batter into the tins. Sprinkle over the remaining coconut. Bake until a skewer inserted in the centre comes out clean, about 50–60 minutes. Leave to stand for 10 minutes before turning out on to a wire rack to cool completely.

American-style Corn Sticks

If you don't have a corn-stick mould, use éclair tins or a bun tray and reduce the cooking time by 10 minutes.

Makes 6

1 egg
120ml/4fl oz/½ cup milk
15ml/1 tbsp vegetable oil
115g/4oz/scant 1 cup cornmeal or polenta
50g/2oz/½ cup plain flour
10ml/2 tsp baking powder
45ml/3 tbsp caster sugar

1 Preheat the oven to 190°C/375°F/Gas 5. Grease a cast-iron corn-stick mould.

2 Beat the egg in a small bowl. Stir in the milk and vegetable oil, and set aside.

3 In a mixing bowl, stir together the cornmeal or polenta, flour, baking powder and sugar. Pour in the egg mixture and stir with a wooden spoon to combine.

4 Spoon the mixture into the prepared mould. Bake until a skewer inserted in the centre of a corn stick comes out clean, about 25 minutes. Cool in the mould on a wire rack for 10 minutes before unmoulding.

Savoury Sweetcorn Bread

For a spicy bread, stir 30ml/2 tbsp chopped fresh chillies into the mixture with the cheese and sweetcorn.

Makes 9

2 eggs, lightly beaten
250ml/8fl oz/1 cup buttermilk
115g/4oz/1 cup plain flour
115g/4oz/scant 1 cup cornmeal or polenta
10ml/2 tsp baking powder
2.5ml/½ tsp salt
15ml/1 tbsp caster sugar
115g/4oz/1 cup Cheddar cheese, grated
225g/8oz/1⅓ cups sweetcorn, fresh or frozen and thawed

1 Preheat the oven to 200°C/400°F/Gas 6. Then grease a 23cm/9in square baking tin.

2 Combine the eggs and buttermilk in a small bowl and whisk until well mixed. Set aside.

3 In another bowl, stir together the flour, cornmeal or polenta, baking powder, salt and sugar. Add the egg mixture and stir with a wooden spoon to combine. Stir in the cheese and sweetcorn.

4 Pour the mixture into the baking tin. Bake until a skewer inserted in the centre comes out clean, about 25 minutes. Unmould the bread on to a wire rack and leave to cool. Cut into squares before serving.

Herb Popovers

Popovers are delicious flavoured with herbs, and served as a snack or starter.

Makes 12

3 eggs
250ml/8fl oz/1 cup milk
25g/1oz/2 tbsp butter, melted
75g/3oz/¾ cup plain flour
1.5ml/¼ tsp salt
1 small sprig each mixed fresh herbs, such as chives, tarragon, dill and parsley

1 Preheat the oven to 220°C/425°F/Gas 7. Grease 12 small ramekins or individual baking cups.

2 With an electric mixer, beat the eggs until blended. Beat in the milk and melted butter. Sift together the flour and salt, then beat into the egg mixture to combine thoroughly.

3 Strip the herb leaves from the stems and chop finely. Mix together and measure out 30ml/2 tbsp. Stir the measured herbs into the batter.

4 Half-fill the prepared ramekins or baking cups. Bake until golden; 25–30 minutes. Do not open the oven door during baking time or the popovers may collapse. For drier popovers, pierce each one with a knife after 30 minutes baking time and then bake for a further 5 minutes. Serve the herb popovers hot.

Cheese Popovers

Serve these popovers simply as an accompaniment to a meal, or make a filling and serve them as a starter.

Makes 12

3 eggs
250ml/8fl oz/1 cup milk
25g/1oz/2 tbsp butter, melted
75g/3oz/¾ cup plain flour
1.5ml/¼ tsp salt
1.5ml/¼ tsp paprika
25g/1oz/⅓ cup freshly grated Parmesan cheese

1 Preheat the oven to 220°C/425°F/Gas 7. Grease 12 small ramekins or individual baking cups.

2 With an electric mixer, beat the eggs until blended. Beat in the milk and melted butter. Sift together the flour, salt and paprika, then beat into the egg mixture. Add the Parmesan cheese and stir in.

3 Half-fill the prepared cups and bake until golden, about 25–30 minutes. Do not open the oven door or the popovers may collapse. For drier popovers, pierce each one with a knife after about 30 minutes baking time and then bake for another 5 minutes. Serve hot.

Sweet Potato and Raisin Bread

Serve buttered slices of this subtly-spiced loaf at coffee or tea time.

Makes one 900g/2lb loaf

350g/12oz/3 cups flour
10ml/2tsp baking powder
2.5ml/½ tsp salt
5ml/1 tsp ground cinnamon
2.5ml/½ tsp grated nutmeg
450g/1lb mashed cooked sweet potatoes
90g/3½ oz light brown sugar
115g/4oz/½ cup butter or margarine, melted and cooled
3 eggs, beaten
75g/3oz/generous ½ cup raisins

1 Preheat the oven to 180°C/350°F/Gas 4. Grease a 900g/2lb loaf dish or tin.

2 Sift the flour, baking powder, salt, cinnamon, and nutmeg into a small bowl. Set aside.

3 With an electric mixer, beat the mashed sweet potatoes with the brown sugar, butter or margarine, and eggs until well mixed.

4 Add the flour mixture and the raisins. Stir with a wooden spoon until the flour is just mixed in.

5 Transfer the batter to the prepared dish or tin. Bake until a skewer inserted in the centre of the loaf comes out clean, about 1–1¼ hours.

6 Let the bread cool in the pan on a wire rack for 15 minutes, then unmould from the dish or tin on to the wire rack and leave to cool completely.

Lemon and Walnut Tea bread

Beaten egg whites give this citrus-flavour loaf a lovely light and crumbly texture.

Makes one 23 x 13cm/9 x 5in loaf

115g/4oz/½ cup butter or margarine, at room temperature
90g/3½oz/½ cup sugar
2 eggs, at room temperature, separated
grated rind of 2 lemons
30ml/2 tbsp lemon juice
215g/7½oz/scant 2 cups plain flour
10ml/2 tsp baking powder
120ml/4fl oz/½ cup milk
50g/2oz/½ cup chopped walnuts
1.5ml/¼ teaspoon salt

1 Preheat the oven to 180°C/350°F/Gas 4. Then line a 23 x 13cm/9 x 5in loaf tin with greaseproof paper and grease the paper.

2 Cream the butter or margarine with the sugar until light and fluffy. Beat in the egg yolks. Add the lemon rind and juice and stir until blended. Set aside.

3 In another bowl, sift together the flour and baking powder three times. Fold into the butter mixture in three batches, alternating with the milk. Fold in the walnuts. Set aside.

4 Beat the egg whites and salt until stiff peaks form. Fold a large spoonful of the egg whites into the walnut mixture to lighten it. Fold in the remaining egg whites carefully until the mixture is just blended.

5 Pour the batter into the prepared tin and bake until a skewer inserted in the centre of the loaf comes out clean, about 45–50 minutes. Cool in the tin for 5 minutes before turning out on to a wire rack to cool completely.

Date and Nut Maltloaf

Choose any type of nut you like to include in this very rich and fruit-packed tea bread.

Makes two 450g/1lb loaves

300g/11oz/2 cups strong plain flour
275g/10oz/2 cups strong plain wholemeal flour
5ml/1 tsp salt
75g/3oz/6 tbsp soft brown sugar
1 sachet easy-blend dried yeast
50g/2oz/4 tbsp butter or margarine
15ml/1 tbsp black treacle
60ml/4 tbsp malt extract
scant 250ml/8fl oz/1 cup lukewarm milk
115g/4oz/½ cup chopped dates
50g/2oz/½ cup chopped nuts
75g/3oz/generous ½ cup sultanas
75g/3oz/generous ½ cup raisins
30ml/2 tbsp clear honey, to glaze

1 Sift the flours and salt into a large bowl, then tip in the wheat flakes from the sieve. Stir in the sugar and yeast.

2 Put the butter or margarine in a small pan with the treacle and malt extract. Stir over a low heat until melted. Leave to cool, then combine with the milk.

3 Stir the milk mixture into the dry ingredients and knead thoroughly for 15 minutes until the dough is elastic.

4 Knead in the fruits and nuts. Transfer the dough to an oiled bowl, cover with clear film and leave in a warm place for about 1½ hours, until the dough has doubled in size.

5 Grease two 450g/1lb loaf tins. Knock back the dough and knead lightly. Divide in half, form into loaves and place in the tins. Cover and leave in a warm place for 30 minutes, until risen. Meanwhile, preheat the oven to 190°C/375°F/Gas 5.

6 Bake for 35–40 minutes, until well risen. Cool on a wire rack. Brush with honey while warm.

Orange Wheatloaf

Perfect just with butter as a breakfast tea bread and lovely for banana sandwiches.

Makes one 450g/1lb loaf

275g/10oz/2¼ cups wholemeal plain flour
2.5ml/½ tsp salt
25g/1oz/2 tbsp butter
25g/1oz/2 tbsp soft light brown sugar
½ sachet easy-blend dried yeast
grated rind and juice of ½ orange

1 Sift the flour into a large bowl and return any wheat flakes from the sieve. Add the salt and rub in the butter lightly with your fingertips.

2 Stir in the sugar, yeast and orange rind. Pour the orange juice into a measuring jug and use hot water to make up to 200ml/7fl oz/scant 1 cup (the liquid should not be more than hand hot).

3 Stir the liquid into the flour and mix to a soft ball of dough. Knead gently on a lightly floured surface until quite smooth and elastic.

4 Place the dough in a greased 450g/1lb loaf tin and leave in a warm place until nearly doubled in size. Preheat the oven to 220°C/425°F/Gas 7.

5 Bake the bread for 30–35 minutes, or until it sounds hollow when tapped underneath. Tip out of the tin and cool on a wire rack.

Orange and Honey Tea bread

Honey gives a special flavour to this tea bread. Serve just with a scraping of butter.

Makes one 23 x 13cm/9 x 5in loaf

385g/13$^1/_2$oz/scant 3$^1/_2$cups plain flour
12.5ml/2$^1/_2$ tsp baking powder
2.5ml/$^1/_2$ tsp bicarbonate of soda
2.5ml/$^1/_2$ tsp salt
25g/1oz/2 tbsp margarine
250ml/8fl oz/1 cup clear honey
1 egg, at room temperature, lightly beaten
25ml/1$^1/_2$ tbsp grated orange rind
175ml/6fl oz/$^3/_4$ cup freshly squeezed orange juice
115g/4oz/1 cup chopped walnuts

1 Preheat the oven to 160°C/325°F/Gas 3. Line the base and sides of a 23 x 13cm/9 x 5in loaf tin with greaseproof paper and grease the paper.

2 Sift the flour, baking powder, bicarbonate of soda and salt together in a bowl.

3 Cream the margarine until soft. Stir in the honey until blended, then stir in the egg. Add the orange rind and stir to combine thoroughly.

4 Fold the flour mixture into the honey and egg mixture in three batches, alternating with the orange juice. Stir in the chopped walnuts.

5 Pour into the prepared tin and bake in the oven until a skewer inserted in the centre comes out clean, about 60–70 minutes. Leave for 10 minutes before turning out on to a wire rack to cool completely.

Apple Loaf

Ring the changes with this loaf by using different nuts and dried fruit.

Makes one 23 x 13cm/9 x 5in loaf

1 egg
250ml/8fl oz/1 cup bottled or home-made apple sauce
50g/2oz/4 tbsp butter or margarine, melted
100g/3$^3/_4$oz/scant $^3/_4$ cup dark brown sugar
45g/1$^3/_4$oz/scant $^1/_4$ cup caster sugar
275g/10oz/2$^1/_2$ cups plain flour
10ml/2 tsp baking powder
2.5ml/$^1/_2$ tsp bicarbonate of soda
2.5ml/$^1/_2$ tsp salt
5ml/1 tsp ground cinnamon
2.5ml/$^1/_2$ tsp grated nutmeg
65g/2$^1/_2$oz/$^1/_2$ cup currants or raisins
50g/2oz/$^1/_2$ cup pecan nuts or walnuts, chopped

1 Preheat the oven to 180°C/350°F/Gas 4. Line the base and sides of a 23 x 13cm/9 x 5in loaf tin with greaseproof paper and grease the paper.

2 Break the egg into a bowl and beat lightly. Stir in the apple sauce, butter or margarine and both sugars. Set aside.

3 In another bowl, sift together the flour, baking powder, bicarbonate of soda, salt, cinnamon and nutmeg. Fold the dry ingredients, including the currants or raisins and the nuts, into the apple sauce mixture in three batches.

4 Pour into the prepared tin and bake in the oven until a skewer inserted in the centre of the loaf comes out clean, about 1 hour. Leave to stand in the tin for 10 minutes, then turn out on to a wire rack to cool completely.

Fruit and Brazil Nut Tea bread

Mashed bananas are a classic ingredient in tea breads, and help to create a moist texture.

Makes one 23 x 13cm/9 x 5in loaf

225g/8oz/2 cups plain flour
10ml/2 tsp baking powder
5ml/1 tsp mixed spice
115g/4oz/½ cup butter, diced
115g/4oz/¾ cup light soft brown sugar
2 eggs, lightly beaten
30ml/2 tbsp milk
30ml/2 tbsp dark rum
2 bananas, peeled and mashed
115g/4oz/½ cup dried figs, chopped
50g/2oz/½ cup brazil nuts, chopped

To decorate

8 whole brazil nuts
4 whole dried figs, halved
30ml/2 tbsp apricot jam
5ml/1 tsp dark rum

1 Preheat the oven to 180°C/350°F/Gas 4. Grease and base-line a 23 x 13cm/9 x 5in loaf tin. Sift the flour, baking powder and mixed spice into a bowl. Rub in the butter until the mixture resembles fine breadcrumbs. Stir in the sugar.

2 Make a well in the centre and work in the eggs, milk and rum until combined. Stir in the remaining ingredients and transfer to the loaf tin.

3 Press the whole brazil nuts and halved figs gently into the mixture, to form an attractive pattern. Bake for 1¼ hours, or until a skewer inserted in the centre comes out clean. Cool in the tin for 10 minutes, then transfer to a wire rack.

4 Heat the jam and rum together in a small saucepan. Increase the heat and boil for 1 minute. Remove from the heat and pass through a fine sieve. Cool the glaze slightly, brush over the warm cake, and leave to cool completely.

Glazed Banana Spiced Loaf

The lemony glaze perfectly sets off the flavours in this banana tea bread.

Makes one 23 x 13cm/9 x 5in loaf

115g/4oz/½ cup butter, at room temperature
165g/5½oz/generous ⅔ cup caster sugar
2 eggs, at room temperature
215g/7½oz/scant 2 cups plain flour
5ml/1 tsp salt
5ml/1 tsp bicarbonate of soda
2.5ml/½ tsp grated nutmeg
1.5ml/¼ tsp mixed spice
1.5ml/¼ tsp ground cloves
175ml/6fl oz/¾ cup soured cream
1 large ripe banana, mashed
5ml/1 tsp vanilla essence

For the glaze

115g/4oz/1 cup icing sugar
15–30ml/1–2 tbsp lemon juice

1 Preheat the oven to 180°C/350°F/Gas 4. Line a 23 x 13cm/9 x 5in loaf tin with greaseproof paper and grease the paper.

2 Cream the butter and sugar until light and fluffy. Add the eggs, one at a time, beating well after each addition.

3 Sift together the flour, salt, bicarbonate of soda, nutmeg, mixed spice and cloves. Add to the butter mixture and stir to combine well. Add the soured cream, banana and vanilla and mix to just blend. Pour into the prepared tin.

4 Bake until the top springs back when touched lightly, about 45–50 minutes. Cool in the tin for 10 minutes. Turn out on to a wire rack.

5 For the glaze, combine the icing sugar and lemon juice, then stir until smooth. Place the cooled loaf on a rack set over a baking sheet. Pour the glaze over the loaf and allow to set.

Banana Bread

For a change, add 50–75g/2–3oz/½–¾ cup chopped walnuts with the dry ingredients or pecan nuts.

Makes one 21 x 11cm/8½ x 4½in loaf

200g/7oz/1¾ cups plain flour
11.5ml/2¼ tsp baking powder
2.5ml/½ tsp salt
4ml/¾ tsp ground cinnamon (optional)
60ml/4 tbsp wheatgerm
65g/2½oz/5 tbsp butter, at room temperature
115g/4oz/generous ½ cup caster sugar
4ml/¾ tsp grated lemon rind
3 ripe bananas, mashed
2 eggs, beaten

1 Preheat the oven to 180°C/350°F/Gas 4. Grease and flour a 21 x 11cm/8½ x 4½in loaf tin.

2 Sift the flour, baking powder, salt and cinnamon, if using, into a bowl. Stir in the wheatgerm.

3 In another bowl, combine the butter with the caster sugar and grated lemon rind. Beat thoroughly until the mixture is light and fluffy.

4 Add the mashed bananas and eggs, and mix well. Add the dry ingredients and blend quickly and evenly.

5 Spoon into the loaf tin. Bake for 50–60 minutes or until a wooden skewer inserted in the centre comes out clean. Cool in the tin for 5 minutes, then turn out on to a wire rack to cool completely.

Banana Orange Loaf

For the best banana flavour and a really good, moist texture, make sure the bananas are ripe for this cake.

Makes one 23 x 13cm/9 x 5in loaf

90g/3½oz/generous ⅔ cup wholemeal plain flour
90g/3½oz/generous ¾ cup plain flour
5ml/1 tsp baking powder
5ml/1 tsp ground mixed spice
45ml/3 tbsp flaked hazelnuts, toasted
2 large ripe bananas
1 egg
30ml/2 tbsp sunflower oil
30ml/2 tbsp clear honey
finely grated rind and juice of 1 small orange
4 orange slices, halved
10ml/2 tsp icing sugar

1 Preheat the oven to 180°C/350°F/Gas 4. Brush a 23 x 13cm/9 x 5in loaf tin with sunflower oil and line the base with non-stick baking paper.

2 Sift the flours with the baking powder and spice into a large bowl, adding any bran that is caught in the sieve. Stir the hazelnuts into the dry ingredients.

3 Peel and mash the bananas. Beat in the egg, oil, honey and the orange rind and juice. Stir evenly into the dry ingredients.

4 Spoon into the prepared tin and smooth the top. Bake for 40–45 minutes, or until firm and golden brown. Turn out on to a wire rack to cool.

5 Sprinkle the orange slices with the icing sugar and grill until golden. Use to decorate the cake.

Marmalade Tea bread

If you prefer, leave the top of the loaf plain and serve sliced and lightly buttered instead.

Makes one 22 x 11cm/8½ x 4½in loaf

200g/7oz/1¾ cups plain flour
5ml/1 tsp baking powder
6.5ml/1¼ tsp ground cinnamon
90g/3½oz/7 tbsp butter or margarine
50g/2oz/⅓ cup soft light brown sugar
60ml/4 tbsp chunky orange marmalade
1 egg, beaten
about 45ml/3 tbsp milk
60ml/4 tbsp glacé icing and shreds of orange and lemon rind, to decorate

1 Preheat the oven to 160°C/325°F/Gas 3. Lightly butter a 22 x 11cm/8½ x 4½in loaf tin, then line the base with greaseproof paper and grease the paper.

2 Sift the flour, baking powder and cinnamon together, toss in the butter, then rub in until the mixture resembles coarse breadcrumbs. Stir in the sugar.

3 In a separate bowl, mix together the marmalade, egg and most of the milk, then stir into the flour mixture to make a soft dropping consistency, adding more milk if necessary.

4 Transfer the mixture to the tin and bake for 1¼ hours, or until firm to the touch. Leave the cake to cool for 5 minutes, then turn on to a wire rack, peel off the lining paper, and leave to cool completely.

5 Drizzle the glacé icing over the top of the cake and decorate with the orange and lemon rind.

Cherry Marmalade Muffins

Purists say you should never serve a muffin cold, so enjoy these fresh from the oven.

Makes 12

225g/8oz/2 cups self-raising flour
5ml/1 tsp ground mixed spice
75g/3oz/scant ½ cup caster sugar
115g/4oz/½ cup glacé cherries, quartered
30ml/2 tbsp orange marmalade
150ml/¼ pint/⅔ cup milk
50g/2oz/4 tbsp sunflower margarine
marmalade, to glaze

1 Preheat the oven to 200°C/400°F/Gas 6. Lightly grease 12 deep muffin cups with oil.

2 Sift together the flour and spice, then stir in the sugar and glacé cherries.

3 Mix the marmalade with the milk and beat into the dry ingredients with the margarine. Spoon into the greased cups. Bake for 20–25 minutes, until golden brown and firm. Turn out on to a wire rack and brush the tops of the muffins, with warmed marmalade.

Spiced Date and Walnut Cake

Nuts and dates are a classic flavour combination. Use pecan nuts instead of walnuts, if you wish.

Makes one 900g/2lb cake

300g/11 oz/2¾ cups wholemeal self-raising flour
10ml/2 tsp mixed spice
150g/5oz/generous ¾ cup chopped dates
50g/2oz/½ cup chopped walnuts
60ml/4 tbsp sunflower oil
115g/4oz/¾ cup dark muscovado sugar
300ml/½ pint/1¼ cups milk
walnut halves, to decorate

1 Preheat the oven to 180°C/350°F/Gas 4. Line a 900g/2lb loaf tin with greaseproof paper and grease the paper.

2 Sift together the flour and spice, adding back any bran from the sieve. Stir in the dates and walnuts.

3 Mix the oil, sugar and milk, then stir evenly into the dry ingredients. Spoon into the loaf tin and arrange the walnut halves on top.

4 Bake the cake in the oven for about 45–50 minutes, or until golden brown and firm. Turn out the cake, remove the lining paper, and leave to cool on a wire rack.

Prune and Peel Rock Buns

The fruit content of these scones gives them plenty of flavour – and they're a low-fat option too!

Makes 12

225g/8oz/2 cups plain flour
10ml/2 tsp baking powder
75g/3oz/½ cup demerara sugar
50g/2oz/½ cup chopped ready-to-eat dried prunes
50g/2oz/⅓ cup chopped mixed peel
finely grated rind of 1 lemon
50ml/2fl oz/¼ cup sunflower oil
75ml/5 tbsp skimmed milk

1 Preheat the oven to 200°C/400°F/Gas 6. Lightly oil a large baking sheet. Sift together the flour and baking powder, then stir in the sugar, prunes, peel and lemon rind.

2 Mix the oil and milk, then stir into the mixture, to make a dough which just binds together.

3 Spoon into rocky heaps on the baking sheet and bake for 20 minutes, until golden. Leave to cool on a wire rack.

Raisin Bran Buns

Serve these buns warm or at room temperature, on their own, with butter, or with cream cheese.

Makes 15

50g/2oz/4 tbsp butter or margarine
40g/1½oz/⅓ cup plain flour
50g/2oz/½ cup wholemeal flour
7.5ml/1½ tsp bicarbonate of soda
1.5ml/¼ tsp salt
5ml/1 tsp ground cinnamon
25g/1oz/generous 1 cup bran
75g/3oz/generous ½ cup raisins
65g/2½oz/scant ½ cup dark brown sugar
50g/2oz/¼ cup caster sugar
1 egg
250ml/8fl oz/1 cup buttermilk
juice of ½ lemon

1 Preheat the oven to 200°C/400°F/Gas 6. Lightly grease 15 bun-tray cups. Put the butter or margarine in a saucepan and melt over a gentle heat. Set aside.

2 In a mixing bowl, sift together the flours, bicarbonate of soda, salt and cinnamon. Add the bran, raisins and sugars and stir until blended.

3 In another bowl, mix together the egg, buttermilk, lemon juice and melted butter. Add the buttermilk mixture to the dry ingredients and stir in lightly and quickly until just moistened. Do not mix until smooth.

4 Spoon the mixture into the prepared bun-tray cups, filling them almost to the top. Half-fill any empty cups with water. Bake until golden, about 15–20 minutes. Remove to a wire rack to cool slightly or serve immediately.

Raspberry Crumble Buns

The crumble topping adds an unusual twist to these lovely fruit buns.

Makes 12

175g/6oz/1½ cups plain flour
50g/2oz/¼ cup caster sugar
45g/1¾ oz/scant ⅓ cup light brown sugar
10ml/2 tsp baking powder
1.5ml/¼ tsp salt
5ml/1 tsp ground cinnamon
115g/4oz/½ cup butter, melted
1 egg
120ml/4fl oz/½ cup milk
150g/5oz/¾ cup fresh raspberries
grated rind of 1 lemon

For the crumble topping

25g/1oz/¼ cup finely chopped pecan nuts or walnuts
50g/2oz/⅓ cup dark brown sugar
45ml/3 tbsp plain flour
5ml/1 tsp ground cinnamon
45ml/3 tbsp butter, melted

1 Preheat the oven to 180°C/350°F/Gas 4. Lightly grease 12 bun-tray cups or use 12 paper cases. Sift the flour into a bowl. Add the sugars, baking powder, salt and cinnamon, and stir to blend.

2 Make a well in the centre. Place the butter, egg and milk in the well and mix until just combined. Stir in the raspberries and lemon rind. Spoon the mixture into the prepared bun tray, filling the cups almost to the top.

3 For the crumble topping, mix the nuts, dark brown sugar, flour and cinnamon in a bowl. Add the melted butter and stir to blend.

4 Spoon some of the crumble over each bun. Bake until browned, about 25 minutes. Transfer to a wire rack to cool slightly. Serve warm.

Banana and Pecan Muffins

As a variation on this recipe, substitute an equal quantity of walnuts for the pecan nuts.

Makes 8

150g/5oz/1¼ cups plain flour
7.5ml/1½ tsp baking powder
50g/2oz/4 tbsp butter or margarine, at room temperature
150g/5oz caster sugar
1 egg
5ml/1tsp teaspoon vanilla essence
3 bananas, mashed
50g/2oz/½ cup pecan nuts, chopped
75ml/5tbsp milk

1 Preheat the oven to 190°C/375°F/Gas 5. Lightly grease 8 deep muffin cups. Sift the flour and baking powder into a small bowl. Set aside.

2 With an electric mixer, cream the butter or margarine and sugar together. Add the egg and vanilla and beat until fluffy. Mix in the banana.

3 Add the pecan nuts. With the mixer on low speed, beat in the flour mixture alternately with the milk.

4 Spoon the mixture into the prepared muffin cups, filling them two-thirds full. Bake until golden brown and a skewer inserted into the centre of a muffin comes out clean, about 20–25 minutes.

5 Let the muffins cool in the cups on a wire rack for about 10 minutes. To loosen, run a knife gently around each muffin and unmould on to the wire rack. Leave to cool 10 minutes longer before serving.

Blueberry and Cinnamon Muffins

These moist and "moreish" muffins appeal equally to adults and children.

Makes 8

115g/4oz/1 cup plain flour
15ml/1tbsp baking powder
pinch of salt
65g/2½ oz/¼ cup light brown sugar
1 egg
175ml/6fl oz/¾ cup milk
45ml/3tbsp vegetable oil
10ml/2tsp ground cinnamon
115g/4oz/⅔ cup fresh or thawed frozen blueberries

1 Preheat the oven to 190°C/375°F/Gas 5. Lightly grease 8 deep muffin cups.

2 With an electric mixer, beat the first eight ingredients together until smooth. Fold in the blueberries.

3 Spoon the mixture into the muffin cups, filling them two-thirds full. Bake until a skewer inserted in the centre of a muffin comes out clean, about 25 minutes.

4 Let the muffins cool in the cups on a wire rack for about 10 minutes, then unmould them on to the wire rack and allow to cool completely, to serve slightly warm.

Carrot Buns

Carrots give these buns a lovely moist consistency, and a delightful taste too.

Makes 12

175g/6oz/$^3/_4$ cup margarine, at room temperature
90g/3$^1/_2$oz/generous $^1/_2$ cup dark brown sugar
1 egg, at room temperature
15ml/1 tbsp water
225g/8oz/1$^1/_2$ cups grated carrots
150g/5oz/1$^1/_4$ cups plain flour
5ml/1 tsp baking powder
2.5ml/$^1/_2$ tsp bicarbonate of soda
5ml/1 tsp ground cinnamon
1.5ml/$^1/_4$ tsp grated nutmeg
2.5ml/$^1/_2$ tsp salt

1 Preheat the oven to 180°C/350°F/Gas 4. Grease a 12-cup bun tray or use paper cases.

2 With an electric mixer, cream the margarine and sugar until light and fluffy. Beat in the egg and water, then stir in the carrots.

3 Sift over the flour, baking powder, bicarbonate of soda, cinnamon, nutmeg and salt. Stir to blend.

4 Spoon the mixture into the prepared bun tray, filling the cups almost to the top. Bake until the tops spring back when touched lightly, about 35 minutes. Leave to stand for about 10 minutes in the bun tray before transferring to a wire rack to cool completely.

Dried Cherry Buns

Dried cherries have a wonderful tart flavour, quite unlike glacé cherries.

Makes 16

250ml/8fl oz/1 cup plain yogurt
175g/6oz/$^3/_4$ cup dried cherries
115g/4oz/$^1/_2$ cup butter, at room temperature
175g/6oz/generous $^3/_4$ cup caster sugar
2 eggs, at room temperature
5ml/1 tsp vanilla essence
200g/7oz/generous 1$^3/_4$ cups plain flour
10ml/2 tsp baking powder
5ml/1 tsp bicarbonate of soda
1.5ml/$^1/_4$ tsp salt

1 In a mixing bowl, combine the yogurt and cherries. Cover and leave to stand for 30 minutes. Preheat the oven to 180°C/350°F/Gas 4. Grease 16 bun-tray cups or use paper cases.

2 With an electric mixer, cream the butter and sugar together until light and fluffy. Add the eggs, one at a time, beating well after each addition. Add the vanilla and the cherry mixture and stir to blend. Set aside.

3 In another bowl, sift together the flour, baking powder, bicarbonate of soda and salt. Fold into the cherry mixture in three batches.

4 Fill the prepared cups two-thirds full. For even baking, half-fill any empty cups with water. Bake until the tops spring back when touched lightly, about 20 minutes. Transfer to a wire rack to cool completely.

Chelsea Buns

A traditional English recipe, Chelsea buns enjoy wide popularity elsewhere in the world.

Makes 12

225g/8oz/2 cups strong white flour
2.5ml/½ tsp salt
40g/1½oz/3 tbsp unsalted butter
7.5ml/1½ tsp easy-blend dried yeast
120ml/4fl oz/½ cup milk
1 egg, beaten
75g/3oz/½ cup mixed dried fruit
25g/1oz/2½ tbsp chopped mixed peel
50g/2oz/⅓ cup soft light brown sugar
clear honey, to glaze

1 Preheat the oven to 190°C/375°F/Gas 5. Grease a 18cm/7in square tin. Sift together the flour and salt; rub in 25g/1oz/2 tbsp of the butter.

2 Stir in the yeast and make a central well. Slowly add the milk and egg, stirring, then beat until the dough leaves the sides of the bowl clean.

3 Knead the dough until smooth. Place in an oiled bowl, cover and set aside until doubled in size. Transfer to a floured surface and roll it out to a rectangle 30 x 23cm/12 x 9in.

4 Mix the dried fruits, peel and sugar. Melt the remaining butter and brush over the dough. Scatter over the fruit mixture, leaving a 2.5cm/1in border. Roll up the dough from a long side. Seal the edges, then cut into 12 slices.

5 Place the slices, cut-sides up, in the greased tin. Cover and set aside until doubled in size. Bake for 30 minutes, until a rich golden brown. Brush with honey and leave to cool slightly in the tin before turning out.

Sticky Nut Buns

These buns will be popular, so save time by making double the recipe and freezing half for another occasion.

Makes 12

160ml/5½ fl oz/generous ⅔ cup lukewarm milk
15ml/1 tbsp easy-blend dried yeast
30ml/2 tbsp caster sugar
450g/1lb/4 cups strong white flour
5ml/1 tsp salt
115g/4oz/½ cup cold butter, cut into small pieces
2 eggs, lightly beaten
finely grated rind of 1 lemon

For the topping and filling

275g/10oz/1¾ cups dark brown sugar
65g/2½oz/5 tbsp butter
120ml/4fl oz/½ cup water
75g/3oz/¾ cup chopped pecan nuts or walnuts
45ml/3 tbsp caster sugar
10ml/2 tsp ground cinnamon
165g/5½oz/generous 1 cup raisins

1 Preheat the oven to 180°C/350°F/Gas 4. Mix the milk, yeast and sugar and leave until frothy. Combine the flour and salt, and rub in the butter. Add the yeast mixture, eggs and lemon rind. Stir to a rough dough. Knead until smooth, then return to the bowl, cover and leave until doubled in size.

2 Cook the brown sugar, butter and water in a heavy saucepan until syrupy, about 10 minutes. Place 15ml/1 tbsp syrup in the base of twelve 4cm/½in muffin cups. Sprinkle a thin layer of nuts in each, reserving the remainder.

3 Punch down the dough; roll out to a 45 x 30cm/18 x 12in rectangle. Combine the caster sugar, cinnamon, raisins and reserved nuts. Sprinkle over the dough. Roll up tightly from a long edge and cut into 2.5cm/1in rounds. Place in the muffin cups, cut-sides up. Leave to rise for 30 minutes.

4 Bake until golden, about 25 minutes. Invert the tins on to a baking sheet, leave for 5 minutes, then remove the tins. Cool on a wire rack, sticky-sides up.

Oatmeal Buttermilk Muffins

These easy-to-make muffins make a healthy treat for breakfast, or a snack at any time.

Makes 12

75g/3oz/1 cup rolled oats
250ml/3fl oz/1 cup buttermilk
115g/4oz/1/2 cup butter, at room temperature
75g/3oz/1/2 cup dark brown sugar, firmly packed
1 egg, at room temperature
115g/4oz/1 cup flour
5ml/1 tsp baking powder
1.5m/1/4 tsp baking soda
25g/1oz/1/4 cup rains

1 In a bowl, combine the oats and buttermilk and leave to soak for 1 hour.

2 Grease a 12-cup muffin pan or use paper cases.

3 Preheat the oven to 200°C/400°F/Gas 6. With an electric mixer, cream the butter and sugar until light and fluffy. Beat in the egg.

4 In another bowl, sift together the flour, baking powder, bicarbonate of soda, and salt. Stir into the butter mixture, alternating with the oat mixture. Fold in the raisins. Do not overmix.

5 Fill the prepared cups two-thirds full. Bake until a cake tester inserted in the centre comes out clean, 20–25 minutes. Transfer to a rack to cool.

Pumpkin Muffins

Molasses adds a delicious flavour to these spicy muffins. For a change, add dried apricots instead of currants.

Makes 14

150g/5oz/2/3 cup butter or margarine, at room temperature
175g/6oz/3/4 cup dark brown sugar, firmly packed
112g/4oz/1/3 cup molasses
1 egg, at room temperature, beaten
225g/8oz/1 cup cooked or canned pumpkin
200g/7oz/1 3/4 cups flour
1.5ml/1/4 tsp salt
5ml/1 tsp bicarbonate of soda
10ml/1 tsp ground cinnamon
5ml/1 tsp grated nutmeg
50g/2oz/1/4 cup currants or raisins

1 Preheat the oven to 200°C/400°F/Gas 6. Grease 14 muffin cups or use paper cases.

2 With an electric mixer, cream the butter or margarine. Add the sugar and molasses and beat until light and fluffy.

3 Add the egg and pumpkin and stir until well blended.

4 Sift over the flour, salt, bicarbonate of soda, cinnamon, and nutmeg. Fold just enough to blend; do not overmix.

5 Fold in the currants or raisins.

6 Spoon the batter into the prepared muffin cups, filling them three-quarters full.

7 Bake for 12–15 minutes until the tops spring back when touched lightly. Serve warm or cold.

Blueberry Muffins

Hot blueberry muffins with a hint of vanilla are an American favourite for breakfast, brunch or tea.

Makes 12

350g/12oz/3 cups plain flour
10ml/2 tsp baking powder
1.5ml/¼ tsp salt
115g/4oz/½ cup caster sugar
2 eggs, beaten
300ml/½ pint/1¼ cups milk
115g/4oz/½ cup butter, melted
5ml/1 tsp vanilla essence
175g/6oz/1½ cups blueberries

1 Preheat the oven to 200°C/400°F/Gas 6. Grease a 12-cup muffin tin.

2 Sift the flour, baking powder and salt into a large mixing bowl and stir in the sugar.

3 Place the eggs, milk, butter and vanilla essence in a separate bowl and whisk together well.

4 Fold the egg mixture into the dry ingredients with a metal spoon, then gently stir in the blueberries.

5 Spoon the mixture into the muffin cups, filling them to just below the top. Place the muffin tin on the top shelf of the oven and bake for 20–25 minutes, until the muffins are well risen and lightly browned. Leave the muffins in the tin for about 5 minutes, and then turn them out on to a wire rack to cool. Serve warm or cold.

Apple and Cranberry Muffins

Not too sweet but good and spicy, these muffins will be a favourite with family and friends.

Makes 12

50g/2oz/4 tbsp butter
1 egg
90g/3½oz/½ cup caster sugar
grated rind of 1 orange
120ml/4fl oz/½ cup fresh orange juice
150g/5oz/1¼ cups plain flour
5ml/1 tsp baking powder
2.5ml/½ tsp bicarbonate of soda
5ml/1 tsp ground cinnamon
2.5ml/½ tsp grated nutmeg
2.5ml/½ tsp mixed spice
1.5ml/¼ tsp ground ginger
1.5ml/¼ tsp salt
1–2 eating apples
175g/6oz/1½ cups cranberries
50g/2oz/½ cup chopped walnuts
icing sugar, for dusting (optional)

1 Preheat the oven to 180°C/350°F/Gas 4. Grease a 12-cup muffin tin or use paper cases. Melt the butter over a gentle heat. Set aside to cool.

2 Place the egg in a mixing bowl and whisk lightly. Add the melted butter and whisk to combine, then add the sugar, orange rind and juice. Whisk to blend.

3 In a large bowl, sift together the flour, baking powder, bicarbonate of soda, spices and salt. Quarter, core and peel the apples. With a sharp knife, chop coarsely.

4 Make a well in the dry ingredients and pour in the egg mixture. With a spoon, stir until just blended. Add the apples, cranberries and walnuts and stir to blend.

5 Fill the cups three-quarters full and bake until the the tops spring back when touched lightly, about 25–30 minutes. Transfer to a wire rack to cool. Dust with icing sugar before serving, if desired.

Yogurt and Honey Muffins

For a more substantial texture, fold in 50g/2oz/½ cup chopped walnuts with the flour.

Makes 12

50g/2oz/4 tbsp butter
75ml/5 tbsp clear honey
250ml/8fl oz/1 cup plain yogurt
1 large egg, at room temperature
grated rind of 1 lemon
50ml/2fl oz/¼ cup lemon juice
150g/5oz/¼ cup plain flour
175g/6oz/½ cup wholemeal flour
7.5ml/1½ tsp bicarbonate of soda
1.5ml/¼ tsp grated nutmeg

1 Preheat the oven to 190°C/375°F/Gas 5. Grease a 12-cup muffin tin or use paper cases.

2 In a saucepan, melt the butter and honey. Remove from the heat and set aside to cool slightly.

3 In a bowl, whisk together the yogurt, egg, lemon rind and juice. Add the butter and honey mixture. Set aside.

4 In another bowl, sift together the dry ingredients. Fold them into the yogurt mixture to blend.

5 Fill the prepared cup two-thirds full. Bake until the tops spring back when touched lightly, about 20–25 minutes. Cool in the tin for 5 minutes before turning out. Serve warm or at room temperature.

Prune Muffins

Prunes bring a delightful moisture to these tasty and wholesome muffins.

Makes 12

1 egg
250ml/8fl oz/1 cup milk
120ml/4fl oz/½ cup vegetable oil
45g/1¾ oz/scant ¼ cup caster sugar
25g/1oz/2 tbsp dark brown sugar
275g/10oz/2½ cups plain flour
10ml/2 tsp baking powder
2.5ml/½ tsp salt
1.5ml/¼ tsp grated nutmeg
115g/4oz/½ cup cooked stoned prunes, chopped

1 Preheat the oven to 200°C/400°F/Gas 6. Grease a 12-cup muffin tin or use paper cases.

2 Break the egg into a mixing bowl and beat with a fork. Beat in the milk and oil. Stir in the sugars and set aside.

3 Sift the flour, baking powder, salt and nutmeg into a mixing bowl. Make a well in the centre, pour in the egg mixture and stir until moistened. Do not overmix; the batter should be slightly lumpy. Finally, fold in the prunes.

4 Fill the prepared cups two-thirds full. Bake until golden brown, about 20 minutes. Leave to stand for 10 minutes before turning out. Serve warm or at room temperature.

Crunchy Muesli Muffins

The muesli in these muffins gives them an unusual texture and makes them ideal to serve for breakfast.

Makes 10

150g/5oz/1¼ cups plain flour
12.5ml/2½ tsp baking powder
30ml/2 tbsp caster sugar
200g/7oz/1½ cups toasted oat cereal with raisins
250ml/8fl oz/1 cup milk
50g/2oz/4tbsp butter, melted, or corn oil
1 egg, beaten

1 Preheat the oven to 200°C/400°F/Gas 6. Grease 10 cups of a muffin tin or use paper cases.

2 Sift the flour, baking powder and sugar together into a large bowl. Add the oat cereal and stir to blend.

3 In a separate bowl, combine the milk, melted butter or corn oil and the beaten egg. Add to the dry ingredients. Stir until moistened, but do not overmix.

4 Spoon the mixture into the cups, leaving room for the muffins to rise. Half-fill any empty cups with water. Bake in the oven for 20 minutes, or until golden brown. Transfer to a wire rack to cool.

Raspberry Muffins

If you are using frozen raspberries, work quickly as the cold berries make the mixture solidify.

Makes 12

115g/4oz/1 cup self-raising flour
115g/4oz/1 cup wholemeal self-raising flour
45ml/3 tbsp caster sugar
2.5ml/½ tsp salt
2 eggs, beaten
200ml/7fl oz/scant 1 cup milk
50g/2oz/4 tbsp butter, melted
175g/6oz/1 cup raspberries, fresh or frozen (defrosted for less than 30 minutes)

1 Preheat the oven to 190°C/375°F/Gas 5. Lightly grease a 12-cup muffin tin, or use paper cases. Sift the dry ingredients together, then tip in any wheat flakes left in the sieve.

2 Beat the eggs, milk and melted butter together and stir into the dry ingredients to make a thick batter.

3 Stir the raspberries in gently. If you mix too much the raspberries begin to disintegrate and colour the dough. Spoon into the cups or paper cases.

4 Bake for 30 minutes, until well risen and just firm. Leave to cool in the tin placed on a wire rack. Serve warm or cool.

Scones

Traditionally, scones should be served with butter, clotted or whipped cream and jam.

Makes 10–12

225g/8oz/2 cups plain flour
15ml/1 tbsp baking powder
50g/2oz/4 tbsp butter, diced
1 egg, beaten
75ml/5 tbsp milk
1 beaten egg, to glaze

1 Preheat the oven to 220°C/425°F/Gas 7. Lightly butter a baking sheet. Sift the flour and baking powder together, then rub in the butter.

2 Make a well in the centre of the flour mixture, add the egg and milk and mix to a soft dough using a round-bladed knife.

3 Turn out the scone dough on to a floured surface, and knead very lightly until smooth.

4 Roll out the dough to about a 2cm/¾ in thickness and cut into 10 or 12 circles using a 5cm/2in plain or fluted cutter dipped in flour.

5 Transfer to the baking sheet, brush with egg, then bake for about 8 minutes, until risen and golden. Cool slightly on a wire rack before serving.

Drop Scones

If you place the cooked scones in a folded dish towel they will stay soft and moist.

Makes 8–10

115g/4oz/1 cup plain flour
5ml/1 tsp bicarbonate of soda
5ml/1 tsp cream of tartar
25g/1oz/2 tbsp butter, diced
1 egg, beaten
150ml/¼ pint/⅔ cup milk

1 Lightly grease a griddle or heavy-based frying pan, then preheat it.

2 Sift the flour, bicarbonate of soda and cream of tartar together, then rub in the butter until the mixture resembles breadcrumbs. Make a well in the centre, then stir in the egg and sufficient milk to give the consistency of double cream.

3 Drop spoonfuls of the mixture, spaced slightly apart, on to the griddle or frying pan. Cook over a steady heat for 2–3 minutes, until bubbles rise to the surface and burst.

4 Turn the scones over and cook for a further 2–3 minutes, until golden underneath. Serve warm with butter and honey.

Wholemeal Scones

Split these wholesome scones in two with a fork while still warm and spread with butter and jam, if you wish.

Makes 16

175g/6oz/¾ cup cold butter
350g/12oz/3 cups wholemeal flour
150g/5oz/1¼ cups plain flour
30ml/2 tbsp sugar
2.5ml/½ tsp salt
12.5ml/2½ tsp bicarbonate of soda
2 eggs
175g/6fl oz/¾ cup buttermilk
35g/1¼oz/¼ cup raisins

1 Preheat the oven to 200°C/400°F/Gas 6. Grease and flour a large baking sheet.

2 Cut the butter into small pieces. Combine all the dry ingredients in a bowl. Add the butter and rub in until the mixture resembles coarse breadcrumbs. Set aside.

3 In another bowl, whisk together the eggs and buttermilk. Set aside 30ml/2 tbsp for glazing, then stir the remaining egg mixture into the dry ingredients until it just holds together. Stir in the raisins.

4 Roll out the dough to about 2cm/¾in thickness. Stamp out circles with a biscuit cutter. Place on the baking sheet and brush with the glaze.

5 Bake until golden, about 12–15 minutes. Allow to cool slightly before serving.

Orange and Raisin Scones

Split these scones when cool and toast them under a preheated grill. Butter them while still hot.

Makes 16

275g/10oz/2½ cups plain flour
25ml/1½ tsp baking powder
60g/2¼oz/generous/¼ cup sugar
2.5ml/½ tsp salt
65g/2½oz/5 tbsp butter, diced
65g/2½oz/5 tbsp margarine, diced
grated rind of 1 large orange
50g/2oz/scant ½ cup raisins
120ml/4fl oz/½ cup buttermilk
milk, to glaze

1 Preheat the oven to 220°C/425°F/Gas 7. Grease and flour a large baking sheet.

2 Combine the dry ingredients in a large bowl. Add the butter and margarine and rub in until the mixture resembles coarse breadcrumbs.

3 Add the orange rind and raisins. Gradually stir in the buttermilk to form a soft dough. Roll out the dough to about a 2cm/¾in thickness. Stamp out circles with a biscuit cutter. Place on the baking sheet and brush the tops with milk.

4 Bake until golden, about 12–15 minutes. Serve hot or warm, with butter, or whipped or clotted cream and jam.

Cheese and Chive Scones

Feta cheese makes an excellent substitute for butter in these tangy savoury scones.

Makes 9

115g/4oz/1 cup self-raising flour
150g/5oz/1 cup wholemeal self-raising flour
2.5ml/½ tsp salt
75g/3oz feta cheese
15ml/1 tbsp chopped fresh chives
150ml/¼ pint/⅔ cup milk, plus extra to glaze
1.5ml/¼ tsp cayenne pepper

1 Preheat the oven to 200°C/400°F/Gas 6. Sift the flours and salt into a mixing bowl. Add any bran left in the sieve.

2 Crumble the feta cheese and rub into the dry ingredients. Stir in the chives, then add the milk and mix to a soft dough.

3 Turn out on to a floured surface and lightly knead until smooth. Roll out to a 2cm/¾ in thickness and stamp out scones with a 6cm/2½in biscuit cutter.

4 Transfer the scones to a non-stick baking sheet. Brush with milk, then sprinkle over the cayenne pepper. Bake in the oven for 15 minutes, or until golden brown. Serve warm or cold.

Sunflower Sultana Scones

Sunflower seeds give these wholesome fruit scones an interesting flavour and appealing texture.

Makes 10–12

225g/8oz/2 cups self-raising flour
5ml/1 tsp baking powder
25g/1oz/2 tbsp soft sunflower margarine
30ml/2 tbsp golden caster sugar
50g/2oz/scant ½ cup sultanas
30ml/2 tbsp sunflower seeds
150g/5oz/½ cup natural yogurt
about 30–45ml/2–3 tbsp skimmed milk

1 Preheat the oven to 230°C/450°F/Gas 8. Lightly oil a baking sheet. Sift the flour and baking powder into a bowl and rub in the margarine evenly.

2 Stir in the sugar, sultanas and half the sunflower seeds, then mix in the yogurt, with just enough milk to make a fairly soft, but not sticky, dough.

3 Roll out on a lightly floured surface to about a 2cm/¾ in thickness. Cut into 6cm/2½ in flower shapes or rounds with a biscuit cutter and lift on to the baking sheet.

4 Brush with milk and sprinkle with the reserved sunflower seeds, then bake for 10–12 minutes, until well risen and golden brown. Cool the scones on a wire rack. Serve split and spread with jam or low-fat spread.

Buttermilk Scones

If time is short, drop heaped tablespoonfuls of the mixture on to the baking sheet.

Makes 10

225g/8oz/2 cups plain flour
5ml/1 tsp baking powder
2.5ml/½ tsp bicarbonate of soda
5ml/1 tsp salt
50g/2oz/4 tbsp butter or margarine, chilled
175ml/6fl oz/¾ cup buttermilk

1 Preheat the oven to 220°C/425°F/Gas 7. Sift the flour, baking powder, bicarbonate of soda and salt into a mixing bowl. Cut in the butter or margarine with a fork until the mixture resembles coarse breadcrumbs.

2 Add the buttermilk and mix until well combined to form a soft dough. Turn the dough on to a lightly floured surface and knead for about 30 seconds.

3 Roll out the dough to a 1cm/½in thickness. Use a floured 6cm/2½in pastry cutter to cut out rounds. Transfer the rounds to a baking sheet and bake until golden brown, about 10–12 minutes. Serve hot with butter and honey.

Date Oven Scones

To ensure light, well-risen scones, don't handle the dough too much or roll it out too thinly.

Makes 12

225g/8oz/2 cups self-raising flour
pinch of salt
50g/2oz/4 tbsp butter
50g/2oz/¼ cup caster sugar
50g/2oz/⅓ cup chopped dates
150ml/¼ pint/⅔ cup milk
1 beaten egg, to glaze

1 Preheat the oven to 230°C/450°F/Gas 8. Sift the flour and salt into a bowl and, using a pastry blender or your fingers, rub in the butter until the mixture resembles fine breadcrumbs. Add the sugar and chopped dates, and stir to blend.

2 Make a well in the centre of the dry ingredients and add the milk. Stir with a fork until the mixture comes together in a fairly soft dough.

3 Turn the dough out on to a lightly floured surface and knead gently for 30 seconds. Roll it out to a 2cm/¾in thickness. Cut out circles with a biscuit cutter. Arrange them, not touching, on an ungreased baking sheet, then glaze with the beaten egg.

4 Bake in the oven for 8–10 minutes, or until well risen and golden brown. Using a palette knife, transfer the scones to a wire rack to cool completely.

Cheese and Marjoram Scones

A great success for a hearty tea. With savoury toppings, these scones can make a good basis for a light lunch.

Makes 18

115g/4oz/1 cup wholemeal flour
115g/4oz/1 cup self-raising flour
pinch of salt
45ml/1½oz/3 tbsp butter
1.5ml/¼ tsp dry mustard
10ml/2 tsp dried marjoram
50–75g/2–3oz/½–¾ cup finely grated Cheddar cheese
120ml/4fl oz/½ cup milk, or as required
50g/2oz/½ cup pecan nuts or walnuts, chopped

1 Gently sift the two flours into a bowl and add the salt. Cut the butter into small pieces, and rub into the flour until the mixture resembles fine breadcrumbs.

2 Add the mustard, marjoram and grated cheese, and mix in sufficient milk to make a soft dough. Knead the dough lightly.

3 Preheat the oven to 220°C/425°F/Gas 7. Lightly grease two or three baking sheets. Roll out the dough on a floured surface to about a 2cm/¾ in thickness and cut it out with a 5cm/2in square biscuit cutter. Place the scones, slightly apart, on the baking sheets.

4 Brush the scones with a little milk and then sprinkle the chopped pecan nuts or walnuts over the top. Bake for about 12 minutes. Serve warm, spread with butter.

Dill and Potato Cakes

The inclusion of dill in these potato cakes makes them quite irresistible.

Makes 10

225g/8oz/2 cups self-raising flour
40g/½oz/3 tbsp butter, softened
pinch of salt
15ml/1 tbsp finely chopped fresh dill
175g/6oz/scant 1 cup mashed potato, freshly made
30–45ml/2–3 tbsp milk

1 Preheat the oven to 230°C/450°F/Gas 8. Grease a baking sheet. Sift the flour into a bowl and add the butter, salt and dill. Mix in the mashed potato and enough milk to make a soft, pliable dough.

2 Roll out the dough on a well-floured surface until fairly thin. Cut into circles with a 7.5cm/3in biscuit cutter.

3 Place the potato cakes on the baking sheet, and bake for 20–25 minutes until risen and golden.

White Bread

There is nothing quite like the smell and taste of home-baked bread, eaten while still warm.

Makes two 23 x 13cm/9 x 5in loaves

50ml/2fl oz/¼ cup lukewarm water
15ml/1 tbsp active dried yeast
30ml/2 tbsp sugar
475ml/16fl oz/2 cups lukewarm milk
25g/1oz/2 tbsp butter or margarine, at room temperature
10ml/2 tsp salt
about 900g/2lb/8 cups strong flour

1 Combine the water, yeast and 15ml/1 tbsp of the sugar in a measuring jug and leave for 15 minutes until frothy.

2 Pour the milk into a large bowl. Add the remaining sugar, the butter or margarine, and salt. Stir in the yeast mixture, then stir in the flour, 150g/5oz/1¼ cups at a time, until a stiff dough is obtained.

3 Transfer the dough to a floured surface. Knead the dough until it is smooth and elastic, then place it in a large greased bowl, cover with a plastic bag, and leave to rise in a warm place until doubled in volume, about 2–3 hours.

4 Grease two 23 x 13cm/9 x 5in loaf tins. Punch down the dough and divide in half. Form into loaf shapes and place in the tins, seam-sides down. Cover and leave to rise again until almost doubled in volume, about 45 minutes. Meanwhile, preheat the oven to 190°C/375°F/Gas 5.

5 Bake until firm and brown, about 45–50 minutes. Turn out and tap the base of a loaf: if it sounds hollow the loaf is done. If necessary, return to the oven and bake for a few minutes longer. Turn out and cool on a wire rack.

Multigrain Bread

Try different flours, such as rye, cornmeal, buckwheat or barley to replace the wheatgerm and the soya flour.

Makes two 22 x 11cm/8½ x 4½in loaves

15ml/1 tbsp active dried yeast
50ml/2fl oz/¼ cup lukewarm water
65g/2½oz/¾ cup rolled oats
475ml/16fl oz/2 cups milk
10ml/2 tsp salt
50ml/2fl oz/¼ cup oil
50g/2oz/⅓ cup light brown sugar
30ml/2 tbsp honey
2 eggs, lightly beaten
25g/1oz wheatgerm
175g/6oz/1½ cups soya flour
350g/12oz/scant 2½ cups wholemeal flour
about 450g/1lb/4 cups strong flour

1 Combine the yeast and water, stir, and leave for about 15 minutes to dissolve. Place the oats in a large bowl. Scald the milk, then pour over the rolled oats. Stir in the salt, oil, sugar and honey. Leave until lukewarm.

2 Stir in the yeast mixture, eggs, wheatgerm, soya and wholemeal flours. Gradually stir in enough strong flour to obtain a rough dough. Transfer the dough to a floured surface and knead, adding flour if necessary, until smooth and elastic. Return to a clean bowl, cover and leave to rise in a warm place until doubled in volume, about 2½ hours.

3 Grease two 22 x 11cm/8½ x 4½in loaf tins. Punch down the risen dough and knead briefly. Then divide the dough into quarters. Roll each quarter into a cylinder 4cm/1½in thick. Twist together two cylinders and place in a tin; repeat for the remaining cylinders. Cover and leave to rise until doubled in volume again, about 1 hour. Meanwhile, preheat the oven to 190°C/375°F/Gas 5.

4 Bake until the bases sound hollow when tapped lightly, about 45–50 minutes. Turn out and cool on a wire rack.

Plaited Loaf

It doesn't take much effort to turn an ordinary dough mix into this work of art.

Makes one loaf

15ml/1 tbsp active dried yeast
5ml/1 tsp honey
250ml/8fl oz/1 cup lukewarm milk
50g/2oz/4 tbsp butter, melted
425g/15oz/3¾ cups strong flour
5ml/1 tsp salt
1 egg, lightly beaten
1 egg yolk, beaten with 5ml/1 tsp milk, to glaze

1 Combine the yeast, honey, milk and butter. Stir and leave for 15 minutes to dissolve.

2 In a large bowl, mix together the flour and salt. Make a central well; add the yeast mixture and egg. With a wooden spoon, stir from the centre, gradually incorporating the flour, to obtain a rough dough.

3 Transfer to a floured surface and knead until smooth and elastic. Place in a clean bowl, cover and leave to rise in a warm place until doubled in volume, about 1½ hours.

4 Grease a baking sheet. Punch down the dough and divide into three equal pieces. Roll each piece into a long thin strip. Begin plaiting with the centre strip, tucking in the ends. Cover loosely and leave to rise in a warm place for 30 minutes. Meanwhile, preheat the oven to 190°C/375°F/Gas 5. Brush the bread with the egg and milk glaze and bake until golden, about 40–45 minutes. Turn out on to a wire rack to cool.

Oatmeal Bread

A healthy, rustic-looking bread made with rolled oats as well as flour.

Makes two loaves

475ml/16fl oz/2 cups milk
25g/1oz/2 tbsp butter
50g/2oz/4 tbsp cup dark brown sugar
10ml/2 tsp salt
15ml/1 tbsp active dried yeast
50ml/2fl oz/¼ cup lukewarm water
400g/14oz/4 cups rolled oats
675–900g/1½–2lb/ 6–8 cups strong white flour

1 Scald the milk. Remove from the heat and stir in the butter, brown sugar and salt. Leave until lukewarm.

2 Combine the yeast and warm water in a large bowl and leave until frothy. Stir in the milk mixture. Add 275g/10oz/ 3 cups of the oats and enough flour to obtain a soft dough.

3 Transfer to a floured surface and knead until smooth and elastic. Place in a greased bowl, cover with a plastic bag, and leave until doubled in volume, about 2–3 hours.

4 Grease a large baking sheet. Transfer the dough to a lightly floured surface and divide in half. Shape into rounds. Place on the baking sheet, cover with a dish towel and leave to rise until doubled in volume, about 1 hour.

5 Preheat the oven to 200°C/400°F/Gas 6. Score the tops and sprinkle with the remaining oats. Bake until the bases sound hollow when tapped, about 45–50 minutes. Turn out on to wire racks to cool.

Country Bread

A filling bread made with a mixture of wholemeal and white flour.

Makes two loaves

350g/12oz/scant 2½ cups wholemeal flour
350g/12oz/3 cups plain flour
150g/5oz/1¼ cups strong plain flour
20ml/4 tsp salt
50g/2oz/4 tbsp butter, at room temperature
475ml/16fl oz/2 cups lukewarm milk

For the starter

15ml/1 tbsp active dried yeast
250ml/8fl oz/1 cup lukewarm water
150g/5oz/1¼ cups plain flour
1.5ml/¼ tsp caster sugar

1 Combine all the starter ingredients in a bowl. Cover and leave in a warm place for 2–3 hours.

2 Place the flours, salt and butter in a food processor and process just until blended, about 1–2 minutes. Stir together the milk and starter, then slowly pour into the processor, with the motor running, until the mixture forms a dough. Knead until smooth.

3 Place in an ungreased bowl, cover with a plastic bag, and leave to rise in a warm place until doubled in size, about 1½ hours. Knead again then return to the bowl and leave until tripled in size, about 1½ hours.

4 Grease a baking sheet. Divide the dough in half. Cut off one-third of the dough from each half and shape into four balls. Top each large ball with a small ball and press the centre with the handle of a wooden spoon to secure. Cover with a plastic bag, slash the top, and leave to rise.

5 Preheat the oven to 200°C/400°F/Gas 6. Dust the loaves with flour and bake until browned and the bases sound hollow when tapped, 45–50 minutes. Cool on a wire rack.

Wholemeal Rolls

To add interest when serving, make these individual rolls into different shapes if you wish.

Makes 12

15ml/2 tbsp active dried yeast
50ml/2fl oz/¼ cup lukewarm water
5ml/1 tsp caster sugar
175ml/6fl oz/¾ cup lukewarm buttermilk
1.5ml/¼ tsp bicarbonate of soda
5ml/1 tsp salt
40g/1½oz/3 tbsp butter, at room temperature
200g/7oz/scant 1½ cups wholemeal flour
150g/5oz/1¼ cups plain flour
1 beaten egg, to glaze

1 In a large bowl, combine the yeast, water and sugar. Stir, and leave for 15 minutes to dissolve.

2 Add the buttermilk, bicarbonate of soda, salt and butter and stir to blend. Stir in the wholemeal flour. Add just enough of the plain flour to obtain a rough dough.

3 Knead on a floured surface until smooth. Divide into three equal parts. Roll each into a cylinder, then cut in four.

4 Grease a baking sheet. Form the pieces into torpedo shapes, place on the baking sheet, cover and leave in a warm place until doubled in size.

5 Preheat the oven to 200°C/400°F/Gas 6. Brush the rolls with the egg. Bake until firm, about 15–20 minutes. Leave to cool on a wire rack.

Wholemeal Bread

A simple wholesome bread to be enjoyed by the whole family at any time.

Makes one 23 x 13cm/9 x 5in loaf

525g/1lb 5oz/generous 4 cups wholemeal flour
10ml/2 tsp salt
20ml/4 tsp active dried yeast
450ml/¾ pint/1¾ cups lukewarm water
30ml/2 tbsp honey
30ml/2 tbsp oil
40g/1½oz wheatgerm
milk, to glaze

1 Warm the flour and salt in a bowl in the oven at its lowest setting for 10 minutes. Meanwhile, combine the yeast with half of the water and leave to dissolve.

2 Make a central well in the flour. Pour in the yeast mixture, the remaining water, honey, oil and wheatgerm. Stir from the centre until smooth.

3 Grease a 23 x 13cm/9 x 5in loaf tin. Knead the dough just enough to shape into a loaf. Put it in the tin and cover with a plastic bag. Leave in a warm place until the dough is about 2.5cm/1in higher than the tin rim, about 1 hour.

4 Preheat the oven to 200°C/400°F/Gas 6. Brush the loaf with milk, and bake until the base sounds hollow when tapped, about 35–40 minutes. Cool on a wire rack.

Two-tone Bread

A tasty, malty bread that, when cut, reveals an attractive swirled interior.

Makes two 350g/12oz loaves

25ml/1½ tbsp active dried yeast
120ml/4fl oz/½ cup warm water
55g/2¼oz/generous ¼ cup caster sugar
675g/1½lb/6 cups strong plain flour
7.5ml/½ tbsp salt
600ml/1 pint/2½ cups warm milk
65g/2½oz/5 tbsp butter or margarine, melted and cooled
45ml/3 tbsp black treacle
275g/10oz/2 cups strong wholemeal plain flour

1 Dissolve the yeast in the water with 5ml/1 tsp of the sugar. Sift 350g/12oz/3 cups of the white flour, the salt and remaining sugar. Make a well and add the yeast, milk and butter. Mix in gradually to form a smooth soft batter.

2 Divide the batter into two bowls. To one bowl, add 275g/10oz/2½ cups of the strong white flour and mix together to a soft dough. Knead until smooth. Shape into a ball, put into a greased bowl and rotate to grease all over. Cover with clear film.

3 Mix the treacle and wholemeal flour into the second bowl. Add enough of the remaining white flour to make a soft dough. Knead until smooth. Shape into a ball, put in a greased bowl and cover. Leave the doughs to rise in a warm place for about 1 hour until doubled in size. Grease two 22 x 11cm/8½ x 4½in loaf tins.

4 Preheat the oven to 220°C/425°F/Gas 7. Punch down the dough and divide each ball in half. Roll out half of the light dough to a 30 x 20cm/12 x 8in rectangle. Roll out half of the dark dough to the same size. Set the dark dough rectangle on the light one. Roll up tightly from a short side. Set in a loaf tin. Repeat. Cover the tins and leave the dough to rise until doubled in size. Bake for 30–35 minutes.

Pleated Rolls

Fancy home-made rolls show that every care has been taken to ensure a welcoming dinner party.

Makes 48 rolls

15ml/1tbsp active dried yeast
475ml/16fl oz/2 cups lukewarm milk
115g/4oz/½ cup margarine
50g/2oz/4tbsp sugar
10ml/2tsp salt
2 eggs
985g–1.2kg/2lb 3oz–2½lb/ scant 7–8 cups strong flour
50g/2oz/4tbsp butter

1 Combine the yeast and 120ml/4fl oz/½ cup milk in a large bowl. Stir and leave for 15 minutes to dissolve. Scald the remaining milk, leave to cool for 5 minutes, then beat in the margarine, sugar, salt and eggs. Leave until lukewarm.

2 Pour the milk mixture into the yeast mixture. Stir in half the flour with a wooden spoon. Add the remaining flour, 190g/5oz/1¼ cups at a time, to obtain a rough dough.

3 Transfer the dough to a floured surface, knead until elastic. Place in a clean bowl, cover with a plastic bag and leave to rise in a warm place until doubled in volume.

4 In a saucepan, melt the butter and set aside. Lightly grease two baking sheets. Punch down the dough and divide into four equal pieces. Roll each piece into a 30 x 20cm/12 x 8in rectangle, about 5mm/¼ in thick. Cut each of the rectangles into four long strips, then cut each strip into three 10 x 5cm/ 4 x 2in rectangles. Brush each rectangle with melted butter, then fold the rectangles in half, so that the top extends about 1cm/½ in over the bottom. Place the rectangles slightly overlapping on the baking sheet, with the longer sides facing up.

5 Cover and chill for 30 minutes. Preheat the oven to 180°C/350°F/Gas 4. Bake until golden, 18–20 minutes. Cool slightly before serving.

Cheese Bread

This flavoured bread is ideal to serve with hot soup for a hearty snack lunch.

Makes one 23 x 13cm/9 x 5in loaf

15ml/1 tbsp active dried yeast
250ml/8fl oz/1 cup lukewarm milk
25g/1oz/2 tbsp butter
425g/15oz/3¾ cups strong white flour
10ml/2 tsp salt
90g/3½ oz/scant 1 cup grated mature Cheddar cheese

1 Combine the yeast and milk. Stir and leave for 15 minutes to dissolve. Meanwhile, melt the butter, leave to cool, then add to the yeast mixture.

2 Mix the flour and salt together in a large bowl. Make a central well and pour in the yeast mixture. With a wooden spoon, stir from the centre to obtain a rough dough. If the dough seems too dry, add 30–45ml/2–3 tbsp water.

3 Transfer to a floured surface and knead until smooth and elastic. Return to the bowl, cover and leave to rise in a warm place until doubled in volume, about 2–3 hours.

4 Grease a 23 x 13cm/9 x 5in loaf tin. Punch down the dough and knead in the cheese to distribute it evenly. Twist the dough, form into a loaf shape and place in the tin, tucking the ends under. Leave in a warm place until the dough rises above the rim of the tin.

5 Preheat the oven to 200°C/400°F/Gas 6. Bake for 15 minutes, then lower the heat to 190°C/375°F/Gas 5 and bake until the base sounds hollow when tapped, about a further 30 minutes.

Poppyseed Knots

The poppyseeds look attractive and add a slightly nutty flavour to these rolls.

Makes 12

300ml/½ pint/1¼ cups lukewarm milk
50g/2oz/4tbsp butter, at room temperature
5ml/1 tsp caster sugar
10ml/2 tsp active dry yeast
1 egg yolk
10ml/2 tsp salt
500–575g/1lb 2oz/4–4½ cup 4oz plain flour
1 egg beaten with 10ml/2 tsp of water, to glaze
poppyseeds, for sprinkling

1 In a large bowl, stir together the milk, butter, sugar and yeast. Leave for 15 minutes to dissolve. Stir in the egg yolk, salt and 275g/10oz/2½ cups of the flour. Add half the remaining flour and stir to obtain a soft dough.

2 Transfer to a floured surface and knead, adding flour if necessary, until smooth and elastic. Place in a bowl, cover and leave in a warm place until the dough doubles in volume, about 1½–2 hours.

3 Grease a baking sheet. Punch down the dough with your fist and cut into 12 pieces the size of golf balls. Roll each piece into a rope, twist to form a knot and place 2.5cm/1in apart on the sheet. Cover loosely and leave to rise in a warm place until doubled in volume, about 1–1½ hours.

4 Preheat the oven to 180°C/350°F/Gas 4. Brush the knots with the egg glaze and sprinkle over the poppyseeds. Bake until the tops are lightly browned, about 30 minutes. Cool slightly on a wire rack before serving.

Clover Leaf Rolls

For a witty touch, make one "lucky four-leaf clover" in the batch.

Makes 24

300ml/½ pint/1¼ cups milk
30ml/2 tbsp caster sugar
50g/2oz/4 tbsp butter, at room temperature
10ml/2 tsp active dried yeast
1 egg
10ml/2 tsp salt
450–500g/1–1¼lb/4–5 cups plain flour
melted butter, to glaze

1 Heat the milk to lukewarm, pour into a large bowl and stir in the sugar, butter and yeast. Leave for 15 minutes. Stir in the egg and salt. Gradually stir in 475g/1lb 2oz/4½ cups of the flour. Add just enough extra to obtain a rough dough. Knead until smooth. Place in a greased bowl, cover and leave in a warm place until doubled in size, about 1½ hours.

2 Grease two 12-cup bun trays. Punch down the dough, and make 72 equal-size balls.

3 Place three balls, in one layer, in each bun cup. Cover loosely and leave to rise in a warm place until doubled in size, about 1½ hours.

4 Preheat the oven to 200°C/400°F/Gas 6. Brush the rolls with glaze. Bake until lightly browned, about 20 minutes. Cool slightly on a wire rack before serving.

French Bread

For truly authentic bread you should use flour grown and milled in France.

Makes 2 loaves

15ml/1 tbsp active dried yeast
475ml/16fl oz/2 cups lukewarm water
15ml/1 tbsp salt
850–900g/1lb 14oz–2lb/ 3½–4 cups plain flour
semolina or flour, for sprinkling

1 In a large bowl, combine the yeast and water, stir, and leave for 15 minutes. Stir in the salt.

2 Add the flour, 150g/5oz/1¼ cups at a time, to obtain a smooth dough. Knead for 5 minutes.

3 Shape into a ball, place in a greased bowl and cover with a plastic bag. Leave to rise in a warm place until doubled in size, about 2–4 hours.

4 On a lightly floured surface shape into two long loaves. Place on a baking sheet sprinkled with semolina or flour and leave to rise for 5 minutes.

5 Score the tops diagonally with a sharp knife. Brush with water and place in a cold oven. Place a pan of boiling water on the base of the oven and set the oven to 200°C/400°F/ Gas 6. Bake until crusty and golden, about 40 minutes. Cool on a wire rack.

Croissants

Enjoy breakfast Continental-style with these melt-in-your-mouth croissants.

Makes 18

15ml/1 tbsp active dried yeast
325ml/11fl oz/1⅓ cups lukewarm milk
10ml/2 tsp caster sugar
12.5ml/1½ tsp salt
450g/1lb/4 cups plain flour
225g/8oz/1 cup cold unsalted butter
1 egg, beaten with 10ml/2 tsp water, to glaze

1 In an electric mixer bowl, stir together the yeast and milk. Leave for about 15 minutes. Stir in the sugar, salt and about 150g/5oz/1¼ cups of the flour.

2 Using a dough hook, slowly add the remaining flour. Beat on a high speed until the dough pulls away from the sides of the bowl. Cover and leave to rise in a warm place until doubled in size, about 1½ hours. Knead until smooth, wrap in greaseproof paper and chill for 15 minutes.

3 Roll out the butter between two sheets of greaseproof paper to make two 15 x 10cm/6 x 4in rectangles. Roll out the dough to 30 x 20cm/12 x 8in. Interleave the butter with the dough. With a short side facing you, roll it out again to 30 x 20cm/12 x 8in. Fold in thirds again, wrap and chill for 30 minutes. Repeat procedure twice, then chill for 2 hours.

4 Roll out the dough to a rectangle about 3mm/⅛ in thick. Trim the sides. Cut into 18 equal-size triangles. Roll up from base to point. Place point-down on baking sheets and form crescents. Cover and leave to rise in a warm place until more than doubled in size, about 1–1½ hours.

5 Preheat the oven to 240°C/475°F/Gas 9. Brush with egg. Bake for 2 minutes. Lower the heat to 190°C/375°F/Gas 5 and bake until golden, about 10–12 minutes. Serve warm.

Individual Brioches

These buttery rolls with their distinctive topknots are delicious served with jam at coffee time.

Makes 8

15ml/1 tbsp active dried yeast
15ml/1 tbsp caster sugar
30ml/2 tbsp warm milk
2 eggs
about 200g/7oz/1¾ cups plain flour
2.5ml/½ tsp salt
75g/3oz/6 tbsp butter, cut into six pieces, at room temperature
1 egg yolk, beaten with 10ml/2 tsp water, to glaze

1 Butter eight individual brioche or muffin tins. Put the yeast and sugar in a small bowl, add the milk and stir until dissolved. Leave to stand for 5 minutes, then beat in the eggs.

2 Put the flour and salt into a food processor, then, with the machine running, slowly pour in the yeast mixture. Scrape down the sides and process until the dough forms a ball. Add the butter and pulse to blend.

3 Transfer the dough to a buttered bowl and cover with a dish towel. Leave to rise in a warm place for 1 hour, then punch down.

4 Shape three-quarters of the dough into eight balls and put into the tins. Shape the last quarter into eight small balls, make a depression in the top of each large ball and set a small ball into it.

5 Leave to rise in a warm place for 30 minutes. Preheat the oven to 200°C/400°F/Gas 6.

6 Brush the brioches with the egg glaze. Bake for about 15–18 minutes, until golden brown. Transfer to a wire rack and leave to cool completely.

Dinner Milk Rolls

Making bread especially for your dinner guests is not only a wonderful gesture, it is also quite easy to do.

Makes 12–16

750g/1½lb/6 cups strong plain flour
10ml/2 tsp salt
25g/1oz/2 tbsp butter
1 sachet easy-blend dried yeast
450ml/¾ pint/1¾ cups lukewarm milk
cold milk, to glaze
poppy, sesame and sunflower seeds, or sea salt flakes, for sprinkling

1 Sift together the flour and salt into a large bowl. Rub in the butter, then stir in the yeast. Mix to a firm dough with the milk (you may not need it all).

2 Knead the dough for 5 minutes, then return to the bowl, cover with oiled clear film and leave to rise until doubled in volume.

3 Grease a baking sheet. Punch down the dough and knead again, then divide into 12–16 pieces and make into shapes of your choice. Place on the baking sheet, glaze the tops with milk, and sprinkle over your chosen seeds or sea salt flakes.

4 Leave to start rising again. Meanwhile, preheat the oven to 230°C/450°F/Gas 8. Bake the rolls for 12 minutes or until golden brown and cooked. Cool on a wire rack. Eat the same day as they will not keep.

Dill Bread

Tasty herb breads such as this are expensive to buy ready-made – if they can be found at all.

Makes two loaves

20ml/4 tsp active dried yeast
475ml/16fl oz/2 cups lukewarm water
30ml/2 tbsp sugar
1.05kg/2lb 5½ oz/scant 9½ cups strong flour
½ onion, chopped
60ml/4 tbsp oil
1 large bunch of dill, finely chopped
2 eggs, lightly beaten
150g/5½ oz/⅔ cup cottage cheese
20ml/4 tsp salt
milk, to glaze

1 Mix together the yeast, water and sugar in a large bowl and leave for 15 minutes to dissolve. Stir in about half of the flour. Cover and leave to rise in a warm place for 45 minutes.

2 In a frying pan, cook the onion in 15ml/1 tbsp of the oil until soft. Set aside to cool, then stir into the yeast mixture. Stir the dill, eggs, cottage cheese, salt and the remaining oil into the yeast. Gradually add the remaining flour until the dough is too stiff to stir.

3 Transfer to a floured surface and knead until smooth and elastic. Place in a bowl, cover and leave to rise until doubled in volume, about 1–1½ hours.

4 Grease a large baking sheet. Cut the dough in half and shape into two rounds. Place on the sheet and leave to rise in a warm place for 30 minutes.

5 Preheat the oven to 190°C/375°F/Gas 5. Score the tops, brush with the milk to glaze and bake until browned, about 50 minutes. Transfer to a wire rack to cool.

Spiral Herb Bread

When you slice this unusual loaf, its herbal secret is revealed inside.

Makes two 23 x 13cm/9 x 5in loaves

30ml/2 tbsp active dried yeast
600ml/1 pint/2½ cups lukewarm water
425g/15oz/3¾ cups strong white flour
500g/1lb 2oz/generous 3½ cups wholemeal flour
15ml/1 tbsp salt
25g/1oz/2 tbsp butter
1 large bunch of parsley, finely chopped
1 bunch of spring onions, chopped
1 garlic clove, finely chopped
salt and ground black pepper
1 egg, lightly beaten
milk, for glazing

1 Combine the yeast and 50ml/2fl oz/¼ cup of the water, stir and leave for 15 minutes to dissolve.

2 Combine the flours and salt in a large bowl. Make a central well and pour in the yeast mixture and the remaining water. With a wooden spoon, stir to a rough dough. Transfer to a floured surface; knead until smooth. Return to the bowl, cover with a plastic bag, and leave until doubled in size.

3 Meanwhile, combine the butter, parsley, spring onions and garlic in a large frying pan. Cook over a low heat, stirring, until softened. Season and set aside.

4 Grease two 23 x 13cm/9 x 5in loaf tins. When the dough has risen, cut in half and roll each half into a rectangle 35 x 23cm/14 x 9in. Brush with the beaten egg; spread with the herb mixture. Roll up to enclose the filling, pinch the short ends to seal. Place in the tins, seam-sides down. Cover, leave in a warm place until the dough rises above the tin rims.

5 Preheat the oven to 190°C/375°F/Gas 5. Brush the loaves with milk and bake until the bases sound hollow when tapped, about 55 minutes. Cool on a wire rack.

Sesame Seed Bread

This delicious bread breaks into individual rolls. It is ideal for entertaining.

Makes one 23cm/9in loaf

10ml/2 tsp active dried yeast
300ml/½ pint/1¼ cups lukewarm water
200g/7oz/1¾ cups plain flour
200g/7oz/scant 1½ cups wholemeal flour
10ml/2 tsp salt
65g/2½oz/5 tbsp toasted sesame seeds
milk, to glaze
30ml/2 tbsp sesame seeds, for sprinkling

1 Combine the yeast and 75ml/5 tbsp of the water and leave to dissolve. Mix the flours and salt in a large bowl. Make a central well and pour in the yeast and water. Stir from the centre to obtain a rough dough.

2 Transfer to a floured surface and knead until smooth and elastic. Return to the bowl and cover with a plastic bag. Leave in a warm place until the dough has doubled in size, about 1½–2 hours.

3 Grease a 23cm/9in round cake tin. Punch down the dough and knead in the sesame seeds. Divide the dough into 16 balls and place in the tin. Cover with a plastic bag and leave in a warm place until risen above the rim.

4 Preheat the oven to 220°C/425°F/Gas 7. Brush the loaf with milk and sprinkle with the sesame seeds. Bake for 15 minutes. Lower the heat to 190°C/375°F/Gas 5 and bake until the base sounds hollow when tapped, about 30 minutes. Cool on a wire rack.

Rye Bread

To bring out the flavour of the caraway seeds, toast them lightly in the oven first.

Makes one loaf

200g/7oz/scant 1½ cups rye flour
475ml/16fl oz/2 cups boiling water
120ml/4fl oz/½ cup black treacle
65g/2½oz/5 tbsp butter, cut into pieces
15ml/1 tbsp salt
30ml/2 tbsp caraway seeds
15ml/1 tbsp active dried yeast
120ml/4fl oz/½ cup lukewarm water
about 850g/1lb 14oz/7½ cups plain flour
semolina or flour, for dusting

1 Mix the rye flour, boiling water, treacle, butter, salt and caraway seeds in a large bowl. Leave to cool.

2 In another bowl, mix the yeast and lukewarm water and leave to dissolve. Stir into the rye flour mixture. Stir in just enough plain flour to obtain a stiff dough. If it becomes too stiff, stir with your hands. Transfer to a floured surface and knead thoroughly until the dough is no longer sticky and is smooth and shiny.

3 Place in a greased bowl, cover with a plastic bag, and leave in a warm place until doubled in volume. Punch down the dough, cover, and leave to rise again for 30 minutes.

4 Preheat the oven to 180°C/350°F/Gas 4. Dust a baking sheet with semolina or flour.

5 Shape the dough into a ball. Place on the sheet and score several times across the top. Bake until the base sounds hollow when tapped, about 40 minutes. Cool on a wire rack.

Rosemary Focaccia

Italian flat bread is easy to make using a packet mix. Additions include olives and sun-dried tomatoes.

Makes two loaves

450g/1lb packet white bread mix
60ml/4 tbsp extra virgin olive oil
10ml/2 tsp dried rosemary, crushed
8 sun-dried tomatoes, chopped
12 black olives, stoned and chopped
200ml/7fl oz/scant 1 cup lukewarm water
sea salt flakes, for sprinkling

1 Combine the bread mix with half the oil, the rosemary, tomatoes, olives and water to form a firm dough.

2 Knead the dough on a lightly floured surface for about 5 minutes. Return to the mixing bowl and cover with a piece of oiled clear film. Leave the dough to rise in a warm place until doubled in size. Meanwhile, lightly grease two baking sheets and preheat the oven to 220°C/425°F/Gas 7.

3 Punch down the dough and knead again. Divide into two and shape into flat rounds. Place on the baking sheet, and make indentations with your fingertips. Trickle over the remaining olive oil and sprinkle with sea salt flakes.

4 Bake the focaccia for 12–15 minutes until golden brown and cooked. Turn out on to wire racks to cool. This bread is best eaten slightly warm.

Saffron Focaccia

A dazzling yellow bread that is both light in texture and distinctive in flavour.

Makes one loaf

pinch of saffron strands
150ml/¼ pint/⅔ cup boiling water
225g/8oz/2 cups plain flour
2.5ml/½ tsp salt
5ml/1 tsp easy-blend dried yeast
15ml/1 tbsp olive oil

For the topping

2 garlic cloves, sliced
1 red onion, cut into thin wedges
rosemary sprigs
12 black olives, stoned and coarsely chopped
15ml/1 tbsp olive oil

1 Place the saffron in a heatproof jug and pour in the boiling water. Leave to infuse until lukewarm.

2 Place the flour, salt, yeast and olive oil in a food processor. Turn on and gradually add the saffron and its liquid. Process until the dough forms a ball.

3 Turn on to a floured surface; knead for 10–15 minutes. Place in a bowl, cover and leave to rise until doubled in size, about 30–40 minutes.

4 Punch down the dough and roll into an oval shape about 1cm/½in thick. Place on a lightly greased baking sheet and leave to rise for 30 minutes.

5 Preheat the oven to 200°C/400°F/Gas 6. With your fingers, press indentations over the surface of the bread.

6 Cover with the topping ingredients, brush lightly with olive oil, and bake for 25 minutes or until the loaf sounds hollow when tapped on the base. Leave to cool on a wire rack.

Rosemary Bread

Sliced thinly, this herb bread is delicious with cheese or soup for a light meal.

Makes one 23 x 13cm/9 x 5in loaf

1 sachet easy-blend dried yeast
175g/6oz/1¼ cups wholemeal flour
175g/6oz/1½ cups self-raising flour
25g/1oz/2 tbsp butter
50ml/2fl oz/¼ cup warm water
250ml/8fl oz/1 cup milk, at room temperature
15ml/1 tbsp sugar
5ml/1 tsp salt
15ml/1 tbsp sesame seeds
15ml/1 tbsp dried chopped onion
15ml/1 tbsp fresh rosemary leaves
115g/4oz/1 cup cubed Cheddar cheese
rosemary leaves and coarse salt, to decorate

1 Mix the yeast with the flours in a large mixing bowl. Melt the butter. Then stir the warm water, milk, sugar, butter, salt, sesame seeds, onion and rosemary into the flour. Knead thoroughly until quite smooth.

2 Flatten the dough, then add the cheese cubes. Knead them in until they are well combined.

3 Place the dough into a clean bowl greased with a little melted butter. Cover with a dish towel and put in a warm place for 1½ hours, or until the dough has doubled in size.

4 Grease a 23 x 13cm/9 x 5in loaf tin with butter. Punch down the dough and shape into a loaf. Place in the tin, cover with the dish towel and leave for about 1 hour until doubled in size. Preheat the oven to 190°C/375°F/Gas 5.

5 Bake for 30 minutes. Cover the loaf with foil for the last 5–10 minutes of baking. Turn the bread out on to a wire rack to cool. Garnish with some rosemary leaves and coarse salt scattered on top.

Potato Bread

Don't add butter or milk to the potatoes when you mash them, or the dough will be too sticky.

Makes two 23 x 13cm/9 x 5in loaves

20ml/4 tsp active dried yeast
250ml/8fl oz/1 cup lukewarm milk
225g/8oz potatoes, boiled (reserve 250ml/8fl oz/1 cup of the cooking liquid)
30ml/2 tbsp oil
20ml/4 tsp salt
850–900g/1lb 4oz–2lb/3½–4 cups plain flour

1 Combine the yeast and milk in a large bowl and leave to dissolve, about 15 minutes. Meanwhile, mash the potatoes.

2 Add the potatoes, oil and salt to the yeast mixture and mix well. Stir in the reserved cooking water, then stir in the flour, in six separate batches, to form a stiff dough. Knead until smooth, return to the bowl, cover, and leave in a warm place until doubled in size, about 1–1½ hours. Punch down, then leave to rise again for 40 minutes.

3 Grease two 23 x 13cm/9 x 5in loaf tins. Roll the dough into 20 small balls. Place two rows of balls in each tin. Leave until the dough has risen above the rims of the tins.

4 Preheat the oven to 200°C/400°F/Gas 6. Bake the dough for 10 minutes, then lower the heat to 190°C/375°F/Gas 5. Bake until the bases of the loaves sound hollow when tapped, about 40 minutes. Cool on a wire rack.

Irish Soda Bread

Easy to make, this distinctive bread goes well with soup, cheese and traditional, rustic-style dishes.

Makes one loaf

275g/10oz/2½ cups plain flour
150g/5oz/1 cup wholemeal flour
5ml/1 tsp bicarbonate of soda
5ml/1 tsp salt
25g/1oz/2 tbsp butter or margarine, at room temperature
300ml/½ pint/1¼ cups buttermilk
15ml/1 tbsp plain flour, for dusting

1 Preheat the oven to 200°C/400°F/Gas 6. Grease a baking sheet. Sift together the flours, bicarbonate of soda and salt. Make a central well and add the butter or margarine and buttermilk. Working from the centre, stir to combine the ingredients until a soft dough is formed.

2 With floured hands, gather the dough into a ball. Knead for 3 minutes. Shape the dough into a large round.

3 Place on the baking sheet. Cut a cross in the top with a sharp knife and dust with the flour. Bake until brown, about 40–50 minutes. Transfer to a wire rack to cool.

Sage Soda Bread

This wonderful loaf, quite unlike bread made with yeast, has a velvety texture and a powerful sage aroma.

Makes one loaf

225g/8oz/⅔ cups wholemeal flour
115g/4oz/1 cup strong white flour
2.5ml/½ tsp salt
5ml/1 tsp bicarbonate of soda
30ml/2 tbsp shredded fresh sage
300–450ml/½–¾ pint/1¼–1¾ cups buttermilk

1 Preheat the oven to 220°C/425°F/Gas 7. Sift the dry ingredients into a bowl. Stir in the sage and add enough buttermilk to make a soft dough.

2 Shape the dough into a round loaf and place on a lightly greased baking sheet.

3 Cut a deep cross in the top. Bake in the oven for about 40 minutes, or until the loaf is well risen and sounds hollow when tapped on the base. Leave to cool on a wire rack.

Breadsticks

If preferred, use other seeds, such as poppy or caraway, in these sticks.

Makes 18–20

15ml/1 tbsp active dried yeast
300ml/½ pint/1¼ cups lukewarm water
425g/15oz/scant 4 cups plain flour
10ml/2 tsp salt
5ml/1 tsp caster sugar
30ml/2 tbsp olive oil
1 egg, beaten, to glaze
150g/5oz/10 tbsp sesame seeds, toasted
coarse salt, for sprinkling

1 Combine the yeast and water, stir and leave for about 15 minutes. Place the flour, salt, sugar and olive oil in a food processor. With the motor running, slowly pour in the yeast mixture and process until the dough forms a ball.

2 Knead until smooth. Place in a bowl, cover and leave to rise in a warm place for 45 minutes. Grease two baking sheets.

3 Roll the dough into 18–20 30cm/12in sticks. Place on the baking sheets, brush with egg then sprinkle with sesame seeds and coarse salt. Leave to rise, uncovered, for 20 minutes.

4 Preheat the oven to 200°C/400°F/Gas 6. Bake until golden, about 15 minutes. Turn off the heat but leave in the oven for a further 5 minutes. Serve warm or cool.

Tomato Breadsticks

Once you've tried this simple recipe you'll never buy manufactured breadsticks again.

Makes 16

225g/8oz/2 cups plain flour
2.5ml/½ tsp salt
7.5ml/½ tbsp easy-blend dried yeast
5ml/1 tsp honey
5ml/1 tsp olive oil
150ml/¼ pint/⅔ cup warm water
6 halves sun-dried tomatoes in olive oil, drained and chopped
15ml/1 tbsp milk
10ml/2 tsp poppyseeds

1 Place the flour, salt and yeast in a food processor. Add the honey and olive oil and, with the machine running, gradually pour in the water until the dough starts to cling together (you may not need all the water). Process for a further 1 minute.

2 Turn out the dough on to a floured surface and knead for 3–4 minutes, until springy and smooth. Knead in the sun-dried tomatoes. Form into a ball and place in a lightly oiled bowl. Leave to rise for 5 minutes.

3 Preheat the oven to 150°C/300°F/Gas 2. Divide the dough into 16 pieces and roll each piece into a 28 x 1cm/11 x ½in stick. Place on a lightly greased baking sheet and leave to rise in a warm place for 15 minutes.

4 Brush the sticks with milk and sprinkle with poppy seeds. Bake for 30 minutes. Leave to cool on a wire rack.

Walnut Bread

This rich bread could be served at a dinner party with the cheese course, or with a rustic ploughman's lunch.

Makes one loaf

420g/15oz/3 cups wholemeal flour
140g/5oz/1¼ cups strong flour
12.5ml/2½ tsp salt
500ml/18fl oz/2¼ cups lukewarm water
15ml/1tbsp clear honey
15ml/1tbsp active dried yeast
140g/5oz/1 cup walnut pieces, plus more to decorate
1 beaten egg, to glaze

1 Combine the flours and salt in a large bowl. Make a well in the centre and add 250ml/8fl oz/1 cup of the water, the honey and the yeast. Set aside until the mixture is frothy.

2 Add the remaining water. With a wooden spoon, stir from the centre, incorporating flour with each turn, to obtain a smooth dough. Add more flour if the dough is too sticky and use your hands if the dough becomes too stiff to stir.

3 Transfer to a floured board and knead, adding flour if necessary, until the dough is smooth and elastic. Place in a greased bowl and roll the dough around in the bowl to coat thoroughly on all sides. Cover with a plastic bag and leave in a warm place until doubled in volume. Punch down the dough and knead in the walnuts evenly.

4 Grease a baking sheet. Shape the dough into a round loaf and place on the baking sheet. Press in walnut pieces to decorate the top. Cover loosely with a damp cloth and leave to rise in a warm place until doubled in size, 25–30 minutes.

5 Preheat the oven to 220°C/425°F/Gas 7. With a sharp knife, score the top. Brush with the beaten egg. Bake for 15 minutes. Lower the heat to 190°C/375°F/Gas 5 and bake until the base sounds hollow when tapped, about 40 minutes. Cool on a rack.

Pecan Nut Rye Bread

A tasty homespun loaf that recalls the old folk cooking of the United States.

Makes two 21.5 x 11.5cm/8½ x 4½in loaves

25ml/1½ tbsp active dried yeast
700ml/22fl oz/2¾ cups lukewarm water
675g/1½lb/6 cups strong flour
500g/1¼lb/5 cups rye flour
30ml/2tbsp salt
15ml/1tbsp clear honey
10ml/2tsp caraway seeds, (optional)
115g/4oz/8tbsp butter, at room temperature
225g/8oz pecan nuts, chopped

1 Combine the yeast and 120ml/4fl oz/½ cup of the water. Stir and leave for 15 minutes to dissolve. In the bowl of an electric mixer, combine the flours, salt, honey, caraway seeds and butter. With the dough hook, mix on low speed until well blended.

2 Add the yeast mixture and the remaining water and mix on medium speed until the dough forms a ball. Transfer to a floured surface and knead in the pecan nuts.

3 Return the dough to a bowl, cover with a plastic bag and leave in a warm place until doubled, about 2 hours. Grease two 21.5 x 11.5cm/8½ x 4½ in loaf tins. Punch down the risen dough.

4 Divide the dough in half and form into loaves. Place in the tins, seam-sides down. Dust the tops with flour. Cover with plastic bags and leave to rise in a warm place until doubled in volume, about 1 hour.

5 Preheat the oven to 190°C/375°F/Gas 5. Bake until the bases sound hollow when tapped, 45–50 minutes. Transfer to wire racks to cool completely.

Prune Bread

Makes 1 loaf

225g/8oz/1 cup dried prunes
15ml/1 tbsp easy-blend dried yeast
75g/3oz/⅔ cup wholemeal flour
385–420g/13½–15oz/3–4cups strong flour
2.5ml/½ tsp bicarbonate of soda
5ml/1 tsp salt
5ml/1 tsp pepper
30g/1oz butter, at room temperature
175ml/6fl oz/⅔ cup buttermilk
55g/2oz/½ cup walnuts, chopped
milk, for glazing

1 Simmer the prunes in water to cover until soft, or soak overnight. Drain, reserving 60ml/4 tbsp of the soaking liquid. Stone and chop the prunes.

2 Combine the yeast and the reserved prune liquid, stir and leave for 15 minutes to dissolve.

3 In a large bowl, stir together the flours, bicarbonate of soda, salt and pepper. Make a well in the centre.

4 Add the prunes, butter, and buttermilk. Pour in the yeast mixture. With a wooden spoon, stir from the centre, folding in more flour with each turn, to obtain a rough dough.

5 Transfer to a floured surface and knead until smooth and elastic. Return to the bowl, cover with a plastic bag and leave to rise in a warm place until doubled in volume, for about 1½ hours. Grease a baking sheet.

6 Punch down the dough with your fist, then knead in the walnuts. Shape the dough into a long, cylindrical loaf. Place on the baking sheet, cover loosely, and leave to rise in a warm place for 45 minutes. Preheat the oven to 220°C/425°F/Gas 7.

7 With a sharp knife, score the top. Brush with milk and bake for 15 minutes. Lower to 190°C/375°F/Gas 5 and bake for 35 minutes more, until the bottom sounds hollow. Cool.

Courgette Crown Bread

Adding grated courgettes and cheese to a loaf mixture will keep it tasting fresher for longer.

Serves 8

450g/1lb/3 cups coarsely grated courgettes
salt
500g/1¼ lb/5 cups plain flour
2 sachets easy-blend dried yeast
60ml/4 tbsp freshly grated Parmesan cheese
ground black pepper
30ml/2 tbsp olive oil
lukewarm water, to mix
milk, to glaze
sesame seeds, to garnish

1 Spoon the courgettes into a colander, sprinkling them lightly with salt. Leave to drain for 30 minutes, then pat dry with kitchen paper.

2 Mix the flour, yeast and Parmesan together and season with black pepper. Stir in the oil and courgettes, and add enough lukewarm water to make a firm dough.

3 Knead the dough on a lightly floured surface until smooth, then return to the mixing bowl, cover it with oiled clear film and leave it to rise in a warm place, until doubled in size. Meanwhile, grease and line a 23cm/9in round sandwich tin. Preheat the oven to 200°C/400°F/Gas 6.

4 Punch down the dough, and knead it lightly. Break into 8 balls, roll each one and arrange them, touching, in the tin. Brush the tops with milk and sprinkle over the sesame seeds.

5 Allow to rise again, then bake for 25 minutes or until golden brown. Cool slightly in the tin, then turn out on to a wire rack.

Raisin Bread

Makes 2 loaves

15ml/1 tbsp easy-blend dried yeast
450ml/¾ pint/1¾ cups lukewarm milk
150g/5oz raisins
65g/2½ oz4 tbsp currants
15ml/1 tbsp sherry or brandy
2.5/½ tsp grated nutmeg
grated rind of 1 large orange
60g/2¼ oz/7 tbsp sugar
15ml/1 tbsp salt
115g/4oz/8 tbsp butter, melted
700–850g/1lb 8oz–1lb 14oz strong flour
1 egg beaten with 15ml/1 tbsp cream

1 Stir the yeast with 120ml/4fl oz/½ cup of the milk and leave to stand for 15 minutes to dissolve. Mix the raisins, currants, sherry or brandy, nutmeg and orange rind together.

2 In another bowl, mix the remaining milk, sugar, salt and half the butter. Add the yeast mixture. With a wooden spoon, stir in half the flour, 150g/5oz at a time, until blended. Add the remaining flour as needed for a stiff dough.

3 Transfer to a floured surface and knead until smooth and elastic. Place in a greased bowl, cover and leave to rise in a warm place until doubled in volume, about 2½ hours.

4 Punch down the dough, return to the bowl, cover and leave to rise in a warm place for 30 minutes. Grease two 21.5 x 11.5cm/8½ x 4½ in bread tins. Divide the dough in half and roll each half into a 50 x 18cm/20 x 7in rectangle.

5 Brush the rectangles with the remaining melted butter. Sprinkle over the raisin mixture, then roll up tightly, tucking in the ends slightly as you roll. Place in the prepared tins, cover, and leave to rise until almost doubled in volume.

6 Preheat the oven to 200°C/400°F/Gas 6. Brush the loaves with the egg and milk. Bake for 20 minutes. Lower to 180°C/350°F/Gas 4 and bake until golden, 25–30 minutes more. Cool on racks.

Coconut Bread

This bread is delicious served with a cup of hot chocolate or a glass of fruit punch.

Makes 1 loaf

175g/6oz/¾ cup butter
115g/4oz/⅔ cup demerara sugar
225g/8oz/2 cups self-raising flour
200g/7oz/scant 2 cups plain flour
115g/4oz desiccated coconut
5ml/1 tsp mixed spice
10ml/2 tsp vanilla essence
15ml/1 tbsp rum
2 eggs
about 150ml/¼ pint/⅔ cup milk
15ml/1 tbsp caster sugar, blended with 30ml/2 tbsp water, to glaze

1 Preheat the oven to 180°C/350°F/Gas 4. Grease two 450g/1lb loaf tins.

2 Place the butter and sugar in a large bowl and sift in the flour. Rub in the ingredients together with your fingertips until the mixture resembles fine breadcrumbs.

3 Add the coconut, mixed spice, vanilla essence, rum, eggs and milk and mix together well with your hands. If the mixture is too dry, moisten with milk. Knead on a floured board until firm and pliable.

4 Halve the mixture and place in the prepared loaf tins. Glaze with sugared water and bake for 1 hour until the loaves are cooked. Test with a skewer, the loaves are ready when the skewer comes out clean.

Danish Wreath

Serves 10–12

5ml/1 tsp easy-blend dried yeast
175ml/6fl oz/¾ cup milk
50g/2oz/4 tbsp sugar
450g/1lb/4 cups strong white flour
2.5ml/½ tsp salt
2.5ml/½ tsp vanilla essence
1 egg, beaten
2 x 115g/4oz/½ cup blocks unsalted butter
1 egg yolk beaten with 10ml/2 tsp water
115g/4oz/1 cup icing sugar

For the filling

200g/7oz/generous 1 cup dark brown sugar
5ml/1 tsp ground cinnamon
50g/2oz/½ cup walnuts or pecans, plus extra

1 Mix the yeast, milk and 2.5ml/½ tsp of the sugar. Leave for 15 minutes to dissolve. Mix the flour, sugar and salt. Make a well; add the yeast, vanilla and egg to make a rough dough. Knead until smooth, wrap and chill.

2 Roll the butter to form two 15 x 10cm/6 x 4in rectangles. Roll the dough to a 30 x 20cm/12 x 8in rectangle. Place one butter rectangle in the centre. Fold the bottom third of dough over and seal the edge. Place the other butter rectangle on top and cover with the top third of the dough.

3 Roll the dough into a 30 x 20cm/12 x 8in rectangle. Fold into thirds. Wrap and chill for 30 minutes. Repeat twice more. After the third fold, chill for 1–2 hours. Grease a baking sheet.

4 Roll out the dough to a 63 x 15cm/25 x 6in strip. Mix the filling ingredients and spread over, leaving a 1cm/½in edge. Roll the dough into a cylinder, place on the sheet in a circle and seal the edges. Cover and leave to rise for 45 minutes.

5 Preheat the oven to 200°C/400°F/Gas 6. Slash the top every 5cm/2in, cutting 1cm/½in deep. Brush with the egg and milk. Bake for 35–40 minutes until golden. Cool. To serve, mix the icing sugar with some water, then drizzle over the wreath. Sprinkle with some nuts.

Kugelhopf

A traditional round moulded bread from Germany, flavoured with Kirsch or brandy.

Makes one ring loaf

100g/3¾ oz/¾ cup raisins
15ml/1 tbsp Kirsch or brandy
15ml/1 tbsp easy-blend dried yeast
120ml/4fl oz/½ cup lukewarm water
115g/4oz/½ cup unsalted butter, at room temperature
90g/3½oz/½ cup sugar
3 eggs, at room temperature
grated rind of 1 lemon
5ml/1 tsp salt
2.5ml/½ tsp vanilla essence
425g/15oz/3¾ cups strong white flour
120ml/4fl oz/½ cup milk
25g/1oz/¼ cup flaked almonds
80g/3¼oz/generous ½ cup whole blanched almonds, chopped
icing sugar, for dusting

1 In a bowl, combine the raisins and Kirsch or brandy. Combine the yeast and water, stir and leave for 15 minutes.

2 Cream the butter and sugar until thick and fluffy. Beat in the eggs, one at a time. Add the lemon rind, salt and vanilla. Stir in the yeast mixture. Add the flour, alternating with the milk, until well blended. Cover and leave to rise in a warm place until doubled in volume, about 2 hours.

3 Grease a 2.75 litre/4½ pint/11¼ cup kugelhopf mould, then sprinkle the flaked almonds evenly over the base. Work the raisins and chopped almonds into the dough, then spoon into the mould. Cover with a polythene bag, and leave to rise in a warm place until the dough almost reaches the top of the tin, about 1 hour.

4 Preheat the oven to 180°C/350°F/Gas 4. Bake until golden brown, about 45 minutes. If the top browns too quickly, cover with foil. Cool in the tin for 15 minutes, then turn out on to a wire rack. Dust the top lightly with icing sugar.

Open Apple Pie

If using eating apples for this pie, make sure they are firm-fleshed rather than soft.

Serves 8

1.5kg/3–3½lb tart eating or cooking apples
45g/1¾oz/scant ¼ cup sugar
10ml/2 tsp ground cinnamon
grated rind and juice of 1 lemon
25g/1oz/2 tbsp butter, diced
30–45ml/2–3 tbsp honey, to glaze

For the pastry

275g/10oz/2½ cups plain flour
2.5ml/½ tsp salt
115g/4oz/½ cup butter, cut into pieces
60g/2¼oz/4½ tbsp vegetable fat or lard, cut into pieces
75–90ml/5–6 tbsp iced water

1 For the pastry, sift the flour and salt into a bowl. Add the butter and fat and rub in until the mixture resembles coarse breadcrumbs. Stir in just enough water to bind the dough. Gather into a ball, wrap and chill for at least 20 minutes.

2 Preheat the oven to 200°C/400°F/Gas 6. Place a baking sheet in the oven.

3 Peel, core and slice the apples. Combine with the sugar, cinnamon, lemon rind and juice.

4 Roll out the pastry to a 30cm/12in circle. Use to line a 23cm/9in pie dish, leaving an overhanging edge. Fill with the apples. Fold in the edges and crimp loosely. Dot the apples with diced butter.

5 Bake on the hot baking sheet until the pastry is golden and the apples are tender, about 45 minutes.

6 Melt the honey in a saucepan and brush over the apples to glaze. Serve warm or at room temperature.

Apple and Cranberry Lattice Pie

Serves 8

grated rind of 1 orange
45ml/3 tbsp orange juice
2 large cooking apples
170g/6oz/1⅓ cups cranberries
70g/2½oz/½ cup raisins
25g/1oz/4 tbsp walnuts, chopped
215g/7½oz/generous 1 cup caster sugar
115g/4oz/½ cup dark brown sugar
15g/½oz/2 tbsp plain flour

For the crust

285g/10oz/2½ cups plain flour
2.5ml/½ tsp salt
85g/3oz/6 tbsp cold butter, cut into pieces
85g/3oz/½ cup cold vegetable fat or lard, cut into pieces
65–125ml/2–4fl oz iced water

1 For the crust, sift the flour and salt, add the butter and fat and rub in well. Stir in enough water to bind the dough. Form into two equal balls, wrap and chill for at least 20 minutes.

2 Put the orange rind and juice into a bowl. Peel and core the apples and grate into the bowl. Stir in the cranberries, raisins, walnuts, all except 1 tbsp of the caster sugar, the brown sugar and flour. Place a baking sheet in the oven and preheat to 200°C/400°F/Gas 6.

3 Roll out one ball of dough about 3mm/⅛in thick. Transfer to a 23cm/9in pie plate and trim. Spoon the cranberry and apple mixture into the shell.

4 Roll out the remaining dough to a circle about 28cm/11in in diameter. With a serrated pastry wheel, cut the dough into 10 strips, 2cm/¾in wide. Place five strips horizontally across the top of the tart at 2.5cm/1in intervals. Weave in five vertical strips and trim. Sprinkle the top with sugar.

5 Bake for 20 minutes. Reduce heat to 180°C/350°F/Gas 4 and bake until the crust is golden and the filling is bubbling, about 15 minutes more.

Peach Leaf Pie

Serves 8
1.1kg/2½lb ripe peaches
juice of 1 lemon
90g/3½oz/½ cup sugar
45ml/3 tbsp cornflour
1.5ml/¼ tsp grated nutmeg
2.5ml/½ tsp ground cinnamon
25g/1oz/2 tbsp butter, diced

For the pastry
275g/10oz/2½ cups plain flour
4ml/¾ tsp salt
115g/4oz/½ cup cold butter, cut into pieces
60g/2¼oz/4½ tbsp cold vegetable fat or lard, cut into pieces
75–90ml/5–6 tbsp iced water
1 egg beaten with 15ml/1 tbsp water

1 Make the pastry as described for Open Apple Pie on page 86. Gather into two balls, one slightly larger than the other. Wrap and chill for at least 20 minutes. Place a baking sheet in the oven and preheat to 220°C/425°F/Gas 7.

2 Drop the peaches into boiling water for 20 seconds, then transfer to a bowl of cold water. When cool, peel off the skins. Slice the flesh and combine with the lemon juice, sugar, cornflour and spices. Set aside.

3 Roll out the larger dough ball to 3mm/⅛in thick. Use to line a 23cm/9in pie tin. Chill. Roll out the remaining dough to 5mm/¼in thick. Cut out leaves 8cm/3in long. Mark veins. With the scraps, roll a few balls.

4 Brush the pastry base with egg glaze. Add the peaches and dot with the butter. To assemble, start from the outside edge and cover the peaches with a ring of leaves. Place a second, staggered ring above. Continue until covered. Place the balls in the centre. Brush with glaze. Bake on the hot baking sheet for 10 minutes. Lower the heat to 180°C/350°F/Gas 4 and bake for 35–40 minutes more.

Walnut and Pear Lattice Pie

For the lattice top, either weave strips of pastry or use a special pastry cutter to create a lattice effect.

Serves 6–8
450g/1lb shortcrust pastry
450g/2lb pears, peeled, cored and thinly sliced
50g/2oz/4 tbsp caster sugar
25g/1oz/2 tbsp plain flour
2.5ml/½ tsp grated lemon rind
25g/1oz/scant ¼ cup raisins or sultanas
25g/1oz/4 tbsp chopped walnuts
2.5ml/½ tsp ground cinnamon
50g/2oz/½ cup icing sugar
15ml/1 tbsp lemon juice
about 10ml/2 tsp cold water

1 Preheat the oven to 190°C/375°F/Gas 5. Roll out half of the pastry and use it to line a 23cm/9in tin that is about 5cm/2in deep.

2 Combine the pears, caster sugar, flour and lemon rind. Toss to coat the fruit. Mix in the raisins, nuts and cinnamon. Put the filling into the pastry case and spread it evenly.

3 Roll out the remaining pastry and use to make a lattice top. Bake the pie for 55 minutes or until the pastry is golden brown on top.

4 Combine the icing sugar, lemon juice and water in a bowl and stir until smooth. Remove the pie from the oven. Drizzle the glaze evenly over the top, on the pastry and filling. Leave the pie to cool in its tin on a wire rack.

Lemon Meringue Pie

A classic dish whose popularity never seems to wane.

Serves 8

225g/8oz shortcrust pastry
grated rind and juice of 1 large lemon
250ml/8fl oz/1 cup plus 15ml/1 tbsp cold water
115g/4oz/generous ½ cup caster sugar plus 90ml/6 tbsp extra
25g/1oz/2 tbsp butter
45ml/3 tbsp cornflour
3 eggs, separated
pinch of salt
pinch of cream of tartar

1 Line a 23cm/9in pie dish with the pastry, folding under a 1cm/½in overhang. Crimp the edge and chill for 20 minutes.

2 Preheat the oven to 200°C/400°F/Gas 6. Prick the pastry case base, line with greaseproof paper and fill with baking beans. Bake for 12 minutes. Remove the paper and beans and bake until golden, 6–8 minutes more.

3 In a saucepan, combine the lemon rind and juice with 250ml/8fl oz/1 cup of the water, 115g/4oz/generous ½ cup of the sugar, and the butter. Bring to the boil.

4 Meanwhile, dissolve the cornflour in the remaining water. Add the egg yolks. Beat into the lemon mixture, return to the boil and whisk until thick, about 5 minutes. Cover the surface with greaseproof paper and leave to cool.

5 For the meringue, beat the egg whites with the salt and cream of tartar until stiffly peaking. Add the remaining sugar and beat until glossy.

6 Spoon the lemon mixture into the pastry case. Spoon the meringue on top, sealing it with the pastry rim. Bake until golden, 12–15 minutes.

Blueberry Pie

Serve this tangy blueberry pie with crème fraîche or double cream.

Serves 6–8

450g/1lb shortcrust pastry
500g/1¼lb/5 cups blueberries
165g/5½oz/generous ⅔ cup caster sugar
45ml/3 tbsp plain flour
5ml/1 tsp grated orange rind
1.5ml/¼ tsp grated nutmeg
30ml/2 tbsp orange juice
5ml/1 tsp lemon juice

1 Preheat the oven to 190°C/375°F/Gas 5. On a lightly floured surface, roll out half of the pastry and use it to line a 23cm/9in pie tin that is 5cm/2in deep.

2 Combine the blueberries, 150g/5oz/¾cup of the sugar, the flour, orange rind and nutmeg. Toss the mixture gently to coat all the fruit.

3 Pour the blueberry mixture into the pastry case and spread evenly. Sprinkle over the citrus juices.

4 Roll out the remaining pastry and cover the pie. Cut out small decorative shapes from the top. Use to decorate the pastry, and finish the edge.

5 Brush the top with water and sprinkle with the remaining caster sugar. Bake for 45 minutes, or until the pastry is golden brown. Serve warm or at room temperature.

Creamy Banana Pie

Do not prepare the topping for this pie too soon before serving or the banana slices will discolour.

Serves 6

200g/7oz/2¼ cups ginger biscuits, finely crushed
65g/2½oz/5 tbsp butter or margarine, melted
2.5ml/½ tsp grated nutmeg or ground cinnamon
175g/6oz/1 ripe banana, mashed
350g/12oz/1½ cups cream cheese, at room temperature
50ml/generous 3 tbsp thick natural yogurt or soured cream
45ml/3 tbsp dark rum or 5ml/1 tsp vanilla essence

For the topping

250ml/8fl oz/1 cup whipping cream
3–4 bananas

1 Preheat the oven to 190°C/375°F/Gas 5. For the crust, combine the crushed biscuits, butter or margarine and spice. Mix thoroughly with a wooden spoon.

2 Press the biscuit mixture into a 23cm/9in pie dish, building up thick sides with a neat edge. Bake for 5 minutes, then leave to cool.

3 Beat the mashed bananas with the cream cheese. Fold in the yogurt or soured cream and rum or vanilla. Spread the filling in the biscuit case. Chill for at least 4 hours or preferably overnight.

4 For the topping, whip the cream until soft peaks form. Spread on the pie filling. Slice the bananas and arrange on top in a decorative pattern.

Red Berry Sponge Tart

When soft berry fruits are in season, serve this delicious tart warm with scoops of vanilla ice cream.

Serves 4

450g/1lb/4 cups soft berry fruits, such as raspberries, blackberries, blackcurrants, redcurrants, strawberries and blueberries
2 eggs
50g/2oz/¼ cup caster sugar, plus extra to taste (optional)
15ml/1 tbsp flour
75g/3oz/¾ cup ground almonds
vanilla ice cream, to serve

1 Preheat the oven to 190°C/375°F/Gas 5. Grease and line a 23cm/9in pie tin with greaseproof paper. Scatter the fruit in the base of the tin with a little sugar if the fruits are tart.

2 Beat the eggs and sugar together for about 3–4 minutes, or until they leave a thick trail across the surface. Combine the flour and almonds, then fold into the egg mixture with a palette knife, retaining as much air as possible.

3 Spread the mixture on top of the fruit base, bake in the preheated oven for 15 minutes, then turn out on to a serving plate .

De Luxe Mincemeat Tart

Serves 8

225g/8oz/2 cups plain flour
10ml/2 tsp ground cinnamon
50g/2oz/½ cup walnuts, finely ground
115g/4oz/½ cup butter
50g/2oz/4 tbsp caster sugar, plus extra for dusting
1 egg
2 drops vanilla essence
15ml/1 tbsp cold water

For the mincemeat

2 eating apples, peeled, cored and grated
225g/8oz/generous 1½ cups raisins
115g/4oz/½ cup dried apricots, chopped
115g/4oz/½ cup ready-to-eat dried figs or prunes, chopped
225g/8oz green grapes, halved and seeded
50g/2oz/½ cup chopped almonds
finely grated rind of 1 lemon
30ml/2 tbsp lemon juice
30ml/2 tbsp brandy or port
1.5ml/¼ tsp mixed spice
115g/4oz/generous ½ cup soft light brown sugar
25g/1oz/2 tbsp butter, melted

1 Process the flour, cinnamon, nuts and butter in a food processor or blender to make fine crumbs. Turn into a bowl and stir in the sugar. Beat the egg with the vanilla and water and stir into the dry ingredients. Form a soft dough, knead until smooth, wrap and chill for 30 minutes.

2 Mix the mincemeat ingredients together. Use two-thirds of the pastry to line a 23cm/9in, loose-based flan tin. Push the pastry well into the edges, then trim. Fill with the mincemeat.

3 Roll out the remaining pastry and cut into 1cm/½in strips. Arrange the strips in a lattice over the top of the pastry, wet the joins and press them together. Chill for 30 minutes.

4 Preheat a baking sheet in the oven at 190°C/375°F/Gas 5. Brush the pastry with water and dust with caster sugar. Bake the tart on the baking sheet for 30–40 minutes. Cool in the tin on a wire rack for 15 minutes. Then remove the tin.

Crunchy Apple and Almond Flan

Don't put sugar with the apples as this produces too much liquid. The sweetness is in the pastry and topping.

Serves 8

75g/3oz/6 tbsp butter
175g/6oz/1½ cups plain flour
25g/1oz/4 tbsp ground almonds
25g/1oz/2 tbsp caster sugar
1 egg yolk
15ml/1 tbsp cold water
1.5ml/¼ tsp almond essence
675g/1½lb cooking apples
25g/1oz/2 tbsp raisins

For the topping

115g/4oz/1 cup plain flour
1.5ml/¼ tsp ground mixed spice
50g/2oz/4 tbsp butter, cut in small cubes
50g/2oz/4 tbsp demerara sugar
50g/2oz/½ cup flaked almonds

1 To make the pastry, rub the butter into the flour until it resembles breadcrumbs. Stir in the almonds and sugar. Whisk the egg yolk, water and almond essence together and mix into the dry ingredients to form a soft dough. Knead until smooth, wrap, and leave to rest for 20 minutes.

2 For the topping, sift the flour and spice into a bowl and rub in the butter. Stir in the sugar and almonds. Roll out the pastry and use to line a 23cm/9in loose-based flan tin. Trim the top and chill for 15 minutes.

3 Preheat a baking sheet in the oven at 190°C/375°F/Gas 5. Peel, core and slice the apples thinly. Arrange in the flan in overlapping, concentric circles, doming the centre. Sprinkle with raisins.

4 Cover with the topping mixture, pressing it on lightly. Bake on the hot baking sheet for 25–30 minutes, or until the top is golden brown and the apples are tender (test them with a fine skewer). Leave the flan to cool in the tin for 10 minutes before serving.

Rhubarb and Cherry Pie

The unusual partnership of rhubarb and cherries works well in this pie.

Serves 8

450g/1lb rhubarb, cut into 2.5cm/1in pieces
450g/1lb canned stoned tart red or black cherries, drained
275g/10oz/scant 1½ cups caster sugar
45ml/3 tbsp quick-cooking tapioca

For the pastry

275g/10oz/2½ cups plain flour
5ml/1 tsp salt
75g/3oz/6 tbsp cold butter, cut in pieces
50g/2oz/4 tbsp cold vegetable fat or lard, cut in pieces
50–120ml/2–4fl oz/¼–½ cup iced water
milk, for glazing

1 For the pastry, sift the flour and salt into a bowl. Add the butter and fat and rub in until the mixture resembles coarse breadcrumbs. Stir in enough water to bind. Form into two balls, wrap and chill for 20 minutes.

2 Preheat a baking sheet in the oven at 200°C/400°F/Gas 6. Roll out one pastry ball and use to line a 23cm/9in pie dish, leaving a 1cm/½in overhang.

3 Mix together the filling ingredients and spoon into the pastry case.

4 Roll out the remaining pastry, cut out four leaf shapes, and use to cover the pie leaving a 2cm/¾in overhang. Fold this under the pastry base and flute. Roll small balls from the scraps, mark veins in the leaves and use to decorate the pie.

5 Glaze the top and bake on the baking sheet until golden, 40–50 minutes.

Festive Apple Pie

Serves 8

900g/2lb cooking apples
15g/½oz/2 tbsp plain flour
115g/4oz/generous ½ cup caster sugar
25ml/1½ tbsp fresh lemon juice
2.5ml/½ tsp ground cinnamon
2.5ml/½ tsp mixed spice
1.5ml/¼ tsp ground ginger
1.5ml/¼ tsp grated nutmeg
1.5ml/¼ tsp salt
50g/2oz/4 tbsp butter, diced

For the pastry

275g/10oz/2½ cups plain flour
5ml/1 tsp salt
75g/3oz/6 tbsp cold butter, cut in pieces
50g/2oz/4 tbsp cold vegetable fat or lard, cut in pieces
50–120ml/2–4fl oz/¼–½ cup iced water

1 For the pastry, sift the flour and salt into a bowl. Add the butter and fat, and rub in until the mixture resembles coarse breadcrumbs. Stir in just enough water to bind. Form two balls, wrap and chill for 20 minutes.

2 Roll out one ball and use to line a 23cm/9in pie dish. Preheat a baking sheet in the oven at 220°C/425°F/Gas 7.

3 Peel, core and slice the apples. Toss with the flour, sugar, lemon juice, spices and salt. Spoon into the pastry case and dot with butter.

4 Roll out the remaining pastry. Place on top of the pie and trim to leave a 2cm/¾in overhang. Fold this under the pastry base and press to seal. Crimp the edge. Form the scraps into leaf shapes and balls. Arrange on the pie and cut steam vents.

5 Bake on the baking sheet for 10 minutes. Reduce the heat to 180°C/350°F/Gas 4 and bake for 40 minutes, until golden.

Black Bottom Pie

Serves 8

10ml/2 tsp gelatine
45ml/3 tbsp cold water
2 eggs, separated
150g/5oz/¾ cup caster sugar
15g/½oz/2 tbsp cornflour
2.5ml/½ tsp salt
475ml/16fl oz/2 cups milk
50g/2oz plain chocolate, finely chopped
30ml/2 tbsp rum
1.5ml/¼ tsp cream of tartar
chocolate curls, to decorate

For the crust

175g/6oz/2 cups gingernuts, crushed
65g/2½oz/5 tbsp butter, melted

1 Preheat the oven to 180°C/350°F/Gas 4. Mix the crushed gingernuts and melted butter. Press evenly over the base and side of a 23cm/9in pie plate. Bake for 6 minutes. Sprinkle the gelatine over the water and leave to soften.

2 Beat the egg yolks in a large mixing bowl and set aside. In a saucepan, combine half the sugar, the cornflour and salt. Gradually stir in the milk. Boil for 1 minute, stirring constantly. Whisk the hot milk mixture into the yolks, pour back into the saucepan and return to the boil, whisking. Cook for 1 minute, still whisking. Remove from the heat.

3 Pour 225g/8oz of the custard mixture into a bowl. Add the chopped chocolate and stir until melted. Stir in half the rum and pour into the pie crust. Whisk the softened gelatine into the plain custard until dissolved, then stir in the remaining rum. Set the pan in cold water to reach room temperature.

4 Beat the egg whites and cream of tartar until they peak stiffly. Add the remaining sugar gradually, beating thoroughly after each addition. Fold the custard into the egg whites, then spoon over the chocolate mixture in the pie crust. Chill until set, about 2 hours. Decorate with chocolate curls.

Pumpkin Pie

A North American classic, this pie is traditionally served at Thanksgiving.

Serves 8

40g/1½oz/scant ½ cup pecan nuts, chopped
250g/9oz puréed pumpkin
475ml/16fl oz/2 cups single cream
130g/4½oz/¾ cup light brown sugar
1.5ml/¼ tsp salt
5ml/1 tsp ground cinnamon
2.5ml/½ tsp ground ginger
1.5ml/¼ tsp ground cloves
1.5ml/¼ tsp grated nutmeg
2 eggs

For the pastry

165g/5½oz/1⅓ cups plain flour
2.5ml/½ tsp salt
115g/4oz/½ cup lard or vegetable fat
30–45ml/2–3 tbsp iced water

1 Preheat the oven to 220°C/425°F/Gas 7. For the pastry, sift the flour and salt into a mixing bowl. Rub in the fat until the mixture resembles coarse breadcrumbs. Sprinkle in enough water to form the mixture into a ball.

2 Roll out the pastry to a 5mm/¼in thickness. Use to line a 23cm/9in pie tin. Trim and flute the edge. Sprinkle the chopped pecan nuts over the base of the case.

3 Beat together the pumpkin, cream, sugar, salt, spices and eggs. Pour the pumpkin mixture into the pastry case. Bake for 10 minutes, then reduce the heat to 180°C/350°F/Gas 4 and continue baking until the filling is set, about 45 minutes. Leave the pie to cool in the tin, set on a wire rack.

Chocolate Nut Tart

This is a sophisticated tart – strictly for grown-ups!

Serves 6–8

225g/8oz sweet shortcrust pastry
200g/7oz/1¾ cups dry amaretti biscuits
90g/3½oz/⅔ cup blanched almonds
50g/2oz/½ cup blanched hazelnuts
45ml/3 tbsp sugar
200g/7oz plain cooking chocolate
45ml/3 tbsp milk
50g/2oz/4 tbsp butter
45ml/3 tbsp amaretto liqueur or brandy
30ml/2 tbsp single cream

1 Grease a shallow loose-based 25cm/10in tart tin. Roll out the pastry and use to line the tin. Trim the edge, prick the base with a fork and chill for 30 minutes.

2 Grind the amaretti biscuits in a blender or food processor. Tip into a mixing bowl. Set eight whole almonds aside and place the rest in the food processor or blender with the hazelnuts and sugar. Grind to a medium texture. Add the nuts to the amaretti, and mix well.

3 Preheat the oven to 190°C/375°F/Gas 5. In the top of a double boiler, melt the chocolate with the milk and butter. Stir until smooth.

4 Pour the chocolate mixture into the dry ingredients, and mix well. Add the liqueur or brandy and cream.

5 Spread the filling evenly in the pastry case. Bake for 35 minutes, or until the crust is golden brown and the filling has puffed up and is beginning to darken. Allow to cool to room temperature. Split the reserved almonds in half and use to decorate the tart.

Pecan Nut Tartlets

These delightful individual tartlets make an elegant dinner-party dessert.

Makes 6 10cm/4in tartlets

450g/1lb shortcrust pastry
175g/6oz/1 cup pecan nut halves
3 eggs, beaten
25g/1oz/2 tbsp butter, melted
275g/10oz/1¼ cups golden syrup
2.5ml/½ tsp vanilla essence
115g/4oz/generous ½ cup caster sugar
15ml/1 tbsp plain flour

1 Preheat the oven to 180°C/350°F/Gas 4. Roll out the pastry and use to line 6 10cm/4in tartlet tins. Divide the pecan nut halves between the pastry cases.

2 Combine the eggs with the butter, and add the golden syrup and vanilla essence. Sift over the caster sugar and flour, and blend. Fill the pastry cases with the mixture and leave until the nuts rise to the surface.

3 Bake for 35–40 minutes, until a skewer inserted in the centre comes out clean. Cool in the tins for 15 minutes, then turn out on to a wire rack.

Pear and Hazelnut Flan

A delicious flan for Sunday lunch. Grind the hazelnuts yourself if you prefer, or use ground almonds instead.

Serves 6–8

115g/4oz/1 cup plain flour
115g/4oz/¾ cup wholemeal flour
115g/4oz/½ cup sunflower margarine
45ml/3 tbsp cold water

For the filling

50g/2oz/½ cup self-raising flour
115g/4oz/1 cup ground hazelnuts
5ml/1 tsp vanilla essence
50g/2oz/4 tbsp caster sugar
50g/2oz/4 tbsp butter, softened
2 eggs, beaten
45ml/3 tbsp raspberry jam
400g/14oz can pears in natural juice
few chopped hazelnuts, to decorate

1 For the pastry, stir the flours together, then rub in the margarine until the mixture resembles fine breadcrumbs. Mix to a firm dough with the water.

2 Roll out the dough and use to line a 23–25cm/9–10in flan tin, pressing it up the sides after trimming, so the pastry sits a little above the tin. Prick the base, line with greaseproof paper and fill with baking beans. Chill for 30 minutes.

3 Preheat the oven to 200°C/400°F/Gas 6. Place the flan tin on a baking sheet and bake blind for 20 minutes. Remove the paper and beans after 15 minutes.

4 Beat all the filling ingredients together except for the jam and pears. If too thick, stir in some of the pear juice. Reduce the oven temperature to 180°C/350°F/Gas 4. Spread the jam on the pastry case and spoon over the filling.

5 Drain the pears and arrange them, cut-side down, in the filling. Scatter over the nuts. Bake for 30 minutes until risen, firm and golden brown.

Latticed Peaches

This elegant dessert may be prepared using canned peach halves when fresh peaches are out of season.

Serves 6

For the pastry

115g/4oz/1 cup plain flour
45ml/3 tbsp butter or sunflower margarine
45ml/3 tbsp natural yogurt
30ml/2 tbsp orange juice
milk, to glaze

For the filling

3 ripe peaches
45ml/3 tbsp ground almonds
30ml/2 tbsp natural yogurt
finely grated rind of 1 small orange
1.5ml/¼ tsp almond essence

For the sauce

1 ripe peach
45ml/3 tbsp orange juice

1 Lightly grease a baking sheet. Sift the flour into a bowl and rub in the butter or margarine. Stir in the yogurt and orange juice to make a firm dough. Roll out half the pastry thinly and stamp out six rounds with a 7.5cm/3in biscuit cutter.

2 Skin the peaches, halve and remove the stones. Mix together the almonds, yogurt, orange rind and almond essence. Spoon into the hollows of each peach half and place, cut-side down, on the pastry rounds.

3 Roll out the remaining pastry thinly and cut into thin strips. Arrange the strips over the peaches to form a lattice, brushing with milk to secure firmly. Trim the ends. Chill for 30 minutes. Preheat the oven to 200°C/400°F/ Gas 6. Brush with milk and bake for 15–18 minutes, until golden brown.

4 For the sauce, skin the peach and halve it to remove the stone. Place the flesh in a food processor or blender, with the orange juice, and purée until smooth. Serve the peaches hot, with the peach sauce spooned around.

Surprise Fruit Tarts

These delicious and simple little tarts are the perfect summer treat.

Serves 6

4 large or 8 small sheets frozen filo pastry, thawed
65g/2½oz/5 tbsp butter or margarine, melted
250ml/8fl oz/1 cup whipping cream
45ml/3 tbsp strawberry jam
15ml/1 tbsp Cointreau or other orange-flavour liqueur
115g/4oz/1 cup seedless black grapes, halved
115g/4oz/1 cup seedless white grapes, halved
150g/5oz fresh pineapple, cubed, or drained canned pineapple chunks
115g/4oz/⅔ cup raspberries
30ml/2 tbsp icing sugar
6 sprigs fresh mint, to decorate

1 Preheat the oven to 180°C/350°F/Gas 4. Grease six cups of a bun tray. Stack the filo sheets and cut with a sharp knife or scissors into 24 squares 11cm/4½in.

2 Lay four squares of pastry in each of the six greased cups. Press the pastry firmly into the cups, rotating slightly to make star-shaped baskets. Brush the pastry baskets lightly with butter or margarine. Bake until the pastry is crisp and golden, 5–7 minutes. Cool on a wire rack.

3 In a bowl, lightly whip the cream until soft peaks form. Gently fold the strawberry jam and Cointreau into the cream.

4 Just before serving, spoon a little of the cream mixture into each pastry basket. Top with the fruit. Sprinkle with icing sugar and decorate each basket with a small sprig of mint.

Truffle Filo Tarts

The cups can be prepared a day ahead and stored in an air-tight container.

Makes 24 cups

3–6 sheets fresh or frozen (thawed) filo pastry, depending on size
45g/1½oz/3 tbsp unsalted butter, melted
sugar, for sprinkling
lemon rind, to decorate

Truffle mixture

250ml/8fl oz/1 cup double cream
225g/8oz bittersweet or semi-sweet chocolate, chopped
50g/2oz/4 tbsp unsalted butter, cut into pieces
30ml/2 tbsp brandy

1 Prepare the truffle mixture. In a saucepan over medium heat, bring the cream to the boil. Remove from the heat and add the chocolate, stirring until melted. Beat in the butter and add the brandy. Sieve into a bowl and chill for 1 hour.

2 Preheat the oven to 200°C/400°F/Gas 6. Grease a bun tray with 24 cups, each 4cm/1½in. Cut each filo sheet into 6cm/2½in squares. Cover with a damp dish towel. Keeping the filo sheets covered, place one square on a work surface. Brush lightly with melted butter, turn over and brush the other side. Sprinkle with a pinch of sugar. Butter another square and place it over the first at an angle. Sprinkle with sugar. Butter a third square and place over the first two, unevenly, so the corners form an uneven edge. Press the layered square into the tray. Continue to fill the tray.

3 Bake the filo cups for 4–6 minutes, until golden. Cool for 10 minutes on a wire rack in the tray. Remove from the tray and cool completely.

4 Stir the chocolate mixture, which should be just thick enough to pipe. Spoon the mixture into a piping bag fitted with a medium star nozzle and pipe a swirl into each cup. Decorate with lemon rind.

Apple Strudel

Ready-made filo pastry makes a good substitute for paper-thin strudel pastry in this classic Austrian dish.

Serves 10–12

75g/3oz/generous ½ cup raisins
30ml/2 tbsp brandy
5 eating apples
3 large cooking apples
90g/3½oz/generous ½ cup dark brown sugar
5ml/1 tsp ground cinnamon
grated rind and juice of 1 lemon
25g/1oz/½ cup dry breadcrumbs
50g/2oz/½ cup chopped pecan nuts or walnuts
12 sheets frozen filo pastry, thawed
175g/6oz/¾ cup butter, melted
icing sugar, for dusting

1 Soak the raisins in the brandy for 15 minutes.

2 Peel, core and thinly slice the apples. Combine with the rest of the filling ingredients, reserving half the breadcrumbs.

3 Preheat the oven to 190°C/375°F/Gas 5. Grease two baking sheets. Unfold the filo pastry and cover with a dish towel. One by one, butter and stack the sheets to make a six-sheet pile.

4 Sprinkle half the reserved breadcrumbs over the last sheet and spoon half the apple mixture at the bottom edge. Roll up from this edge, Swiss roll style. Place on a baking sheet, seam-side down and fold under the ends to seal. Repeat to make a second strudel. Brush both with butter.

5 Bake in the oven for 45 minutes, cool slightly, then dust with icing sugar.

Cherry Strudel

A refreshing variation on traditional apple strudel. Serve with whipped cream, if you like.

Serves 8

65g/2½oz/1¼ cups fresh breadcrumbs
175g/6oz/¾ cup butter, melted
200g/7oz/1 cup sugar
15ml/1 tbsp ground cinnamon
5ml/1 tsp grated lemon rind
450g/1lb/2 cups sour cherries, stoned
8 sheets filo pastry
icing sugar, for dusting

1 In a frying pan, fry the breadcrumbs in 65g/2½oz/5 tbsp of the butter until golden. Set aside.

2 In a large mixing bowl, toss together the sugar, cinnamon and lemon rind. Stir in the cherries.

3 Preheat the oven to 190°C/375°F/Gas 5. Grease a baking sheet. Unfold the filo sheets. Keep the unused sheets covered with damp kitchen paper. Lift off one sheet and place on a piece of greaseproof paper. Brush the pastry with butter. Sprinkle an eighth of the breadcrumbs over the surface.

4 Lay a second sheet of filo pastry on top, brush with butter and sprinkle with breadcrumbs. Continue until you have used up all the pastry.

5 Spoon the cherry mixture at the bottom edge of the strip. Starting at the cherry-filled end, roll up the dough Swiss roll style. Use the paper to flip the strudel on to the baking sheet, seam-side down. Carefully fold under the ends to seal. Brush the top with melted butter.

6 Bake the strudel for 45 minutes. Cool slightly, then dust with a fine layer of icing sugar.

Strawberry Tart

This tart is best assembled just before serving, but you can bake the pastry case and make the filling ahead.

Serves 6

350g/12oz rough-puff or puff pastry
225g/8oz/1 cup cream cheese
grated rind of ½ orange
30ml/2 tbsp orange liqueur or juice
45–60ml/3–4 tbsp icing sugar, plus extra for dusting (optional)
450g/1lb/4 cups ripe strawberries, hulled

1 Preheat the oven to 200°C/400°F/Gas 6. Roll out the pastry to about a 3mm/⅛in thickness and use to line a 28 x 10cm/11 x 4in rectangular flan tin. Trim the edges, then chill for 30 minutes.

2 Prick the base of the pastry all over. Line with foil, fill with baking beans and bake for 15 minutes. Remove the foil and beans and bake for 10 minutes, until the pastry is browned. Gently press down on the pastry base to deflate, then leave to cool on a wire rack.

3 Beat together the cheese, orange rind, liqueur or orange juice and icing sugar to taste. Spread the cheese filling in the pastry case. Halve the strawberries and arrange them on top of the filling. Dust with icing sugar, if you like.

Alsatian Plum Tart

Fruit and custard tarts, similar to a fruit quiche, are typical in Alsace. Sometimes they have a yeast dough base instead of pastry. You can use other seasonal fruits in this tart, or a mixture of fruit.

Serves 6–8

450g/1lb ripe plums, halved and stoned
30ml/2 tbsp kirsch or plum brandy
350g/12oz shortcrust or sweet shortcrust pastry
30ml/2 tbsp seedless raspberry jam

For the custard filling

2 eggs
25g/1oz/4 tbsp icing sugar
175ml/6 fl oz/¾ cup double cream
grated rind of ½ lemon
1.5ml/¼ tsp vanilla essence

1 Preheat the oven to 200°C/400°F/Gas 6. Mix the plums with the kirsch or brandy and set aside for about 30 minutes.

2 Roll out the pastry thinly and use to line a 23cm/9in pie tin. Prick the base of the pastry case all over and line with foil. Add a layer of baking beans and bake for 15 minutes until slightly dry and set. Remove the foil and the baking beans.

3 Brush the base of the pastry case with a thin layer of jam, then bake for a further 5 minutes. Remove the pastry case from the oven and transfer to a wire rack. Reduce the oven temperature to 180°C/350°F/Gas 4.

4 To make the custard filling, beat the eggs and sugar until well combined, then beat in the cream, lemon rind, vanilla and any juice from the plums.

5 Arrange the plums, cut-side down, in the pastry case and pour over the custard mixture. Bake for about 30–35 minutes until a knife inserted in the centre comes out clean. Serve the tart warm or at room temperature.

Almond Mincemeat Tartlets

Makes 36

275g/10oz/2½ cups plain flour
75g/3oz/¾ cup icing sugar
5ml/1 tsp ground cinnamon
175g/6oz/¾ cup butter
50g/2oz/½ cup ground almonds
1 egg yolk
45ml/3 tbsp milk
450g/1lb jar mincemeat
15ml/1 tbsp brandy or rum

For the lemon filling

115g/4oz/½ cup butter or margarine
115g/4oz/½ cup caster sugar
175g/6oz/1½ cups self-raising flour
2 large eggs
finely grated rind of 1 large lemon

For the lemon icing

115g/4oz/1 cup icing sugar
15ml/1 tbsp lemon juice

1 Sift the flour, sugar and cinnamon into a bowl and rub in the butter until it resembles breadcrumbs. Add the ground almonds and bind with the egg yolk and milk to a soft, pliable dough. Knead until smooth, wrap and chill for 30 minutes.

2 Preheat the oven to 375°F/190°C/Gas 5. On a lightly floured surface, roll out the pastry and cut out 36 fluted rounds with a pastry cutter. Mix the mincemeat with the brandy or rum and put a small teaspoonful in the bottom of each pastry case. Chill.

3 For the lemon sponge filling, whisk the butter or margarine, sugar, flour, eggs and lemon rind together until smooth. Spoon on top of the mincemeat, dividing it evenly, and level the tops. Bake for 20–30 minutes, or until golden brown and springy to the touch. Remove and leave to cool on a wire rack.

4 For the lemon icing, sift the icing sugar and mix with the lemon juice to a smooth coating consistency. Spoon into a piping bag and drizzle a zig-zag pattern over each tart. If you're short of time, simply dust the tartlets with icing sugar.

Mince Pies with Orange Pastry

Homemade mince pies are so much nicer than shop-bought, especially with this flavoursome pastry.

Makes 18

225g/8oz/2 cups plain flour
30g/1½oz/scant ⅓ cup icing sugar
10ml/2 tsp ground cinnamon
150g/5oz/generous 1 cup butter
grated rind of 1 orange
about 60ml/4 tbsp iced water
225g/8oz/1½ cups mincemeat
1 egg, beaten, to glaze
icing sugar, for dusting

1 Sift together the flour, icing sugar and cinnamon. Rub in the butter until it resembles fine breadcrumbs. Stir in the grated orange rind.

2 Mix to a firm dough with the water. Knead lightly, then roll out to a 5mm/¼in thickness. Using a 7cm/2½in round biscuit cutter, stamp out 18 circles, then stamp out 18 smaller 5cm/2in circles.

3 Line two bun tins with the larger circles. Place a small spoonful of mincemeat into each pastry case and top with the smaller pastry circles, pressing the edges to seal.

4 Glaze the tops with egg and leave to rest in the fridge for 30 minutes. Preheat the oven to 200°C/400°F/Gas 6.

5 Bake for 15–20 minutes, or until golden brown. Remove to wire racks. Serve just warm, dusted with icing sugar.

Glacé Fruit Pie

Use half digestive and half gingernut biscuits for the crust, if you prefer.

Serves 10

15ml/1 tbsp rum
50g/2oz/4 tbsp mixed glacé fruit, chopped
475ml/16fl oz/2 cups milk
20ml/4 tsp gelatine
90g/3½oz/½ cup sugar
2.5ml/½ tsp salt
3 eggs, separated
250ml/8fl oz/1 cup whipping cream, whipped
chocolate curls, to decorate

For the crust

175g/6oz/2 cups digestive biscuits, crushed
75g/2½oz/5 tbsp butter, melted
15ml/1 tbsp sugar

1 Mix the digestive biscuits, butter and sugar. Press evenly over the base and sides of a 23cm/9in pie plate. Chill.

2 Stir together the rum and glacé fruit. Set aside. Pour 120ml/4fl oz/½ cup of the milk into a small bowl. Sprinkle over the gelatine and leave for 5 minutes to soften.

3 In the top of a double boiler, combine 50g/2oz/4 tbsp of the sugar, the remaining milk and salt. Stir in the gelatine mixture. Cook, stirring, until the gelatine dissolves. Whisk in the egg yolks and cook, stirring, until thick enough to coat the spoon. Pour the custard over the glacé fruit mixture, set in a bowl of iced water.

4 Beat the egg whites until they peak softly. Add the remaining sugar and beat just to blend. Fold a large dollop of the egg whites into the cooled gelatine mixture. Pour into the remaining egg whites and fold together. Fold in the cream.

5 Pour into the pie crust and chill until firm. Decorate with chocolate curls.

Chocolate Chiffon Pie

As the name suggests, this is a wonderfully smooth and light-textured pie.

Serves 8

200g/7oz plain chocolate, chopped
250ml/8fl oz/1 cup milk
15ml/1 tbsp gelatine
90g/3½oz/1 cup sugar
2 extra-large eggs, separated
5ml/1 tsp vanilla essence
1.5ml/¼ tsp salt
350ml/12fl oz/1½ cups whipping cream, whipped
whipped cream and chocolate curls, to decorate

For the crust

200g/7oz/2⅓ cups digestive biscuits, crushed
75g/3oz/6 tbsp butter, melted

1 Place a baking sheet in the oven and preheat to 180°C/350°F/Gas 4. Mix the biscuits and butter together and press over the base and sides of a 23cm/9in pie plate. Bake for 8 minutes.

2 Grate the chocolate in a blender or food processor. Place the milk in the top of a double boiler. Sprinkle over the gelatine and leave for 5 minutes to soften.

3 In the top of a double boiler, put 40g/1½oz/6 tbsp sugar, the chocolate and egg yolks. Stir until dissolved. Add the vanilla. Place the top in a bowl of ice and stir until the mixture reaches room temperature. Remove from the ice.

4 Beat the egg whites and salt until they peak softly. Add the remaining sugar and beat just to blend. Fold a dollop of egg whites into the chocolate mixture, then pour back into the whites and fold in.

5 Fold in the cream and pour into the pie crust. Freeze until just set, about 5 minutes, then chill for 3–4 hours. Decorate with whipped cream and chocolate curls.

Chocolate Pear Tart

Chocolate and pears have a natural affinity, well used in this luxurious pudding.

Serves 8
115g/4oz plain chocolate, grated
3 large firm, ripe pears
1 egg
1 egg yolk
120ml/4fl oz/½ cup single cream
2.5ml/½ tsp vanilla essence
45ml/3 tbsp caster sugar

For the pastry
150g/5oz/1¼ cups plain flour
1.5ml/¼ tsp salt
30ml/2 tbsp sugar
115g/4oz/½ cup cold unsalted butter, cut into pieces
1 egg yolk
15ml/1 tbsp lemon juice

1 For the pastry, sift the flour and salt into a bowl. Add the sugar and butter. Rub in until the mixture resembles coarse breadcrumbs. Stir in the egg yolk and lemon juice. Form a ball, wrap, and chill for 20 minutes.

2 Preheat the oven to 200°C/400°F/Gas 6. Roll out the pastry and use to line a 25cm/10in tart dish.

3 Sprinkle the pastry case with the grated chocolate.

4 Peel, halve and core the pears. Cut in thin slices crossways, then fan out slightly. Transfer the pears to the tart using a palette knife and arrange like wheel spokes.

5 Whisk together the egg and egg yolk, cream and vanilla. Ladle over the pears and sprinkle with sugar.

6 Bake on a baking sheet for 10 minutes. Reduce the heat to 180°C/350°F/Gas 4 and cook until the custard is set and the pears begin to caramelize, about 20 minutes more. Serve while still warm.

Pear and Apple Crumble Pie

You could use just one fruit in this pie if you prefer.

Serves 8
3 firm pears
4 cooking apples
175g/6oz/scant 1 cup caster sugar
30ml/2 tbsp cornflour
1.5ml/¼ tsp salt
grated rind of 1 lemon
30ml/2 tbsp fresh lemon juice
75g/3oz/generous ½ cup raisins
75g/3oz/¾ cup plain flour
5ml/1 tsp ground cinnamon
75g/3oz/6 tbsp cold butter, cut in pieces

For the pastry
150g/5oz/1¼ cups plain flour
2.5ml/½ tsp salt
65g/2½oz/5 tbsp cold vegetable fat or lard, cut in pieces
30ml/2 tbsp iced water

1 For the pastry, sift the flour and salt into a bowl. Add the fat and rub in until the mixture resembles breadcrumbs. Stir in enough water to bind. Form into a ball, roll out, and use to line a 23cm/9in pie dish, leaving a 1cm/½in overhang. Fold this under for double thickness. Flute the edge, then chill.

2 Preheat a baking sheet at 230°C/450°F/Gas 8. Peel, core and slice the fruit. Combine in a bowl with one-third of the sugar, the cornflour, salt, lemon rind and juice, and raisins.

3 For the crumble topping, combine the remaining sugar, flour, cinnamon and butter in a bowl. Rub in until the mixture resembles coarse breadcrumbs.

4 Spoon the filling into the pastry case. Sprinkle the crumbs over the top.

5 Bake on the baking sheet for 10 minutes, then reduce the heat to 180°C/350°F/Gas 4. Cover the pie loosely with foil and bake until browned, 35–40 minutes more.

Chocolate Lemon Tart

The unusual chocolate pastry complements the lemon filling superbly in this rich tart.

Serves 8–10

245g/8¾oz/1¼ cups caster sugar
6 eggs
grated rind of 2 lemons
160ml/5½fl oz/generous ⅔ cup fresh lemon juice
160ml/5½fl oz/generous ⅔ cup whipping cream
chocolate curls, to decorate

For the pastry

180g/6¼oz/generous 1½ cups plain flour
30ml/2 tbsp cocoa powder
25g/1oz/4 tbsp icing sugar
2.5ml/½ tsp salt
115g/4oz/½ cup butter or margarine
15ml/1 tbsp water

1 Grease a 25cm/10in tart tin. For the pastry, sift the flour, cocoa powder, icing sugar and salt into a bowl. Set aside.

2 Melt the butter and water over a low heat. Pour over the flour mixture and stir until the dough is smooth.

3 Press the dough evenly over the base and sides of the tart tin. Chill while preparing the filling.

4 Preheat a baking sheet in the oven at 190°C/375°F/Gas 5. Whisk the sugar and eggs until the sugar is dissolved. Add the lemon rind and juice and mix well. Add the cream.

5 Pour the filling into the pastry case and bake on the hot baking sheet until the filling is set, 20–25 minutes. Cool on a wire rack, then decorate with chocolate curls.

Kiwi Ricotta Cheese Tart

A delicious filling in a rich pastry case creates an elegant dinner-party dessert.

Serves 8

75g/3oz/½ cup blanched almonds, ground
130g/3½ oz/½ cup sugar
900g/2lb/4 cups ricotta cheese
250ml/8fl oz/1 cup whipping cream
1 egg and 3 egg yolks
15ml/1 tbsp plain flour
pinch of salt
30ml/2 tbsp rum
grated rind of 1 lemon
30ml/2 tbsp lemon juice
30ml/2 tbsp honey
5 kiwi fruit

For the pastry

150g/5oz/1¼ cups plain flour
15ml/1 tbsp sugar
2.5ml/½ tsp each salt and baking powder
75g/3oz/6 tbsp butter
1 egg yolk
45–60ml/3–4 tbsp whipping cream

1 For the pastry, mix the flour, sugar, salt and baking powder. Add the butter and rub in. Mix in the egg yolk and cream to bind the pastry. Wrap and chill for 30 minutes.

2 Preheat the oven to 220°C/425°F/Gas 7. On a lightly floured surface, roll out the dough to a 3mm/⅛in thickness. Use to line a 23cm/9in springform tin. Prick the pastry all over with a fork. Line with crumpled greaseproof paper and fill with dried beans. Bake for 10 minutes. Remove the paper and beans and bake for another 6–8 minutes until golden. Reduce the oven temperature to 180°C/350°F/Gas 4.

3 Mix the almonds with 15ml/1 tbsp of the sugar. Beat the ricotta until creamy then add the cream, egg, yolks, remaining sugar, flour, salt, rum, lemon rind and 30ml/2 tbsp lemon juice. Beat, add the almonds and mix. Pour into pastry case and bake for 1 hour, until golden. Cool and chill. Mix the honey and remaining lemon juice. Halve the kiwis lengthways then slice. Arrange over tart and brush with the honey glaze.

Lime Tart

Use lemons instead of limes, with yellow food colouring, if you prefer.

Serves 8

3 large egg yolks
400g/14oz can sweetened condensed milk
15ml/1 tbsp grated lime rind
120ml/4fl oz/½ cup fresh lime juice
green food colouring (optional)
120ml/4fl oz/½ cup whipping cream

For the base

115g/4oz/1⅓ cups crushed digestive biscuits
65g/2½oz/5 tbsp butter or margarine, melted

1 Preheat the oven to 180°C/350°F/Gas 4. For the base, place the crushed biscuits in a bowl and add the butter or margarine. Mix to combine.

2 Press the mixture evenly over the base and sides of a 23cm/9in pie dish. Bake for 8 minutes, then cool.

3 Beat the yolks until thick. Beat in the milk, lime rind and juice and colouring, if using. Pour into the pastry case and chill until set, about 4 hours. To serve, whip the cream. Pipe a lattice pattern on top, or spoon dollops around the edge.

Fruit Tartlets

You could make one large fruit tart for an elegant dessert, if you like.

Makes 8

175ml/6fl oz/¾ cup redcurrant jelly
15ml/1 tbsp fresh lemon juice
175ml/6fl oz/¾ cup whipping cream
675g/1½lb fresh fruit, such as strawberries, raspberries, kiwi fruit, peaches, grapes or currants, peeled and sliced as necessary

For the pastry

150g/5oz/generous ½ cup cold butter, cut in pieces
65g/2½oz/scant ½ cup dark brown sugar
45ml/3 tbsp cocoa powder
200g/7oz/1¾ cups plain flour
1 egg white

1 For the pastry, melt the butter, brown sugar and cocoa over a low heat. Remove from the heat and sift over the flour. Stir, then add enough egg white to bind. Form into a ball, wrap, and chill for 30 minutes.

2 Grease eight 8cm/3in tartlet tins. Roll out the pastry between two sheets of greaseproof paper. Stamp out eight 10cm/4in rounds with a fluted biscuit cutter.

3 Line the tartlet tins and prick the bases with a fork. Chill for 15 minutes. Preheat the oven to 180°C/350°F/Gas 4.

4 Bake the pastry cases until firm, 20–25 minutes. Cool, then turn out.

5 Melt the jelly with the lemon juice. Brush over the tartlet bases. Whip the cream and spread thinly in the tartlet cases. Arrange the fruit on top. Brush with the jelly glaze and serve.

Chocolate Cheesecake Tart

You can use just digestive biscuits for the base of this tart, if you prefer.

Serves 8

350g/12oz/1½ cups cream cheese
60ml/4 tbsp whipping cream
225g/8oz/generous 1 cup caster sugar
50g/2oz/½ cup cocoa powder
2.5ml/½ tsp ground cinnamon
3 eggs
whipped cream and chocolate curls, to decorate

For the base

75g/3oz/1 cup crushed digestive biscuits
40g/1½oz/scant 1 cup crushed amaretti biscuits
75g/3oz/6 tbsp butter, melted

1 Preheat a baking sheet in the oven at 180°C/350°F/Gas 4. For the base, mix the crushed biscuits and butter in a bowl. Press the mixture over the base and sides of a 23cm/9in pie dish. Bake for 8 minutes. Leave to cool. Keep the oven on.

2 Beat the cream cheese and cream together until smooth. Beat in the sugar, cocoa and cinnamon until blended.

3 Add the eggs, one at a time, beating just enough to blend.

4 Pour into the biscuit base and bake on the baking sheet for 25–30 minutes. The filling will sink down as it cools. Decorate with whipped cream and chocolate curls.

Frozen Strawberry Tart

For a frozen raspberry tart, use raspberries in place of the strawberries.

Serves 8

225g/8oz/1 cup cream cheese
250ml/8fl oz/1 cup soured cream
500g/1¼lb/5 cups frozen strawberries, thawed and sliced

For the base

115g/4oz/1⅓ cups crushed digestive biscuits
15ml/1 tbsp caster sugar
65g/2½oz/5 tbsp butter, melted

1 For the base, mix together the biscuits, sugar and butter. Press the mixture over the base and sides of a 23cm/9in pie dish. Freeze until firm.

2 Blend together the cream cheese and soured cream. Reserve 90ml/6 tbsp of the strawberries. Add the rest to the cream cheese mixture.

3 Pour the filling into the biscuit base and freeze until firm, about 6–8 hours. To serve, spoon some of the reserved strawberries on top.

Treacle Tart

A very rich dessert, popular with all the family.

Serves 4–6

175ml/6fl oz/¾ cup golden syrup
75g/3oz/1½ cups fresh white breadcrumbs
grated rind of 1 lemon
30ml/2 tbsp fresh lemon juice

For the pastry

175g/6oz/1½ cups plain flour
2.5ml/½ tsp salt
75g/3oz/6 tbsp cold butter, cut in pieces
40g/1½oz/3 tbsp cold margarine, cut in pieces
45–60ml/3–4 tbsp iced water

1 For the pastry, sift together the flour and salt, add the fats and rub in until the mixture resembles coarse breadcrumbs. Stir in enough water to bind. Form into a ball, wrap and chill for 20 minutes.

2 Roll out the pastry and use to line a 20cm/8in pie dish. Chill for 20 minutes. Reserve the pastry trimmings.

3 Preheat a baking sheet in the oven at 200°C/400°F/Gas 6. In a saucepan, warm the syrup until thin and runny. Stir in the breadcrumbs and lemon rind. Leave for 10 minutes, then stir in the lemon juice. Spread in the pastry case.

4 Roll out the pastry trimmings and cut into 12 thin strips. Lay six strips on the filling, then lay the other six at an angle over them to form a lattice.

5 Bake on the baking sheet for 10 minutes. Lower the heat to 190°C/375°F/Gas 5. Bake until golden, about 15 minutes more. Serve warm or cold.

Almond Syrup Tart

Serves 6

75g/3oz/1½ cups fresh white breadcrumbs
225g/8oz/1 cup golden syrup
finely grated rind of ½ lemon
10ml/2 tsp lemon juice
23cm/9in pastry case, made with basic, nut or rich shortcrust pastry
25g/1oz/4 tbsp flaked almonds
milk, to glaze (optional)
cream, custard, ice cream, to serve

1 Preheat the oven to 200°C/400°F/Gas 6. Combine the breadcrumbs with the syrup and the lemon rind and juice.

2 Spoon into the pastry case and spread out evenly. Sprinkle the flaked almonds evenly over the top.

3 Brush the pastry with milk to glaze, if you like. Bake for 25–30 minutes, until the pastry and filling are golden brown.

4 Transfer to a wire rack to cool. Serve warm or cold, with cream, custard or ice cream.

Tarte Tatin

A special *tarte tatin* tin is ideal, but an ovenproof frying pan can be used quite successfully.

Serves 8–10

225g/½lb puff or shortcrust pastry
10–12 large Golden Delicious apples
115g/4oz/½ cup butter, cut into pieces
115g/4oz/½ cup caster sugar
2.5ml/½ tsp ground cinnamon
crème fraîche or whipped cream, to serve

1 On a lightly floured surface, roll out the pastry to a 28cm/11in round less than 5mm/¼in thick. Transfer to a lightly floured baking sheet and chill.

2 Peel, halve and core the apples, sprinkle with lemon juice.

3 In a 25cm/10in *tarte tatin* tin, cook the butter, sugar and cinnamon until the butter has melted and the sugar has dissolved. Cook for 6–8 minutes until the mixture is a medium caramel colour. Remove from the heat and arrange the apple halves, standing on their edges, in the tin.

4 Return the tin to the heat and simmer for 20–25 minutes until the apples are tender and coloured. Remove from the heat and cool slightly.

5 Preheat the oven to 230°C/450°F/Gas 8. Place the pastry over the apples and tuck the edges inside the tin around the apples. Pierce the pastry in two or three places, then bake for 25–30 minutes until the pastry is golden and the filling is bubbling. Cool in the tin for 10–15 minutes.

6 To serve, run a sharp knife around the edge of the tin to loosen the pastry. Cover with a serving plate and carefully invert the tin and plate together. It is best to do this over a sink in case any caramel drips. Lift off the tin and loosen any apples that stick with a palette knife. Serve the tart warm with crème fraîche or whipped cream.

Rich Chocolate Pie

A delicious pie generously decorated with chocolate curls.

Serves 8

75g/3oz plain chocolate
50g/2oz/4 tbsp butter or margarine
45ml/3 tbsp golden syrup
3 eggs, beaten
150g/5oz/⅔ cup caster sugar
5ml/1 tsp vanilla essence
115g/4oz milk chocolate
475ml/16fl oz/2 cups whipping cream

For the pastry

165g/5½oz/1⅓ cups plain flour
2.5ml/½ tsp salt
115g/4oz/½ cup lard or vegetable fat
30–45ml/2–3 tbsp iced water

1 Preheat the oven to 220°C/425°F/Gas 7. For the pastry, sift the flour and salt into a bowl. Rub in the fat until the mixture resembles coarse breadcrumbs. Add water until the pastry forms a ball.

2 Roll out the pastry and use to line a 20–23cm/8–9in pie tin. Flute the edge. Prick the base and sides of the pastry case with a fork. Bake until lightly browned, 10–15 minutes. Cool in the tin on a wire rack.

3 Reduce the oven temperature to 180°C/350°F/Gas 4. In the top of a double boiler, melt the plain chocolate, the butter or margarine and syrup. Remove from the heat and stir in the eggs, sugar and vanilla. Pour the chocolate mixture into the pastry case. Bake until the filling is set, 35–40 minutes. Cool in the tin on a wire rack.

4 For the decoration, use the heat of your hands to soften the milk chocolate slightly. Use a swivel-headed vegetable peeler to shave off short, wide curls. Chill until needed.

5 Before serving, lightly whip the cream until soft peaks form. Spread the cream over the surface of the chocolate filling. Decorate with the milk chocolate curls.

Red Berry Tart with Lemon Cream

This flan is best filled just before serving so the pastry remains mouth-wateringly crisp.

Serves 6–8

150g/5oz/1¼ cups plain flour
25g/1oz/4 tbsp cornflour
30g/1½oz/scant ⅓ cup icing sugar
90g/3½oz/7 tbsp butter
5ml/1 tsp vanilla essence
2 egg yolks, beaten

For the filling

200g/7oz/scant 1 cup cream cheese, softened
45ml/3 tbsp lemon curd
grated rind and juice of 1 lemon
icing sugar, to taste (optional)
225g/8oz/2 cups mixed red berry fruits
45ml/3 tbsp redcurrant jelly

1 Sift the flour, cornflour and icing sugar together. Rub in the butter until the mixture resembles fine breadcrumbs.

2 Beat the vanilla into the egg yolks, then stir into the flour mixture to make a firm dough. Add cold water if necessary.

3 Roll out the pastry and use it to line a 23cm/9in round flan tin. Trim the edges. Prick the base and leave to rest in the fridge for 30 minutes.

4 Preheat the oven to 200°C/400°F/Gas 6. Line the flan with greaseproof paper and fill with baking beans. Place on a baking sheet and bake for 20 minutes, removing the paper and beans after 15 minutes. Leave to cool, then remove the pastry case from the flan tin.

5 Cream the cheese, lemon curd and lemon rind and juice, adding icing sugar if you wish. Spread the mixture into the base of the flan. Top with the fruits. Warm the redcurrant jelly and trickle over the fruits just before serving.

Peach Tart with Almond Cream

Serves 8–10

4 large ripe peaches, peeled
115g/4oz blanched almonds
15g/½oz/2 tbsp plain flour
100g/3¼oz/scant ¼ cup unsalted butter
115g/4oz/1 cup, plus 2 tbsp caster sugar
1 egg, plus 1 egg yolk
1.5ml/¼ tsp vanilla essence, or 10ml/2 tsp rum

For the pastry

190g/6¼oz/generous 1½ cups plain flour
2.5ml/½ tsp salt
100g/3¼oz/scant ¼ cup cold unsalted butter, diced
1 egg yolk
10–45ml/2–3 tbsp iced water

1 Sift the flour and salt into a bowl. Rub in the butter until the mixture resembles coarse breadcrumbs. Stir in the egg yolk and enough water to bind the pastry. Gather into a ball, wrap and chill for at least 20 minutes. Preheat a baking sheet in the centre of a 200°C/400°F/Gas 6 oven.

2 Roll out the pastry 3mm/⅛in thick. Transfer to a 25cm/10in pie dish. Trim the edge, prick the base and chill.

3 Grind the almonds with the flour. With an electric mixer, cream the butter and 115g/4oz/scant ¾ cup of the sugar until light and fluffy. Gradually beat in the egg and yolk. Stir in the almonds and vanilla or rum. Spread in the pastry case.

4 Halve the peaches and remove the stones. Cut crossways in thin slices and arrange on top of the almond cream like the spokes of a wheel. Keep the slices of each peach-half together. Fan out by pressing down gently at a slight angle.

5 Bake until the pastry browns, 10–15 minutes. Lower the heat to 180°C/350°F/Gas 4 and bake until the almond cream sets, about 15 minutes more. 10 minutes before the end of the cooking time, sprinkle with the remaining sugar.

Pear and Almond Cream Tart

This tart is equally successful made with nectarines, peaches, apricots or apples.

Serves 6

350g/12oz shortcrust or sweet shortcrust pastry
3 firm pears
lemon juice
15ml/1 tbsp peach brandy or cold water
60ml/4 tbsp peach jam, sieved

For the filling

90g/3½oz/generous ½ cup blanched whole almonds
50g/2oz/4 tbsp caster sugar
65g/2½oz/5 tbsp butter
1 egg, plus 1 egg white
few drops almond essence

1 Roll out the pastry and use to line a 23cm/9in flan tin. Chill. For the filling, put the almonds and sugar in a food processor or blender and pulse until finely ground but not pasty. Add the butter and process until creamy, then add the egg, egg white and almond essence and mix well.

2 Preheat a baking sheet in the oven at 190°C/375°F/Gas 5. Peel the pears, halve them, remove the cores and rub with lemon juice. Put the pear halves, cut-side down, on a board and slice thinly crossways, keeping the slices together.

3 Pour the filling into the pastry case. Slide a palette knife under one pear half and press the top to fan out the slices. Transfer to the tart, placing the fruit on the filling like spokes of a wheel.

4 Bake the tart on the baking sheet for 50–55 minutes, until the filling is set and well browned. Cool on a wire rack.

5 Heat the brandy or water with the jam. Brush over the top of the hot tart to glaze. Serve at room temperature.

Lemon Tart

This tart, a classic of France, has a refreshing tangy flavour.

Serves 8–10

350g/12oz shortcrust or sweet shortcrust pastry
grated rind of 2–3 lemons
150ml/¼ pint/⅔ cup freshly squeezed lemon juice
100g/3½oz/½ cup caster sugar
60ml/4 tbsp crème fraîche or double cream
4 eggs, plus 3 egg yolks
icing sugar, for dusting

1 Preheat the oven to 190°C/375°F/Gas 5. Roll out the pastry and use to line a 23cm/9in flan tin. Prick the base, line with foil and fill with baking beans. Bake for 15 minutes, or until the edges are dry. Remove the foil and beans, and bake for a further 5–7 minutes, until golden.

2 Beat together the lemon rind, juice and sugar, then gradually add the crème fraîche or double cream and beat until well blended. Beat in the eggs, one at a time, then beat in the egg yolks.

3 Pour the filling into the baked pastry case. Bake for about 15–20 minutes, until the filling is set. If the pastry begins to brown too much, cover the edges with foil. Leave to cool. Dust with icing sugar before serving.

Maple Walnut Tart

Makes sure you use 100 per cent pure maple syrup in this decadent tart.

Serves 8

3 eggs
1.5ml/¼ tsp salt
50g/2oz/4 tbsp caster sugar
50g/2oz/4 tbsp butter, melted
250ml/8fl oz/1 cup pure maple syrup
115g/4oz/1 cup chopped walnuts
whipped cream, to decorate

For the pastry

65g/2½oz/9 tbsp plain flour
65g/2½oz/½ cup wholemeal flour
1.5ml/¼ tsp salt
50g/2oz/4 tbsp cold butter, cut in pieces
40g/1½oz/3 tbsp cold vegetable fat or lard, cut in pieces
1 egg yolk

1 For the pastry, mix the flours and salt in a bowl. Add the fats and rub in until the mixture resembles coarse breadcrumbs. Stir in the egg yolk and 30–45ml/2–3 tbsp iced water to bind. Form into a ball, wrap and chill for 20 minutes.

2 Preheat the oven to 220°C/425°F/Gas 7. Roll out the pastry and use to line a 23cm/9in pie dish. Use the trimmings to stamp out heart shapes. Arrange on the pastry case rim with a little water.

3 Prick the pastry base, line with greaseproof paper and fill with baking beans. Bake for 10 minutes. Remove the paper and beans and bake until golden, 3–6 minutes more.

4 Whisk together the eggs, salt and sugar. Stir in the butter and maple syrup. Set the pastry case on a baking sheet. Pour in the filling, then sprinkle with the nuts.

5 Bake until just set, about 35 minutes. Cool on a wire rack. Decorate with piped whipped cream.

Pecan Tart

Serve this tart warm, accompanied by ice cream or whipped cream, if you wish.

Serves 8

3 eggs
pinch of salt
200g/7oz/generous 1 cup dark brown sugar
120ml/4fl oz/½ cup golden syrup
30ml/2 tbsp fresh lemon juice
75g/3oz/6 tbsp butter, melted
150g/5oz/1¼ cups chopped pecan nuts
50g/2oz/½ cup pecan nut halves

For the pastry

175g/6oz/1½ cups plain flour
15ml/1 tbsp caster sugar
5ml/1 tsp baking powder
2.5ml/½ tsp salt
75g/3oz/6 tbsp cold unsalted butter, cut in pieces
1 egg yolk
45–60ml/3–4 tbsp whipping cream

1 For the pastry, sift together the flour, sugar, baking powder and salt. Add the butter and rub in until the mixture resembles coarse breadcrumbs.

2 Blend the egg yolk and whipping cream, then stir into the flour mixture.

3 Form the pastry into a ball, then roll out and use to line a 23cm/9in pie dish. Flute the edge and chill for 20 minutes.

4 Preheat a baking sheet in the oven at 200°C/400°F/Gas 6. Lightly whisk the eggs and salt. Mix in the sugar, syrup, lemon juice and butter. Stir in the chopped nuts.

5 Pour into the pastry case and arrange the pecan nut halves in concentric circles on top.

6 Bake on the baking sheet for 10 minutes. Reduce the heat to 160°C/325°F/Gas 3 and bake for 25 minutes more.

Velvety Mocha Tart

A creamy smooth filling tops a dark light-textured base in this wondrous dessert.

Serves 8

10ml/2 tsp instant espresso coffee
30ml/2 tbsp hot water
175g/6oz plain chocolate
25g/1oz bitter cooking chocolate
350ml/12fl oz/1½ cups whipping cream, slightly warmed
120ml/4fl oz/½ cup whipped cream, to decorate
chocolate coated coffee beans, to decorate

For the base

150g/5oz/2½cups crushed chocolate wafers
30ml/2 tbsp caster sugar
65g/2½oz/5 tbsp butter, melted

1 Combine the base ingredients. Press the mixture over the base and sides of a 23cm/9in pie dish. Chill.

2 Dissolve the coffee in the water. Set aside.

3 Melt the chocolates in the top of a double boiler. Set the base of the pan in cold water to cool.

4 Whip the cream until light and fluffy. Add the coffee and whip until the cream just holds its shape.

5 When the chocolate is at room temperature, fold it gently into the cream.

6 Pour into the biscuit base and chill until firm. Decorate with piped whipped cream and chocolate coated coffee beans just before serving.

Coconut Cream Tart

Serves 8

140g/5oz desiccated coconut
140g/5oz/¾ cup caster sugar
25g/1oz/4 tbsp cornflour
1.5ml/¼ tsp salt
625ml/1 pint/2½ cups milk
65ml/2fl oz whipping cream
2 egg yolks
30g/1oz/2 tbsp unsalted butter
10ml/2 tsp vanilla essence

For the pastry

140g/5oz/1¼ cups plain flour
1.5ml/¼ tsp salt
45g/1½oz/3 tbsp cold butter, cut in pieces
30g/1oz/3 tbsp cold vegetable fat or lard
30–45ml/2 – 3 tbsp iced water

1 Sift the flour and salt into a bowl, add the fats and rub in until it resembles coarse breadcrumbs. With a fork, stir in just enough water to bind the pastry. Gather into a ball, wrap and chill for 20 minutes. Preheat the oven to 220°C/425°F/Gas 7.

2 Roll out the pastry 3mm/⅛in thick. Line a 23cm/9in pie dish. Trim and flute the edges, prick the base, line with crumpled greaseproof paper and fill with baking beans. Bake for 10 – 12 minutes. Remove the paper and beans, reduce heat to 180°C/350°F/Gas 4 and bake until brown, 10 – 15 minutes.

3 Spread 55g/2oz of the coconut on a baking sheet and toast in the oven until golden, 6 – 8 minutes.

4 Put the sugar, cornflour and salt in a pan. In a bowl, whisk the milk, cream and yolks. Add the egg mixture to the pan.

5 Cook over a low heat, stirring, until the mixture comes to the boil. Boil for 1 minute, then remove from the heat. Add the butter, vanilla and remaining coconut.

6 Pour into the pre-baked pastry case. When cool, sprinkle toasted coconut in a ring in the centre.

Orange Tart

If you like oranges, this is the dessert for you!

Serves 8

200g/7oz/1 cup sugar
250ml/8fl oz/1 cup fresh orange juice, strained
2 large navel oranges
165g/5½oz/scant 1 cup whole blanched almonds
50g/2oz/4 tbsp butter
1 egg
15ml/1 tbsp plain flour
45ml/3 tbsp apricot jam

For the pastry

210g/7½oz/scant 2 cups plain flour
2.5ml/½ tsp salt
50g/2oz/4 tbsp cold butter, cut into pieces
40g/1½oz/3 tbsp cold margarine, cut into pieces
45–60ml/3–4 tbsp iced water

1 For the pastry, sift the flour and salt into a bowl. Add the butter and margarine and rub in until the mixture resembles coarse breadcrumbs. Stir in just enough water to bind the dough. Wrap and chill for 20 minutes. Roll out the pastry to a 5mm/¼in thickness. Use to line a 20cm/8in tart tin. Trim and chill until needed.

2 In a saucepan, combine 165g/5½oz/¾ cup of the sugar and the orange juice and boil until thick and syrupy. Cut the unpeeled oranges into 5mm/¼in slices. Add to the syrup. Simmer gently for 10 minutes. Put on a wire rack to dry. When cool, cut in half. Reserve the syrup. Place a baking sheet in the oven and heat to 200°C/400°F/Gas 6.

3 Grind the almonds finely in a blender or food processor. Cream the butter and remaining sugar until light and fluffy. Beat in the egg and 30ml/2 tbsp of the orange syrup. Stir in the almonds and flour.

4 Melt the jam over a low heat, then brush over the pastry case. Pour in the almond mixture. Bake on the baking sheet until set, about 20 minutes, then cool. Arrange overlapping orange slices on top. Boil the remaining syrup until thick and brush on top to glaze.

Raspberry Tart

A luscious tart with a custard topped with juicy berries.

Serves 8

4 egg yolks
65g/2½oz/generous 4 tbsp caster sugar
45ml/3 tbsp plain flour
300ml/10fl oz/1¼ cups milk
1.5ml/¼ tsp salt
2.5ml/½ tsp vanilla essence
450g/1lb/2⅔ cups fresh raspberries
75ml/5 tbsp redcurrant jelly
15ml/1 tbsp orange juice

For the pastry

185g/6½oz/1⅔ cups plain flour
2.5ml/½ tsp baking powder
1.5ml/¼ tsp salt
15ml/1 tbsp sugar
grated rind of ½ orange
75g/3oz/6 tbsp cold butter, cut in pieces
1 egg yolk
45–60ml/3–4 tbsp whipping cream

1 For the pastry, sift the flour, baking powder and salt into a bowl. Stir in the sugar and orange rind. Add the butter and rub in until the mixture resembles breadcrumbs. Stir in the egg yolk and cream to bind. Form into a ball, wrap and chill.

2 For the filling, beat the egg yolks and sugar until thick and creamy. Gradually stir in the flour. Bring the milk and salt just to the boil, then remove from the heat. Whisk into the egg yolk mixture, return to the pan and continue whisking over a moderately high heat until just bubbling. Cook for 3 minutes to thicken. Transfer to a bowl. Stir in the vanilla, then cover with greaseproof paper.

3 Preheat the oven to 200°C/400°F/Gas 6. Roll out the pastry and use to line a 25cm/10in pie dish. Prick the base, line with greaseproof paper and fill with baking beans. Bake for 15 minutes. Remove the paper and beans, and bake until golden, 6–8 minutes more. Leave to cool. Spread an even layer of the custard filling in the pastry case and arrange the raspberries on top. Melt the jelly and orange juice in a pan and brush on top to glaze.

Lattice Berry Pie

Choose any berries you like for this handsome pie.

Serves 8

450g/1lb/about 4 cups berries, such as bilberries, blueberries and blackcurrants
115g/4oz/generous ½ cup caster sugar
45ml/3 tbsp cornflour
30ml/2 tbsp fresh lemon juice
25g/1oz/2 tbsp butter, diced

For the pastry

275g/10oz/2½ cups plain flour
4ml/¾ tsp salt
115g/4oz/½ cup cold butter, diced
40g/1½oz/3 tbsp cold vegetable fat or lard, diced
75–90ml/5–6 tbsp iced water
1 egg, beaten with 15ml/1 tbsp water, for glazing

1 For the pastry, sift the flour and salt into a bowl. Add the butter and fat and rub in until the mixture resembles coarse breadcrumbs. Stir in just enough water to bind. Form into two balls, wrap and chill for 20 minutes. Roll out one ball and use to line a 23cm/9in pie dish, leaving a 1cm/½in overhang. Brush the base with egg

2 Mix all the filling ingredients together, except the butter (reserve a few berries for decoration). Spoon into the pastry case and dot with the butter. Brush egg around the pastry rim.

3 Preheat a baking sheet at 220°C/425°F/Gas 7. Roll out the remaining pastry on a baking sheet lined with greaseproof paper. With a serrated pastry wheel, make 24 thin strips. Use the scraps to cut out leaf shapes, and mark veins. Weave the strips in a close lattice and transfer to the pie. Seal the edges and trim. Arrange the leaves around the rim. Brush with egg and bake for 10 minutes.

4 Reduce the heat to 180°C/350°F/Gas 4 and bake the pie for a further 40–45 minutes. Decorate with berries.

Plum Pie

Treat someone special with this lightly spiced plum pie.

Serves 8

900g/2lb red or purple plums
grated rind of 1 lemon
15ml/1 tbsp fresh lemon juice
115–175g/4–6oz/1–1¼ cups caster sugar
45ml/3 tbsp quick-cooking tapioca
1.5ml/¼ tsp salt
2.5ml/½ tsp ground cinnamon
1.5ml/¼ tsp grated nutmeg

For the pastry

275g/10oz/2½ cups plain flour
5ml/1 tsp salt
75g/3oz/6 tbsp cold butter, diced
50g/2oz/4 tbsp cold vegetable fat or lard, diced
50–120ml/2–4fl oz/¼–½ cup iced water
milk, for glazing

1 For the pastry, sift the flour and salt into a bowl. Add the butter and fat and rub in until the mixture resembles coarse breadcrumbs. Stir in just enough water to bind the pastry. Form into two balls, wrap and chill for 20 minutes.

2 Preheat a baking sheet in the oven at 220°C/425°F/Gas 7. Roll out a pastry ball and use to line a 23cm/9in pie dish.

3 Halve and stone the plums, and chop roughly. Mix all the filling ingredients together, then transfer to the pastry case.

4 Roll out the remaining pastry, place on a baking sheet lined with greaseproof paper, and stamp out four hearts. Transfer the pastry lid to the pie using the paper.

5 Trim to leave a 2cm/¾in overhang. Fold this under the pastry base and pinch to seal. Arrange the hearts on top. Brush with milk and bake for 15 minutes. Reduce the heat to 180°C/350°F/Gas 4 and bake for a further 30–35 minutes.

Dorset Apple Cake

Serve this fruity apple cake warm, and spread with butter if liked.

Makes one 18cm/7in round cake

225g/8oz cooking apples, peeled, cored and chopped
juice of ½ lemon
225g/8oz/2 cups plain flour
7.5ml/1½ tsp baking powder
115g/4oz/½ cup butter, diced
165g/5½oz/scant 1 cup soft light brown sugar
1 egg, beaten
about 30–45ml/2–3 tbsp milk, to mix
2.5ml/½ tsp ground cinnamon

1 Preheat the oven to 180°C/350°F/Gas 4. Grease and line an 18cm/7in round cake tin.

2 Toss the apple with the lemon juice and set aside. Sift the flour and baking powder together, then rub in the butter, until the mixture resembles breadcrumbs.

3 Stir in 115g/4oz/¾ cup of the brown sugar, the apple and the egg, and mix well, adding sufficient milk to make a soft dropping consistency.

4 Transfer the dough to the prepared tin. In a bowl, mix together the remaining sugar and the cinnamon. Sprinkle over the cake mixture, then bake for 45–50 minutes, until golden. Leave to cool in the tin for 10 minutes, then transfer to a wire rack.

Parkin

The flavour of the cake will improve if it is stored in an airtight container for several days or a week before serving.

Makes 16–20 squares

300ml/½ pint/1¼ cups milk
225g/8oz/5 tbsp golden syrup
225g/8oz/4 tbsp black treacle
115g/4oz/½ cup butter or margarine, diced
50g/2oz/scant ¼ cup dark brown sugar
450g/1lb/4 cups plain flour
2.5ml/½ tsp bicarbonate of soda
6.5ml/1¼ tsp ground ginger
350g/12oz/4 cups medium oatmeal
1 egg, beaten
icing sugar, for dusting

1 Preheat the oven to 180°C/350°F/Gas 4. Grease and line the base of a 20cm/8in square cake tin. Gently heat together the milk, syrup, treacle, butter or margarine and sugar, stirring until smooth. Do not allow the mixture to boil.

2 Stir together the flour, bicarbonate of soda, ginger and oatmeal. Make a well in the centre, pour in the egg, then slowly pour in the warmed mixture, stirring to make a smooth batter.

3 Pour the batter into the tin and bake for about 45 minutes, until firm to the touch. Cool slightly in the tin, then cool completely on a wire rack. Cut into squares and dust with icing sugar.

Banana Ginger Parkin

Parkin keeps well and really improves with keeping. Store it in a covered container for up to two months.

Makes 16–20 squares

200g/7oz/scant 2 cups plain flour
10ml/2 tsp bicarbonate of soda
10ml/2 tsp ground ginger
150g/5oz/1¼ cups medium oatmeal
50g/2oz/4 tbsp dark muscovado sugar
75g/3oz/6 tbsp sunflower margarine
150g/5oz/3 tbsp golden syrup
1 egg, beaten
3 ripe bananas, mashed
75g/3oz/¾ cup icing sugar
stem ginger, to decorate (optional)

1 Preheat the oven to 160°C/325°F/Gas 3. Grease and line an 18 x 28cm/7 x 11in cake tin.

2 Sift together the flour, bicarbonate of soda and ginger, then stir in the oatmeal. Melt the sugar, margarine and syrup in a saucepan, then stir into the flour mixture. Beat in the egg and mashed bananas.

3 Spoon into the tin and bake for about 1 hour, or until firm to the touch. Allow to cool in the tin, then turn out and cut into squares.

4 Sift the icing sugar into a bowl and stir in just enough water to make a smooth, runny icing. Drizzle the icing over each square and top with a piece of stem ginger, if you like.

Gooseberry Cake

This cake is delicious served warm with whipped cream.

Makes one 18cm/7in square cake

115g/4oz/½ cup butter
165g/5½oz/1⅓ cups self-raising flour
5ml/1 tsp baking powder
2 eggs, beaten
115g/4oz/generous ½ cup caster sugar
5–10ml/1–2 tsp rose water
pinch of freshly grated nutmeg
115g/4oz jar gooseberries in syrup, drained, juice reserved
caster sugar, to decorate
whipped cream, to serve

1 Preheat the oven to 180°C/350°F/Gas 4. Grease an 18cm/7in square cake tin, line the base and sides with greaseproof paper and grease the paper. Gently melt the butter, then transfer to a mixing bowl and allow to cool.

2 Sift together the flour and baking powder and add to the butter. Beat in the eggs, one at a time, the sugar, rose water and grated nutmeg, to make a smooth batter.

3 Mix in 15–30ml/1–2 tbsp of the reserved gooseberry juice, then pour half of the batter mixture into the prepared tin. Scatter over the gooseberries and pour over the remaining batter mixture.

4 Bake for about 45 minutes, or until a skewer inserted into the centre of the cake comes out clean.

5 Leave in the tin for 5 minutes, then turn out on a wire rack, peel off the lining paper and allow to cool for a further 5 minutes. Dredge with caster sugar and serve immediately with whipped cream, or leave the cake to cool completely before decorating.

Crunchy-topped Sponge Loaf

This light sponge makes a perfect tea-time treat.

Makes one 450g/1lb loaf

200g/7oz/scant 1 cup butter, softened
finely grated rind of 1 lemon
150g/5oz/5 tbsp caster sugar
3 eggs
75g/3oz/¾ cup plain flour, sifted
150g/5oz/1¼ cups self-raising flour, sifted

For the topping

45ml/3 tbsp clear honey
115g/4oz/¾ cup mixed peel
50g/2oz/½ cup flaked almonds

1 Preheat the oven to 180°C/350°F/Gas 4. Grease and line a 450g/1lb loaf tin with greaseproof paper. Grease the paper.

2 Beat together the butter, lemon rind and sugar until light and fluffy. Blend in the eggs, one at a time.

3 Sift together the flours, then stir into the egg mixture. Fill the loaf tin.

4 Bake for 45 minutes, or until a skewer inserted into the centre comes out clean. Stand in the tin for 5 minutes. Turn the loaf out on to a wire rack, peel off the lining paper and leave to cool.

5 For the topping, melt the honey with the mixed peel and almonds. Remove from the heat, stir briefly, then spread over the cake top. Cool before serving.

Irish Whiskey Cake

Other whiskies could be used in this cake.

Makes one 23 x 13cm/9 x 5in cake

175g/6oz/1½ cups chopped walnuts
75g/3oz/generous ½ cup raisins, chopped
75g/3oz/scant ½ cup currants
115g/4oz/1 cup plain flour
5ml/1 tsp baking powder
1.5ml/¼ tsp salt
115g/4oz/½ cup butter
225g/8oz/scant 1½ cups caster sugar
3 eggs, separated, at room temperature
5ml/1 tsp grated nutmeg
2.5ml/½ tsp ground cinnamon
85ml/5 tbsp Irish whiskey
icing sugar, for dusting

1 Preheat the oven to 160°C/325°F/Gas 3. Base-line and grease a 23.x 13cm/9 x 5in loaf tin. Mix the nuts and dried fruit with 30ml/2 tbsp of the flour and set aside. Sift together the remaining flour, baking powder and salt.

2 Cream the butter and sugar until light and fluffy. Beat in the egg yolks.

3 Mix the nutmeg, cinnamon and whiskey. Fold into the butter mixture, alternating with the flour mixture.

4 Beat the egg whites until stiff. Fold into the whiskey mixture until just blended. Fold in the walnut mixture.

5 Fill the loaf tin and bake until a skewer inserted in the centre comes out clean, about 1 hour. Cool in the tin. To serve, dust with icing sugar over a template.

Autumn Dessert Cake

Greengages, plums or semi-dried prunes are delicious in this recipe.

Serves 6–8
115g/4oz/½ cup butter, softened
150g/5oz/5 tbsp caster sugar
3 eggs, beaten
75g/3oz/¾ cup ground hazelnuts
150g/5oz/1¼ cups shelled pecan nuts, chopped
50g/2oz/½ cup plain flour
5ml/1 tsp baking powder
2.5ml/½ tsp salt
675g/1½lb/3 cups stoned plums, greengages or semi-dried prunes
60ml/4 tbsp lime marmalade
15ml/1 tbsp lime juice
30ml/2 tbsp blanched almonds, chopped, to decorate

1 Preheat the oven to 180°C/350°F/Gas 4. Grease a 23cm/9in round, fluted tart tin.

2 Beat the butter and sugar until light and fluffy. Gradually beat in the eggs, alternating with the ground hazelnuts.

3 Stir in the pecan nuts, then sift and fold in the flour, baking powder and salt. Spoon into the tart tin.

4 Bake for 45 minutes, or until a skewer inserted into the centre comes out clean.

5 Arrange the fruit on the base. Return to the oven and bake for 10–15 minutes until the fruit has softened. Transfer to a wire rack to cool, then turn out.

6 Warm the marmalade and lime juice gently. Brush over the fruit, then sprinkle with the almonds. Allow to set, then chill before serving.

Apple Crumble Cake

In the autumn use windfall apples. Served warm with thick cream or custard, this cake doubles as a dessert.

Serves 8–10

For the topping
75g/3oz/⅔ cup self-raising flour
½ tsp ground cinnamon
40g/1½oz/3 tbsp butter
25g/1oz/2 tbsp caster sugar

For the base
50g/2oz/4 tbsp butter, softened
75g/3oz/6 tbsp caster sugar
1 size 3 egg, beaten
115g/4oz/1 cup self-raising flour, sifted
2 cooking apples, peeled, cored and sliced
50g/2oz/4 tbsp sultanas

To decorate
1 red dessert apple, cored, thinly sliced and tossed in lemon juice
25g/1oz/2 tbsp caster sugar, sifted
pinch of ground cinnamon

1 Preheat the oven 180°C/350°F/Gas 4. Grease a deep 18cm/7in springform tin, line the base with greaseproof paper and grease the paper.

2 To make the topping, sift the flour and cinnamon into a mixing bowl. Rub the butter into the flour until it resembles breadcrumbs, then stir in the sugar. Set aside.

3 To make the base, put the butter, sugar, egg and flour into a bowl and beat for 1–2 minutes until smooth. Spoon into the prepared tin.

4 Mix together the apple slices and sultanas and spread them evenly over the top. Sprinkle with the topping.

5 Bake in the centre of the oven for about 1 hour. Cool in the tin for 10 minutes before turning out on to a wire rack and peeling off the lining paper. Serve warm or cool, decorated with slices of red dessert apple and caster sugar and cinnamon sprinkled over.

Light Fruit Cake

For the best flavour, wrap this cake in foil and store for a week before cutting.

Makes two 23 x 13cm/9 x 5in cakes

225g/8oz/1 cup prunes
225g/8oz/1⅓ cups dates
225g/8oz/1 cup currants
225g/8oz/generous 1½ cups sultanas
250ml/8fl oz/1 cup dry white wine
250ml/8fl oz/1 cup rum
350g/12oz/3 cups plain flour
10ml/2 tsp baking powder
5ml/1 tsp ground cinnamon
2.5ml/½ tsp grated nutmeg
225g/8oz/1 cup butter, at room temperature
225g/8oz/scant 1¼ cups caster sugar
4 eggs, lightly beaten
5ml/1 tsp vanilla essence

1 Stone the prunes and dates and chop finely. Place in a bowl with the currants and sultanas. Stir in the wine and rum and leave, covered, for 2 days. Stir occasionally.

2 Preheat the oven to 150°C/300°F/Gas 2 with a tray of hot water in the bottom. Line two 23 x 13cm/9 x 5in loaf tins with greaseproof paper and grease the paper.

3 Sift together the flour, baking powder, ground cinnamon and grated nutmeg.

4 Cream the butter and sugar together until light and fluffy. Gradually add the eggs and vanilla. Fold in the flour mixture in three batches. Fold in the dried fruit mixture and its liquid.

5 Divide the mixture between the tins and bake until a skewer inserted in the centre comes out clean, about 1½ hours. Stand for 20 minutes, then unmould on to a wire rack.

Rich Fruit Cake

Makes one 23 x 8cm/9 x 3in cake

140g/5oz/½ cup currants
170g/6oz/generous 1 cup raisins
50g/2oz/½ cup sultanas
55g/2oz/4 tbsp glacé cherries, halved
3 tbsp sweet sherry
170g/6oz/¾ cup butter
200g/7oz/scant 1 cup dark brown sugar
2 size 1 eggs, at room temperature
200g/7oz/1¾ cups plain flour
10ml/2 tsp baking powder
10ml/2 tsp each ground ginger, allspice, and cinnamon
15ml/1 tbsp golden syrup
15ml/1 tbsp milk
55g/2oz/5 tbsp cut mixed peel
115g/4oz/1 cup chopped walnuts

For the decoration

120ml/4fl oz/½ cup orange marmalade
crystallized citrus fruit slices
glacé cherries

1 A day in advance, combine the dried fruit and cherries in a bowl. Stir in the sherry, cover and soak overnight.

2 Preheat the oven to 150°C/300°F/Gas 2. Line and grease a 23 x 8cm/9 x 3in springform tin with greaseproof paper. Place a tray of hot water on the bottom of the oven.

3 Cream the butter and sugar. Beat in the eggs, 1 at a time. Sift the flour, baking powder and spices together three times. Fold into the butter mixture in three batches. Fold in the syrup, milk, dried fruit and liquid, mixed peel and nuts.

4 Spoon into the tin, spreading out so there is a slight depression in the centre. Bake for about 2½–3 hours. Cover with foil when the top is golden to prevent over-browning. Cool in the tin on a rack.

5 Melt the marmalade over a low heat, then brush over the top of the cake. Decorate with the crystallized citrus fruit slices and glacé cherries.

Creole Christmas Cake

Makes one 23cm/9in cake

450g/1lb/3 cups raisins
225g/8oz/1 cup currants
115g/4oz/¾ cup sultanas
115g/4oz/½ cup no-soak prunes, chopped
115g/4oz/1 cup candied orange peel, chopped
115g/4oz/1 cup chopped walnuts
60ml/4 tbsp dark brown sugar
5ml/1 tsp vanilla essence
5ml/1 tsp ground cinnamon
1.5ml/¼ tsp each ground nutmeg and cloves
5ml/1 tsp salt
60ml/4 tbsp each rum, brandy and whisky

For the second stage

225g/8oz/2 cups plain flour
5ml/1 tsp baking powder
225g/8oz demerara sugar
225g/8oz/1 cup butter
4 eggs, beaten

For the topping

225g/8oz apricot jam, sieved
pecan halves and crystallized kumquat slices, to decorate

1 Put the first set of ingredients into a pan, mix and heat gently. Simmer over low heat for 15 minutes. Remove from the heat and cool. Transfer to a lidded jar and leave in the fridge for 7 days, stirring at least once a day.

2 Preheat the oven to 140°C/275°F/Gas 1. Line a 23cm/9in round cake tin with a double thickness of non-stick baking paper and grease it well. Beat the flour, baking powder, sugar and butter together until smooth, then gradually beat in the eggs until the mixture is well blended and smooth.

3 Fold in the fruit mixture and stir well to mix. Spoon the mixture into the prepared tin, level the surface and bake in the centre of the oven for 3 hours. Cover with foil and continue baking for 1 hour, until the cake feels springy. Cool on a wire rack then remove from the tin. Wrap in foil until needed. The cake will keep well for 1 year.

4 To decorate , heat the jam with 30ml/2 tbsp water, brush half over the cake. Arrange the nuts and fruit over the cake and brush with the remaining apricot glaze.

Light Jewelled Fruit Cake

If you want to cover this cake with marzipan and icing, omit the almond decoration.

Makes one 20cm/8in round or 18cm/7in square cake

115g/4oz/½ cup currants
115g/4oz/¾ cup sultanas
225g/8oz/1 cup mixed glacé cherries, quartered
50g/2oz/½ cup mixed peel, finely chopped
30ml/2 tbsp rum, brandy or sherry
225g/8oz/1 cup butter
225g/8oz/generous 1 cup caster sugar
finely grated rind of 1 orange
grated rind of 1 lemon
4 eggs
50g/2oz/½ cup chopped almonds
50g/2oz/5 tbsp ground almonds
225g/8oz/2 cups plain flour

To decorate

50g/2oz/5 tbsp whole blanched almonds (optional)
15ml/1 tbsp apricot jam

1 A day in advance, soak the currants, sultanas, glacé cherries and mixed peel in the rum, brandy or sherry, cover and leave to soak overnight.

2 Grease and line a 20cm/8in round cake tin or an 18cm/7in square cake tin with a double thickness of greaseproof paper. Preheat the oven to 160°C/325°F/Gas 3. Beat the butter, sugar and orange and lemon rinds together until light and fluffy. Beat in the eggs, one at a time. Mix in the chopped almonds, ground almonds, soaked fruits (with the liquid) and the flour. Spoon into the cake tin and level the top. Bake for 30 minutes.

3 Arrange the almonds, if using, on top of the cake (do not press them into the cake or they will sink during cooking). Return the cake to the oven and cook for 1½–2 hours, or until the centre is firm to the touch. Let the cake cool in the tin for 30 minutes, then turn it out in its paper on to a wire rack. When cold, wrap foil over the paper and store in a cool place. To finish, warm, then sieve the jam and use to glaze the cake.

Angel Cake

This heavenly cake tastes simply divine!

Makes one 25cm/10in cake

130g/4½oz/generous 1 cup sifted plain flour
30ml/2 tbsp cornflour
285g/10½oz/1½ cups caster sugar
10–11 egg whites
6.5ml/1¼ tsp cream of tartar
1.5ml/¼ tsp salt
5ml/1 tsp vanilla essence
1.5ml/¼ tsp almond essence
icing sugar, for dusting

1 Preheat the oven to 160°C/325°F/Gas 3. Sift the flours before measuring, then sift them four times together with 90g/3½oz/½ cup of the sugar.

2 Beat the egg whites until foamy. Sift over the cream of tartar and salt and continue to beat until the egg whites form soft peaks.

3 Add the remaining sugar in three batches, beating well after each addition. Stir in the vanilla and almond essences. Fold in the flour mixture in two batches.

4 Transfer to an ungreased 25cm/10in cake tin and bake until just browned on top, about 1 hour.

5 Turn the tin upside-down on to a wire rack and cool for 1 hour. Then invert on to a serving plate. Lay a star-shaped template on top of the cake, sift over some icing sugar and remove the template.

Spice Cake with Ginger Frosting

A rich three-layer cake with a creamy ginger frosting.

Makes one 20cm/8in round cake

300ml/10fl oz/1¼ cups milk
30ml/2 tbsp golden syrup
10ml/2 tsp vanilla essence
75g/3oz/¾ cup chopped walnuts
175g/6oz/¾ cup butter, at room temperature
285g/10½oz/1½ cups sugar
1 whole egg, plus 3 egg yolks
275g/10oz/2½ cups plain flour
15ml/1 tbsp baking powder
5ml/1 tsp grated nutmeg
5ml/1 tsp ground cinnamon
2.5ml/½ tsp ground cloves
1.5ml/¼ tsp ground ginger
1.5ml/¼ tsp mixed spice
stem ginger pieces, to decorate

For the frosting

175g/6oz/¾ cup cream cheese
25g/1oz/2 tbsp unsalted butter
200g/7oz/1⅓ cups icing sugar
30ml/2 tbsp finely chopped stem ginger
30ml/2 tbsp syrup from stem ginger

1 Preheat the oven to 180°C/350°F/Gas 4. Line and grease three 20cm/8in cake tins with greaseproof paper. In a bowl, combine the milk, golden syrup, vanilla and walnuts.

2 Cream the butter and sugar until light and fluffy. Beat in the egg and egg yolks. Add the milk mixture and stir well. Sift together the flour, baking powder and spices three times. Add to the butter mixture in four batches, folding in carefully.

3 Divide the cake mixture between the tins. Bake until the cakes spring back when touched lightly, about 25 minutes. Leave in the tins for 5 minutes, then cool on a wire rack. For the frosting, combine all the ingredients and beat until smooth. Spread the frosting between the layers and over the top. Decorate with pieces of stem ginger.

Lemon Coconut Layer Cake

Makes one 20cm/8in round cake

150g/5oz/1¼ cups plain flour, sifted with 1.5ml/¼ tsp salt
8 eggs
370g/12¾oz/scant 2 cups caster sugar
15ml/1 tbsp grated orange rind
grated rind of 2 lemons
juice of 1 lemon
65g/2½oz/1¼ cups sweetened, shredded coconut
30ml/2 tbsp cornflour
250ml/8fl oz/1 cup water
75g/3oz/6 tbsp butter

For the frosting
115g/4oz/½ cup unsalted butter
115g/4oz/1 cup icing sugar
grated rind of 1 lemon
90–120ml/6–8 tbsp lemon juice
115g/4oz/2 cups sweetened shredded coconut

1 Preheat the oven to 180°C/350°F/Gas 4. Line and grease three 20cm/8in cake tins with greaseproof paper.

2 Place 6 of the eggs in a bowl set over hot water and beat until frothy. Beat in 165g/5½oz/¾ cup sugar until the mixture doubles in volume. Remove from the heat. Fold in the orange rind, half the lemon rind, 15ml/1 tbsp of the lemon juice and the coconut. Sift over the flour mixture and fold in well.

3 Divide the mixture between the cake tins. Bake until the cakes pull away from the sides of the tins, 25–30 minutes. Leave in the tins for 5 minutes, then cool on a wire rack.

4 Blend the cornflour with cold water to dissolve. Whisk in the remaining eggs until blended. In a pan, mix the remaining lemon rind and juice, water, remaining sugar and butter. Bring to the boil. Whisk in the cornflour, and return to the boil. Whisk until thick. Remove and cover with clear film.

5 Cream the butter and icing sugar. Stir in the lemon rind and enough lemon juice to obtain a spreadable consistency. Sandwich the cake layers with the lemon custard. Spread the frosting over the top and sides. Cover with the coconut.

Lemon Yogurt Ring

The glaze gives this dessert a refreshing finishing touch.

Serves 12

225g/8oz/1 cup butter, at room temperature
285g/10½oz/1½ cups caster sugar
4 eggs, separated
10ml/2 tsp grated lemon rind
90ml/6 tbsp lemon juice
250ml/8fl oz/1 cup natural yogurt
275g/10oz/2½ cups plain flour
10ml/2 tsp baking powder
5ml/1 tsp bicarbonate of soda
2.5ml/½ tsp salt

For the glaze
115g/4oz/1 cup icing sugar
30ml/2 tbsp lemon juice
45–60ml/3–4 tbsp natural yogurt

1 Preheat the oven to 180°C/350°F/Gas 4. Grease a 3-litre/5-pint/12½-cup *bundt* or fluted tube tin and dust with flour.

2 Cream the butter and caster sugar until light and fluffy. Add the egg yolks, one at a time, beating well after each addition. Add the lemon rind, juice and yogurt and stir .

3 Sift together the flour, baking powder and bicarbonate of soda. In another bowl, beat the egg whites and salt until they hold stiff peaks.

4 Fold the dry ingredients into the butter mixture, then fold in a dollop of egg whites. Fold in the remaining whites.

5 Pour into the tin and bake until a skewer inserted in the centre comes out clean, about 50 minutes. Leave in the tin for 15 minutes, then turn out and cool on a wire rack.

6 For the glaze, sift the icing sugar into a bowl. Stir in the lemon juice and just enough yogurt to make a smooth glaze.

7 Set the cooled cake on the wire rack over a sheet of greaseproof paper. Pour over the glaze and allow to set.

Carrot Cake with Geranium Cheese

Makes one 23 x 12cm/9 x 5in cake

115g/4oz/1 cup self-raising flour
5ml/1 tsp bicarbonate of soda
2.5ml/½ tsp ground cinnamon
2.5ml/½ tsp ground cloves
200g/7oz/generous 1 cup soft brown sugar
225g/8oz/generous 1½ cups grated carrot
150g/5oz/1 cup sultanas
150g/5oz/½ cup finely chopped preserved stem ginger
150g/5oz/generous 1 cup pecan nuts
150ml/¼ pint/⅔ cup sunflower oil
2 eggs, lightly beaten

For the topping

2–3 lemon-scented geranium leaves
225g/8oz/2 cups icing sugar
60g/2¼oz/generous 4 tbsp cream cheese
30g/1¼oz/generous 2 tbsp softened butter
5ml/1 tsp grated lemon rind

1 For the topping, put the geranium leaves, torn into small pieces, in a small bowl and mix with the icing sugar. Leave in a warm place overnight for the sugar to take up the scent.

2 For the cake, sift the flour, bicarbonate of soda and spices together. Add the sugar, carrots, sultanas, ginger and pecan nuts. Stir well, then add the oil and beaten eggs. Mix with an electric mixer for 5 minutes.

3 Preheat the oven to 180°C/350°F/Gas 4. Then grease a 23 x 12cm/9 x 5in loaf tin, line the base with greaseproof paper, and grease the paper. Pour the mixture into the tin and bake for about 1 hour. Remove the cake from the oven, leave to stand for a few minutes, and then cool on a wire rack.

4 Meanwhile, make the cream cheese topping. Remove the pieces of geranium leaf from the icing sugar and discard. Place the cream cheese, butter and lemon rind in a bowl. Using an electric mixer, gradually add the icing sugar, beating well until smooth. Spread over the top of the cooled cake.

Carrot and Courgette Cake

If you can't resist the lure of a slice of iced cake, you'll love this spiced sponge with its delicious creamy topping.

Makes one 18cm/7in square cake

1 carrot
1 courgette
3 eggs, separated
115g/4oz/¾ cup soft light brown sugar
30ml/2 tbsp ground almonds
finely grated rind of 1 orange
150g/5oz/1¼ cups self-raising wholemeal flour
5ml/1 tsp ground cinnamon
5ml/1 tsp icing sugar, for dusting
fondant carrots and courgettes, to decorate

For the topping

175g/6oz/¾ cup low-fat soft cheese
5ml/1 tsp clear honey

1 Preheat the oven to 180°C/350°F/Gas 4. Line an 18cm/7in square tin with non-stick baking paper. Coarsely grate the carrot and courgette.

2 Put the egg yolks, sugar, ground almonds and orange rind into a bowl and whisk until very thick and light. Sift together the flour and cinnamon and fold into the mixture together with the grated vegetables. Add any bran left in the sieve.

3 Whisk the egg whites until stiff and carefully fold them in, a half at a time. Spoon into the tin. Bake in the oven for 1 hour, covering the top with foil after 40 minutes. Leave to cool in the tin for 5 minutes, then turn out on to a wire rack and remove the lining paper.

4 For the topping, beat together the cheese and honey and spread over the cake. Dust with icing sugar and decorate with fondant carrots and courgettes.

Banana Coconut Cake

Slightly over-ripe bananas are best for this perfect coffee-morning cake.

Makes one 18cm/7in square cake

115g/4oz/½ cup butter, softened
115g/4oz/generous ½ cup caster sugar
2 eggs
115g/4oz/1 cup self-raising flour
50g/2oz/½ cup plain flour
5ml/1 tsp bicarbonate of soda
120ml/4fl oz/½ cup milk
2 large bananas, peeled and mashed
75g/3oz/1½ cups desiccated coconut, toasted

For the topping

25g/1oz/2 tbsp butter
30ml/2 tbsp clear honey
115g/4oz/2 cups shredded coconut

1 Preheat the oven to 190°C/375°F/Gas 5. Grease a deep 18cm/7in square cake tin, line with greaseproof paper and grease the paper.

2 Beat the butter and sugar until smooth and creamy. Beat in the eggs, one at a time. Sift together the flours and bicarbonate of soda, sift half into the butter mixture and stir to mix.

3 Combine the milk and mashed banana and beat half into the egg mixture. Stir in the remaining flour and banana mixtures and toasted coconut. Transfer to the cake tin and smooth the surface.

4 Bake for 1 hour, or until a skewer inserted into the centre of the cake comes out clean. Leave in the tin for 5 minutes, then turn out on to a wire rack, peel off the paper and cool.

5 For the topping, gently melt the butter and honey. Stir in the shredded coconut and cook, stirring, for 5 minutes or until lightly browned. Remove from the heat and allow to cool slightly. Spoon the topping over the cake and allow to cool.

St Clement's Cake

A tangy orange-and-lemon cake makes a spectacular centrepiece when decorated with fruits and flowers.

Makes one 23cm/9in ring cake

175g/6oz/¾ cup butter
75g/3oz/⅓ cup soft light brown sugar
3 eggs, separated
grated rind and juice of 1 orange and 1 lemon
150g/5oz/1¼ cups self-raising flour
75g/3oz/6 tbsp caster sugar
15g/½ oz/2 tbsp ground almonds
350ml/12fl oz/1½ cups double cream
15ml/1 tbsp Grand Marnier
16 crystallized orange and lemon slices, silver dragées, sugared almonds and fresh flowers, to decorate

1 Preheat the oven to 180°C/350°F/Gas 4. Grease and flour a 900ml/1½ pint/3¾ cup ring mould.

2 Cream half the butter and all of the brown sugar until pale and light. Beat in the egg yolks, orange rind and juice and fold in 75g/3oz/⅔ cup flour.

3 Cream the remaining butter and caster sugar. Stir in the lemon rind and juice and fold in the remaining flour and ground almonds. Whisk the egg whites until stiff, and fold in.

4 Spoon the two mixtures alternately into the prepared tin. Using a skewer or small spoon, swirl through the mixture to create a marbled effect. Bake for 45–50 minutes until risen, and a skewer inserted in the cake comes out clean. Cool in the tin for 10 minutes then transfer to a wire rack to cool.

5 Whip the cream and Grand Marnier together until lightly thickened. Spread over the cake and swirl a pattern over the icing with a palette knife. Decorate the ring with the crystallized fruits, dragées and sugared almonds to resemble a jewelled crown. Arrange a few fresh flowers in the centre.

Apple Cake

Makes one ring cake

675g/1½lb apples, peeled, cored and quartered
500g/1lb 2oz/generous 2½ cups caster sugar
15ml/1 tbsp water
350g/12oz/3 cups plain flour
9ml/1¾ tsp bicarbonate of soda
5ml/1 tsp ground cinnamon
5ml/1 tsp ground cloves
175g/6oz/generous 1 cup raisins
150g/5oz/1¼ cups chopped walnuts
225g/8oz/1 cup butter or margarine, at room temperature
5ml/1 tsp vanilla essence

For the icing

115g/4oz/1 cup icing sugar
1.5ml/¼ tsp vanilla essence
30–45ml/2–3 tbsp milk

1 Put the apples, 50g/2oz/4 tbsp of the sugar and the water in a saucepan and bring to the boil. Simmer for 25 minutes, stirring occasionally to break up any lumps. Leave to cool. Preheat the oven to 160°C/325°F/Gas 3. Thoroughly butter and flour a 1.75-litre/3-pint/7½-cup tube tin.

2 Sift the flour, bicarbonate of soda and spices into a bowl. Remove 30ml/2 tbsp of the mixture to another bowl and toss with the raisins and 115g/4oz/1 cup of the walnuts.

3 Cream the butter or margarine and remaining sugar together until light and fluffy. Fold in the apple mixture gently. Fold the flour mixture into the apple mixture. Stir in the vanilla and the raisin and walnut mixture. Pour into the tube tin. Bake until a skewer inserted in the centre comes out clean, about 1½ hours. Cool completely in the tin on a wire rack, then unmould on to the rack.

4 For the icing, put the sugar in a bowl and stir in the vanilla and 15ml/1 tbsp milk. Add more milk until the icing is smooth and has a thick pouring consistency. Transfer the cake to a serving plate and drizzle the icing on top. Sprinkle with the remaining nuts. Allow the icing to set.

Chocolate Amaretto Marquise

This light-as-air marquise is perfect for a special occasion, served with Amaretto cream.

Makes one heart-shaped cake

15ml/1 tbsp sunflower oil
75g/3oz/7–8 amaretti biscuits, crushed
25g/1oz/2 tbsp unblanched almonds, toasted and finely chopped
450g/1lb plain chocolate, broken into pieces
75ml/5 tbsp Amaretto liqueur
75ml/5 tbsp golden syrup
475ml/16fl oz/2 cups double cream
cocoa powder, to dust

For the Amaretto cream

350ml/12fl oz 1½ cups whipping or double cream
30–45 ml/2–3 tbsp Amaretto liqueur

1 Lightly oil a 23cm/9in heart-shaped or springform cake tin. Line the base with non-stick baking paper and oil the paper. In a small bowl, combine the crushed amaretti biscuits and the chopped almonds. Sprinkle evenly over the base of the tin.

2 Place the chocolate, Amaretto liqueur and golden syrup in a saucepan over very low heat. Stir frequently until the chocolate is melted and the mixture is smooth. Allow to cool for 6–8 minutes, until the mixture just feels warm.

3 Beat the cream until it just begins to hold its shape. Stir a large spoonful into the chocolate mixture, then quickly add the remaining cream and gently fold into the chocolate mixture. Pour into the prepared tin and tap the tin gently on the work surface to release any large air bubbles. Cover the tin with clear film and leave in the fridge overnight.

4 To unmould, run a thin-bladed sharp knife under hot water and dry carefully. Run the knife around the edge of the tin to loosen, place a serving plate over the tin, then invert to unmould. Carefully peel off the paper then dust with cocoa. Whip the cream and liqueur and serve separately.

Tangy Lemon Cake

The lemon syrup forms a crusty topping when completely cooled. Leave in the tin until ready to serve.

Makes one 900g/2lb loaf

175g/6oz/¾ cup butter
175g/6oz/scant 1 cup caster sugar
3 eggs, beaten
175g/6oz/1½ cups self-raising flour
grated rind of 1 orange
grated rind of 1 lemon

For the syrup

115g/4oz/generous ½ cup caster sugar
juice of 2 lemons

1 Preheat the oven to 180°C/350°F/Gas 4. Then grease a 900g/2lb loaf tin.

2 Beat the butter and sugar together until light and fluffy, then gradually beat in the eggs. Fold in the flour and the orange and lemon rinds.

3 Turn the cake mixture into the cake tin and bake for 1¼–1½ hours, until set in the centre, risen and golden. Remove the cake from the oven, but leave in the tin.

4 To make the syrup, gently heat the sugar in the lemon juice until melted, then boil for 15 seconds. Pour the syrup over the cake in the tin and leave to cool.

Pineapple and Apricot Cake

This is not a long-keeping cake, but it does freeze, well-wrapped in greaseproof paper and then foil.

Makes one 18cm/7in square or 20cm/8in round cake

175g/6oz/¾ cup unsalted butter
150g/5oz/generous ¾ cup caster sugar
3 eggs, beaten
few drops vanilla essence
225g/8oz/2 cups plain flour
1.5ml/¼ tsp salt
7.5ml/1½ tsp baking powder
225g/8oz/1¼ cups ready-to-eat dried apricots, chopped
115g/4oz/½ cup each chopped crystallized ginger and crystallized pineapple
grated rind and juice of ½ orange
grated rind and juice of ½ lemon
a little milk

1 Preheat the oven to 180°C/350°F/Gas 4. Double line an 18cm/7in square or 20cm/8in round cake tin. Cream the butter and sugar together until light and fluffy.

2 Gradually beat in the eggs with the vanilla essence, beating well after each addition. Sift together the flour, salt and baking powder, add a little with the last of the egg, then fold in the rest.

3 Gently fold in the apricots, ginger and pineapple and the fruit rinds, then add sufficient fruit juice and milk to give a fairly soft dropping consistency.

4 Spoon into the cake tin and smooth the top with a wet spoon. Bake for 20 minutes, then reduce the oven temperature to 160°C/325°F/Gas 3 and bake for a further 1½–2 hours, or until firm to the touch and a skewer comes out of the centre clean. Leave the cake to cool completely in the tin. Wrap in fresh paper before storing in an airtight tin.

Soured Cream Crumble Cake

The consistency of this cake, with its two layers of crumble, is sublime.

Makes one 23cm/9in square cake

115g/4oz/½ cup butter, at room temperature
130g/4½oz/scant ¾ cup caster sugar
3 eggs
210g/7½oz/scant 2 cups plain flour
5ml/1 tsp bicarbonate of soda
5ml/1 tsp baking powder
250ml/8fl oz/1 cup soured cream

For the topping

225g/8oz/1 cup dark brown sugar
10ml/2 tsp ground cinnamon
115g/4oz/1 cup finely chopped walnuts
50g/2oz/4 tbsp cold butter, cut into pieces

1 Preheat the oven to 180°C/350°F/Gas 4. Line the base of a 23cm/9in square cake tin with greaseproof paper and grease the paper and sides.

2 For the topping, place the brown sugar, cinnamon and walnuts in a bowl. Mix, then add the butter and rub in until the mixture resembles breadcrumbs.

3 To make the cake, cream the butter until soft. Add the sugar and beat until light and fluffy. Add the eggs, one at a time, beating well after each addition.

4 In another bowl, sift the flour, bicarbonate of soda and baking powder together three times. Fold the dry ingredients into the butter mixture in three batches, alternating with the soured cream. Fold until blended after each addition.

5 Pour half of the batter into the prepared tin and sprinkle over half of the topping. Pour the remaining batter on top and sprinkle over the remaining topping. Bake until browned, 60–70 minutes. Leave in the tin for 5 minutes, then turn out and cool on a wire rack.

Plum Crumble Cake

This cake can also be made with the same quantity of apricots or cherries.

Serves 8–10

150g/5oz/generous ½ cup butter or margarine, at room temperature
150g/5oz/¾ cup caster sugar
4 eggs, at room temperature
7.5ml/1½ tsp vanilla essence
150g/5oz/1¼ cups plain flour
5ml/1 tsp baking powder
675g/1½lb red plums, halved and stoned

For the topping

115g/4oz/1 cup plain flour
130g/4½oz/generous ¾ cup light brown sugar
7.5ml/1½ tsp ground cinnamon
75g/3oz/6 tbsp butter, cut in pieces

1 Preheat the oven to 180°C/350°F/Gas 4. Using greaseproof paper, line a 25 x 5cm/10 x 2in tin and grease the paper. For the topping, combine the flour, light brown sugar and cinnamon in a bowl. Add the butter and rub in until it resembles coarse breadcrumbs.

2 Cream the butter or margarine and sugar until light and fluffy. Beat in the eggs, one at a time. Stir in the vanilla. In three batches, sift, then fold in the flour and baking powder.

3 Pour the mixture into the tin. Arrange the plums on top and sprinkle with the topping.

4 Bake until a skewer inserted in the centre comes out clean, about 45 minutes. Cool in the tin.

5 To serve, run a knife around the inside edge and invert on to a plate. Invert again on to a serving plate so the topping is uppermost.

Pineapple Upside-down Cake

For an apricot cake, replace the pineapple slices with 225g/8oz/1¾ cups dried ready-to-eat apricots.

Makes one 25cm/10in round cake

115g/4oz/½ cup butter
200g/7oz/generous 1 cup dark brown sugar
450g/1lb canned pineapple slices, drained
4 eggs, separated
grated rind of 1 lemon
pinch of salt
115g/4oz/generous ½ cup caster sugar
75g/3oz/¾ cup plain flour
5ml/1 tsp baking powder

1 Preheat the oven to 180°C/350°F/Gas 4. Melt the butter in a 25cm/10in ovenproof cast-iron frying pan. Then reserve 15ml/1 tbsp butter. Add the brown sugar to the pan and stir to blend. Place the pineapple on top in one layer. Set aside.

2 Whisk together the egg yolks, reserved butter and lemon rind until well blended. Set aside.

3 Beat the egg whites and salt until stiff. Gradually fold in the caster sugar, then the egg yolk mixture.

4 Sift the flour and baking powder together. Carefully fold into the egg mixture in three batches.

5 Pour the mixture over the pineapple. Bake until a skewer inserted in the centre comes out clean, about 30 minutes.

6 While still hot, invert on to a serving plate. Serve hot or cold.

Upside-down Pear and Ginger Cake

This light spicy sponge, topped with glossy baked fruit and ginger, makes an excellent pudding.

Serves 6–8

900g/2lb can pear halves, drained
120ml/8 tbsp finely chopped stem ginger
120ml/8 tbsp ginger syrup from the jar
175g/6oz/1½ cups self-raising flour
2.5ml/½ tsp baking powder
5ml/1 tsp ground ginger
175g/6oz/1 cup soft light brown sugar
175g/6oz/¾ cup butter, softened
3 eggs, lightly beaten

1 Preheat the oven to 180°C/350°F/Gas 4. Base-line and grease a deep 20cm/8in round cake tin.

2 Fill the hollow in each pear with half the chopped stem ginger. Arrange, flat-sides down, in the base of the cake tin, then spoon over half the ginger syrup.

3 Sift together the flour, baking powder and ground ginger. Stir in the sugar and butter, add the eggs and beat until creamy, 1–2 minutes.

4 Spoon the mixture into the cake tin. Bake in the oven for 50 minutes, or until a skewer inserted in the centre of the cake comes out clean. Leave the cake in the tin for 5 minutes. Turn out on to a wire rack, peel off the lining paper and leave to cool completely.

5 Add the reserved ginger to the pear halves and drizzle over the remaining syrup.

Cranberry and Apple Ring

Tangy cranberries add an unusual flavour to this cake which is best eaten very fresh.

Makes one ring cake

225g/8oz/2 cups self-raising flour
5ml/1 tsp ground cinnamon
75g/3oz/½ cup light muscovado sugar
1 eating apple, cored and diced
75g/3oz/¾ cup fresh or frozen cranberries
60ml/4 tbsp sunflower oil
150ml/¼ pint/⅔ cup apple juice
cranberry jelly and apple slices, to decorate

1 Preheat the oven to 180°C/350°F/Gas 4. Lightly grease a 1-litre/1¾-pint/4-cup ring tin with oil.

2 Sift together the flour and ground cinnamon, then stir in the muscovado sugar.

3 Toss together the diced apple and cranberries. Stir into the dry ingredients, then add the oil and apple juice and beat together well.

4 Spoon the mixture into the prepared ring tin and bake for 35–40 minutes, or until the cake is firm to the touch. Turn out and leave to cool completely on a wire rack.

5 To serve, drizzle warmed cranberry jelly over the cake and decorate with apple slices.

Greek Honey and Lemon Cake

A wonderfully moist and tangy cake, you could ice it if you wished.

Makes one 19cm/7½in square cake

40g/1½oz/3 tbsp sunflower margarine
60ml/4 tbsp clear honey
finely grated rind and juice of 1 lemon
150ml/¼ pint/⅔ cup milk
150g/5oz/1¼ cups plain flour
7.5ml/1½ tsp baking powder
2.5ml/½ tsp grated nutmeg
50g/2oz/¼ cup semolina
2 egg whites
10ml/2 tsp sesame seeds

1 Preheat the oven to 200°C/400°F/Gas 6. Lightly oil and base-line a 19cm/7½in square deep cake tin.

2 Place the margarine and 45ml/3 tbsp of the honey in a saucepan and heat gently until melted. Reserve 15ml/1 tbsp lemon juice, then stir in the rest with the lemon rind and milk.

3 Sift together the flour, baking powder and nutmeg, then beat in with the semolina. Whisk the egg whites until they form soft peaks, then fold evenly into the mixture.

4 Spoon into the cake tin and sprinkle with sesame seeds. Bake for 25–30 minutes, until golden brown. Mix the reserved honey and lemon juice and drizzle over the cake while warm. Cool in the tin, then cut into fingers to serve.

Pear and Cardamom Spice Cake

Fresh pears and cardamoms – a classic combination – are used together in this moist fruit and nut cake.

Makes one 20cm/8in round cake

115g/4oz/½ cup butter
115g/4oz/generous ½ cup caster sugar
2 eggs, lightly beaten
225g/8oz/2 cups plain flour
15ml/1 tbsp baking powder
30ml/2 tbsp milk
crushed seeds from 2 cardamom pods
50g/2oz/½ cup walnuts, chopped
15ml/1 tbsp poppy seeds
500g/1¼lb dessert pears, peeled, cored and thinly sliced
3 walnut halves, to decorate
clear honey, to glaze

1 Preheat the oven to 180°C/350°F/Gas 4. Grease and base-line a 20cm/8in round, loose-based cake tin.

2 Cream the butter and sugar until pale and light. Gradually beat in the eggs. Sift over the flour and baking powder and fold in with the milk.

3 Stir in the cardamom seeds, chopped nuts and poppy seeds. Reserve one-third of the pear slices, and chop the rest. Fold into the creamed mixture.

4 Transfer to the cake tin. Smooth the surface, making a small dip in the centre. Place the walnut halves in the centre of the cake and fan the reserved pear slices around the walnuts, covering the cake mixture. Bake for 1¼ – 1½ hours, or until a skewer inserted in the centre comes out clean.

5 Remove the cake from the oven and brush with the honey. Leave in the tin for 20 minutes, then transfer to a wire rack to cool before serving.

Spiced Honey Nut Cake

A combination of ground pistachio nuts and breadcrumbs replaces flour in this recipe, resulting in a light, moist sponge cake.

Makes one 20cm/8in square cake

115g/4oz/generous ½ cup caster sugar
4 eggs, separated
grated rind and juice of 1 lemon
130g/4½oz/generous 1 cup ground pistachios
50g/2oz/scant 1 cup dried breadcrumbs

For the glaze

1 lemon
90ml/6 tbsp clear honey
1 cinnamon stick
15ml/1 tbsp brandy

1 Preheat the oven to 180°C/350°F/Gas 4. Grease and base-line a 20cm/8in square cake tin.

2 Beat the sugar, egg yolks, lemon rind and juice together until pale and creamy. Fold in 115g/4oz/1 cup of the ground pistachios and the breadcrumbs.

3 Whisk the egg whites until stiff and fold into the creamed mixture. Transfer to the cake tin and bake for 15 minutes, until risen and springy to the touch. Cool in the tin for 10 minutes, then transfer to a wire rack.

4 For the syrup, peel the lemon and cut the rind into very thin strips. Squeeze the juice into a small pan and add the honey and cinnamon stick. Bring to the boil, add the shredded rind, and simmer fast for 1 minute. Cool slightly and stir in the brandy.

5 Place the cake on a serving plate, prick all over with a skewer, and pour over the cooled syrup, lemon shreds and cinnamon stick. Sprinkle over the reserved pistachios.

Clare's American Carrot Cake

Makes one 20cm/8in round cake

250ml/8fl oz/1 cup corn oil
175g/6oz/1¼ cups granulated sugar
3 eggs
175g/6oz/1½ cups plain flour
7.5ml/1½ tsp baking powder
7.5ml/1½ tsp bicarbonate of soda
1.5ml/¼ tsp salt
7.5ml/1½ tsp ground cinnamon
good pinch of grated nutmeg
1.5ml/¼ tsp ground ginger
115g/4oz/1 cup chopped walnuts
225g/8oz/generous 1½ cups finely grated carrots
5ml/1 tsp vanilla essence
30ml/2 tbsp soured cream
8 tiny marzipan carrots, to decorate

For the frosting

175g/6oz/1 cup full fat soft cheese
25g/1oz/2 tbsp butter, softened
225g/8oz/2 cups icing sugar, sifted

1 Preheat the oven to 180°C/350°F/Gas 4. Grease and line two 20cm/8in loose-based round cake tins.

2 Put the corn oil and sugar into a bowl and beat well. Add the eggs, one at a time, and beat thoroughly. Sift the flour, baking powder, bicarbonate of soda, salt, cinnamon, nutmeg and ginger into the bowl and beat well. Fold in the chopped walnuts and grated carrots and stir in the vanilla essence and soured cream.

3 Divide the mixture between the cake tins and bake in the centre of the oven for about 65 minutes, or until a skewer inserted into the centre of the cakes comes out clean. Leave to cool in the tins on a wire rack. Meanwhile, beat all the frosting ingredients together until smooth.

4 Sandwich the cakes together with a little frosting. Spread the remaining frosting over the top and sides of the cake. Just before serving, decorate with the marzipan carrots.

Passion Cake

This cake is associated with Passion Sunday. The carrot and banana give it a rich, moist texture.

Makes one 20cm/8in round cake

200g/7oz/1¾ cups self-raising flour
10ml/2 tsp baking powder
5ml/1 tsp cinnamon
2.5ml/½ tsp freshly grated nutmeg
150g/5oz/10 tbsp butter, softened, or sunflower margarine
150g/5oz/¾ cup soft brown sugar
grated rind of 1 lemon
2 eggs, beaten
2 carrots, coarsely grated
1 ripe banana, mashed
115g/4oz/¾ cup raisins
50g/2oz/½ cup chopped walnuts or pecan nuts
30ml/2 tbsp milk
6–8 walnuts, halved, to decorate
coffee crystal sugar, to decorate

For the frosting

200g/7oz/scant 1 cup cream cheese, softened
30g/1½oz/scant ⅓ cup icing sugar
juice of 1 lemon
grated rind of 1 orange

1 Line and grease a deep 20cm/8in round cake tin. Preheat the oven to 180°C/350°F/Gas 4. Sift the flour, baking powder and spices into a bowl. In another bowl, cream the butter and sugar with the lemon rind until it is light and fluffy, then beat in the eggs. Fold in the flour mixture, then the carrots, banana, raisins, chopped nuts and milk.

2 Spoon the mixture into the cake tin, level the top and bake for about 1 hour, until risen and the top is springy to touch. Turn the tin upside-down and allow the cake to cool in the tin for 30 minutes. Then turn out on to a wire rack. When cold, split the cake in half.

3 Cream the cheese with the icing sugar, lemon juice and orange rind, then sandwich the two halves of the cake together with half of the frosting. Spread the rest of the frosting on top and decorate with walnut halves and sugar.

Caribbean Fruit and Rum Cake

Definitely a festive treat, this spicy cake contains both rum and sherry.

Makes one 25cm/10in round cake

450g/1lb/2 cups currants
450g/1lb/2¾ cups raisins
225g/8oz/1 cup prunes, stoned
115g/4oz/¾ cup mixed peel
400g/14oz/2⅔ cups dark soft brown sugar
5ml/1 tsp mixed spice
90ml/6 tbsp rum, plus more if needed
300ml/½ pint/1¼ cups sherry, plus more if needed
450g/1lb/4 cups self-raising flour
450g/1lb/2 cups butter, softened
10 eggs, beaten
5ml/1 tsp vanilla essence

1 Finely chop the dried fruits and peel in a food processor. Combine them in a bowl with 115g/4oz/generous ½ cup of the sugar, the mixed spice, rum and sherry. Cover and leave for 2 weeks. Stir daily and add more alcohol if you wish.

2 Preheat the oven to 160°C/325°F/Gas 3. Grease and then line a 25cm/10in round cake tin with a double layer of greaseproof paper.

3 Sift the flour, and set aside. Cream together the butter and remaining sugar and beat in the eggs until the mixture is smooth and creamy.

4 Add the fruit mixture, then gradually stir in the flour and vanilla essence. Mix well, adding more sherry if the mixture is too stiff; it should just fall off the back of the spoon.

5 Spoon the mixture into the prepared tin, cover loosely with foil and bake for about 2½ hours, until the cake is firm and springy. Leave to cool in the tin overnight.

Thai Rice Cake

A celebration gâteau made from fragrant Thai rice covered with a tangy cream icing and topped with fresh fruits.

Makes one 25cm/10in round cake

225g/8oz/1¼ cups Thai fragrant rice
1 litre/1¾ pints/4½ cups milk
115g/4oz/½ cup caster sugar
6 cardamom pods, crushed open
2 bay leaves
300ml/½ pint/1¼ cups whipping cream
6 eggs, separated

For the topping

300ml/½ pint/1¼ cups double cream
200g/7oz/scant 1 cup quark
5ml/1 tsp vanilla essence
grated rind of 1 lemon
30g/1½oz/scant ¼ cup caster sugar
soft berry fruits and sliced star or kiwi fruit, to decorate

1 Grease and line a deep 25cm/10in round cake tin. Boil the rice in unsalted water for 3 minutes, then drain.

2 Return the rice to the pan with the milk, sugar, cardamom pods and bay leaves. Bring to the boil, then simmer for 20 minutes, stirring occasionally.

3 Allow to cool, then remove the bay leaves and any cardamom husks. Turn into a bowl. Beat in the cream and then the egg yolks. Preheat the oven to 180°C/350°F/Gas 4.

4 Whisk the egg whites until they form soft peaks and fold into the rice mixture. Spoon into the cake tin and bake for 45–50 minutes, until risen and golden brown. The centre should be slightly wobbly – it will firm up as it cools.

5 Chill overnight in the tin. Turn out on to a large serving plate. Whip the double cream until stiff, then mix in the quark, vanilla essence, lemon rind and sugar. Cover the top and sides of the cake with the cream, swirling it attractively. Decorate with soft berry fruits and sliced star or kiwi fruit.

Luxurious Chocolate Cake

This delicious chocolate cake contains no flour and has a light mousse-like texture.

Makes one 20cm/8in round cake

175g/6oz/¾ cup butter, softened
130g/3½oz/⅔ cup caster sugar
9 x 25g/1oz squares plain chocolate, melted
225g/8oz/2 cups ground almonds
4 eggs, separated
4 x 25g/1oz squares white chocolate, melted, to decorate

1 Preheat the oven to 180°C/350°F/Gas 4. Grease and base-line a 20cm/8in springform cake tin. Beat 115g/4oz butter and all the sugar until light and fluffy. Add two-thirds of the plain chocolate, the almonds and egg yolks and beat well.

2 Whisk the egg whites in another clean, dry bowl until stiff. Fold them into the chocolate mixture, then transfer to the tin and smooth the surface. Bake for 50–55 minutes or until a skewer inserted into the centre comes out clean. Cool in the tin for 5 minutes, then remove from the tin and transfer to a wire rack. Remove the lining paper and cool completely.

3 Place the remaining butter and remaining melted chocolate in a saucepan. Heat very gently, stirring constantly, until melted. Place a large sheet of greaseproof paper under the wire rack to catch any drips. Pour the chocolate topping over the cake, allowing the topping to coat the top and sides. Leave to set for at least 1 hour.

4 To decorate, fill a paper piping bag with the melted white chocolate and snip the end. Drizzle the white chocolate around the edges. Use any remaining chocolate to make leaves. Allow to set then place on top of the cake.

One-stage Chocolate Sponge

For family teas, quick and easy favourites like this chocolate cake are invaluable.

Makes one 18cm/7in round cake

175g/6oz/¾ cup soft margarine, at room temperature
115g/4oz/½ cup caster sugar
50g/2oz/4 tbsp golden syrup
175g/6oz/1½ cups self-raising flour, sifted
45ml/3 tbsp cocoa powder, sifted
2.5ml/½ tsp salt
3 eggs, beaten
a little milk, as required
150ml/¼ pint/⅔ cup whipping cream
15–30ml/1–2 tbsp fine shred marmalade
icing sugar, for dusting

1 Preheat the oven to 180°C/350°F/Gas 4. Lightly grease or line two 18cm/7in sandwich tins. Place the margarine, sugar, syrup, flour, cocoa, salt and eggs in a large bowl, and cream together until well blended. If the mixture seems a little thick, stir in 15–30ml/1–2 tbsp milk, until you have a soft dropping consistency.

2 Spoon the mixture into the prepared sandwich tins and bake for about 30 minutes, changing shelves if necessary after 15 minutes, until the tops are just firm and the cakes are springy to the touch.

3 Leave the cakes to cool for 5 minutes, then remove from the tins and leave to cool completely on a wire rack.

4 Whip the cream and fold in the marmalade, then use to sandwich the two cakes together. Sprinkle the top with sifted icing sugar.

One-stage Victoria Sandwich

This versatile sponge recipe can be used for all sorts of cakes.

Makes one 18cm/7in round cake

175g/6oz/1½ cups self-raising flour
pinch of salt
175g/6oz/¾ cup butter, softened
175g/6oz/scant 1 cup caster sugar
3 eggs

To finish

60–90ml/4–6 tbsp raspberry jam
caster sugar or icing sugar

1 Preheat the oven to 180°C/350°F/Gas 4. Grease two 18cm/7in sandwich tins, line the bases with greaseproof paper and grease the paper.

2 Whisk all the cake ingredients together until smooth and creamy. Divide the mixture between the cake tins and smooth the surfaces. Bake for 25–30 minutes, or until a skewer inserted into the centre of the cakes comes out clean. Turn out on to a wire rack, peel off the lining paper and leave to cool.

3 Place one of the cakes on a serving plate and spread with the raspberry jam. Place the other cake on top.

4 Cut out paper star shapes, place on the cake and dredge with sugar. Remove the paper to reveal the pattern.

Mocha Victoria Sponge

A light coffee- and cocoa-flavoured sponge with a rich buttercream topping.

Makes one 18cm/7in round cake

175g/6oz/¾ cup butter
175g/6oz/generous ¾ cup caster sugar
3 eggs
175g/6oz/1½ cups self-raising flour, sifted
15ml/1 tbsp strong black coffee
15ml/1 tbsp cocoa powder mixed with 15–30ml/1–2 tbsp boiling water

For the coffee buttercream

150g/5oz/generous ½ cup butter
15ml/1 tbsp coffee essence or 10ml/2 tsp instant coffee powder dissolved in 15–30ml/1–2 tbsp warm milk
275g/10oz/2½ cups icing sugar

1 Preheat the oven to 180°C/350°F/Gas 4. Grease and base-line two 18cm/7in round sandwich tins. For the sponge, cream the butter and sugar until light and fluffy. Add the eggs, one at a time, beating well after each addition. Fold in the flour.

2 Divide the mixture into two bowls. Fold the coffee into one and the cocoa mixture into the other.

3 Place alternate spoonfuls of each mixture side by side in the cake tins. Bake for 25–30 minutes. Turn out on to a wire rack to cool.

4 For the buttercream, beat the butter until soft. Gradually beat in the remaining ingredients until smooth.

5 Sandwich the cakes, base-sides together, with a third of the buttercream. Cover the top and side with the rest.

Lemon and Apricot Cake

This cake is soaked in a tangy lemon syrup after baking to keep it really moist.

Makes one 23 x 13cm/9 x 5in loaf

175g/6oz/¾ cup butter, softened
175g/6oz/1½ cups self-raising flour
2.5ml/½ tsp baking powder
175g/6oz/¾ cup caster sugar
3 eggs, lightly beaten
finely grated rind of 1 lemon
175g/6oz/1½ cups ready-to-eat dried apricots, finely chopped
75g/3oz/¾ cup ground almonds
40g/1½oz/6 tbsp pistachio nuts, chopped
50g/2oz/½ cup flaked almonds
15g/½oz/2 tbsp whole pistachio nuts

For the syrup

45ml/3 tbsp caster sugar
freshly squeezed juice of 1 lemon

1 Preheat the oven to 180°C/350°F/Gas 4. Grease and line a 23 x 13cm/9 x 5in loaf tin with greaseproof paper and grease the paper.

2 Place the butter in a mixing bowl. Sift over the flour and baking powder, then add the sugar, eggs and lemon rind. Beat for 1–2 minutes until smooth and glossy, then stir in the apricots, ground almonds and chopped pistachio nuts.

3 Spoon the mixture into the loaf tin and smooth the surface. Sprinkle with the flaked almonds and the whole pistachio nuts. Bake for 1¼ hours, or until a skewer inserted into the centre of the cake comes out clean. Check the cake after 45 minutes and cover with a piece of foil when the top is nicely browned. Leave the cake to cool in the tin.

4 For the lemon syrup, gently dissolve the sugar in the lemon juice. Spoon the syrup over the cake. When the cake is completely cooled, turn it carefully out of the tin and peel off the lining paper.

Cherry Batter Cake

This colourful tray bake looks pretty cut into neat squares or fingers.

Makes one 33 x 23cm/13 x 9in cake

225g/8oz/2 cups self-raising flour
5ml/1 tsp baking powder
75g/3oz/6 tbsp butter, softened
150g/5oz/scant 1 cup soft light brown sugar
1 egg, lightly beaten
150ml/¼ pint/⅔ cup milk
icing sugar, for dusting
whipped cream, to serve (optional)

For the topping

675g/1½lb jar black cherries or blackcurrants, drained
175g/6oz/1 cup soft light brown sugar
50g/2oz/½ cup self-raising flour
50g/2oz/¼ cup butter, melted

1 Preheat the oven to 190°C/375°F/Gas 5. Grease and line a 33 x 23cm/13 x 9in Swiss roll tin with greaseproof paper and grease the paper.

2 To make the base, sift the flour and baking powder into a mixing bowl. Add the butter, sugar, egg and milk. Beat until the mixture becomes smooth, then turn into the prepared tin and smooth the surface.

3 Scatter the drained fruit evenly over the batter mixture.

4 Mix together the remaining topping ingredients and spoon evenly over the fruit. Bake for 40 minutes, or until golden brown and the centre is firm to the touch.

5 Leave to cool, then dust with icing sugar. Serve with whipped cream, if wished.

Fruit Salad Cake

You can use any combination of dried fruits in this rich, dark fruit cake.

Makes one 18cm/7in round cake

175g/6oz/1 cup roughly chopped mixed dried fruit, such as apples, apricots, prunes and peaches
250ml/8fl oz/1 cup hot tea
225g/8oz/2 cups wholemeal self-raising flour
5ml/1 tsp grated nutmeg
50g/2oz/⅓ cup dark muscovado sugar
45ml/3 tbsp sunflower oil
45ml/3 tbsp skimmed milk
demerara sugar, for sprinkling

1 Soak the dried fruits in the tea for several hours or overnight. Drain and reserve the liquid.

2 Preheat the oven to 180°C/350°F/Gas 4. Grease an 18cm/7in round cake tin and line the base with non-stick baking paper.

3 Sift the flour into a bowl with the nutmeg. Stir in the muscovado sugar, fruit and tea. Add the oil and milk, and mix well.

4 Spoon the mixture into the cake tin and sprinkle with demerara sugar. Bake for 50–55 minutes or until firm. Turn out on to a wire rack to cool.

Fairy Cakes with Blueberries

This luxurious treatment of fairy cakes means they will be as popular with adults as with children.

Makes 8–10

115g/4oz/½ cup soft margarine
115g/4oz/½ cup caster sugar
5ml/1 tsp grated lemon rind
pinch of salt
2 eggs, beaten
115g/4oz/1 cup self-raising flour, sifted
120ml/4fl oz/½ cup whipping cream
75–115g/3–4oz/¾–1 cup blueberries
icing sugar, for dusting

1 Preheat the oven to 190°C/375°F/Gas 5. Cream the margarine, sugar, lemon rind and salt in a large bowl until pale and fluffy.

2 Gradually beat in the eggs, then fold in the flour until well mixed. Spoon the mixture into eight to ten paper cases on baking sheets and bake for 15–20 minutes, until just golden.

3 Leave the cakes to cool, then scoop out a circle of sponge from the top of each using the point of a small sharp knife, and set them aside.

4 Whip the cream and place a spoonful in each cake, plus a couple of blueberries. Replace the lids at an angle and sift over some icing sugar.

Jewel Cake

This pretty cake is excellent served as a tea-time treat.

Makes one 23 x 13cm/9 x 5in cake

115g/4oz/½ cup mixed glacé cherries, halved, washed and dried
50g/2oz/4 tbsp stem ginger in syrup, chopped, washed and dried
50g/2oz/5 tbsp chopped mixed peel
115g/4oz/1 cup self-raising flour
75g/3oz/¼ cup plain flour
25g/1oz/3 tbsp cornflour
175g/6oz/¾ cup butter
175g/6oz/scant 1 cup caster sugar
3 eggs
grated rind of 1 orange

To decorate

175g/6oz/1½ cups icing sugar, sifted
30–45ml/2–3 tbsp freshly squeezed orange juice
50g/2oz/¼ cup mixed glacé cherries, chopped
25g/1oz/2½ tbsp mixed peel, chopped

1 Preheat the oven to 180°C/350°F/Gas 4. Grease and line a 23 x 13cm/9 x 5in loaf tin and grease the paper.

2 Place the cherries, stem ginger and mixed peel in a polythene bag with 25g/1oz/4 tbsp of the self-raising flour and shake to coat evenly. Sift together the remaining flours and cornflour.

3 Beat together the butter and sugar until light and fluffy. Beat in the eggs, one at a time. Fold in the sifted flours with the orange rind, then stir in the dried fruit.

4 Transfer the mixture to the cake tin and bake for 1¼ hours, or until a skewer inserted into the centre comes out clean. Leave in the tin for 5 minutes, then cool on a wire rack.

5 For the decoration, mix the icing sugar with the orange juice until smooth. Drizzle the icing over the cake. Mix together the chopped glacé cherries and mixed peel, then use to decorate the cake. Allow the icing to set before serving.

Iced Paradise Cake

Makes one 23 x 13cm/9 x 5in cake

3 eggs
75g/3oz/scant ½ cup caster sugar
65g/12½oz/9 tbsp plain flour
15g/½oz/1 tbsp cornflour
90ml/6 tbsp dark rum
250g/9oz/1½ cups plain chocolate chips
30ml/2 tbsp golden syrup
30ml/2 tbsp water
400ml/14fl oz/1¾ cups double cream
115g/4oz/scant 1 cup desiccated coconut, toasted
25g/1oz/2 tbsp unsalted butter
30ml/2 tbsp single cream
50g/2oz/5 tbsp white chocolate chips, melted
coconut curls, to decorate
cocoa powder, for dusting

1 Preheat the oven to 200°C/400°F/Gas 6. Grease and flour two baking sheets. Line a 23 x 13cm/9 x 5in tin with clear film.

2 Whisk the eggs and sugar in a heatproof bowl until blended. Place over a pan of simmering water and whisk until pale and thick. Whisk off the heat until cool. Sift over the flour and cornflour and fold in. Pipe 30 8cm/3in sponge fingers on to the baking sheets. Bake for 8–10 minutes. Cool slightly on the sheets, then on a wire rack.

3 Line the base and sides of the loaf tin with sponge fingers. Brush with rum. Melt 75g/3oz/½ cup chocolate chips, syrup, water and 30ml/2 tbsp rum in a bowl over simmering water.

4 Whip the double cream until it holds its shape, stir in the chocolate mixture and toasted coconut. Pour into the tin and top with the remaining sponge fingers. Brush over the remaining rum. Cover with clear film and freeze until firm.

5 Melt the remaining chocolate, butter and cream as before, then cool slightly. Turn the cake out on to a wire rack. Pour over the icing to coat. Chill.

6 Drizzle the white chocolate in zigzags over the cake. Chill. Sprinkle with coconut curls and dust with cocoa powder.

Pound Cake with Red Fruit

This orange-scented cake is good for tea, or serve as a dessert with a fruit coulis.

Makes one 20 x 10cm/8 x 4in cake

450g/1lb/about 4 cups fresh raspberries, strawberries or stoned cherries, or a combination of any of these
175g/6oz/¾ cup caster sugar, plus 15–30ml/1–2 tbsp, plus extra for sprinkling
15ml/1 tbsp lemon juice
175g/6oz/1½ cups plain flour
10ml/2 tsp baking powder
pinch of salt
175g/6oz/¾ cup unsalted butter, softened
3 eggs
grated rind of 1 orange
15ml/1 tbsp orange juice

1 Reserve a few whole fruits for decorating. In a blender or food processor, process the fruit until smooth. Add 15–30ml/1–2 tbsp sugar and the lemon juice, and process again. Strain the sauce and chill.

2 Grease the base and sides of a 20 x 10cm/8 x 4in loaf tin and line the base with non-stick baking paper. Grease the paper. Sprinkle with sugar and tip out any excess. Preheat the oven to 180°C/350°F/Gas 4.

3 Sift together the flour, baking powder and a pinch of salt. Beat the butter until creamy. Add the sugar and beat until light and fluffy. Add the eggs, one at a time, beating well after each addition. Beat in the orange rind and juice. Gently fold the flour mixture into the butter mixture in three batches, then spoon the mixture into the loaf tin and tap gently to release any air bubbles.

4 Bake for 35–40 minutes, until the top is golden and it is springy to the touch. Leave the cake in its tin on a wire rack for 10 minutes, then remove the cake from the tin and cool for 30 minutes. Remove the paper and serve slices of cake with a little of the fruit sauce, decorated with the reserved fruit.

Madeleine Cakes

These little tea cakes, baked in a special tin with shell-shaped cups, are best eaten on the day they are made.

Makes 12

165g/5½oz/generous 1¼ cups plain flour
5ml/1 tsp baking powder
2 eggs
75g/3oz/½ cup icing sugar, plus extra for dusting
grated rind of 1 lemon or orange
15ml/1 tbsp lemon or orange juice
75g/3oz/6 tbsp unsalted butter, melted and slightly cooled

1 Preheat the oven to 190°C/375°F/Gas 5. Generously grease a 12-cup madeleine cake tin. Sift together the flour and the baking powder.

2 Beat the eggs and icing sugar until the mixture is thick and creamy and leaves ribbon trails. Gently fold in the lemon or orange rind and juice.

3 Beginning with the flour mixture, alternately fold in the flour and melted butter in four batches. Leave to stand for 10 minutes, then spoon into the tin. Tap gently to release any air bubbles. Bake for 12–15 minutes, rotating the tin halfway through cooking, until a skewer inserted in the centre comes out clean. Tip out on to a wire rack to cool completely and dust with icing sugar before serving.

Chocolate-orange Battenburg Cake

A tasty variation on the traditional pink-and-white Battenburg cake.

Makes one 18cm/7in long rectangular cake

115g/4oz/½ cup soft margarine
115g/4oz/½ cup caster sugar
2 eggs, beaten
few drops vanilla essence
15g/½oz/1 tbsp ground almonds
115g/4oz/1 cup self-raising flour, sifted
grated rind and juice of ½ orange
15g/½oz/2 tbsp cocoa powder, sifted
30–45ml/2–3 tbsp milk
1 jar chocolate and nut spread
225g/8oz white almond paste

1 Preheat the oven to 180°C/350°F/Gas 4. Grease and line an 18cm/7in square cake tin. Put a double piece of foil across the middle of the tin, to divide it into two equal oblongs.

2 Cream the margarine and sugar. Beat in the eggs, vanilla and almonds. Divide the mixture evenly into two halves. Fold half of the flour into one half, with the orange rind and enough juice to give a soft dropping consistency. Fold the rest of the flour and the cocoa into the other half, with enough milk to give a soft dropping consistency. Fill the tin with the two mixes and level the top.

3 Bake for 15 minutes, reduce the heat to 160°C/325°F/Gas 3 and cook for 20–30 minutes, until the top is just firm. Leave to cool in the tin for a few minutes. Turn out on to a board, cut each cake into two strips and trim evenly. Leave to cool.

4 Using the spread, sandwich the cakes together, Battenburg-style. Roll out the almond paste on a board lightly dusted with cornflour to a rectangle 18cm/7in wide and long enough to wrap around the cake. Wrap the paste around the cake, putting the join underneath. Press to seal.

Best-ever Chocolate Sandwich

A three-layered cake that would be ideal for a birthday party or a special high tea.

Makes one 20cm/8in round cake

115g/4oz/1cup plain flour
50g/2oz/½ cup cocoa powder
5ml/1 tsp baking powder
pinch of salt
6 eggs
225g/8oz/generous 1 cup caster sugar
10ml/2 tsp vanilla essence
115g/4oz/½ cup unsalted butter, melted
225g/8oz plain chocolate, chopped
75g/3oz/6 tbsp unsalted butter
3 eggs, separated
250ml/8fl oz/1 cup whipping cream
45ml/3 tbsp caster sugar

1 Preheat the oven to 180°C/350°F/Gas 4. Line three 20cm/8in round tins with greaseproof paper, grease the paper and dust with flour. Sift the flour, cocoa, baking powder and salt together three times.

2 Place the eggs and sugar in a heatproof bowl set over a pan of simmering water. Beat until doubled in volume, about 10 minutes. Add the vanilla. Fold in the flour mixture in three batches, then the butter.

3 Put the mixture in the tins. Bake until the cakes pull away from the tin sides, about 25 minutes. Transfer to a wire rack.

4 For the icing, melt the chocolate in the top of a double boiler. Off the heat, stir in the butter and egg yolks. Return to the heat and stir until thick.

5 Whip the cream until firm. In another bowl, beat the egg whites until stiff. Add the sugar and beat until glossy. Fold the cream, then the egg whites, into the chocolate mixture. Chill for about 20 minutes, then sandwich together and cover the cake with icing.

Chocolate Layer Cake

Makes one 23cm/9in cake

225g/8oz can cooked whole beetroot, drained and juice reserved
115g/4oz/½ cup unsalted butter, softened
550g/1lb 6oz/2½ cups light brown sugar
3 eggs
15ml/1 tbsp vanilla essence
75g/3oz unsweetened chocolate, melted
285g/10oz/2 cups plain flour
10ml/2 tsp baking powder
2.5ml/½ tsp salt
120ml/4fl oz/½ cup buttermilk
chocolate curls, to decorate (optional)

For the frosting

450ml/16fl oz/2 cups double cream
500g/1lb 2oz plain chocolate, chopped
15ml/1 tbsp vanilla essence

1 Preheat the oven to 180°C/350°F/Gas 4. Grease two 23cm/9in cake tins and dust with cocoa powder. Grate the beetroot and add it to its juice. Beat the butter, brown sugar, eggs and vanilla until pale and fluffy. Beat in the chocolate.

2 Sift together the flour, baking powder and salt. With the mixer on low speed and beginning and ending with flour mixture, alternately beat in flour and buttermilk. Add the beetroot and juice and beat for 1 minute. Fill the tins and bake for 30–35 minutes, until a skewer inserted in the centre comes out clean. Cool for 10 minutes, then unmould and cool.

3 To make the frosting, heat the cream until it just begins to boil, stirring occasionally to prevent scorching. Remove from the heat and stir in the chocolate, until melted and smooth. Stir in the vanilla. Strain into a bowl and chill, stirring every 10 minutes, for 1 hour.

4 Sandwich and cover the cake with frosting, and top with chocolate curls, if using. Allow to set for 20–30 minutes, then chill before serving.

Marbled Chocolate-peanut Cake

Serves 12–14

115g/4oz unsweetened chocolate, chopped
225g/8oz/1 cup unsalted butter, softened
225g/8oz/1 cup peanut butter
200g/6½oz/1 cup granulated sugar
220g/7oz/1 cup light brown sugar
5 eggs
285g/10oz/2 cups plain flour
10ml/2 tsp baking powder
2.5ml/½ tsp salt
125ml/4fl oz/½ cup milk
50g/2oz/5 tbsp chocolate chips

For the chocolate-peanut butter glaze

25g/1oz/2 tbsp butter, diced
25g/1oz/2 tbsp smooth peanut butter
45ml/3 tbsp golden syrup
5ml/1 tsp vanilla essence
175g/6oz plain chocolate, broken into pieces

1 Preheat the oven to 180°C/350°F/Gas 4. Grease and flour a 3-litre/5-pint/12-cup tube tin or ring mould. In the top of a double boiler, melt the chocolate.

2 Beat the butter, peanut butter and sugars until light and creamy. Add the eggs, one at a time, beating well after each addition. Sift together the flour, baking powder and salt. Add to the butter mixture alternately with the milk.

3 Pour half the batter into another bowl. Stir the melted chocolate into one half and stir the chocolate chips into the other half. Drop alternate large spoonfuls of the two batters into the tin or mould. Using a knife, pull through the batters to create a swirled marbled effect; do not let the knife touch the side or base of the tin. Bake for 50–60 minutes, until the top springs back when touched. Cool in the tin on a wire rack for 10 minutes. Then unmould on to the wire rack.

4 Combine the glaze ingredients and 15ml/1 tbsp water in a small saucepan. Melt over a low heat, stirring. Cool slightly, then drizzle over the cake, allowing it to run down the side.

Chocolate Fairy Cakes

Makes 24

115g/4oz good-quality plain chocolate, cut into small pieces
15ml/1 tbsp water
300g/10oz/2½ cups plain flour
5ml/1 tsp baking powder
2.5ml/½ tsp bicarbonate of soda
pinch of salt
300g/10oz/scant 1½ cups caster sugar
170g/6oz/¾ cup butter or margarine, at room temperature
150ml/¼ pint/⅔ cup milk
5ml/1 tsp vanilla essence
3 eggs
1 recipe quantity buttercream, flavoured to taste

1 Preheat the oven to 180°C/350°F/Gas 4. Grease and flour 24 deep bun tins, about 6.5cm/2¾in in diameter, or use paper cases in the tins.

2 Put the chocolate and water in a bowl set over a pan of almost simmering water. Heat until melted and smooth, stirring. Remove from the heat and leave to cool.

3 Sift the flour, baking powder, bicarbonate of soda, salt and sugar into a large bowl. Add the chocolate mixture, butter or margarine, milk and vanilla essence.

4 With an electric mixer on medium-low speed, beat until smoothly blended. Increase the speed to high and beat for 2 minutes. Add the eggs and beat for 2 more minutes.

5 Divide the mixture evenly among the prepared bun tins and bake for 20–25 minutes, or until a skewer inserted into the centre of a cake comes out clean. Cool in the tins for 10 minutes, then turn out to cool completely on a wire rack.

6 Ice the top of each cake with buttercream, swirling it into a peak in the centre.

Chocolate Mint-filled Cupcakes

For extra mint flavour, chop eight thin mint cream-filled after-dinner mints and fold into the cake batter.

Makes 12

225g/8oz/2 cups plain flour
5ml/1 tsp bicarbonate of soda
pinch of salt
50g/2oz/½ cup cocoa powder
150g/5oz/10 tbsp unsalted butter, softened
300g/10½oz/1½ cups caster sugar
3 eggs
5ml/1 tsp peppermint essence
250ml/8fl oz/1 cup milk

For the filling

300ml/10fl oz/1¼ cups double or whipping cream
5ml/1 tsp peppermint essence

For the glaze

170g/6oz plain chocolate
115g/4oz/½ cup unsalted butter
5ml/1 tsp peppermint essence

1 Preheat the oven to 180°C/350°F/Gas 4. Line a 12-cup bun tray with paper cases. Sift together the flour, bicarbonate of soda, salt and cocoa powder. In another bowl, beat the butter and sugar until light and creamy. Add the eggs, one at a time, beating well after each addition; beat in the peppermint. On low speed, beat in the flour mixture alternately with the milk, until just blended. Spoon into the paper cases.

2 Bake for 12–15 minutes, until a skewer inserted in the centre of a cake comes out clean. Transfer to a wire rack to cool. When cool, remove the paper cases.

3 For the filling, whip the cream and peppermint until stiff. Spoon into a piping bag fitted with a small plain nozzle. Pipe about 15ml/1 tbsp into each cake through the base.

4 For the glaze, melt the chocolate and butter, stirring until smooth. Remove from the heat and stir in the peppermint essence. Cool, then spread on top of each cake.

Rich Chocolate Nut Cake

Use walnuts or pecan nuts for the cake sides if you prefer.

Makes one 23cm/9in round cake

225g/8oz/1 cup butter
225g/8oz plain chocolate
115g/4oz/1 cup cocoa powder
350g/12oz/1¾ cups caster sugar
6 eggs
85ml/3fl oz/5 tbsp brandy
225g/8oz/2 cups finely chopped hazelnuts

For the glaze

50g/2oz/4 tbsp butter
150g/5oz bitter cooking chocolate
30ml/2 tbsp milk
5ml/1 tsp vanilla essence

1 Preheat the oven to 180°C/350°F/Gas 4. Line a 23 x 5cm/ 9 x 2in round tin with greaseproof paper and grease the paper. Melt the butter and chocolate in the top of a double boiler. Leave to cool.

2 Sift the cocoa into a bowl. Add the sugar and eggs and stir until just combined. Pour in the chocolate mixture and brandy. Fold in three-quarters of the nuts, then pour the mixture into the cake tin.

3 Set the tin in a roasting tin and pour 2.5cm/1in hot water into the outer tin. Bake until the cake is firm to the touch, about 45 minutes. Leave for 15 minutes, then unmould on to a wire rack. When cool, wrap in greaseproof paper and chill for at least 6 hours.

4 For the glaze, melt the butter and chocolate with the milk and vanilla in the top of a double boiler.

5 Place the cake on a wire rack over a plate. Drizzle the glaze over, letting it drip down the sides. Cover the cake sides with the remaining nuts. Transfer to a serving plate when set.

Multi-layer Chocolate Cake

For a change, sandwich the cake layers with softened vanilla ice cream. Freeze before serving.

Makes one 20cm/8in round cake

115g/4oz plain chocolate
175g/6oz/¾ cup butter
450g/1lb/2¼ cups caster sugar
3 eggs
5ml/1 tsp vanilla essence
175g/6oz/1½ cups plain flour
5ml/1 tsp baking powder
115g/4oz/1 cup chopped walnuts

For the filling and topping

350ml/12fl oz/1½ cups whipping cream
225g/8oz plain chocolate
15ml/1 tbsp vegetable oil

1 Preheat the oven to 180°C/350°F/Gas 4. Line two 20cm/8in round cake tins with greaseproof paper and grease the paper.

2 Melt the chocolate and butter in the top of a double boiler. Transfer to a bowl and stir in the sugar. Add the eggs and vanilla and mix well. Sift over the flour and baking powder. Stir in the walnuts.

3 Pour the mixture into the cake tins. Bake until a skewer inserted in the centre comes out clean, about 30 minutes. Stand for 10 minutes, then unmould on to a wire rack to cool.

4 Whip the cream until firm. Slice the cakes in half horizontally. Sandwich them together and cover the cake with the cream. Chill.

5 To make the chocolate curls, melt the chocolate and oil in the top of a double boiler. Spread on to a non-porous surface. Just before it sets, hold the blade of a knife at an angle to the chocolate and scrape across the surface to make curls. Use to decorate the cake.

Chocolate Frosted Layer Cake

The contrast between the frosting and the sponge creates a dramatic effect when the cake is cut.

Makes one 20cm/8in round cake

225g/8oz/1 cup butter or margarine, at room temperature
285g/10½oz/1½ cups sugar
4 eggs, separated
10ml/2 tsp vanilla essence
385g/13½oz/3½ cups plain flour
10ml/2 tsp baking powder
1.5ml/¼ tsp salt
250ml/8fl oz/1 cup milk

For the frosting

150g/5oz plain chocolate
120ml/4fl oz/½ cup soured cream
1.5ml/¼ tsp salt

1 Preheat the oven to 180°C/350°F/Gas 4. Line two 20cm/8in round cake tins with greaseproof paper and grease the paper. Dust the tins with flour. Tap to remove any excess.

2 Cream the butter or margarine until soft. Gradually add the sugar and beat until light and fluffy. Beat the egg yolks, then add to the butter mixture with the vanilla.

3 Sift the flour with the baking powder three times. Set aside. Beat the egg whites with the salt until they peak stiffly.

4 Fold the dry ingredients into the butter mixture in three batches, alternating with the milk. Add a dollop of the egg white and fold in to lighten the mixture. Fold in the rest until just blended.

5 Spoon into the cake tins and bake until the cakes pull away from the sides, about 30 minutes. Leave in the tins for 5 minutes, then turn out on to a wire rack.

6 For the frosting, melt the chocolate in the top of a double boiler. When cool, stir in the soured cream and salt. Sandwich the layers with frosting, then spread on the top and side.

Devil's Food Cake with Orange

Makes one 23cm/9in round cake

50g/2oz/½ cup cocoa powder
175ml/6fl oz/¾ cup boiling water
175g/6oz/¾ cup butter, at room temperature
350g/12oz/2 cups dark brown sugar
3 eggs
275g/10oz/2½ cups plain flour
7.5ml/1½ tsp bicarbonate of soda
1.5ml/¼ tsp baking powder
120ml/4fl oz/½ cup soured cream
blanched orange rind shreds, to decorate

For the frosting

285g/10½oz/1½ cups caster sugar
2 egg whites
60ml/4 tbsp frozen orange juice concentrate
15ml/1 tbsp lemon juice
grated rind of 1 orange

1 Preheat the oven to 180°C/350°F/Gas 4. Line two 23cm/9in cake tins with greaseproof paper and grease the paper. In a bowl, mix the cocoa and water until smooth.

2 Cream the butter and sugar until light and fluffy. Add the eggs, one at a time, beating well after each addition. When the cocoa mixture is lukewarm, add to the butter mixture. Sift together the flour, soda and baking powder twice. Fold into the cocoa mixture in three batches, alternating with the soured cream. Pour into the tins and bake until the cakes pull away from the sides, 30–35 minutes. Stand for 15 minutes, then turn out on to a wire rack.

3 For the frosting, place all the ingredients in the top of a double boiler. With an electric mixer, beat until the mixture holds soft peaks. Continue beating off the heat until thick enough to spread.

4 Sandwich the cake layers with frosting, then spread over the top and side. Decorate with orange rind shreds.

French Chocolate Cake

This is typical of a French home-made cake – dense, dark and delicious. Serve with cream or a fruit coulis.

Makes one 24cm/9½in round cake

150g/5oz/5 tbsp caster sugar
275g/10oz plain chocolate, chopped
175g/6oz/¾ cup unsalted butter, cut into pieces
10ml/2 tsp vanilla essence
5 eggs, separated
40g/1½oz/¼ cup plain flour, sifted
pinch of salt
icing sugar, for dusting

1 Preheat the oven to 160°C/325°F/Gas 3. Butter a 24cm/9½in springform tin, sprinkle with sugar and tap out the excess.

2 Set aside 45ml/3 tbsp of the sugar. Place the chocolate, butter and remaining sugar in a heavy saucepan and cook over a low heat until melted. Remove from the heat, stir in the vanilla essence and leave to cool slightly.

3 Beat the egg yolks, one at a time, into the chocolate mixture, then stir in the flour.

4 Beat the egg whites with the salt until soft peaks form. Sprinkle over the reserved sugar and beat until stiff and glossy. Beat one-third of the whites into the chocolate mixture, then fold in the rest.

5 Pour the mixture into the tin and tap it gently to release any air bubbles.

6 Bake the cake for 35–45 minutes, until well risen and the top springs back when touched lightly. Transfer to a wire rack, remove the sides of the tin and leave to cool. Remove the tin base, dust the cake with icing sugar and transfer to a serving plate.

Almond Cake

Serve this wonderfully nutty cake with coffee, or, for a treat, with a glass of almond liqueur.

Makes one 23cm/9in round cake

225g/8oz/1⅓ cups blanched, toasted whole almonds
75g/3oz/5 tbsp icing sugar
3 eggs
25g/1oz/2 tbsp butter, melted
2.5ml/½ tsp almond essence
25g/1oz/4 tbsp plain flour
3 egg whites
15ml/1 tbsp caster sugar
toasted whole almonds, to decorate

1 Preheat the oven to 160°C/325°F/Gas 3. Line a 23cm/9in round cake tin with greaseproof paper and grease the paper.

2 Coarsely chop the almonds and grind them with half the icing sugar in a blender or food processor. Transfer to a mixing bowl.

3 Beat in the whole eggs and remaining icing sugar until the mixture forms ribbon trails. Mix in the butter and almond essence. Sift over the flour and fold in.

4 Beat the egg whites until they peak softly. Add the caster sugar and beat until stiff and glossy. Fold into the almond mixture in four batches.

5 Spoon the mixture into the cake tin and bake until golden brown, 15–20 minutes. Decorate with toasted almonds.

Caramel Layer Cake

Makes one 20cm/8in round cake

275g/10oz/2½ cups plain flour
7.5ml/1½ tsp baking powder
175g/6oz/¾ cup butter, at room temperature
165g/5½oz/generous ⅔ cup caster sugar
4 eggs, beaten
5ml/1 tsp vanilla essence
120ml/4fl oz/½ cup milk
whipped cream, to decorate
caramel threads, to decorate (optional)

For the frosting

285g/10½oz/1⅓ cups dark brown sugar
250ml/8fl oz/1 cup milk
25g/1oz/2 tbsp unsalted butter
45–75ml/3–5 tbsp whipping cream

1 Preheat the oven to 180°C/350°F/Gas 4. Line two 20cm/8in cake tins with greaseproof paper and grease the paper. Sift the flour and baking powder together three times.

2 Cream the butter and caster sugar until light and fluffy. Slowly mix in the beaten eggs. Add the vanilla. Fold in the flour mixture, alternating with the milk. Divide the batter between the cake tins and spread evenly. Bake until the cakes pull away from the sides of the tin, about 30 minutes. Stand in the tins for 5 minutes, then turn out and cool on a wire rack.

3 For the frosting, bring the brown sugar and milk to the boil, cover and cook for 2 minutes. Uncover and continue to boil, without stirring, until the mixture reaches 119°C/238°F (soft ball stage) on a sugar thermometer.

4 Remove the pan from the heat and add the butter, but do not stir it in. Leave to cool until lukewarm, then beat until the mixture is smooth. Stir in enough cream to obtain a spreadable consistency.

5 Sandwich the cake together with frosting and then cover the top and sides. Decorate with whipped cream, and caramel threads if liked.

Marbled Spice Cake

You could bake this cake in a 20cm/8in round tin if you do not have a kugelhopf.

Makes one ring cake

75g/3oz/6 tbsp butter, softened
115g/4oz/generous ½ cup caster sugar
2 eggs, lightly beaten
few drops vanilla essence
130g/4½oz/generous 1 cup plain flour
7.5ml/1½ tsp baking powder
45ml/3 tbsp milk
45ml/3 tbsp black treacle
5ml/1 tsp mixed spice
2.5ml/½ tsp ground ginger
175g/6oz/1½ cups icing sugar, sifted, to decorate

1 Preheat the oven to 180°C/350°F/Gas 4. Grease and flour a 900g/2lb kugelhopf or ring mould.

2 Cream together the butter and sugar until light and fluffy. Beat in the eggs and vanilla.

3 Sift together the flour and baking powder, then fold into the butter mixture, alternating with the milk.

4 Add the treacle and spices to one-third of the mixture. Drop alternating spoonfuls of the two mixtures into the tin. Run a knife through them to give a marbled effect.

5 Bake for 50 minutes, or until a skewer inserted into the centre comes out clean. Leave in the tin for 10 minutes, then turn out on to a wire rack to cool.

6 To decorate, make a smooth icing with the icing sugar and some warm water. Drizzle over the cake and leave to set.

Raspberry Meringue Gâteau

A rich hazelnut meringue filled with cream and raspberries makes a delicious combination of textures and tastes.

Serves 8

4 egg whites
225g/8oz/1 cup caster sugar
few drops vanilla essence
5ml/1 tsp malt vinegar
115g/4oz/1 cup toasted chopped hazelnuts, ground
300ml/½ pint/1¼ cups double cream
350g/12oz /2 cups raspberries
icing sugar, for dusting
raspberries and mint sprigs, to decorate

For the sauce

225g/8oz/1⅓ cups raspberries
45ml/3 tbsp icing sugar
15ml/1 tbsp orange liqueur

1 Preheat the oven to 180°C/350°F/Gas 4. Grease two 20cm/8in cake tins and line the bases with greaseproof paper.

2 Whisk the egg whites in a large bowl until they hold stiff peaks, then gradually whisk in the caster sugar a tablespoon at a time, whisking well after each addition.

3 Continue whisking the meringue mixture for a minute or two until very stiff, then fold in the vanilla essence, vinegar and the ground hazelnuts. Divide the meringue mixture between the prepared tins and spread level. Bake for 50–60 minutes, until crisp. Remove the meringues from the tins and leave to cool on a wire rack.

4 Meanwhile, make the sauce. Purée the raspberries with the icing sugar and orange liqueur in a blender or food processor, then press the purée through a nylon sieve to remove any pips. Chill the sauce until ready to serve.

5 Whip the cream then fold in the raspberries. Sandwich the meringue rounds with the raspberry cream. Dust with icing sugar, decorate with fruit and mint and serve with the sauce.

Strawberry Mint Sponge

This combination of fruit, mint and ice cream will prove popular with everyone.

Makes one 20cm/8in round cake

6–10 fresh mint leaves, plus extra to decorate
175g/6oz/¾ cup caster sugar
175g/6oz/¾ cup butter
175g/6oz/1½ cups self-raising flour
3 eggs
1.2 litres/2 pints/5 cups strawberry ice cream, softened
600ml/1 pint/2½ cups double cream
30ml/2 tbsp mint liqueur
350g/12oz/2 cups fresh strawberries

1 Tear the mint into pieces, mix with the sugar, and leave overnight. (Remove the leaves from the sugar before use.)

2 Preheat the oven to 190°C/375°F/Gas 5. Grease and line a 20cm/8in deep springform cake tin. Cream the butter and sugar, add the flour, and then the eggs. Pour the mixture into the tin.

3 Bake for 20–25 minutes, or until a skewer inserted in the centre comes out clean. Turn out on to a wire rack to cool. When cool, split into two layers.

4 Wash the cake tin and line with clear film. Put the cake base back in the tin. Spread with the ice cream, then cover with the top half of the cake. Freeze for 3–4 hours.

5 Whip the cream with the liqueur. Turn the cake out on to a serving plate and quickly spread a layer of whipped cream all over it, leaving a rough finish. Freeze until 10 minutes before serving. Decorate the cake with the strawberries and place fresh mint leaves around it.

Chestnut Cake

This rich, moist cake can be made up to 1 week in advance and kept, undecorated and wrapped, in an airtight tin.

Serves 8–10

150g/5oz/1¼ cups plain flour
pinch of salt
225g/8oz/1 cup butter, softened
150g/5oz/¾ cup caster sugar
425g/15oz can chestnut purée
9 eggs, separated
105ml/7 tbsp dark rum
300ml/½ pint/1¼ cups double cream
marron glacés and icing sugar, to decorate

1 Preheat the oven to 180°C/350°F/Gas 4. Grease and line a 20cm/8in springform cake tin.

2 Sift the flour and salt and set aside. Beat the butter and sugar together until light and fluffy. Fold in two-thirds of the chestnut purée, with the egg yolks. Fold in the flour and salt.

3 Whisk the egg whites in a clean, dry bowl until stiff.Beat a little of the egg whites into the chestnut mixture, until evenly blended, then fold in the remainder. Transfer the cake mixture to the tin and smooth the surface. Bake in the centre of the oven for about 1¼ hours, or until a skewer comes out clean. Leave in the tin and place on a wire rack.

4 Using a skewer, pierce holes over the cake. Sprinkle with 60ml/4 tbsp of rum, then cool. Remove the cake from the tin, peel off the lining paper and cut horizontally into two layers. Place bottom layer on a serving plate. Whisk the cream with the remaining rum, sugar and chestnut purée until smooth.

5 To assemble, spread two-thirds of the chestnut cream mixture over the bottom layer and place other layer on top. Spread some chestnut cream over the top and sides of the cake, pipe the remainder in large swirls round the edge of the cake. Decorate with chopped marron glacés and icing sugar.

Marbled Ring Cake

Glaze this cake with running icing if you prefer.

Makes one 25cm/10in ring cake

115g/4oz plain chocolate
350g/12oz/3 cups plain flour
5ml/1 tsp baking powder
450g/1lb/2 cups butter, at room temperature
725g/1lb 10oz/3¾ cups caster sugar
15ml/1 tbsp vanilla essence
10 eggs, at room temperature
icing sugar, for dusting

1 Preheat the oven to 180°C/350°F/Gas 4. Line a 25 x 10cm/10 x 4in ring mould with greaseproof paper and grease the paper. Dust with flour. Melt the chocolate in the top of a double boiler, stirring occasionally. Set aside.

2 Sift together the flour and baking powder. In another bowl, cream the butter, sugar and vanilla essence until light and fluffy. Add the eggs, two at a time, then gradually blend in the flour mixture.

3 Spoon half of the mixture into the ring mould. Stir the chocolate into the remaining mixture, then spoon into the tin. With a palette knife, swirl the mixtures for a marbled effect.

4 Bake until a skewer inserted in the centre comes out clean, about 1¾ hours. Cover with foil halfway through baking. Stand for 15 minutes, then unmould and transfer to a wire rack. To serve, dust with icing sugar.

Chocolate and Nut Gâteau

Hazelnuts give an interesting crunchy texture to this delicious iced dessert.

Serves 6–8

75g/3oz/½ cup shelled hazelnuts
about 32 sponge fingers
150ml/¼ pint/⅔ cup cold strong black coffee
30ml/2 tbsp brandy
450ml/¾ pint/1⅞ cups double cream
75g/3oz/6 tbsp icing sugar, sifted
150g/5oz plain chocolate
icing sugar and cocoa powder, for dusting

1 Preheat the oven to 200°C/400°F/Gas 6. Spread out the hazelnuts on a baking sheet and toast them in the oven for 5 minutes until golden. Transfer the nuts to a clean dish towel and rub off the skins while still warm. Cool, then chop finely.

2 Line a 1.2 litre/2 pint/5 cup loaf tin with clear film and cut enough sponge fingers to fit the base and sides. Reserve the remaining fingers.

3 Mix the coffee and brandy in a shallow dish. Dip the sponge fingers briefly into the coffee mixture and return to the tin, sugary side down.

4 Whip the cream with the icing sugar until it forms soft peaks. Roughly chop 75g/3oz of the chocolate, and fold into the cream with the hazelnuts. Melt the remaining chocolate in a bowl set over a pan of barely simmering water. Cool, then fold into the cream mixture. Spoon into the tin.

5 Moisten the remaining biscuits in the coffee mixture and lay over the filling. Wrap and freeze until firm.

6 Remove from the freezer 30 minutes before serving. Turn out on to a serving plate and dust with icing sugar and cocoa.

Chocolate and Orange Angel Cake

This light-as-air sponge with its fluffy icing is the answer to a cake-lover's prayer.

Makes one 20cm/8in ring cake

25g/1oz/¼ cup plain flour
15g/½oz/2 tbsp cocoa powder
15g/½oz/2 tbsp cornflour
pinch of salt
5 egg whites
2.5ml/½ tsp cream of tartar
115g/4oz/scant ½ cup caster sugar
blanched and shredded rind of 1 orange, to decorate

For the icing

200g/7oz/1 cup caster sugar
1 egg white

1 Preheat the oven to 180°C/350°F/Gas 4. Sift the flour, cocoa powder, cornflour and salt together three times. Beat the egg whites in a large bowl until foamy. Add the cream of tartar, then whisk until soft peaks form.

2 Add the caster sugar to the egg whites a spoonful at a time, whisking after each addition. Sift a third of the flour and cocoa mixture over the meringue and gently fold in. Repeat twice more.

3 Spoon the mixture into a non-stick 20cm/8in ring mould and level the top. Bake for 35 minutes, or until springy when lightly pressed. Turn upside-down on to a wire rack and leave to cool in the tin. Carefully ease out of the tin.

4 For the icing, put the sugar in a pan with 75ml/5 tbsp cold water. Stir over a low heat until dissolved. Boil until the syrup reaches soft ball stage (119°C/238°F on a sugar thermometer). Remove from the heat. Whisk the egg white until stiff. Add the syrup in a thin stream, whisking all the time, until the mixture is very thick and fluffy.

5 Spread the icing over the top and sides of the cooled cake. Sprinkle the orange rind over the top of the cake and serve.

Chocolate Date Cake

A stunning cake that tastes wonderful. Rich and gooey – it's a chocoholic's delight!

Serves 8

200g/7oz/scant 1 cup fromage frais
200g/7oz/scant 1 cup mascarpone
5ml/1 tsp vanilla essence, plus few extra drops
icing sugar, to taste
4 egg whites
115g/4oz/½ cup caster sugar
200g/7oz plain chocolate
175g/6oz/scant 1 cup Medjool dates, stoned and chopped
175g/6oz/1½ cups walnuts or pecan nuts, chopped

1 Preheat the oven to 180°C/350°F/Gas 4. Grease and base-line a 20cm/8in springform cake tin.

2 To make the frosting, mix together the fromage frais and mascarpone, add a few drops of vanilla essence and icing sugar to taste, then set aside.

3 Whisk the egg whites until they form stiff peaks. Whisk in 30ml/2 tbsp of the caster sugar until the meringue is thick and glossy, then fold in the remainder.

4 Chop 175g/6oz of the chocolate. Carefully fold into the meringue with the dates, nuts and 5ml/1 tsp of the vanilla essence. Pour into the prepared tin, spread level and bake for about 45 minutes, until risen around the edges.

5 Allow to cool in the tin for about 10 minutes, then unmould, peel off the lining paper and leave until completely cold. Swirl the frosting over the top of the cake.

6 Melt the remaining chocolate in a bowl over hot water. Spoon into a small paper piping bag and drizzle the chocolate over the cake. Chill before serving.

Warm Lemon and Syrup Cake

This delicious cake is the perfect winter dessert for both children and adults.

Serves 8

3 eggs
175g/6oz/¾ cup butter, softened
175g/6oz/¾ cup caster sugar
175g/6oz/1½ cups self-raising flour
50g/2oz/½ cup ground almonds
1.25ml/¼ tsp freshly grated nutmeg
50g/2oz/5 tbsp candied lemon peel, finely chopped
grated rind of 1 lemon
30ml/2 tbsp lemon juice
poached pears, to serve

For the syrup

175g/6oz/¾ cup caster sugar
juice of 3 lemons

1 Preheat the oven to 180°C/350°F/Gas 4. Grease and base-line a deep, round 20cm/8in cake tin.

2 Place all the cake ingredients in a large bowl and beat well for 2–3 minutes, until light and fluffy.

3 Tip the mixture into the prepared tin, spread level and bake for 1 hour, or until golden and firm to the touch.

4 Meanwhile, make the syrup. Put the sugar, lemon juice and 75ml/5 tbsp water in a pan. Heat gently, stirring, until the sugar has dissolved, then boil, without stirring, for a further 1–2 minutes.

5 Turn out the cake on to a plate with a rim. Prick the surface of the cake all over with a fork, then pour over the hot syrup. Leave to soak for about 30 minutes. Serve the cake warm with thin wedges of poached pears.

Strawberry Shortcake Gâteau

A light biscuit-textured sponge forms the base of this summertime dessert.

Makes one 20cm/8in round cake

225g/8oz/2 cups fresh strawberries, hulled
30ml/2 tbsp ruby port
225g/8oz/2 cups self-raising flour
10ml/2 tsp baking powder
75g/3oz/6 tbsp unsalted butter, diced
40g/1½oz/3 tbsp caster sugar
1 egg, lightly beaten
15–30ml/1–2 tbsp milk
melted butter, for brushing
250ml/8fl oz/1 cup double cream
icing sugar, for dusting

1 Preheat the oven to 220°C/425°F/Gas 7. Grease and base-line two 20cm/8in round, loose-based cake tins. Reserve 5 strawberries, slice the rest and marinate in the port for about 1–2 hours. Strain, reserving the port.

2 Sift the flour and baking powder into a bowl. Rub in the butter until the mixture resembles fine breadcrumbs and stir in the sugar. Work in the egg and 15ml/1 tbsp of the milk to form a soft dough, adding more milk if needed.

3 Knead on a lightly floured surface and divide in two. Roll out each half, mark one half into eight wedges, and transfer to the cake tins. Brush with a little melted butter and bake for 15 minutes until risen and golden. Cool in the tins for 10 minutes, then transfer to a wire rack.

4 Cut the marked cake into wedges. Reserving a little cream for decoration, whip the rest until it holds its shape, and fold in the reserved port and strawberry slices. Spread over the cake. Place the wedges on top and dust with icing sugar.

5 Whip the remaining cream and use to pipe swirls on each wedge. Halve the reserved strawberries and use to decorate the cake.

Almond and Raspberry Swiss Roll

A light and airy sponge cake is rolled up with a fresh cream and raspberry filling for a decadent tea-time treat.

Makes one 23cm/9in long roll

3 eggs
75g/3oz/⅓ cup caster sugar
50g/2oz/½ cup plain flour
30ml/2 tbsp ground almonds
caster sugar, for dusting
250ml/8fl oz/1 cup double cream
225g/8oz/generous 1 cup fresh raspberries
16 flaked almonds, toasted, to decorate

vanilla -

1 Preheat the oven to 200°C/400°F/Gas 6. Grease a 33 x 23cm/13 x 9in Swiss roll tin and line with greaseproof and grease the paper.

2 Whisk the eggs and sugar in a heatproof bowl until blended. Place over a pan of simmering water and whisk until thick and pale. Whisk off the heat until cool. Sift over the flour and almonds and fold in gently.

3 Transfer to the prepared tin and bake for 10–12 minutes, until risen and springy to the touch. Invert the cake in its tin on to greaseproof paper dusted with caster sugar. Leave to cool, then remove the tin and lining paper.

4 Reserve a little cream, then whip the rest until it holds its shape. Fold in all but 8 raspberries and spread the mixture over the cooled cake, leaving a narrow border. Roll the cake up and sprinkle with caster sugar.

5 Whip the reserved cream until it just holds its shape, and spoon along the cake centre. Decorate with the reserved raspberries and toasted flaked almonds.

Orange and Walnut Swiss Roll

This unusual cake is tasty enough to serve alone, but you could also pour over some single cream.

Makes one 24cm/9½in long roll

4 eggs, separated
115g/4oz/generous ½ cup caster sugar
115g/4oz/1 cup very finely chopped walnuts
pinch of cream of tartar
pinch of salt
icing sugar, for dusting

For the filling

300ml/10fl oz/1¼ cups whipping cream
15ml/1 tbsp caster sugar
grated rind of 1 orange
15ml/1 tbsp orange-flavour liqueur

1 Preheat the oven to 180°C/350°F/Gas 4. Line a 30 x 24cm/12 x 9½in Swiss roll tin with greaseproof paper and grease the paper.

2 Beat the egg yolks and sugar until thick. Stir in the walnuts. Beat the egg whites with the cream of tartar and salt until stiffly peaking. Fold into the walnut mixture.

3 Pour the mixture into the prepared tin and level. Bake for 15 minutes. Invert the cake on to greaseproof paper dusted with icing sugar. Peel off the lining paper. Roll up the cake with the sugared paper. Leave to cool.

4 For the filling, whip the cream until softly peaking. Fold in the caster sugar, orange rind and liqueur.

5 Unroll the cake. Spread with the filling, then re-roll. Chill. To serve, dust with icing sugar.

Chocolate Swiss Roll

Makes one 33cm/13in long roll

225g/8oz plain chocolate
45ml/3 tbsp water
30ml/2 tbsp rum, brandy or strong coffee
7 eggs, separated
170g/6oz/scant 1 cup caster sugar
1.5ml/¼ tsp salt
350ml/12fl oz/1½ cups whipping cream
icing sugar, for dusting

1 Preheat the oven to 180°C/350°F/Gas 4. Line and grease a 38 x 33cm/15 x 13in Swiss roll tin with greaseproof paper.

2 Combine the chocolate, water and rum or other flavouring in the top of a double boiler, or in a heatproof bowl set over simmering water. Heat until melted. Set aside.

3 With an electric mixer, beat the egg yolks and sugar until thick. Stir in the melted chocolate.

4 In another bowl, beat the egg whites and salt until they hold stiff peaks. Fold a large dollop of egg whites into the yolk mixture to lighten it, then carefully fold in the rest of the egg whites.

5 Pour the mixture into the tin and smooth evenly with a palette knife. Bake for 15 minutes. Remove from the oven, cover with greaseproof paper and a damp cloth. Leave to stand for 1–2 hours. With an electric mixer, whip the cream until stiff. Set aside.

6 Run a knife along the inside edge of the tin to loosen the cake, then invert the cake on to a sheet of greaseproof paper that has been dusted with icing sugar.

7 Peel off the lining paper. Spread with an even layer of whipped cream, then roll up the cake with the help of the sugared paper. Chill for several hours. Before serving, dust with an even layer of icing sugar.

Apricot Brandy-snap Roulade

A magnificent combination of soft and crisp textures, this cake looks impressive and is easy to prepare.

Makes one 33cm/13in long roll

4 eggs, separated
7.5ml/1½ tsp fresh orange juice
115g/4oz/generous ½ cup caster sugar
175g/6oz/1½ cups ground almonds
4 brandy snaps, crushed, to decorate

For the filling

150g/5oz canned apricots, drained
300ml/½ pint/1¼ cups double cream
25g/1oz/¼ cup icing sugar

1 Preheat the oven to 190°C/375°F/Gas 5. Base-line and grease a 33 x 23cm/13 x 9in Swiss roll tin. Beat together the egg yolks, orange juice and sugar until thick and pale, about 10 minutes. Fold in the ground almonds.

2 Whisk the egg whites until they hold stiff peaks. Fold into the almond mixture, then transfer to the Swiss roll tin and smooth the surface. Bake for 20 minutes, or until a skewer inserted into the centre comes out clean. Leave to cool in the tin, covered with a just-damp dish towel.

3 For the filling, process the apricots in a blender or food processor until smooth. Whip the cream and icing sugar until it holds soft peaks. Fold in the apricot purée.

4 Spread the crushed brandy snaps on a sheet of greaseproof paper. Spread one-third of the cream mixture over the cake, then invert on to the brandy snaps. Peel off the lining paper.

5 Use the remaining cream mixture to cover the whole cake, then roll up the roulade from a short end. Transfer to a serving dish.

Apricot and Orange Roulade

This sophisticated dessert is very good served with a spoonful of Greek yogurt or crème fraîche.

Makes one 33cm/13in long roll

For the roulade

4 egg whites
115g/4oz/½ cup golden caster sugar
50g/2oz/½ cup plain flour
finely grated rind of 1 small orange
45ml/3 tbsp orange juice

For the filling

115g/4oz/½ cup ready-to-eat dried apricots
150ml/¼ pint/⅔ cup orange juice

To decorate

10ml/2 tsp icing sugar
shredded orange rind

1 Preheat the oven to 200°C/400°F/Gas 6. Base-line and grease a 33 x 23cm/13 x 9in Swiss roll tin.

2 To make the roulade, place the egg whites in a large bowl and whisk until they hold soft peaks. Gradually add the sugar, whisking hard between each addition. Fold in the flour, orange rind and juice. Spoon the mixture into the tin and spread it evenly.

3 Bake for 15–18 minutes, or until the sponge is firm and light golden in colour. Turn out on to a sheet of greaseproof paper and roll it up loosely from one short side. Leave to cool.

4 Roughly chop the apricots and place them in a pan with the orange juice. Cover and leave to simmer until most of the liquid has been absorbed. Purée the apricots in a food processor or blender.

5 Unroll the roulade and spread with the apricot mixture. Roll up, arrange strips of paper diagonally across the roll, sprinkle lightly with icing sugar, remove the paper and scatter with orange rind.

Classic Cheesecake

Dust the top of the cheesecake with icing sugar to decorate, if you wish.

Serves 8

50g/2oz/⅔ cup digestive biscuits, crushed
900g/2lb/4 cups cream cheese, at room temperature
245g/8¾oz/generous 1¼ cups sugar
grated rind of 1 lemon
45ml/3 tbsp lemon juice
5ml/1 tsp vanilla essence
4 eggs

1 Preheat the oven to 160°C/325°F/Gas 3. Grease a 20cm/8in springform tin. Place on a 30cm/12in circle of foil. Press it up the sides to seal tightly. Press the crushed biscuits into the base of the tin.

2 Beat the cream cheese until smooth. Add the sugar, lemon rind and juice, and vanilla, and beat until blended. Beat in the eggs, one at a time.

3 Pour into the prepared tin. Set the tin in a larger baking tray and place in the oven. Pour enough hot water in the outer tray to come 2.5cm/1in up the side of the tin.

4 Bake until the top is golden brown, about 1½ hours. Cool in the tin.

5 Run a knife around the edge to loosen, then remove the rim of the tin. Chill for at least 4 hours before serving.

Chocolate Cheesecake

Substitute digestive biscuits for the base to create a slightly different pudding.

Serves 10–12

275g/10oz plain chocolate
1.1kg/2½lb/5 cups cream cheese, at room temperature
200g/7oz/1 cup sugar
10ml/2 tsp vanilla essence
4 eggs
15ml/1 tbsp cocoa powder
175ml/6fl oz/¾ cup soured cream

For the base

200g/7oz/2⅓ cups chocolate biscuits, crushed
75g/3oz/6 tbsp butter, melted
2.5ml/½ tsp ground cinnamon

1 Preheat the oven to 180°C/350°F/Gas 4. Grease the base and sides of a 23 x 7.5cm/9 x 3in springform tin.

2 For the base, mix the biscuits with the butter and cinnamon. Press into the base of the tin.

3 Melt the chocolate in the top of a double boiler. Set aside.

4 Beat the cream cheese until smooth, then beat in the sugar and vanilla. Add the eggs, one at a time.

5 Stir the cocoa powder into the soured cream. Add to the cream cheese mixture. Stir in the melted chocolate.

6 Pour over the crust. Bake for 1 hour. Cool in the tin, then remove the rim. Chill before serving.

Marbled Cheesecake

Serves 10

900g/2lb/4 cups cream cheese, at room temperature
200g/7oz/1 cup caster sugar
4 eggs
5ml/1 tsp vanilla essence
50g/2oz/½ cup cocoa powder, dissolved in 75ml/5 tbsp hot water
70g/2½oz/1 cup digestive biscuits, crushed

1 Preheat the oven to 180°C/350°F/Gas 4. Grease and base-line a 20 x 7.5cm/8 x 3in cake tin.

2 With an electric mixer, beat the cheese until smooth and creamy. Add the sugar and beat to incorporate. Beat in the eggs, one at a time. Do not overmix.

3 Divide the mixture between two bowls. Stir the vanilla into one, then add the chocolate mixture to the other. Pour a cupful of the vanilla mixture into the centre of the tin to make an even layer. Slowly pour over a cupful of chocolate mixture in the centre. Repeat, alternating cupfuls of the batter in a circular pattern until both are used up.

4 Set the tin in a larger baking tray and pour in hot water to come 3cm/1½in up the sides of the cake tin. Bake until the top of the cake is golden, about 1½ hours. It will rise during baking but will sink later. Leave to cool in the tin on a rack.

5 To turn out, run a knife around the inside edge. Place a flat plate, bottom-side up, over the tin and invert on to the plate.

6 Sprinkle the crushed biscuits evenly over the base, gently place another plate over them, and invert again. Cover and chill for at least 3 hours, or overnight. To serve, cut slices with a sharp knife dipped in hot water.

Baked Cheesecake with Fresh Fruits

Vary the fruit decoration to suit the season for this rich, creamy dessert.

Serves 12

175g/6oz/2 cups digestive biscuits, crushed
50g/2oz/¼ cup unsalted butter, melted
450g/1lb/2 cups curd cheese
150ml/¼ pint/⅔ cup soured cream
115g/4oz/generous ½ cup caster sugar
3 eggs, separated
grated rind of 1 lemon
30ml/2 tbsp Marsala
2.5ml/½ tsp almond essence
50g/2oz/½ cup ground almonds
50g/2oz/scant ½ cup sultanas
450g/1lb prepared mixed fruits, such as figs, cherries, peaches and strawberries, to decorate

1 Preheat the oven to 180°C/350°F/Gas 4. Grease and line the sides of a 25cm/10in round springform tin. Combine the biscuits and butter and press into the base of the tin. Chill for 20 minutes.

2 For the cake mixture, beat together the cheese, cream, sugar, egg yolks, lemon rind, Marsala and almond essence until smooth and creamy.

3 Whisk the egg whites until stiff and fold into the cheese mixture with all the remaining ingredients, except the fruit, until evenly combined. Pour over the biscuit base and bake for 45 minutes, until risen and just set in the centre.

4 Leave in the tin until completely cold. Carefully remove the tin and peel away the lining paper.

5 Chill the cheesecake for at least 1 hour before decorating with the prepared fruits, just before serving.

Tofu Berry "Cheesecake"

Strictly speaking, this summery "cheesecake" is not a cheesecake at all, as it's based on tofu – but who would guess?

Serves 6

For the base
50g/2oz/4 tbsp margarine
30ml/2 tbsp apple juice
115g/4oz/1 cup bran flakes

For the filling
275g/10oz/1½ cups tofu or low fat soft cheese
200g/7oz/scant 1 cup natural yogurt
15ml/1 tbsp/1 sachet powdered gelatine
60ml/4 tbsp apple juice

For the topping
175g/6oz/1½ cups mixed summer soft fruit, such as strawberries, raspberries, redcurrants, blackberries
30ml/2 tbsp redcurrant jelly
30ml/2 tbsp hot water

1 For the base, place the margarine and apple juice in a pan and heat gently until melted. Crush the cereal and stir it into the pan. Tip into a 23cm/9in round flan tin and press down firmly. Leave to set.

2 For the filling, place the tofu or cheese and yogurt in a food processor or blender and process until smooth. Dissolve the gelatine in the apple juice and stir into the tofu mixture.

3 Spread the tofu mixture over the chilled base, smoothing it evenly. Chill until set.

4 Remove the flan tin and place the "cheesecake" on a serving plate. Arrange the fruits over the top. Melt the redcurrant jelly with the hot water. Let it cool, and then spoon over the fruit to serve.

Baked Blackberry Cheesecake

This light cheesecake is best made with wild blackberries; if they're not available, use cultivated ones.

Serves 6
175g/6oz/¾ cup cottage cheese
150g/5oz/¾ cup natural yogurt
15ml/1 tbsp plain wholemeal flour
25g/1oz/2 tbsp golden caster sugar
1 egg
1 egg white
finely grated rind and juice of ½ lemon
200g/7oz/scant 2 cups fresh or frozen and thawed blackberries

1 Preheat the oven to 180°C/350°F/Gas 4. Lightly grease and base-line an 18cm/7in sandwich tin.

2 Place the cottage cheese in a food processor or blender and process until smooth. Place in a bowl, then add the yogurt, flour, sugar, egg and egg white, and mix. Add the lemon rind, juice and blackberries, reserving a few.

3 Tip the mixture into the tin and bake for 30–35 minutes, or until just set. Turn off the oven and leave the cake in it for a further 30 minutes.

4 Run a knife around the edge of the cheesecake and turn it out. Remove the lining paper and place the cheesecake on a warm serving plate.

5 Decorate the cheesecake with the reserved blackberries and serve warm.

Coffee, Peach and Almond Daquoise

Makes one 23cm/9in gâteau

5 eggs, separated
425g/15oz/scant 2 cups caster sugar
15ml/1 tbsp cornflour
175g/6oz/1½ cups ground almonds, toasted
135ml/4½fl oz/generous ½ cup milk
275g/10oz/1¼ cups unsalted butter, diced
45–60ml/3–4 tbsp coffee essence
2 x 400g/14oz cans peach halves in juice, drained
65g/2½oz/generous ½ cup flaked almonds, toasted
icing sugar, for dusting
few fresh mint leaves, to decorate

1 Preheat the oven to 150°C/300°F/Gas 2. Draw three 23cm/9in circles on to some greaseproof paper and place on baking sheets.

2 Whisk the egg whites until stiff. Gradually whisk in 275g/10oz/scant 1½ cups of the sugar until thick and glossy. Fold in the cornflour and almonds. Using a 1cm/½in plain nozzle, pipe circles of the mixture on to the paper. Bake for 2 hours. Turn on to wire racks to cool.

3 For the buttercream, beat together the egg yolks and remaining sugar until thick and pale. Heat the milk to boiling point and beat into the egg mixture. Return to the pan and heat until the mixture coats the back of a spoon. Strain into a large bowl and beat until lukewarm. Gradually beat in the butter until glossy. Beat in the coffee essence.

4 Trim the meringues and crush the trimmings. Reserve 3 peach halves, chop the rest and fold into half the buttercream with the crushed meringue. Use to sandwich the meringues together and place on a serving plate.

5 Ice the cake with the plain buttercream. Cover the top with flaked almonds and dust generously with icing sugar. Thinly slice the reserved peaches and use to decorate the cake edge with some mint leaves.

Mocha Brazil Layer Torte

Makes one 20cm/8in round cake

For the meringue
3 egg whites
115g/4oz/generous ½ cup caster sugar
15ml/1 tbsp coffee essence
75g/3oz/¾ cup Brazil nuts, toasted and finely ground
20cm/8in chocolate sponge cake

For the icing
175g/6oz/1 cup plain chocolate chips
30ml/2 tbsp coffee essence
30ml/2 tbsp water
600ml/1 pint/2½ cups double cream, whipped

To decorate
12 chocolate triangles
12 chocolate-coated coffee beans

1 Preheat the oven to 150°C/300°F/Gas 2. Draw two 20cm/8in circles on greaseproof paper and place on a baking sheet. Grease, base-line and flour a 20cm/8in round springform tin.

2 For the meringue, whisk the egg whites until stiff. Whisk in the sugar until glossy. Fold in the coffee essence and nuts. Using a 1cm/½in plain nozzle, pipe circles of the mixture on to the paper. Bake for 2 hours. Cool. Increase the oven temperature to 180°C/350°F/Gas 4.

3 For the icing, melt the chocolate chips, coffee essence and water in a bowl over a pan of simmering water. Remove from the heat and fold in the whipped cream.

4 Cut the cake into three equal layers. Trim meringue discs to the same size and assemble the cake with a layer of sponge, a little icing and a meringue disc, ending with sponge.

5 Reserve a little of the remaining icing, use the rest to cover the cake completely, forming a swirling pattern over the top. Using the reserved icing, and a piping bag with a star nozzle, pipe 24 small rosettes on top of the cake. Top alternately with the coffee beans and the chocolate triangles.

Fresh Fruit Genoese

This Italian classic can be made with any selection of seasonal fruits.

Serves 8–10

For the sponge
175g/6oz/1½ cups plain flour
pinch of salt
4 eggs
115g/4oz/½ cup caster sugar
90ml/6 tbsp orange-flavoured liqueur

For the filling and topping
600ml/1 pint/2½ cups double cream
60ml/4 tbsp vanilla sugar
450g/1lb mixed fresh fruits
150g/5oz/1¼ cups pistachio nuts, chopped
60ml/4 tbsp apricot jam, warmed and sieved

1 Preheat the oven to 180°C/350°F/Gas 4. Grease and line the base of a 20cm/ 8in springform cake tin.

2 Sift the flour and salt together three times, then set aside. Using an electric mixer, beat the eggs and sugar together for 10 minutes until thick and pale.

3 Fold the flour mixture gently into the egg and sugar mixture. Transfer the cake mixture to the prepared tin and bake for 30–35 minutes. Leave the cake in the tin for about 5 minutes, then transfer to a wire rack, remove paper and cool.

4 Cut the cake horizontally in to two layers, place the bottom layer on a plate. Sprinkle both layers with liqueur.

5 Add the vanilla sugar to the cream and whisk until the cream holds peaks. Spread two-thirds of the cream over the bottom layer and top with half of the fruit. Top with the second layer and spread the top and sides with the remaining cream. Press the nuts around the sides, arrange remaining fruit on top and brush with the apricot jam.

Fruit Gâteau with Heartsease

This gâteau would be lovely to serve as a dessert at a summer lunch party in the garden.

Makes one ring cake
90g/3½oz/½ cup soft margarine
100g/3½oz/scant ½ cup sugar
10ml/2 tsp clear honey
150g/5oz/1¼ cups self-raising flour
2.5ml/½ tsp baking powder
30ml/2 tbsp milk
2 eggs
15ml/1 tbsp rose water
15ml/1 tbsp Cointreau

To decorate
16 heartsease pansy flowers
1 egg white, lightly beaten
caster sugar
icing sugar
450g/1lb/4 cups strawberries
strawberry leaves

1 Preheat the oven to 190°C/375°F/Gas 5. Grease and lightly flour a ring mould. Put the soft margarine, sugar, honey, flour, baking powder, milk and eggs into a mixing bowl and beat well for 1 minute. Add the rose water and the Cointreau and mix well.

2 Pour the mixture into the mould and bake for 40 minutes. Allow to stand for a few minutes, and then turn out on to a serving plate.

3 Crystallize the heartsease pansies by painting them with the lightly beaten egg white and sprinkling with caster sugar. Leave to dry.

4 Sift icing sugar over the cake. Fill the centre of the ring with strawberries – if they will not all fit, place some around the edge. Decorate with the crystallized heartsease flowers and some strawberry leaves.

Nut and Apple Gâteau

Makes one 23cm/9in round cake

115g/4oz/1 cup pecan nuts or walnuts, toasted
50g/2oz/½ cup plain flour
10ml/2 tsp baking powder
1.5ml/¼ tsp salt
2 large cooking apples
3 eggs
225g/8oz/scant 1¼ cups caster sugar
5ml/1 tsp vanilla essence
175ml/6fl oz/¾ cup whipping cream

1 Preheat the oven to 160°C/325°F/Gas 3. Line two 23cm/9in cake tins with greaseproof paper and grease the paper.

2 Finely chop the nuts. Reserve 25ml/1½ tbsp of them and place the rest in a mixing bowl. Sift over the flour, baking powder and salt and stir.

3 Peel and core the apples. Cut into 3mm/⅛in dice, then stir into the flour mixture.

4 Beat the eggs until frothy. Gradually add the sugar and vanilla and beat until ribbon trails form, about 8 minutes. Fold in the flour mixture.

5 Pour into the cake tins and bake until a skewer inserted in the centre comes out clean, about 35 minutes. Leave to stand for 10 minutes, then turn out on to a wire rack to cool.

6 Whip the cream until firm. Use half for the filling. Pipe rosettes on the top and sprinkle over the reserved nuts.

Chocolate Pecan Nut Torte

This torte uses finely ground nuts instead of flour. Toast, then cool the nuts before grinding finely in a processor.

Makes one 20cm/8in round cake

200g/7oz plain chocolate, chopped
150g/5oz/10 tbsp unsalted butter, cut into pieces
4 eggs
100g/3½oz/½ cup caster sugar
10ml/2 tsp vanilla essence
115g/4oz/1 cup ground pecan nuts
10ml/2 tsp ground cinnamon
24 toasted pecan nut halves, to decorate (optional)

For the chocolate honey glaze

115g/4oz plain chocolate, chopped
60g/2oz/¼ cup unsalted butter, cut into pieces
30ml/2 tbsp honey
pinch of ground cinnamon

1 Preheat the oven to 180°C/350°F/Gas 4. Grease a 20cm/8in springform tin, line with greaseproof paper, then grease the paper. Wrap the tin with foil.

2 Melt the chocolate and butter over a low heat, stirring until smooth. Set aside. Beat the eggs, sugar and vanilla until frothy. Stir in the melted chocolate and butter, ground nuts and cinnamon. Pour into the tin. Place in a large roasting tin and pour boiling water into the roasting tin, to come 2cm/¾in up the side of the springform tin. Bake for 25–30 minutes, until the edge of the cake is set, but the centre soft. Remove the foil and set on a wire rack.

3 For the glaze, melt the chocolate, butter, honey and cinnamon, stirring until smooth. Remove from the heat. If using, dip toasted pecan halves halfway into the glaze and place on greaseproof paper to set. Remove the cake from its tin and invert on to a wire rack. Remove the paper. Pour the glaze over the cake, tilting the rack to spread it. Use a palette knife to smooth the sides. Arrange the nuts on top.

Coconut Lime Gâteau

Makes one 23cm/9in round cake

225g/8oz/2 cups plain flour
12.5ml/2½ tsp baking powder
1.5ml/¼ tsp salt
225g/8oz/1 cup butter, at room temperature
225g/8oz/generous 1 cup caster sugar
grated rind of 2 limes
4 eggs
60ml/4 tbsp fresh lime juice
75g/3oz/1½ cups desiccated coconut

For the frosting

450g/1lb/generous 2 cups granulated sugar
60ml/4 tbsp water
pinch of cream of tartar
1 egg white, whisked stiffly

1 Preheat the oven to 180°C/350°F/Gas 4. Grease and base-line two 23cm/9in sandwich tins. Sift together the flour, baking powder and salt.

2 Beat the butter until soft. Add the sugar and lime rind and beat until pale and fluffy. Beat in the eggs, one at a time.

3 Gradually fold in the dry ingredients, alternating with the lime juice, then stir in two-thirds of the coconut.

4 Divide the mixture between the cake tins, even the tops and bake for 30–35 minutes. Cool in the tins on a wire rack for 10 minutes, then turn out and peel off the lining paper.

5 Bake the remaining coconut until golden brown, stirring occasionally. For the frosting, heat the sugar, water and cream of tartar until dissolved, stirring. Boil to reach 120°C/250°F on a sugar thermometer. Remove from the heat and, when the bubbles subside, whisk in the egg white until thick.

6 Sandwich and cover the cake with the frosting. Sprinkle over the toasted coconut. Leave to set.

Exotic Celebration Gâteau

Use any tropical fruits you can find to make a spectacular display of colours and tastes.

Makes one 20cm/8in ring gâteau

175g/6oz/¾ cup butter, softened
175g/6oz/scant 1 cup caster sugar
3 eggs, beaten
250g/9oz/2¼ cups self-raising flour
30–45ml/2–3 tbsp milk
90–120ml/6–8 tbsp light rum
425ml/14fl oz/scant 2 cups double cream
25g/1oz/¼ cup icing sugar, sifted

To decorate

450g/1lb mixed fresh exotic and soft fruits, such as figs, redcurrants, star fruit and kiwi fruit
90ml/6 tbsp apricot jam, warmed and sieved
30ml/2 tbsp warm water
icing sugar

1 Preheat the oven to 190°C/375°F/Gas 5. Grease and flour a deep 20cm/8in ring mould.

2 Beat together the butter and sugar until light and fluffy. Gradually beat in the eggs, then fold in the flour and milk.

3 Spoon the mixture into the ring mould. Bake the cake for 45 minutes, or until a skewer inserted into the centre comes out clean. Turn out on to a wire rack and leave to cool.

4 Place the cake on a serving plate. Make holes randomly over the cake with a skewer. Drizzle over the rum and allow to soak in.

5 Beat together the cream and icing sugar until the mixture holds soft peaks. Spread all over the cake. Arrange the fruits in the hollow centre of the cake. Mix the apricot jam and water, then brush over the fruit. Sift over some icing sugar.

Chocolate and Fresh Cherry Gâteau

Makes one 20cm/8in round cake

115g/4oz/½ cup butter
150g/5oz/⅔ cup caster sugar
3 eggs, lightly beaten
175g/6oz/1 cup plain chocolate chips, melted
60ml/4 tbsp kirsch
150g/5oz/1¼ cups self-raising flour
5ml/1 tsp ground cinnamon
2.5ml/½ tsp ground cloves
350g/12oz fresh cherries, stoned and halved
45ml/3 tbsp morello cherry jam, warmed
5ml/1 tsp lemon juice

For the frosting

115g/4oz/⅔ cup plain chocolate chips
50g/2oz/¼ cup unsalted butter
60ml/4 tbsp double cream

To decorate

75g/3oz/½ cup white chocolate chips, melted
18 fresh cherries
few rose leaves, washed and dried

1 Preheat the oven to 160°C/325°F/Gas 3. Grease, base-line and flour a 20cm/8in round springform tin.

2 Cream the butter and 115g/4oz/½ cup of the sugar until pale. Beat in the eggs. Stir in the chocolate and half the kirsch. Fold in the flour and spices. Transfer to the tin and bake for 55–60 minutes, or until a skewer inserted in the centre comes out clean. Cool for 10 minutes then transfer to a wire rack.

3 For the filling, bring the cherries, remaining kirsch and sugar to the boil, cover, and simmer for 10 minutes. Uncover for a further 10 minutes until syrupy. Leave to cool.

4 Halve the cake horizontally. Cut a 1cm/½in deep circle from the base, leaving a 1cm/½in edge. Crumble into the filling and stir to form a paste. Fill and cover the cake base.

5 Sieve the jam and lemon juice. Brush all over the cake. For the frosting, melt all the ingredients. Cool, pour over the cake. Decorate with chocolate-dipped cherries and leaves.

Coffee Almond Flower Gâteau

This delicious cake can be made quite quickly. Ring the changes by using a coffee-flavoured sponge.

Makes one 20cm/8in round cake

475g/1lb 2oz/2¼ cups coffee-flavour butter icing
2 x 20cm/8in round sponge cakes with chopped nuts
75g/3oz plain chocolate
20 blanched almonds
4 chocolate-coated coffee beans

1 Reserve 60ml/4 tbsp of the butter icing for piping and use the rest to sandwich the sponges together and cover the top and side of the cake. Smooth the top with a palette knife and serrate the side with a scraper.

2 Melt the chocolate in a heatproof bowl over a pan of hot water. Remove from the heat, then dip in half of each almond at a slight angle. Leave to dry on greaseproof paper. Return the chocolate to the pan of hot water (off the heat) so it does not set. Remove and allow to cool slightly.

3 Arrange the almonds on top of the cake to represent flowers. Place a chocolate-coated coffee bean in the flower centres. Spoon the remaining melted chocolate into a greaseproof paper piping bag. Cut a small piece off the end in a straight line. Pipe the chocolate in wavy lines over the top of the cake and in small beads around the top edge.

4 Transfer the cake to a serving plate. Place the reserved buttercream in a fresh piping bag fitted with a No 2 writing nozzle. Pipe beads of icing all around the bottom of the cake, then top with small beads of chocolate.

Vegan Chocolate Gâteau

A rare treat for vegans, this gâteau tastes really delicious.

Makes one 20cm/8in gâteau

275g/10oz/2½ cups self-raising wholemeal flour
50g/2oz/½ cup cocoa powder
15ml/1 tbsp baking powder
250g/9oz/1¼ cups caster sugar
a few drops of vanilla essence
135ml/9 tbsp sunflower oil
350ml/12fl oz/1½ cups water
sifted cocoa powder, to decorate
25g/1oz/¼ cup chopped nuts, to decorate

For the chocolate fudge

50g/2oz/¼ cup soya margarine
45ml/3 tbsp water
250g/9oz/2¼ cups icing sugar
30ml/2 tbsp cocoa powder

1 Preheat the oven to 160°C/325°F/Gas 3. Grease and line a deep 20cm/8in round cake tin, and grease the paper.

2 Sift the flour, cocoa and baking powder into a large mixing bowl. Add the sugar and vanilla, then gradually beat in the oil and water to make a smooth batter. Pour the mixture into the cake tin and smooth the surface. Bake for 45 minutes, or until a skewer inserted into the centre of the cake comes out clean. Leave in the tin for 5 minutes, then turn out on to a wire rack and leave to cool. Cut the cake in half.

3 For the chocolate fudge, gently melt the margarine with the water. Remove from the heat, add the icing sugar and cocoa, and beat until smooth and shiny. Allow to cool until firm enough to spread and pipe.

4 Place a layer of cake on a serving plate and spread over two-thirds of the chocolate fudge. Top with the other layer of cake. Using a star nozzle, pipe chocolate fudge stars over the cake. Sprinkle with cocoa powder and chopped nuts.

Black Forest Gâteau

A perfect gâteau for a special tea party, or for serving as a sumptuous dinner-party dessert.

Makes one 20cm/8in gâteau

5 eggs
175g/6oz/scant 1 cup caster sugar
50g/2oz/½ cup plain flour
50g/2oz/½ cup cocoa powder
75g/3oz/6 tbsp butter, melted

For the filling

75–90ml/5–6 tbsp kirsch
600ml/1 pint/2½ cups double cream
425g/15oz can black cherries, drained, stoned and chopped

To decorate

chocolate curls
15–20 fresh cherries, preferably with stems
icing sugar

1 Preheat the oven to 180°C/350°F/Gas 4. Base-line and grease two deep 20cm/8in round cake tins.

2 Beat together the eggs and sugar for 10 minutes, or until thick and pale. Sift over the flour and cocoa, and fold in gently. Trickle in the melted butter and fold in gently.

3 Transfer the mixture to the cake tins. Bake for 30 minutes, or until springy to the touch. Leave in the tins for 5 minutes, then turn out on to a wire rack, peel off the lining paper and leave to cool. Cut each cake in half horizontally and sprinkle with the kirsch.

4 Whip the cream until softly peaking. Combine two-thirds of the cream with the chopped cherries. Place a layer of cake on a serving plate and spread with one-third of the filling. Repeat twice, and top with a layer of cake. Use the reserved cream to cover the top and sides of the gâteau.

5 Decorate the gâteau with chocolate curls, fresh cherries and dredge with icing sugar.

Walnut Coffee Gâteau

Serves 8–10

140g/5oz/1¼ cups walnuts
150g/5½oz/generous ¾ cup caster sugar
5 eggs, separated
55g/2oz/scant 1 cup dry breadcrumbs
15ml/1 tbsp cocoa powder
15ml/1 tbsp instant coffee
30ml/2 tbsp rum or lemon juice
1.5ml/¼ tsp salt
90ml/6 tbsp redcurrant jelly, warmed
chopped walnuts, for decorating

For the frosting

225g/8oz plain chocolate
750ml/1¼ pint/3 cups whipping cream

1 For the frosting, combine the chocolate and cream in the top of a double boiler until the chocolate melts. Cool, then cover and chill overnight, or until the mixture is firm.

2 Preheat the oven to 180°C/350°F/Gas 4. Line and grease a 23 x 5cm/9 x 2in cake tin. Grind the nuts with 45ml/3 tbsp of the sugar in a food processor, blender or coffee grinder.

3 With an electric mixer, beat the egg yolks and remaining sugar until thick and lemon-coloured. Fold in the walnuts. Stir in the breadcrumbs, cocoa, coffee and rum or lemon juice.

4 In another bowl, beat the egg whites with the salt until they hold stiff peaks. Fold carefully into the walnut mixture. Pour the meringue batter into the tin and bake until the top of the cake springs back when touched, about 45 minutes. Allow the cake to stand for 5 minutes, then turn out and cool, before slicing the cake in half horizontally.

5 With an electric mixer, beat the chocolate frosting mixture on low speed until it becomes lighter, about 30 seconds. Brush some of the jelly over the cut cake layer. Spread with some of the chocolate frosting, then sandwich with the remaining cake layer. Brush the top of the cake with jelly, then cover the side and top with the remaining frosting. Make a starburst pattern with a knife and sprinkle chopped walnuts around the edge.

Sachertorte

A rich cake, ideal to serve as a treat for anyone who is a self-confessed chocoholic.

Makes one 23cm/9in round cake

115g/4oz plain chocolate
90g/3oz/⅓ cup unsalted butter, at room temperature
50g/2oz/¼ cup sugar
4 eggs, separated, plus 1 egg white
1.5ml/¼ tsp salt
65g/2½oz/9 tbsp plain flour, sifted

For the topping

75ml/5 tbsp apricot jam
250ml/8fl oz/1 cup plus 15ml/1 tbsp water
15g/½oz/1 tbsp unsalted butter
175g/6oz plain chocolate
75g/3oz/⅓ cup sugar
ready-made chocolate decorating icing

1 Preheat the oven to 160°C/325°F/Gas 3. Line and grease a 23cm/9in cake tin. Melt the chocolate in the top of a double boiler and set aside.

2 Cream the butter and sugar until light and fluffy. Stir in the chocolate, then beat in the egg yolks, one at a time.

3 Beat the egg whites with the salt until stiff. Fold a dollop of whites into the chocolate mixture to lighten it. Fold in the remaining whites in three batches, alternating with the sifted flour. Pour into the tin and bake until a skewer comes out clean, about 45 minutes. Turn out on to a wire rack.

4 Meanwhile, melt the jam with 15ml/1 tbsp of the water, then strain for a smooth consistency. For the frosting, melt the butter and chocolate in the top of a double boiler. In a heavy saucepan, dissolve the sugar in the remaining water, then boil until it reaches 107°C/225°F (thread stage) on a sugar thermometer. Plunge the base of the pan into cold water for 1 minute. Stir into the chocolate. Cool for a few minutes.

5 Brush the warm jam over the cake. Pour over the frosting and spread over the top and sides. Leave to set overnight. Decorate with chocolate icing.

Dundee Cake

This is the perfect recipe for a festive occasion when a lighter fruit cake is required.

Makes one 20cm/8in round cake

175g/6oz/¾ cup butter
175g/6oz/1 cup light soft brown sugar
3 eggs
225g/8oz/2 cups plain flour
10ml/2 tsp baking powder
5ml/1 tsp ground cinnamon
2.5ml/½ tsp ground cloves
1.5ml/¼ tsp grated nutmeg
225g/8oz/generous 1½ cups sultanas
175g/6oz/generous 1 cup raisins
175g/6oz/¾ cup glacé cherries, halved
115g/4oz/¾ cup chopped mixed peel
50g/2oz/½ cup blanched almonds, chopped
grated rind of 1 lemon
30ml/2 tbsp brandy
115g/4oz/1 cup whole blanched almonds, to decorate

1 Preheat the oven to 160°C/325°F/Gas 3. Grease and line a 20cm/8in round deep cake tin. Cream the butter and sugar until pale and light. Add the eggs, 1 at a time, beating well after each addition.

2 Sift together the flour, baking powder and spices. Fold into the egg mixture alternately with the remaining ingredients, until evenly combined. Transfer to the cake tin. Smooth the surface, then make a small dip in the centre.

3 Decorate the top of the cake by pressing the blanched almonds in decreasing circles over the entire surface. Bake for 2–2¼ hours, until a skewer inserted in the centre of the cake comes out clean.

4 Leave to cool in the tin for 30 minutes then transfer the cake to a wire rack.

Vegan Dundee Cake

As it contains neither eggs nor dairy products, this cake is suitable for vegans.

Makes one 20cm/8in square cake

350g/12oz/scant 2½ cups wholemeal flour
5ml/1 tsp mixed spice
175g/6oz/¾ cup soya margarine
175g/6oz/1 cup dark muscovado sugar, plus 30ml/2 tbsp
175g/6oz/generous 1 cup sultanas
175g/6oz/1 cup currants
175g/6oz/generous 1 cup raisins
75g/3oz/½ cup chopped mixed peel
150g/5oz/generous ½ cup glacé cherries, halved
finely grated rind of 1 orange
30ml/2 tbsp ground almonds
25g/1oz/¼ cup blanched almonds, chopped
5ml/1 tsp bicarbonate of soda
120ml/4fl oz/½ cup soya milk
75ml/3fl oz/⅓ cup sunflower oil
30ml/2 tbsp malt vinegar

To decorate

mixed nuts, such as pistachios, pecan nuts and macadamia nuts
glacé cherries
angelica
60ml/4 tbsp clear honey, warmed

1 Preheat the oven to 150°C/300°F/Gas 2. Grease and double-line a deep 20cm/8in square loose-based cake tin.

2 Sift together the flour and mixed spice. Rub in the soya margarine. Stir in the sugar, dried fruits, mixed peel, cherries, orange rind, ground almonds and blanched almonds.

3 Dissolve the bicarbonate in a little of the milk. Warm the remaining milk with the oil and vinegar and add the bicarbonate mixture. Stir into the flour mixture.

4 Spoon into the tin and smooth. Bake for 2½ hours. Leave in the tin for 5 minutes, then cool on a rack. Decorate with the nuts, cherries and angelica and brush with the honey.

Panforte

This rich, spicy nougat-type cake is a Christmas speciality of Siena in Italy.

Makes one 20cm/8in round cake

275g/10oz/1⅔ cups mixed chopped exotic peel, to include lemon orange, citron, papaya and pineapple
115g/4oz/1 cup unblanched almonds
50g/2oz/½ cup walnut halves
50g/2oz/½ cup plain flour
5ml/1 tsp ground cinnamon
1.5ml/¼ tsp each grated nutmeg, ground cloves and ground coriander
175g/6oz/1 cup caster sugar
60ml/4 tbsp water
icing sugar, for dusting

1 Preheat the oven to 180°C/350°F/Gas 4. Grease and base-line a 20cm/8in round loose-based cake tin with rice paper. Put the mixed peel and nuts in a bowl. Sift in the flour and spices and mix well.

2 Dissolve the caster sugar and water in a small saucepan, then boil until the mixture reaches 107°C/225°F on a sugar thermometer (thread stage). Pour on to the fruit mixture, stirring to coat well. Transfer to the cake tin, pressing into the sides with a metal spoon.

3 Bake for 25–30 minutes, until the mixture is bubbling. Cool in the tin for 5 minutes.

4 Use a lightly oiled palette knife to work around the edges of the cake to loosen it. Remove the cake from the tin, leaving the base in place. Leave to go cold, then remove the base and dust generously with icing sugar.

Kulich

This Russian yeast cake is traditionally made at Eastertime.

Makes two cakes

15ml/1 tbsp easy-blend dried yeast
90ml/6 tbsp lukewarm milk
75g/3oz/scant ½ cup caster sugar
500g/1¼lb/5 cups plain flour
pinch of saffron strands
30ml/2 tbsp dark rum
2.5ml/½ tsp ground cardamom seeds
2.5ml/½ tsp ground cumin
50g/2oz/4 tbsp unsalted butter
2 eggs plus 2 egg yolks
½ vanilla pod, finely chopped
25g/1oz/2 tbsp each crystallized ginger, mixed peel, almonds and currants, chopped

To decorate

75g/3oz/¾ cup icing sugar, sifted
7.5–10ml/1½–2 tsp warm water
drop of almond essence
2 candles
blanched almonds
mixed peel

1 Blend together the yeast, milk, 25g/1oz/2 tbsp sugar and 50g/2oz/½ cup flour. Leave in a warm place for 15 minutes, until frothy. Soak the saffron in the rum for 15 minutes.

2 Sift together the remaining flour and spices and rub in the butter. Stir in the rest of the sugar. Add the yeast mixture, saffron liquid and remaining ingredients. Knead until smooth. Put in an oiled bowl, cover and leave until doubled in size.

3 Preheat the oven to 190°C/375°F/Gas 5. Grease, line and flour two 500g/1¼lb coffee tins or 15cm/6in clay flowerpots.

4 Punch down the dough and form into two rounds. Press into the tins or pots, cover and leave for 30 minutes. Bake for 35 minutes for the pots or 50 minutes for the tins. Cool.

5 Mix together the icing sugar, water and almond essence. Pour over the cakes. Decorate with the candles, nuts and peel.

Yule Log

This rich seasonal treat could provide an economical alternative to a traditional iced fruit cake.

Makes one 28cm/11in long roll

4 eggs, separated
150g/5oz/¾ cup caster sugar
5ml/1 tsp vanilla essence
pinch of cream of tartar (optional)
115g/4oz/1 cup plain flour, sifted
250ml/8fl oz/1 cup whipping cream
300g/11oz plain chocolate, chopped
30ml/2 tbsp rum or Cognac
icing sugar, for dusting

1 Preheat the oven to 190°C/375°F/Gas 5. Grease, line and flour a 40 x 28cm/16 x 11in Swiss roll tin.

2 Whisk the egg yolks with all but 25g/1oz/2 tbsp of the sugar until pale and thick. Add the vanilla essence.

3 Whisk the egg whites (with the cream of tartar if not using a copper bowl) until they form soft peaks. Add the reserved sugar and continue whisking until stiff and glossy.

4 Fold half the flour into the yolk mixture. Add a quarter of the egg whites and fold in to lighten the mixture. Fold in the remaining flour, then the remaining egg whites.

5 Spread the mixture in the tin. Bake for 15 minutes. Turn on to paper sprinkled with caster sugar. Roll up and leave to cool.

6 Bring the cream to the boil. Put the chocolate in a bowl and add the cream. Stir until the chocolate has melted, then beat until it is fluffy and has thickened to a spreading consistency. Mix a third of the chocolate cream with the rum or Cognac.

7 Unroll the cake and spread with the rum mixture. Re-roll and cut off about a quarter, at an angle. Arrange to form a branch. Spread the chocolate cream over the cake. Mark with a fork, add Christmas decorations and dust with icing sugar.

Chocolate Chestnut Roulade

A traditional version of Bûche de Nôel, the delicious French Christmas gâteau.

Makes one 33cm/13in long roll

225g/8oz plain chocolate
50g/2oz white chocolate
4 eggs, separated
115g/4oz/generous ½ cup caster sugar

For the chestnut filling

150ml/¼ pint/⅔ cup double cream
225g/8oz can chestnut purée
50–65g/2–2½oz/4–5 tbsp icing sugar, plus extra for dusting
15–30ml/1–2 tbsp brandy

1 Preheat the oven to 180°C/350°F/Gas 4. Line and grease a 23 x 33cm/9 x 13in Swiss roll tin.

2 For the chocolate curls, melt 50g/2oz of the plain and all of the white chocolate in separate bowls set over saucepans of hot water. When melted, spread on a non-porous surface and leave to set. Hold a long sharp knife at a 45-degree angle to the chocolate and push it along the chocolate, turning the knife in a circular motion. Put the curls on greaseproof paper.

3 Melt the remaining plain chocolate. Beat the egg yolks and caster sugar until thick and pale. Stir in the chocolate.

4 Whisk the whites until they form stiff peaks, then fold into the mixture. Turn into the tin and bake for 15–20 minutes. Cool, covered with a just-damp dish towel, on a wire rack.

5 Sprinkle a sheet of greaseproof paper with caster sugar. Turn the roulade out on to it. Peel off the lining paper and trim the edges of the roulade. Cover with the dish towel.

6 For the filling, whip the cream until softly peaking. Beat together the chestnut purée, icing sugar and brandy until smooth, then fold in the cream. Spread over the roulade and roll it up. Top with chocolate curls and dust with icing sugar.

Chocolate Christmas Cups

To crystallize cranberries for decoration, beat an egg white until frothy. Dip each berry in egg white then in sugar.

Makes about 35 cups

70–80 foil or paper sweet cases
275g/10oz plain chocolate, broken into pieces
175g/6oz cooked, cold Christmas pudding
75ml/3fl oz/⅓ cup brandy or whisky
chocolate leaves and a few crystallized cranberries, to decorate

1 Place the chocolate in a bowl over a saucepan of hot water. Heat gently until the chocolate is melted, stirring until the chocolate is smooth.

2 Using a pastry brush, brush or coat the base and sides of about 35 sweet cases. Allow to set, then repeat, reheating the melted chocolate if necessary, and apply a second coat. Leave to cool and set completely, 4–5 hours or overnight. Reserve the remaining chocolate.

3 Crumble the Christmas pudding in a small bowl, sprinkle with the brandy or whisky and allow to stand for 30–40 minutes, until the spirit is absorbed.

4 Spoon a little of the pudding mixture into each cup, smoothing the top. Reheat the remaining chocolate and spoon over the top of each cup to cover the surface of each cup to the edge. Leave to set.

5 When completely set, carefully peel off the cases and place in clean foil cases. Decorate with chocolate leaves and crystallized cranberries.

Eggless Christmas Cake

This simple cake contains a wealth of fruit and nuts to give it that traditional Christmas flavour.

Makes one 18cm/7in square cake

75g/3oz/½ cup sultanas
75g/3oz/½ cup raisins
75g/3oz/½ cup currants
75g/3oz/scant ½ cup glacé cherries, halved
50g/2oz/¼ cup mixed peel
250ml/8fl oz/1 cup apple juice
25g/1oz/scant ¼ cup toasted hazelnuts
30ml/2 tbsp pumpkin seeds
2 pieces stem ginger in syrup, chopped
finely grated rind of 1 lemon
120ml/4fl oz/½ cup milk
50ml/2fl oz/¼ cup sunflower oil
225g/8oz/2 cups wholemeal self-raising flour
10ml/2 tsp mixed spice
45ml/3 tbsp brandy or dark rum
apricot jam, for brushing
glacé fruits, to decorate

1 Soak the sultanas, raisins, currants, cherries and mixed peel in the apple juice overnight.

2 Preheat the oven to 150°C/300°F/Gas 2. Grease and line an 18cm/7in square cake tin.

3 Add the hazelnuts, pumpkin seeds, ginger and lemon rind to the fruit. Stir in the milk and oil. Sift the flour and spice, then stir in with the brandy or rum.

4 Spoon into the cake tin and bake for about 1½ hours, or until the cake is golden brown and firm to the touch.

5 Turn out and cool on a wire rack. Brush with sieved apricot jam and decorate with glacé fruits.

Flourless Fruit Cake

This makes the perfect base for a birthday cake for anyone who needs to avoid eating flour.

Makes one 25cm/10in round cake

450g/1lb/1⅓ cups mincemeat
350g/12oz/2 cups dried mixed fruit
115g/4oz/½ cup ready-to-eat dried apricots, chopped
115g/4oz/⅔ cup ready-to-eat dried figs, chopped
115g/4oz/½ cup glacé cherries, halved
115g/4oz/1 cup walnut pieces
225g/8oz/8 – 10 cups cornflakes, crushed
4 eggs, lightly beaten
410g/14½oz can evaporated milk
5ml/1 tsp mixed spice
5ml/1 tsp baking powder
mixed glacé fruits, chopped, to decorate

1 Preheat the oven to 150°C/300°F/Gas 2. Grease a 25cm/10in round cake tin, line the base and sides with a double thickness of greaseproof paper and grease the paper.

2 Put all the ingredients into a large mixing bowl. Beat together well.

3 Turn into the cake tin and smooth the surface.

4 Bake for about 1¾ hours or until a skewer inserted in the centre of the cake comes out clean. Allow the cake to cool in the tin for 10 minutes, then turn out on to a wire rack, peel off the lining paper and leave to cool completely. Decorate with the chopped glacé fruits.

Glazed Christmas Ring

Makes one 25cm/10in ring cake

225g/8oz/generous 1½ cups sultanas
175g/6oz/generous 1 cup raisins
175g/6oz/generous 1 cup currants
175g/6oz/1 cup dried figs, chopped
90ml/6 tbsp whisky
45ml/3 tbsp orange juice
225g/8oz/1 cup butter
225g/8oz/1cup dark soft brown sugar
5 eggs
250g/9oz/2¼ cups plain flour
15ml/1 tbsp baking powder
15ml/1 tbsp mixed spice
115g/4oz/⅔ cup glacé cherries, chopped
115g/4oz/1 cup brazil nuts, chopped
50g/2oz/⅓ cup chopped mixed peel
50g/2oz/½ cup ground almonds
grated rind and juice 1 orange
30ml/2 tbsp thick-cut orange marmalade

To decorate

150ml/¼ pint/⅔ cup thick-cut orange marmalade
15ml/1 tbsp orange juice
175g/6oz/1 cup glacé cherries
115g/4oz/⅔ cup dried figs, halved
75g/3oz/½ cup whole brazil nuts

1 Put the dried fruits in a bowl, pour over 60ml/4 tbsp of the whisky and all the orange juice and marinate overnight.

2 Preheat the oven to 160°C/325°F/Gas 3. Grease and line a 25cm/10in ring mould. Cream the butter and sugar. Beat in the eggs. Sift together the remaining flour, baking powder and mixed spice. Fold into the egg mixture, alternating with the rest of the ingredients, except the whisky. Transfer to the tin and bake for 1 hour, then reduce the oven temperature to 150°C/300°F/Gas 2 and bake for a further 1¾–2 hours.

3 Prick the cake all over and pour over the reserved whisky. Cool in the tin for 30 minutes, then transfer to a wire rack. Boil the marmalade and orange juice for 3 minutes. Stir in the fruit and nuts. Cool, then spoon over the cake and leave to set.

Noel Christmas Cake

If you like a traditional royal-iced cake, this is a simple design using only one icing and easy-to-pipe decorations.

Makes one 20cm/8in round cake

20cm/8in round rich fruit cake
30ml/2 tbsp apricot jam, warmed and sieved
750g/1¼lb/5¼ cups marzipan
900g/2lb/6 cups royal icing
red and green food colouring

Materials/equipment

23cm/9in round silver cake board
3 greaseproof paper piping bags
No 1 writing nozzle bags
2 x No 0 writing nozzles
44 large gold dragées
2.5m/2½yd gold ribbon, 2cm/¾in wide
2.5m/2½yd red ribbon, 5mm/¼in wide

1 Brush the fruit cake with apricot jam, cover with the marzipan and place on the cake board.

2 Flat-ice the top of the cake with two layers of royal icing and leave to dry. Ice the sides of the cake and peak the royal icing, leaving a space around the centre for the ribbon. Leave to dry. Reserve the remaining royal icing.

3 Pipe beads of icing around the top edge of the cake and place a gold dragée on alternate beads. Using a No 1 writing nozzle, write "NOEL" across the cake and pipe holly leaves, stems and berries around the top.

4 Secure the ribbons around the side of the cake. Tie a red bow and attach to the front of the cake. Use the remaining ribbon for the board. Leave to dry overnight.

5 Tint 30ml/2 tbsp of the royal icing bright green and 15ml/1 tbsp bright red. Using a No 0 writing nozzle, over-pipe "NOEL" in red, then the edging beads and berries. Overpipe the holly in green. Leave to dry.

Christmas Tree Cake

No piping is involved in this bright and colourful cake, making it an easy choice.

Makes one 20cm/8in round cake

45ml/3 tbsp apricot jam
20cm/8in round rich fruit cake
900g/2lb/6 cups marzipan
green, red, yellow and purple food colouring
225g/8oz/1½ cups royal icing
edible silver balls

Materials/equipment

25cm/10in round cake board

1 Warm, then sieve the apricot jam and brush the cake with it. Colour 675g/1½lb/4½ cups of the marzipan green. Use to cover the cake. Leave to dry overnight.

2 Secure the cake to the board with royal icing. Spread the icing halfway up the cake side. Press the flat side of a palette knife into the icing, then pull away sharply to form peaks.

3 Make three different-size Christmas tree templates. Tint half the remaining marzipan a deeper green than the top. Using the templates, cut out three tree shapes and arrange them on the cake.

4 Divide the remaining marzipan into three and colour red, yellow and purple. Use a little of each marzipan to make five 9cm/3in rolls. Loop them alternately around the top edge of the cake. Make small red balls and press on to the loop ends.

5 Use the remaining marzipan to make the tree decorations. Arrange on the trees, securing with water, if necessary. Finish the cake by adding silver balls to the Christmas trees.

Christmas Stocking Cake

A bright and happy cake that is sure to delight children at Christmas time.

Makes one 20cm/8in square cake

20cm/8in square rich fruit cake
45ml/3 tbsp apricot jam, warmed and sieved
900g/2lb/6 cups marzipan
1.2kg/2½lb/7½ cups sugarpaste icing
15ml/1 tbsp royal icing
red and green food colouring

Materials/equipment

25cm/10in square silver cake board
1.25m/1½yd red ribbon, 2cm/¾in wide
1m/1yd green ribbon, 2cm/¾in wide

1 Brush the cake with the apricot jam and place on the cake board. Cover with marzipan.

2 Set aside 225g/8oz/1½ cups of the sugarpaste icing. Cover the cake with the rest. Leave to dry. Secure the red ribbon around the board and the green ribbon around the cake with royal icing.

3 Divide the icing in half and roll out one half. Using a template, cut out two sugarpaste stockings, one 5mm/¼in larger all round. Put the smaller one on top of the larger one.

4 Divide the other half of the sugarpaste into two and tint one red and the other green. Roll out and cut each colour into seven 1 cm/½in strips. Alternate the strips on top of the stocking. Roll lightly to fuse and press the edges together. Leave to dry.

5 Shape the remaining white sugarpaste into four parcels. Trim with red and green sugarpaste ribbons. Use the remaining red and green sugarpaste to make thin strips to decorate the cake sides. Secure in place with royal icing. Stick small sugarpaste balls over the joins. Arrange the stocking and parcels on the cake top.

Marbled Cracker Cake

Here is a Christmas cake that is decorated in a most untraditional way!

Makes one 20cm/8in round cake

20cm/8in round rich fruit cake
45ml/3 tbsp apricot jam, warmed and sieved
675g/1½lb/4½ cups marzipan
750g/1¾lb/5¼ cups sugarpaste icing
red and green food colouring
edible gold balls

Materials /equipment

wooden cocktail sticks
25cm/10in round cake board
red, green and gold thin gift-wrapping ribbon
3 red and 3 green ribbon bows

1 Brush the cake with the jam. Roll out the marzipan and use to cover the cake. Leave to dry overnight.

2 Form a roll with 500g/1¼lb/3¾ cups of the sugarpaste icing. With a cocktail stick, dab a few drops of red colouring on to the icing. Repeat with the green. Knead lightly. Roll out the icing until marbled. Brush the marzipan with water and cover with the icing. Position the cake on the cake board.

3 Colour half of the remaining sugarpaste icing red and the rest green. Use half of each colour to make five crackers, about 6cm/2½in long. Decorate each with a gold ball. Leave to dry on greaseproof paper.

4 Roll out the remaining red and green icings, and cut into 1cm/½in wide strips. Then cut into 12 red and 12 green diamonds. Attach them alternately around the top and base of the cake with water.

5 Cut the ribbons into 10cm/4in lengths. Arrange them with the crackers on the cake top. Attach the bows with softened sugarpaste icing, between the diamonds at the top cake edge.

Greek New Year Cake

A "good luck", foil-wrapped gold coin is traditionally baked into this cake.

Makes one 23cm/9in square cake

275g/10oz/2½ cups plain flour
10ml/2 tsp baking powder
50g/2oz/½ cup ground almonds
225g/8oz/1 cup butter, softened
175g/6oz/generous ¾ cup caster sugar, plus extra for sprinkling
4 eggs
150ml/¼ pint/⅔ cup fresh orange juice
50g/2oz/½ cup blanched almonds
15g/½oz/1 tbsp sesame seeds

1 Preheat the oven to 180°C/350°F/Gas 4. Grease a 23cm/9in square cake tin, line with greaseproof paper and grease the paper.

2 Sift together the flour and baking powder and stir in the ground almonds.

3 Cream the butter and sugar until light and fluffy. Beat in the eggs, 1 at a time. Fold in the flour mixture, alternating with the orange juice.

4 Spoon the mixture into the cake tin. Arrange the blanched almonds on top, then sprinkle over the sesame seeds. Bake for 50 minutes, or until a skewer inserted in the centre comes out clean. Leave in the tin for 5 minutes, then turn out on to a wire rack and peel off the lining paper. Sprinkle with caster sugar before serving.

Starry New Year Cake

Makes one 23cm/9in round cake

23cm/9in round Madeira cake
675g/1½lb/3 cups butter icing
750g/1¾lb/5¼ cups sugarpaste icing
grape violet and mulberry food colouring
gold, lilac shimmer and primrose sparkle powdered food colouring

Materials/equipment

fine paintbrush
star-shaped cutter
florist's wire, cut into short lengths
28cm/11in round cake board
purple ribbon with gold stars

1 Cut the cake into three layers. Sandwich together with three-quarters of the butter icing. Spread the rest thinly over the top and sides of the cake.

2 Tint 500g/1¼lb/3¼ cups of the sugarpaste icing purple with the grape violet and mulberry food colouring. Roll out and use to cover the cake. Leave to dry overnight.

3 Place the cake on a sheet of greaseproof paper. Water down some gold and lilac food colouring. Use a paintbrush to flick each colour in turn over the cake. Leave to dry.

4 For the stars, divide the remaining sugarpaste icing into three pieces. Tint one portion purple with the grape violet food colouring, one with the lilac shimmer and one with the primrose sparkle. Roll out each colour to 3mm/⅛in thick. Cut out ten stars in each colour and highlight the stars by flicking on the watered-down gold and lilac colours.

5 While the icing is soft, push the florist's wire through the middle of 15 of the stars. Leave to dry overnight. Put the cake on the board. Arrange the stars on top of the cake. Secure the unwired ones with water. Secure the ribbon around the base.

Simnel Cake

This is a traditional cake to celebrate Easter, but it is delicious at any time of the year.

Makes one 20cm/8in round cake

225g/8oz/1 cup butter, softened
225g/8oz/generous 1 cup caster sugar
4 eggs, beaten
500g/1¼lb/3⅓ cups mixed dried fruit
115g/4oz/½ cup glacé cherries
45ml/3 tbsp sherry (optional)
275g/10oz/2½ cups plain flour
15ml/1 tbsp mixed spice
5ml/1 tsp baking powder
675g/1½lb/4½ cups yellow marzipan
1 egg yolk, beaten
ribbons, sugared eggs and sugarpaste animals, to decorate

1 Preheat the oven to 160°C/325°F/Gas 3. Grease a deep 20cm/8in round cake tin, line with a double thickness of greaseproof paper and grease the paper.

2 Beat together the butter and sugar until light and fluffy. Gradually beat in the eggs. Stir in the dried fruit, glacé cherries and sherry, if using. Sift over the flour, mixed spice and baking powder, then fold in.

3 Roll out half the marzipan to a 20cm/8in round. Spoon half of the cake mixture into the cake tin and place the round of marzipan on top. Add the other half of the cake mixture and smooth the surface.

4 Bake for 2½ hours, or until golden and springy to the touch. Leave in the tin for 15 minutes, then turn out on to a wire rack, peel off the lining paper and leave to cool.

5 Roll out the reserved marzipan to fit the cake. Brush the cake top with egg yolk and place the marzipan on top. Flute the edges and make a pattern on top with a fork. Brush with more egg yolk. Put the cake on a baking sheet and grill for 5 minutes to brown the top lightly. Cool before decorating.

Easter Sponge Cake

This light lemon quick-mix sponge cake is decorated with lemon butter icing and cut-out marzipan flowers.

Makes one 20cm/8in round cake

3-egg quantity lemon-flavour quick-mix sponge cake
675g/1½lb/3 cups lemon-flavour butter icing
50g/2oz/½ cup flaked almonds, toasted

To decorate

50g/2oz/⅜ cup homemade or commercial white marzipan
green, orange and yellow food colouring

1 Preheat the oven to 160°C/325°F/Gas 3. Bake the cakes in two lined and greased 20cm/8in round sandwich tins for 35–40 minutes until they are golden brown and spring back when lightly pressed in the centre. Loosen the edges of the cakes with a palette knife, turn out, remove the lining paper and cool on a wire rack.

2 Sandwich the cakes together with one-quarter of the butter icing. Spread the side of the cake evenly with another one-quarter of butter icing.

3 Press the almonds on to the sides to cover evenly. Spread the top of the cake evenly with another one-quarter of icing. Finish with a palette knife dipped in hot water, spreading backwards and forwards to give an even lined effect.

4 Place the remaining icing into a nylon piping bag fitted with a medium-size gâteau nozzle and pipe a scroll edging.

5 Using the marzipan and food colouring, make six cut-out daffodils and ten green and eight orange cut-out marzipan flowers. Arrange them on the cake and leave the icing to set.

Easter Egg Nest Cake

Celebrate Easter with this colourfully adorned, fresh-tasting lemon sponge cake.

Makes one 20cm/8in ring cake

20cm/8in lemon sponge ring cake
350g/12oz/1½ cups lemon-flavour butter icing
225g/8oz/1½ cups marzipan
pink, green and purple food colouring
small foil-wrapped chocolate eggs

Materials/equipment
25cm/10in cake board

1 Cut the cake in half horizontally and sandwich together with one-third of the butter icing. Place on the cake board. Use the remaining icing to cover the cake. Smooth the top and swirl the side with a palette knife.

2 For the marzipan plaits, divide the marzipan into three and tint pink, green and purple. Cut each portion in half. Using one-half of each colour, roll thin sausages long enough to go around the base. Pinch the ends together, then twist the strands into a rope. Pinch the other ends to seal.

3 Place the coloured marzipan rope on the cake board around the cake.

4 For the nests, take the remaining portions of coloured marzipan and divide each into five. Roll each piece into a 16cm/6½in rope. Take a rope of each colour, pinch the ends together, twist to form a multi-coloured rope and pinch the other ends. Form into a circle. Repeat to make five nests.

5 Space the nests evenly on the cake. Place small chocolate eggs in the nests.

Mother's Day Bouquet

A piped bouquet of flowers can bring as much pleasure as a fresh one for a Mother's Day treat.

Makes one 18cm/7in round cake

675g/1½lb/3 cups butter icing
2 x 18cm/7in round sponge cakes
green, blue, yellow and pink food colouring

Materials/equipment
serrated scraper
No 3 writing and petal nozzles
5 greaseproof paper piping bags

1 Reserve one-third of the butter icing for decorating. Sandwich together the two sponges with butter icing and place on a serving plate. Cover the top and side with the rest of the butter icing, smoothing the top with a palette knife and serrating the side using a scraper.

2 Divide the remaining butter icing into four bowls. Tint them green, blue, yellow and pink.

3 Decorate the top of the cake first. Use No 3 writing nozzles for the blue and green icing and petal nozzles for the yellow and pink. Pipe on the vase and flowers.

4 For the side decoration, spoon the remaining yellow icing into a fresh piping bag fitted with a No 3 writing nozzle. Pipe the stems, then the flowers and flower centres. Finish by piping green beads at the top and base edges of the cake.

Mother's Day Basket

Makes one 15cm/6in cake

175g/6oz/1½ cups self-rising flour, sifted
175g/6oz/scant 1 cup caster sugar
175g/6oz/¾ cup soft margarine
3 eggs
900g/2lb/4 cups orange-flavour butter icing

Materials/equipment

thin 15cm/6in round silver cake board
greaseproof paper piping bag
basketweave nozzle
foil
1m/1yd mauve ribbon, 1cm/½in wide
fresh flowers
0.5m/½yd spotted mauve ribbon, 3mm/⅛in wide

1 Preheat the oven to 160°C/325°F/Gas 3. Lightly grease and base-line a 15cm/6in brioche mould. Place all the cake ingredients in a bowl, mix together then beat for 1–2 minutes until smooth. Transfer to the prepared mould and bake for about 1¼ hours, or until risen and golden.

2 Place the cooled cake upside-down on the board. Cover the sides with one-third of the butter icing. Using a basketweave nozzle, pipe the sides with a basketweave pattern.

3 Invert the cake on the board and spread the top with butter icing. Pipe a shell edging with the basketweave nozzle. Pipe the basketweave pattern over the cake top, starting at the edge. Leave to set.

4 Fold a strip of foil several layers thick. Wrap the plain ribbon around the strip and bend up the ends to secure the ribbon. Form the foil into a handle and press into the icing.

5 Finish by tying a posy of fresh flowers with the spotted ribbon and making a mixed ribbon bow for the handle.

Basket Cake

This is a perfect cake for a retirement gathering or other special occasion.

Makes one basket-shaped cake

20cm/8in round Madeira cake
450g/1lb/2 cups coloured butter icing
chocolates or sweets and ribbon for decoration

Materials/equipment

pastillage (gum paste)
2 greaseproof paper piping bags, fitted with a plain tube and a basketweave tube
powder food colour

1 Cut a template from card to the same size as the top of the cake, fold it in half and cut along the fold. Roll out pastillage fairly thinlyand cut out two pieces for the lid, using the templates as a guide. Leave to dry.

2 Coat the top of the cake with butter icing. Fill both piping bags with butter icing and on the side of the cake and about 2.5cm/1in on to the top of the cake, pipe a plain vertical line, then pipe short lengths of basketweave across the line. Pipe another plain line along the ends of the basketweave strips. Pipe the next row of basketweave strips in the spaces left between the existing strips and over the new plain line. Continue until the side of the cake and the area on the top is completely covered.

3 Brush the underside of the pastillage lid with powder food colour, then pipe a basketweave on top of the lid.

4 Divide the top of the cake in half and pipe a line of basketweave along this central line. Use two or three pieces of pastillage to support each lid half in an open position on the cake. Fill the area under each lid half with chocolates or sweets and decorate with ribbon

Valentine's Heart Cake

This cake could also be used to celebrate a special birthday or anniversary.

Makes one 20cm/8in square cake

20cm/8in square light fruit cake
45ml/3 tbsp apricot jam, warmed and sieved
900g/2lb/6 cups marzipan
1.5kg/3lb/9 cups royal icing
115g/4oz/¾ cup sugarpaste icing
red food colouring

Materials/equipment

25cm/10in square cake board
5cm/2in heart-shaped cutter
2.5cm/1in heart-shaped cutter
4 greaseproof paper piping bags
No 1 and No 2 writing and No 42 star nozzles
heart-patterned ribbon

1 Brush the cake with the apricot jam. Roll out the marzipan and use to cover the cake. Leave to dry overnight.

2 Secure the cake on the cake board with a little royal icing. Flat-ice the cake with three or four layers of smooth icing. Set aside some royal icing in an airtight container for piping.

3 Tint the sugarpaste icing red. Roll it out and cut 12 hearts with the larger cutter. Stamp out the middles with the smaller cutter. Cut four extra small hearts. Dry on greaseproof paper.

4 Using a No 1 writing nozzle, pipe wavy lines in royal icing around the four small hearts. Leave to dry. Using a fresh bag and a No 42 nozzle, pipe swirls around the top and base of the cake. Colour 15ml/1 tbsp of the remaining royal icing red and pipe red dots on top of each white swirl with the No 1 nozzle.

5 Secure the ribbon in place. Using a No 2 writing nozzle, pipe beads down each corner, avoiding the ribbon. Decorate the cake with the hearts, using royal icing to secure them.

Valentine's Box of Chocolates Cake

This cake would also make a wonderful surprise for Mother's Day.

Makes one 20cm/8in heart-shaped cake

20cm/8in heart-shaped chocolate sponge cake
275g/10oz/generous 2 cups marzipan
120ml/8 tbsp apricot jam, warmed and sieved
900g/2lb/6 cups sugarpaste icing
red food colouring
225g/8oz/about 16–20 hand-made chocolates

Materials/equipment

23cm/9in square piece of stiff card
pencil and scissors
23cm/9in square cake board
piece of string
small heart-shaped cutter
length of ribbon and a pin
small paper sweet cases

1 Place the cake on the card, draw around it and cut the heart shape out. It will be used to support the box lid. Cut through the cake horizontally just below the dome. Place the top section on the card and the base on the board.

2 Use the string to measure around the outside of the base. Roll the marzipan into a long sausage to the measured length. Place on the cake around the outside edge. Brush both sections of the cake with apricot jam. Tint the sugarpaste icing red and cut off one-third. Cut another 50g/2oz/8 tbsp portion from the larger piece. Set aside. Use the large piece to cover the base section of cake.

3 Stand the lid on a raised surface. Use the reserved one-third of sugarpaste icing to cover the lid. Roll out the remaining piece of icing and stamp out small hearts with the cutter. Stick them around the edge of the lid with water. Tie the ribbon in a bow and secure on top of the lid with the pin.

4 Place the chocolates in the paper cases and arrange in the cake base. Position the lid slightly off-centre, to reveal the chocolates. Remove the ribbon and pin before serving.

Double Heart Engagement Cake

For a celebratory engagement party, these sumptuous cakes make the perfect centrepiece.

Makes two 20cm/8in heart-shaped cakes

350g/12oz plain chocolate
2 x 20cm/8in heart-shaped chocolate sponge cakes
675g/1½lb/3 cups coffee-flavour butter icing
icing sugar, for dusting
fresh raspberries, to decorate

Materials/equipment

2 x 23cm/9in heart-shaped cake boards

1 Melt the chocolate in a heatproof bowl over a saucepan of hot water. Pour the chocolate on to a smooth, non-porous surface and spread it out with a palette knife. Leave to cool until just set, but not hard.

2 To make the chocolate curls, hold a large sharp knife at a 45-degree angle to the chocolate and push it along the chocolate in short sawing movements. Leave to set on greaseproof paper.

3 Cut each cake in half horizontally. Use one-third of the butter icing to sandwich the cakes together. Use the remaining icing to coat the tops and sides of the cakes.

4 Place the cakes on the cake boards. Generously cover the tops and sides of the cakes with the chocolate curls, pressing them gently into the butter icing.

5 Sift a little icing sugar over the top of each cake and decorate with raspberries. Chill until ready to serve.

Sweetheart Cake

Makes one 20cm/8in heart-shaped cake

20cm/8in heart-shaped light fruit cake
30ml/2 tbsp apricot jam, warmed and sieved
900g/2lb/6 cups marzipan
900g/2lb/6 cups sugarpaste icing
red food colouring
225g/8oz/1½ cups royal icing

Materials/equipment

25cm/10in silver heart-shaped cake board
large and medium heart-shaped plunger cutters
1m/1yd red ribbon, 2.5cm/1in wide
1m/1yd looped red ribbon, 1cm/½in wide
0.5m/½yd red ribbon, 5mm/¼in wide
greaseproof paper piping bag
medium star nozzle
fresh red rosebud

1 Brush the cake with apricot jam, place on the cake board and cover with marzipan. Cover the cake and board with sugarpaste icing. Leave to dry overnight.

2 Tint the sugarpaste icing red. Cut out 18 large and 21 medium-size hearts. Leave to dry on greaseproof paper.

3 Secure the wide ribbon around the cake board. Secure a band of the looped ribbon around the side of the cake with a bead of icing. Tie a bow with long tails and attach to the side of the cake with a bead of icing.

4 Using the star nozzle, pipe a row of royal icing stars around the base of the cake and attach a medium-size heart to every third star. Pipe stars around the cake top, and arrange large red hearts on each one.

5 Tie a bow on to the rosebud stem and place on the cake top just before serving.

Cloth-of-Roses Cake

This cake simply says "congratulations". It is a very pretty cake that is bound to impress your guests.

Makes one 20cm/8in round cake

20cm/8in round light fruit cake
45ml/3 tbsp apricot jam, warmed and sieved
675g/1½lb/4½ cups marzipan
900g/2lb/6 cups sugarpaste icing
yellow, orange and green food colouring
115g/4oz/¾ cup royal icing

Materials/equipment

25cm/10in cake board
5.5cm/2¼in plain cutter
petal cutter
thin yellow ribbon

1 Brush the cake with apricot jam. Cover with marzipan and leave to dry overnight.

2 Cut off 675g/1½lb/4½ cups of the sugarpaste icing and divide in half. Colour pale yellow and pale orange.

3 Make a greaseproof paper template for the orange icing by drawing a 25cm/10in circle round the cake board then, using the plain cutter, draw scallops around the circle.

4 Cover the cake side with yellow sugarpaste icing. Place the cake on the board. Using the template, cut out the orange sugarpaste icing. Place on the cake and bend the scallops slightly. Leave to dry overnight.

5 For the roses and leaves, cut off three-quarters of the remaining sugarpaste icing and divide into four. Tint pale yellow, deep yellow, orange, and marbled yellow and orange. Make 18 roses. Tint the remaining icing green. Cut out 24 leaves with a petal cutter. Dry on greaseproof paper.

6 Secure the leaves and roses with royal icing. Decorate the cake with the ribbon.

Rose Blossom Wedding Cake

Serves 80

23cm/9in square rich fruit cake
15cm/6in square rich fruit cake
75ml/5 tbsp apricot jam, warmed and sieved
1.5kg/3½lb/10½ cups marzipan
1.5kg/3½lb/10½ cups royal icing, to coat
675g/1½lb/4½ cups royal icing, to pipe
pink and green food colouring

Materials/equipment

28cm/11in square cake board
20cm/8in square cake board
No 1 writing and No 42 nozzles
greaseproof paper piping bags
thin pink ribbon
8 pink bows
3–4 cake pillars
12 miniature roses
few fern sprigs

1 Brush the cakes with the jam and cover with marzipan. Leave to dry overnight, then secure to their boards with icing. Flat-ice the cakes with three or four layers, allowing each to dry overnight. Dry for several days.

2 For the sugar pieces, use the No 1 writing nozzle to pipe the double-triangle design in white icing on greaseproof paper. You will need 40 pieces, but make extra. Tint some icing pale pink and some very pale green. Using No 1 writing nozzles, pipe pink dots on the corners of the top triangles and green on the corners of the lower triangles. Leave to dry.

3 Use a pin to mark out the triangles on the tops and sides of each cake. Using a No 1 writing nozzle, pipe double white lines over the pin marks, then pipe cornelli inside all the triangles. With a No 42 nozzle, pipe white shells around the top and base edges of each cake, between the triangles.

4 Using No 1 writing nozzles, pipe pink and green dots on the cake corners. Secure the sugar pieces to the cakes and boards with icing. Attach the ribbons and bows. Assemble the cake with the pillars and decorate with roses and fern sprigs.

Basketweave Wedding Cake

This wonderful wedding cake can be made in any flavour.

Serves 150

25cm/10in, 20cm/8in and 15cm/6in square Madeira cakes
2.75kg/6lb/12 cups butter icing

Materials/equipment

30cm/12in square silver cake board
20cm/8in and 15cm/6in thin silver cake board
smooth scraper
12 small greaseproof piping bags
No 4 writing and basketweave nozzles
1.5m/1½yd pale lilac ribbon, 2.5cm/1in wide
2.5m/2½yd deep lilac ribbon, 5mm/¼in wide
30 fresh lilac-coloured freesias

1 Level the cake tops, then invert the cakes on to the boards and cover with butter icing. Use a smooth scraper on the sides and a palette knife to smooth the top. Leave to set for 1 hour.

2 Pipe a line of icing with the No 4 writing nozzle on to the corner of the large cake, from the base to the top. Using the basketweave nozzle, pipe a basketweave pattern (see above photograph). Pipe all around the side of the cake and neaten the top edge with a shell border, using the basketweave nozzle. Repeat for the second cake.

3 To decorate the top of the small cake, start at the edge with a straight plain line, then pipe across with the basketweave nozzle, spacing the lines equally apart. When the top is complete, work the design around the sides, making sure the top and side designs align. Leave the cakes overnight to set.

4 Fit the wide and narrow lilac ribbons around the board. Use the remaining narrow ribbon to tie eight small bows with long tails. Trim off the flower stems.

5 Assemble the cakes. Decorate with the bows and flowers.

Chocolate-iced Anniversary Cake

This attractive cake is special enough to celebrate any wedding anniversary.

Makes one 20cm/8in round cake

20cm/8in round Madeira cake
475g/1lb 2oz/2¼ cups chocolate-flavour butter icing

For the chocolate icing

175g/6oz plain chocolate
150ml/¼ pint/⅔ cup single cream
2.5ml/½ tsp instant coffee powder

To decorate

chocolate buttons, quartered
selection of fresh fruits, such as kiwi fruit, nectarines, peaches, apricots and Cape gooseberries, peeled and sliced as necessary

Materials/equipment

No 22 star nozzle
greaseproof paper piping bag
gold ribbon, about 5mm/¼in wide
florist's wire

1 Cut the cake horizontally into three and sandwich together with three-quarters of the butter icing. Place on a wire rack over a baking sheet.

2 To make the satin chocolate icing, put all of the ingredients in a saucepan and melt over a very low heat until smooth. Immediately pour over the cake to coat completely. Use a palette knife, if necessary. Allow to set.

3 Transfer the cake to a serving plate. Using a No 22 star nozzle, pipe butter icing scrolls around the top edge. Decorate with chocolate button pieces and fruit.

4 Make seven ribbon decorations. For each one, make two small loops from ribbon and secure the ends with a twist of florist's wire . Cut the wire to the length you want and use to position the decoration in the fruit. Remove before serving.

Silver Wedding Cake

Makes one 25cm/10in round cake

25cm/10in round rich or light fruit cake
60ml/4 tbsp apricot jam, warmed and sieved
1.2kg/2½lb/7½ cups marzipan
1.5kg/3lb/9 cups royal icing

For the petal paste

10ml/2 tsp gelatine
75ml/5 tbsp cold water
10ml/2 tsp liquid glucose
10ml/2 tsp white vegetable fat
450g/1lb/4 cups icing sugar, sifted
5ml/1 tsp gum tragacanth, sifted
1 egg white

Materials/equipment

30cm/12in round silver cake board
1.5m/1½yd white ribbon, 2.5cm/1in wide
2m/2yd silver ribbon, 2.5cm/1in wide
club cocktail cutter
tiny round cutter
greaseproof piping bag
No 1 writing nozzle
50 large silver dragées
1.5m/1½yd silver ribbon, 5mm/¼in wide
7 silver leaves
"25" silver cake decoration

1 Brush the cake with apricot jam and cover with marzipan. Place on the board. Flat-ice the top and side of the cake with three or four layers of royal icing. Leave to dry overnight, then ice the board. Reserve the remaining royal icing. Secure the wider ribbons around the board and cake with icing.

2 For the petal paste, melt the first four ingredients in a pan set over a bowl of hot water. Mix the sugar, gum tragacanth, egg white and gelatine mixture to a paste and knead until smooth. Leave for 2 hours, then re-knead. Make 65 cut-outs using the two cutters. Leave to dry overnight.

3 Arrange 25 cut-outs around the top and secure with icing beads piped with a No 1 writing nozzle. Repeat at the base. Pipe icing beads between and press a dragée in each. Leave to dry. Thread the thin ribbon through. Arrange seven cut-outs and seven dragées in the centre. Position the leaves and "25".

Golden Wedding Heart Cake

Makes one 23cm/9in round cake

60ml/4 tbsp apricot jam
23cm/9in round rich fruit cake
900g/2lb/6 cups marzipan
900g/2lb/6 cups sugarpaste icing
cream food colouring
115g/4oz/¾ cup royal icing

Materials/equipment

28cm/11in round cake board
crimping tool
pins
small heart-shaped plunger tool
7.5cm/3in plain cutter
dual large and small blossom cutter
stamens
frill cutter
wooden cocktail stick
foil-wrapped chocolate hearts

1 Warm, then sieve the apricot jam and brush over the cake. Cover with marzipan and leave to dry overnight.

2 Tint 675g/1½lb/4½ cups of the sugarpaste icing very pale cream and cover the cake. Put on the board. Crimp the top edge. With pins, mark eight equidistant points around the top edge. Crimp slanting lines to the base. Emboss the base edge with the plunger. Use the plain cutter to emboss a circle on top.

3 Divide the remaining sugarpaste icing into two and tint cream and pale cream. Using half of each colour, make flowers with the blossom cutter. Make pinholes in the large flowers. Leave to dry then secure the stamens in the holes with royal icing.

4 Make eight frills with the rest of the sugarpaste icing using the frill cutter, and a cocktail stick to trim and fill the edges. Attach the frills with water next to the crimped lines on the cake side. Crimp the edges of the deeper coloured frills.

5 Secure the flowers on the top and side of the cake with royal icing. Place the chocolate hearts in the centre.

Marzipan Bell Cake

This cake can be easily adapted to make a christening cake if you leave out the holly decorations.

Makes one 18cm/7in round cake

18cm/7in round rich or light fruit cake
30ml/2 tbsp apricot jam, warmed and sieved
900g/2lb/6 cups marzipan
green, yellow and red food colouring

Materials/equipment

20cm/8in round silver cake board
crimping tool
bell and holly leaf cutter
1m/1yd red ribbon, 2cm/¾in wide
1m/1yd green ribbon, 5mm/¼in wide
0.25m/¼yd red ribbon, 5mm/¼in wide

1 Brush the cake with apricot jam and place on the cake board. Tint two-thirds of the marzipan pale green. Use to cover the cake. Crimp the top edge of the cake to make a scalloped pattern.

2 Tint a small piece of remaining marzipan bright yellow, another bright red and the rest bright green. Make two yellow bells and clappers, 11 green holly leaves (veins marked with the back of a knife), two green bell ropes, 16 red holly berries and two bell-rope ends. Leave to dry.

3 Secure the wide red and fine green ribbons around the side of the cake with a pin. Tie a double bow from red and green fine ribbon and attach to the side with a pin.

4 Arrange the bells, clappers, bell ropes, holly leaves and berries on top of the cake and secure with apricot jam.

Christening Sampler

Serves 30

20cm/8in square rich fruit cake
45ml/3 tbsp apricot jam, warmed and sieved
450g/1lb/3cups marzipan
675g/1½lb/4½ cups sugarpaste icing
brown, yellow, orange, purple, cream, blue, green and pink food colouring

Materials/equipment

25cm/10in square cake board
fine paintbrush
small heart-shaped biscuit cutter

1 Brush the cake with apricot jam. Roll out the marzipan, cover the cake and leave to dry overnight. Roll out 150g/5oz/1 cup of the sugarpaste icing to fit the cake top. Brush the top with water and cover with the icing.

2 Colour 300g/10oz/2 cups of the icing brown and roll out four pieces to the length and about 1cm/½in wider than the cake sides. Brush the sides with water and cover with icing, folding over the extra width at the top and cutting the corners at an angle to make the picture frame. Place on a cake board. With a fine paintbrush, paint over the sides with watered-down brown food colouring to represent wood grain.

3 Take the remaining icing and colour small amounts yellow, orange, brown, purple and cream and two shades of blue, green and pink. Leave a little white. Use these colours to shape the ducks, teddy bear, bulrushes, water, branch and leaves. Cut out a pink heart and make the baby's initial from white icing.

4 Mix the white and pink icings together for the apple blossom flowers. Make the shapes for the border. Attach the decorations to the cake with a little water.

5 Use the leftover colours to make "threads". Arrange in loops around the base of the cake on the board.

Teddy Bear Christening Cake

To personalize the cake, make a simple plaque for the top and pipe on the name of the new baby.

Makes one 20cm/8in square cake

20cm/8in square light fruit cake
45ml/3 tbsp apricot jam, warmed and sieved
900g/2lb/6 cups marzipan
800g/1¾lb/5¼ cups sugarpaste icing
peach, yellow, blue and brown food colouring
115g/4oz/¾ cup royal icing

Materials/equipment

25cm/10in square cake board
crimping tool
cornflour, for dipping
fine paintbrush
wooden cocktail stick
peach ribbon
small blue ribbon bow

1 Brush the cake with the apricot jam. Roll out the marzipan and use to cover the cake. Leave to dry overnight.

2 Colour 500g/1¼lb/3¾ cups of the sugarpaste icing peach, then roll it out. Brush the marzipan with water and cover the cake with the icing. Place the cake on the board. Using a crimping tool dipped in cornflour, crimp the top and base edges of the cake.

3 Divide the remaining sugarpaste into three. Leave one-third white and tint one-third yellow. Divide the last third in two, tint one half peach and the other blue.

4 Make flowers from the peach and blue sugarpaste. Leave to dry. Reserve the blue trimmings. Make a yellow teddy bear. Paint on its face with brown food colouring. Give it a blue button. Leave to dry. Make a blue blanket. Frill the white edge with a cocktail stick. Secure the frill to the blanket with water.

5 Decorate the cake with the ribbon, place the bear on top under its blanket, securing with royal icing. Secure the flowers and the bear's bow-tie in the same way.

Daisy Christening Cake

A ring of daisies sets off this pretty pink christening cake.

Makes one 20cm/8in round cake

20cm/8in round rich fruit cake
45ml/3 tbsp apricot jam, warmed and sieved
675g/1½lb/4½ cups marzipan
900g/2lb/6 cups royal icing
115g/4oz/¾ cup sugarpaste icing
pink and yellow food colouring

Materials/equipment

25cm/10in round cake board
fine paintbrush
5cm/2in fluted cutter
wooden cocktail stick
2 greaseproof paper piping bags
No 42 nozzle
pink and white ribbon

1 Brush the cake with the apricot jam. Roll out the marzipan and use to cover the cake. Leave to dry overnight.

2 Use a little royal icing to secure the cake to the board. Tint three-quarters of the royal icing pink. Flat-ice the cake with three or four layers, using white for the top and pink for the side. Allow each layer to dry overnight before applying the next. Set aside a little of both icings in airtight containers.

3 Make 28 daisies. For each daisy, shape a small piece of sugarpaste icing to look like a golf tee. Snip the edges and curl them slightly. Dry on greaseproof paper. Trim the stems and paint the edges pink and the centres yellow.

4 To make the plaque, roll out the remaining sugarpaste icing and cut out a circle with the fluted cutter. Roll a cocktail stick around the edge until it frills. Dry on greaseproof paper, then paint the name and the edges with pink food colouring.

5 Pipe twisted ropes around the top and base of the cake with the reserved white royal icing. Then pipe a row of stars around the top of the cake. Stick the plaque in the centre with royal icing. Stick on the daisies and decorate with the ribbons.

Birthday Parcel

Serves 10

15cm/6in square Madeira cake
275g/10oz/1⅓ cup orange-flavour butter icing
45ml/3 tbsp apricot jam, warmed and sieved
450g/1lb/3cups sugarpaste icing
blue, orange and green food colouring
icing sugar, for dusting

Materials/equipment

15–18cm/7–8in square cake board
small triangular and round cocktail cutters

1 Cut the cake in half horizontally and sandwich together with the butter icing. Brush the cake with apricot jam. Colour three-quarters of the sugarpaste icing blue. Divide the remaining sugarpaste icing in half and colour one half orange and the other half green. Wrap the orange and green sugarpaste separately in clear film and set aside. Roll out the blue icing on a work surface lightly dusted with icing sugar and use it to cover the cake. Position on the cake board.

2 While the sugarpaste covering is still soft, use the cocktail cutters to cut out triangles and circles from the blue icing, lifting out the shapes to expose the cake.

3 Roll out the orange and green icings and cut out circles and triangles to fill the exposed holes in the blue icing. Roll out the trimmings and cut three orange strips, 2cm/¾in wide and long enough to go over the corner of the cake and 3 very thin green strips the same length as the orange ones. Place the strips next to each other to make three striped ribbons, and secure the pieces together with a little water.

4 Place one striped ribbon over one corner of the cake, securing with a little water. Place a second strip over the opposite corner. Cut the remaining ribbon in half. Bend each half to make loops and attach both to one corner of the cake with water to form a loose bow.

Chocolate Fruit Birthday Cake

The marzipan fruits on this moist chocolate Madeira cake make an eye-catching decoration.

Makes one 18cm/7in square cake

18cm/7in square deep chocolate Madeira cake
45ml/3 tbsp apricot jam, warmed and sieved
450g/1lb/3 cups marzipan
450g/1lb/2cups chocolate fudge icing
red, yellow, orange, green and purple food colouring
whole cloves
angelica strips

Materials/equipment

20cm/8in square silver cake board
medium gâteau nozzle
nylon piping bag
0.75m/¾yd yellow ribbon, 1cm/½in wide

1 Level the cake top and invert. Brush with apricot jam.

2 Use two-thirds of the marzipan to cover the cake. Reserve the trimmings.

3 Place the cake on a wire rack over a tray and pour three-quarters of the chocolate fudge icing over, spreading with a palette knife. Leave for 10 minutes, then place on the board.

4 Using the reserved icing and a medium-size gâteau nozzle, pipe stars around the top edge and base of the cake. Leave to set.

5 Using the reserved marzipan, food colouring, cloves and angelica strips, model a selection of fruits.

6 Secure the ribbon around the sides of the cake. Decorate the top with the marzipan fruits.

Eighteenth Birthday Cake

A really striking cake for an eighteenth birthday. Change the shape if you don't have the tin.

Serves 80

33.5 x 20cm/13½ x 8in diamond-shaped deep rich or light fruit cake
45ml/3 tbsp apricot jam, warmed and sieved
1.1kg/2½lb/7½ cups marzipan
1.6kg/3½lb/10½ cups sugarpaste
black food colouring
30ml/2 tbsp royal icing

Materials/equipment

38 x 23cm/15 x 9in diamond-shaped cake board
"18" template
small greaseproof paper piping bag
No 1 writing nozzle
2m/2yd white ribbon, 2.5cm/1in wide
2m/2yd black ribbon, 3mm/⅛in wide

1 Make the cake using quantities for a 23cm/9in round cake. Brush with apricot jam. Cover in marzipan. Place on the cake board. Cover the cake using 1.2kg/2½lb/7½ cups sugarpaste icing. Knead the trimmings into the remaining sugarpaste and tint black.

2 Use two-thirds of the black sugarpaste to cover the board.

3 Use a quarter of the remaining sugarpaste to cut out a number "18" using a template. Use the rest to cut out a variety of bow ties, wine glasses and music notes. Leave to dry on greaseproof paper.

4 Tint the royal icing black. Using a No 1 writing nozzle, attach the cut-outs to the cake top and sides.

5 Tie four small bows with the black ribbon. Secure with icing to the top corners. Position and secure black ribbon around the cake base and white ribbon around the board.

Flickering Birthday Candle Cake

Flickering stripy candles are ready to blow out on this birthday cake for all ages.

Makes one 20cm/8in square cake

20cm/8in square Madeira cake
350g/12oz/1½ cups butter icing
45ml/3 tbsp apricot jam, warmed and sieved
800g/1¾lb/5¼ cups sugarpaste icing
pink, yellow, purple and jade food colouring
edible silver balls

Materials/equipment

23cm/9in square cake board
small round cutter
pink and purple food colouring pens
5mm/¼in wide jade-coloured ribbon

1 Cut the cake into three layers. Sandwich together with the butter icing and brush the cake with the apricot jam. Roll out 500g/1¼lb/3¾ cups of the sugarpaste icing and use to cover the cake. Position on the cake board.

2 Divide the remaining sugarpaste into four pieces and tint them pink, yellow, pale purple and jade.

3 Make the candles from jade and the flames from yellow icing. Press a silver ball into their bases. Position the candles and flames on the cake with a little water. Mould strips in yellow and purple icing to go round the candles. Secure with water. Cut small wavy pieces from the pink and purple icing for smoke, and arrange them, using water, above the candles.

4 Cut out yellow circles with the cutter for the side decorations. Mould small pink balls and press a silver ball into their centres. Attach using water.

5 Using food colouring pens, draw wavy lines and dots coming from the purple and pink wavy icings. Decorate the sides of the cake board with the ribbon, securing at the back with a little softened sugarpaste.

Flower Birthday Cake

A simple birthday cake decorated with piped yellow and white flowers and ribbons.

Makes one 18cm/7in round cake

18cm/7in round light fruit cake
30ml/2 tbsp apricot jam, warmed and sieved
675g/1½lb/4½ cups marzipan
1.2kg/2½lb/7½ cups royal icing
yellow and orange food colouring

Materials/equipment

23cm/9in round silver cake board
petal nozzle, No 1 and 2 writing nozzles, and medium star nozzle
greaseproof paper piping bags
1m/1yd white ribbon, 2cm/¾in wide
2m/2yd coral ribbon, 1cm/½in wide
25cm/10in coral ribbon, 5mm/¼in wide

1 Brush the cake with apricot jam and cover with marzipan. Place on the board.

2 Flat-ice the top and side of the cake with three layers of royal icing. Leave to dry, then ice the board. Reserve the remaining royal icing.

3 Tint one-third of the reserved royal icing yellow and 15ml/1 tbsp of it orange. Using the petal nozzle for the petals and No 1 writing nozzle for the centres, make four white narcissi with yellow centres and nine yellow narcissi with orange centres. Make nine plain white flowers with a snipped piping bag with yellow centres. When dry, secure to the top.

4 Use the star nozzle to pipe shell edgings to the cake top and base. Pipe "Happy Birthday" using the No 2 writing nozzle. Overlay in orange using the No 1 writing nozzle.

5 Secure the ribbons around the board and cake side. Finish with a coral bow.

Jazzy Chocolate Gâteau

This cake is made with Father's Day in mind, though you can make it for anyone who loves chocolate.

Serves 12–15

2 x quantity chocolate-flavour quick-mix sponge cake mix
75g/3oz/3 squares plain chocolate
75g/3oz/3 squares white chocolate
175g/6oz fudge frosting
115g/4oz/1 cup glacé icing
5ml/1 tsp weak coffee
8 tbsp chocolate hazelnut spread

Materials/equipment

2 x 20cm/8in round cake tins
greaseproof paper piping bag
No 1 writing nozzle

1 Preheat the oven to 160°C/325°F/Gas 3. Grease the cake tins, line the bases with greaseproof paper and grease the paper. Divide the cake mixture evenly between the tins and smooth the surfaces. Bake in the centre of the oven for about 20–30 minutes, or until firm to the touch. Turn out on to a wire rack, peel off the lining paper and leave to cool.

2 Melt the chocolates in two separate bowls, pour on to baking paper and spread evenly. As it begins to set, place another sheet of baking paper on top and turn the chocolate "sandwich" over. When set, peel off the paper and turn the chocolate sheets over. Cut out haphazard shapes of chocolate and set aside.

3 Sandwich the two cakes together using the fudge frosting. Place the cake on a stand or plate. Colour the glacé icing using the weak coffee and add enough water to form a spreading consistency. Spread the icing on top of the cake almost to the edges. Cover the side of the cake with chocolate hazelnut spread.

4 Press the chocolate pieces around the side of the cake and, using a piping bag fitted with a No 1 nozzle, decorate the top of the cake with "jazzy" lines over the glacé icing.

Petal Retirement Cake

Makes one 20cm/8in petal-shaped cake

20cm/8in petal-shaped deep light fruit cake
45ml/3 tbsp apricot jam, warmed and sieved
900g/2lb/6 cups marzipan
mulberry and pink food colouring
900g/2lb/6 cups sugarpaste icing
275g/10oz petal paste
15ml/1 tbsp royal icing

Materials/equipment

23cm/9in petal-shaped silver cake board
foam sponge
large and small blossom plunger cutters
2m/2yd white ribbon, 2cm/¾in wide
2m/2yd fuchsia ribbon, 1cm/½in wide
2m/2yd fuchsia ribbon, 3mm/⅛in wide
greaseproof paper piping bag
No 1 writing nozzle
pink food colouring pen
fresh flowers

1 Brush the cake with jam and put on the board. Cover with marzipan. Knead mulberry colouring into the sugarpaste icing. Use to cover the cake and board. Dry overnight.

2 Tint the petal paste with pink colouring. Roll and cut out a 5 x 2.5cm/2 x 1in rectangle. Fold in half and dry over a foam sponge to make the card. Make holes in the top edges of the fold for the ribbon. Cut out 30 large and four small plunger blossom flowers. Leave to dry.

3 Using the royal icing and a No 1 writing nozzle, secure the white and narrow fuchsia ribbons around the board and the medium ribbon around the cake base. Tie six small bows from the narrow ribbon for the base.

4 Attach the large flowers to the side of the cake with icing. Secure the small flowers to the board. Draw a design and write a message inside the card with the pen. Thread ribbon through the holes and tie a bow. Place on the cake top with the fresh flowers.

Pansy Retirement Cake

You can use other edible flowers such as nasturtiums, roses or tiny daffodils for this cake, if you prefer.

Makes one 20cm/8in round cake

20cm/8in round light fruit cake
45ml/3 tbsp apricot jam, warmed and sieved
675g/1½lb/4½ cups marzipan
1.1kg/2½lb/7½ cups royal icing
orange food colouring
about 7 sugar-frosted pansies (orange and purple)

Materials/equipment

25cm/10in round cake board
2 greaseproof paper piping bags
No 19 star and No 1 writing nozzles
2cm/¾in wide purple ribbon
3mm/⅛in wide dark purple ribbon

1 Brush the cake with the apricot jam. Roll out the marzipan and use to cover the cake. Leave to dry overnight.

2 Secure the cake to the cake board with a little royal icing. Tint a quarter of the royal icing pale orange. Flat-ice the cake with three layers of smooth icing. Use the orange icing for the top and the white for the side. Set aside a little of both icings in airtight containers for decoration.

3 Spoon the reserved white royal icing into a greaseproof paper piping bag fitted with a No 19 star nozzle. Pipe a row of scrolls around the cake top. Pipe a second row directly underneath the first row in the reverse direction. Pipe another row of scrolls around the base of the cake.

4 Spoon the reserved orange icing into a fresh piping bag fitted with a No 1 writing nozzle. Pipe around the outline of the top of each scroll. Pipe a row of single orange dots below the lower row of reverse scrolls at the top and a double row of dots above the base row of scrolls. Arrange the sugar-frosted pansies on top of the cake. Decorate the side with the ribbons.

Hallowe'en Pumpkin Patch Cake

Celebrate Hallowe'en with this autumn-coloured cake, colourfully decorated with sugarpaste pumpkins.

Makes one 20cm/8in round cake

175g/6oz/generous 1 cup sugarpaste icing
brown and orange food colouring
2 x 20cm/8in round chocolate sponge cakes
675g/1 ½lb/3 cups orange-flavour butter icing
chocolate chips
angelica

Materials/equipment

wooden cocktail stick
fine paintbrush
23cm/9in round cake board
serrated scraper
No 7 writing nozzle
greaseproof paper piping bag

1 For the pumpkins, tint a very small piece of the sugarpaste icing brown, and the rest orange. Shape some balls of the orange icing the size of walnuts and some a bit smaller. Make ridges with a cocktail stick. Make stems from the brown icing and secure with water. Paint highlights on the pumpkins in orange. Leave to dry on greaseproof paper.

2 Cut both cakes in half horizontally. Use one-quarter of the butter icing to sandwich the cakes together. Place the cake on the board. Use two-thirds of the remaining icing to cover the cake. Texture the icing with a serrated scraper.

3 Using a No 7 writing nozzle, pipe a twisted rope pattern around the top and base edges of the cake with the remaining butter icing. Decorate with chocolate chips.

4 Cut the angelica into diamond shapes and arrange on the cake with the pumpkins.

Fudge-frosted Starry Roll

Whether it's for a birthday or another occasion, this sumptuous-looking cake is sure to please.

Makes one 33cm/13in long roll

23 x 33cm/9 x 13in Swiss roll sponge
175g/6oz/¾ cup chocolate butter icing
50g/2oz white chocolate
50g/2oz plain chocolate

For the fudge frosting

75g/3oz plain chocolate, broken into pieces
350g/12oz/3 cups icing sugar, sifted
75g/3oz/6 tbsp butter or margarine
65ml/4½ tbsp milk or single cream
7.5ml/1½ tsp vanilla essence

Materials/equipment

small star cutter
several greaseproof paper piping bags
No 19 star nozzle

1 Unroll the sponge and spread with the butter icing. Re-roll and set aside.

2 For the decorations, melt the white chocolate in a bowl set over a pan of hot water and spread on to a non-porous surface. Leave to firm, then cut out stars with the cutter. Leave to set on greaseproof paper. To make lace curls, melt the plain chocolate and then cool slightly. Cover a rolling pin with greaseproof paper. Pipe zigzags on the paper and leave on the rolling pin until cool.

3 For the frosting, stir all the ingredients over a low heat until melted. Remove from the heat and beat frequently until cool and thick. Cover the cake with two-thirds of the frosting, swirling with a palette knife.

4 With a No 19 star nozzle, use the remaining frosting to pipe diagonal lines on the cake.

5 Position the lace curls and stars. Transfer the cake to a serving plate and decorate with more stars.

Lucky Horseshoe Cake

This horseshoe-shaped cake, made to wish "good luck", is made from a round cake and the shape is then cut out.

Makes one 25cm/10in horseshoe cake

25cm/10in rich fruit cake
60ml/4 tbsp apricot jam, warmed and sieved
800g/1¾lb/5¼ cups marzipan
1kg/2¼lb/6¾ cups sugarpaste icing
peach and blue food colouring
edible silver balls
115g/4oz/¾ cup royal icing

Materials/equipment

30cm/12in round cake board
crimping tool
pale blue ribbon, 3mm/⅛in wide
scalpel
large and small blossom cutters

1 Make a horseshoe template and use to shape the cake. Brush the cake with the apricot jam. Roll out 350g/12oz/ 2¼ cups of the marzipan to a 25cm/10in circle. Using the template, cut out the shape and place on the cake. Measure the inside and outside of the cake. Cover with the remaining marzipan. Place the cake on the board and leave overnight.

2 Tint 800g/1¾lb/5¼ cups of the sugarpaste icing peach. Cover the cake in the same way. Crimp the top edge.

3 Draw and measure the ribbon insertion on the template. Cut 13 pieces of ribbon fractionally longer than each slit. Make the slits through the template with a scalpel. Insert the ribbon with a painted tool. Leave to dry overnight.

4 Make a small horseshoe template. Tint half the remaining sugarpaste icing pale blue. Using the template, cut out nine blue shapes. Mark each horseshoe with a sharp knife. Cut out 12 large and 15 small blossoms. Press a silver ball into the centres of the larger blossoms. Leave to dry. Repeat with the white icing. Decorate the cake and board with the ribbon, horseshoes and blossoms, securing with royal icing.

Bluebird Bon-voyage Cake

This cake is sure to see someone off on an exciting journey in a very special way.

Makes one 20cm/8in round cake

450g/1lb/3 cups royal icing
blue food colouring
800g/1¾lb/5¼ cups sugarpaste icing
20cm/8in round Madeira cake
350g/12oz/1½ cups butter icing
45ml/3 tbsp apricot jam, warmed and sieved
edible silver balls

Materials/equipment

No 1 writing nozzle
greaseproof paper piping bags
25cm/10in round cake board
thin pale blue ribbon

1 Make two-thirds of the royal icing softer to use for the run-outs. Make the rest stiffer for the outlines and further piping. Tint the softer icing bright blue. Cover and leave overnight.

2 Make two different-size bird templates, and use to pipe the run-outs on greaseproof paper. Using a No 1 writing nozzle, pipe the outlines, and then fill in. You need four large and five small birds. Leave to dry for at least 2 days.

3 Tint two-thirds of the sugarpaste icing blue. Form all the icing into small rolls and place them alternately together on a work surface. Form into a round and lightly knead to marble.

4 Cut the cake horizontally into three and sandwich together with the butter icing. Place the cake on the board, flush with an edge, and brush with apricot jam. Roll out the marbled icing and use to cover the cake and board.

5 Using the No 1 writing nozzle and the stiffer royal icing, pipe a wavy line around the edge of the board. Position the balls evenly in the icing. Secure the birds to the cake with royal icing. Pipe beads of white icing for eyes and stick on a ball. Drape the ribbon between the beaks, securing with icing.

Ghost Cake

This children's cake is really simple to make yet very effective. It is ideal for a Hallowe'en party.

Serves 15–20

900g/2lb/6 cups sugarpaste icing
black food colouring
2 Madeira cakes, baked in an 18cm/7in square cake tin and a 300ml/½ pint/1¼ cup pudding basin
350g/12oz/1½ cups butter icing

Materials/equipment

23cm/9in round cake board
fine paintbrush

1 Tint 115g/4oz/¾ cup of the sugarpaste icing dark grey and use to cover the cake board.

2 Cut two small corners off the large cake. Cut two larger wedges off the other two corners, then stand the cake on the board. Divide the larger trimmings in half and wedge around the base of the cake.

3 Secure the small cake to the top of the larger cake with butter icing. Completely cover both of the cakes with the remaining butter icing.

4 Roll out the remaining sugarpaste icing to an oval shape 50 x 30cm/20 x 12in. Lay it over the cake, letting the icing fall into folds around the sides. Gently smooth the icing over the top half of the cake and trim off any excess.

5 Using black food colouring and a fine paintbrush, paint two oval eyes on to the head.

Cat-in-a-Basket Cake

Makes one 15cm/6in round cake

800g/1¾lb/5¼ cups marzipan
red, green, yellow and brown food colouring
15cm/6in round deep sponge cake
30ml/2 tbsp apricot jam, warmed and sieved
50g/2oz/4 tbsp butter icing
50g/2oz/4 tbsp white sugarpaste icing

Materials/equipment

20cm/8in round cake board
fine paintbrush

1 Tint 350g/12oz/2 cups of the marzipan pink. Divide the rest in half and tint one half green and the other yellow. Brush the cake with the apricot jam and place it on the board.

2 Roll out the pink marzipan to a rectangle measuring 15 x 25cm/6 x 10in. Cut five 1cm/½in wide strips, about 24cm/9½in long, keeping them attached to the rectangle at one end. Roll out the green marzipan and cut it into 7.5cm/3in lengths of the same width. Fold back alternate pink strips and lay a green strip across widthways. Bring the pink strips over the green strip to form the weave. Keep repeating the process until the entire length is woven. Press lightly to join. Repeat with the rest of the rectangle and more strips of green marzipan.

3 Press the two pieces of basketweave on to the side of cake, joining them neatly. Model a yellow marzipan cat about 7.5cm/3in across. Leave to dry overnight.

4 Roll out the sugarpaste icing and place on the centre of the cake. Put the cat on top and arrange the icing in folds around it. Trim the edges neatly.

5 Make long ropes from any leftover pink and green marzipan. Twist together and press on to the top edge of the cake. Paint the cat's features in brown food colouring.

Fish-shaped Cake

A very easy, but colourful cake, perfect for a small child's birthday party.

Makes one fish-shaped cake

450g/1lb/3 cups sugarpaste icing
blue, orange, red, mauve and green food colouring
sponge cake, baked in a 3.5 litre/6 pint/15 cup ovenproof mixing bowl
350g/12oz/1½ cups butter icing
1 blue Smartie

Materials/equipment

large oval cake board
2.5cm/1in plain biscuit cutter
greaseproof paper piping bag

1 Tint two-thirds of the sugarpaste icing blue, roll out very thinly and use to cover the dampened cake board.

2 Invert the cake and trim into the fish shape. Slope the sides. Place on the cake board.

3 Tint all but 15ml/1 tbsp of the butter icing orange. Use to cover the cake, smoothing with a palette knife. Score curved lines for scales, starting from the tail end.

4 Tint half the remaining sugarpaste icing red. Shape and position two lips. Cut out the tail and fins. Mark with lines using a knife and position on the fish. Make the eye from white sugarpaste and the blue Smartie.

5 Tint a little sugarpaste mauve, cut out crescent-shaped scales using a biscuit cutter and place on the fish. Tint the remaining sugarpaste green and cut into long thin strips. Twist each strip and arrange around the board.

6 To make the bubbles around the fish, place the reserved butter icing in a piping bag, snip off the end and pipe small circles on to the board.

Pink Monkey Cake

This cheeky little monkey could be made in any colour icing you wish.

Makes one 20cm/8in cake

20cm/8in round sponge cake
115g/4oz/½ cup butter icing
45ml/3 tbsp apricot jam, warmed and sieved
450g/1lb/3 cups marzipan
500g/1¼lb/scant 3¾ cups sugarpaste icing
red, blue and black food colouring

Materials/equipment

25cm/10in round cake board
2 candles and holders

1 Trace the outline and paws of the monkey from the photograph. Enlarge to fit the cake and cut a template.

2 Split and fill the cake with butter icing. Place on the cake board and use the template to cut out the basic shape of the monkey. Use the trimmings to shape the nose and tummy. Brush with apricot jam and cover with a layer of marzipan.

3 Tint 450g/1lb/3 cups of the sugarpaste icing pale pink and use to cover the cake. Leave to dry overnight.

4 Mark the position of the face and paws. Tint a little of the sugarpaste icing blue and use for the eyes. Tint a little icing black and cut out the pupils and tie.

5 Tint the remaining sugarpaste icing dark pink and cut out the nose, mouth, ears and paws. Stick all the features in place with water. Roll the trimmings into balls and place on the board to hold the candles.

Porcupine Cake

Melt-in-the-mouth strips of chocolate flake give this porcupine its spiky coating.

Serves 15–20

2 chocolate sponge cakes, baked in a 1.2 litre/ 2 pint/5 cup and a 600ml/1 pint/2½ cup pudding basin
500g/1¼lb/2½ cups chocolate-flavour butter icing
cream, black, green, brown and red food colouring
5–6 chocolate flakes
50g/2oz/⅓ cup white marzipan

Materials/equipment

36cm/14in long rectangular cake board
wooden cocktail stick
fine paintbrush

1 Use the smaller cake for the head and shape a pointed nose at one end. Reserve the trimmed wedges.

2 Place the cakes side-by-side on the board, inverted, and use the trimmings to fill in the sides and top where they meet. Secure with butter icing.

3 Cover the cake with the remaining butter icing and mark the nose with a cocktail stick.

4 Make the spikes by breaking the chocolate flakes into thin strips and sticking them into the butter icing all over the body part of the porcupine.

5 Reserve a small portion of marzipan. Divide the remainder into three and tint cream, black and green. Tint a tiny portion of the reserved marzipan brown. Shape cream ears and feet, black-and-white eyes, and black claws and nose. Arrange all the features on the cake. Make green apples and highlight in red with a fine paintbrush. Make the stalks from the brown marzipan and push them in to the apples.

Mouse-in-Bed Cake

This cake is suitable for almost any age. Make the mouse well in advance to give it time to dry.

Makes one 20 x 15cm/8 x 6in cake

20cm/8in square sponge cake
115g/4oz/½ cup butter icing
45ml/3 tbsp apricot jam, warmed and sieved
450g/1lb/3 cups marzipan
675g/1½lb/4½ cups sugarpaste icing
blue and red food colouring

Materials/equipment

25cm/10in square cake board
flower cutter
blue and red food colouring pens

1 Cut 5cm/2in off one side of the cake. Split and fill the main cake with butter icing. Place on the cake board, brush with apricot jam and cover with a layer of marzipan. With the cake off-cut, shape a hollowed pillow, the torso and the legs of the mouse. Cover with marzipan and leave to dry overnight.

2 Cover the cake and pillow with white sugarpaste icing. Lightly frill the edge of the pillow with a fork. To make the valance, roll out 350g/12oz/2¼ cups of sugarpaste icing and cut into four 7.5cm/3in wide strips. Attach to the bed with water. Arrange the pillow and mouse body on the cake.

3 For the quilt, tint 75g/3oz/½ cup of sugarpaste icing blue and roll out to an 18cm/7in square. Mark with a diamond pattern and the flower cutter. Cover the mouse with the quilt.

4 Cut a 2.5 x 19cm/1 x 7½in white sugarpaste icing strip for the sheet, mark the edge and place over the quilt, tucking it under at the top edge.

5 Tint 25g/1oz/2 tbsp of marzipan pink and make the head and paws of the mouse. Put the head on the pillow, tucked under the sheet, and the paws over the edge of the sheet. Use food colouring pens to draw on the face of the mouse.

Teddy's Birthday

After the pieces have been assembled and stuck into the cake, an icing smoother is useful to flatten the design.

Makes one 20cm/8in round cake

20cm/8in round cake
115g/4oz/½ cup butter icing
45ml/3 tbsp apricot jam, warmed and sieved
350g/12oz/2 cups marzipan
450g/1lb/3 cups sugarpaste icing
brown, red, blue and black food colouring
115g/4oz/¾ cup royal icing
edible silver balls

Materials/equipment

25cm/10in round cake board
small greaseproof paper piping bags
No 7 shell and No 7 star nozzle
1.5m/1½yd red ribbon
2 candles and holders

1 Split and fill the cake with butter icing. Place on the cake board and brush with apricot jam. Cover with a layer of marzipan then a layer of sugarpaste icing. Using a template, mark the design on top of the cake.

2 Colour one-third of the remaining sugarpaste icing pale brown. Colour a piece pink, a piece red, some blue and a tiny piece black. Using the template, cut out the pieces and place in position on the cake. Stick down by lifting the edges carefully and brushing the undersides with a little water. Roll small ovals for the eyes and stick in place with the nose and eyebrows. Cut out a mouth and press flat.

3 Tie the ribbon around the cake. Colour the royal icing blue and pipe the border around the base of the cake with the shell nozzle and tiny stars around the small cake with the star nozzle, inserting silver balls. Put the candles on the cake.

Party Teddy Bear Cake

The teddy on this cake is built up with royal icing and coloured coconut.

Makes one 20cm/8in square cake

20cm/8in square sponge cake
115g/4oz/½ cup butter icing
45ml/3 tbsp apricot jam, warmed and sieved
450g/1lb/3 cups marzipan
350g/12oz/2 cups white sugarpaste icing
25g/1oz/½ cup desiccated coconut
blue and black food colouring
115g/4oz/¾ cup royal icing

Materials/equipment

25cm/10in square cake board
2 small greaseproof paper piping bags
small red bow
No 7 shell nozzle
1.5m/1½yd red ribbon
6 candles and holders

1 Cut the cake in half and sandwich together with butter icing. Place on the cake board and brush with apricot jam. Cover with a thin layer of marzipan and then white sugarpaste icing. Leave to dry overnight. Using a template, carefully mark the position of the teddy on to the cake.

2 Put the coconut into a bowl and mix in a drop of blue colouring to colour it pale blue. Spread a thin layer of royal icing within the outline of the teddy. Before the icing dries, sprinkle on some pale blue coconut and press it down lightly.

3 Roll out the sugarpaste trimmings and cut out a nose, ears and paws. Stick in place with a little royal icing. Tint some royal icing black and pipe on the eyes, nose and mouth. Use the bow as a tie and stick it in place. Pipe a white royal icing border around the base of the cake, tie the ribbon around the cake and position the candles on top.

Iced Fancies

These cakes are ideal for a children's tea-party. Ready-made cake decorating products may be used instead, if preferred.

Makes 16

115g/4oz/½ cup butter, at room temperature
225g/8oz/generous 1 cup caster sugar
2 eggs, at room temperature
175g/6oz/1½ cups plain flour
1.5ml/¼ tsp salt
7.5ml/1½ tsp baking powder
120ml/4fl oz/½ cup milk
5ml/1 tsp vanilla essence

For the icing

2 large egg whites
400g/14oz/3½ cups sifted icing sugar
1–2 drops glycerine
juice of 1 lemon
food colourings
coloured vermicelli, to decorate
crystallized lemon and orange slices, to decorate

1 Preheat the oven to 190°C/375°F/Gas 5. Line a 16-bun tray with paper cases.

2 Cream the butter and sugar until light and fluffy. Add the eggs, 1 at a time, beating well after each addition. Sift over and stir in the flour, salt and baking powder, alternating with the milk. Add the vanilla essence.

3 Half-fill the cups and bake for about 20 minutes, or until the tops spring back when touched. Stand in the tray to cool for 5 minutes, then unmould on to a wire rack.

4 For the icing, beat the egg whites until stiff. Gradually add the sugar, glycerine and lemon juice, and beat for 1 minute.

5 Tint the icing with different food colourings. Ice the cakes.

6 Decorate the cakes with coloured vermicelli and crystallized lemon and orange slices. Make freehand decorations using a paper piping bag.

Fairy Castle Cake

If the icing on this cake dries too quickly, dip a palette knife into hot water to help smooth the surface.

Makes one castle-shaped cake

20cm/8in round sponge cake
115g/4oz/½ cup butter icing
45ml/3 tbsp apricot jam, warmed and sieved
675g/1½lb/4½ cups marzipan
8 mini Swiss rolls
675g/1½lb/4½ cups royal icing
red, blue and green food colouring
jelly diamonds
4 ice cream cones
2 ice cream wafers
50g/2oz/1 cup desiccated coconut
8 marshmallows

Materials/equipment

30cm/12in square cake board
wooden cocktail stick

1 Split and fill the cake with butter icing, place in the centre of the board and brush with apricot jam. Cover with a layer of marzipan. Cover each of the Swiss rolls with marzipan. Stick four of them around the cake and cut the other four in half.

2 Tint two-thirds of the royal icing pale pink and cover the cake. Ice the extra pieces of Swiss roll and stick them around the top of the cake. Use a cocktail stick to score the walls with a brick pattern. Make windows on the corner towers from jelly diamonds. Cut the ice cream cones to make the tower spires and stick them in place. Leave to dry overnight.

3 Tint half the remaining royal icing pale blue and cover the cones. Use a fork to pattern the icing. Shape the wafers for the gates, stick to the cake and cover with blue icing. Use the back of a knife to mark planks.

4 Tint the coconut with a few drops of green colouring. Spread the board with the remaining royal icing and sprinkle over the coconut. Stick on the marshmallows with a little royal icing to make the small turrets.

Sailing Boat

For chocoholics, make this cake using chocolate sponge.

Makes one boat-shaped cake

20cm/8in square sponge cake
225g/8oz/1 cup butter icing
15ml/1 tbsp cocoa powder
4 large chocolate flakes
115g/4oz/¾ cup royal icing
blue food colouring

Materials/equipment

25cm/10in square cake board
rice paper
blue and red powder tints
paint brush
plastic drinking straw
wooden cocktail stick
2 small cake ornaments

1 Split and fill the cake with half of the butter icing. Cut 7cm/2¾in from one side of the cake. Shape the larger piece to resemble the hull of a boat. Place diagonally across the cake board. Mix the cocoa powder into the remaining butter icing and spread evenly over the top and sides of the boat.

2 Make the rudder and tiller from short lengths of flake and place them at the stern of the boat. Split the rest of the flakes lengthways and press on to the sides of the boat, horizontally, to resemble planks of wood. Sprinkle the crumbs over the top.

3 Cut two rice paper rectangles, one 14 x 16cm/5¾ x 6½in and the other 15 x 7.5cm/6 x 3in. Cut the bigger one in a gentle curve to make the large sail and the smaller one into a triangle. Brush a circle of blue powder tint on to the large sail. Wet the edges of the sails and stick on to the straw. Make a hole for the straw 7.5cm/3in from the bow of the boat and push into the cake.

4 Cut a rice paper flag and brush with red powder tint. Stick the flag on to a cocktail stick and insert into the top of the straw. Tint the royal icing blue and spread on the board in waves. Place the small ornaments on the boat.

Spiders' Web Cake

A spooky cake for any occasion, fancy dress or otherwise.

Makes one 900g/2lb cake

900g/2lb dome-shaped lemon sponge cake
225g/8oz/¾ cup lemon-flavour glacé icing
black and yellow food colouring
cocoa powder, for dusting
chocolate vermicelli
2–3 liquorice wheels, sweet centres removed
15g/½oz/2 tbsp sugarpaste icing

For the spiders

115g/4oz plain chocolate, broken into pieces
150ml/¼ pint/⅔ cup double cream
45ml/3 tbsp ground almonds

Materials/equipment

greaseproof paper
small greaseproof paper piping bag
wooden skewer
20cm/8in cake board

1 Place the cake on greaseproof paper. Tint 45ml/3 tbsp of the glacé icing black. Tint the rest yellow and pour it over the cake, letting it run down the side.

2 Fill a piping bag with the black icing and, starting at the centre top, drizzle it round the cake in an evenly-spaced spiral. Finish the web by drawing downwards through the icing with a skewer. When set, place on the cake board.

3 For the spiders, gently melt the chocolate with the cream, stirring frequently. Transfer to a bowl, allow to cool, then beat the mixture for 10 minutes, or until thick and pale. Stir in the ground almonds, then chill until firm enough to handle. Dust your hands with a little cocoa, then make walnut-size balls with the mixture. Roll the balls in chocolate vermicelli.

4 For the legs, cut the liquorice into 4cm/1½in lengths. Make holes in the sides of the spiders and insert the legs. For the spiders' eyes, tint a piece of sugarpaste icing black and form into tiny balls. Make larger balls with white icing. Stick on using water. Arrange the spiders on and around the cake.

Toy Telephone Cake

The child's name could be piped in a contrasting colour of icing, if you wish.

Makes one telephone-shaped cake

15cm/6in square sponge cake
50g/2oz/¼ cup butter icing
30ml/2 tbsp apricot jam, warmed and sieve
275g/10oz/2 cups marzipan
350g/12oz/2 cups sugarpaste icing
yellow, blue, red and black food colouring
liquorice strips
115g/4oz/¾ cup royal icing

Materials/equipment

20cm/8in square cake board
piping nozzle
small greaseproof paper piping bag
No 1 writing nozzle

1 Split and fill the cake with butter icing. Trim to the shape of a telephone. Round off the edges and cut a shallow groove where the receiver rests on the telephone. Place the cake on the board and brush with apricot jam.

2 Cover the cake with marzipan then sugarpaste icing. Tint half the remaining sugarpaste icing yellow, a small piece blue and the rest of the icing red. To make the dial, cut out an 8cm/3½in diameter circle in yellow and a 4cm/1½in diameter circle in blue. Stamp out 12 red discs for the numbers with the end of a piping nozzle and cut out a red receiver. Position on the cake with water.

3 Twist the liquorice around to form a curly cord and use royal icing to stick one end to the telephone and the other end to the receiver. Tint the royal icing black and pipe the numbers on the discs and the child's name on the telephone.

Bumble Bee Cake

The edible sugar flowers that are used to decorate this cake were bought ready-made.

Makes one bee-shaped cake

20cm/8in round sponge cake
115g/4oz/½ cup butter icing
45ml/3 tbsp apricot jam, warmed and sieved
350g/12oz/2¼ cups marzipan
500g/1¼ lb/3¾ cups sugarpaste icing
yellow, black, blue and red food colouring
115g/4oz/¾ cup royal icing
50g/2oz/1 cup desiccated coconut

Materials/equipment

25cm/10in square cake board
6 sugarpaste daisies
1 paper doily
sticky tape
1 pipe cleaner

1 Split and fill the cake with butter icing. Cut in half to make semicircles, sandwich the halves together and stand upright on the cake board. Trim the ends to shape the head and tail. Brush with apricot jam and cover with a layer of marzipan. Tint 350g/12oz/2¼ cups of the sugarpaste icing yellow and use to cover the cake.

2 Tint 115g/4oz/¾cup of the sugarpaste icing black. Roll out and cut three stripes, each 2.5 x 25cm/1 x 10in. Space evenly on the cake and stick on with water. Use the remaining icing to make the eyes and mouth, tinting the icing blue for the pupils and pink for the mouth. Stick on with water.

3 Tint the coconut with a drop of yellow colouring. Cover the cake board with royal icing then sprinkle with coconut. Place the daisies on the board.

4 To make the wings, cut the doily in half, wrap each half into a cone shape and stick together with sticky tape. Cut the pipe cleaner in half and stick the pieces into the cake, just behind the head. Place the wings over the pipe cleaners.

Toy Car Cake

You can add a personalized number plate with the child's name and age to the back of this car.

Makes one car-shaped cake

20cm/8in round sponge cake
115g/4oz/½ cup butter icing
45ml/3 tbsp apricot jam, warmed and served
450g/1lb/3 cups marzipan
500g/1¼lb/3¾ cups sugarpaste icing
yellow, red and black food colouring
30ml/2 tbsp royal icing
red and green sweets

Materials/equipment

25cm/10in round cake board
wooden cocktail stick
cutters, 4cm/1½in and 2.5cm/1in
small greaseproof paper piping bag
No 1 writing nozzle
2 candles and holders

1 Split and fill the cake with the butter icing. Cut in half and sandwich the halves together. Stand upright and slice off pieces to create the windscreen and bonnet. Place on the cake board and brush with apricot jam.

2 Cut a strip of marzipan to cover the top of the cake to level the joins. Then cover the cake all over with marzipan. Tint 450g/1lb/3 cups of the sugarpaste icing yellow and use to cover the cake. Leave to dry overnight.

3 Mark the outlines of the doors and windows on to the car with a cocktail stick.

4 Tint the remaining sugarpaste icing red. Cut out four wheels with the larger cutter. Stick in place with water. Mark the hubs in the centre of each wheel with the smaller cutter.

5 Tint the royal icing black and pipe over the outline marks of the doors and windows. Stick on sweets for headlights with royal icing. Press the candles into sweets and stick to the board with royal icing.

Fire Engine Cake

This jolly fire engine is simplicity itself as the decorations are mainly bought sweets and novelties.

Makes one 20 x 10cm/8 x 4in cake

20cm/8in square sponge cake
115g/4oz/½ cup butter icing
45ml/3 tbsp apricot jam, warmed and sieved
350g/12oz/2¼ cups marzipan
450g/1lb/3 cups sugarpaste icing
red, black and green food colouring
liquorice strips
115g/4oz/4 tbsp royal icing
sweets
50g/2oz/1 cup desiccated coconut

Materials/equipment

25cm/10in round cake board
small greaseproof paper piping bag
No 2 plain nozzle
2 silver bells
3 candles and holders

1 Split and fill the cake with the butter icing. Cut in half and sandwich one half on top of the other. Place on the cake board and brush with apricot jam.

2 Trim a thin wedge off the front edge to make a sloping windscreen. Cover with marzipan. Tint 350g/12oz/2¼ cups of the sugarpaste icing red and use to cover the cake.

3 For the ladder, cut the liquorice into two strips and some short pieces for the rungs. Tint half the royal icing black and use some to stick the ladder to the top of the cake. Roll out the remaining sugarpaste icing, cut out windows and stick them on with a little water.

4 Pipe around the windows in black royal icing. Stick sweets in place for headlights, lamps and wheels and stick the silver bells on the roof. Tint the coconut green, spread a little royal icing over the cake board and sprinkle with the coconut. Stick sweets to the board with royal icing and press the candles into the sweets.

Sandcastle Cake

Crushed digestive biscuits make convincing-looking sand when used to cover this fun cake.

Makes one 15cm/6in round cake

2 x 15cm/6in round sponge cakes
115g/4oz/½ cup butter icing
45ml/3 tbsp apricot jam, warmed and sieved
115g/4oz/¾ cup digestive biscuits
115g/4oz/¾ cup royal icing
blue food colouring
shrimp-shaped sweets

Materials/equipment

25cm/10in square cake board
rice paper
plastic drinking straw
4 candles and holders

1 Split both of the cakes, then sandwich all the layers together with the butter icing. Place in the centre of the cake board. Cut 3cm/1¼in off the top just above the filling and set aside. Shape the rest of the cake with slightly sloping sides.

2 Cut four 3cm/1¼in cubes from the reserved piece of cake. Stick on the cubes for the turrets and brush with apricot jam.

3 Crush the digestive biscuits and press through a sieve to make the "sand". Press some crushed biscuits on to the cake, using a palette knife to get a smooth finish.

4 Colour some royal icing blue and spread on the board around the sandcastle to make a moat. Spread a little royal icing on the board around the outside edge of the moat and sprinkle on some crushed biscuit.

5 To make the flag, cut a small rectangle of rice paper and stick on to half a straw with water. Push the end of the straw into the cake. Stick candles into each turret and arrange the shrimp-shaped sweets on the board.

Clown Face Cake

Children love this happy clown whose frilly collar is surprisingly simple to make.

Makes one 20cm/8in cake

20cm/8in round sponge cake
115g/4oz/½ cup butter icing
45ml/3 tbsp apricot jam, warmed and sieved
450g/1lb/3 cups marzipan
450g/1lb/3 cups sugarpaste icing
115g/4oz/¾ cup royal icing
edible silver balls
red, green, blue and black food colouring

Materials/equipment

25cm/10in round cake board
small greaseproof paper piping bag
No 8 star nozzle
wooden cocktail stick
cotton wool
two candles and holders

1 Split and fill the cake with butter icing. Place on the cake board and brush with apricot jam. Cover with a thin layer of marzipan then with white sugarpaste icing. Mark the position of the features. Pipe stars around the base of the cake with some royal icing, placing silver balls as you work, and leave to dry overnight.

2 Make a template for the face and features. Tint half the remaining sugarpaste icing pink and cut out the face base.Tint and cut out all the features, rolling a sausage to make the mouth. Cut thin strands for the hair. Stick all the features and hair in place with a little water.

3 Tint the remaining sugarpaste icing green. Cut three strips 4cm/1½ in wide. Give each a scalloped edge and stretch by rolling a cocktail stick along it to make the frill. Stick on with water and arrange the frills, holding them in place with cotton wool until dry. Place the candles at the top of the head.

Pinball Machine

Serves 8–10

25cm/10in square sponge cake
225g/8oz/1½ cups butter icing
45ml/3 tbsp apricot jam, warmed and sieved
450g/1lb/3 cups marzipan
115g/4oz/¾ cup royal icing
450g/1lb/3 cups sugarpaste icing
yellow, blue, green and red food colouring
sweets
2 ice cream fan wafers

Materials/equipment

20cm/8in round cake tin
30cm/12in square cake board
small greaseproof paper piping bag
No 1 writing nozzle

1 Split and fill the sponge cake with butter icing. Cut off a 5cm/2in strip from one side and reserve. Cut a thin wedge off the top of the cake, diagonally along its length, to end just above the halfway mark. This will give a sloping table.

2 Using the cake tin as a guide, cut the reserved strip of cake to make a rounded back for the pinball table. Brush the back and table with apricot jam, then cover separately with marzipan and place on the board. Stick them together with royal icing. Leave to dry overnight.

3 Cover with a layer of sugarpaste icing and leave to dry. Use a template to mark out the pinball design on the top of the cake. Colour the remaining sugarpaste icing yellow, blue, green and pink. Roll out the colours and cut to fit the design. Stick on the pieces with water and smooth the joins carefully.

4 Using royal icing, stick sweets on the cake as buffers, flippers, lights and knobs. Roll some blue sugarpaste icing into a long sausage and edge the pinball table and divider. Cut zig-zags for the sides and a screen for the back. Stick on with water. Stick the ice cream fans at the back of the screen. Load the pinball sweets. Add the child's name on the screen with run-out letters or piping.

Pirate's Hat

If you prefer, buy ready-made black sugarpaste icing rather than tinting it yourself.

Serves 8–10

25cm/10in round sponge cake
225g/8oz/1 cup butter icing
45ml/3 tbsp apricot jam, warmed and sieved
450g/1lb/3 cups marzipan
500g/1¼lb/3¾ cups sugarpaste icing
black and gold food colouring
chocolate money
jewel sweets

Materials/equipment

30cm/12in square cake board
fine paint brush

1 Split and fill the cake with butter icing. Cut in half and sandwich the halves together. Stand upright diagonally across the cake board and cut shallow dips from each end to create the brim of the hat. Brush with apricot jam.

2 Cut a strip of marzipan to lay over the top of the cake. Then cover the whole of the cake with a layer of marzipan. Tint 450g/1lb/3 cups of the sugarpaste icing black. Use to cover the cake.

3 Roll out the remaining sugarpaste icing and cut some 1cm/½in strips. Stick the strips in place with a little water around the brim of the pirate's hat and mark with the prongs of a fork to make a braid.

4 Make a skull and crossbones template and mark on to the hat. Cut the shapes out of the white sugarpaste icing and stick in place with water. Paint the braid strip gold and arrange the chocolate money and jewel sweets on the board.

Noah's Ark Cake

This charming cake is decorated with small animals, about 4cm/1½in high, available from cake decorating shops.

Makes one 20 x 13cm/8 x 5in cake

20cm/8in square sponge cake
115g/4oz/½ cup butter icing
45ml/3 tbsp apricot jam, warmed and sieved
450g/1lb/3 cups marzipan
450g/1lb/3 cups sugarpaste icing
brown, yellow and blue food colouring
115g/4oz/¾ cup royal icing
chocolate mint stick

Materials/equipment

25cm/10in square cake board
skewer
rice paper flag
small animal cake ornaments

1 Split and fill the cake with butter icing. Cut off and set aside a 7.5cm/3in strip. Shape the remaining piece of cake to form the hull of the boat. Place diagonally on the cake board.

2 Use the set-aside piece of cake, to cut a rectangle 10 x 6cm/4 x 2½in for the cabin and a triangular piece for the roof. Sandwich together with butter icing or apricot jam.

3 Cover the three pieces with a layer of marzipan. Tint the sugarpaste icing brown and use most of it to cover the hull and cabin. Use the remaining brown icing to make a long sausage. Stick around the edge of the hull with water. Mark planks with the back of a knife. Leave to dry overnight.

4 Tint one-third of the royal icing yellow and spread it over the cabin roof with a palette knife. Roughen it with a skewer to create a thatch effect.

5 Tint the remaining royal icing blue and spread over the cake board, making rough waves. Stick a rice paper flag on to the chocolate mint stick and press on the back of the boat. Stick the small animals on to the boat with a dab of icing.

Balloons Cake

This is a simple yet effective cake design that can be adapted to suit any age.

Makes one 20cm/8in round cake

20cm/8in round cake
115g/4oz/½ cup butter icing
45ml/3 tbsp apricot jam, warmed and sieved
450g/1lb/3 cups marzipan
450g/1lb/3 cups sugarpaste icing
red, blue, green and yellow food colouring
115g/4oz/¾ cup royal icing

Materials/equipment

25cm/10in round cake board
2 small greaseproof paper piping bags
No 2 plain and No 7 star nozzles
1.5m/1½yd blue ribbon
3 candles and holders

1 Split and fill the cake with butter icing. Place on the cake board and brush with apricot jam. Cover with a layer of marzipan then sugarpaste icing.

2 Divide the remaining sugarpaste icing into three pieces and tint pink, blue and green. Make a balloon template, roll out the coloured sugarpaste and cut out one balloon from each colour. Stick on to the cake with water and rub the edges gently to round them off.

3 Tint the royal icing yellow. With a plain nozzle, pipe on the balloon strings and a number on each balloon. Using the star nozzle, pipe a border around the base of the cake.

4 Tie the ribbon round the cake and place the candles on top.

Horse Stencil Cake

Use a fairly dry brush when painting the design on this cake and allow each colour to dry before adding the next.

Makes one 20cm/8in round cake

20cm/8in round sponge cake
115g/4oz/½ cup butter icing
45ml/3 tbsp apricot jam, warmed and sieved
450g/1lb/3 cups marzipan
450g/1lb/3 cups sugarpaste icing
yellow, brown, black, red, orange and blue food colouring

Materials/equipment

25cm/10in round cake board
spoon with decorative handle
fine paintbrush
horse and letter stencils
1.5m/1½yd blue ribbon
7 candles and holders

1 Split and fill the cake with butter icing. Place on the cake board and brush with apricot jam. Cover with a layer of marzipan. Tint the sugarpaste icing yellow, roll out and use to cover the cake. Roll the trimmings into two thin ropes, long enough to go halfway round the cake. Brush water in a thin band around the base of the cake, lay on the ropes and press together. Pattern the border with the decorative spoon handle. Leave to dry overnight.

2 If you do not have a stencil, make one by tracing a simple design on to a thin piece of card and cutting out the shape with a craft knife. Place the horse stencil in the centre of the cake. With a fairly dry brush, gently paint over the parts you want to colour first. Allow these to dry completely before adding another colour, otherwise the colours will run into each other. Clean the stencil between colours.

3 When the horse picture is finished carefully paint on the lettering. Tie the ribbon around the side of the cake and place the candles on top.

Doll's House Cake

Serves 8–10

25cm/10in square sponge cake
225g/8oz/1 cup butter icing
45ml/3 tbsp apricot jam, warmed and sieved
450g/1lb/3 cups marzipan
450g/1lb/3 cups sugarpaste icing
red, yellow, blue, black, green and gold food colouring
115g/4oz/¾ cup royal icing

Materials/equipment

30cm/12in square cake board
pastry wheel
large and fine paintbrushes
wooden cocktail stick
small greaseproof paper piping bags
No 2 writing nozzle
flower decorations

1 Split and fill the cake with butter icing. Cut triangles off two corners and use the pieces to make a chimney. Place on the cake board and brush with apricot jam. Cover with a layer of marzipan then sugarpaste icing.

2 Mark the roof with a pastry wheel and the chimney with the back of a knife. Paint the chimney red and the roof yellow.

3 Tint 25g/1oz/2 tbsp of sugarpaste icing red and cut out a 7.5 x 12cm/3 x 4½in door. Tint enough sugarpaste icing blue to make a fanlight. Stick to the cake with water. Mark windows, 6cm/2½in square, with a cocktail stick. Paint on curtains with blue food colouring. Tint half the royal icing black and pipe around the windows and the door.

4 Tint the remaining royal icing green. Pipe the flower stems and leaves under the windows and the climber up on to the roof. Stick the flowers in place with a little icing and pipe green flower centres. Pipe the house number or child's age, the knocker and handle on the door. Leave to dry for 1 hour, then paint with gold food colouring.

Treasure Chest Cake

Allow yourself a few days before the party to make this cake as the lock and handles need to dry for 48 hours.

Makes one 20 x 10cm/8 x 4in cake

20cm/8in square sponge cake
115g/4oz/½ cup butter icing
45ml/3 tbsp apricot jam, warmed and sieved
350g/12oz/2cups marzipan
400g/14oz/2½ cups sugarpaste icing
brown and green food colouring
50g/2oz/1 cup desiccated coconut
115g/4oz/¾ cup royal icing
edible gold dusting powder
edible silver balls
chocolate money

Materials/equipment

30cm/12in round cake board
fine paintbrush

1 Split and fill the cake with butter icing. Cut the cake in half and sandwich the halves on top of each other with butter icing. Place on the cake board.

2 Shape the top into a rounded lid and brush with apricot jam. Cover with a layer of marzipan. Tint 350g/12oz/2¼ cups of the sugarpaste icing brown and use to cover the cake.

3 Use the brown sugarpaste trimmings to make strips. Stick on to the chest with water. Mark the lid with a sharp knife.

4 Tint the coconut with a few drops of green colouring. Spread a little royal icing over the cake board and press the green coconut lightly into it to make the grass.

5 From the remaining sugarpaste icing, cut out the padlock and handles. Cut a keyhole shape from the padlock and shape the handles over a small box. Leave to dry. Stick the padlock and handles in place with royal icing and paint them gold. Stick silver balls on to look like nails. Arrange the chocolate money on the board.

Lion Cake

For an animal lover or a celebration cake for a Leo horoscope sign, this cake is ideal.

Makes one 28 x 23cm/11 x 9in oval cake

25 x 30cm/10 x 12in sponge cake
350g/12oz/1½ cups orange flavour butter icing
orange and red food colouring
675g/1½lb/4½ cups yellow marzipan
50g/2oz/generous 4 tbsp sugarpaste icing
red and orange liquorice bootlaces
long and round marshmallows

Materials/equipment

30cm/12in square cake board
cheese grater
small heart-shaped cutter

1 With the flat side of the cake uppermost, cut it to make an oval shape with an uneven scallop design around the edge. Turn the cake over and trim the top level.

2 Place the cake on the cake board. Tint the butter icing orange and use it to cover the cake.

3 Roll 115g/4oz/¾ cup of marzipan to a 15cm/6in square. Place in the centre of the cake for the lion's face.

4 Grate the remaining marzipan and use to cover the sides and the top of the cake up to the face panel.

5 Tint the sugarpaste icing red. Use the heart-shaped cutter to stamp out the lion's nose and position on the cake with water. Roll the remaining red icing into two thin, short strands to make the lion's mouth, and stick on with water.

6 Cut the liquorice into graduated lengths, and place on the cake for the whiskers. Use two flattened round marshmallows for the eyes and two snipped long ones for the eyebrows.

Train Cake

This cake is made in a train-shaped tin, so all you need to do is decorate it.

Makes one train-shaped cake

train-shaped sponge cake, about 35cm/14in long
675g/1½lb/3 cups butter icing
yellow food colouring
red liquorice bootlaces
90–120ml/6–8 tbsp coloured vermicelli
4 liquorice wheels

Materials/equipment

25 x 38cm/10 x 15in cake board
2 fabric piping bags
small round and small star nozzles
pink and white cotton wool balls

1 Slice off the top surface of the cake to make it flat. Place diagonally on the cake board.

2 Tint the butter icing yellow. Use half of it to cover the cake.

3 Using a round nozzle and a quarter of the remaining butter icing, pipe a straight double border around the top edge of the cake.

4 Place the red liquorice bootlaces on the piped border. Snip the bootlaces around the curves on the train.

5 Using a small star nozzle and the remaining butter icing, pipe small stars over the top of the cake. Add extra liquorice and piping, if you like. Use a palette knife to press on the coloured vermicelli all around the sides of the cake.

6 Pull a couple of balls of cotton wool apart for the steam and stick on the cake board with butter icing. Press the liquorice wheels in place for the wheels.

Number 7 Cake

Any combination of colours will work well for this cake with its marbled effect.

Makes one 30cm/12in long cake

23 x 30cm/9 x 12in sponge cake
350g/12oz/1½ cups orange-flavour butter icing
60ml/4 tbsp apricot jam, warmed and sieved
675g/1½lb/4½ cups sugarpaste icing
blue and green food colouring
rice paper sweets

Materials /equipment

25 x 33cm/10 x 13in cake board
small "7" cutter

1 Place the cake flat-side up and cut out the number seven. Slice the cake horizontally, sandwich together with the butter icing and place on the board.

2 Brush the cake evenly with apricot jam. Divide the sugarpaste icing into three and tint one of the pieces blue and another green. Set aside 50g/2oz/scant ½cup from each of the coloured icings. Knead together the large pieces of blue and green icing with the third piece of white icing to marble. Use to cover the cake.

3 Immediately after covering, use the cutter to remove sugarpaste shapes in a random pattern from the covered cake.

4 Roll out the reserved blue and green sugarpaste icing and stamp out shapes with the same cutter. Use these to fill the stamped-out shapes from the cake. Decorate the board with some rice paper sweets.

Musical Cake

Creating a sheet of music on a cake requires very delicate piping work, so it is best to practise first.

Makes one 20 x 25cm/8 x 10in cake

25cm/10in square sponge cake
225g/8oz/1 cup butter icing
45ml/3 tbsp apricot jam, warmed and sieved
450g/1lb/3 cups marzipan
450g/1lb/3 cups sugarpaste icing
115g/4oz/¾ cup royal icing
black food colouring

Materials/equipment

25 x 30cm/10 x 12in cake board
wooden cocktail stick
2 small greaseproof paper piping bags
No 0 writing and No 7 shell nozzles
1.5m/1½yd red ribbon

1 Split and fill the cake with a little butter icing. Cut a 5cm/2in strip off one side of the cake. Place the cake on the cake board and brush with apricot jam. Cover with a layer of marzipan then sugarpaste icing. Leave to dry overnight.

2 Make a template and mark out the sheet of music and child's name with a cocktail stick.

3 Using white royal icing and a No 0 nozzle, begin by piping the lines and bars. Leave to dry.

4 Tint the remaining icing black and pipe the clefs, name and notes. With the shell nozzle, pipe a royal icing border around the base of the cake and tie a ribbon around the side.

Magic Rabbit Cake

Makes one 15cm/6in tall round cake

2 x 15cm/6in round cakes
225g/8oz/1 cup butter icing
115g/4oz/¾ cup royal icing
45ml/3 tbsp apricot jam, warmed and sieved
675g/1½lb/4½ cups marzipan
675g/1½lb/4½ cups sugarpaste icing
black and pink food colouring
edible silver balls

Materials/equipment

25cm/10in square cake board
2 small greaseproof paper piping bags
star nozzle
1.5m/1½yd pink ribbon

1 Split and fill the cakes with butter icing, then sandwich them one on top of the other. Stick on the centre of the cake board with a little royal icing. Brush with apricot jam. Use 450g/1lb/3 cups of the marzipan to cover the cake.

2 Tint the sugarpaste icing grey. Use about two-thirds of it to cover the cake. Roll out the rest to a 20cm/8in round. Cut a 15cm/6in circle from its centre. Lower the brim over the cake. Shape the brim sides over wooden spoon handles until dry.

3 Cut a cross in the 15cm/6in grey circle and place on the hat. Curl the triangles over a wooden spoon handle to shape. Smooth the join at the top and sides of the hat.

4 Tint the remaining marzipan pink and make the rabbit's head, about 5cm/2in wide with a pointed face. Mark the position of the eyes, nose and mouth. Leave to dry overnight.

5 Stick the rabbit in the centre of the hat with a little royal icing. Pipe a border of royal icing around the top and base of the hat and decorate with silver balls while still wet. Tint the remaining royal icing black and pipe the rabbit's eyes and mouth. Tie the ribbon round the hat.

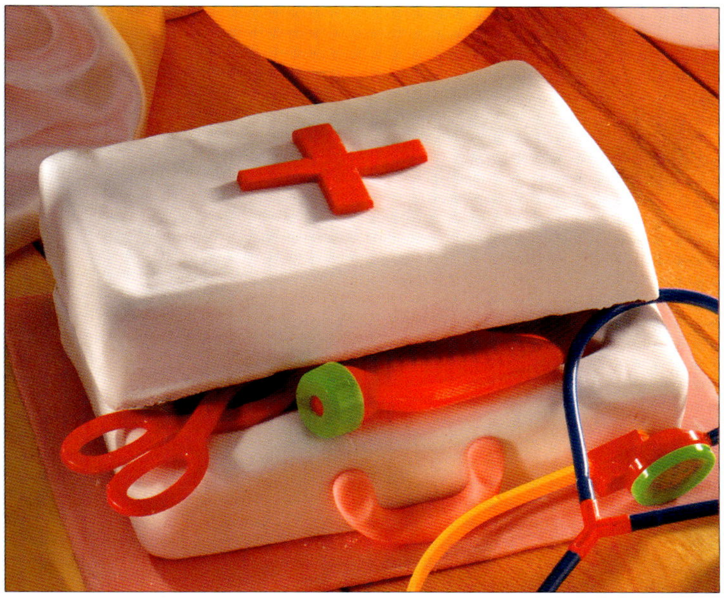

Nurse's Kit Cake

The box is easy to make and is simply filled with toy kit.

Makes one 20 x 17cm/8 x 6½in cake

35 x 20cm/14 x 8in chocolate sponge cake
120ml/4fl oz/½ cup apricot jam, warmed and sieved
675g/1½lb/4½ cups sugarpaste icing
red food colouring

Materials/equipment
25cm/10in square cake board
selection of toy medical equipment

1 Place the cake dome-side down and cut in half widthways.

2 To make the base of the nurse's box, turn one cake half dome-side up and hollow out the centre to a depth of 1cm/½in, leaving a 1cm/½in border on the three uncut edges. Brush the tops and sides of both halves with jam.

3 Tint 150g/5oz/generous ½ cup sugarpaste icing deep pink. Use a little to make a small handle for the box. Wrap in clear film and set aside. Cover the cake board with the rest of the pink icing. Tint 25g/1oz/2 tbsp of the sugarpaste icing red. Cover with clear film and set aside.

4 Tint the remaining icing light pink and divide into two portions, one slightly bigger than the other. Roll out the bigger portion and use to cover the base of the box, easing it into the hollow and along the edges. Trim, then position the base on the cake board.

5 Roll out the other portion and use to cover the lid of the box. Trim, then place on top of the base at a slight angle.

6 Stick the handle to the base of the box using water. Cut a small cross out of red icing and stick it on the lid. Place a few toy items under the lid, protruding slightly. Arrange some more items around the board and cake.

Ballerina Cake

Use flower cutters with ejectors to make the tiny flowers.

Makes one 20cm/8in round cake

20cm/8in round sponge cake
115g/4oz/½ cup butter icing
45ml/3 tbsp apricot jam, warmed and sieved
450g/1lb/3 cups marzipan
450g/1lb/3 cups sugarpaste icing
pink, yellow, blue and green food colouring
115g/4oz/¾ cup royal icing

Materials/equipment
25cm/10in round cake board
small flower cutter
small circle cutter
wooden cocktail stick
cotton wool
fine paintbrush
3 small greaseproof paper piping bags
No 7 shell nozzle
1.5m/1½yd pink ribbon

1 Split and fill the cake with butter icing. Place on the board and brush with apricot jam. Cover with marzipan then sugarpaste icing. Leave to dry overnight. Divide the rest of the sugarpaste into three. Tint flesh tone, light pink and dark pink. Stamp out 15 pale pink flowers. Leave to dry.

2 Make a template of the ballerina. Mark her position on the cake. Cut out a flesh-tone body and dark pink bodice. Stick on with water, rounding off the edges.

3 Cut two dark pink underskirts, a pale pink top skirt and a dark pink bodice extension to make the tutu. Stamp out hollow, fluted circles, divide the circles into four and frill the fluted edges with a cocktail stick. Stick the tutu in place, supported with cotton wool. Cut out and stick on pale pink shoes. Leave to dry overnight.

4 Paint the ballerina's face and hair. Position 12 hoop and three headdress flowers. Tint some royal icing green and dark pink to complete the flowers and ballet shoes. Pipe a border around the base with the shell nozzle. Tie round the ribbon.

Monsters on the Moon

A great cake for little monsters! This cake is best eaten on the day of making.

Serves 12–15

1 quantity quick-mix sponge cake
500g/1¼lb/3¾ cups sugarpaste icing
225g/8oz/1½ cups marzipan
black food colouring
edible silver glitter powder (optional)
375g/12oz/¾ cups caster sugar
2 egg whites
60ml/4 tbsp water

Materials/equipment

ovenproof wok
various sizes of plain round and star cutters
30cm/12in round cake board
small monster toys

1 Preheat the oven to 180ºC/350ºF/Gas 4. Grease and line the wok. Spoon in the cake mixture and smooth the surface. Bake in the centre of the oven for 35–40 minutes. Leave for 5 minutes, then turn out on to a rack and peel off the paper.

2 With the cake dome-side up, use the round cutters to cut out craters. Press in the cutters to about 2.5cm/1in deep, then remove and cut the craters out of the cake with a knife.

3 Use 115g/4oz/¾ cup of the sugarpaste icing to cover the cake, pulling off small pieces and pressing them in uneven strips around the edges of the craters. Tint the remaining sugarpaste icing black. Roll out and cover the board. Stamp out stars and replace with marzipan stars of the same size. Dust with glitter powder, if using and place on the board.

4 Put the sugar, egg whites and water in a heatproof bowl over a pan of simmering water. Beat until thick and peaky. Spoon the icing over the cake, swirling it into the craters and peaking it unevenly. Sprinkle over the silver glitter powder, if using, then position the monsters on the cake.

Circus Cake

This colourful design is easy to achieve and is sure to delight young children.

Makes one 20cm/8in cake

20cm/8in round sponge cake
115g/4oz/½ cup butter icing
45ml/3 tbsp apricot jam, warmed and sieved
450g/1lb/3 cups marzipan
450g/1lb/3 cups sugarpaste icing
red and blue food colouring
115g/4oz/¾ cup royal icing
edible silver balls
3 digestive biscuits

Materials/equipment

25cm/10in round cake board
small greaseproof paper piping bag
No 5 star nozzle
5cm/2in plastic circus ornaments

1 Split and fill the cake with butter icing. Place on the cake board and brush with apricot jam. Cover with a layer of marzipan then sugarpaste icing.

2 Tint 115g/4oz/¾ cup sugarpaste icing pink, then roll into a rope and stick around the top edge of the cake with a little water.

3 Tint half the remaining sugarpaste icing red and half blue. Roll out each colour and cut into twelve 2.5cm/1in squares. Stick the squares alternately at an angle around the side of the cake with a little water. Pipe stars around the base of the cake with royal icing and stick in the edible silver balls.

4 Crush the digestive biscuits by pressing through a sieve to make the "sand" for the circus ring. Scatter over the top of the cake and place small circus ornaments on top.

Frog Prince Cake

Serves 8–10

20cm/8in round sponge cake
115g/4oz/½ cup butter icing
45ml/3 tbsp apricot jam, warmed and sieved
450g/1lb/3 cups marzipan
cornflour, for dusting
400g/1¼lb/3¾ cups sugarpaste icing
115g/4oz/¾ cup royal icing
green, red, black and gold food colouring

Materials/equipment

25cm/10in square cake board
glass
fine paintbrush

1 Split and fill the cake with butter icing. Cut in half and sandwich the halves together with apricot jam. Stand upright diagonally across the cake board. Brush the cake with apricot jam and cover with marzipan.

2 Tint 450g/1lb/3 cups of the sugarpaste icing green and cover the cake. Roll the remaining green sugarpaste icing into 1cm/½in diameter sausages. You will need two folded 20cm/8in lengths for the back legs and 14 10cm/4in lengths for the front legs and feet. Stick in place with a little royal icing. Roll balls for the eyes and stick in place.

3 Roll out the reserved sugarpaste icing and cut a 5 x 19cm/2 x 7½in strip. Cut out triangles along one edge to make the crown shape. Wrap around a glass dusted with cornflour and moisten the edges to join. Leave to dry.

4 Cut a 10cm/4in circle for the white shirt. Stick in place and trim the base edge. Cut white circles and stick to the eyes. Tint a little sugarpaste pink, roll into a sausage and stick on for the mouth. Tint the rest black and use for the pupils and the bow tie. Stick in place.

5 Paint the crown with gold food colouring, leave to dry, then stick into position with royal icing.

Ladybird Cake

Children will love this colourful and appealing ladybird, and it is very simple to make.

Serves 10–12

3-egg quantity quick-mix sponge cake
175g/6oz butter icing
60ml/4 tbsp lemon curd, warmed
icing sugar, for dusting
1kg/2¼ lb sugarpaste icing
food colourings
5 marshmallows
50g/2oz marzipan
2 pipe cleaners

1 Preheat the oven to 180°C/350°F/Gas 4. Grease and line the base of a 1.2 litre/2 pint/5 cup ovenproof bowl. Spoon in the cake mixture and smooth the surface. Bake for 55–60 minutes until a skewer comes out clean. Cool.

2 Cut the cake in half crossways and sandwich together with the butter icing. Cut vertically through the cake, about a third of the way in. Brush both pieces with the lemon curd.

3 Colour 450g/1lb of the sugarpaste icing red. Dust a work surface with icing sugar and roll out the icing to about 5mm/¼ in thick. Use to cover the larger piece of cake to make the body. Using a wooden skewer, make an indentation down the centre for the wings. Colour 350g/12oz of icing black, roll out three-quarters and use to cover the smaller piece of cake for the head. Place both cakes on a cakeboard, press together.

4 Roll out 50g/2oz icing and cut out two 5cm/2in circles for the eyes, stick to the head with water. Roll out the remaining black icing and cut out eight 4cm/1½ in circles. Use two of these for the eyes and stick the others on to the body.

5 Colour some icing green and squeeze through a garlic crusher to make grass. Flatten the marshmallows and stick a marzipan round in the centre of each. Colour pipe cleaners black and press a ball of black icing on to the end of each. Arrange grass on board, with the ladybird and decorations.

Spaceship Cake

Serves 10–12

25cm/10in square sponge cake
225g/8oz/1 cup butter icing
60ml/4 tbsp apricot jam, warmed and sieved
350g/12oz/2¼ cups marzipan
450g/1lb/3 cups sugarpaste icing
blue, red and black food colouring

Materials/equipment

30cm/12in square cake board
4 silver candles and holders
gold paper stars

1 Split and fill the sponge cake with butter icing. Cut a 10cm/4in wide piece diagonally across the middle of the cake, about 25cm/10in long. Shape the nose end and straighten the other end.

2 From the off-cuts make three 7.5cm/3in triangles for the wings and top of the ship. Cut two smaller triangles for the booster jets. Position the main body, wings and top of the cake diagonally across the board. Add extra pieces of cake in front of the top triangle. Brush the cake and booster jets with apricot jam, then cover with a layer of marzipan and sugarpaste icing.

3 Divide the remaining sugarpaste icing into three. Tint blue, pink and black. Roll out the blue icing and cut it into 1cm/½in strips. Stick around the base of the cake with water and outline the boosters. Cut a 2.5cm/1in strip and stick down the centre of the spaceship.

4 Roll out the pink and black sugarpaste icing separately and cut shapes, numbers and the child's name to finish the design. When complete, position the boosters.

5 Make small cubes with the off-cuts of sugarpaste icing and use to stick the candles to the cake board. Decorate the board with gold stars.

Racing Track Cake

This cake will delight eight-year-old racing car enthusiasts.

Serves 10–12

2 x 15cm/6in round sponge cakes
115g/4oz/½ cup butter icing
60ml/4 tbsp apricot jam, warmed and sieved
450g/1lb/3 cups marzipan
500g/1¼lb/3¾ cups sugarpaste icing
blue and red food colouring
115g/4oz/¾ cup royal icing

Materials/equipment

25 x 35cm/10 x 14in cake board
5cm/2in fluted cutter
2 small greaseproof paper piping bags
No 8 star and No 2 plain nozzles
8 candles and holders
2 small racing cars

1 Split and fill the cakes with a little butter icing. Cut off a 1cm/½in piece from the side of each cake and place the cakes on the cake board, cut edges together.

2 Brush the cake with apricot jam and cover with a layer of marzipan. Tint 450g/1lb/3 cups of the sugarpaste icing pale blue and use to cover the cake.

3 Mark a 5cm/2in circle in the centre of each cake. Roll out the remaining white sugarpaste icing and cut out two fluted 5cm/2in circles and stick them in the marked spaces.

4 Tint the royal icing red. Pipe a shell border around the base of the cake using the star nozzle. Pipe a track for the cars on the cake using the plain nozzle and stick the candles into the two white circles. Place the cars on the track.

Floating Balloons Cake

Makes one 20cm/8in round cake

20cm/8in round sponge or fruit cake, covered with 800g/1¾lb/5½ cups marzipan, if liked
900g/2lb/6 cups sugarpaste icing
red, green and yellow food colouring
3 eggs
2 egg whites
450g/1lb/4 cups icing sugar

Materials/equipment
25cm/10in round cake board
3 bamboo skewers, 25cm/10in, 24cm/9½in and 23cm/9in long
small star cutter
greaseproof paper piping bags
fine writing nozzle
1m/1yd fine coloured ribbon
8 candles

1 Place the cake on the board. Tint 50g/2oz/scant ½ cup of the sugarpaste icing red, 50g/2oz/scant ½ cup green and 115g/4oz/1 cup yellow. Cover the cake with the remaining icing. Use just under half the yellow icing to cover the board.

2 Using a skewer, pierce the eggs and carefully empty the contents. Wash and dry the shells. Cover them carefully with the tinted sugarpaste and insert a bamboo skewer in each. Use the trimmings to stamp out a star shape of each colour. Thread on to the skewers for the balloon knots.

3 Trace 16 balloon shapes on to baking paper. Beat the egg whites with the icing sugar until smooth and divide among four bowls. Leave one white and tint the others red, green and yellow. With the fine writing nozzle and white icing, trace round the balloon shapes. Thin the tinted icings with water. Fill the run-outs using snipped piping bags. Dry overnight.

4 Stick the run-outs around the side of the cake with icing. Pipe white balloon strings. Push the large balloons into the centre and decorate with the ribbon. Push the candles into the icing around the edge.

Number 6 Cake

Use the round cake tin as a guide to cut the square cake to fit neatly around the round cake.

Serves 10–12

15cm/6in round and 15cm/6in square sponge cakes
115g/4oz/½ cup butter icing
60ml/4 tbsp apricot jam, warmed and sieved
450g/1lb/3 cups marzipan
500g/1¼lb/3¾ cups sugarpaste icing
yellow and green food colouring
115g/4oz/¾ cup royal icing

Materials/equipment
25 x 35cm/10 x 14in cake board
2 small greaseproof paper piping bags
7.5cm/3in fluted cutter
No 1 plain and No 8 star nozzles
plastic train set with 6 candles

1 Split and fill the cakes with butter icing. Cut the square cake in half and cut, using the round cake tin as a guide, a rounded end from one rectangle to fit around the round cake. Trim the cakes to the same depth and assemble the number on the cake board. Brush with apricot jam and cover with a thin layer of marzipan.

2 Tint 450g/1lb/3 cups of the sugarpaste icing yellow and the rest green. Cover the cake with the yellow icing. With the cutter, mark a circle in the centre of the round cake. Cut out a green sugarpaste icing circle. Stick in place with water and leave to dry overnight.

3 Mark a track the width of the train on the top of the cake. Tint the royal icing yellow and pipe the track with the plain nozzle. Use the star nozzle to pipe a border around the base and top of the cake. Pipe the name on the green circle and attach the train and candles with royal icing.

Spider's Web Cake

Make the marzipan spider several days before you need the cake to give it time to dry.

Makes one 20cm/8in round cake

20cm/8in round deep sponge cake
225g/8oz/1 cup butter icing
45ml/3 tbsp apricot jam, warmed and sieved
30ml/2 tbsp cocoa powder
chocolate vermicelli
40g/1½oz/4 tbsp marzipan
yellow, red, black and brown food colouring
225g/8oz/1½ cups icing sugar
15–30ml/1–2 tbsp water

Materials/equipment

25cm/10in round cake board
2 small greaseproof paper piping bags
wooden cocktail stick
star nozzle
8 candles and holders

1 Split and fill the cake with half the butter icing. Brush the sides with apricot jam, add the cocoa to the remaining butter icing then smooth a little over the sides of the cake. Roll the sides of the cake in chocolate vermicelli. Place on the board.

2 For the spider, tint the marzipan yellow. Roll half of it into two balls for the head and body. Tint a small piece red and make three balls and a mouth. Tint a tiny piece black for the eyes. Roll the rest of the marzipan into eight legs and two smaller feelers. Stick together.

3 Gently heat the icing sugar and water over a pan of hot water. Use two-thirds of the glacé icing to cover the cake top.

4 Tint the remaining glacé icing brown and use it to pipe concentric circles on to the cake. Divide the web into eighths by drawing lines across with a cocktail stick. Leave to set.

5 Put the rest of the chocolate butter icing into a piping bag fitted with a star nozzle and pipe a border around the web. Put candles around the border and the spider in the centre.

Dart Board Cake

Makes one 25cm/10in round cake

25cm/10in round sponge cake
175g/6oz/¾ cup butter icing
5ml/3 tbsp apricot jam, warmed and sieved
450g/1lb/3 cups marzipan
450g/1lb/3 cups sugarpaste icing
115g/4oz/¾ cup royal icing
black, red, yellow and silver food colouring

Materials/equipment

30cm/12in round cake board
icing smoother
1cm/½in plain circle cutter
small greaseproof paper piping bag
No 1 writing nozzle
3 candles and holders

1 Split and fill the cake with butter icing and put on to the board. Brush with jam and cover with marzipan. Colour some of the sugarpaste icing black, a small piece red and the remaining yellow. Cover the cake with black sugarpaste icing. Cut a 20cm/8in circular template out of greaseproof paper. Fold it in quarters, then divide each quarter into fifths.

2 Using the template, mark the centre and wedges on the top of the cake with a sharp knife. Cut out ten wedges from the yellow sugarpaste, using the template as a guide. Place on alternate sections but do not stick in place yet. Repeat with the black sugarpaste. Cut 3mm/⅛in off each wedge and swop the colours. Mark a 13cm/5in circle in the centre of the board and cut out 3mm/⅛in pieces to swop with adjoining colours. Stick in place and use an icing smoother to flatten.

3 Use the cutter to remove the centre for the bull's eye. Replace with a circle of red sugarpaste, cut with the same cutter. Surround it with a strip of black sugarpaste. Roll the remaining black sugarpaste into a long sausage to fit round the base of the cake and stick in place with a little water. Mark numbers on the board and pipe on with royal icing. Leave to dry then paint with silver food colouring. Stick candles in at an angle to resemble darts.

Camping Tent Cake

Makes one 20 x 10cm/8 x 4in cake

20cm/8in square sponge cake
115g/4oz/½ cup butter icing
45ml/3 tbsp apricot jam, warmed and sieved
450g/1lb/3 cups marzipan
500g/1¼lb/3¾ cups sugarpaste icing
brown, orange, green, red and blue food colouring
115g/4oz/¾ cup royal icing
50g/2oz/1 cup desiccated coconut
chocolate mint sticks

Materials/equipment

25cm/10in square cake board
wooden cocktail sticks
fine paintbrush
4 small greaseproof paper piping bags
No 1 basketweave and plain nozzles

1 Split and fill the cake with butter icing. Cut the cake in half. Cut one half in two diagonally from the top right edge to the bottom left edge to form the roof of the tent. Stick the two wedges, back-to-back, on top of the rectangle with jam. Trim to 10cm/4in high and use the trimmings on the base. Place the cake diagonally on the board and brush with jam.

2 Cover with marzipan, reserving some for modelling. Tint 50g/2oz/scant ½ cup of the sugarpaste icing brown and cover one end of the tent. Tint the rest orange and cover the rest of the cake. Cut a semicircle for the tent opening and a central 7.5cm/3in slit. Lay over the brown end. Secure the flaps with royal icing. Put halved cocktail sticks in the corners and ridge.

3 Tint the coconut green. Spread the board with a thin layer of royal icing and sprinkle with the coconut.

4 Tint the reserved marzipan flesh-colour and use to make a model of a child. Paint on a blue T-shirt and leave to dry. Tint some royal icing brown and pipe on the hair with a basketweave nozzle. Tint the icing and pipe on the mouth and eyes. Make a bonfire with broken chocolate mint sticks.

Army Tank Cake

Create an authentic camouflaged tank by combining green and brown sugarpaste icing.

Makes one 25 x 15cm/10 x 6in cake

25cm/10in square sponge cake
225g/8oz/1 cup butter icing
45ml/3 tbsp apricot jam, warmed and sieved
450g/1lb/3 cups marzipan
450g/1lb/3 cups sugarpaste icing
brown, green and black food colouring
chocolate flake
liquorice strips
60ml/4 tbsp royal icing
round biscuits
sweets

Materials/equipment

25 x 35cm/10 x 14in cake board

1 Split and fill the sponge cake with butter icing. Cut off a 10cm/4in strip from one side of the cake. Use the off-cut to make a 15 x 7.5cm/6 x 3in rectangle, and stick on the top.

2 Shape the sloping top and cut a 2.5cm/1in piece from both ends between the tracks. Shape the rounded ends for the wheels and tracks. Place on the cake board and brush with apricot jam. Cover with a layer of marzipan.

3 Tint a quarter of the sugarpaste icing brown and the rest green. Roll out the green to a 25cm/10in square. Break small pieces of brown icing and place all over the green. Flatten and roll out together to give a camouflage effect. Turn the icing over and repeat.

4 Continue to roll out until the icing is 3mm/⅛in thick. Lay it over the cake and gently press to fit. Cut away the excess. Cut a piece into a 6cm/2½in disc and stick on the top with a little water. Cut a small hole in it for the gun and insert the chocolate flake. Stick liquorice on for the tracks, using a little black royal icing. Stick on biscuits for the wheels and sweets for the lights and portholes.

Computer Game Cake

Making a cake look like a computer is easier than you think. This cake is ideal for a computer game fanatic.

Makes one 14 x 13cm/5½ x 5in cake

15cm/6in square sponge cake
115g/4oz/½ cup butter icing
45ml/3 tbsp apricot jam, warmed and sieved
225g/8oz/1½ cups marzipan
275g/10oz/scant 2 cups sugarpaste icing
black, blue, red and yellow food colouring
royal icing, to decorate

Materials/equipment

20cm/8in square cake board
wooden cocktail stick
fine paintbrush
small greaseproof paper piping bag

1 Split and fill the cake with a little butter icing. Cut 2.5cm/1in off one side of the cake and 1cm/½in off the other side. Round the corners slightly. Place on the cake board and brush with apricot jam. Cover with a layer of marzipan.

2 Tint 225g/8oz/1½ cups of the sugarpaste black. Use to cover the cake. Reserve the trimmings. With a cocktail stick, mark the speaker holes and position of the screen and knobs.

3 Tint half the remaining sugarpaste pale blue, roll out and cut out a 6cm/2½in square for the screen. Stick in the centre of the game with a little water. Tint a small piece of sugarpaste red and the rest yellow. Use to cut out the switch and controls. Stick them in position with water. Roll the reserved black sugarpaste icing into a long, thin sausage and edge the screen and base of the cake.

4 With a fine paintbrush, draw the game on to the screen with a little blue colouring. Pipe letters on to the buttons with royal icing.

Chessboard Cake

To make this cake look most effective, ensure that the squares have very sharp edges.

Makes one 25cm/10in square cake

25cm/10in square sponge cake
225g/8oz/1 cup butter icing
60ml/4 tbsp apricot jam, warmed and sieved
800g/1¾lb/5¼ cups marzipan
500g/1¼lb/3¾ cups sugarpaste icing
black and red food colouring
edible silver balls
115g/4oz/¾ cup royal icing

Materials/equipment

30cm/12in square cake board
small greaseproof paper piping bag
No 8 star nozzle

1 Split and fill the cake with butter icing. Place on the board and brush with jam. Roll out 450g/1lb/3 cups of marzipan and use to cover the cake. Then cover with 450g/1lb/3 cups of the sugarpaste icing. Leave to dry overnight.

2 Divide the remaining marzipan into two, and tint black and red. To shape the chess pieces, roll 50g/2oz/4 tbsp of each colour into a sausage and cut into eight equal pieces. Shape into pawns.

3 Divide 75g/3oz/generous 4 tbsp of each colour into six equal pieces and use to shape into two castles, two knights and two bishops.

4 Divide 25g/1oz/2 tbsp of each colour marzipan in half and shape a queen and a king. Decorate with silver balls. Leave to dry overnight.

5 Cut 1cm/½in black strips of marzipan to edge the board and stick in place with water. Pipe a border round the base of the cake with royal icing. Place the chess pieces in position.

Kite Cake

The happy face on this cheerful kite is a great favourite with children of all ages.

Serves 10–12

25cm/10in square sponge cake
225g/8oz/1 cup butter icing
45ml/3 tbsp apricot jam, warmed and sieved
675g/1½lb/4½ cups sugarpaste icing
yellow, red, green, blue and black food colouring
450g/1lb/3 cups marzipan
115g/4oz/¾ cup royal icing

Materials/equipment

30cm/12in square cake board
wooden cocktail stick
small greaseproof paper piping bag
No 8 star nozzle
6 candles and holders

1 Trim the cake into a kite shape, then split and fill with butter icing. Place diagonally on the cake board and brush with apricot jam. Cover with a layer of marzipan

2 Tint 225g/8oz/1½ cups of the sugarpaste icing pale yellow and cover the cake. Make a template of the face, tie and buttons and mark on to the cake with a cocktail stick. Divide the rest of the sugarpaste icing into four and tint red, green, blue and black. Cut out the features and stick on with water.

3 Pipe a royal icing border around the base of the cake.

4 For the kite's tail, roll out each colour separately and cut two 4 x 1cm/1½ x ½in lengths in blue, red and green. Pinch each length to shape into a bow.

5 Roll the yellow into a long rope and lay it on the board in a wavy line from the narrow end of the kite. Stick the bows in place with water. Roll balls of yellow sugarpaste, stick on the board with a little royal icing and press in the candles.

Hotdog Cake

Makes one 23cm/9in long cake

23 x 33cm/9 x 13in Swiss roll sponge
175g/6oz/¾ cup coffee flavour butter icing
90ml/6 tbsp apricot jam, warmed and sieved
450g/1lb/3 cups sugarpaste icing
brown and red food colouring
15–30ml/1–2 tbsp toasted sesame seeds
115g/4oz/¾ cup glacé icing

Filling

175g/6oz sponge cake pieces
50g/2oz/¼ cup dark brown sugar
45ml/3tbsp orange juice
75ml/5tbsp honey

Materials/equipment

fine paintbrush
2 small greaseproof paper piping bags
napkin, plate, knife and fork

1 Unroll the Swiss roll, spread with butter icing, then roll up again. Slice the Swiss roll along the centre lengthways, almost to the base and ease the two halves apart.

2 Mix all the filling ingredients in a food processor or blender until smooth. Shape the mixture with your hands to a 23cm/9in sausage shape.

3 Tint all the sugarpaste icing brown. Set aside 50g/2oz/scant ½ cup and use the rest to cover the cake.

4 Paint the top of the "bun" with diluted brown food colouring to give a toasted effect. Position the "sausage".

5 Divide the glacé icing in half. Tint one half brown and the other red. Pipe red icing along the sausage, then overlay with brown icing. Sprinkle the sesame seeds over the "bun".

6 Cut the reserved brown sugarpaste icing into thin strips. Place on the cake with the joins under the "sausage". Place the cake on a napkin on a serving plate, with a knife and fork.

Drum Cake

This is a colourful cake for very young children. It even comes complete with drumsticks.

Makes one 15cm/6in round cake

15cm/6in round sponge cake
50g/2oz/4 tbsp butter icing
45ml/3 tbsp apricot jam, warmed and served
350g/12oz/2cups marzipan
450g/1lb/3 cups sugarpaste icing
red, blue and yellow food colouring
royal icing, for sticking

Materials/equipment

20cm/8in round cake board

1 Split and fill the cake with a little butter icing. Place on the cake board and brush with apricot jam. Cover with a layer of marzipan and leave to dry overnight.

2 Tint half of the sugarpaste icing red and roll it out to 25 x 30cm/10 x 12in. Cut in half and stick to the side of the cake with water.

3 Roll out a circle of white sugarpaste icing to fit the top of the cake and divide the rest in half. Tint one half blue and the other yellow. Divide the blue into four pieces and roll into sausages long enough to go halfway round the cake. Stick around the base and top of the cake with a little water.

4 Mark the cake into six around the top and base. Roll the yellow sugarpaste icing into 12 strands long enough to cross diagonally from top to base to form the drum strings. Roll the rest of the yellow icing into 12 small balls and stick where the strings join the drum.

5 Knead together the red and white sugarpaste icing until streaky, then roll two balls and sticks 15cm/6in long. Leave to dry overnight. Stick together with royal icing to make the drumsticks and place on top of the cake.

Ice Cream Cones

Individual cakes make a change for a party. Put a candle in the special person's one.

Makes 9

115g/4oz/¾ cup marzipan
9 ice cream cones
9 sponge fairy cakes
350g/12oz/1½ cups butter icing
red, green and brown food colouring
coloured and chocolate vermicelli, wafers and chocolate sticks
sweets

Materials/equipment

3 12-egg egg boxes
foil

1 Make the stands for the cakes by turning the egg boxes upside down and pressing three balls of marzipan into evenly spaced holes in each box. Wrap the boxes in foil. Pierce the foil above the marzipan balls and insert the cones, pressing them in gently.

2 Gently push a fairy cake into each cone. If the bases of the cakes are too large, trim them down with a small, sharp knife. The cakes should be quite secure in the cones.

3 Divide the butter icing into three bowls and tint them pale red, green and brown.

4 Using a small palette knife, spread each cake with some of one of the icings, making sure that the finish on the icing is a little textured so it looks like ice cream.

5 To insert a wafer or chocolate stick into an ice cream, use a small, sharp knife to make a hole through the icing and into the cake, then insert the wafer or stick. Add the finishing touches to the cakes by sprinkling over some coloured and chocolate vermicelli. Arrange sweets around the cones.

Treasure Map

Makes one 20 x 25cm/8 x 10in cake

25cm/10in square sponge cake
225g/8oz/1½ cups butter icing
45ml/3 tbsp apricot jam, warmed and sieved
450g/1lb/3 cups marzipan
675g/1½lb/4½ cups sugarpaste icing
yellow, brown, paprika, green, black and red food colouring
115g/4oz/¾ cup royal icing

Materials/equipment

25 x 35cm/10 x 14in cake board
fine paintbrush
kitchen paper
4 small greaseproof paper piping bags
No 7 shell and No 1 writing nozzles
6 candles and holders

1 Split and fill the cake with butter icing, cut it into a 20 x 25cm/8 x 10in rectangle and place on the cake board. Brush with apricot jam. Cover with a layer of marzipan then with 450g/1lb/3cups sugarpaste icing.

2 Colour the remaining sugarpaste icing yellow and cut out with an uneven outline. Stick on to the cake with water and leave to dry overnight. Mark the island, river, lake, mountains and trees on the map.

3 With brown and paprika colours and a fine paintbrush, paint the edges of the map to look old, smudging the colours together with kitchen paper. Paint the island pale green and the water around the island, the river and the lake pale blue. Dry overnight before painting on the other details, otherwise the colours will run.

4 Pipe a border of royal icing around the base of the cake with a shell nozzle. Colour a little royal icing red and pipe the path to the treasure, marked with an "X". Colour some icing green and pipe on grass and trees. Finally colour some icing black and pipe on a North sign with the writing nozzle.

Royal Crown Cake

This regal cake is sure to delight any prince or princess.

Serves 16–20

20cm/8in and 15cm/6in round sponge cake
175g/6oz/¾ cup butter icing
45ml/3 tbsp apricot jam, warmed and sieved
450g/1lb/3 cups marzipan
500g/1¼lb/3¾ cups sugarpaste icing
red food colouring
450g/1lb/3 cups royal icing
small black jelly sweets
4 ice cream fan wafers
edible silver balls
jewel sweets

Materials/equipment

30cm/12in square cake board
wooden cocktail sticks

1 Split and fill the cakes with butter icing. Sandwich one on top of the other and place on the board. Shape the top cake into a dome.

2 Brush the cake with apricot jam and cover with marzipan. Set aside 115g/4oz/¾ cup of the sugarpaste icing and use the rest to cover the cake.

3 Tint the reserved sugarpaste icing red, and use to cover the dome of the cake. Trim away the excess.

4 Spoon rough mounds of royal icing around the base of the cake and stick a black jelly sweet on each mound.

5 Cut the ice cream wafers in half. Spread both sides of the wafers with royal icing and stick to the cake, smoothing the icing level with the sides of the cake.

6 Use cocktail sticks to support the wafers until they are dry. Put silver balls on top of each point and stick jewel sweets around the side of the crown with a little royal icing.

Box of Chocolates Cake

This sophisticated cake is perfect for an adult's birthday and will delight chocolate lovers.

Makes one 15cm/6in square cake

15cm/6in square sponge cake
50g/2oz/4 tbsp butter icing
30ml/2 tbsp apricot jam, warmed and sieved
350g/12oz/2¼ cups marzipan
350g/12oz/2¼ cups sugarpaste icing
red food colouring
wrapped chocolates

Materials/equipment

20cm/8in square cake board
small paper sweet cases
1.30m/1½yd x 4cm/1½in-wide gold and red ribbon

1 Split and fill the cake with butter icing. Cut a shallow square from the top of the cake, leaving a 1cm/¼in border around the edge. Place on the cake board and brush with apricot jam. Cover with a layer of marzipan.

2 Roll out the sugarpaste icing and cut an 18cm/7in square. Ease it into the hollow dip and trim. Tint the remaining sugarpaste icing red and use to cover the sides.

3 Put the chocolates into paper cases and arrange in the box. Tie the ribbon around the sides and tie a big bow.

Strawberry Cake

Makes one 900g/2lb cake

650g/1lb 7oz/scant 4½ cups marzipan
green, red and yellow food colouring
30ml/2 tbsp apricot jam, warmed and sieved
900g/2lb heart-shaped sponge cake
caster sugar, for dusting

Materials/equipment

30cm/12in round cake board
icing smoother
teaspoon

1 Tint 175g/6oz/generous 1 cup of the marzipan green. Brush the cake board with apricot jam, roll out the green marzipan and use to cover the board. Trim the edges. Use an icing smoother to flatten and smooth the marzipan.

2 Brush the remaining apricot jam over the top and sides of the cake. Position the cake on the cake board. Tint 275g/10oz/scant 2 cups of the remaining marzipan red. Roll it out to 5mm/¼in thick and use to cover the cake, smoothing down the sides. Trim the edges. Use the handle of a teaspoon to indent the "strawberry" evenly and lightly all over.

3 For the stalk, tint 175g/6oz/generous 1 cup of the marzipan bright green. Cut it in half and roll out one portion into a 10 x 15cm/4 x 6in rectangle. Cut "V" shapes out of the rectangle, leaving a 2.5cm/1in border across the top, to form the calyx. Position on the cake, curling the "V" shapes to make them look realistic.

4 Roll the rest of the green marzipan into a sausage shape 13cm/5in long. Bend it slightly, then position it on the board to form the stalk.

5 For the strawberry pips, tint the remaining marzipan yellow. Pull off tiny pieces and roll them into tear-shaped pips. Place them in the indentations all over the strawberry. Dust the cake and board with sifted caster sugar.

Gift-wrapped Parcel

If you don't have a tiny flower cutter for the "wrapping paper" design, then press a small decorative button into the icing while still soft to create a pattern.

Makes one 15cm/6in square cake

15cm/6in square cake
50g/2oz/4 tbsp butter icing
45ml/3 tbsp apricot jam, warmed and served
450g/1lb/3 cups marzipan
350g/12oz/2¼ cups pale lemon yellow fondant icing
red and green food colouring
30ml/2 tbsp royal icing

Materials/equipment

20cm/8in square cake board
small flower cutter (optional)

1 Split and fill the cake with butter icing. Place on the cake board and brush with jam. Cover with half the marzipan, then yellow fondant and mark with a small flower cutter.

2 Divide the remaining marzipan in half, colour one half pink and the other pale green. Roll out the pink marzipan and cut into four 2.5 x 18cm/1 x 7in strips. Roll out the green marzipan and cut into four 1cm/½in strips the same length. Centre the green strips on top of the pink strips and stick on to the cake with a little water. Cut two 5cm/2in strips from each colour and cut a "V" from the ends to form the ends of the ribbon. Stick in place and leave to dry overnight.

3 Cut the rest of the green into four 2.5 x 7.5cm/1 x 3in lengths and the pink into four 1 x 7.5cm/½ x 3in lengths. Centre the pink on top of the green, fold in half, stick ends together and slip over the handle of a wooden spoon, dusted with cornflour. Leave to dry overnight.

4 Cut the ends in "V" shapes to fit neatly together on the cake. Cut two pieces for the join in the centre. Remove the bows from the spoon and stick in position with royal icing.

Sweetheart Cake

The heart-shaped run-outs can be made a week before the cake is made to ensure that they are completely dry.

Makes one 20cm/8in round cake

20cm/8in round sponge cake
115g/4oz/½ cup butter icing
45ml/3 tbsp apricot jam, warmed and served
450g/1lb/3 cups marzipan
675g/1½lb/4½ cups sugarpaste icing
red food colouring
115g/4oz/¾ cup royal icing

Materials/equipment

25cm/10in round cake board
spoon with decorative handle
small greaseproof paper piping bag
No 1 writing nozzle
8 candles and holders
1.5m/1½yd x 2.5cm/1in wide ribbon

1 Split and fill the cake with butter icing. Place on the cake board and brush with apricot jam. Cover with a layer of marzipan. Tint the sugarpaste icing pale pink and cover the cake and board. Mark the edge with the decorative handle of a spoon.

2 Tint the royal icing dark pink. Make a heart-shaped template and use to pipe the run-outs on greaseproof paper. Using a No 1 writing nozzle, pipe the outlines in a continuous line. Then fill in until the hearts are rounded. You will need eight for the cake top. Leave to dry for at least 2 days.

3 Arrange the hearts on top of the cake and place the candles in the centre. Tie the ribbon round the cake.

Rosette Cake

This cake is quick to decorate and looks truly professional.

Makes one 20cm/8in square cake

20cm/8in square sponge cake
450g/1lb/2 cups butter icing
60ml/4 tbsp apricot jam, warmed and sieved
mulberry red food colouring
crystallized violets

Materials/equipment

25cm/10in square cake board
serrated scraper
piping bag
No 8 star nozzle
4 candles and holders

1 Split and fill the cake with a little butter icing. Place in the centre of the cake board and brush with apricot jam. Tint the remaining butter icing dark pink. Spread the top and sides with butter icing.

2 Using the serrated scraper, hold it against the cake and move it from side to side across the top to make waves. Hold the scraper against the side of the cake, resting the flat edge on the board and draw it along to give straight ridges along each side.

3 Put the rest of the butter icing into a piping bag fitted with a No 8 star nozzle. Mark a 15cm/6in circle on the top of the cake and pipe stars around it and around the base of the cake. Place the candles and violets in the corners.

Number 10 Cake

This is a very simple cake to decorate. If you can't master the shell edge, pipe stars instead.

Makes one 20cm/8in tall round cake

20cm/8in and 15cm/6in round sponge cakes
450g/1lb/2 cups butter icing
75ml/5 tbsp apricot jam, warmed and sieved
coloured vermicelli
cream food colouring

Materials/equipment

25cm/10in round cake board
wooden cocktail stick
plastic "10" cake decoration
small greaseproof paper piping bag
No 7 shell and No 7 star nozzles
10 candles and holders

1 Split and fill both cakes with a little butter icing. Brush the sides with apricot jam. When cold, spread a layer of butter icing on the sides then roll in coloured vermicelli to cover.

2 Tint the rest of the icing cream, spread over the top of each cake. Place the small cake on top of the large cake. Using a cocktail stick, make a pattern in the icing on top of the cake.

3 Using the remaining icing, pipe around the base of the cakes and around the edge. Stick the "10" decoration in the centre of the top tier and two candles on either side. Arrange the other candles evenly around the base cake.

Shirt and Tie Cake

Makes one 19 x 26.5cm/7½ x 10½in cake

coffee sponge cake, baked in a 19 x 26.5cm/ 7½ x 5in loaf tin
350g/12oz/1½ cups coffee-flavour butter icing
90ml/6 tbsp apricot jam, warmed and sieved
good 1kg/2lb 6oz/7 cups sugarpaste icing
blue food colouring
125g/4oz/1 cup icing sugar, sifted
45–60ml/3–4 tbsp water

Materials/equipment
30 x 39cm/15½ x 12in cake board
steel ruler
small greaseproof paper piping bag
small round nozzle
card collar template
"Happy Birthday" decoration
tissue paper (optional)

1 Cut the cake in half horizontally and sandwich together with the butter icing. Brush the cake with apricot jam. Colour 675g/1½lb/4½ cups sugarpaste icing light blue and roll out to about 5mm/¼in thick. Use to cover the whole cake. Trim away any excess icing. Place the cake on the cake board.

2 Using a steel ruler, make grooves down the length and sides of the cake, about 2.5cm/1in apart. Mix the icing sugar and water to make a glacé icing to pipe into the grooves.

3 To make the collar, roll out 225g/8oz/1½ cups sugarpaste icing to a 40.5 x 10cm/16½ x 4in rectangle. Lay the piece of card for the collar on top. Brush water around the edges, then carefully lift one edge over the card to encase it completely. Trim the two short ends to match the angles of the card. Lift the collar and gently bend it round and position on the cake.

4 Colour 175g/6oz/1 cup sugarpaste icing dark blue. Cut off one-third and shape into a tie knot. Position the knot. Roll out the rest to about 5mm/½in thick. Cut out a tie piece to fit under the knot and long enough to hang over the edge of the cake. Position the tie piece, tucking it under the knot and securing in place with a little water. Finish the cake with the "Happy Birthday" decoration and tissue paper, if using.

Mobile Phone Cake

Makes one 23 x 13cm/9 x 5in cake

sponge cake, baked in a 23 x 13cm/9 x 5in loaf tin
30ml/2 tbsp apricot jam, warmed and sieved
375g/13oz/2¼ cups sugarpaste icing
black food colouring
10 small square sweets
2 striped liquorice sweets
30–45ml/2–3 tbsp icing sugar
2.5–5ml/½–1 tsp water

Materials/equipment
25 x 18cm/10 x 7in cake board
diamond-shaped biscuit cutter
small piece of foil
small greaseproof paper piping bag
small round nozzle

1 Turn the cake upside-down. Make a 2.5cm/1in diagonal cut 2.5cm/1in from one end. Cut down vertically to remove the wedge. Remove the middle of the cake to the wedge depth up to 4cm/1½in from the other end.

2 Place the cake on the board and brush with apricot jam. Tint 275g/10oz/1¼ cups of the sugarpaste icing black. Use to cover the cake, smoothing it over the carved shape. Reserve the trimmings.

3 Tint 75g/3oz/ ½ cup of the sugarpaste icing grey. Cut a piece to fit the hollowed centre, leaving a 1cm/ ½in border, and another piece 2.5cm/1in square. Stamp out the centre of the square with the cutter. Secure all the pieces on the cake with water.

4 Position the sweets and the foil for the display pad. For the glacé icing, mix the icing sugar with the water and tint black. With the small round nozzle, pipe border lines around the edges of the phone, including the grey pieces of sugarpaste. Pipe the numbers on the keys.

5 Roll a sausage shape from the reserved black sugarpaste for the aerial. Indent one side of the top with a knife and secure the aerial with water.

Heart Cake

Makes one 20cm/8in heart-shaped cake

3 egg whites
350g/12oz/1¾ cups caster sugar
30ml/2 tbsp cold water
30ml/2 tbsp fresh lemon juice
1.5ml/¼ tsp cream of tartar
red food colouring
20cm/8in heart-shaped sponge cake
85–115g/3–4oz/¾–1 cup icing sugar

Materials/equipment

30cm/12in square cake board
small greaseproof piping bag
small nozzle

1 Make the icing by combining 2 of the egg whites, the caster sugar, water, lemon juice and cream of tartar in the top of a double boiler or in a bowl set over simmering water. With an electric mixer, beat until thick and holding soft peaks, about 7 minutes. Remove from the heat and continue beating until the mixture is thick enough to spread. Colour the icing pale pink.

2 Put the cake on the cake board and spread the icing evenly on the cake. Smooth the top and sides. Leave to set for 3–4 hours, or overnight.

3 Place 1 tbsp of the remaining egg white in a bowl and whisk until frothy. Gradually beat in enough icing sugar to make a stiff mixture suitable for piping.

4 Spoon the white icing into a piping bag and pipe the decorations on the top and sides of the cake as shown in the photograph above.

Bowl-of-Strawberries Cake

The strawberry theme of the painting is carried on into the moulded decorations on this summery birthday cake.

Makes one 20cm/8in petal-shaped cake

350g/12oz/1½ cups butter icing
red, yellow, green and claret food colouring
20cm/8in petal-shaped Madeira cake
45ml/3 tbsp apricot jam, warmed and sieved
675g/1½lb/4½ cups sugarpaste icing
yellow powder tint

Materials/equipment

25cm/10in petal-shaped cake board
paint palette or small saucers
fine paintbrushes
thin red and green ribbons

1 Tint the butter icing pink. Cut the cake horizontally into three. Sandwich together with the butter icing. Brush the cake with apricot jam. Use 500g/1¼lb/3¾ cups of the sugarpaste icing to cover the cake. Place on the cake board and leave to dry overnight.

2 For the strawberries, tint three-quarters of the remaining sugarpaste icing red, and equal portions of the rest yellow and green. Make the strawberries, securing with water if necessary. Leave to dry on greaseproof paper.

3 Put the red, green, yellow and claret food colouring in a palette and water them down slightly. Paint the bowl and strawberries, using yellow powder tint to highlight the bowl.

4 Decorate the cake with the ribbons. Secure two strawberries to the top of the cake, and arrange the others around the base.

Barley Twist Cake

Makes one 20cm/8in round cake

20cm/8in round sponge cake
115g/4oz/½ cup butter icing
45ml/3 tbsp apricot jam, warmed and sieved
450/1lb/3 cups marzipan
450g/1lb/3 cups pale yellow sugarpaste icing
115g/4oz/¾ cup white sugarpaste icing
115g/4oz/¾ cup royal icing
blue food colouring
pink dusting powder

Materials/equipment

25cm/10in round cake board
wooden cocktail stick
fine paintbrush
No 1 plain nozzle
small greaseproof paper piping bags
6 small blue bows

1 Split and fill the cake with butter icing. Place on the board and brush with jam. Cover with marzipan, then yellow sugarpaste icing, extending it over the board. Mark six equidistant points around the cake with a cocktail stick.

2 Colour 40g/½oz/1 tbsp of white sugarpaste icing pale blue and roll out thinly. Moisten a paintbrush with water and brush lightly over it. Roll out the same quantity of white icing, lay on top and press together. Roll out to a 20cm/8in square.

3 Cut 5mm/¼in strips, carefully twist each one, moisten the six marked points around the cake with water and drape each barley twist into place, pressing lightly to stick to the cake.

4 Cut out a jersey shape from white icing and stick on with water. Roll some icing into a ball and colour a small amount dark blue. Roll into two tapering 7.5cm/3in needles with a small ball at the end. Dry overnight. Stick the needles and ball in position. Using royal icing and a No 1 nozzle, pipe the stitches and wool in position. Pipe a white border around the base of the cake. Stick small bows around the edge of the cake with a little royal icing and carefully brush the knitting with red powder tint.

Tablecloth Cake

Makes one 20cm/8in round cake

20cm/8in round sponge cake
115g/4oz/½ cup butter icing
45ml/3 tbsp apricot jam, warmed and sieved
450g/1lb/3 cups marzipan
675g/1½lb/4½ cups sugarpaste icing
115g/4oz/¾ cup royal icing
red food colouring

Materials/equipment

25cm/10in round cake board
spoon with decorative handle
8 wooden cocktail sticks
sharp needle
skewer
8 red ribbon bows
small greaseproof paper piping bags
No 2 and No 0 plain nozzles

1 Split and fill the cake with butter icing. Place on the board and brush with apricot jam. Cover with a layer of marzipan. Tint 450g/1lb/3 cups of the sugarpaste icing red and cover the cake and board. Roll the rest of the red fondant into a thin rope long enough to go round the cake. Stick around the base of the cake with water. Mark with the decorative handle of a spoon. Leave to dry overnight.

2 Roll out the remaining icing to a 25cm/10in circle and trim. Lay this icing over the cake and drape the "cloth" over the wooden cocktail sticks set at equidistant points.

3 Mark a 10cm/4in circle in the centre of the cake. Make a template of the flower design and transfer to the cake with a needle. Use a skewer to make the flowers; the red colour should show through.

4 Remove the cocktail sticks and stick on the bows with royal icing. With a No 2 plain nozzle and white royal icing pipe around the circle in the centre. With a No 0 plain nozzle, pipe small dots around the edge of the cloth. Colour some royal icing red and pipe a name in the centre.

Pizza Cake

Quick and easy, this really is a definite winner for pizza fanatics everywhere.

Makes one 23cm/9in round cake

23cm/9in shallow sponge cake
350g/12oz/1½ cups butter icing
red and green food colouring
175g/6oz/generous 1 cup yellow marzipan
25g/1oz/4 tbsp sugarpaste icing
15ml/1 tbsp desiccated coconut

Materials/equipment

25cm/10in pizza plate
cheese grater
leaf cutter

1 Place the cake on the pizza plate. Tint the butter icing red and spread evenly over the cake, leaving a 1cm/ ½in border.

2 Knead the marzipan for a few minutes, to soften slightly, then grate it like cheese, and sprinkle all over the top of the red butter icing.

3 Tint the sugarpaste icing green. Use the leaf cutter to cut out two leaf shapes. Mark the veins with the back of a knife and place on the pizza cake.

4 For the chopped herbs, tint the desiccated coconut dark green. Then scatter over the pizza cake.

Flowerpot Cake

Makes one round cake

Madeira cake, baked in a 1.2-litre/2-pint/5-cup pudding basin
175g/6oz/½ cup jam
175g/6oz/¾ cup butter icing
30ml/2 tbsp apricot jam, warmed and sieved
575g/1¼lb/4¼ cups sugarpaste icing
125g/4oz/¾ cup royal icing
dark orange-red, red, silver, green, purple and yellow food colouring
2 chocolate flakes, coarsely crushed

Materials/equipment

fine paintbrush
wooden spoon

1 Slice the cake into three layers and stick together again with jam and butter icing. Cut out a shallow circle from the cake top, leaving a 1cm/ ½in rim. Brush the outside of the cake and rim with apricot jam. Tint 400g/14oz/2¼ cups of the sugarpaste orange-red and cover the cake, moulding it over the rim. Reserve the trimmings. Leave to dry.

2 Use the trimmings to make decorations and handles for the flowerpot. Leave to dry on greaseproof paper. Sprinkle the chocolate flakes into the pot for soil.

3 Tint a small piece of sugarpaste very pale orange-red. Use to make a seed bag. When dry, paint on a pattern in food colouring. Tint two small pieces of icing red and silver. Make a trowel and dry over a wooden spoon handle.

4 Tint the remaining icing green, purple and a small piece yellow. Use to make the flowers and leaves, attaching together with royal icing. Score leaf veins with the back of a knife. Leave to dry on greaseproof paper.

5 Attach all the decorations to the flowerpot and arrange the plant, seed bag and trowel with soil, seeds and grass made from leftover tinted sugarpaste.

Glittering Star Cake

With a quick flick of a paintbrush you can give a sparkling effect to this glittering cake.

Makes one 20cm/8in round cake

20cm/8in round rich fruit cake
40ml/2½ tbsp apricot jam, warmed and sieved
675g/1½lb/4½ cups marzipan
450g/1lb/4 cups sugarpaste icing
115g/4oz/¾ cup royal icing
silver, gold, lilac shimmer, red sparkle, glitter green and primrose sparkle food colouring and powder tints

Materials/equipment

paintbrush
25cm/10in round cake board

1 Brush the cake with the apricot jam. Use two-thirds of the marzipan to cover the cake. Leave to dry overnight.

2 Cover the cake with the sugarpaste icing. Leave to dry.

3 Place the cake on a large sheet of greaseproof paper. Dilute a little powdered silver food colouring and, using a loaded paintbrush, flick it all over the cake to give a spattered effect. Allow to dry.

4 Make templates of two different-size moon shapes and three irregular star shapes. Divide the remaining marzipan into six pieces and tint silver, gold, lilac, pink, green and yellow. Cut into stars and moons using the templates as a guide, cutting some of the stars in half.

5 Place the cut-outs on greaseproof paper, brush each with its own colour powder tint. Allow to dry.

6 Secure the cake on the board with royal icing. Arrange the stars and moons at different angles all over the cake, attaching with royal icing, and position the halved stars upright as though coming out of the cake. Allow to set.

Racing Ring Cake

Serves 12

ring mould sponge cake
350g/12oz/1½ cups butter icing
500g/1lb 2oz/4⅛ cups sugarpaste icing
125g/4oz/¾ cup royal icing, for fixing
black, blue, yellow, green, orange, red, purple food colouring
selection of liquorice sweets, dolly mixtures and teddy bears
113g/4½oz packet liquorice Catherine wheels

Materials/equipment

25cm/10in round cake board
wooden kebab skewer
fine paintbrush

1 Cut the cake in half horizontally and fill with some butter icing. Cover the outside with the remaining butter icing.

2 Use 350g/12oz/2¼ cups of sugarpaste icing to coat the top and inside of the cake. Use the trimmings to roll an oblong for the flag. Cut the skewer to 12.5cm/5in and fold one end of the flag around it, securing with water. Paint on the pattern with black food colouring. Colour a ball of icing black, and stick on top of the skewer. Make a few folds and leave to dry.

3 Colour the remaining sugarpaste icing blue, yellow, green, orange, red and a very small amount purple. Shape each car in two pieces, attaching in the centre with royal icing where the seat joins the body of the car. Add decorations and headlights and attach dolly mixture wheels with royal icing. Place a teddy bear in each car and leave to set.

4 Unwind the Catherine wheels and remove the centre sweets. Fix them to the top of the cake with royal icing. Secure one strip round the bottom. Cut some of the liquorice into small strips and attach round the middle of the outside of the cake with royal icing. Arrange small liquorice sweets around the bottom of the cake. Position the cars on top of the cake on the tracks and attach the flag to the outside with royal icing.

Artist's Cake

Making cakes is an art in itself, and this cake proves it!

Makes one 20cm/8in square cake

20cm/8in square rich fruit cake
45ml/3 tbsp apricot jam, warmed and sieved
450g/1lb/3 cups marzipan
800g/1¾lb/5¼ cups sugarpaste icing
115g/4oz/¾ cup royal icing
chestnut, yellow, blue, black, silver, paprika, green and mulberry food colouring

Materials/equipment

25cm/10in square cake board
fine paintbrush

1 Brush the cake with the apricot jam. Cover in marzipan and leave to dry overnight.

2 Make a template of a painter's palette that will fit the cake top. Tint 175g/6oz/generous 1 cup of the sugarpaste very pale chestnut. Cut out the palette shape, place on greaseproof paper and leave to dry overnight.

3 Tint 450g/1lb/3 cups of the sugarpaste icing dark chestnut. Use to cover the cake. Secure the cake on the board with royal icing. Leave to dry.

4 Divide half the remaining sugarpaste icing into seven equal parts and tint yellow, blue, black, silver, paprika, green and mulberry. Make all the decorative pieces for the box and palette, using the remaining white sugarpaste for the paint tubes. Leave to dry on greaseproof paper.

5 Paint black markings on the paint tubes and chestnut wood markings on the box.

6 Position all the sugarpaste pieces on the cake and board using royal icing. Leave to dry.

Liquorice Sweet Cake

Makes one 20cm/8in square cake

20cm/8in and 15cm/6in square Madeira cakes
675g/1½lb/3 cups butter icing
45ml/3 tbsp apricot jam, warmed and sieved
350g/12oz/2¼ cups marzipan
800g/1¾lb/5¼ cups sugarpaste icing
egg-yellow, black, blue and mulberry food colouring

Materials/equipment

25cm/10in square cake board
4.5cm/1¾in round cutter

1 Cut both cakes horizontally into three. Fill with butter icing, reserving a little to coat the smaller cake. Wrap and set aside the smaller cake. Brush the larger cake with apricot jam. Cover with marzipan and secure on the cake board with butter icing. Leave to dry overnight.

2 Tint 350g/12oz/2¼ cups of the sugarpaste icing yellow. Take 115g/4oz/¾ cup of the sugarpaste icing and tint half black and leave the other half white. Cover the top and one-third of the sides of the cake with yellow sugarpaste icing.

3 Use the white icing to cover the lower third of the sides of the cake. Use the black icing to fill the central third.

4 Cut the smaller cake into three equal strips. Divide two of the strips into three squares each. Cut out two circles from the third strip, using a cutter as a guide.

5 Tint 115g/4oz/¾ cup of the remaining sugarpaste black. Divide the rest into four equal portions, leave one white and tint the others blue, pink and yellow.

6 Coat the outsides of the cake cut-outs with the reserved butter icing. Use the tinted and white sugarpaste to cover the pieces to resemble sweets. Make small rolls from the trimmings. Arrange on and around the cake.

Sun Cake

Makes one 20cm/8in star-shaped cake

2 x 20 x 5cm/8 x 2in sponge cakes
25g/1oz/2 tbsp unsalted butter
450g/1lb/4 cups sifted icing sugar
120ml/4fl oz/½ cup apricot jam
30ml/2 tbsp water
2 large egg whites
1–2 drops glycerine
juice of 1 lemon
yellow and orange food colouring

Materials/equipment

40cm/16in square cake board
fabric piping bag
small star nozzle

1 Cut one of the cakes into eight wedges. Trim the outsides to fit round the other cake. Make butter icing with the butter and 25g/1oz/2 tbsp of the icing sugar. Place the whole cake on a 40cm/16in board and attach the sunbeams with the butter icing.

2 Melt the jam with the water and brush over the cake.

3 For the icing, beat the egg whites until stiff. Gradually add the icing sugar, glycerine and lemon juice, and beat for 1 minute. Tint yellow and spread over the cake. Tint the remaining icing bright yellow and orange. Pipe the details on to the cake.

Strawberry Basket Cake

Makes one small rectangular cake

sponge cake baked in a 450g/1lb/3 cup loaf tin
45ml/3 tbsp apricot jam, warmed and sieved
675g/1½lb/4½ cups marzipan
350g/12oz/1½ cups chocolate-flavour butter icing
red food colouring
50g/2oz/4 tbsp caster sugar

Materials/equipment

small star nozzle
small greaseproof paper piping bag
10 plastic strawberry stalks
30 x 7.5cm/12 x 3in strip foil
30cm/12in thin red ribbon

1 Level the top of the cake and make it perfectly flat. Score a 5mm/¼in border around the edge and scoop out the inside to make a shallow hollow.

2 Brush the sides and border edges of the cake with apricot jam. Roll out 275g/10oz/scant 2 cups of the marzipan, cut into rectangles and use to cover the sides of the cake, overlapping the borders. Press the edges together to seal.

3 Using the star nozzle, pipe vertical lines 2.5cm/1in apart all around the sides of the cake. Pipe short horizontal lines of butter icing alternately crossing over and then stopping at the vertical lines to give a basketweave effect. Pipe a decorative line of icing around the top edge of the basket to finish.

4 Tint the remaining marzipan red and mould it into ten strawberry shapes. Roll in the caster sugar and press a plastic stalk into each top. Arrange in the "basket".

5 For the basket handle, fold the foil into a thin strip and wind the ribbon around it to cover. Bend up the ends and then bend into a curve. Push the ends into the sides of the cake. Decorate with bows made from the ribbon.

Banana Gingerbread Slices

Bananas make this spicy bake delightfully moist. The flavour develops on keeping, so store the gingerbread for a few days before cutting, if possible.

Makes 20 slices

275g/10oz/2½ cups plain flour
20ml/4 tsp ground ginger
10ml/2 tsp mixed spice
5ml/1 tsp bicarbonate of soda
115g/4oz/½ cup soft light brown sugar
60ml/4 tbsp corn oil
30ml/2 tbsp molasses or black treacle
30ml/2 tbsp malt extract
2 eggs, beaten
60ml/4 tbsp orange juice
3 ripe bananas
115g/4oz/scant 1 cup raisins or sultanas

1 Preheat the oven to 180°C/350°F/Gas 4. Line and grease a 28 x 18cm/11 x 7in baking tin.

2 Sift the flour, spices and bicarbonate of soda into a mixing bowl. Spoon some of the mixture back into the sieve, add the brown sugar and sift the mixture back into the bowl.

3 Make a well in the centre of the dry ingredients and add the oil, molasses or treacle, malt extract, eggs, and orange juice. Mix thoroughly.

4 Mash the bananas in a bowl. Add to the gingerbread mixture with the raisins or sultanas. Mix well.

5 Scrape the mixture into the prepared tin. Bake for 35–40 minutes or until the centre springs back when the surface of the cake is lightly pressed.

6 Leave the gingerbread in the tin to cool for 5 minutes, then turn onto a wire rack, remove the lining paper and leave to cool completely. Cut into 20 slices to serve.

Banana and Apricot Chelsea Buns

Old favourites get a new twist with a delectable filling.

Serves 9

225g/8oz/2 cups strong plain flour
10ml/2 tsp mixed spice
2.5ml/½ tsp salt
25g/1oz/2 tbsp soft margarine
7.5ml/1½ tsp easy-blend dried yeast
50g/2oz/¼ cup caster sugar
90ml/6 tbsp hand-hot milk
1 egg, beaten

For the filling

1 large ripe banana
175g/6oz/1 cup ready-to-eat dried apricots
30ml/2tbsp soft light brown sugar

For the glaze

30ml/2tbsp caster sugar
30ml/2tbsp water

1 Grease an 18cm/7in square cake tin. Prepare the filling. Mash the banana in a bowl. Using kitchen scissors, snip in the apricots, then stir in the brown sugar. Mix well.

2 Sift the flour, spice and salt into a mixing bowl. Rub in the margarine, then stir in the yeast and sugar. Make a well in the centre and pour in the milk and the egg. Mix to a soft dough, adding a little extra milk if necessary.

3 Turn the dough onto a floured surface and knead for 5 minutes until smooth and elastic. Roll out to a 30 x 23cm/12 x 9in rectangle. Spread the filling over the dough and roll up lengthways like a Swiss roll, with the join underneath. Cut into 9 pieces and place cut side downwards in the prepared tin. Cover and leave in a warm place until doubled in size.

4 Preheat the oven to 200°C/400°F/Gas 6. Bake the buns for 20–25 minutes until golden brown. Meanwhile make the glaze: mix the caster sugar and water in a small saucepan. Heat, stirring, until dissolved, then boil for 2 minutes. Brush the glaze over the buns while still hot, then remove from the tin and cool on a wire rack.

Lemon Sponge Fingers

These sponge fingers are perfect for serving with fruit salads or light, creamy desserts.

Makes about 20

2 eggs
75g/3oz/6 tbsp caster sugar
grated rind of 1 lemon
50g/2oz/½ cup plain flour, sifted
caster sugar, for sprinkling

1 Preheat the oven to 190°C/375°F/Gas 5. Line two baking sheets with non-stick baking paper. Whisk the eggs, sugar and lemon rind together with a hand-held electric whisk until thick and mousse-like: when the whisk is lifted, a trail should remain on the surface of the mixture for at least 30 seconds.

2 Carefully fold in the flour with a large metal spoon using a figure-of-eight action.

3 Place the mixture in a piping bag fitted with a 1cm/½in plain nozzle. Pipe into finger lengths on the prepared baking sheets, leaving room for spreading.

4 Sprinkle the fingers with caster sugar. Bake for 6–8 minutes until golden brown, then remove to a wire rack to cool completely.

Variation

To make Hazelnut Fingers, omit the lemon rind and fold in 25g/1oz/¼ cup toasted ground hazelnuts and 5ml/1 tsp mixed spice with the flour.

Apricot and Almond Fingers

These delicious almond fingers will stay moist for several days, thanks to the addition of apricots.

Makes 18

225g/8oz/2 cups self-raising flour
115g/4oz/½ cup soft light brown sugar
50g/2oz/⅓ cup semolina
175g/6oz/1 cup ready-to-eat dried apricots, chopped
30ml/2 tbsp clear honey
30ml/2 tbsp malt extract
2 eggs, beaten
60ml/4 tbsp skimmed milk
60ml/4 tbsp sunflower oil
few drops of almond essence
30ml/2 tbsp flaked almonds

1 Preheat the oven to 160°C/325°F/Gas 3. Grease and line a 28 x 18cm/11 x 7in baking tin. Sift the flour into a bowl and stir in the sugar, semolina and apricots. Make a well in the centre and add the honey, malt extract, eggs, milk, oil and almond essence. Mix well until combined.

2 Turn the mixture into the prepared tin, spread to the edges and sprinkle with the flaked almonds.

3 Bake for 30–35 minutes or until the centre springs back when lightly pressed. Invert the cake on a wire rack to cool. Remove the lining paper if necessary and cut into 18 slices with a sharp knife.

Cook's Tip

If you cannot find ready-to-eat dried apricots, soak chopped dried apricots in boiling water for 1 hour, then drain them and add to the mixture. This works well with other dried fruit too. Try ready-to-eat dried pears or peaches for a change.

Raspberry Muffins

Unlike English muffins, which are made from a yeast mixture and cooked on a griddle, these American muffins are baked, giving them a light and spongy texture.

Makes 10 – 12

275g/10oz/2½ cups plain flour	*1 egg*
15ml/1 tbsp baking powder	*250ml/8fl oz/1 cup buttermilk*
115g/4oz/½ cup caster sugar	*60ml/4 tbsp sunflower oil*
	150g/5oz/1 cup raspberries

1 Preheat the oven to 200°C/400°F/Gas 6. Arrange 12 paper cases in a deep muffin tin. Sift the flour and baking powder into a mi[illegible] in the cen[illegible]

2 Mix th[illegible] to the bowl [illegible]

3 Add th[illegible] n. Spoon int[illegible]

4 Bake th[illegible] and firm i[illegible] while still [illegible]

***Cook**[illegible]*
This i[illegible] lightl[illegible] breaks[illegible] blackc[illegible] if you prefer.

Currant Buns.
(15)
190°
12-15 mins
4oz marg.
4oz sugar) cream
8oz self raising
2 eggs
4oz fruit. (milk.)

Date and Apple Muffins

These tasty muffins are delicious with morning coffee or breakfast. You will only need one or two per person as they are very filling.

Makes 12

150g/5oz/1¼ cups self-raising wholemeal flour	*brown sugar*
150g/5oz/1¼ cups self-raising white flour	*250ml/8fl oz/1 cup apple juice*
5ml/1 tsp ground cinnamon	*30ml/2 tbsp pear and apple spread*
5ml/1 tsp baking powder	*1 egg, lightly beaten*
25g/1oz/2 tbsp soft margarine	*1 eating apple*
75g/3oz/6 tbsp soft light	*75g/3oz/½ cup chopped dates*
	15ml/1 tbsp chopped pecan nuts

1 Preheat the oven to 200°C/400°F/Gas 6. Arrange 12 paper cases in a deep muffin tin. Put the wholemeal flour in a mixing bowl. Sift in the white flour with the cinnamon and baking powder. Rub in the margarine until the mixture resembles breadcrumbs, then stir in the brown sugar.

2 In a bowl, stir a little of the apple juice with the pear and apple spread until smooth. Add the remaining juice, mix well, then add to the rubbed-in mixture with the egg. Peel and core the apple, chop the flesh finely and add it to the bowl with the dates. Mix quickly until just combined.

3 Divide the mixture among the muffin cases. Sprinkle with the chopped pecans.

4 Bake the muffins for 20 – 25 minutes until golden brown and firm in the middle. Turn onto a wire rack and serve while still warm.

Filo and Apricot Purses

Filo pastry is very easy to use and is low in fat. Always keep a packet in the freezer ready for rustling up a speedy teatime treat.

Makes 12

115g/4oz/1 cup ready-to-eat dried apricots
45ml/3 tbsp apricot compôte
3 amaretti biscuits, crushed
3 sheets of filo pastry
20ml/4 tsp soft margarine, melted
icing sugar, for dusting

1 Preheat the oven to 180°C/350°F/Gas 4. Grease two baking sheets. Chop the apricots, put them in a bowl and stir in the apricot compôte. Mix in the amaretti biscuits.

2 Cut the filo pastry into 24 13cm/5in squares, pile the squares on top of each other and cover with a clean dish towel to prevent the pastry from drying out.

3 Lay one pastry square on a flat surface, brush lightly with melted margarine and lay another square diagonally on top. Brush the top square with melted margarine. Spoon a small mound of apricot mixture in the centre of the pastry, bring up the edges and pinch together in a money-bag shape. The margarine will help to make the pastry stick.

4 Repeat with the remaining filo squares and filling to make 12 purses in all. Arrange on the prepared baking sheets and bake for 5–8 minutes until golden brown. Dust with icing sugar and serve warm.

Cook's Tip
The easiest way to crush the amaretti biscuits is to put them in a plastic bag and roll with a rolling pin.

Filo Scrunchies

Quick and easy to make, these are ideal to serve at teatime. Eat them warm or they will lose their crispness.

Makes 6

5 apricots or plums
4 sheets of filo pastry
20ml/4 tsp soft margarine, melted
50g/2oz/¼ cup demerara sugar
30ml/2 tbsp flaked almonds
icing sugar, for dusting

1 Preheat the oven to 190°C/375°F/Gas 5. Cut the apricots or plums in half, remove the stones and slice the fruit thinly.

2 Cut the filo pastry into 12 18cm/7in squares. Pile the squares on top of each other and cover with a clean dish towel to prevent the pastry from drying out. Remove one square and brush it with melted margarine. Lay a second filo square on top, then, using your fingers, mould the pastry into neat folds.

3 Lay the scrunched filo square on a baking sheet. Make five more scrunchies in the same way, working quickly so that the pastry does not dry out.Arrange a few slices of fruit in the folds of each scrunchie, then sprinkle generously with demerara sugar and almonds.

4 Bake the scrunchies for 8–10 minutes until golden brown, then loosen from the baking sheet with a palette knife. Place on a platter, dust with icing sugar and serve immediately.

Cook's Tip
Filo pastry dries out very quickly. Keep it covered as much as possible with clear film or a dry cloth to limit exposure to the air, or it will become too brittle to use.

Coffee Sponge Drops

These light biscuits are delicious on their own, but taste even better with a filling made by mixing low-fat soft cheese with chopped stem ginger.

Makes about 24

50g/2oz/½ cup plain flour
15ml/1 tbsp instant coffee powder
2 eggs
75g/3oz/6 tbsp caster sugar

For the filling (optional)

115g/4oz/½ cup low fat soft cheese
40g/1½oz/¼ cup chopped stem ginger

1 Preheat the oven to 190°C/375°F/Gas 5. Line two baking sheets with non-stick paper. Sift the flour and coffee powder together.

2 Combine the eggs and caster sugar in a heatproof bowl. Place over a saucepan of simmering water. Beat with a hand-held electric whisk until thick and mousse-like: when the whisk is lifted a trail should remain on the surface of the mixture for at least 30 seconds.

3 Carefully fold in the sifted flour mixture with a large metal spoon, being careful not to knock out any air.

4 Spoon the mixture into a piping bag fitted with a 1cm/½in plain nozzle and pipe 4cm/1½in rounds on the prepared baking sheets. Bake for 12 minutes. Cool on a wire rack. Sandwich together in pairs with a ginger-cheese filling (above) or a coffee icing, if you like.

Variation

To make Chocolate Sponge Drops, replace the coffee with 30ml/2 tbsp reduced-fat cocoa powder.

Oaty Crisps

These biscuits are very crisp and crunchy – ideal to serve with morning coffee.

Makes 18

175g/6oz/1½ cups rolled oats
75g/3oz/6 tbsp soft light brown sugar
1 egg
60ml/4 tbsp sunflower oil
30ml/2 tbsp malt extract

1 Preheat the oven to 190°C/375°F/Gas 5. Grease two baking sheets. Mix the oats and brown sugar in a bowl, breaking up any lumps in the sugar.

2 Add the egg, oil and malt extract, mix well, then leave to soak for 15 minutes.

3 Using a teaspoon, place small heaps of the mixture on the prepared baking sheets, leaving room for spreading. Press into 7.5cm/3in rounds with a dampened fork.

4 Bake the biscuits for 10–15 minutes until golden brown. Leave to cool for 1 minute, then remove with a palette knife and cool on a wire rack.

Variation

Add 50g/2oz/½ cup chopped almonds or hazelnuts to the mixture. You can also add some jumbo oats to give a coarser texture.

Snowballs

These light and airy morsels make a good accompaniment to yogurt ice cream.

Makes about 20

2 egg whites
115g/4oz/½ cup caster sugar
15ml/1 tbsp cornflour, sifted
5ml/1 tsp white wine vinegar
1.5ml/¼ tsp vanilla essence

1 Preheat the oven to 150°C/300°F/Gas 2 and line two baking sheets with non-stick baking paper. Whisk the egg whites in a grease-free bowl, using a hand-held electric whisk, until very stiff.

2 Add the caster sugar, a little at a time, whisking until the meringue is very stiff. Whisk in the cornflour, vinegar and vanilla essence.

3 Using a teaspoon, mound the mixture into snowballs on the prepared baking sheets. Bake for 30 minutes.

4 Cool on the baking sheets, then remove the snowballs from the paper with a palette knife.

Variation

Make Pineapple Snowballs by lightly folding about 50g/2oz/⅓ cup finely chopped semi-dried pineapple into the meringue.

Caramel Meringues

Muscovado sugar gives these meringues a marvellous caramel flavour. Take care not to overcook them, so that they stay chewy in the middle.

Makes about 20

115g/4oz/½ cup muscovado sugar
2 egg whites
5ml/1 tsp finely chopped walnuts

1 Preheat the oven to 160°C/325°F/Gas 3. Line two baking sheets with non-stick paper. Press the sugar through a metal sieve into a bowl. Whisk the egg whites in a grease-free bowl until very stiff and dry, then add the sieved brown sugar, about 15ml/1 tbsp at a time, whisking it in the meringue until it is thick and glossy.

2 Spoon small mounds of the mixture onto the prepared baking sheets. Sprinkle with the walnuts.

3 Bake for 30 minutes, then leave to cool for 5 minutes on the baking sheets. Transfer the meringues to a wire rack to cool completely.

Cook's Tip

For an easy sophisticated filling, mix 115g/4oz/½ cup low-fat soft cheese with 15ml/1 tbsp icing sugar. Chop 2 slices of fresh pineapple and add to the mixture. Sandwich the meringues together in pairs.

Chocolate Banana Cake

A delicious sticky chocolate cake, moist enough to eat without the icing if you want to cut down on the calories.

Serves 8

225g/8oz/2 cups self-raising flour
45ml/3 tbsp fat-reduced cocoa powder
115g/4oz/½ cup soft light brown sugar
30ml/2 tbsp malt extract
30ml/2 tbsp golden syrup
2 eggs, beaten
60ml/4 tbsp skimmed milk
60ml/4 tbsp sunflower oil
2 large ripe bananas

For the icing

175g/6oz/1½ cups icing sugar, sifted
30ml/2 tbsp fat-reduced cocoa powder, sifted
15–30ml/1–2 tbsp warm water

1 Preheat the oven to 160°C/325°F/Gas 3. Line and grease a deep 20cm/8in round cake tin. Sift the flour into a mixing bowl with the cocoa powder. Stir in the sugar.

2 Make a well in the centre and add the malt extract, golden syrup, eggs, milk and oil. Mix well. Mash the bananas thoroughly and stir them into the mixture until thoroughly combined.

3 Spoon the mixture into the prepared tin and bake for 1–1¼ hours or until the centre of the cake springs back when lightly pressed. Remove the cake from the tin and turn on to a wire rack to cool.

4 Make the icing: put the icing sugar and cocoa in a mixing bowl and gradually add enough water to make a mixture thick enough to coat the back of a wooden spoon. Pour over the top of the cake and ease to the edges, allowing the icing to dribble down the sides.

Spiced Apple Cake

Grated apple and dates give this cake a natural sweetness. It may not be necessary to add all the sugar.

Serves 8

225g/8oz/2 cups self-raising wholemeal flour
5ml/1 tsp baking powder
10ml/2 tsp ground cinnamon
175g/6oz/1 cup chopped dates
75g/3oz/scant ½ cup soft light brown sugar
15ml/1 tbsp pear and apple spread
120ml/4fl oz/½ cup apple juice
2 eggs, beaten
90ml/6 tbsp sunflower oil
2 eating apples, cored and grated
15ml/1 tbsp chopped walnuts

1 Preheat the oven to 180°C/350°F/Gas 4. Line and grease a 20cm/8in deep round cake tin. Sift the flour, baking powder and cinnamon into a mixing bowl, then mix in the dates and make a well in the centre.

2 Mix the sugar with the pear and apple spread in a small bowl. Gradually stir in the apple juice. Add to the dry ingredients with the eggs, oil and apples. Mix thoroughly.

3 Spoon into the prepared cake tin, sprinkle with the walnuts and bake for 60–65 minutes or until a skewer inserted into the centre of the cake comes out clean. Invert on a wire rack, remove the lining paper and leave to cool.

Cook's Tip

It is not necessary to peel the apples – the skin adds extra fibre and softens on cooking.

Irish Whiskey Cake

This moist rich fruit cake is drizzled with whiskey as soon as it comes out of the oven.

Serves 10

115g/4oz/scant 1 cup sultanas
115g/4oz/scant 1 cup raisins
115g/4oz/½ cup currants
115g/4oz/½ cup glacé cherries
175g/6oz/1 cup soft light brown sugar
300ml/½ pint/1¼ cups cold tea
1 egg, beaten
300g/11oz/2½ cups self-raising flour, sifted
45ml/3 tbsp Irish whiskey

1 Mix the dried fruit, cherries, sugar and tea in a large bowl. Leave to soak overnight until the tea has been absorbed.

2 Preheat the oven to 180°C/350°F/Gas 4. Line and grease a 1kg/2¼lb loaf tin. Add the egg and flour to the fruit mixture and beat thoroughly until well mixed.

3 Pour into the prepared tin and bake for 1½ hours or until a skewer inserted into the centre comes out clean.

4 Prick the top of the cake with a skewer and drizzle over the whiskey while still hot. Allow to stand for 5 minutes, then remove from the tin and cool on a wire rack.

Cook's Tip

If time is short use hot tea and soak the fruit for two hours instead of overnight.

Fruit and Nut Cake

A rich fruit cake that matures with keeping.

Serves 12–14

175g/6oz/1½ cups self-raising wholemeal flour
175g/6oz/1½ cups self-raising white flour
10ml/2 tsp mixed spice
15ml/1 tbsp apple and apricot spread
45ml/3 tbsp clear honey
15ml/1 tbsp molasses
90ml/6 tbsp sunflower oil
175ml/6fl oz/¾ cup orange juice
2 eggs, beaten
675g/1½lb/4 cups luxury mixed fruit
115g/4oz/½ cup glacé cherries, halved
45ml/3 tbsp split almonds

1 Preheat the oven to 160°C/325°F/Gas 3. Line and grease a deep 20cm/8in cake tin. Tie a band of newspaper around the outside of the tin and stand it on a pad of newspaper on a baking sheet.

2 Combine the flours in a mixing bowl. Stir in the mixed spice and make a well in the centre.

3 Put the apple and apricot spread in a small bowl. Gradually stir in the honey and molasses. Add to the bowl with the oil, orange juice, eggs and mixed fruit. Stir with a wooden spoon to mix thoroughly.

4 Scrape the mixture into the prepared tin and smooth the surface. Arrange the cherries and almonds in a decorative pattern over the top. Bake for 2 hours or until a skewer inserted into the centre of the cake comes out clean. Turn on to a wire rack to cool, then remove the lining paper.

Cook's Tip

For a less elaborate cake, omit the cherries, chop the almonds roughly and sprinkle them over the top.

Angel Cake

Served with fromage frais and fresh raspberries, this makes a light dessert.

Serves 10

40g/1½oz/scant ½ cup cornflour
40g/1½oz/scant ½ cup plain flour
8 egg whites
225g/8oz/1 cup caster sugar, plus extra for sprinkling
5ml/1 tsp vanilla essence
icing sugar, for dusting

1 Preheat the oven to 180°C/350°F/Gas 4. Sift both flours into a bowl.

2 Whisk the egg whites in a large grease-free bowl until very stiff, then gradually add the sugar and vanilla essence, whisking until the mixture is thick and glossy.

3 Fold in the flour mixture with a large metal spoon. Spoon into an ungreased 25cm/10in angel cake tin, smooth the surface and bake for 40–45 minutes.

4 Sprinkle a piece of greaseproof paper with caster sugar and set an egg cup in the centre. Invert the cake tin over the paper, balancing it carefully on the egg cup. When cold, the cake will drop out of the tin. Transfer it to a plate, dust generously with icing sugar and serve.

Variation
Make a lemon icing by mixing 175g/6oz/1½ cups icing sugar with 15–30ml/1–2 tbsp lemon juice. Drizzle the icing over the cake and decorate with lemon slices and mint sprigs or physalis.

Peach Swiss Roll

This is the perfect cake for a summer afternoon tea in the garden.

Serves 6–8

3 eggs
115g/4oz/½ cup caster sugar
75g/3oz/¾ cup plain flour, sifted
15ml/1 tbsp boiling water
90ml/6 tbsp peach jam
icing sugar, for dusting (optional)

1 Preheat the oven to 200°C/400°F/Gas 6. Line and grease a 30 x 20cm/12 x 8in Swiss roll tin. Combine the eggs and sugar in a bowl. Beat with a hand-held electric whisk until thick and mousse-like: when the whisk is lifted a trail should remain on the surface of the mixture for at least 30 seconds.

2 Carefully fold in the flour with a large metal spoon, then add the boiling water in the same way.

3 Spoon into the prepared tin, spread evenly to the edges and bake for 10–12 minutes until the cake springs back when lightly pressed.

4 Spread a sheet of greaseproof paper on a flat surface, sprinkle it with caster sugar, then invert the cake on top. Peel off the lining paper.

5 Make a neat cut two-thirds of the way through the cake, about 1 cm/½ in from the short edge nearest you – this will make it easier to roll. Trim the remaining edges.

6 Spread the cake with the peach jam and roll up quickly from the partially-cut end. Hold in position for a minute, making sure the join is underneath. Cool on a wire rack. Dust with icing sugar before serving, if you like.

Pear and Sultana Tea Bread

This is an ideal tea bread to make when pears are plentiful. There's no better use for autumn windfalls.

Serves 6–8

25g/1oz/3 cups rolled oats
50g/2oz/¼ cup soft light brown sugar
30ml/2 tbsp pear or apple juice
30ml/2 tbsp sunflower oil
1 large or 2 small pears
115g/4oz/1 cup self-raising flour
115g/4oz/scant 1 cup sultanas
2.5ml/½ tsp baking powder
10ml/2 tsp mixed spice
1 egg

1 Preheat the oven to 180°C/350°F/Gas 4. Line a 450g/1lb loaf tin with non-stick paper. Put the oats in a bowl with the sugar, pour over the pear or apple juice and oil, mix well and leave to stand for 15 minutes.

2 Quarter, core and grate the pear(s). Add to the bowl with the flour, sultanas, baking powder, spice and egg. Using a wooden spoon, mix thoroughly.

3 Spoon the tea bread mixture into the prepared loaf tin. Bake for 55–60 minutes or until a skewer inserted into the centre comes out clean.

4 Invert the tea bread on a wire rack and remove the lining paper. Leave to cool.

Cook's Tip
Health-food shops sell concentrated pear juice, ready for diluting as required.

Banana and Ginger Tea Bread

The bland creaminess of banana is given a delightful lift with chunks of stem ginger in this tasty tea bread. If you like a strong ginger flavour add 5ml/1 tsp ground ginger with the flour.

Serves 6–8

175g/6oz/1½ cups self-raising flour
5ml/1 tsp baking powder
40g/1½oz/3 tbsp soft margarine
50g/2oz/¼ cup soft light brown sugar
50g/2oz/⅓ cup drained stem ginger, chopped
60ml/4 tbsp skimmed milk
2 ripe bananas, mashed

1 Preheat the oven to 180°C/350°F/Gas 4. Line and grease a 450g/1lb loaf tin. Sift the flour and baking powder into a mixing bowl.

2 Rub in the margarine until the mixture resembles breadcrumbs, then stir in the sugar.

3 Add the ginger, milk and mashed bananas and mix to a soft dough.

4 Spoon into the prepared tin and bake for 40–45 minutes. Run a palette knife around the edges to loosen them, turn the tea bread onto a wire rack and leave to cool.

Variation
To make Banana and Walnut Tea Bread, add 5ml/1 tsp mixed spice and omit the chopped stem ginger. Stir in 50g/2oz/½ cup chopped walnuts and add 50g/2oz/scant ½ cup sultanas.

Olive and Oregano Bread

This is an excellent accompaniment to all salads and is very good with grilled goat's cheese.

Serves 8–10

15ml/1 tbsp olive oil
1 onion, chopped
450g/1lb/4 cups strong white flour
10ml/2 tsp easy-blend dried yeast
5ml/1 tsp salt
1.5ml/1/4 tsp black pepper
50g/2oz/1/3 cup pitted black olives, roughly chopped
15ml/1 tbsp black olive paste
15ml/1 tbsp chopped fresh oregano
15ml/1 tbsp chopped fresh parsley
300ml/1/2 pint/1 1/4 cups hand-hot water

1 Lightly oil a baking sheet. Heat the olive oil in a frying pan and fry the onion until golden brown.

2 Sift the flour into a mixing bowl. Add the yeast, salt and pepper. Make a well in the centre. Add the fried onion (with the oil), the olives, olive paste, herbs and water. Gradually incorporate the flour and mix to a soft dough, adding a little extra water if necessary.

3 Turn the dough onto a floured surface and knead for 5 minutes until smooth and elastic. Shape into a 20cm/8in round and place on the prepared baking sheet. Using a sharp knife, make criss-cross cuts over the top, cover and leave in a warm place until doubled in size. Preheat the oven to 220°C/425°F/Gas 7.

4 Bake the olive and oregano loaf for 10 minutes, then lower the oven temperature to 200°C/400°F/Gas 6. Bake for 20 minutes more, or until the loaf sounds hollow when tapped underneath. Cool on a wire rack.

Sun-dried Tomato Plait

This makes a marvellous centrepiece for a summer buffet.

Serves 8–10

225g/8oz/2 cups wholemeal flour
225g/8oz/2 cups strong white flour
5ml/1 tsp salt
1.5ml/1/4 tsp black pepper
10ml/2 tsp easy-blend dried yeast
pinch of sugar
300ml/1/2 pint/1 1/4 cups hand-hot water
115g/4oz/3/4 cup drained sun-dried tomatoes in oil, chopped, plus 15ml/1 tbsp oil from the jar
25g/1oz/1/4 cup freshly grated Parmesan cheese
30ml/2 tbsp red pesto
2.5ml/1/2 tsp coarse sea salt

1 Lightly oil a baking sheet. Put the wholemeal flour in a mixing bowl. Sift in the white flour, salt and pepper. Add the yeast and sugar. Make a well in the centre and add the water, the sun-dried tomatoes, oil, Parmesan and pesto. Gradually incorporate the flour and mix to a soft dough, adding a little extra water if necessary.

2 Turn the dough onto a floured surface and knead for 5 minutes until smooth and elastic. Shape into 3 33cm/13in long sausages.

3 Dampen the ends of the three sausages. Press them together at one end, plait them loosely, then press them together at the other end. Place on the baking sheet, cover and leave in a warm place until doubled in size. Preheat the oven to 220°C/425°F/Gas 7.

4 Sprinkle the plait with coarse sea salt. Bake for 10 minutes, then lower the oven temperature to 200°C/400°F/Gas 6 and bake for a further 15–20 minutes, or until the loaf sounds hollow when tapped underneath. Cool on a wire rack.

Cheese and Onion Herb Stick

An extremely tasty bread which is very good with soup or salads. Use a strong cheese to give plenty of flavour.

Makes 2 sticks, each serving 4–6

15ml/1 tbsp sunflower oil
1 red onion, chopped
450g/1lb/4 cups strong white flour
5ml/1 tsp salt
5ml/1 tsp mustard powder
10ml/2 tsp easy-blend dried yeast
45ml/3 tbsp chopped fresh herbs, such as thyme, parsley, marjoram or sage
75g/3oz/¾ cup grated reduced-fat Cheddar cheese
300ml/½ pint/1¼ cups hand-hot water

1 Lightly oil two baking sheets. Heat the oil in a frying pan and fry the onion until well browned.

2 Sift the flour, salt and mustard powder into a mixing bowl. Stir in the yeast and herbs. Set aside 30ml/2 tbsp of the cheese. Add the rest to the flour mixture and make a well in the centre. Add the water with the fried onions and oil; gradually incorporate the flour and mix to a soft dough, adding a little extra water if necessary.

3 Turn the dough onto a floured surface and knead for 5 minutes until smooth and elastic. Divide the mixture in half and roll each piece into a stick 30cm/12in in length.

4 Place each bread stick on a baking sheet, make diagonal cuts along the top and sprinkle with the reserved cheese. Cover and leave until doubled in size. Preheat the oven to 220°C/425°F/Gas 7.

5 Bake the loaves for 25 minutes or until the bread sounds hollow when tapped underneath.

Focaccia

This Italian flatbread is best served warm. It makes a delicious snack with olives and feta cheese.

Serves 8

450g/1lb/4 cups strong white flour
5ml/1 tsp salt
1.5ml/¼ tsp freshly ground black pepper
10ml/2 tsp easy-blend dried yeast
300ml/½ pint/1¼ cups hand-hot water
pinch of sugar
15ml/1 tbsp pesto
115g/4oz/⅔ cup pitted black olives, chopped
25g/1oz/3 tbsp drained sun-dried tomatoes in oil, chopped, plus 15ml/1 tbsp oil from the jar
5ml/1 tsp coarse sea salt
5ml/1 tsp chopped fresh rosemary

1 Lightly oil a 30 x 20cm/12 x 8in Swiss roll tin. Sift the flour, salt and pepper into a bowl. Add the yeast and sugar and make a well in the centre.

2 Add the water with the pesto, olives and sun-dried tomatoes (reserve the oil). Mix to a soft dough, adding a little extra water if necessary.

3 Turn the dough onto a floured surface and knead for 5 minutes until smooth and elastic. Roll into a rectangle measuring 33 x 23cm/13 x 9in. Lop over the rolling pin and place in the prepared tin. Leave to rise until doubled in size. Preheat the oven to 220°C/425°F/Gas 7.

4 Using your fingertips, make indentations all over the dough. Brush with the oil from the sun-dried tomatoes, then sprinkle with the salt and rosemary. Bake for 20–25 minutes until golden. Remove to a wire rack and serve warm.

Spinach and Bacon Bread

This bread is so good that it is a good idea to make double the quantity and freeze one of the loaves.

Makes 2 loaves, each serving 8

15ml/1 tbsp olive oil
1 onion, chopped
115g/4oz rindless smoked bacon rashers, chopped
675g/1½lb/6 cups plain flour
7.5ml/1½ tsp salt
2.5ml/½ tsp grated nutmeg
1 sachet easy-blend dried yeast
475ml/16fl oz/2 cups hand-hot water
225g/8oz chopped spinach, thawed if frozen
25g/1oz/¼ cup grated reduced-fat Cheddar cheese

1 Lightly oil two 23cm/9in cake tins. Heat the oil in a frying pan and fry the onion and bacon for 10 minutes until golden brown.

2 Sift the flour, salt and nutmeg into a mixing bowl, add the yeast and make a well in the centre. Add the water. Tip in the fried bacon and onion, with the oil, then add the well-drained spinach. Gradually incorporate the flour and mix to a soft dough.

3 Turn the dough onto a floured surface and knead for 5 minutes until smooth and elastic. Divide the mixture in half. Shape each half into a ball, flatten slightly and place in a tin, pressing the dough so that it extends to the edges.

4 Mark each loaf into six wedges and sprinkle with the cheese. Cover loosely with a plastic bag and leave in a warm place until each loaf has doubled in size. Preheat the oven to 200°C/400°F/Gas 6.

5 Bake the loaves for 25–30 minutes or until they sound hollow when tapped underneath. Cool on a wire rack.

Parma Ham and Parmesan Bread

This nourishing bread can be made very quickly, and is a meal in itself when served with a tomato and feta salad.

Serves 8

225g/8oz/2 cups self-raising wholemeal flour
225g/8oz/2 cups self-raising plain flour
5ml/1 tsp salt
5ml/1 tsp freshly ground black pepper
75g/3oz Parma ham, chopped
30ml/2 tbsp chopped fresh parsley
25g/1oz/2 tbsp freshly grated Parmesan cheese
45ml/3 tbsp Meaux mustard
350ml/12fl oz/1½ cups buttermilk
skimmed milk, to glaze

1 Preheat the oven to 200°C/400°F/Gas 6. Flour a baking sheet. Put the wholemeal flour in a bowl and sift in the plain flour, salt and pepper. Stir in the ham and parsley. Set aside about half of the grated Parmesan and add the rest to the flour mixture. Make a well in the centre.

2 Mix the mustard and buttermilk in a jug, pour into the bowl and quickly mix to a soft dough.

3 Turn onto a well-floured surface and knead very briefly. Shape into an oval loaf and place on the baking sheet.

4 Brush the loaf with milk, sprinkle with the reserved Parmesan and bake for 25–30 minutes until golden brown. Cool on a wire rack.

Cook's Tip

When chopping the ham, sprinkle it with flour so that it does not stick together. Do not knead the mixture as for a yeast dough, or it will become tough. It should be mixed quickly and kneaded very briefly before shaping.

Austrian Three-Grain Bread

A mixture of grains gives this close-textured bread a delightful nutty flavour.

Makes 1 large loaf

225g/8oz/2 cups strong white flour
7.5ml/1½ tsp salt
225g/8oz/2 cups malted brown flour
225g/8oz/2 cups rye flour
75g/3oz/½ cup medium oatmeal
1 sachet easy-blend dried yeast
45ml/3 tbsp sunflower seeds
30ml/2 tbsp linseeds
475ml/16fl oz/2 cups hand-hot water
30ml/2 tbsp malt extract

1 Sift the plain flour and salt into a mixing bowl and add the remaining flours, oatmeal, yeast and sunflower seeds. Set aside 5ml/1 tsp of the linseeds and add the rest to the flour mixture. Make a well in the centre.

2 Add the water to the bowl with the malt extract. Gradually incorporate the flour and mix to a soft dough, adding extra water if necessary.

3 Flour a baking sheet. Turn the dough onto a floured surface and knead for 5 minutes until smooth and elastic. Divide it in half. Roll each half into a sausage, about 30cm/12in in length. Twist the two pieces together, dampen each end and press together firmly.

4 Lift the loaf onto the prepared baking sheet. Brush with water, sprinkle with the remaining linseeds and cover loosely with a large plastic bag (balloon it to trap the air inside). Leave in a warm place until doubled in size. Preheat the oven to 220°C/425°F/Gas 7.

5 Bake the bread for 10 minutes, then lower the oven temperature to 200°C/400°F/Gas 6 and cook for 20 minutes more, or until the loaf sounds hollow when tapped underneath. Allow to cool on a wire rack.

Rye Bread

Rye bread is popular in Northern Europe and makes an excellent base for open sandwiches.

Makes 2 loaves, each serving 10

350g/12oz/3 cups wholemeal flour
225g/8oz/2 cups rye flour
115g/4oz/1 cup strong white flour
7.5ml/1½ tsp salt
1 sachet easy-blend dried yeast
30ml/2 tbsp caraway seeds
475ml/16fl oz/2 cups hand-hot water
30ml/2 tbsp molasses
30ml/2 tbsp sunflower oil

1 Grease a baking sheet. Put the flours in a bowl with the salt and yeast. Set aside 5ml/1 tsp of the caraway seeds and add the rest to the bowl. Mix well, then make a well in the centre.

2 Add the water to the bowl with the molasses and oil. Gradually incorporate the flour and mix to a soft dough, adding a little extra water if necessary.

3 Turn the dough on to a floured surface and knead for 5 minutes until smooth and elastic. Divide the dough in half and shape into two 23cm/9in long oval loaves.

4 Flatten the loaves slightly and place them on the baking sheet. Brush them with water and sprinkle with the remaining caraway seeds. Cover and leave in a warm place until doubled in size. Preheat the oven to 220°C/425°F/Gas 7.

5 Bake the loaves for 30 minutes until they sound hollow when tapped underneath. Allow to cool on a wire rack.

Soda Bread

Finding the bread bin empty need never be a problem when your repertoire includes a recipe for soda bread. It takes only a few minutes to make and needs no rising or proving. If possible, eat soda bread warm from the oven as it does not keep well.

Serves 8

450g/1lb/4 cups plain flour
5ml/1 tsp salt
5ml/1 tsp bicarbonate of soda
5ml/1 tsp cream of tartar
350ml/12fl oz/1½ cups buttermilk

1 Preheat the oven to 220°C/425°F/Gas 7. Flour a baking sheet. Sift the dry ingredients into a mixing bowl and make a well in the centre.

2 Add the buttermilk and mix quickly to a soft dough. Turn onto a floured surface and knead lightly. Shape into a round about 18cm/7in in diameter; place on the baking sheet.

3 Cut a deep cross on top of the loaf and sprinkle with a little flour. Bake for 25–30 minutes, then transfer to a wire rack to cool.

Cook's Tip

Soda bread needs a light hand. The ingredients should be bound together quickly in the bowl and kneaded very briefly. The aim is just to get rid of the largest cracks, as the dough becomes tough if handled for too long.

Malt Loaf

This is a rich and sticky loaf. If it lasts long enough to go stale, try toasting it for a delicious teatime treat.

Serves 8

350g/12oz/3 cups plain flour
1.5ml/¼ tsp salt
5ml/1 tsp easy-blend dried yeast
pinch of caster sugar
30ml/2 tbsp soft light brown sugar
175g/6oz/generous 1 cup sultanas
150ml/¼ pint/⅔ cup hand-hot skimmed milk
15ml/1 tbsp sunflower oil
45ml/3 tbsp malt extract

To glaze

30ml/2 tbsp caster sugar
30ml/2 tbsp water

1 Sift the flour and salt into a mixing bowl, stir in the yeast, pinch of sugar, brown sugar and sultanas, and make a well in the centre. Add the hot milk with the oil and malt extract. Gradually incorporate the flour and mix to a soft dough, adding a little extra milk if necessary.

2 Turn onto a floured surface and knead for about 5 minutes until smooth and elastic. Lightly oil a 450g/1lb loaf tin.

3 Shape the dough and place it in the prepared tin. Cover with a damp dish cloth and leave in a warm place until doubled in size. Preheat the oven to 190°C/375°F/Gas 5.

4 Bake the loaf for 30–35 minutes or until it sounds hollow when tapped underneath.

5 Meanwhile, make the glaze by dissolving the sugar in the water in a small pan. Bring to the boil, stirring, then lower the heat and simmer for 1 minute. Brush the loaf while hot, then transfer it to a wire rack to cool.

Banana and Cardamom Bread

The combination of banana and cardamom is delicious in this soft-textured moist loaf.

Serves 6

10 cardamom pods
400g/14oz/3½ cups strong white flour
5ml/1 tsp salt
5ml/1 tsp easy-blend dried yeast
150ml/¼ pint/⅔ cup hand-hot water
30ml/2 tbsp malt extract
2 ripe bananas, mashed
5ml/1 tsp sesame seeds

1 Grease a 450g/1lb loaf tin. Split the cardamom pods. Remove the seeds and chop the pods finely.

2 Sift the flour and salt into a mixing bowl, add the yeast and make a well in the centre. Add the water with the malt extract, chopped cardamom pods and bananas. Gradually incorporate the flour and mix to a soft dough, adding a little extra water if necessary.

3 Turn the dough onto a floured surface and knead for 5 minutes until smooth and elastic. Shape into a plait and place in the prepared tin. Cover loosely with a plastic bag (ballooning it to trap the air) and leave in a warm place until well risen. Preheat the oven to 220°C/425°F/Gas 7.

4 Brush the plait lightly with water and sprinkle with the sesame seeds. Bake for 10 minutes, then lower the oven temperature to 200°C/400°F/Gas 6. Cook for 15 minutes more, or until the loaf sounds hollow when tapped underneath. Remove to a wire rack to cool.

Swedish Sultana Bread

A lightly sweetened bread that goes very well with the cheeseboard and is also excellent toasted as a tea bread.

Serves 10

225g/8oz/2 cups wholemeal flour
225g/8oz/2 cups strong white flour
5ml/1 tsp easy-blend dried yeast
5ml/1 tsp salt
115g/4oz/scant 1 cup sultanas
50g/2oz/½ cup walnuts, chopped
15ml/1 tbsp clear honey
150ml/¼ pint/⅔ cup hand-hot water
175ml/6fl oz/¾ cup hand-hot skimmed milk, plus extra for glazing

1 Grease a baking sheet. Put the flours in a bowl with the yeast, salt and sultanas. Set aside 15ml/1 tbsp of the walnuts and add the rest to the bowl. Mix lightly and make a well in the centre.

2 Dissolve the honey in the water and add it to the bowl with the milk. Gradually incorporate the flour, mixing to a soft dough and adding a little extra water if necessary.

3 Turn the dough onto a floured surface and knead for 5 minutes until smooth and elastic. Shape into a 28cm/11in long sausage shape. Place on the prepared baking sheet.

4 Make diagonal cuts down the length of the loaf, brush with milk, sprinkle with the remaining walnuts and leave in a warm place until doubled in size. Preheat the oven to 220°C/425°F/Gas 7.

5 Bake the loaf for 10 minutes, then lower the oven temperature to 200°C/400°F/Gas 6 and bake for 20 minutes more or until the loaf sounds hollow when tapped underneath. Remove to a wire rack to cool.

Poppy Seed Rolls

Pile these soft rolls in a basket and serve them for breakfast or with dinner.

Makes 12

oil for greasing
450g/1lb/4 cups strong white flour
5ml/1 tsp salt
5ml/1 tsp easy-blend dried yeast
300ml/½ pint/1¼ cups hand-hot skimmed milk
1 egg, beaten

For the topping

1 egg, beaten
poppy seeds

1 Lightly grease two baking sheets with the oil. Sift the flour and salt into a mixing bowl. Add the yeast. Make a well in the centre and pour in the milk and the egg. Gradually incorporate the flour and mix to a soft dough.

2 Turn the dough on to a floured surface and knead for 5 minutes until smooth and elastic. Cut into 12 pieces and shape into rolls.

3 Place the rolls on the prepared baking sheets, cover loosely with a large plastic bag (ballooning it to trap the air inside) and leave in a warm place until the rolls have doubled in size. Preheat the oven to 220°C/425°F/Gas 7.

4 Glaze the rolls with beaten egg, sprinkle with poppy seeds and bake for 12–15 minutes until golden brown.

Variations

Vary the toppings. Linseed, sesame and caraway seeds all look good; try adding caraway seeds to the dough, too, for extra flavour.

Granary Baps

These make excellent picnic fare and are also good buns for hamburgers.

Makes 8

oil for greasing
450g/1lb/4 cups malted brown flour
5ml/1 tsp salt
10ml/2 tsp easy-blend dried yeast
15ml/1 tbsp malt extract
300ml/½ pint/1¼ cups hand-hot water
15ml/1 tbsp rolled oats

1 Lightly oil a large baking sheet. Put the malted flour, salt and yeast in a mixing bowl and make a well in the centre. Dissolve the malt extract in the water and add it to the well. Gradually incorporate the flour and mix to a soft dough.

2 Turn the dough on to a floured surface and knead for 5 minutes until smooth and elastic. Divide it into eight pieces. Shape into balls and flatten with the palm of your hand to make 10cm/4in rounds.

3 Place the rounds on the prepared baking sheet, cover loosely with a large plastic bag (ballooning it to trap the air inside), and leave in a warm place until the baps have doubled in size. Preheat the oven to 220°C/425°F/Gas 7.

4 Brush the baps with water, sprinkle with the oats and bake for 20–25 minutes or until they sound hollow when tapped underneath. Cool on a wire rack.

Variation

To make a large loaf, shape the dough into a round, flatten it slightly and bake for 30–40 minutes. Test by tapping the base of the loaf – if it sounds hollow, it is cooked.

Wholemeal Herb Triangles

These make a good lunchtime snack when stuffed with ham and salad and also taste good when served with soup.

Makes 8

225g/8oz/2 cups wholemeal flour
115g/4oz/1 cup strong plain flour
5ml/1 tsp salt
2.5ml/½ tsp bicarbonate of soda
5ml/1 tsp cream of tartar
2.5ml/½ tsp chilli powder
50g/2oz/¼ cup soft margarine
250ml/8fl oz/1 cup skimmed milk
60ml/4 tbsp chopped mixed fresh herbs
15ml/1 tbsp sesame seeds

1 Preheat the oven to 220°C/425°F/Gas 7. Flour a baking sheet. Put the wholemeal flour in a mixing bowl. Sift in the remaining dry ingredients, including the chilli powder, then rub in the margarine.

2 Add the milk and herbs and mix quickly to a soft dough. Turn onto a lightly floured surface. Knead very briefly or the dough will become tough.

3 Roll out to a 23cm/9in circle and place on the prepared baking sheet. Brush lightly with water and sprinkle with the sesame seeds.

4 Cut the dough round into 8 wedges, separate slightly and bake for 15–20 minutes. Transfer the triangles to a wire rack to cool. Serve warm or cold.

Variation
Sun-dried Tomato Triangles: replace the mixed herbs with 30ml/2 tbsp chopped, drained sun-dried tomatoes in oil, and add 15ml/1 tbsp mild paprika, 15ml/1 tbsp chopped fresh parsley and 15ml/1 tbsp chopped fresh marjoram.

Caraway Bread Sticks

Ideal to nibble with drinks, these can be made in a wide variety of flavours, including cumin seed, poppy seed and celery seed, as well as the coriander and sesame variation given below.

Makes about 20

225g/8oz/2 cups plain flour
2.5ml/½ tsp salt
2.5ml/½ tsp easy-blend dried yeast
10ml/2 tsp caraway seeds
150ml/¼ pint/⅔ cup hand-hot water
pinch of sugar

1 Grease two baking sheets. Sift the flour, salt, yeast and sugar into a mixing bowl, stir in the caraway seeds and make a well in the centre. Add the water and gradually mix the flour to make a soft dough, adding a little extra water if necessary.

2 Turn onto a lightly floured surface and knead for 5 minutes until smooth and elastic. Divide the mixture into 20 pieces and roll each one into a 30cm/12in stick.

3 Arrange the bread sticks on the baking sheets, leaving room to allow for rising. Leave for 30 minutes until well risen. Meanwhile, preheat the oven to 220°C/425°F/Gas 7.

4 Bake the bread sticks for 10–12 minutes until golden brown. Cool on the baking sheets.

Variation
Coriander and Sesame Sticks: replace the caraway seeds with 15ml/1 tbsp crushed coriander seeds. Dampen the bread sticks lightly and sprinkle them with sesame seeds before baking.

Curry Crackers

These spicy, crisp little biscuits are ideal for serving with drinks or cheese.

Makes 12

50g/2oz/½ cup plain flour
5ml/1 tsp curry powder
1.5ml/¼ tsp chilli powder
1.5ml/¼ tsp salt
15ml/1 tbsp chopped fresh coriander
30ml/2 tbsp water

1 Preheat the oven to 180°C/350°F/Gas 4. Sift the flour, curry powder, chilli powder and salt into a mixing bowl and make a well in the centre. Add the chopped coriander and water. Gradually incorporate the flour and mix to a fine dough.

2 Turn onto a lightly floured surface, knead until smooth, then leave to rest for 5 minutes.

3 Cut the dough into 12 pieces and knead into small balls. Roll each ball out very thinly to a 10cm/4in round.

4 Arrange the rounds on two ungreased baking sheets. Bake for 15 minutes, turning over once during cooking.

Variations

These can be flavoured in many different ways. Omit the curry and chilli powders and add 15ml/1 tbsp caraway, fennel or mustard seeds. Any of the stronger spices such as nutmeg, cloves or ginger will give a good flavour but you will only need to add 5ml/1 tsp.

Oatcakes

These are traditionally served with cheese, but are also delicious topped with thick honey for breakfast.

Makes 8

175g/6oz/1 cup medium oatmeal, plus extra for sprinkling
pinch of bicarbonate of soda
2.5ml/½ tsp salt
15g/½oz/1 tbsp butter
75ml/5 tbsp water

1 Preheat the oven to 150°C/300°F/Gas 2. Grease a baking sheet. Put the oatmeal, bicarbonate of soda and salt in a mixing bowl.

2 Melt the butter with the water in a small saucepan. Bring to the boil, then add to the oatmeal and mix to a moist dough.

3 Turn on to a surface sprinkled with oatmeal and knead to a smooth ball. Turn a large baking sheet upside down, sprinkle it lightly with oatmeal and place the ball of dough on top. Dust with oatmeal; roll out thinly to a 25cm/10in round.

4 Cut the round into eight sections, ease apart slightly and bake for 50–60 minutes until crisp. Leave to cool on the baking sheet, then remove the oatcakes with a palette knife.

Cook's Tip

To get a neat circle, place a 25cm/10in cake board or plate on top of the oatcake. Cut away any excess dough with a palette knife, then remove the board or plate.

Chive and Potato Scones

These little cakes should be fairly thin, soft and crisp. They are delicious served for breakfast.

Makes 20

450g/1lb potatoes
115g/4oz/1 cup plain flour, sifted
30ml/2 tbsp olive oil
30ml/2 tbsp snipped chives
salt and freshly ground black pepper
low-fat spread, for topping

1 Cook the potatoes in a saucepan of boiling salted water for 20 minutes, then drain thoroughly. Return the potatoes to the clean pan and mash them. Preheat a griddle or heavy-based frying pan over low heat.

2 Tip the hot mashed potatoes into a bowl. Add the flour, olive oil and chives, with a little salt and pepper. Mix to a soft dough.

3 Roll out the dough on a well-floured surface to a thickness of 5 mm/¼ in and stamp out rounds with a 5cm/2in scone cutter, re-rolling and cutting the trimmings.

4 Cook the scones, in batches, on the hot griddle or frying pan for about 10 minutes until they are golden brown. Keep the heat low and turn the scones once. Spread with a little low-fat spread and serve immediately.

Cook's Tip

Use floury potatoes such as King Edwards. The potatoes must be freshly cooked and mashed and should not be allowed to cool before mixing. Cook the scones over low heat so that the outside does not burn before the inside is cooked.

Ham and Tomato Scones

These make an ideal accompaniment for soup. If you have any left over the next day, halve them, sprinkle with cheese, and toast under the grill.

Makes 12

225g/8oz/2 cups self-raising flour
5ml/1 tsp mustard powder
5ml/1 tsp paprika, plus extra for topping
2.5ml/½ tsp salt
25g/1oz/2 tbsp soft margarine
50g/2oz Black Forest ham, chopped
15ml/1 tbsp snipped fresh basil
50g/2oz/⅓ cup drained sun-dried tomatoes in oil, chopped
90–120ml/3–4fl oz/⅓–½ cup skimmed milk, plus extra for brushing

1 Preheat the oven to 200°C/400°F/Gas 6. Flour a large baking sheet. Sift the flour, mustard, paprika and salt into a bowl. Rub in the margarine until the mixture resembles breadcrumbs.

2 Stir in the ham, basil and sun-dried tomatoes; mix lightly. Pour in enough milk to mix to a soft dough.

3 Turn the dough onto a lightly floured surface, knead lightly and roll out to a 20 x 15cm (8 x 6in) rectangle. Cut into 5cm/2in squares and arrange on the baking sheet.

4 Brush sparingly with milk, sprinkle with paprika and bake for 12–15 minutes. Transfer to a wire rack to cool.

Cook's Tip

Scone dough should be soft and moist and mixed for just long enough to bind the ingredients together. Too much kneading makes the scones tough.

Drop Scones

Children love making – and eating – these little scones.

Makes 18

225g/8oz/2 cups self-raising flour
2.5ml/½ tsp salt
15ml/1 tbsp caster sugar
1 egg, beaten
300ml/½ pint/1¼ cups skimmed milk
oil for brushing

1 Preheat a griddle, heavy-based frying pan or an electric frying pan. Sift the flour and salt into a mixing bowl. Stir in the sugar and make a well in the centre.

2 Add the egg and half the milk and gradually incorporate the surrounding flour to make a smooth batter. Beat in the remaining milk.

3 Lightly grease the griddle or pan. Drop tablespoons of the batter onto the surface, leaving them until they bubble and the bubbles begin to burst.

4 Turn the drop scones with a palette knife and cook until the underside is golden brown. Keep the cooked drop scones warm and moist by wrapping them in a clean napkin while cooking successive batches. Serve with jam.

Variation
For a savoury version of these tasty scones, add 2 chopped spring onions and 15ml/1 tbsp freshly grated Parmesan cheese to the batter. Serve with cottage cheese.

Pineapple and Spice Drop Scones

Making the batter with pineapple or orange juice instead of milk cuts down on fat and adds to the taste. Semi-dried pineapple has an intense flavour that makes it ideal to use in baking.

Makes 24

115g/4oz/1 cup self-raising wholemeal flour
115g/4oz/1 cup self-raising white flour
5ml/1 tsp ground cinnamon
15ml/1 tbsp caster sugar
1 egg, beaten
300ml/½ pint/1¼ cups pineapple juice
75g/3oz/½ cup semi-dried pineapple, chopped
oil for greasing

1 Preheat a griddle, heavy-based frying pan or an electric frying pan. Put the wholemeal flour in a mixing bowl. Sift in the white flour, ground cinnamon and sugar and make a well in the centre.

2 Add the egg with half the pineapple juice and gradually incorporate the surrounding flour to make a smooth batter. Beat in the remaining juice with the chopped pineapple.

3 Lightly grease the griddle or pan. Drop tablespoons of the batter onto the surface, leaving them until they bubble and the bubbles begin to burst.

4 Turn the drop scones with a palette knife and cook until the underside is golden brown. Keep the cooked scones warm and moist by wrapping them in a clean napkin while cooking successive batches.

Cook's Tip
Drop scones do not keep well and are best eaten freshly cooked. These taste good with cottage cheese.

Peach and Amaretto Cake

Try this delicious cake for dessert, with reduced-fat fromage frais, or serve it solo for afternoon tea.

Serves 8

3 eggs, separated
175g/6oz/¾ cup caster sugar
grated rind and juice of 1 lemon
50g/2oz/⅓ cup semolina
40g/1½oz/scant ½ cup ground almonds
25g/1oz/¼ cup plain flour

For the syrup

75g/3oz/6 tbsp caster sugar
90ml/6 tbsp water
30ml/2 tbsp Amaretto liqueur
2 peaches or nectarines, halved and stoned
60ml/4 tbsp apricot jam, sieved, to glaze

1 Preheat the oven to 180°C/350°F/Gas 4. Grease a 20cm/8in round loose-bottomed cake tin. Whisk the egg yolks, caster sugar, lemon rind and juice in a bowl until thick, pale and creamy, then fold in the semolina, almonds and flour until smooth.

2 Whisk the egg whites in a grease-free bowl until fairly stiff. Using a metal spoon, stir a generous spoonful of the whites into the semolina mixture to lighten it, then fold in the remaining egg whites. Spoon into the prepared cake tin.

3 Bake for 30–35 minutes, then remove the cake from the oven and carefully loosen the edges. Prick the top with a skewer and leave to cool slightly in the tin.

4 Meanwhile, make the syrup. Heat the sugar and water in a small pan, stirring until dissolved, then boil without stirring for 2 minutes. Add the Amaretto liqueur and drizzle slowly over the cake.

5 Remove the cake from the tin and transfer it to a serving plate. Slice the peaches or nectarines, arrange them in concentric circles over the top and brush with the glaze.

Chestnut and Orange Roulade

A very moist roulade – ideal to serve as a dessert.

Serves 8

3 eggs, separated
115g/4oz/½ cup caster sugar
½ x 439g/15½oz can unsweetened chestnut purée
grated rind and juice of 1 orange
icing sugar, for dusting

For the filling

225g/8oz/1 cup low-fat soft cheese
15ml/1 tbsp clear honey
1 orange

1 Preheat the oven to 180°C/350°F/Gas 4. Line and grease a 30 x 20cm/12 x 8in Swiss roll tin. Whisk the egg yolks and sugar in a mixing bowl until thick and creamy. Put the chestnut purée in a separate bowl. Whisk the orange rind and juice into the purée, then whisk into the egg mixture.

2 Whisk the egg whites until fairly stiff. Stir a generous spoonful of the whites into the chestnut mixture to lighten it, then fold in the remaining egg whites. Spoon the mixture into the prepared tin and bake for 30 minutes until firm. Cool for 5 minutes, then cover with a clean damp dish cloth and leave until cold.

3 Meanwhile, make the filling. Put the soft cheese in a bowl with the honey. Finely grate the orange rind and add to the bowl. Peel away all the pith from the orange, cut the fruit into segments, chop roughly and set aside. Add any juice to the bowl, then beat until smooth. Mix in the orange segments.

4 Sprinkle a sheet of greaseproof paper with icing sugar. Turn the roulade out onto the paper; peel off the lining paper. Spread the filling over the roulade and roll up like a Swiss roll. Transfer to a plate and dust with icing sugar.

Cinnamon and Apple Gâteau

Make this lovely gâteau for an autumn teatime treat.

Serves 8

3 eggs
115g/4oz/½ cup caster sugar
75g/3oz/¾ cup plain flour
5ml/1 tsp ground cinnamon

For the filling and topping

4 large eating apples
15ml/1 tbsp water
60ml/4 tbsp clear honey
75g/3oz/½ cup sultanas
2.5ml/½ tsp ground cinnamon
350g/12oz/1½ cups low-fat soft cheese
60ml/4 tbsp reduced-fat fromage frais
10ml/2 tsp lemon juice

1 Preheat the oven to 190°C/375°F/Gas 5. Line and grease a 23cm/9in sandwich cake tin. Whisk the eggs and sugar until thick, then sift the flour and cinnamon over the surface and carefully fold in with a large metal spoon.

2 Pour into the prepared tin and bake for 25–30 minutes or until the cake springs back when lightly pressed. Cool on a wire rack.

3 To make the filling, peel, core and slice three of the apples and cook them in a covered pan with the water and half the honey until softened. Add the sultanas and cinnamon, stir well, replace the lid and leave to cool.

4 Put the soft cheese in a bowl with the fromage frais, the remaining honey and half the lemon juice; beat until smooth. Split the sponge cake in half, place the bottom half on a plate and drizzle over any liquid from the apples. Spread with two-thirds of the cheese mixture, then top with the apple filling. Fit the top of the cake in place.

5 Swirl the remaining filling over the top of the sponge. Quarter, core and slice the remaining apple, dip the slices in the remaining lemon juice and use to decorate the edges.

Lemon Chiffon Cake

Lemon mousse makes a tangy and delicious sponge filling.

Serves 8

1 lemon sponge cake mix
lemon glacé icing
shreds of blanched lemon rind

For the filling

2 eggs, separated
75g/3oz/6 tbsp caster sugar
grated rind and juice of 1 small lemon
20ml/4 tsp water
10ml/2 tsp gelatine
120ml/4fl oz/½ cup reduced-fat fromage frais

1 Preheat the oven to 180°C/350°F/Gas 4. Line and grease a 20cm/8in loose-bottomed cake tin, add the sponge mixture and bake for 20–25 minutes until firm and golden. Cool on a wire rack, then split in half. Return the lower half of the cake to the clean cake tin and set aside.

2 Make the filling. Whisk the egg yolks, sugar, lemon rind and juice in a bowl until thick, pale and creamy. In a grease-free bowl, whisk the egg whites to soft peaks.

3 Sprinkle the gelatine over the water in a bowl. When spongy, dissolve over simmering water. Cool slightly, then whisk into the yolk mixture. Fold in the fromage frais. When the mixture begins to set, fold in a generous spoonful of the egg whites to lighten it, then fold in the remaining whites.

4 Spoon the lemon mousse over the sponge in the cake tin. Set the second layer of sponge on top and chill until set.

5 Carefully transfer the cake to a serving plate. Pour the glacé icing over the cake and spread it evenly to the edges. Decorate with the lemon shreds.

Strawberry Gâteau

It is difficult to believe that a cake that tastes so delicious can be low fat.

Serves 6

2 eggs
75g/3oz/6 tbsp caster sugar
grated rind of 1/2 orange
50g/2oz/1/2 cup plain flour

For the filling

275g/10oz/1 1/4 cups low-fat soft cheese
grated rind of 1/2 orange
30ml/2 tbsp caster sugar
60ml/4 tbsp reduced-fat fromage frais
225g/8oz strawberries, halved and chopped
25g/1oz/1/4 cup chopped almonds, toasted

1 Preheat the oven to 190°C/375°F/Gas 5. Line a 30 x 20cm/12 x 8in Swiss roll tin with non-stick baking paper.

2 In a bowl, whisk the eggs, sugar and orange rind until thick and mousse-like, then fold in the flour lightly. Turn the mixture into the prepared tin. Bake for 15–20 minutes or until firm and golden. Cool on a wire rack, removing the lining paper.

3 Meanwhile, make the filling. In a bowl, mix the soft cheese with the orange rind, sugar and fromage frais until smooth. Divide between two bowls. Add half the strawberries to one bowl. Cut the sponge widthways into three equal pieces and sandwich together with the strawberry filling. Place on a serving plate.

4 Spread the plain filling over the top and sides of the cake. Press the toasted almonds over the sides and decorate the top with the remaining strawberry halves.

Tia Maria Gâteau

A feather-light coffee sponge with a creamy liqueur-flavoured filling spiked with stem ginger.

Serves 8

75g/3oz/3/4 cup plain flour
30ml/2 tbsp instant coffee powder
3 eggs
115g/4oz/1/2 cup caster sugar

For the filling

175g/6oz/3/4 cup low-fat soft cheese
15ml/1 tbsp clear honey
15ml/1 tbsp Tia Maria
50g/2oz/1/3 cup stem ginger, chopped

For the icing

225g/8oz/2 cups icing sugar, sifted
10ml/2 tsp coffee essence
5ml/1 tsp fat-reduced cocoa
coffee beans (optional)

1 Preheat the oven to 190°C/375°F/Gas 5. Line and grease a 20cm/8in round cake tin. Sift the flour and coffee powder together.

2 Whisk the eggs and sugar in a bowl until thick and mousse-like, then fold in the flour mixture lightly. Turn the mixture into the prepared tin. Bake for 30–35 minutes or until firm and golden. Cool on a wire rack.

3 Make the filling. Mix the soft cheese with the honey in a bowl. Beat until smooth, then stir in the Tia Maria and ginger. Split the cake in half horizontally and sandwich together with the Tia Maria filling.

4 Make the icing. In a bowl, mix the icing sugar and coffee essence with enough water to make an icing which will coat the back of a wooden spoon. Pour three-quarters of the icing over the cake. Stir the cocoa into the remaining icing, spoon it into a piping bag fitted with a writing nozzle and drizzle the mocha icing over the coffee icing. Decorate with coffee beans, if desired.

Quick-mix Sponge Cake

Choose either chocolate or lemon flavouring for this light and versatile sponge cake, or leave it plain.

Makes 1 x 20cm/8in round cake

115g/4oz/1 cup self-raising flour
5ml/1 tsp baking powder
115g/4oz/½ cup soft margarine
115g/4oz/½ cup caster sugar
2 eggs

For the flavourings

Chocolate: 15ml/1 tbsp cocoa powder blended with 15ml/1 tbsp boiling water
Lemon: 10ml/2 tsp grated lemon rind

1 Preheat the oven to 160°C/325°F/Gas 3. Grease a 20cm/8in round cake tin, line the base with greaseproof paper and grease the paper.

2 Sift the flour and baking powder into a bowl. Add the margarine, sugar and eggs with the chosen flavourings, if using.

3 Beat with a wooden spoon for 2–3 minutes. The mixture should be pale in colour and slightly glossy.

4 Spoon the mixture into the cake tin and smooth the surface. Bake in the centre of the oven for 30–40 minutes, or until a skewer inserted into the centre of the cake comes out clean. Turn out onto a wire rack, remove the lining paper and leave to cool completely.

Genoese Sponge Cake

This sponge cake has a firm texture due to the addition of butter and is suitable for cutting into layers for gâteaux.

Makes 1 x 20cm/8in round cake

4 eggs
125g/4oz/½ cup caster sugar
75g/3oz/6tbsp unsalted butter, melted and cooled slightly
75g/3oz/¾ cup plain flour

For the flavourings

Citrus: 10ml/2 tsp grated orange, lemon or lime rind
Chocolate: 50g/2oz plain chocolate, melted
Coffee: 10ml/2 tsp coffee granules, dissolved in 5ml/1 tsp boiling water

1 Preheat the oven to 180°C/350°F/Gas 4. Base line and grease a 20cm/8in round cake tin.

2 Whisk the eggs and caster sugar together in a heatproof bowl until thoroughly blended. Place the bowl over a saucepan of simmering water and continue to whisk the mixture until thick and pale.

3 Remove the bowl from the saucepan and continue to whisk until the mixture is cool and leaves a thick trail on the surface when beaters are lifted.

4 Pour the butter carefully into the mixture, leaving any sediment behind.

5 Sift the flour over the surface. Using a plastic spatula, carefully fold the flour, butter and any flavourings into the mixture until smooth and evenly blended. Scrape the mixture into the prepared tin, tilt to level and bake for 30–40 minutes, until firm to the touch and golden. Cool on a wire rack.

Madeira Cake

Enjoy this cake in the traditional way with a large glass of Madeira or a schooner of sherry.

Serves 6–8

225g/8oz/2 cups plain flour
5ml/1 tsp baking powder
225g/8oz/1 cup butter or margarine, at room temperature
225g/8oz/1 cup caster sugar
grated rind of 1 lemon
5ml/1 tsp vanilla essence
4 eggs

1 Preheat the oven to 160°C/325°F/Gas 3. Base line and grease a 20cm/8in cake tin.

2 Sift the flour and baking powder into a bowl. Set the mixture aside.

3 Cream the butter or margarine, adding the caster sugar about 30ml/2 tbsp at a time, until light and fluffy. Stir in the lemon rind and vanilla. Add the eggs one at a time, beating for 1 minute after each addition. Add the flour mixture and stir until just combined.

4 Pour the cake mixture into the prepared tin and tap lightly to level. Bake for about 1¼ hours, or until a metal skewer inserted in the centre comes out clean.

5 Cool in the tin on a wire rack for 10 minutes, then turn the cake out onto a wire rack and leave to cool completely.

Swiss Roll

Vary the flavour of the Swiss roll by adding a little grated orange, lime or lemon rind to the mixture.

Serves 6–8

4 eggs, separated
115g/4oz/½ cup caster sugar
115g/4oz/1 cup plain flour
5ml/1 tsp baking powder

For a chocolate flavouring

Replace 25ml/1½ tbsp of the flour with 25ml/1½ tbsp cocoa powder

1 Preheat the oven to 180°C/350°F/Gas 4. Base line and grease a 33 x 23cm/13 x 9in Swiss roll tin. Whisk the egg whites until stiff. Beat in 30ml/2 tbsp of the caster sugar.

2 Beat the egg yolks with the remaining caster sugar and 15ml/1 tbsp water for about 2 minutes until the mixture is pale and leaves a thick ribbon trail.

3 Sift together the flour and baking powder. Carefully fold the beaten egg yolks into the egg whites, then fold in the flour mixture.

4 Pour the mixture into the prepared tin and gently smooth the surface. Bake in the centre of the oven for 12–15 minutes, or until the cake starts to come away from the edges of the tin.

5 Turn out onto a piece of greaseproof paper lightly sprinkled with caster sugar. Peel off the lining paper and cut off any crisp edges. Spread with jam, if wished, and roll up, using the greaseproof paper as a guide. Leave to cool completely on a wire rack.

Rich Fruit Cake

Make this cake a few weeks before icing, wrap well and store in an airtight container to mature.

Makes 1 x 20cm/8in round or 18cm/7in square cake

375g/12oz/1¾ cups currants
250g/9oz/scant 2 cups sultanas
150g/5oz/1 cup raisins
90g/3½ oz/scant ½ cup glacé cherries, halved
90g/3½ oz/scant 1 cup almonds, chopped
65g/2½ oz/scant ½ cup mixed peel
grated rind of 1 lemon
40ml/2½ tbsp brandy
250g/9oz/2¼ cups plain flour, sifted
6.5ml/1¼ tsp mixed spice
2.5ml/½ tsp grated nutmeg
65g/2½ oz/generous ½ cup ground almonds
200g/7oz/scant 1 cup soft margarine or butter
225g/8oz/1¼ cups soft brown sugar
15ml/1 tbsp black treacle
5 eggs, beaten

1 Preheat the oven to 140°C/275°F/Gas 1. Grease a deep 20cm/8in round or 18cm/7in square cake tin, line the base and sides with a double thickness of greaseproof paper and grease the paper.

2 Combine the ingredients in a large mixing bowl. Beat with a wooden spoon for 5 minutes until well mixed.

3 Spoon the mixture into the prepared cake tin. Make a slight depression in the centre.

4 Bake in the centre of the oven for 3–3½ hours. Test the cake after 3 hours. If it is ready it will feel firm and a skewer inserted in the centre will come out clean. Cover the top loosely with foil if it starts to brown too quickly.

5 Leave the cake to cool completely in the tin. Then turn out. The lining paper can be left on to help keep the cake moist.

Light Fruit Cake

For those who prefer a slightly less dense fruit cake, here is one that is still ideal for marzipanning and icing.

Makes 1 x 20cm/8in round or 18cm/7in square cake

225g/8oz/1 cup soft margarine or butter
225g/8oz/1 cup caster sugar
grated rind of 1 orange
5 eggs, beaten
300g/11oz/2¾ cups plain flour
2.5ml/½ tsp baking powder
10ml/2 tsp mixed spice
175g/6oz/¾ cup currants
175g/6oz/generous 1 cup raisins
175g/6oz/generous 1 cup sultanas
50g/2oz/⅓ cup dried, ready-to-eat apricots
115g/4oz/⅔ cup mixed peel

1 Preheat the oven to 150°C/300°F/Gas 2. Grease a deep 20cm/8in round or 18cm/7in square cake tin, line the base and sides with a double thickness of greaseproof paper and grease the paper.

2 Combine all the ingredients in a large mixing bowl, snipping in the apricots in strips, using kitchen scissors. Beat thoroughly with a wooden spoon for 3–4 minutes, until thoroughly mixed.

3 Spoon the mixture into the cake tin. Make a slight depression in the centre. Bake in the centre of the oven for 2½–3¼ hours. Test the cake after 2½ hours. If it is ready it will feel firm and a skewer inserted in the centre will come out clean. Test at intervals if necessary. Cover the top loosely with foil if it starts to brown too quickly.

4 Leave the cake to cool completely in the tin. Then turn out. The lining paper can be left on to help keep the cake moist.

Marzipan

Marzipan can be used on its own, under an icing or for modelling.

Makes 450g/1lb/3 cups

225g/8oz/2 cups ground almonds
115g/4oz/½ cup caster sugar
115g/4oz/1 cup icing sugar, sifted
5ml/1 tsp lemon juice
a few drops of almond essence
1 (size 4) egg, or 1 (size 2) egg white

1 Stir the ground almonds and sugars together in a bowl until evenly mixed. Make a well in the centre and add the lemon juice, almond essence and enough egg or egg white to mix to a soft but firm dough, using a wooden spoon.

2 Form the marzipan into a ball. Lightly dust a surface with icing sugar and knead the marzipan until smooth. Wrap in clear film or store in a polythene bag until needed. Tint with food colouring if required.

Sugarpaste Icing

Sugarpaste icing is wonderfully pliable and can be coloured, moulded and shaped in imaginative ways.

Makes 350g/12oz/2¼ cups

1 egg white
15ml/1 tbsp liquid glucose, warmed
350g/12oz/3 cups icing sugar, sifted

1 Put the egg white and glucose in a mixing bowl. Stir them together to break up the egg white.

2 Add the icing sugar and mix together with a palette knife, using a chopping action, until well blended and the icing begins to bind together. Knead the mixture with your fingers until it forms a ball.

3 Knead the sugarpaste on a work surface lightly dusted with icing sugar for several minutes until smooth, soft and pliable. If the icing is too soft, knead in some more sifted sugar until it reaches the right consistency.

Marzipan Roses

To decorate a cake, shape the roses in a variety of colours and sizes then arrange on top.

Form a small ball of coloured marzipan into a cone shape. This forms the central core which supports the petals. To make the petals, take a piece of marzipan about the size of a large pea, and make a petal shape which is thicker at the base. Wrap the petal around the cone, pressing the petal to the cone to secure. Bend back the ends of the petal to curl. Repeat with more petals, each overlapping. Make some petals bigger until the required size is achieved.

Royal Icing

Royal icing gives a professional finish. This recipe makes enough icing to cover the top and sides of an 18cm/7in cake.

Makes 675g/1½ lb/4½ cups

3 egg whites
about 675g/1½ lb/6 cups icing sugar, sifted
7.5ml/1½ tsp glycerine
a few drops of lemon juice
food colouring (optional)

1 Put the egg whites in a bowl and stir lightly with a fork to break them up.

2 Add the icing sugar gradually, beating well with a wooden spoon after each addition. Add enough icing sugar to make a smooth, shiny icing that has the consistency of very stiff meringue.

3 Beat in the glycerine, lemon juice and food colouring, if using. Leave for 1 hour before using, covered with damp clear film, then stir to burst any air bubbles.

Storing
The icing will keep for up to three days, stored in a plastic container with a tight-fitting lid in a fridge.

Icing consistencies
This recipe is for an icing consistency suitable for flat icing a marzipanned rich fruit cake. When the spoon is lifted, the icing should form a sharp point, with a slight curve at the end, known as "soft peak". For piping, the icing needs to be slightly stiffer. It should form a fine sharp peak when the spoon is lifted.

Butter Icing

The creamy rich flavour and silky smoothness of butter icing is popular with both children and adults.

Makes 350g/12oz/1½ cups

75g/3oz/6 tbsp soft margarine or butter, softened
225g/8oz/2 cups icing sugar, sifted
5ml/1 tsp vanilla essence
10–15ml/2–3 tsp milk

For the flavourings

Chocolate: Blend 15ml/1 tbsp cocoa powder with 15ml/1 tbsp hot water. Cool before beating into the icing.

Coffee: Blend 10ml/2 tsp coffee powder with 15ml/1 tbsp boiling water. Omit the milk. Cool before beating the mixture into the icing.

Lemon, orange or lime: Substitute the vanilla essence and milk with lemon, orange or lime juice and 10ml/2 tsp of finely grated citrus rind. Omit the rind if using the icing for piping. Lightly tint the icing with food colouring, if wished.

1 Put the margarine or butter, icing sugar, vanilla essence and 5ml/1 tsp of the milk in a bowl.

2 Beat with a wooden spoon or an electric mixer, adding sufficient extra milk to give a light, smooth and fluffy consistency. For flavoured butter icing, follow the instructions above for the flavour of your choice.

Storing
The icing will keep for up to three days in an airtight container stored in a fridge.

Fudge Frosting

A darkly delicious frosting, this can transform a simple sponge cake into one worthy of a very special occasion. Spread fudge frosting smoothly over the cake or swirl it. Or be even more elaborate with a little piping – it really is very versatile. This recipe makes enough to fill and coat the top and sides of a 20cm/ 8in or 23cm/ 9in round sponge cake.

Makes 350g/12oz/1½ cups

50g/2oz squares plain chocolate
225g/8oz icing sugar, sifted
50g/2oz/4 tbsp butter
45ml/3 tbsp milk or single cream
5ml/1 tsp vanilla essence

1 Break or chop the chocolate into small pieces. Put the chocolate, icing sugar, butter, milk or cream and vanilla essence in a heavy-based saucepan.

2 Stir over a very low heat until both the chocolate and the butter have melted. Remove the mixture from the heat and stir until evenly blended.

3 Beat the icing frequently as it cools until it thickens sufficiently to use for spreading or piping. Use the icing immediately and work quickly once it has reached the right consistency.

Storing
This icing should be used straightaway.

Crème au Beurre

The rich, smooth, light texture of this icing makes it ideal for spreading, filling or piping onto cakes and gâteaux for all occasions.

Makes 350g/12oz/1½ cups

60ml/4 tbsp water
75g/3oz/6 tbsp caster sugar
2 egg yolks
150g/5oz/generous ½ cup unsalted butter, softened

For the flavourings

Citrus: replace water with orange, lemon or lime juice and 10ml/2 tsp grated rind
Chocolate: add 50g/2oz plain chocolate, melted
Coffee: add 10ml/2 tsp instant coffee granules, dissolved in 5ml/1 tsp boiling water, cooled

1 Bring the water to the boil, remove from the heat and stir in the sugar. Heat gently, stirring, until the sugar has dissolved. Then boil rapidly until the mixture becomes syrupy, or reaches the "thread" stage. To test, place a little syrup on the back of a dry teaspoon. Press a second teaspoon on to the syrup and gently pull apart. The syrup should form a fine thread. If not, return to the heat, boil rapidly and re-test a minute later.

2 Whisk the egg yolks together in a bowl. Continue to whisk while slowly adding the sugar syrup. Whisk until thick, pale and cool.

3 Beat the butter until light and fluffy. Add the egg mixture gradually, beating well after each addition, until thick and fluffy. For Chocolate or Coffee Crème au Beurre, fold in the flavouring at the end. If you prefer a citrus flavour, follow the instructions above.

American Frosting

A light marshmallow icing which crisps on the outside when left to dry, this versatile frosting may be swirled or peaked into a soft coating.

Makes 350g/12oz/1½ cups

1 egg white
30ml/2 tbsp water
15ml/1 tbsp golden syrup
5ml/1 tsp cream of tartar
175g/6oz/1½ cups icing sugar, sifted

1 Place the egg white with the water, golden syrup and cream of tartar in a heatproof bowl. Whisk together well until thoroughly blended.

2 Stir the icing sugar into the mixture and place the bowl over a saucepan of simmering water. Whisk until the mixture becomes thick and white.

3 Remove the bowl from the saucepan and continue to whisk the frosting until cool and thick, and the mixture stands up in soft peaks. Use immediately to fill or cover cakes.

Glacé Icing

An instant icing for quickly finishing the tops of large or small cakes.

Makes 350g/12oz/1½ cup

225g/8oz/2 cups icing sugar
30–45ml/2–3 tbsp hot water
food colouring (optional)

For the flavourings

Citrus: replace the water with orange, lemon or lime juice
Chocolate: sift 10ml/2 tsp cocoa powder with the icing sugar
Coffee: replace the water with strong, liquid coffee

1 Sift the icing sugar into a bowl. Using a wooden spoon, gradually stir in enough water to obtain the consistency of thick cream.

2 Beat until white and smooth, and the icing thickly coats the back of the spoon. Tint with a few drops of food colouring, if desired, or flavour the icing as suggested above. Use immediately to cover the top of the cake.

Simple Piped Flowers

Bouquets of iced blossoms, such as roses, pansies and bright summer flowers make colourful cake decorations.

For a rose, make a fairly firm icing. Colour the icing. Fit a petal nozzle into a paper piping bag, half-fill with icing and fold over top to seal. Hold the piping bag so the wider end is pointing at what will be the base of the rose and hold a cocktail stick in the other hand. Pipe a small cone shape around the tip of the stick, pipe a petal half way around the cone, lifting it so it is at an angle and curling outwards, turning the stick at the same time. Repeat with more petals so they overlap. Remove from stick and leave until dry.

Butterscotch Frosting

Makes 675g/1½ lb/3 cups

75g/3oz/6 tbsp unsalted butter
45ml/3 tbsp milk
25g/1oz/2 tbsp soft light brown sugar
15ml/1 tbsp black treacle
350g/12oz/3 cups icing sugar, sifted

For the flavourings

Citrus: replace the treacle with golden syrup and add 10ml/2 tsp finely grated orange, lemon or lime rind
Chocolate: sift 15ml/1 tbsp cocoa powder with the icing sugar
Coffee: replace the treacle with 15ml/1 tbsp coffee granules

1 Place the butter, milk, sugar and treacle in a bowl over a pan of simmering water. Stir until the butter and sugar melt.

2 Remove the bowl and stir in the icing sugar. Beat until smooth and glossy. For flavouring, follow instructions above.

3 Pour over the cake, or cool for a thicker consistency.

Chocolate Fudge Icing

A rich glossy icing which sets like chocolate fudge, this is versatile enough to smoothly coat, swirl or pipe, depending on the temperature of the icing when it is used.

Makes 450g/1lb/2 cups

115g/4oz plain chocolate, in squares
50g/2oz/¼ cup unsalted butter
1 egg, beaten
175g/6oz/1½ cups icing sugar, sifted

1 Place the chocolate and butter in a heatproof bowl over a saucepan of hot water.

2 Stir occasionally with a wooden spoon until both the chocolate and butter are melted. Add the egg and beat well.

3 Remove the bowl from the saucepan and stir in the icing sugar, then beat until smooth and glossy.

4 Pour immediately over the cake for a smooth finish, or leave to cool for a thicker spreading or piping consistency.

Making Caramel

Caramel has endless uses – for dipping fruits and nuts, crushing for cake coating, or drizzling into shapes.

Place 150ml/¼ pint/⅔ cup water in a saucepan. Bring to the boil, remove from the heat and stir in 175g/6oz/¾cup caster sugar. Heat gently until the sugar has dissolved. Bring the syrup to the boil, boil rapidly until the bubbles begin to subside and the syrup begins to turn a pale golden brown. For praline, add 75g/3oz/¾ cup toasted almonds to the caramel, shake to mix, then pour onto a sheet of oiled foil on a baking sheet. Cool, then crush with a rolling pin, or process in a food processor until finely ground.

Apricot Glaze

It is a good idea to make a large quantity of apricot glaze, especially when making celebration cakes.

Makes 450g/1lb/1½ cups
450g/1lb/1½ cups apricot jam
45ml/3 tbsp/ water

1 Place the jam and water in a saucepan. Heat gently, stirring occasionally until melted. Boil rapidly for 1 minute, then rub through a sieve, pressing the fruit against the sides of the sieve with the back of a wooden spoon. Discard the skins left in the sieve. Use the warmed glaze to brush cakes before applying marzipan, or use for glazing fruits on gâteaux and cakes.

Glossy Chocolate Icing

A rich smooth glossy icing, this can be made with plain or milk chocolate.

Makes 350g/12oz/1¼ cups
175g/6oz plain chocolate
150ml/¼ pint/⅔ cup single cream

1 Break up the chocolate into small pieces and place it in a saucepan with the cream.

2 Heat gently, stirring occasionally, until the chocolate has melted and the mixture is smooth.

3 Allow the icing to cool until it is thick enough to coat the back of a wooden spoon. Use it at this stage for a smooth glossy icing, or allow it to thicken to obtain an icing which can be swirled or patterned with a cake decorating scraper.

Sugar-frosting Flowers

Choose edible flowers such as pansies, primroses, violets, roses, freesias, tiny daffodils or nasturtiums.

Lightly beat an egg white in a small bowl and sprinkle some caster sugar on a plate. Wash the flowers then dry on kitchen paper. If possible leave some stem attached. Evenly brush both sides of the petals with the egg white. Hold the flower by its stem over a plate lined with kitchen paper, sprinkle it evenly with the sugar, then shake off any excess. Place on a flat board or wire rack covered with kitchen paper and leave to dry in a warm place. Use to decorate a cake.

Petal Paste

Makes 500g/1¼lb

10ml/2 tsp gelatine
25ml/1½ tsp cold water
10ml/2 tsp liquid glucose
10ml/2 tsp white vegetable fat
450g/1lb/4 cups icing sugar, sifted
5ml/1 tsp gum tragacanth
1 egg white

1 Place the gelatine, water, liquid glucose and white fat in a heatproof bowl over a saucepan of hot water until melted, stirring occasionally. Remove the bowl from the heat.

2 Sift the icing sugar and gum tragacanth into a bowl. Make a well in the centre and add the egg white and the gelatine mixture. Mix together to form a soft malleable white paste.

3 Knead on a surface dusted with icing sugar until smooth, white and free from cracks. Place in a plastic bag or wrap in clear film, sealing well to exclude all the air. Leave for about two hours before use, then knead again and use small pieces at a time, leaving the remaining petal paste well sealed.

Meringue Frosting

Makes 450g/1lb/1½ cups

2 egg whites
115g/4oz/1 cup icing sugar, sifted
150g/5oz/⅔ cup unsalted butter, softened

For the flavourings

Citrus: 10ml/2 tsp finely grated orange, lemon or lime rind.
Chocolate: 50g/2oz plain chocolate, melted
Coffee: 10ml/2 tsp coffee granules, blended with 5ml/1 tsp boiling water, cooled

1 Whisk the egg whites in a clean, heatproof bowl, add the icing sugar and gently whisk to mix well. Place the bowl over a saucepan of simmering water and whisk until thick and white. Remove the bowl from the saucepan and continue to whisk until cool and the meringue stands up in soft peaks.

2 Beat the butter in a separate bowl until light and fluffy. Add the meringue gradually, beating well after each addition, until thick and fluffy. Fold in the chosen flavouring, using a palette knife, until evenly blended. Use immediately for coating, filling and piping onto cakes.

Marbling

Sugarpaste, or fondant, lends itself to tinting in all shades and marbling is a good way to colour the paste.

Using a cocktail stick, add a few drops of the chosen edible food colour to some sugarpaste icing. Do not knead the food colouring fully into the icing.
When the sugarpaste is rolled out, the colour is dispersed in such a way that it gives a marbled appearance.
Marbled sugarpaste icing can be used to cover novelty cakes. Several colours can be used in the same icing to give an interesting multi-coloured effect.

THE CAKE DECORATOR'S BIBLE

THE CAKE DECORATOR'S BIBLE

A Complete Guide to Cake Decorating Techniques, with Over 100 Projects, from Traditional Classics to the Latest in Contemporary Designs

ANGELA NILSEN AND SARAH MAXWELL

PHOTOGRAPHY BY TIM HILL

HERMES HOUSE

This Paperback edition published by Hermes House
an imprint of
Anness Publishing Limited
Hermes House
88-89 Blackfriars Road
London SE1 8HA

A CIP catalogue record for this book is available from the British Library

ISBN 1-84038-726-2

Publisher: Joanna Lorenz
Project Editors: Judith Simons and Clare Nicholson
Photographer: Tim Hill
Home Economists: Sarah Maxwell and Angela Nilsen
Assistant Home Economist: Teresa Goldfinch
Stylist: Sarah Maxwell
Assistant Stylist: Timna Rose
Design: Axis Design

1 3 5 7 9 10 8 6 4 2

Contents

Introduction

This book is not only an invaluable foundation course in cake decorating techniques, but also a wonderful reference for a host of tried-and-tested recipes for classic cake bases and icings, as well as inspirational cake projects, which you will use again and again.

Clearly structured, the decorating course leads you through all the different decorating techniques which can be applied to royal icing, sugarpaste, marzipan, chocolate and other icings. There are step-by-step instructions and photographs for piping, crimping, embossing, frills, plaques, coloring, run-outs, modeling, stenciling, flowers, using purchased decorations, such as sweet confections, ribbons and fresh flowers, and much more.

The wonderful decorated cakes featured in the project sections on Classic Cakes, Special Occasion Cakes, Novelty Cakes and Children's Party Cakes are a feast for the eye and the palate. Moreover, they provide wonderful working examples which you can follow step-by-step, giving you the opportunity to practice and develop the techniques described in the first section of the book with professional results.

Do follow each recipe as closely as possible. Baking is one area of cooking in which accuracy will greatly improve the likelihood of achieving good results. When whisking egg whites, make sure the bowl and whisk are perfectly clean. For best results, use eggs at room temperature. If you sift flour from a height, it will have more chance to aerate and lighten.

No two ovens are alike. If possible, buy a reliable oven thermometer and test the temperature of your oven. Always bake in the center of the oven where the heat is more likely to be constant. If using a fan assisted oven, follow the manufacturer's guidelines for baking. Good quality cake pans will also improve results, as they conduct heat more efficiently.

Finally, there are some current health concerns about the use of raw egg in uncooked recipes. Homemade royal icing, marzipan and sugarpaste icing do include raw egg. An alternative recipe for royal icing, using pure albumen powder, has been provided in light of this. If you prefer to avoid raw egg, do buy ready-made marzipan and sugarpaste. Store-bought versions are usually good quality products and, of course, very quick and easy to use.

Basic Cake Recipes

Cakes are the highlight of many celebrations. What birthday would be complete without a cake with candles to blow out, or a wedding without a beautiful cake to cut? Some of the most traditional cake recipes provide the best bases for decorating. Recipes can be found in this chapter, and are used as bases for the decorated cakes later in the book. None of the cakes involve complicated techniques, and several are as simple as putting the ingredients into a bowl, and mixing them together.

Fruit cake is one of our most popular special occasion cakes. Among its advantages is that it keeps really well and in fact improves with storage, so it can be baked well ahead of time and decorated in easy stages. It also provides a wonderfully firm base for all sorts of elegant or novelty decorations. There are other ideas, too, for those who prefer a less rich tasting cake, such as the Madeira or a light fruit cake, as well as a quick-mix sponge for those last-minute, spontaneous celebrations.

Baking Equipment

A selection of basic equipment is needed for cake making. Here are a few of the more necessary items:

Scales For good, consistent results, ingredients for cake making require precise measuring. An accurate set of scales is therefore essential.
Bowls Various sizes of glass or china heatproof bowls with rounded sides make mixing easier and are useful when baking.
Measuring Jug Whether you are working in imperial, metric or cup measurements, a glass measuring jug is easy to read and means liquids are calculated accurately.
Measuring Spoons These are available in a standard size, making the measuring of small amounts more accurate.
Sieves These are used to aerate flour, making cakes lighter, and to remove lumps from icing sugar.
Electric Whisks These whisks are particularly useful for beating egg whites for Swiss rolls.
Balloon Whisks Useful for beating smaller amounts of either egg or cream mixtures.
Greaseproof Paper Used to line cake tins to prevent cakes from sticking.
Wooden and Metal Spoons Wooden spoons in various sizes are essential

for beating mixtures together when not using an electric mixer, while metal spoons are necessary for folding in ingredients and for smoothing over mixtures to give a flat surface before baking.
Spatulas Because they are so pliable, plastic spatulas are particularly useful for scraping all the cake mixture from a bowl.
Cake Tins These are available in all shapes and sizes, and the thicker the metal the less likely the cake will be to overcook. Most cake icing specialists hire out cake tins, useful when very large or unusual shaped tins are required.
Oven Gloves Essential when removing anything hot from the oven. It is worth choosing a good quality, well lined pair of gloves.
Wire Racks Made from wire mesh, these are available in different sizes and shapes and allow cakes to 'breathe' as they cool.
Cake Boards Choose the shape and size to fit the cake. Thick boards are for large, heavy cakes, royal iced cakes and any other fruit cake coated in icing. The board should be 5 cm/2 inches larger than the size of the cake. Thinner boards are for small Madeira cakes and other lighter cakes covered with icings such as butter, glacé or fudge. These can be about 2.5 cm/1 inch larger than the cake size.

1 glass mixing bowls
2 balloon whisk
3 large round cake tin
4 electric hand mixer
5 small round cake tin
6 scales
7 large square cake tin
8 measuring jug
9 measuring spoons
10 cake boards
11 pastry brush
12 pre-cut greaseproof paper tin liners
13 scissors
14 wooden mixing spoons
15 wire rack
16 sieve
17 oven gloves
18 plastic spatula
19 metal spoon

Quick-mix Sponge Cake

Here's a no-fuss, foolproof all-in-one cake, where the ingredients are quickly mixed together. The following quantities and baking instructions are for a deep 20cm/8 inch round cake tin or a 20 cm/ 8 inch ring mould. For other quantities and tin sizes, follow the baking instructions given in the decorated cake recipes.

INGREDIENTS

115 g/4oz/1 cup self-raising flour
1 tsp baking powder
115 g/4 oz/½ cup soft margarine
115 g/4 oz/½ cup caster sugar
2 size 3 eggs

STORING AND FREEZING

The cake can be made up to two days in advance, wrapped in clear film or foil and stored in an airtight container. The cake can be frozen for up to three months.

FLAVOURINGS

The following amounts are for a 2-egg, single quantity cake, as above. Increase the amounts proportionally for larger cakes.
Chocolate *Fold 1 tbsp cocoa powder blended with 1 tbsp boiling water into the cake mixture.*
Citrus *Fold 2 tsp of finely grated lemon, orange or lime zest into the cake mixture.*

1 Preheat the oven to 160°C/325°F/ Gas 3. Grease the round cake tin, line the base with greaseproof paper and grease the paper, or grease and flour the ring mould.

2 ▲ Sift the flour and baking powder into a bowl. Add the margarine, sugar and eggs.

3 ▲ Beat with a wooden spoon for 2–3 minutes. The mixture should be pale in colour and slightly glossy.

4 Spoon the cake mixture into the prepared tin and then smooth the surface. Bake for 20–30 minutes. To test if cooked, press the cake lightly in the centre. If firm, the cake is done, if soft, cook for a little longer. Alternatively, insert a skewer into the centre of the cake. If it comes out clean the cake is ready. Turn out on to a wire rack, remove the lining paper and leave to cool completely.

This quick-mix sponge cake can be filled and simply decorated with icing for a special occasion.

Swiss Roll

Swiss rolls are traditionally made without fat, so they don't keep as long as most other cakes. However, they have a deliciously light texture and provide the cook with the potential for all sorts of luscious fillings and tasty toppings.

Ingredients

4 size 3 eggs, separated
115 g/4 oz/½ cup caster sugar
115 g/4 oz/1 cup plain flour
1 tsp baking powder

STORING AND FREEZING
Swiss rolls and other fat-free sponges do not keep well, so if possible bake on the day of eating. Otherwise, wrap in clear film or foil and store in an airtight container overnight or freeze for up to three months.

1 Preheat the oven to 180°C/350°F/ Gas 4. Grease a 33 x 23 cm/ 13 x 9 inch Swiss roll tin, line with greaseproof paper and grease the paper.

2 Whisk the egg whites in a clean, dry bowl until stiff. Beat in 2 tbsp of the sugar.

3 ▲ Place the egg yolks, remaining sugar and 1 tbsp water in a bowl and beat for about 2 minutes until the mixture is pale and leaves a thick trail when the beaters are lifted.

4 ▼ Carefully fold the beaten egg yolks into the egg white mixture with a metal spoon.

5 Sift together the flour and baking powder. Carefully fold the flour mixture into the egg mixture with a metal spoon.

6 ▲ Pour the cake mixture into the prepared tin and then smooth the surface, being careful not to press out any air.

7 Bake in the centre of the oven for 12 –15 minutes. To test if cooked, press lightly in the centre. If the cake springs back it is done. It will also start to come away from the edges of the tin.

8 Turn the cake out on to a piece of greaseproof paper lightly sprinkled with caster sugar. Peel off the lining paper and cut off any crisp edges of the cake with a sharp knife. Spread with jam, if wished, and roll up, using the greaseproof paper as a guide. Leave to cool on a wire rack.

Vary the flavour of a traditional Swiss roll by adding a little grated orange, lime or lemon rind to the basic mixture.

Madeira Cake

This fine-textured cake makes a good base for decorating and is therefore a useful alternative to fruit cake, although it will not keep as long. It provides a firmer, longer-lasting base than a Victoria sponge, and can be covered with butter icing, fudge frosting, a thin layer of marzipan or sugarpaste icing. For the ingredients, decide what size and shape of cake you wish to make and then follow the chart shown opposite.

STORING AND FREEZING
The cake can be made up to a week in advance, wrapped in clear film or foil and stored in an airtight container. The cake can be frozen for up to three months.

Madeira cake provides a firmer base for icing than a Victoria sponge. It can be covered with a thin layer of sugarpaste, as here, or marzipan, and is a great alternative for anyone who does not like fruit cake.

1 Preheat the oven to 160°C/325°F/ Gas 3. Grease a deep cake tin, line the base and sides with a double thickness of greaseproof paper and grease the paper.

2 ▲ Sift together the flour and baking powder into a mixing bowl. Add the margarine, sugar, eggs and lemon juice.

3 ▲ Stir the ingredients together with a wooden spoon until they are all well combined.

4 ▲ Beat the mixture for about 2 minutes until smooth and glossy.

5 Spoon the mixture into the prepared tin and smooth the top. Bake in the centre of the oven, following the chart opposite as a guide for baking times. If the cake browns too quickly, cover the top loosely with foil. To test if baked, press lightly in the centre. If the cake springs back it is done. Alternatively, test by inserting a skewer into the centre of the cake. If it comes out clean the cake is done. Leave the cake to cool in the tin for 5 minutes and then turn out on to a wire rack. Remove the lining paper and leave to cool.

Madeira Cake Chart

Cake tin sizes	18 cm/7 in round	20 cm/8 in round	23 cm/9 in round	25 cm/10 in round	30 cm/12 in round
	15 cm/6 in square	18 cm/7 in square	20 cm/8 in square	23 cm/9 in square	28 cm/11 in square
Plain flour	225 g/ 8 oz/ 2 cups	350 g/ 12 oz/ 3 cups	450 g/ 1 lb/ 4 cups	500 g/ 1 lb 2 oz/ 4½ cups	625g/ 1½ lb/ 6 cups
Baking powder	1½ tsp	2 tsp	2½ tsp	1 tbsp	4 tsp
Soft margarine	175 g/ 6 oz/ ¾ cup	250 g/ 9 oz/ 1¼ cups	350 g/ 12 oz/ 1½ cups	400 g/ 14 oz/ 1¾ cups	550g/ 1 lb 3 oz 2¼ cups
Caster sugar	175 g/ 6 oz/ ¾ cup	250 g/ 9 oz/ 1¼ cups	350 g/ 12 oz/ 1½ cups	400 g/ 14 oz/ 1¾ cups	550g/ 1 lb 3 oz/ 2½ cups
Eggs, size 3, beaten	3	4	6	7	10
Lemon juice	1 tbsp	1½ tbsp	2 tbsp	2½ tbsp	4 tbsp
Approx. baking time	1¼ – 1½ hours	1½ – 1¾ hours	1¾ – 2 hours	1¾ – 2 hours	2¼ – 2½ hours

A traditional Madeira cake peaks and cracks slightly on the top. For a flat surface on which to ice, simply level the top with a sharp knife.

Rich Fruit Cake

This is the traditional cake mixture for many cakes made for special occasions such as weddings, Christmas, anniversaries and christenings. Make the cake a few weeks before icing, keep it well wrapped and stored in an airtight container and it should mature beautifully. Because of all its rich ingredients, this fruit cake will keep moist and fresh for several months. Follow the ingredients guide in the chart opposite for the size of cake you wish to make.

STORING

When the cake is cold, wrap in a double thickness of greaseproof paper or foil. Store in an airtight container in a cool dry place where it will keep for several months. During storage, the cake can be unwrapped and the bottom brushed with brandy (about half the amount used in the recipe). Re-wrap before storing again. As the cake keeps so well, there is no need to freeze.

A long-lasting cake which is full of rich flavours.

1 Preheat the oven to 140°C/275°F Gas 1. Grease a deep cake tin, line the base and sides with a double thickness of greaseproof paper and grease the paper.

2 ▲ Place all the ingredients in a large mixing bowl.

3 ▲ Stir to combine, then beat thoroughly with a wooden spoon for 3–6 minutes (depending on size), until well mixed.

4 ▲ Spoon the mixture into the prepared tin and smooth the surface with the back of a wet metal spoon. Make a slight impression in the centre to help prevent the cake from doming.

5 Bake in the centre of the oven. Use the chart opposite as a guide for timing the cake you are baking. Test the cake about 30 minutes before the end of the baking time. If the cake browns too quickly, cover the top loosely with foil. To test if baked, press lightly in the centre. If the cake feels firm and when a skewer inserted in the centre comes out clean, it is done. Test again at intervals if necessary.

6 Leave the cake to cool in the tin. When completely cool, turn out of the tin. The lining paper can be left on to help keep the cake moist.

Rich Fruit Cake Chart

Cake tin sizes	15 cm/6 in round 13 cm/5 in square	18 cm/7 in round 15 cm/6 in square	20 cm/8 in round 18 cm/7 in square	23 cm/9 in round 20 cm/8 in square	25 cm/10 in round 23 cm/9 in square	28 cm/11 in round 25 cm/10 in square	30 cm/12 in round 28 cm/11 in square	33 cm/13 in round 30 cm/12 in square
Currants	200 g/ 7 oz/ 1¼ cups	275 g/ 10 oz/ 1¾ cups	375 g/ 13 oz/ 2¼ cups	450 g/ 1 lb/ 3 cups	575 g/ 1¼ lb/ 3½ cups	675 g/ 1½ lb/ 4½ cups	800 g/ 1¾ lb/ 5¼ cups	900 g/ 2 lb/ 6 cups
Sultanas	115 g/ 4 oz/ ⅔ cup	200 g/ 7 oz/ 1 cup	250 g/ 9 oz/ 1½ cups	300 g/ 11 oz/ 1¾ cups	375 g/ 13 oz/ 2 cups	450 g/ 1 lb/ 2½ cups	550 g/ 1 lb 3 oz/ 3 cups	625 g/ 1 lb 6 oz/ 3½ cups
Raisins	65 g/ 2½ oz/ ⅓ cup	115 g/ 4 oz/ ⅔ cup	150 g/ 5 oz/ ¾ cup	175 g/ 6 oz/ 1 cup	200 g/ 7 oz/ 1 cup	225 g/ 8 oz/ 1⅓ cups	250 g/ 9 oz/ 1½ cups	275 g/ 10 oz/ 1½ cups
Glacé cherries, halved	40 g/ 1½ oz/ ¼ cup	65 g/ 2½ oz/ ⅓ cup	90 g/ 3½ oz/ ½ cup	115 g/ 4 oz/ ½ cup	150 g/ 5 oz/ ⅔ cup	175 g/ 6 oz/ ¾ cup	200 g/ 7 oz/ 1 cup	225 g/ 8 oz/ 1¼ cups
Almonds, chopped	40 g/ 1½ oz/ ⅓ cup	65 g/ 2½ oz/ ½ cup	90 g/ 3½ oz/ ¾ cup	115 g/ 4 oz/ 1 cup	150 g 5 oz/ 1¼ cups	175 g/ 6 oz/ 1½ cups	200 g/ 7 oz/ 1⅔ cups	225 g/ 8 oz/ 2 cups
Mixed peel	40 g/ 1½ oz/ ¼ cup	65 g/ 2½ oz/ ½ cup	65 g/ 2½ oz/ ½ cup	90 g/ 3½ oz/ ⅔ cup	115 g/ 4 oz/ ¾ cup	150 g/ 5 oz/ 1 cup	175 g/ 6 oz/ 1 cup	200 g/ 7 oz/ 1⅓ cups
Lemon, grated rind	½	1	1	2	2	2	3	3
Brandy	1½ tbsp	2 tbsp	2½ tbsp	3 tbsp	3½ tbsp	4 tbsp	4½ tbsp	5 tbsp
Plain flour	150 g/ 5 oz/ 1⅓ cups	200 g/ 7 oz/ 1¾ cups	250 g/ 9 oz/ 2 cups	300 g/ 11 oz/ 2¾ cups	400 g/ 14 oz/ 3½ cups	450 g/ 1 lb/ 4 cups	550 g/ 1 lb 3 oz/ 4½ cups	625 g/ 1 lb 6 oz/ 5½ cups
Ground mixed spice	1 tsp	1 tsp	1¼ tsp	1½ tsp	1½ tsp	2 tsp	2½ tsp	1 tbsp
Ground nutmeg	¼ tsp	½ tsp	½ tsp	1 tsp	1 tsp	1 tsp	1½ tsp	2 tsp
Ground almonds	40 g/ 1½ oz/ ½ cup	50 g/ 2 oz/ ⅔ cup	65 g/ 2½ oz/ ¾ cup	75 g/ 3 oz/ 1 cup	90 g/ 3½ oz/ 1¼ cups	115 g/ 4 oz/ 1⅓ cups	130 g/ 4½ oz/ 1½ cups	150 g/ 5 oz/ 1⅔ cups
Soft margarine or butter	115 g/ 4 oz/ ½ cup	150 g/ 5 oz/ ⅔ cup	200 g/ 7 oz/ scant 1 cup	250 g/ 9 oz/ scant 1¼ cups	300 g/ 11 oz/ scant 1½ cups	375 g/ 13 oz/ scant 1¾ cups	425 g/ 15 oz/ scant 2 cups	500 g/ 1 lb 2 oz/ 2¼ cups
Soft brown sugar	130 g 4½ oz/ ⅔ cup	175 g/ 6 oz/ ¾ cup	225 g/ 8 oz/ 1 cup	275 g/ 10 oz/ 1⅓ cups	350 g/ 12 oz 1½ cups	400 g/ 14 oz/ scant 2 cups	450 g/ 1 lb/ 2 cups	500 g/ 1 lb 2 oz/ 2¼ cups
Black treacle or molasses	1 tbsp	1 tbsp	1 tbsp	1½ tbsp	2 tbsp	2 tbsp	2 tbsp	2½ tbsp
Eggs, size 3, beaten	3	4	5	6	7	8	9	10
Approx. baking time	2¼–2½ hours	2½–2¾ hours	3–3½ hours	3¼–3¾ hours	3¾–4¼ hours	4–4½ hours	4½–5¼ hours	5¼–5¾ hours

Light Fruit Cake

For those who prefer a lighter fruit cake, here is a less rich version, still ideal for marzipanning and covering with sugarpaste or royal icing. Follow the ingredients guide in the chart opposite according to the size of cake you wish to make.

STORING AND FREEZING
When the cake is cold, wrap well in greaseproof paper, clear film or foil. It will keep for several weeks, stored in an airtight container. As the cake keeps so well, there is no need to freeze, but, if wished, freeze for up to three months.

1 Preheat the oven to 150°C/300°F/ Gas 2. Grease a deep cake tin, line the sides and base with a double thickness of greaseproof paper and grease the paper.

2 ▲ Measure and prepare all the ingredients, then place them all together in a large mixing bowl.

3 ▲ Stir to combine, then beat thoroughly with a wooden spoon for 3–4 minutes, depending on the size, until well mixed.

4 ▲ Spoon the mixture into the prepared tin and smooth the surface with the back of a wet metal spoon. Make a slight impression in the centre to help prevent the cake from doming.

5 Bake in the centre of the oven. Use the chart opposite as a guide according to the size of cake you are baking. Test the cake about 15 minutes before the end of the baking time. If the cake browns too quickly, cover the top loosely with foil. To test if baked, press lightly in the centre. If the cake feels firm, and when a skewer inserted in the centre comes out clean, it is done. Test again at intervals if necessary.

6 Leave the cake to cool in the tin. When completely cool, turn out of the tin. The lining paper can be left on to help keep the cake moist.

Round, square, ring or heart-shaped – the shape of this light fruit cake can be varied to suit the occasion.

LIGHT FRUIT CAKE CHART

Cake tin sizes	15 cm/6 in round 13 cm/5 in square	18 cm/7 in round 15 cm/6 in square	20 cm/8 in round 18 cm/7 in square	23 cm/9 in round 20 cm/8 in square
Soft margarine or butter	115 g/ 4 oz/ ½ cup	175 g/ 6 oz/ ¾ cup	225 g/ 8 oz/ 1 cup	275 g/ 10 oz/ 1⅓ cups
Caster sugar	115 g/ 4 oz/ ½ cup	175 g/ 6 oz/ ¾ cup	225 g/ 8 oz/ 1 cup	275 g/ 10 oz/ 1⅓ cups
Orange, grated rind	½	½	1	1
Eggs, size 3, beaten	3	4	5	6
Plain flour	165 g 5½ oz/ 1½ cups	200 g/ 7 oz/ 1¾ cups	300 g/ 11 oz/ 2¾ cups	400 g/ 14 oz/ 3½ cups
Baking powder	¼ tsp	½ tsp	½ tsp	1 tsp
Ground mixed spice	1 tsp	1½ tsp	2 tsp	2½ tsp
Currants	50 g/ 2 oz/ ⅓ cup	115 g/ 4 oz/ ⅔ cup	175 g/ 6 oz/ 1 cup	225 g/ 8 oz/ 1½ cups
Sultanas	50 g/ 2 oz/ ⅓ cup	115 g/ 4 oz/ ⅔ cup	175 g/ 6 oz/ 1 cup	225 g/ 8 oz/ 1⅓ cups
Raisins	50 g/ 2 oz/ ⅓ cup	115 g/ 4 oz/ ⅔ cup	175 g/ 6 oz/ 1 cup	225 g/ 8 oz/ 1⅓ cups
Dried apricots, chopped	25 g/ 1 oz/ 7	50 g/ 2 oz/ 14	50 g/ 2 oz/ 14	75 g/ 3 oz/ 21
Mixed cut peel	50 g/ 2 oz/ scant ½ cup	75 g/ 3 oz/ good ½ cup	115 g/ 4 oz/ ¾ cup	150 g/ 5 oz/ 1 cup
Approx. baking time	2¼ – 2½ hours	2½ – 2¾ hours	2¾ – 3¼ hours	3¼ – 3¾ hours

Truffle Cake Mix

This is a no-cook recipe, using leftover pieces of sponge cake or plain shop-bought sponge to make a moist, rich cake mixture, which is used in several of the novelty cakes.

Ingredients

175 g/6 oz plain sponge cake pieces
175 g/6 oz/2 cups ground almonds
75 g/3oz/scant 1/3 cup dark brown muscovado sugar
1 tsp ground mixed spice
pinch of ground cinnamon
finely grated zest of 1 orange
3 tbsp freshly squeezed orange juice
5 tbsp clear honey

STORING AND FREEZING
The mixture can be made up to two days in advance, wrapped in clear film and stored in an airtight container. Not suitable for freezing.

1 Place the sponge cake pieces into the bowl of a food processor or blender and process for a few seconds to form fine crumbs.

2 Place the cake crumbs, ground almonds, sugar, spices, orange zest, orange juice and honey in a large mixing bowl. Stir well to combine into a thick, smooth mixture.

3 ▲ Use the mixture as directed in the novelty cake recipes. The truffle mixture can be made and moulded into any simple shape, such as a log or round balls. The moulded mixture can be covered with marzipan or sugarpaste icing.

Tip

Dampen your hands slightly before handling the truffle mixture, as it is very sticky.

Here the truffle mixture has been rolled into a log shape to form the sausage in this sweet-tasting novelty Hot Dog cake.

Lining Cake Tins

Greaseproof paper is normally used for lining cake tins. The paper lining prevents the cakes from sticking to the tins and makes them easier to turn out. Different cake recipes require slightly different techniques of lining, depending on the shape of the tin, the type of cake mixture, and how long the cake needs to cook. Quick-mix sponge cakes require only one layer of paper to line the base, for example, whereas rich fruit cakes that often bake for several hours if they are large in size need to be lined with a double layer of paper on the base and sides. This extra protection also helps cakes to cook evenly.

Lining a shallow round tin

This technique is used for a quick-mix sponge cake.

1 Put the tin on a piece of greaseproof paper and draw around the base of the tin. Cut out the circle just inside the marked line.

2 ▲ Lightly brush the inside of the tin with a little vegetable oil and position the paper circle in the base of the tin. Brush the paper with a little more vegetable oil.

Tip

Softened butter or margarine can be used as a greasing agent in place of vegetable oil, if wished.

Lining a Swiss roll tin

1 Put the tin on a piece of greaseproof paper and draw around the base. Increase the rectangle by 2.5 cm/1 inch on all sides. Cut out this rectangle and snip each corner diagonally down to the original rectangle.

2 ▲ Lightly brush the inside of the tin with a little vegetable oil and fit the paper into the tin, overlapping the corners slightly so that they fit neatly. Brush the paper with a little more vegetable oil.

Lining a deep round cake tin

This technique should be used for all rich or light fruit cakes and Madeira cakes. Use this method for a square tin, but cut out the sides separately.

1 Put the tin on a double thickness of greaseproof paper and draw around the base. Cut out just inside the line.

2 For the sides of the tin, cut out a double thickness strip of greaseproof paper that will wrap around the outside of the tin, allowing a slight overlap, and which is 2.5 cm/1 inch taller than the depth of the tin.

3 Fold over 2.5 cm/1 inch along the length of the side lining. Snip the paper along its length, inside the fold, at short intervals.

4 Brush the inside of the tin with vegetable oil. Slip the side lining into the tin so the snipped edge fits into the curve of the base and sits flat.

5 ▲ Position the base lining in the tin and brush the paper with a little more vegetable oil.

Basic Icing Recipes

Cakes can take on many guises, and nothing enhances their appearance more for that extra special occasion than a little icing. This chapter offers a range of simple classic icing recipes to suit the type of cake you have made and which can be adapted according to the occasion. Ideas range from quick-mix icings, such as butter icing and satin chocolate icing, which may be instantly poured, spread, swirled or piped on to sponge and Madeira cakes or Swiss rolls, to the more regal icings, such as royal icing and sugarpaste icing. These are ideal for covering and decorating fruit cakes intended for more formal occasions, such as anniversaries, christenings and weddings.

The icings in this section are all fairly traditional. However, if you want to substitute any of them with a favourite icing recipe when decorating, make sure that it suits the cake on which you are working.

Decorating Equipment

With a few simple tools, it is possible to create the most stunning of cake decorations. Thick swirls of butter icing formed with a palette knife, or stark white icing sugar dusted over a contrastingly dark chocolate icing, instantly provide an impressive effect. As your skills develop, however, you will probably want to invest in some specialized pieces of icing equipment, such as those listed here.

Icing Turntable This is one of the most expensive but useful items for either the novice or more advanced cake decorator. Because it revolves, it is particularly handy for piping, or for icing the sides of a round cake with royal icing.
Straight-edge Ruler Choose one made of stainless steel so that it will not bend as you pull it across a layer of royal icing, to give a smooth, flat surface to a cake.
Plastic Scrapers These can have straight or serrated edges for giving a smooth or patterned surface to the sides or tops of cakes coated with royal, butter or fudge icing.
Small Rolling Pin Made in a handy size for rolling out small amounts of marzipan or sugarpaste icing for decorations.
Nozzles There are numerous shapes and sizes to choose from, but it is best to start off with some of the basic shapes. Small straight-sided nozzles fit home-made greaseproof paper piping bags. Larger ones are more suitable for the commercially-made material bags when piping large amounts of icing.
Nozzle Brush A small wire brush which makes the job of cleaning out nozzles a lot easier.
Flower Nail Used as a support when piping flowers.
Crimping Tools These are available with different end-shapes which produce varied patterns and offer a quick way of giving a professional finish to a cake.
Paintbrushes Brushes for painting designs on to cakes, adding highlights to flowers or modelled shapes, or for making run-outs are available at cake icing specialists, stationers or art supply shops.
Florist's Wire, Tape and Stamens All available from cake icing specialists, the wire, available in different gauges, is handy for wiring small sugarpaste flowers together to form floral sprays. The tape is used to neaten the stems, and the stamens, available in many colours, form the centres of the flowers.

Papers There are several papers used in cake decorating. Greaseproof paper is used for making piping bags and for drying sugar-frosted flowers and fruits, while baking parchment is used for spreading melted chocolate and for icing run-outs.
Cutters Small cocktail cutters are useful for making cut-out shapes from chocolate, sugarpaste and marzipan. Blossom cutters, available in different shapes and sizes, are good for making small flowers, while a special frill cutter can be used to cut out quick-and-easy frills.

1 food colourings
2 greaseproof paper and baking parchment
3 piping nozzles
4 fabric piping bag
5 nozzle brush
6 paintbrushes
7 icing turntable
8 florist's wire
9 stamens
10 florist's tape
11 straight-edge ruler
12 cake pillars
13 cake pillar supports
14 crimping tools
15 food colouring pens
16 flower nail
17 frill cutter
18 textured rolling pin
19 foam pad
20 shaped cutters
21 modelling tool
22 plunger cutters
23 dual blossom cutter
24 cocktail cutters
25 plain and serrated side scrapers

Marzipan

With its smooth, pliable texture, marzipan has been popular for centuries in cake making, especially for large cakes such as wedding and christening cakes. It is also excellent for making a variety of cake decorations. The following recipe is sufficient to cover the top and sides of an 18 cm/7 inch round or a 15 cm/6 inch square cake. Make half the amount if only the top is to be covered.

INGREDIENTS
Makes 450 g/1 lb
225 g/8 oz/2¼ cups ground almonds
115 g/4 oz/1 cup icing sugar, sifted
115 g/4 oz/½ cup caster sugar
1 tsp lemon juice
2 drops almond essence
1 size 4 egg, beaten

STORING
The marzipan will keep for up to four days, wrapped in clear film in an airtight container, and stored in the refrigerator.

1 ▲ Put the ground almonds, icing and caster sugars into a bowl and mix together.

2 ▲ Add the lemon juice, almond essence and enough beaten egg to mix to a soft but firm dough. Gather together with your fingers to form a ball.

3 ▲ Knead the marzipan on a work surface lightly dusted with sifted icing sugar until smooth.

Using Marzipan

Marzipan is applied to the sides and top of a cake, particularly rich fruit cakes, to prevent moisture seeping through the cake and to provide a smooth under-coat for the top covering of royal icing or sugarpaste icing.

Once the marzipan has been applied, leave it to dry for a day or two before applying the icing. For a richer taste you can mix up your own marzipan. However, if you have any concerns about using raw eggs in uncooked recipes, especially in light of current health warnings, do buy ready-made marzipan. It is very good quality, does not contain raw egg and is available in two colours, white and yellow. White is the best choice if you want to add your own colours and create different moulded shapes.

Marzipan can be used as an attractive cake coating in its own right as well as providing a base for other icings.

Sugarpaste Icing

Sugarpaste icing has opened up a whole new concept in cake decorating. It is wonderfully pliable, easy to make and use, and can be coloured, moulded and shaped in the most imaginative fashion. Though quick to make at home, shop-bought sugarpaste, also known as easy-roll or ready-to-roll icing, is very good quality and handy to use. This recipe makes sufficient to cover the top and sides of an 18 cm/7 inch round or a 15 cm/6 inch square cake.

INGREDIENTS
Makes 350 g/12 oz
1 size 3 egg white
1 tbsp liquid glucose, warmed
350 g/12 oz/3 cups icing sugar, sifted

STORING
The icing will keep for up to a week, wrapped in clear film or a plastic bag and stored in the refrigerator. Bring to room temperature before using. If a thin crust forms, trim off before using or it will make the icing lumpy. Also, if the icing dries out or hardens, knead in a little boiled water to make it smooth and pliable again.

1 Put the egg white and glucose in a bowl. Stir together with a wooden spoon to break up the egg white.

2 ▲ Add the icing sugar and mix together with a palette knife or knife, using a chopping action, until well blended and the icing begins to bind together.

3 Knead the mixture with your fingers until it forms a ball.

4 ▲ Knead the sugarpaste on a work surface lightly dusted with sifted icing sugar for several minutes until smooth, soft and pliable. If the icing is too soft, knead in some more sifted icing sugar until it is firm and pliable.

Tip

Ready-made shop-bought sugarpaste does not contain raw egg, so do use if you prefer to avoid uncooked egg in recipes in light of current health warnings.

Tinted or left pure white, sugarpaste icing can be used to cover cakes, and moulded to make decorations to suit any shape of cake.

Royal Icing

Royal icing has gained a regal position in the world of icing. Any special occasion cake which demands a classical, professional finish uses this smooth, satin-like icing. The following recipe makes sufficient to cover the top and sides of an 18 cm/7 inch round or a 15 cm/6 inch square cake.

INGREDIENTS
Makes 675 g/1½ lb
3 size 3 egg whites
about 675 g/1½ lb/6 cups icing sugar, sifted
1½ tsp glycerine
few drops lemon juice
colouring (optional)

STORING
Royal icing will keep for up to three days in an airtight container, stored in the refrigerator. Stir the icing well before using.

Tips

- Always sift the icing sugar before using, to get rid of any lumps.
- Never add more than the stated amount of glycerine. Too much will make the icing crumbly and too fragile to use.
- A little lemon juice is added to prevent the icing from discolouring, but too much will make the icing become hard.

1 ▲ Put the egg whites in a bowl and stir lightly with a wooden spoon to break them up.

2 ▲ Add the icing sugar gradually in small quantities, beating well with a wooden spoon between each addition. Add sufficient icing sugar to make a smooth, white, shiny icing with the consistency of very stiff meringue. It should be thin enough to spread, but thick enough to hold its shape.

3 ▲ Beat in the glycerine, lemon juice and food colouring, if using.

4 It is best to let the icing sit for about 1 hour before using. Cover the surface with a piece of damp clear film or a lid so the icing does not dry out. Before using, stir the icing to burst any air bubbles. Even when working with royal icing, always keep it covered.

Royal Icing Using Pure Albumen Powder

If you are concerned about current health warnings advising against the use of raw eggs in uncooked recipes, try the following recipe.

INGREDIENTS
Makes 450 g/1 lb
450 g/1 lb/4 cups icing sugar, sifted
6 tbsp water
12.5g/½ oz/7 tsp pure albumen powder

STORING
This royal icing will keep for up to a week in an airtight container, stored in a cool place.

1 Mix the pure albumen powder with the water. Leave to stand for 15 minutes, then stir until the powder dissolves.

2 Sieve the albumen solution into a mixing bowl. Add half the icing sugar and beat until smooth. Add the remaining sugar and beat again for 12–14 minutes or until smooth.

3 Adjust the consistency as needed, adding a little more icing sugar for a stiffer icing or a little water for a thinner one. If storing, transfer to an airtight container, cover the surface of the royal icing with clear film and then close the lid.

Icing Consistencies

For flat icing

▲ The recipes on the opposite page are for a consistency of icing suitable for flat icing a rich fruit cake covered in marzipan. When the spoon is lifted out of the icing, it should form a sharp point, with a slight curve at the end, known as a 'soft peak'.

For peaking

▲ Make the royal icing as before, but to a stiffer consistency so that when the spoon is lifted out of the bowl the icing stands in straight peaks.

For piping

For piping purposes, the icing needs to be slightly stiffer than for peaked icing so that it forms a fine, sharp peak when the spoon is lifted out. This allows the icing to flow easily for piping, at the same time enabling it to keep its definition.

For run-outs

For elegant and more elaborate cakes, you may want to pipe outlines of shapes and then fill these in with different coloured icing. These are known as run-outs. For the outlines, you need to make the icing to a piping consistency, while for the insides you need a slightly thinner icing with a consistency of thick cream, so that with a little help it will flow within the shapes. Ideally the icing should hold its shape and be slightly rounded after filling the outlines.

The right consistency

If you need to change the consistency of your icing, add a little sifted icing sugar to make it stiffer, or beat in a little egg white for a thinner icing. Be sure to do this carefully, as a little of one or the other will change the consistency fairly quickly.

A traditional look for a classic royal icing. This square rich fruit cake has been marzipanned and then flat iced with three, ultra-smooth layers of royal icing. It is simply, but elegantly, decorated with piped borders, a crisp, white ribbon and fresh roses.

Butter Icing

The creamy, rich flavour and silky smoothness of butter icing are popular with both children and adults. The icing can be varied in colour and flavour and makes a decorative filling and coating for sponge and Madeira cakes or Swiss rolls. Simply swirled, or more elaborately piped, butter icing gives a delicious and attractive finish. The following quantity makes enough to fill and coat the sides and top of a 20 cm/8 inch sponge cake.

Ingredients

Makes 350 g/12 oz

75 g/3 oz/6 tbsp butter, softened, or soft margarine
225 g/8 oz/2 cups icing sugar, sifted
1 tsp vanilla essence
2–3 tsp milk

STORING

The icing will keep for up to three days, in an airtight container stored in the refrigerator.

1 ▲ Put the butter or margarine, icing sugar, vanilla essence and 1 tsp of the milk in a bowl.

2 ▲ Beat with a wooden spoon or an electric mixer, adding sufficient extra milk to give a light, smooth and fluffy consistency.

FLAVOURINGS

The following amounts are for a single quantity of icing. Increase or decrease the amounts proportionally as needed.

Chocolate *Blend 1 tbsp cocoa powder with 1 tbsp hot water. Allow to cool before beating into the icing.*

Coffee *Blend 2 tsp instant coffee powder or granules with 1 tbsp boiling water. Allow to cool before beating into the icing.*

Lemon, orange or lime *Substitute the vanilla essence and milk for lemon, orange or lime juice and 2 tsp of finely grated citrus zest. Omit the zest if using the icing for piping. Lightly colour the icing with the appropriate shade of food colouring, if wished.*

Generous swirls of butter icing give a mouth-watering effect to a cake.

Glacé Icing

This icing can be made in just a few minutes and can be varied by adding a few drops of food colouring or flavouring. The following quantity makes enough to cover the top and decorate a 20 cm/8 inch round sponge cake.

Ingredients
Makes 225 g/8 oz
225 g/8 oz/2 cups icing sugar
2–3 tbsp warm water or fruit juice
food colouring, optional

STORING
Not suitable for storing. The icing must be used immediately after making.

1 ▲ Sift the icing sugar into a mixing bowl to get rid of any lumps.

2 ▲ Using a wooden spoon, gradually stir in enough water to make an icing with the consistency of thick cream. Beat until the icing is smooth. It should be thick enough to coat the back of the spoon. If it is too runny, beat in a little more sifted icing sugar.

3 To colour the icing, beat in a few drops of food colouring. Use the icing immediately for coating or piping.

Drizzled or spread, glacé icing can quickly turn a plain cake into something special.

Fudge Frosting

A rich, darkly delicious frosting, this can transform a simple sponge cake into one worthy of a very special occasion. Spread fudge frosting smoothly over the cake or swirl it. Or be even more elaborate with a little piping - it is very versatile. The following amount will fill and coat the top and sides of a 20 cm/8 inch or 23 cm/9 inch round sponge cake.

INGREDIENTS
Makes 350 g/12 oz
50 g/2 oz plain chocolate
225 g/8 oz/2 cups icing sugar, sifted
50 g/2 oz/4 tbsp butter or margarine
3 tbsp milk or single cream
1 tsp vanilla essence

STORING
Not suitable for storing. The icing must be used immediately after making.

1 ▲ Break or chop the chocolate into small pieces. Put the chocolate, icing sugar, butter, milk and vanilla essence in a heavy-based saucepan.

2 ▲ Stir over a very low heat until the chocolate and butter or margarine melt. Remove from the heat and stir until evenly blended.

3 ▲ Beat the icing frequently as it cools until it thickens sufficiently to use for spreading or piping. Use immediately and work quickly once it has reached the right consistency.

Thick glossy swirls of fudge icing almost make a decoration in themselves on this cake.

Satin Chocolate Icing

Shiny as satin and smooth as silk, this dark chocolate icing can be poured over a sponge cake. A few fresh flowers, pieces of fresh fruit, simple chocolate shapes or white chocolate piping add the finishing touch. Use this recipe to cover a 20 cm/8 inch square or a 23 cm/9 inch round quick-mix sponge or Madeira cake.

Ingredients
Makes 225 g/8 oz
175g/6 oz plain chocolate
150 ml/¼ pint/⅔ cup single cream
½ tsp instant coffee powder

STORING
Not suitable for storing. The icing must be used immediately after making.

Tip

Before using the icing, place the cake on a wire rack positioned over a baking sheet or a piece of greaseproof paper. This will avoid unnecessary mess.

1 ▲ Break or chop the chocolate into small pieces. Put the chocolate, cream and coffee in a small heavy-based saucepan. Place the cake to be iced on a wire rack.

2 ▲ Stir over a very low heat until the chocolate melts and the mixture is smooth and evenly blended.

3 Remove from the heat and immediately pour the icing over the cake, letting it slowly run down the sides to coat it completely. Spread the icing with a palette knife as necessary, working quickly before the icing has time to thicken.

Satin chocolate icing brings a real touch of sophistication to the most humble of cakes.

Covering Cakes

Covering cakes with icing – whether marzipan, royal or sugarpaste – not only provides a wonderful surface for decorating but also helps to keep the cake moist. The icings need to be applied with care to ensure that the finish is beautifully smooth. Always plan ahead; it will take several days to marzipan and royal ice a cake, allowing for the drying out times.

Marzipanning a Cake for Sugarpaste Icing

Marzipan can be applied as an icing in its own right, but is mainly used as a base for sugarpaste or royal icing. Unlike a cake covered in royal icing which traditionally has sharp, well defined corners, a cake covered in sugarpaste has much smoother lines with rounded corners and edges. There are therefore two different techniques depending on how you wish to ice the cake.

1 If the cake is not absolutely flat, fill any hollows or build up the top edge (if it is lower than the top of the cake) with a little marzipan. Brush the top of the cake with a little warmed and sieved apricot jam.

2 ▲ Lightly dust a work surface with icing sugar. Knead the marzipan into a smooth ball. Roll out to a 5 mm/¼ inch thickness and large enough to cover the top and sides of the cake, allowing about an extra 7.5 cm/3 inches all around for trimming. Make sure the marzipan does not stick to the work surface and moves freely.

3 ▲ Lift the marzipan using your hands, or place it over a rolling pin to support it, and position over the top of the cake. Drape the marzipan over the cake to cover it evenly.

4 ▲ Smooth the top with the palm of your hand to eliminate any air bubbles. Then carefully lift up the edges of the marzipan and let them fall against the sides of the cake, being careful not to stretch the marzipan. Ensure the marzipanned sides are flat and there are no creases - all the excess marzipan should fall on to the work surface. Use the palms of your hands to smooth the sides and eliminate air bubbles.

5 ▲ With a sharp knife, trim the excess marzipan, cutting it flush with the base of the cake.

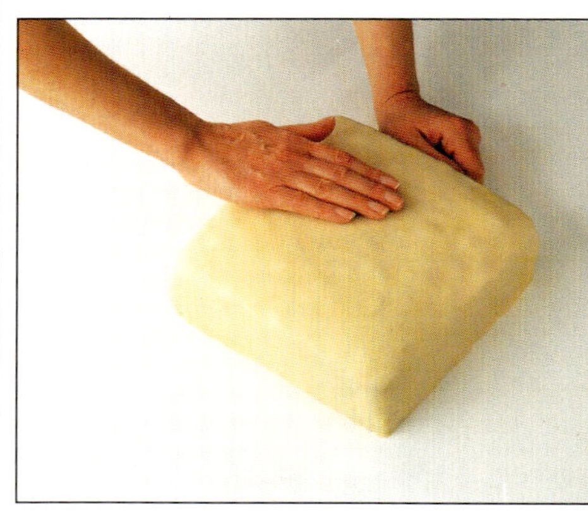

6 ▲ With your hands, work in a circular motion over the surface of the marzipan to give it a smooth finish. Spread a little royal icing over the middle of a cake board and place the cake in the centre to secure. Lay a piece of greaseproof paper over the top to protect the surface, then leave for at least 12 hours to dry before covering with icing.

Marzipanning a Round Cake for Royal Icing

1 ▲ If the cake is not absolutely flat, fill any hollows or build up the top edge (if it is lower than the top of the cake) with a little marzipan.

2 Brush the top of the cake with warmed and sieved apricot jam.

3 Lightly dust a work surface with icing sugar. Using one-third of the marzipan, knead it into a ball. Roll out to a round 5 mm/¼ inch thickness and 1 cm/½ inch larger than the top of the cake. Make sure that the marzipan does not stick to the work surface and moves freely.

4 ▲ Invert the top of the cake on to the marzipan. Trim the marzipan almost to the edge of the cake. With a small metal palette knife, press the marzipan inwards so it is flush with the edge of the cake.

5 Carefully turn the cake the right way up. Check the sides of the cake. If there are any holes, fill them with marzipan to make a flat surface. Brush the sides with apricot jam.

6 Knead the remaining marzipan and any trimmings (making sure there are no cake crumbs on the work surface) to form a ball. For the sides of the cake, measure the circumference with a piece of string, and the height of the sides with another piece.

7 ▲ Roll out a strip of marzipan to the same thickness as the top, matching the length and width to the measured string. Hold the cake on its side, being careful to touch the marzipanned top as lightly as possible. Roll the cake along the marzipan strip, pressing the marzipan into position to cover the sides. Trim if necessary to fit.

8 ▲ Smooth the joins together with a palette knife. Spread a little royal icing into the middle of a cake board and place the cake in the centre to secure. Lay a piece of greaseproof paper very loosely over the top to protect the surface, then leave for at least 24 hours to dry before covering with icing.

Tip

When buying marzipan, it is best to choose the white kind for covering a cake, as the bright yellow marzipan may discolour pale coloured sugarpaste or royal icing.

▶ The method for marzipanning a square cake for royal icing is the same as for a round one, except for the sides. Measure the length and height of the sides with string and roll out the marzipan in four separate pieces, using the string measurements as a guide.

Covering a Round Cake with Royal Icing

A cake which is coated with royal icing is always covered with marzipan first. The marzipan should be applied one to two days before the royal icing so it has time to dry out slightly, giving a firm surface on which to work. The royal icing is then built up in two or three layers, each one being allowed to dry out before covering with the next. The final coat should be perfectly flat and smooth, with no air bubbles.

Tip

It is difficult to calculate the exact amount of icing required, but if you work with 450 g/1 lb/⅔ quantity batches, it should always be fresh. While working, keep the royal icing in a bowl and cover with a clean, damp cloth or clear film so it does not dry out.

1 The icing should be of 'soft peak' consistency. Put about 2 tbsp of icing in the centre of the marzipanned cake (the amount will depend on the size of cake you are icing).

2 ▲ Using a small palette knife, spread the icing over the top of the cake, working back and forth with the flat of the knife to eliminate any air bubbles. Keep working the icing in this way until the top of the cake is completely covered. Trim any icing that extends over the edge of the cake with the palette knife.

3 ▲ Position a straight-edge ruler on the top edge of the cake furthest away from you. Slowly and smoothly pull the ruler across the surface of the icing, holding it at a slight angle. Do this without stopping to prevent ridges forming. You may need several attempts to get a smooth layer, in which case simply re-spread the top of the cake with icing and try again.

4 ▲ Trim any excess icing from the top edges of the cake with the palette knife to give a straight, neat edge. Leave the icing to dry for several hours, or overnight, in a dry place before continuing.

5 ▲ Place the cake on a turntable. To cover the sides, spread some icing on to the side of the cake with a palette knife. Rock the knife back and forth as you spread the icing to eliminate air bubbles. Rotate the turntable as you work your way around the cake.

6 ▲ Using a plain side-scraper, hold it firmly in one hand against the side of the cake at a slight angle. Turn the turntable round in a continuous motion and in one direction with the other hand, while pulling the scraper smoothly in the opposite direction to give a smooth surface to the iced sides. When you have completed the full turn, carefully lift off the scraper to leave a neat join. Trim off any excess icing from the top edge and the cake board.

7 Leave the cake to dry, uncovered, then apply the icing in the same way to give the cake two or three more coats of icing. For a really smooth final layer, use a slightly softer consistency of icing.

Covering a Square Cake

The method is essentially the same as for icing a round cake.

1 Cover the top with icing as for the round cake. Leave to dry.

2 ▲ Cover the sides as for the round cake, but work on one side at a time and allow the icing to dry out before continuing with the next side. You will not need a turntable. Simply pull the scraper firmly and smoothly across each side in a single movement, repeating if necessary, for a really smooth finish.

3 ▲ Trim off any excess icing from the cake board with a knife.

4 Leave the cake to dry, uncovered, then apply the icing in the same way to give the cake two or three more coats of icing. For a really smooth final layer, use a slightly softer consistency.

Rough Icing a Cake

Peaking the icing to give it a rough appearance, like that of snow, is a much quicker and simpler way of applying royal icing to a cake. It is also much quicker to apply as you only need one covering of icing.

1 ▲ Spread the icing evenly over the cake, bringing the icing right to the edges so the cake is completely covered.

2 ▲ Starting at the bottom of the cake, press the flat side of a palette knife into the icing, then pull away sharply to form a peak. Repeat until the whole cake is covered with peaks. Alternatively, flat ice the top of the cake and rough ice the sides - or vice versa.

This colourful Christmas Tree cake shows an interesting version of peaked, or rough, icing. The fruit cake is first covered with coloured marzipan and left to dry for 12 hours, then royal icing is peaked around the lower half of the sides. The decorations are also made of coloured marzipan.

Covering with Sugarpaste Icing

Sugarpaste icing is a quick, professional way to cover a cake. Although fruit cakes are usually covered with marzipan first, this is not necessary if you are using a sponge base. The sugarpaste can be applied in one coating, unlike royal icing which requires several coats for a really smooth finish. Keep the icing white or knead in a little food colouring to tint. Ready-made sugarpaste is extremely good quality and is available in various colours for fast and professional results.

1 Carefully brush a little water or sherry over the marzipanned surface to help the icing stick to the marzipan. (If you miss a patch, unsightly air bubbles may form.)

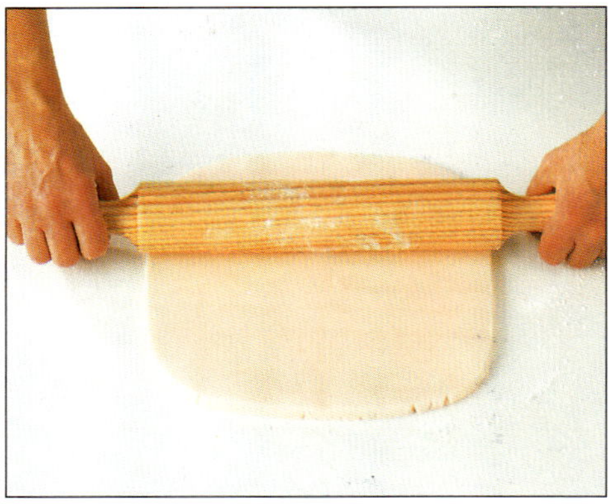

2 ▲ Lightly dust a work surface with icing sugar. Roll out the sugarpaste to a 5 mm/¼ inch thickness and large enough to cover the top and sides of the cake plus a little extra for trimming. Make sure the icing does not stick to the surface and moves freely.

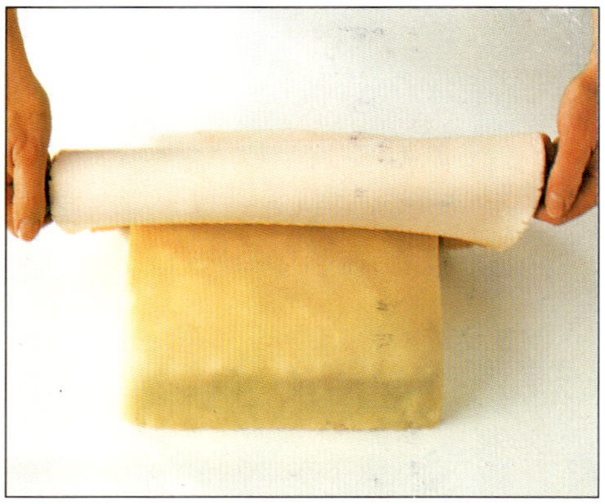

3 ▲ Lift the sugarpaste using your hands, or place it over a rolling pin to support it, and position over the top of the cake. Drape the sugarpaste over the cake to cover it evenly.

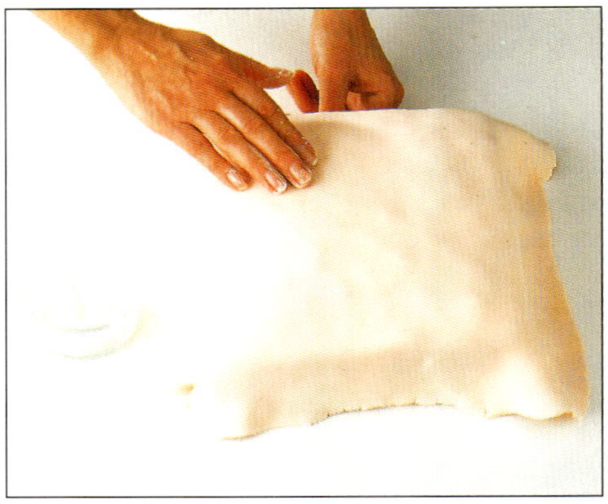

4 ▲ Dust your hands with a little cornflour. Smooth the top and sides of the cake with your hands, working from top to bottom, to eliminate any air bubbles.

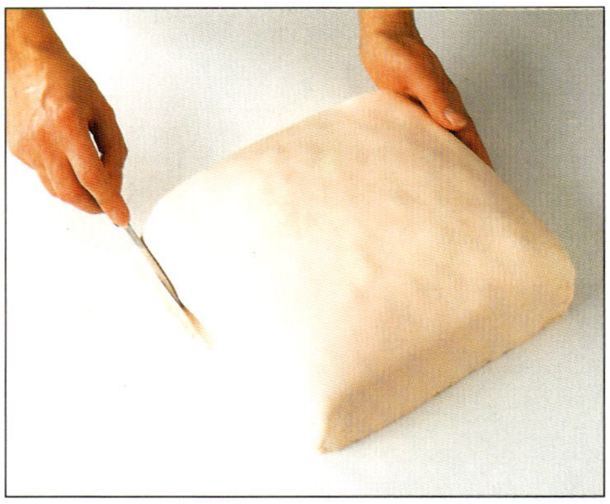

5 ▲ With a sharp knife, trim off the excess sugarpaste, cutting flush with the base of the cake.

6 Spread a little royal icing into the middle of a cake board and place the cake in the centre to secure.

Tip

To avoid damaging the surface of the cake while you move it, slide the cake to the edge of the work surface and support it underneath with your hand. Lift it and place on the cake board.

Covering Awkward Shapes

Although most shapes of cake can be covered smoothly with one piece of sugarpaste icing, there are some which need to be covered in sections. A cake baked in a ring mould is one such. The top and outer side of the cake is covered with two identical pieces of sugarpaste, and the inner side with a third piece.

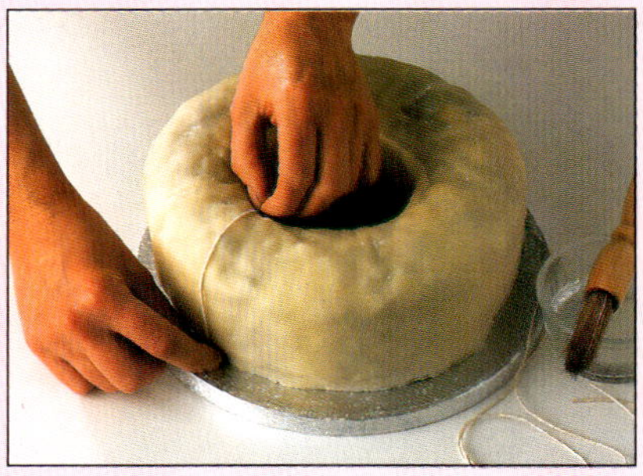

1 ▲ Measure half of the outer circumference of the cake with a piece of string, then measure the side and rounded top with another piece of string.

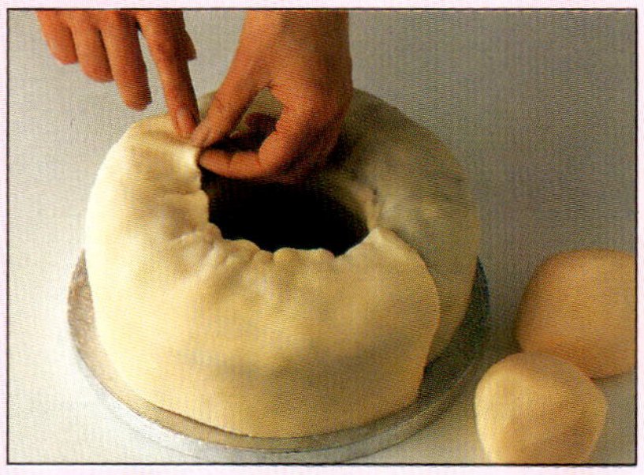

2 ▲ Take three-quarters of the sugarpaste icing and cut in half. Keep the remaining icing well wrapped until needed. Brush the marzipan lightly with water. Roll out each half of the icing into a rectangle, matching the string measurements. Cover the top and side of the cake in two halves.

3 Measure the circumference and the height of the inner side with two pieces of string. Roll out the reserved sugarpaste icing into a rectangle matching the string measurements, and use to cover the inside of the ring. Trim the sugarpaste to fit and press the joins together securely.

Food Colourings & Tints

Food colourings and tints for cake making are available today in almost as large a range as those found on an artist's palette. This has opened up endless possibilities for the cake decorator to create the most imaginative and colourful designs. Liquid colours are only suitable for marzipan and sugarpaste icing if a few drops are required to tint the icing a very pale shade. If used in large amounts they will soften the icings too much. So for vibrant, stronger colours, as well as for subtle sparkling tints, use pastes or powders, available from cake icing specialists. When choosing colours for icings, ensure that they are harmonious, and complement your design.

Colouring icings

How you apply the colour to an icing depends on whether it is in liquid form, a paste or powder. While working with the colourings it is best to stand them on a plate or washable board so they do not mark your work surface. When using cocktail sticks for transferring the colour to the icing, select a fresh stick for each colour so the colours do not become mixed.

1 ▲ Add liquid colour to the icing a few drops at a time until the required shade is reached. Stir into softer icings, such as butter, royal or glacé.

2 ▲ To colour firmer icings, such as sugarpaste and marzipan, use paste colourings. Dip a cocktail stick into the colouring and streak it on to the surface of a ball of the icing.

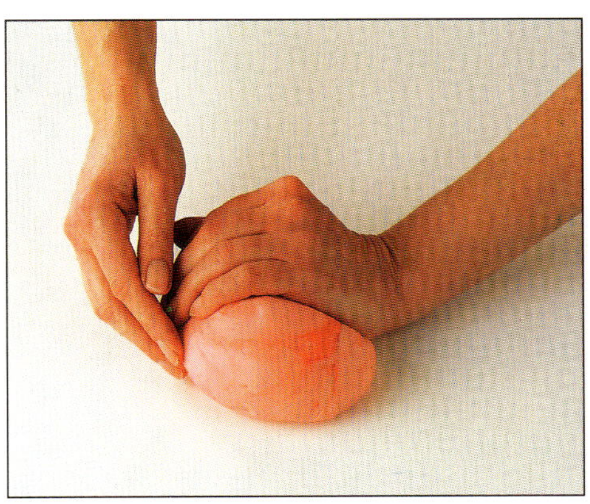

3 ▲ Knead thoroughly until the colour is evenly worked in and there is no streaking. Add sparingly at first, remembering that the colour becomes more intense as the icing stands, then leave for about 10 minutes to see if it is the shade you need.

4 ▲ To create subtle tints in specific areas, brush powdered colourings on to the surface of the icing.

A cake decorator's palette – a vivid array of food colourings to help bring out the artist in you.

Decorating with Royal Icing

Of all the icings, royal icing is probably the most complex and hardest to work with. But once the techniques are mastered, it provides a classic backdrop for both traditional as well as more contemporary cake designs. Traditionally it is used for decorating white wedding and Christmas cakes, but as colour is being introduced more and more into cake decorating, royal icing can now be used in many imaginative ways. This chapter demonstrates how to introduce a modern look using a wide variety of classic techniques.

Making and Using Piping Bags

A piping bag is an essential tool when working with royal icing. You can buy piping bags made of washable fabric and icing syringes, which are ideal for the beginner or for piping butter icing in bold designs. However, for more intricate piping, particularly if using several icing colours and nozzles, home-made greaseproof paper or baking parchment piping bags are more practical and flexible to handle. Make up several ahead of time, following the instructions given here, then fit them with straight-sided nozzles. Do not use nozzles with ridges as they do not have such a tight fit in the bag. To prevent the icing drying out when working with several bags, cover the nozzle ends with a damp cloth when not in use.

1 ▲ Cut out a 25 cm/10 inch square of greaseproof paper or baking parchment. Fold it in half diagonally to make a triangle.

2 ▶ With the point of the triangle facing away from you, hold the triangle with your thumb in the middle of the longest edge. Take the left corner and bring it over to meet the point of the triangle, as shown.

3 ▼ Hold in position and bring the remaining corner round and back over to meet the other two points, forming a cone shape. Holding all the points together, position them to make the cone tight and the point of it sharp, as shown.

4 ▲ With the cone open, turn the points neatly inside the top edge, creasing firmly down. Secure the cone with a staple.

5 For using with a nozzle, cut off the pointed end of the bag and position the nozzle so it fits snugly into the point. Half-fill the bag with icing and fold over the top to seal. To use without a nozzle, add the icing, seal, then cut a small straight piece off the end of the bag to pipe lines.

6 For ease and control, it is important to hold the bag in a relaxed position. You may find it easier to hold it with one or both hands. For one hand, hold the bag between your middle and index fingers and push out the icing with your thumb.

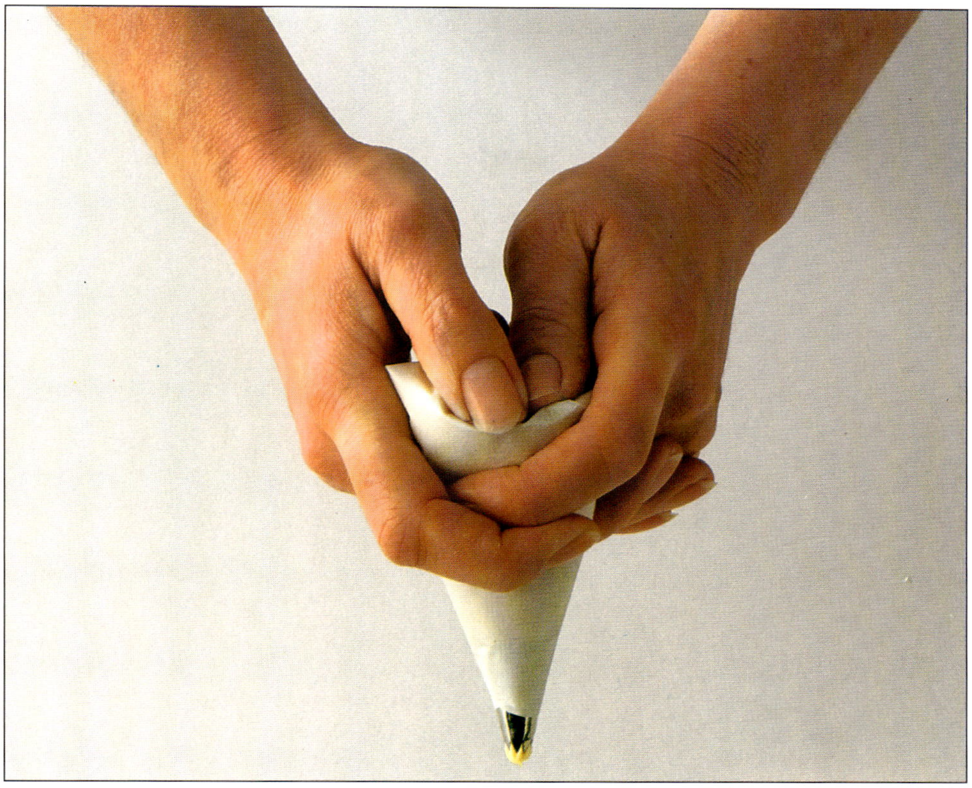

7 ▲ If using both hands, simply wrap the other hand around the bag in the same manner, so both thumbs can push the icing out.

8 ▲ To pipe, hold the bag so the nozzle is directly over the area you want to pipe on. The bag will be held straight or at an angle, depending on the shape you are piping. Gently press down with your thumb on the top of the bag to release the icing, and lift your thumb to stop the flow of icing. Use a small palette knife to cut off any excess icing from the tip of the nozzle as you lift the bag from each piped shape, to keep the shapes neat.

Royal icing is the perfect icing for piping. This cake shows how you can achieve pretty effects with shells, stars, lines and beads. Piped roses in full bloom complement the colour chosen for the top of the cake, and the petal tips have been highlighted with food colouring. Carry the design on to the cake board for a classic celebratory cake.

Piping Shapes

Royal icing gives cakes a professional finish, and is often used in decorating to give a formal and ornate character to a cake. However, simple piping skills can easily be achieved given a little practice. This section shows you how, with just a few piping nozzles, you can enhance the look of your cakes. Remember that the icing must be of the correct consistency – not too firm or it will be difficult to squeeze out of the piping bag, and not too soft or the piping will not hold its shape. Small nozzles are used for the delicate designs made with royal icing. Larger ones are more suitable for butter icing and frostings.

Piping Twisted Ropes and Leaves

For the ropes, fit nozzles Nos 43 or 44, or a writing nozzle, into a greaseproof paper piping bag and half-fill with icing. Hold the bag at a slight angle and pipe in a continuous line with even pressure, twisting the bag as you pipe. For leaves, you can use a No 18 petal nozzle or simply cut off the point of the bag in the shape of an arrow. Place the tip of the bag on the cake, holding the bag at a slight angle. Pipe out the icing, then pull away quickly to make the tapering end of a leaf.

Stars, swirls and scrolls

Piping Stars

For a simple star shape, choose a star-shaped nozzle in a size to suit your design. Hold the piping bag upright directly over the area to be iced. Gently squeeze the bag to release the icing and to form a star. Pull off quickly and sharply, keeping the bag straight, to give a neat point to the star.

Piping Swirls

Choose a star-shaped nozzle in a size to suit your design. Hold the piping bag directly over the area to be iced. Pipe a swirl in a circular movement, then pull off quickly and sharply, keeping the bag straight to leave a neat point.

Piping Scrolls

Choose star or rope nozzles in a size to suit your design. Hold the piping bag at a slight angle and place the tip of the nozzle on the cake. Pipe the icing lightly upwards and outwards, then come down in a circular movement, tailing off the icing so the end rests on the cake to make a scroll. The action is a little like piping a large 'comma'. For a reverse scroll, repeat as before, but pipe in the opposite direction, going inwards to reverse the shape. A scroll border can be particularly effective if you alternate two colours of icing.

Piping Cornelli

Cornelli is a fun technique which can be carried out in one or more colours. It is a little like doodling. Use writing nozzles Nos 1 or 2 and pipe a continuous flow of icing, squiggling the lines in the shape of W's and M's.

Piping Simple Embroidery

Piped embroidery is very fine work, requiring writing nozzles Nos 0 or 1. Keep the design simple and work in one or several colours. Pipe little circles, lines and dots to make a delicate pattern for your cake. Look at textile embroidery designs for some ideas.

Twisted ropes and leaves

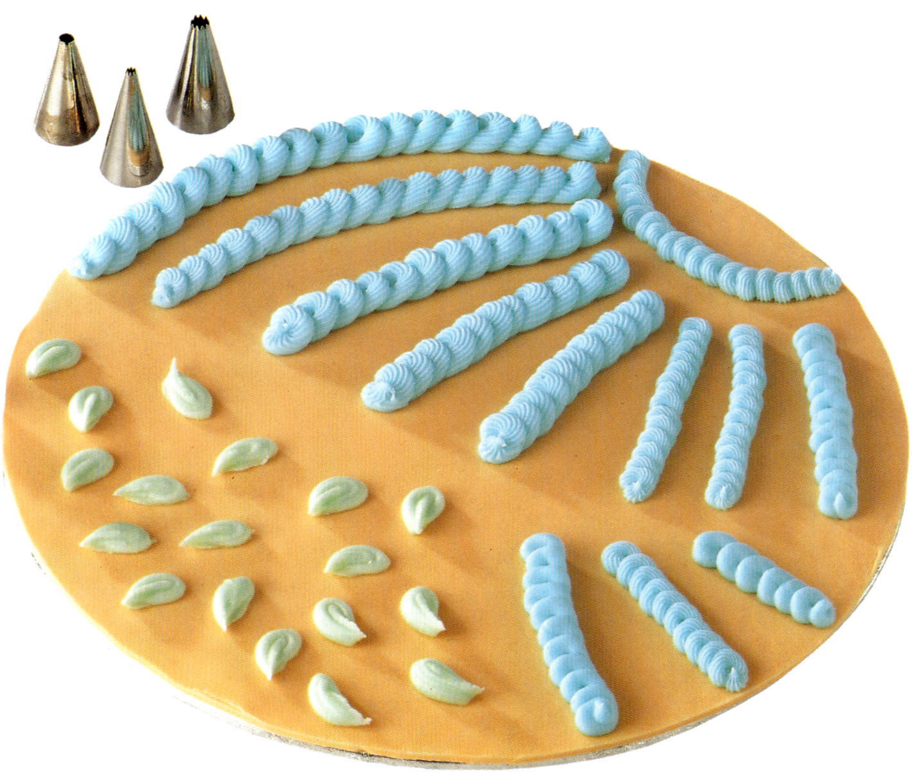

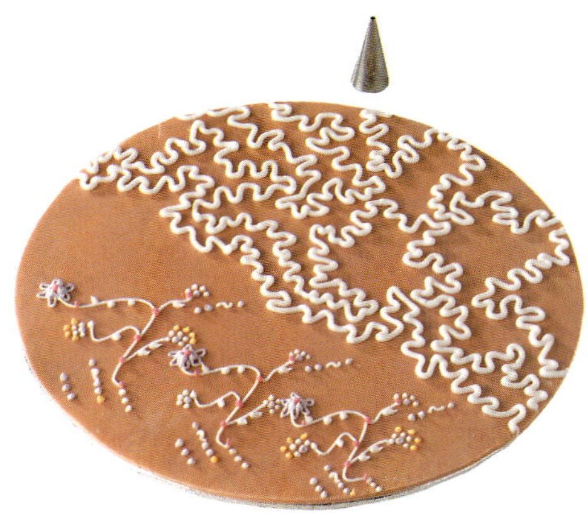

Cornelli and simple embroidery

PIPING DOTS OR BEADS

Use writing nozzles Nos 1, 2 or 3. Hold the piping bag directly over the area you wish to pipe. Press out the icing so it forms a bead, then release the pressure on the bag and take it off gently to one side. The smaller size nozzle will make simple dots. Neither dots nor beads should end in a sharp point. If this happens, lightly press any sharp points back into the bead with a small damp brush, or try making the icing a little softer.

PIPING SHELLS

Use star nozzles Nos 5 or 8. Rest the tip of the nozzle on the cake and pipe out a little icing to secure it to the surface. Gently squeeze out the icing while lifting the bag slightly up and then down, ending with the nozzle back on the surface of the cake. Pull off to release the icing. Repeat, allowing the beginning of the next shell to touch the end of the first one and continue in this way until you have completed a continuous line of shells.

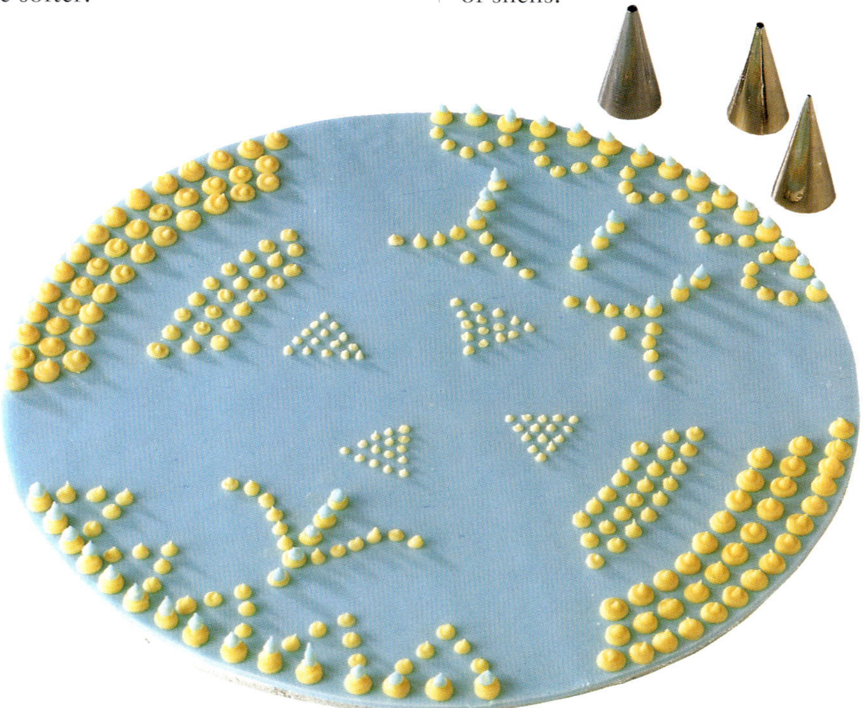

Dots and beads

Shells

PIPING LINES

Use a writing nozzle, remembering that the smaller the hole, the finer the line. Hold the bag at an angle, rest the nozzle on the cake and pipe out a little icing to secure it to the surface. Pipe the icing, lifting the bag slightly as you work, so it is just above the surface of the cake. Continue to pipe, allowing the line of piping to fall in a straight line. Do not pull or the line will break. At the end of the line, release the pressure, rest the nozzle on the surface of the cake and pull off to break the icing. The line can be varied by curving or looping it.

PIPING TRELLISES

To pipe trellises, use the same technique as above to pipe a set of parallel lines. Then overpipe a set in the opposite direction for squares, or horizontally across the lines for diamonds. You can also get different effects by using different widths of writing nozzles.

PIPING ZIGZAGS

Use a No 2 or 3 writing nozzle and pipe either one continuous zigzag, or stop and start at the end of each point to make them sharper.

Lines, trellises and zigzags

Piped Sugar Pieces

These little piped sugar pieces are very fragile and have the appearance of fine lace. They must be made ahead of time, and left to dry. The sugar pieces need to be handled carefully, and it is a good idea to make plenty in case of breakages.

1 ▲ On a piece of greaseproof paper, draw your chosen design several times with pencil. The designs should be kept fairly small.

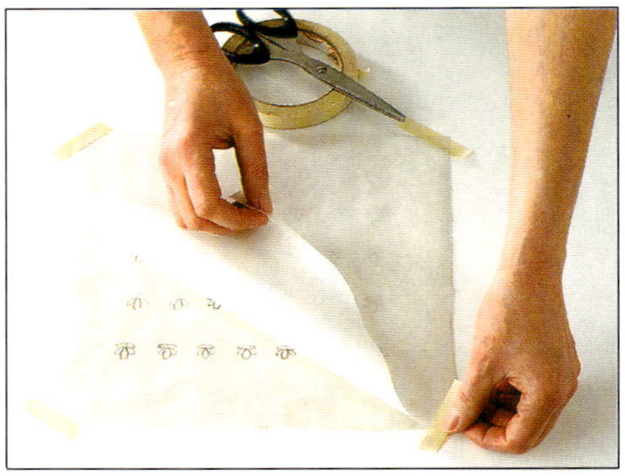

2 ▲ Tape the paper to the work surface or a flat board and secure a piece of greaseproof paper or baking parchment over the top. Tape the paper down at the corners with masking tape.

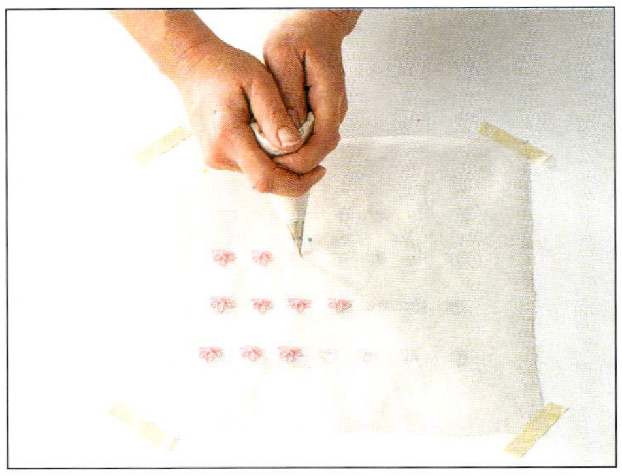

3 ▲ Fit a piping bag with a No 1 writing nozzle. Half-fill with royal icing, and fold over the top to seal. Pipe over each design, carefully following the pencilled lines with a continuous thread of icing. Repeat, piping as many pieces as you need plus a few extra in case of any breakages.

4 Leave to dry for at least two hours. Remove from the paper by carefully turning it back and lifting off each piece with a palette knife. When dry, store in a box between layers of tissue paper.

Shapely forms – delicate piped sugar pieces can be made in all kinds of designs and colours and attached to the sides, tops or edges of cakes with a dab of royal icing.

Simple Piped Flowers

To make these pretty piped flowers, you will need a petal nozzle – either small, medium or large depending on how big you want the flowers to be –a paper piping bag, a cocktail stick and a flower nail. Make the flowers ahead of time and, when dry, store in a box between layers of tissue paper.

Rose

1 For a tightly formed rose, make a fairly firm icing. Colour the icing, or leave it white. Fit the petal nozzle into a paper piping bag, half-fill with royal icing and fold over the top to seal.

2 Hold the piping bag so the wider end of the nozzle is pointing into what will be the base of the flower, and hold a cocktail stick in the other hand. Pipe a small cone shape around the tip of a cocktail stick. Pipe a petal half way around the cone, lifting it so it is at an angle and curling outwards, not flat, and turning the cocktail stick at the same time.

3 ▲ Repeat with more petals so they overlap each other slightly. The last petals can lie flatter and be more open. Remove the rose from the cocktail stick by threading the stick through a large hole on a grater. The rose will rest on the grater. Leave until dry and firm.

Pansy

1 Colour the icing. Fit the petal nozzle into a paper piping bag, half-fill with royal icing and fold over the top to seal. Cut out a small square of greaseproof paper and secure to the flower nail with a little icing.

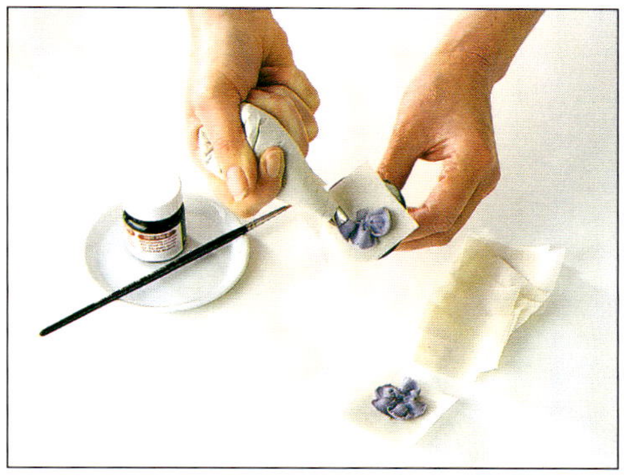

2 ▲ Holding the nozzle flat, pipe the petal shape in a curve, turning the flower nail at the same time. Pipe five petals in all. Pipe beads of yellow icing in the centre with a small writing nozzle, or use stamens.

3 Remove the paper from the flower nail, but leave the pansy on the paper until it is dry and firm. Coloured details can be added by painting with food colouring, or using food colouring pens, once the flower has dried. Lift the pansy from the paper by carefully slipping a palette knife underneath the base of the flower.

Coloured Summer Flowers

1 Colour the icing. Make up the flowers in a variety of shades for a colourful arrangement. Fit the petal nozzle into a paper piping bag, half-fill with royal icing and fold over the top to seal. Cut out a small square of greaseproof paper and secure to the flower nail with a little icing.

2 ▲ Pipe five flat petals in a circle so they slightly overlap each other. Pipe beads of yellow icing in the centre of each flower or sprinkle with hundreds and thousands. Leave to dry and add coloured details as for the pansy.

Bouquet of iced blossoms, including roses, pansies and bright summer flowers – arrangements of piped flowers make colourful cake decorations.

Run-outs

Designs for run-outs can be as complicated or as simple as you like. It is best to start off with a fairly solid shape for your first attempt, as these decorations can be quite fragile to handle. Always make a few more run-outs than you think you will need in case of breakages.

1 Make up the royal icings to the correct consistencies: a stiffer one for the outline, and a softer one for filling in (see the basic recipe for Royal Icing). Leave the icing to stand, preferably overnight, to allow any air bubbles to come to the surface. Stir the icing before using. On a piece of greaseproof paper, draw your chosen design several times.

2 ▲ Tape the paper to the work surface or a flat board and lay a piece of baking parchment over the top. Tape the paper down at the corners with masking tape.

3 ▲ Fit a paper piping bag with a No 1 writing nozzle, and half-fill with the stiffer icing for piping the outline. Carefully pipe over the outline of your design with a continuous thread of icing.

4 ▲ Add the softer icing for filling in into a second paper piping bag. Cut the pointed end off the bag in a straight line. Do not make it too big, or the icing will flow out too quickly. Pipe the icing into the outlines to fill, working from the outline into the centre, being careful not to touch the outline or it may break. To prevent air bubbles forming, keep the end of the bag in the icing. The icing should look overfilled and rounded, as it will shrink slightly as it dries.

5 ▲ You now need to work quickly while the icing is still soft. Move a paintbrush carefully through the icing to fill in any gaps and to ensure it goes right to the edge of the outline, keeping the icing smooth. If any air bubbles do appear, smooth them out with the brush or burst with a pin.

6 ▲ Leave the run-outs on the paper to dry; the drying time will vary depending on their size, but leave for at least one day and preferably longer. When completely dry, remove by carefully slipping a palette knife under the shapes and easing them off the paper. Decorative details can then be piped on to the dried run-outs. Allow these to dry before using or storing.

7 Store the run-outs in a box between layers of greaseproof paper.

When royal icing is presented in bright colours it takes on a lively new look. The hearts and brilliant butterflies are made using the run-out technique. The wings are made separately, then joined with a line of piping to form the body of each butterfly. This also secures them to the cake. Piped sugar pieces, scroll borders and polka dots complete the design.

Decorating with Sugarpaste Icing

As a covering, sugarpaste icing gives a softer look to a cake than royal icing. It is much quicker to work with, requiring only one rolled out layer. This is then placed in position so it curves itself over the edges of the cake. Because it is so pliable, sugarpaste can also be used for a wide range of decorative effects. When making sugarpaste decorations, always wrap any icing you are not using immediately in clear film to stop it drying out.

Marbling

As an alternative to covering a cake in a single colour, sugarpaste icing can be marbled for a multi-coloured effect. Use several colours and keep them quite vibrant, or use one or two delicate tones. Marbled sugarpaste icing can also be used to make effective moulded flowers and other modelled decorations.

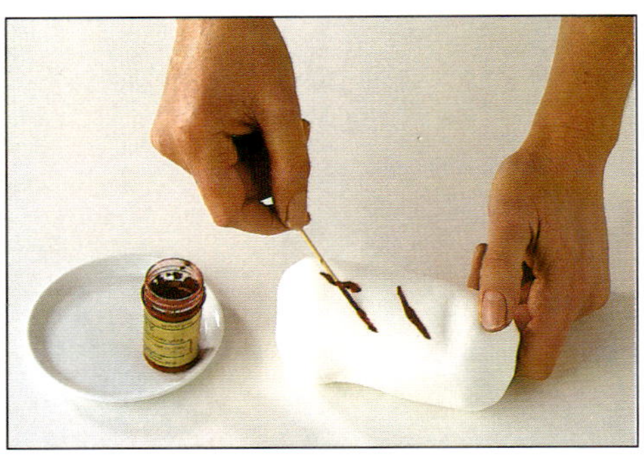

1 ▲ Form the sugarpaste icing into a smooth roll or ball. Dip the end of a cocktail stick into the food colouring and dab a few drops on to the icing. Repeat with more colours if wished.

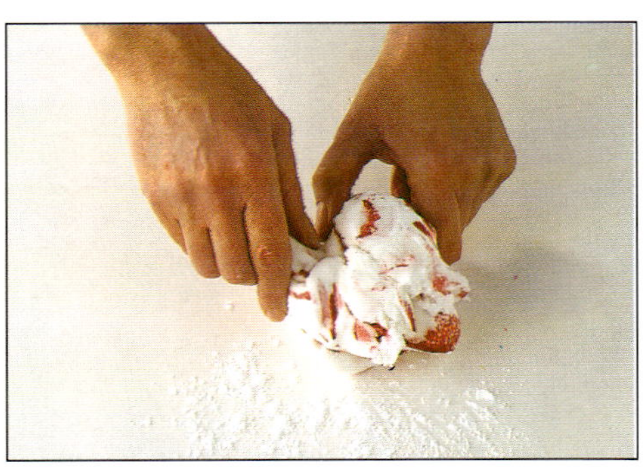

2 ▲ Knead the sugarpaste icing just a few times. The colouring should look very patchy.

3 ▲ On a work surface lightly sprinkled with icing sugar, roll out the sugarpaste icing to reveal the marbled effect.

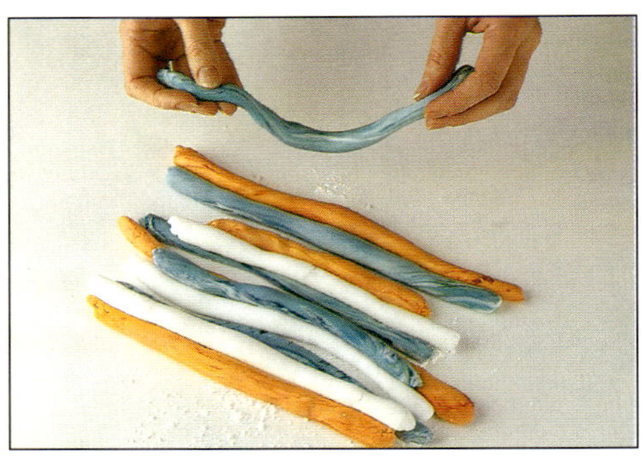

4 ▲ Alternatively, for a very bold interweaving of colours, use the following technique. Divide the sugarpaste icing into three or four equal portions, depending on how many colours you want to use. Colour with food colouring. Divide each colour into four or five portions and roll out with your hands into sausage shapes. You could even put two colours together for an instant marbled sausage. Place the different-coloured sausages side-by-side on the work surface.

5 ▲ Twist the colours together and knead for several seconds until the strips of colour are fused together but retain their individual colours.

6 ▲ Roll out the marbled icing on a work surface lightly dusted with icing sugar.

Crimping

Crimping tools are similar to large tweezers with patterned ends and are available in a good variety of styles. Crimping is a very quick and efficient way of giving decorative edges and borders to sugarpaste-coated cakes – the effect is similar to the embroidery technique of smocking. For a simple finish to the crimped cake, top with a small posy of edible flowers, a ribbon, or other bought decorations.

1 ▲ Cover the cake with sugarpaste icing. For crimping, the icing must still be soft, so do not allow it to dry out before decorating. Dip the crimping tool in a little cornflour.

2 ▼ Position the crimping tool on the cake in the place you wish to start the design and squeeze the teeth together to make the pattern.

3 ▲ Slowly release the crimper so as not to tear the icing. Repeat the pattern, either touching the last one or spacing them evenly apart. The pattern can be varied by using different crimping tools.

4 ▲ The same technique can be used to crimp decorative designs down the sides of a cake. If applying sugarpaste frills to a cake, crimp the edges for a neat and pretty finish.

Embossing

Special embossing tools can be purchased from cake icing specialists, but you can also use any other patterned items such as cookie stamps, cutters or icing nozzles.

1 ▲ Cover the cake with sugarpaste icing. For embossing, the icing must still be soft, so do not allow it to dry out. Brush a little cornflour on to the embossing tool and press firmly on to the soft icing. Repeat, brushing with cornflour each time.

2 ▲ To add colour, brush a little powdered food colouring on to the embossing tool instead of the cornflour and press on to the icing as before. Highlights can also be added with food colouring pens, as shown.

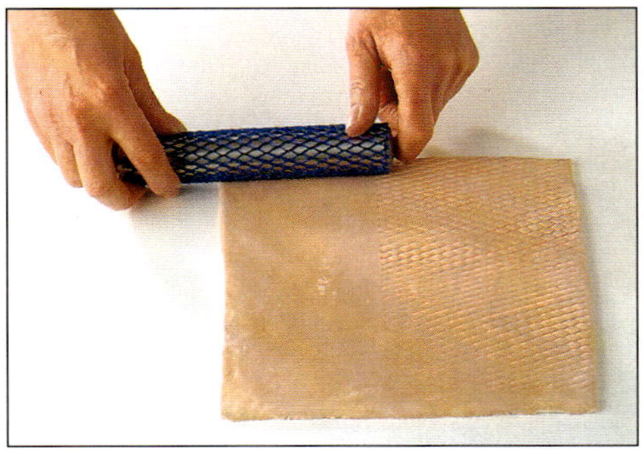

3 ▲ Textured rolling pins are also available from cake icing specialists. Cover the cake with sugarpaste icing as before and smooth over with your hand. Roll over the surface of the icing with the textured rolling pin. This rolling pin gives a basketweave effect.

Modelling

Sugarpaste is wonderfully adaptable, and can be used to model almost any shape you can think of. Choose small objects, such as flowers, fruits, vegetables, animals, or whatever is going to suit your cake. Using this technique, every cake you make will be unique. Remember to dust the work surface lightly with icing sugar before you start, to prevent sticking. Leave the modelled shapes to dry on greaseproof paper, before applying to the cake.

Smart Teddy Bear

▲ Mould each part of the bear's body separately in cream-coloured sugarpaste icing. Roll out the waistcoat to fit the body and cut out the bow tie in purple icing. Mould the buttons and eyes in black icing. Attach the head to the body with a little water, pressing together to secure. Brush the body lightly with water and wrap the waistcoat round, folding back the top two corners. Attach the arms, legs and ears with a little water, pressing to secure, then bend into shape. Attach the bow tie, buttons and eyes with a little water, then paint on any details such as nose and mouth with brown food colouring.

Frosty Snowman

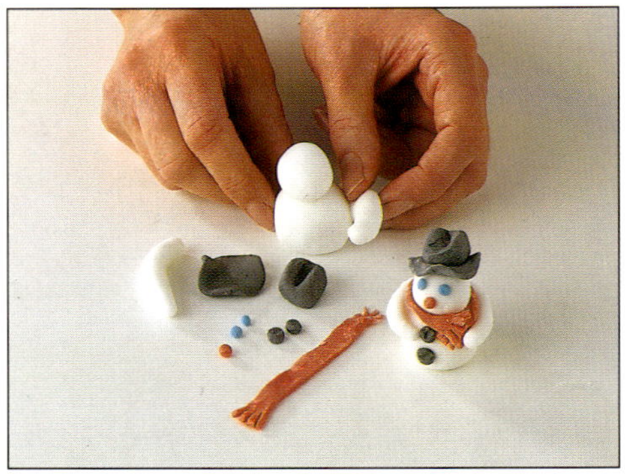

▲ Mould the snowman's body, head and arms in white sugarpaste icing. Roll out the scarf in red icing, cutting the ends with a sharp knife to represent the tassels. Shape two small balls of blue icing for the eyes, one of red for the nose and two of black for buttons. Using black icing, shape the hat in two pieces, as shown. Attach the head to the body with a little water, then the arms, pressing lightly to secure. Attach the scarf, eyes, nose, buttons and hat in the same way.

Hungry Rabbit

▼ Mould the rabbit's body and head, legs, tail and ears in light brown sugarpaste icing. Shape two small balls of blue icing for the eyes. Attach the tail, legs and ears to the rabbit's body with a little water, pressing lightly to secure. Paint the nose and details on the eyes with brown food colouring. For the carrots, shape long ovals out of orange icing, tapering at one end, then make markings on them with the back of a knife. Attach small pieces of green icing on to the ends.

Cat on a Mat

▲ Mould and shape the cat's body, head, legs, tail and ears in grey marbled sugarpaste icing. Shape two small ovals in black for the eyes and a small pink ball for the nose. Roll out a piece of green icing for the mat. Attach the head to the body with a little water, then the legs, tail, ears, eyes and nose, pressing lightly to secure and bending into shape where necessary. Press four short lengths of florist's wire into the head to represent whiskers (these must be removed before serving the cake). Paint the mouth with black food colouring and place the cat on the mat.

Let your imagination run riot when it comes to using sugarpaste icing. All the inhabitants of this water-lily pond are moulded or cut out of sugarpaste. The water lilies are formed with a small petal-shaped cocktail cutter, then bent into shape. The lily pads are formed with a small round cutter, and then snipped with a knife to make them more lifelike. A blossom cutter creates the flowers on the grassy bank, and the irises, bulrushes, frog and goldfish are modelled by hand.

Cut-out Shapes

Using a variety of shaped cutters, sugarpaste icing can be stamped out to make all kinds of colourful shapes for decorating cakes.

1 Colour the sugarpaste icing to the desired shade, then roll out evenly on a work surface lightly dusted with icing sugar.

2 ▲ Dip the ends of the cutter in icing sugar and cut out the shapes. Leave to dry flat on greaseproof paper, then attach the shapes to the cake with a little royal icing.

The sky's the limit – use cutters or make your own templates for creating a variety of cut-out images.

Cut-out Borders

Borders on the cutting edge – cut-out shapes can also be positioned around the edge of a cake to add a decorative border. Make the borders in bold or delicate designs so that they fit the character of the cake.

1 ▲ Roll out the sugarpaste icing thinly and cut out with a medium-sized cutter - a round, fluted biscuit cutter has been used here. Leave whole or cut in half, depending on the shape.

2 ▲ Use smaller cutters to cut out inside shapes for a filigree effect, or make up your own shapes and use templates cut out of card.

3 Leave the shapes to dry flat on greaseproof paper, then attach them around the top edges of the cake with a little royal icing.

Plunger Blossoms

A special plunger blossom cutter, available in different sizes, is used to make these dainty flowers. The cutter contains a plunger for ejecting the delicate shapes once they have been cut out.

1 ▲ Roll out the icing thinly on a work surface lightly dusted with icing sugar. Dip the cutter in cornflour and cut out the flower shapes.

2 ▲ The flower should remain on the end of the cutter. To remove the flower, hold the cutter on a foam pad and depress the plunger. As it goes into the foam it will bend the flower into shape and release it.

3 The flowers can be simply finished with a little bead of royal icing piped into the centre when they are dry, or you can make a spray of flowers using florist's wire and stamens.

4 ▲ To make a spray, push a pin through the centre of each flower. Leave the flowers to dry on the foam.

5 ▲ When dry, pipe a little royal icing on to a stamen and thread it through the hole. This will hold it in position. Repeat with all the flowers.

6 ▲ When the individual flowers are completely dry, twist a piece of florist's wire on to the end of each stamen. Group the flowers and twist the wires together to make a spray.

This pretty Teddy Bear Christening cake is simply decorated with a modelled bear and delicate plunger blossoms.

Frills

Sugarpaste frills give a particularly elaborate finish to a cake and are especially appropriate for decorating wedding, christening and anniversary cakes. Try layering two different coloured frills together for a very special occasion.

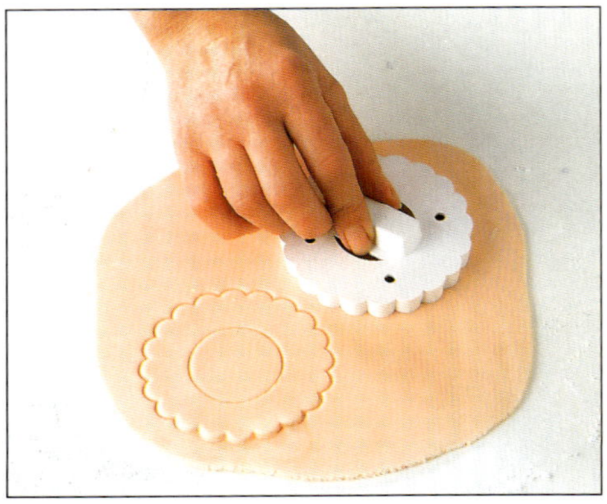

1 ▲ Roll out the sugarpaste icing thinly on a work surface lightly dusted with icing sugar. Use a special frill cutter to cut out the rings for the frills. One ring will make one large or two smaller frills.

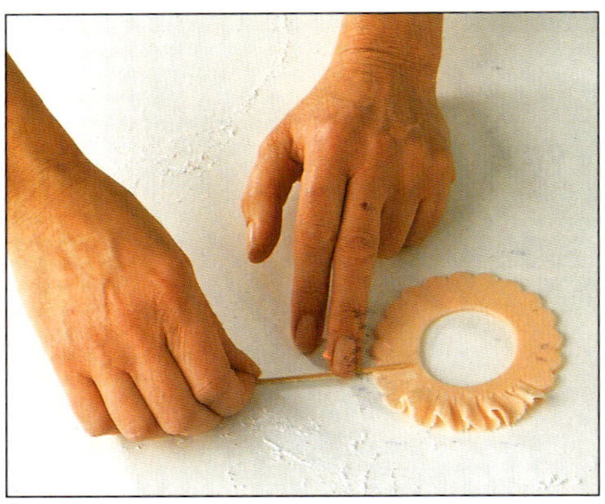

2 ▲ Position the end of a wooden cocktail stick over about 5 mm/ $\frac{1}{4}$ inch of the outer edge of the ring. Roll the stick back and forth firmly around the edge with your finger. The edge will become thinner and start to frill. Continue in this way until the ring is completely frilled.

3 ▲ Using a sharp knife, cut through the ring once to open it up. Gently ease it open. For shorter frills, cut the ring in half to make two frills.

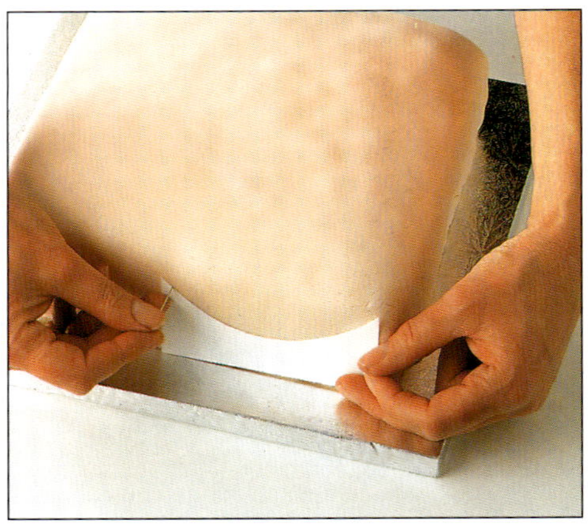

4 ▲ Cut out a template the size of the opened frill and hold against the side of a covered cake. Mark with a pin to show where to attach the frill, and repeat all around the cake.

5 ▲ To attach the frill, either pipe a line of royal icing on to the cake or brush a line of water. Carefully secure the frill on to the line of royal icing or water. Overlay with a second frill in the same or a different coloured icing if wished. Repeat around the cake. The top edge of each frill can be decorated with piping or with a crimping tool.

Tip

If you do not have a special frill cutter you can use individual pastry cutters instead. Use a 7.5–10 cm/ 3–4 inch plain or fluted cutter to cut out the outer circle and a 4–5 cm/ $1\frac{1}{2}$–2 inch plain cutter to cut out the inner circle.

Design Variations

1 ▲ Looped frills look very pretty attached to the cake 'upside-down' as shown here. They are made and attached in the same way as described for looped frills, except that you need to cut out a larger hole from the middle of the ring to make the frills thinner. They will drape more effectively this way.

2 ▲ Frills look equally attractive applied diagonally to the cake sides at regular intervals. They are made and attached to the cake in exactly the same way as described for looped frills, although each ring will probably be large enough to make two frills.

Plaques

A plaque can simply be a plain cut-out shape, or it can be more decorative with, for example, a frilled edge and delicate piping work. Use a plaque as a focal point on a cake to dedicate it to someone special, for weddings, christenings, anniversaries and birthdays, or as a base on which to paint a picture with food colourings.

1 ▲ For a plain plaque, roll out the sugarpaste thinly on a work surface lightly dusted with icing sugar. Dip a cutter (round, oval, heart-shaped or fluted) in a little cornflour. Cut out the shape and leave it to dry flat on greaseproof paper.

2 ▲ Using royal or glacé icing, pipe on a decoration or name. Alternatively, write or draw on the plaque with a food colouring pen, or with food colourings and a fine paintbrush.

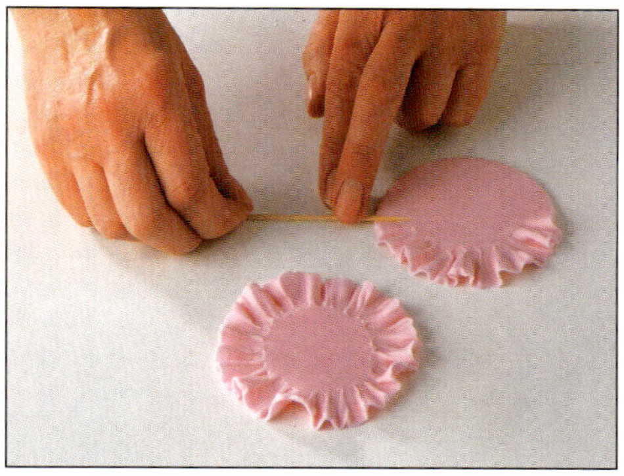

3 ▲ For a frilled plaque, cut out the shape as described above. While the icing is still soft, position the end of a wooden cocktail stick over about 5 mm/¼ inch of the outer edge of the plaque. Roll the stick back and forth firmly around the edge with your finger. The edge will become thinner and start to frill. Continue until the edge of the plaque is completely frilled.

Endlessly versatile, sugarpaste icing can be embossed, crimped, cut out and marbled, techniques which are all displayed on this unusual diamond-shaped cake. Small cutters have been used for the embossed pattern on the sides, and different crimping tools for the designs at the corners. 'Paprika' food colouring has been used for the sugarpaste covering for a contemporary terracotta shade, and the trimmings have been marbled with a little blue icing both for the unusual cut-out edging and the star decorations.

Decorating with Marzipan

Marzipan can be a decorative icing in its own right, or it can provide a firm undercoat for a royal icing or sugarpaste icing covering. It is extremely pliable, and the white variety in particular takes colour well.

Marzipan can be moulded and shaped, crimped and embossed, and cut out or modelled into all kinds of animal shapes, figures, flowers, fruits, and even edible Christmas decorations, to name just a few possibilities.

Embossing

A 'pattern in relief' can be created on cakes by using special embossing tools, or any piece of kitchen equipment that will leave a patterned indentation on the marzipan. To make the embossed picture more interesting, paint on highlights with food colouring.

1 Cover the cake with marzipan, then emboss straight away before the icing dries. Dust the embossing tool with a little cornflour, press firmly into the marzipan, then lift off carefully to reveal the pattern. Alternatively, for a coloured design, brush a little powdered food colouring on to the embossing tool instead of the cornflour and press on to the marzipan as before.

2 ▼ Paint on coloured highlights with food colouring, if you wish.

Very simple versions of crimping and embossing have been applied to the marzipan top of this Simnel cake. The edges are crimped – or fluted – with the fingers and the top is embossed using the back of the fork.

Crimping

As with sugarpaste icing, marzipan can be crimped to give simple, pretty edgings and patterns to cakes.

1 Cover a cake with marzipan, but do not allow to dry out. To prevent the crimping tool from sticking, dip it in a little cornflour.

2 Place the crimping tool on the edge of the cake where it is to be decorated and then squeeze the teeth together to make the design. Slowly release the crimping tool, being careful not to let it open quickly or it will tear the marzipan.

3 ▲ Re-position the crimper and repeat to complete the design. You can decorate both the top and base edges of the cake, or the whole side of the cake, if you wish. The crimping tool can also be used to make a pattern on top of the cake.

Marzipan Cut-outs

Small flower and other shaped cutters can be purchased from cake icing specialists for cutting out marzipan shapes. Aspic, cocktail or biscuit cutters can also be used. Once you have cut out the basic shapes, you can decorate them with different coloured marzipan trims, small sweets or piping. Here are some ideas for cut-out marzipan flowers.

Colourful Blossoms

▲ Colour the marzipan to the desired shades. Roll out evenly on a work surface lightly dusted with icing sugar. Dip the ends of a leaf cutter or a small round cutter in icing sugar, and cut out five petals for each flower. Overlap the petals in a circle, securing with a little water. Shape small balls of yellow or orange marzipan and place one in the centre of each flower.

Frilly Blossoms and Leaves

▲ Colour and roll out the marzipan as for the Colourful Blossoms. For each flower, cut out two circles using two fluted cutters, one slightly smaller than the other. (The sizes will depend on the size of flower you are making.) To frill the edges, position the end of a wooden cocktail stick over 3 mm/⅛ inch of the outer edge of each circle. Roll the stick firmly back and forth around the edges with your finger so the edges become thinner and begin to frill. Continue until the circles are completely frilled.

Place the smaller frill on top of the larger, and lightly press together to secure. Take a small ball of the deeper shade of marzipan and press through a fine sieve. Cut off the marzipan which has been pushed through the sieve and place in the centre of the flower.

Cut out leaves from green marzipan with a leaf cutter. Bend the leaves slightly to make them look more life-like. Larger leaves can be left to bend over the handle of a wooden spoon until firm.

Violets

▲ Colour the marzipan purple and roll out as for the Colourful Blossoms. Cut out each flower with a four-petal cocktail cutter. With a little yellow marzipan, shape small balls and then position in the centre of each flower.

Creative cut-outs – marzipan can be used in unusual ways to make imaginative shapes and borders.

Modelling

Marzipan is a wonderful icing to use for modelling. Work with either coloured marzipan, or use white and highlight it with colour after shaping. If colouring your own marzipan, tint it to the required shade, then paint on extra tones and details when the model is assembled to make the objects more life-like. Here are just a few suggestions for shaping fruits and vegetables.

RED-HOT CHILLI PEPPERS

▲ Colour equal portions of marzipan red and green. Mould the chilli shapes, tapering them to a point towards the ends. Shape the stems from green marzipan and attach to the chillies, pressing together lightly to secure.

BUNCH OF GRAPES

▲ Colour the marzipan purple. Shape a cone for the main body of the grape bunch, then mould small individual balls for the grapes. Mould the stem, using a little brown marzipan. Arrange the grapes until the cone is completely covered. Use a little water if necessary to make them stick and press lightly to secure. Make a small indentation in the top of the cone and press in the stem to secure.

RIPE BANANAS

▲ Colour the marzipan yellow or use yellow marzipan. Mould and bend small pieces of the icing into the shapes of bananas. Paint on highlights with brown food colouring.

ROSY APPLES

▲ Colour the marzipan green for the apples and brown for the stems. Shape the green marzipan into rounds and make an indent at one end with a modelling tool. Shape small pieces of brown icing for the stems. Paint a rosy bloom on the apples with red food colouring and press the stems into the indents.

More familiar as an undercoat for a cake, marzipan should not be neglected as a decoration in itself. It takes colour well, and when used to coat this light fruit ring cake, it should certainly not be covered up. Marzipan's plasticity also makes it ideal for moulding flowers, such as this colourful collection of roses, and for twisting into ropes to make a colourful edging.

Plaiting and Weaving

Use these techniques with marzipan to make colourful edgings and decorations for cakes.

CANDY-STRIPE ROPE

1 Take two pieces of different coloured marzipan. On a work surface lightly dusted with icing sugar, roll out two or three ropes of even length and width with your fingers.

2 ▲ Pinch the ends together at the top, then twist into a rope. Pinch the other ends to seal neatly.

PLAIT

1 Take three pieces of different coloured marzipan. On a work surface lightly dusted with icing sugar, roll out three ropes of even length and width with your fingers.

2 ▲ Pinch the ends together at the top, then plait the ropes neatly and pinch the other ends to seal neatly.

MARZIPAN TWIST

1 Colour the marzipan (working with one or two colours). On a work surface lightly dusted with icing sugar, roll out each piece of marzipan to a 5 mm/ ¼ inch thickness, then cut each piece into 1 cm/ ½ inch wide strips.

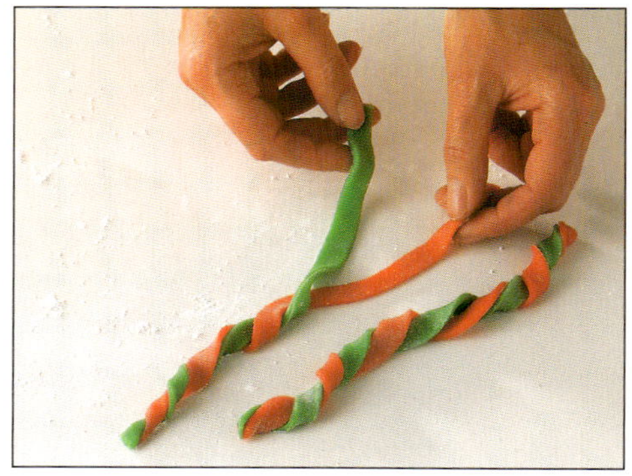

2 ▲ Take two different coloured strips and pinch the ends together at the top. Twist the strips together, joining on more strips with water, if needed.

BASKET-WEAVE

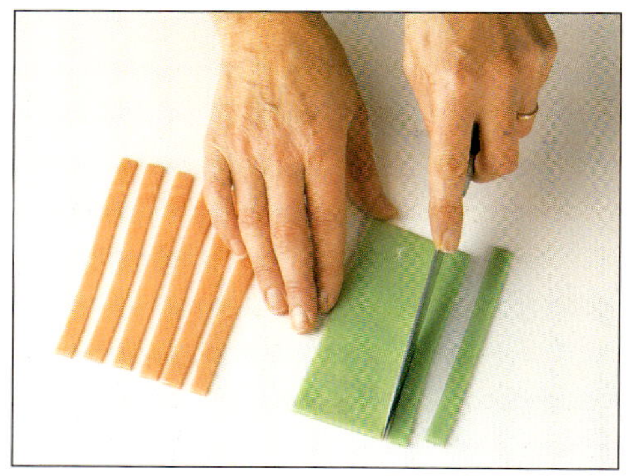

1 ▲ On a work surface lightly dusted with icing sugar, roll out a piece of marzipan (or work with two colours and roll out each one separately) to a 5 mm/ ¼ inch thickness. Cut into 5 mm/ ¼ inch wide strips.

2 ◀ Arrange the strips, evenly spaced, in parallel lines, then weave the strips in and out. Alternate the colours if using two, as shown. This decoration looks stunning on top of a cake. The edges can be trimmed to fit the shape of the cake.

Marzipan Roses

Not only do these roses smell sweet, they taste good too. Though they may look difficult to make, marzipan roses are quite simple to mould. For a formally decorated cake, shape the roses in a variety of colours and sizes, then arrange flamboyantly on top.

1 ▲ Take a small ball of coloured marzipan and form it into a cone shape. This forms the central core which supports the petals.

2 ▲ To make each petal, take a small piece of marzipan about the size of a large pea, and work it with your fingers to a petal shape which is slightly thicker at the base. If the marzipan sticks, dust your fingers in icing sugar or cornflour.

3 ▲ Wrap the petal around the cone as shown. Press the petal to the cone to secure. Bend the ends of the petal back slightly, to curl.

4 ▲ Mould the next petal in the same way and attach as before, so it just overlaps the first one. Curl the ends back slightly. Repeat with several more petals, making them slightly bigger until you have the size of rose you want. Overlap each petal and curl the ends back as before. Make sure all the petals are securely attached, then cut off the base of the cone. This provides a flat surface so the rose will stand on the cake.

5 For rosebuds, make just a few smaller petals and do not curl the ends back.

6 To add more detail to the rose, paint tints on to the petals using a paintbrush and food colouring. Leave to stand on greaseproof paper until firm.

Blooming roses – moulded roses can add glamour to any cake.

Decorating with Butter Icing

Butter icing is very quick to make up and is easy to use for quick and simple decorations. It can be used to sandwich cakes together, or to coat the top and sides with a thick, creamy layer of icing. To make your butter-iced cakes a little more individual, texture the icing on the tops or sides – or both if you wish. To finish, you can pipe the icing in swirls.

Cake Sides

For decorating cake sides, all you need is a plain or serrated scraper, depending on whether you want a smooth or a textured finish to the icing. If you have an icing turntable, it will make icing cake sides a much simpler task, but it is not essential.

Here a chocolate-flavoured and green-coloured butter icing have been realistically swirled to imitate tree bark and leaves in this delightful novelty cake idea.

1 ▲ Secure the cake to a cake board with a little icing. Cover the top and sides of the cake with icing and put it on an icing turntable. Using a plain or serrated scraper, hold it with one hand firmly against the side of the cake at a slight angle.

2 ▲ Turn the turntable round in a steady continuous motion and in one direction with the other hand, while pulling the scraper smoothly in the opposite direction to give a smooth or serrated surface to the iced sides. When you have completed the full turn, stop the turntable and carefully lift off the scraper to leave a neat join. Trim off any excess icing from the top edge and the cake board.

Cake Tops

More intricate patterns can be made on the tops of cakes with a few simple tools. Use a small palette knife, a plain or serrated scraper or a fork to give a silky smooth finish to the cake, or to make a variety of patterned ridges or some deep, generous swirls.

SWIRLS

1 ▲ Spread the icing smoothly over the top of the cake, then work over the icing with the tip of a palette knife from side to side to create a series of swirled grooves.

2 For a more formal appearance, draw the tip of a palette knife through the swirled grooves in evenly spaced lines.

RIDGED SPIRAL

1 Spread the icing smoothly over the top of the cake, then place the cake on a turntable.

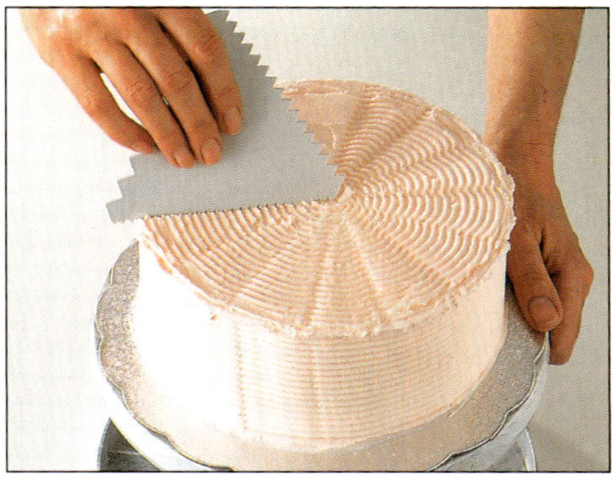

2 ▲ Hold a serrated scraper at a slight angle, pointing it towards the centre of the cake. Rotate the cake with your other hand, while moving the scraper sideways to make undulations and a ridged spiral pattern.

FEATHERED SPIRAL

1 Spread the icing smoothly over the top of the cake and place the cake on a turntable. Rotate the turntable slowly, drawing the flat tip of a palette knife in a continuous curved line, starting from the edge of the cake and working in a spiral into the centre.

2 ▲ Pull out lines with the tip of the knife, radiating out from a central point to the edge of the cake.

RIDGED SQUARES

1 Spread the icing smoothly over the top of the cake. Pull a fork across the cake four or five times, depending on the size of the cake, to produce groupings of evenly spaced lines.

2 ▲ Pull the fork across the cake four or five times as before, but at right angles to the first lines, to give a series of large squares.

DIAMONDS

1 Spread the icing smoothly over the top of the cake. Then lightly dredge with cocoa powder, if using white or lightly tinted butter icing, or icing sugar if using chocolate icing.

2 ▲ Draw a series of lines with the flat side of a knife to expose the butter icing and to make a diamond pattern over the top.

Piping with Butter Icing

The butter icing needs to be of the correct consistency for piping. To check, dip a palette knife and then lift out - the icing should form a sharp point. If too stiff, the icing will be difficult to pipe, if too soft, it will not hold its shape. Add a little extra milk or fruit juice if the consistency is too stiff, or more icing sugar if it is too thin.

DRAMATIC TOUCHES

Piping butter icing in bold, swirling designs with large nozzles can produce dramatic effects.

1 ▲ Cover the top of the cake with a smooth, thin layer of butter icing and smooth the sides with a plain scraper. Using a No 13 plain piping nozzle fitted in a material piping bag, pipe large overlapping spirals to cover the top of the cake. For each spiral, start in the centre and work outwards, until they are the required size.

2 ▼ Pipe large beads of icing around the edges of the cake, using a large writing nozzle. Lightly sprinkle the spirals with either a little sifted cocoa or icing sugar, depending on the colour of the butter icing.

DAINTY DESIGNS

For a more delicate effect, use small nozzles to pipe shapes such as dots and beads, stars or scrolls, as demonstrated for royal icing.

1 Cover the top of the cake with a smooth, thin layer of butter icing. Make a ridged pattern with a serrated scraper around the sides of the cake and a swirled spiral with a palette knife over the top.

2 Using a writing nozzle fitted in a paper piping bag, pipe loops and beads of icing in a contrasting colour.

3 ▲ Pipe beads of icing at the ends of each loop in the same colour as used to cover the cake.

BASKET-WEAVE DESIGN

Butter icing can be piped very effectively with a ribbon nozzle to make a basket-weave design. You can use different colours for the vertical and horizontal lines.

1 Fit a ribbon nozzle into a paper piping bag. Add the icing and fold over the top of the bag to secure. Pipe a vertical line the length of the area you wish to cover with basket weave.

2 Pipe 2 cm/¾ inch horizontal lines over the vertical line (slightly longer each side than the width of the vertical line) at 1 cm/½ inch intervals.

3 ▲ Pipe another vertical line so that it just covers one end of all the horizontal lines.

4 ▲ Fill in the spaces between the horizontal lines with an alternating row of horizontal lines to make the basket-weave design. Repeat until the area you wish to cover is completed.

Few can resist the glossy smoothness of butter icing. If you add flavouring and food colouring, the colour of the icing should reflect the taste, as with this tangy lemon-iced cake. Use a serrated scraper to create ridges in the icing on the sides and a palette knife to make the swirled and feathered effect on the top of the cake. Finish off with generous swirls of piped white butter icing.

Decorating with Glacé Icing

Using white and coloured glacé icing, simple but effective patterns can be created for decorating sponges, Madeira cakes or Swiss rolls. To vary the ideas shown here using one colour of icing, make up two colours of icing and pipe them alternately. Glacé icing sets quickly but needs to be very soft to create the following designs, so make a batch just before you want to decorate the cake and work quickly before it hardens.

Cobweb, Feather and Fan Icing

Cobweb, feather and fan effects are created using the same basic technique. For the cobweb, the coloured lines are piped in circles. For the fan, the colour is applied in straight lines and the skewer is pulled across in radiating lines. For feather icing the skewer is pulled at right angles through them.

Cobweb Icing

1 Make the glacé icing, colour a portion and put in a paper piping bag, as for feather icing. Coat the top of the cake evenly with the remaining white icing.

2 ▲ Work quickly before the icing has a chance to set. Pipe evenly spaced circles on top of the icing, starting from the centre of the cake and moving towards the edge.

3 ▲ Using a skewer, pull it in straight lines from the edge of the cake to the centre so that it is evenly divided into four sections.

4 ▲ Working from the centre of the cake to the edge, pull the skewer between the four lines to divide the cake evenly into eight. Leave to set.

For an effective Spider's web cake, use the cobweb icing technique. First cover the cake with yellow glacé icing. Pipe a continuous spiral of black glacé icing, then draw a skewer down from the top at regular intervals.

FEATHER ICING

1 Make the glacé icing (see Basic Icing Recipes). Put 2 tbsp of the icing in a small bowl and colour with a little food colouring.

2 Fit a paper piping bag with a No 2 writing nozzle, then spoon in the coloured icing and fold over the top of the bag to secure.

3 ▼ Coat the top of the cake evenly with the remaining white icing. Working quickly so the icing does not set, pipe the coloured icing in straight lines across the cake. You may find it easier to work from the centre outwards when doing this.

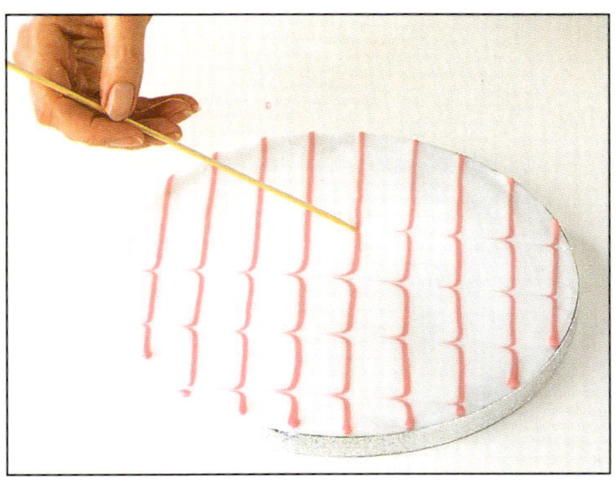

4 ▲ Using a skewer, pull it at right angles through the coloured lines in one direction, leaving an even spacing between the lines.

5 ▲ Working in the space between the lines, pull the skewer in the opposite direction, to give a feather pattern. Leave to set.

FAN ICING

1 Make the glacé icing, colour a portion and put in a paper piping bag. Ice the top of the cake as for the Feather and Cobweb techniques.

2 Working quickly so the icing does not set, pipe the coloured icing in evenly spaced straight lines across the cake. You may find it easier to work from the centre outwards.

3 ▲ Using a skewer, pull it through the coloured lines, starting from a point at one edge of the cake and radiating the lines out from it.

4 ▲ Working in the space between the lines, pull the skewer through the piped lines in the opposite direction to give a fan pattern. Leave to set.

Squiggle Icing

Here a random patterning of icing, similar to cornelli (see Decorating with Royal Icing), is lightly feathered or marbled. The technique is shown here using white icing on a chocolate-tinted background, but would be equally effective using one or two colours on a white icing background.

1 Make the glacé icing. Put 2 tbsp of the icing into a paper piping bag fitted with a No 2 writing nozzle, and colour the rest with cocoa mixed with a little water. Coat the top of the cake evenly with the chocolate icing.

2 ▲ Working quickly before the icing has a chance to set, pipe haphazard squiggles all over the top of the cake in a continuous line.

3 ▼ Using a cocktail stick, pull it through the lines in short, swirling movements and in different directions, to create a random feathered effect.

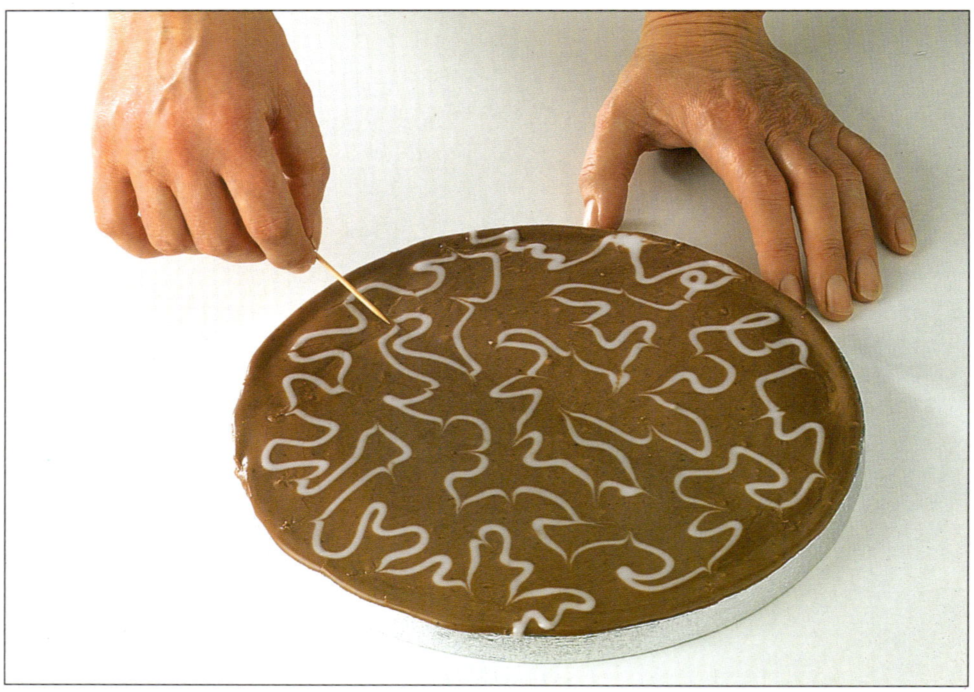

Marbling Flowers and Leaves

The feathering technique can also be used to give a marbled effect to piped decorations. The technique has been used here for a pretty flower and leaf design. The method is also effective for holly leaves, with the lines being pulled outwards to create the spiky points on the leaves.

1 Make the glacé icing, colour a small portion green and a portion red and put each in a paper piping bag fitted with a No 2 writing nozzle. Coat the top of the cake evenly with the remaining white icing.

2 ▲ Working quickly before the icing sets, pipe a floral design on to the cake, piping circles for flowers in the red icing, and ovals for leaves in the green icing.

3 ▲ To marble the flowers, pull a skewer through the lines from the outer edge almost to the middle. The number of petals will be determined by the number of lines you pull. Do the same for the leaves.

Tip

If the top of the cake is not perfectly flat for piping on, simply turn the cake upside down and use the flat base as the top.

Piping with Glacé Icing

All kinds of imaginative designs can be created, using the following method, to decorate the tops and edges of cakes.

This cake is covered with white glacé icing and the side is then coated with green-tinted desiccated coconut. The bold, exotic flowers are piped in red and green glacé icing and then marbled with a small cocktail stick, before the white or coloured icings have time to set, for a delicate finish.

1 Make the glacé icing, reserving a few tablespoons for piping. Coat the top of the cake evenly with the remaining icing (either white or coloured) and leave to set.

2 Divide the reserved icing into two equal portions and colour each in contrasting but complementary shades. Spoon the icings into two separate paper piping bags, each fitted with a No 2 writing nozzle. Use one colour to pipe geometric shapes or other simple designs over the icing.

3 ▲ Pipe a border around the edge of the cake with the other colour.

Decorating with Chocolate

Nothing adds a luxurious touch to a cake quite like chocolate, whether it is poured over to form a glossy icing, or piped, shaved, dipped or curled. There are several types of chocolate to choose from, and all should be used with care. Couverture is the best and used for professional chocolate work, but it is expensive and requires particularly careful handling. For the following techniques, good-quality baking or eating chocolate is suitable. Chocolate-flavoured cake covering is easy to use but is inferior both in taste and texture.

Chocolate decorations can look particularly interesting if different kinds of chocolate - dark, milk and white - are used in combination. White chocolate can be coloured, but make sure you use powdered food colouring for this as liquid colourings will thicken it. Store chocolate decorations in the refrigerator in a plastic container between layers of greaseproof paper until ready to use. Also, handle the decorations as little as possible with your fingers, as they will leave dull marks on the shiny surface of the chocolate.

Melting

For most of the decorations described in this section, the chocolate must be melted first.

1 ▼ Break the chocolate into small pieces and place in a bowl set over a pan of hot water. Do not allow the bowl to touch the water and do not let the water boil; the chocolate will spoil if overheated. Melt the chocolate slowly and stir occasionally. Be careful not to let water or steam near the chocolate or it will become too thick.

2 ▲ When the chocolate is completely melted, remove the pan from the heat and stir.

Coating Cakes

1 ▲ Stand the cake on a wire rack. It is a good idea to place a sheet of greaseproof paper or a baking sheet underneath the rack to catch any chocolate drips. Pour the chocolate icing over the cake quickly, in one smooth motion, to coat the top and sides.

2 Use a palette knife to smooth the chocolate over the sides, if necessary. Allow the chocolate to set, then coat with another layer, if wished.

Piping with Chocolate

Chocolate can be piped directly on to a cake, or it can be piped on to baking parchment to make run-outs, small outlined shapes or irregular designs. After melting the chocolate, allow it to cool slightly so it just coats the back of a spoon. If it still flows freely it will be too runny to hold its shape when piped. When it is the right consistency, you then need to work fast as the chocolate will set quickly.

CHOCOLATE OUTLINES

Pipe the chocolate in small, delicate shapes to use as elegant decorations on cakes. Or pipe random squiggles and loosely drizzle a contrasting chocolate over the top.

1 Melt 115 g/4 oz chocolate and allow to cool slightly. Tape a piece of baking parchment to a baking sheet or flat board.

2 ▼ Fill a paper piping bag with the chocolate. Cut a small piece off the pointed end of the bag in a straight line. Pipe your chosen shape in a continuous line, and repeat or vary. Leave to set in a cool place, then carefully lift off the paper with a palette knife.

PIPING ON TO CAKES

This looks effective on top of a cake iced with coffee glacé icing.

1 Melt 50 g/2 oz each of white and dark chocolate in separate bowls and allow to cool slightly. Place the chocolates in separate paper piping bags. Cut a small piece off the pointed end of each bag in a straight line.

2 ▲ Hold each piping bag in turn above the surface of the cake and pipe the chocolates all over. Here, the chocolates have been piped in overlapping semi-circles of different sizes. Try your own designs, too.

CHOCOLATE LACE CURLS

Make lots of these curly shapes and store them in a cool place ready for using as cake decorations. Try piping the lines in contrasting colours of chocolate to vary the effect.

1 ▲ Melt 115 g/4 oz chocolate and allow to cool slightly. Cover a rolling pin with baking parchment and attach it with tape. Fill a paper piping bag with the chocolate and cut a small piece off the pointed end in a straight line.

2 ▲ Pipe lines of chocolate backwards and forwards over the baking parchment, as shown.

3 ▲ Leave the chocolate lace curls to set in a cool place, then carefully peel off the paper.

Marbling Chocolate

Here, dark chocolate is swirled over a white glacé-iced cake for a stunningly simple effect. Before melting the chocolate, make the icing, then work very quickly while both the chocolate and the icing are still soft.

1 Melt 50 g/2 oz of dark chocolate. Coat the top of the cake evenly with white glacé icing.

2 ▲ Spoon the chocolate into a paper piping bag, cut a small piece off the pointed end in a straight line and then quickly pipe the chocolate in large, loose loops.

3 ▼ Pull a cocktail stick through the chocolate in short, swirling movements and in different directions, to create a random marbled effect.

Chocolate Run-Outs

The same basic method used for making royal icing run-outs is used here with chocolate. Try piping the outline in one colour of chocolate and filling in the middle with another.

1 ▲ Tape a piece of greaseproof paper to a baking sheet or flat board. Draw around a shaped biscuit cutter on to the paper, or trace or draw a shape of your choice freehand. Repeat the design several times.

2 Secure a piece of baking parchment over the top of the pencilled design. Tape it down securely at the corners with masking tape.

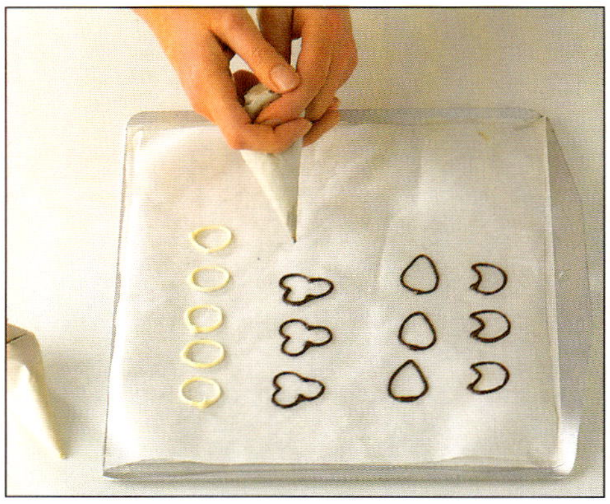

3 ▲ Fill two paper piping bags with melted chocolate. Cut a small piece off the pointed end of one of the bags in a straight line and pipe over the outline of your design in a continuous thread.

4 ▲ Cut the end off the other bag, slightly wider than before, and pipe the chocolate to fill in the outline so it looks slightly rounded. Leave to set in a cool place, then carefully lift off the paper with a palette knife.

Chocolate icing and decorating techniques are demonstrated in all their glory on this sumptuous chocolate gâteau. The cake is covered with fudge frosting. A neat ring of cocoa is then dusted around the edge, using a round stencil to protect the centre of the cake. The cake is decorated with mottled white and plain chocolate leaves. Chocolate curls adorn the top, and haphazardly piped white chocolate shapes, loosely overpiped with dark chocolate, complete the ultimate chocoholic extravaganza.

Chocolate Leaves

Chocolate leaves are made by coating real leaves with dark, white or milk chocolate or any combination of the three. Choose small freshly-picked leaves with simple shapes and well-defined veins, such as rose leaves. Leave a short stem on the leaves so you have something to hold.

1 ▲ Wash and dry the leaves well on kitchen paper. Melt 115 g/4 oz chocolate. Using a paintbrush, brush the underside of each leaf with chocolate. Take care not to go over the edge of the leaf or the chocolate will be difficult to peel off.

2 ▲ Using different chocolates for a mottled effect, brush the leaves in the same way, partly with plain or milk and partly with white chocolate.

3 Place the leaves chocolate-side up on baking parchment. Leave to set.

4 ▲ Carefully peel the leaf from the chocolate, handling the chocolate as little as possible. If the chocolate seems too thin, re-coat with more melted chocolate. Leave to set.

Chocolate Cut-Outs

You can make abstract shapes, or circles, squares and diamonds, by cutting them out freehand with a sharp knife. Alternatively, use a large biscuit cutter or ruler as a guide, or cut out the shapes with small biscuit or cocktail cutters. These shapes look equally attractive whether evenly positioned around the sides of the cake, spaced apart or overlapping each other, or simply arranged haphazardly.

1 ▲ Cover a baking sheet with baking parchment and tape down at each corner. Melt 115 g/4 oz dark, milk or white chocolate. Pour the chocolate on to the baking parchment.

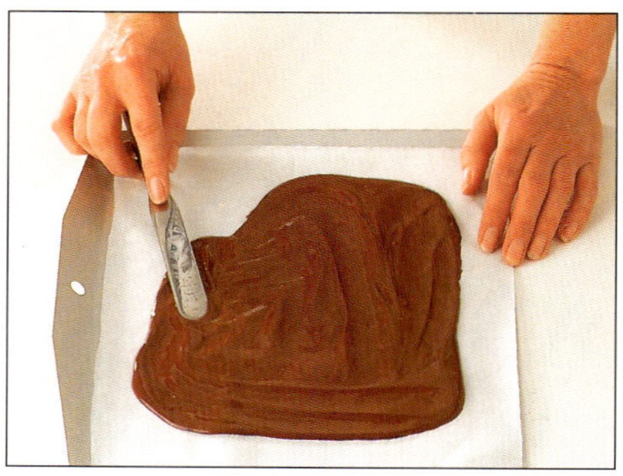

2 ▲ Spread the chocolate evenly with a palette knife. Allow to stand until the surface is firm enough to cut, but not so hard that it will break. It should no longer feel sticky when touched with your finger.

3 ▲ Press the cutter firmly through the chocolate and lift off the paper with a palette knife. Try not to touch the surface of the chocolate or you will leave marks on it.

4 ▲ The finished shapes can be left plain or piped with a contrasting chocolate if you wish.

5 ▲ Abstract shapes can be cut with a knife freehand. They look particularly effective pressed on to the sides of a butter iced cake.

Chocolate-dipped Fruit and Nuts

Use small, fresh fruit such as strawberries, grapes and kumquats for dipping, and whole nuts such as almonds, cashews, brazils or macadamias. Make sure that the fruit and nuts are at room temperature, or the chocolate will set too quickly.

1 Line a baking sheet with baking parchment. Wash the fruit and dry well on kitchen paper. Hold the fruit by its stem, then dip into the chocolate. You can either coat the piece of fruit completely, or just dip half of it, leaving the line of chocolate straight or at a slight angle. Remove the fruit, shake it gently and let any excess chocolate fall back into the bowl. Place on baking parchment and leave to set.

2 ▲ For nuts, place a nut on the end of a long kitchen fork or dipping fork. Lower into the chocolate and coat completely. Lift out of the chocolate and shake off any excess, then leave to set as for fruit. To coat just half of the nut, hold it between your fingers and dip part way into the chocolate.

3 For a two-tone effect, melt dark and white chocolate in separate bowls. Dip the fruit or nuts into one colour to coat completely, then, when set, half-dip into the other colour.

Chocolate Curls

1 Melt 115 g/4 oz chocolate. Pour the chocolate on to a firm, smooth surface such as a marble, wood or plastic laminate, set on a slightly damp cloth to prevent slipping. Spread the chocolate evenly over the surface with a large palette knife.

2 ▲ Leave the chocolate to cool slightly. It should feel just set, but not hard. Hold a large sharp knife at a 45° angle to the chocolate and push it along the chocolate in short sawing movements from right to left and left to right to make curls.

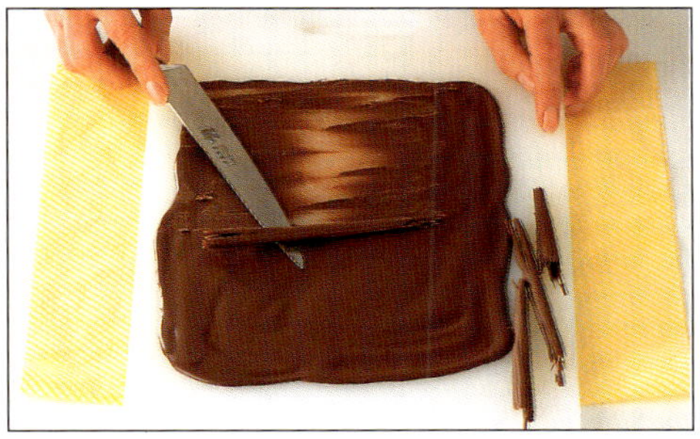

3 ▲ Remove the curls by sliding the point of the knife underneath each one and lifting off. Leave until firm.

Chocolate Shavings

The quickest way to turn chocolate into a decoration is simply to grate or shave it. The chocolate should be at room temperature for this.

1 ▲ For fine shavings, grate the chocolate on the coarse side of a grater. For coarser shavings, peel off curls with a vegetable peeler.

This sophisticated heart-shaped cake is a wonderful idea for Valentine's Day or to celebrate an engagement. It is completely covered with rich, dark chocolate curls.

Colour Effects

If you think of the surface of a cake as an artist's canvas, it opens up all sorts of decorating ideas using painting and drawing techniques. This is made possible by the wide range of colours available in the form of food colourings and food colouring pens.

Using Stencils

Cards with stencil patterns on them can be found at cake icing specialists or at stationers, or you can make your own stencils out of thin card.

1 Coat the cake with sugarpaste, royal or marzipan icing and leave to dry.

2 ▲ Lay the stencil over the surface of the cake. Dip a dry, clean paintbrush into powdered food colouring and dab into the stencil. Lift off the stencil to reveal the design. You could also fill in the colour with a food colouring pen.

Flicking

Use one colour or several. This is almost a decoration in itself.

1 Cover the cake with sugarpaste, royal or marzipan icing and leave to dry. Place the cake on a fairly large sheet of greaseproof paper to protect the work surface.

2 ▲ Water down the food colouring, and then load up the end of the paintbrush with the colour. Position the brush over the area you wish to colour, then flick your wrist in the direction of the cake, so the colour falls on to it in small beads.

Linework

Food colouring pens are a quick way to add simple line designs to the tops and sides of cakes. Use a ruler to achieve straight lines, and a pair of compasses for large curved lines.

1 Cover the cake and leave to dry. Royal icing gives the firmest surface for the pens. Work out the design.

2 ▲ For small circles, curves or semi-circles, draw around the edge of a plain round cutter.

3 ▼ Add details to the design with small dots.

Painting and Drawing

Food colourings can be used like water-colours and food colouring pens like crayons or felt-tip pens on iced cakes. Let the icing dry before applying the design. Before working on the cake, you might find it easier to practise on a spare piece of icing. When painting different colours next to each other, allow the first colour to dry before applying the second to prevent colours running into each other - unless that is the effect you wish to achieve.

1 ▲ Dilute food colourings with a little water or use straight from the bottle. A small plastic palette is useful for mixing the colours. Work out the design and either paint it straight on to the cake, or draw it out first with a food colouring pen.

2 ▲ Food colouring pens look like felt-tip pens, but are filled with edible food colourings. They are a speedy way to add lively highlights to designs. They can also be used to colour in patterned borders, to draw personalized pictures or to write messages on cakes.

3 ▶ Look to the great artists, such as Matisse and Picasso, for inspiration, either for a painting style or theme.

Stippling

This is normally used as a background decoration, so it is best to keep the colours delicate. Try blending two soft shades together.

1 Cover the cake with sugarpaste, royal or marzipan icing and leave until the icing is dry.

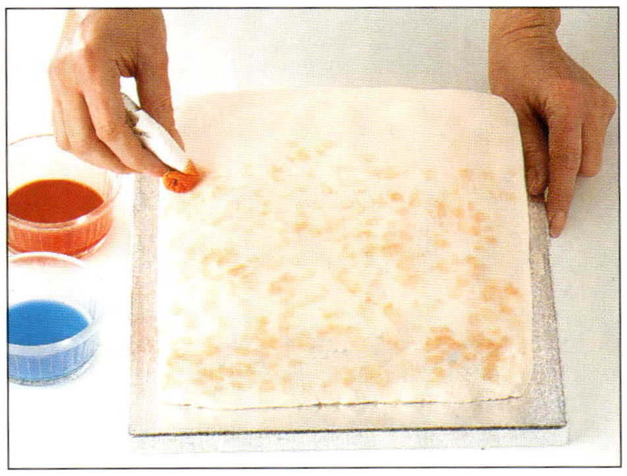

2 ▲ Water down the food colouring and apply with a dry, clean piece of sponge or kitchen paper, by dabbing it on to the surface of the cake.

Powdered Tints

These can be brushed on dry, either with a paintbrush for detail, or with a clean, dry piece of sponge when you wish to cover larger areas.

1 Cover the cake with sugarpaste, royal or marzipan icing and leave until the icing is dry.

2 ▲ Draw on the design with different coloured food colouring pens, and then brush in the colours with powdered tints.

Using Bought Decorations

When you want to put a cake together in a hurry for a last-minute celebration, or even if you do not have much time to spend on decorating cakes, remember there are all kinds of easy-to-use edible items and ready-to-use decorations that can be found in supermarkets, health food shops, and in confectionery and specialist cake icing shops.

Edible Decorations

Here are just some of the delicious edible decorations which can be used for quick-and-easy cake decorating. Keep a few of these in your cupboard, ready for an impromptu celebration cake.

Sweets Choose small, colourful, simple shapes such as jelly babies, jelly beans, coloured chocolate beans, chocolate buttons, liquorice allsorts, chocolate-coated espresso beans, yogurt-coated nuts and raisins, small moulded chocolate shapes or sugared almonds. These are just a few of the sweets which, used with imagination and flair, turn a cake into something special.
Jellied Shapes Packaged jellied orange and lemon slices are also useful, either whole or cut into wedges, as are jelly diamonds, available in several colours.
Nuts Use these chopped or whole, plain or toasted, for decorating the tops and to coat the sides of cakes.
Glacé and Crystallized Fruits Glacé cherries and angelica are probably the most familiar of these popular quick cake decorations, but there are many other tasty varieties to choose from, such as pineapple and ginger – even diced papaya. Depending on their size, the fruits can be halved, sliced, chopped or cut into shapes ready for arranging on the cake.
Coconut Desiccated coconut is another useful cake decoration, particularly as it can also be tinted with a few drops of food colouring to give an attractive coating for the sides of a cake. Other more unusual kinds of coconut are also available; such as coconut threads, coconut chips and coconut slices. All can be used raw or toasted.
Marzipan Fruits and Sugar Flowers Both can be bought ready-made if you do not wish to shape your own.
Citrus Fruits Fresh lemon, lime and orange zest can be transformed into attractive cake decorations. Cut off thin, curly strips of rind with a sharp knife or zester. Alternatively, use tiny aspic cutters to cut out shapes from the rinds, but be careful not to include the white pith. The shapes can be grouped together or linked to form a border around the cake.

MAKING PATTERNS WITH EDIBLE DECORATIONS

1 ▲ Arrange jelly diamonds and jellied orange slices on a square or round cake to form a pretty stylized design such as the one shown.

2 ▲ This jazzy design is ideal for a child's cake. It is made from whole and halved coloured chocolate beans.

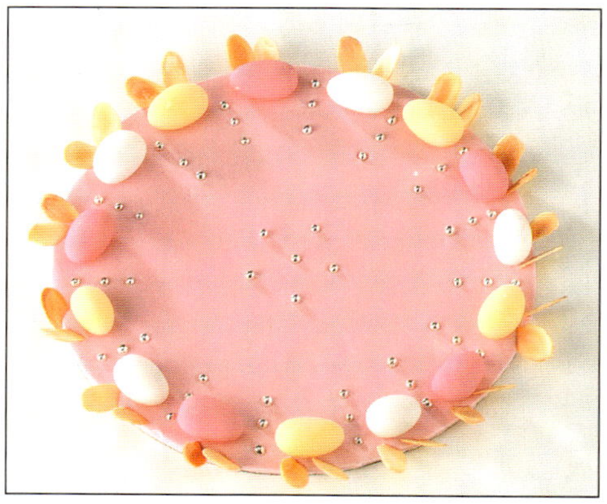

3 ▲ Sugared almonds, flaked toasted almonds and silver balls add life to any cake iced in pastel shades, and are ideal for Easter.

Decorative edibles help to make cake decorating fun as well as easy.

Sweet Flowers

Edible decorations can be used in different combinations to make attractive floral designs for cakes.

1 ▲ Use jelly diamonds for the petals and leaves, slices of dolly mixtures for the centres and strips of angelica for the stems.

2 ▲ Arrange halved coloured chocolate beans, cut-side down, to form a flower. Use different colours, with a silver ball for the centre.

3 ▲ Dip blanched whole almonds in melted chocolate to form the petals of a flower, then arrange with a chocolate button or chocolate bean for the centre.

Stencilling

For this technique you can use icing sugar, cocoa or even finely ground nuts to create the stencilling effect.

1 ▲ For a quick stencilled pattern, lay a patterned doiley on the cake and sift icing sugar over the top. Lift off the doiley to reveal the pattern. The centre can be cut out of the doiley to create another stencilled area. For maximum contrast, use icing sugar on a chocolate cake and cocoa on a plain cake.

2 ▼ Another stencilling method is to lay strips of paper over the cake, either in straight lines, diagonally or in a lattice pattern. Use fairly thick paper so it lies flat. For more dramatic effects, cut out strips of paper in wavy, zigzag or other geometric patterns.

It's time to have fun. Load up a paintbrush with orange food colouring and then flick it over a sugarpaste-iced cake. Cut out bears with the icing and paint on their features. Line up jelly teddy bears, jelly beans and other colourful sweets, paint a bright design on the iced board and you have a cake that is surprisingly easy to decorate.

Ribbon Decorations

Stripy ones, dotty ones, sparkly ones, wide and pencil-thin ones - ribbons are a lovely way to add height, colour and a special celebratory look to a cake. They can be wrapped around the cake, using varying widths and colours for different effects, made into simple shapes, or threaded into the icing. Tiny coloured bows can be purchased from cake icing specialists, or you can make your own decorations as suggested here.

Ribbon Loops

These look pretty if one or several loops are attached to florist's wire, or if alternating colours are looped together.

1 Use thin ribbon, about 5 mm/¼ inch wide. Make two or three small loops of ribbon.

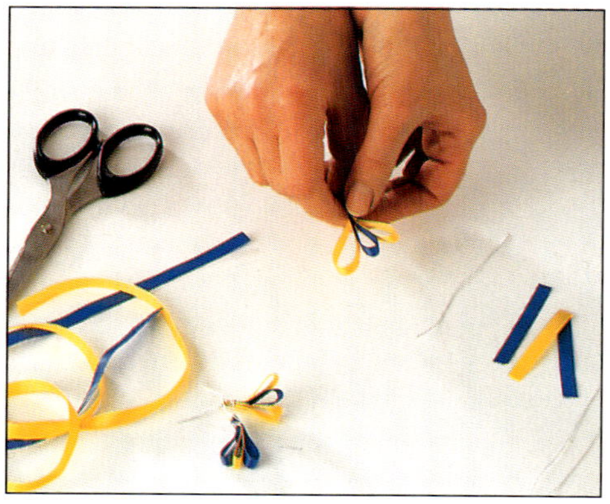

2 ▲ Using a piece of florist's wire, twist it around the ends of the ribbon to secure the loops together. Trim the ends of the ribbon. The wire will form a stem for the loops, so cut it to the required length and use it to put the loops in position on the cake. The loops must be removed from the cake before serving.

Ribbon Curls

▲ Use a thin piece of gift wrapping ribbon, about 5 mm/¼ inch wide, and cut into the chosen lengths. Run the blade of a pair of scissors or a sharp knife down the length of the ribbons to make them curl.

Multiple Curls

▲ Use a thick piece of gift wrapping ribbon, about 2 cm/¾ inch wide, and cut into the chosen lengths. Tear the ribbon into four or five thin strips, almost to the end. Run the blade of a pair of scissors or a sharp knife down the length of each strip to curl.

Ovals

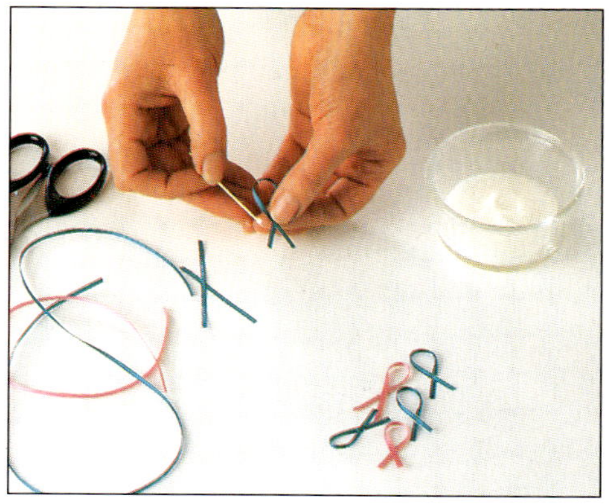

▲ Hold both ends of a thin piece of ribbon. With your left hand bring the end up and twist it over to cross and form an oval with two straight ends hanging down. Where the ribbon crosses, secure with a little royal icing. Cut the ends diagonally to neaten.

Ribbon Designs

▲ Use combinations of colours and widths of ribbons and bows to create special patterns on the tops and sides of cakes. Secure with a little royal icing.

A riot of ribbons - let the colours or patterns of ribbon you choose complement the shade and design of the cake without dominating it.

RIBBON INSERTION

This technique looks much more difficult than it actually is. A cake covered with sugarpaste icing provides the best surface for this decoration. Leave the icing to dry until it is soft underneath and just firm on the top.

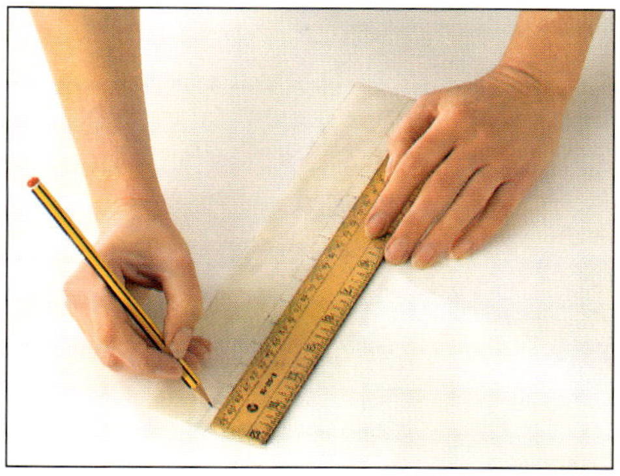

1 ▲ Work out your design for the number and size of slits, and whether the design is to be straight or curved. Draw the design on a piece of greaseproof paper.

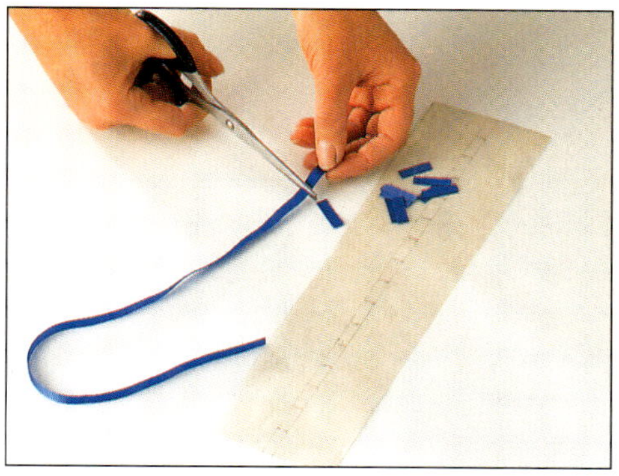

2 ▲ Cut pieces of ribbon which are fractionally longer than the size of each slit.

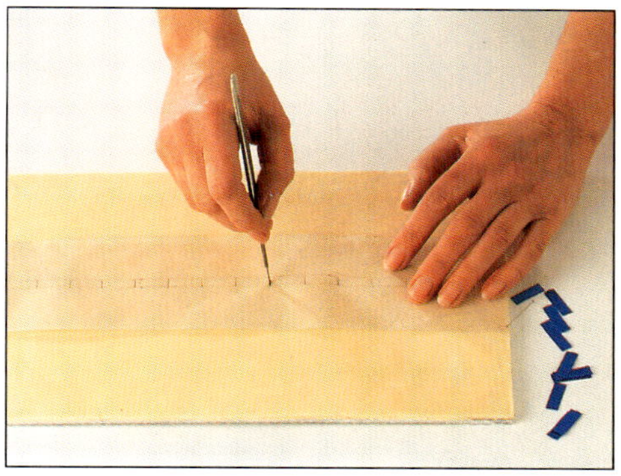

3 ▲ Secure the template to the cake with pins. Cut through the drawn lines to make the slits in the icing using a scalpel. Remove the template.

4 ▲ With the aid of a pointed tool, insert one end of the ribbon into the first slit and the other end into the second slit.

5 ▲ Leave a space and repeat, filling all the slits with the pieces of ribbon in the same way.

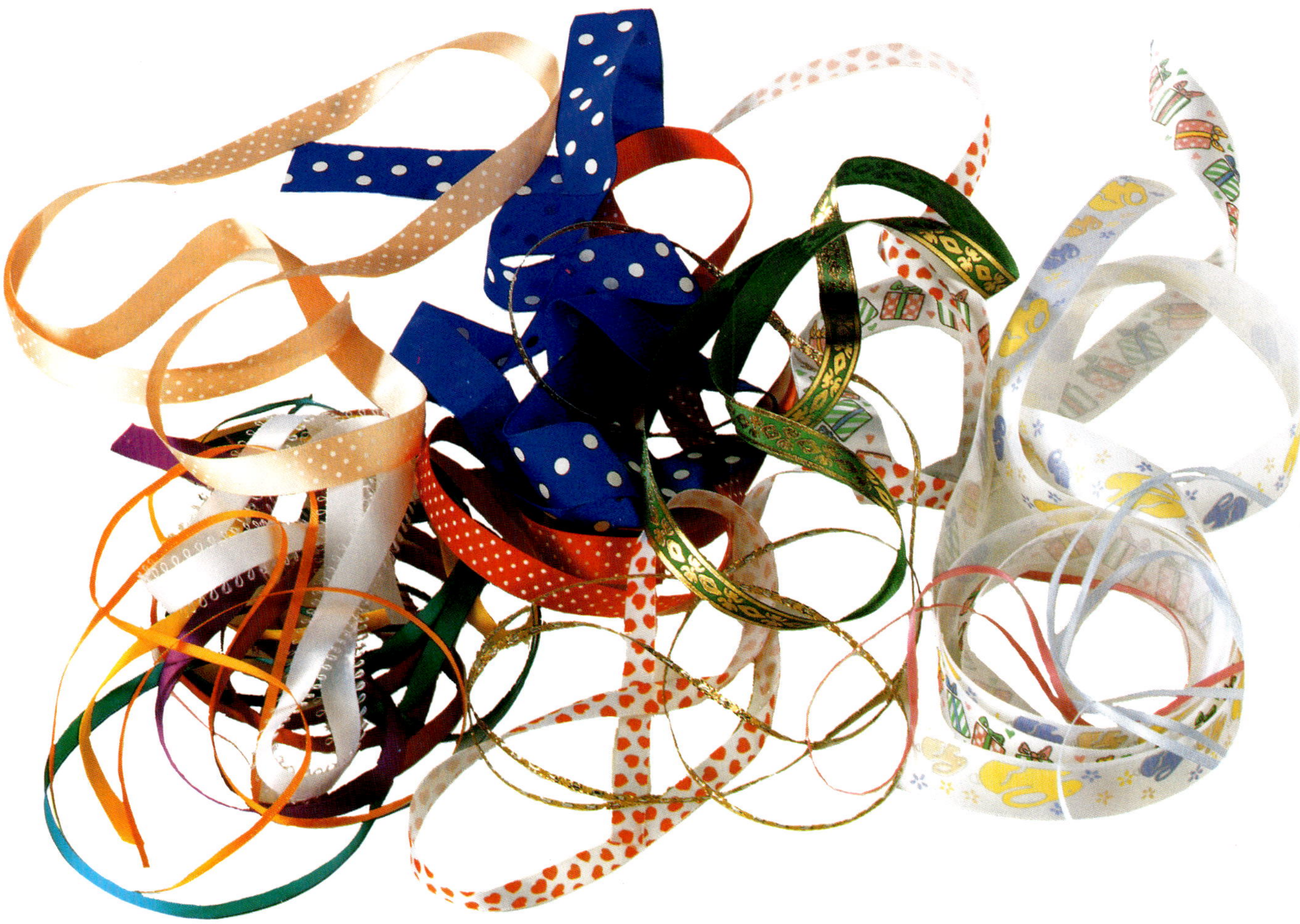

Sugar-frosting Flowers and Fruit

Something as simple as a spray of fresh sugar-frosted flowers or a grouping of small fruits is often all that is needed to decorate a cake. When frosting flowers choose ones that are edible, such as pansies, primroses, violets, roses, freesias, tiny daffodils or nasturtiums.

Flowers

Sugar-frosted flowers keep surprisingly well, and you may want to make the most of springtime primroses and violets to liven up cakes later in the year. Once the flowers are dry, store them in a single layer between sheets of tissue paper in a small box. Keep the box in a cool, dry place.

1 ▲ Lightly beat an egg white in a small bowl, and sprinkle some caster sugar on to a plate. Dry the flower on kitchen paper. If possible, leave some stem attached. Evenly brush both sides of the petals with the egg white.

2 ▲ Holding the flower by its stem over a plate lined with kitchen paper, sprinkle it evenly with the sugar, then shake off any excess.

3 ▲ Place on a flat board or wire rack covered with kitchen paper and leave to dry in a warm place.

Frosty florals - whole flowers or individual petals can be frosted in the same way.

Fruits

When frosting fruits, choose really fresh ones which are small and firm such as kumquats, cherries, grapes or strawberries. Frosted fruits will only keep as long as the fruits themselves stay fresh. Place on a lined tray and keep in the refrigerator. Eat within two days.

1 Wash the fruit and pat dry on kitchen paper.

2 ▲ Lightly beat an egg white in a small bowl, and sprinkle some caster sugar on to a plate. Hold the fruit by the stem if possible and evenly brush all over with the egg white.

Sometimes the simplest cakes can be the most elegant. The stark white background of sugarpaste icing is all that is needed to show off a sweeping spray of frosted flowers, an interlocking design of ribbons and a few ribbon curls and bows.

3 ▲ Holding the fruit over a plate lined with kitchen paper, sprinkle it evenly with the sugar, then shake off any excess.

4 Place on a flat board or wire rack covered with kitchen paper and leave to dry in a warm place.

Frosty fruits - make a pile of these luscious fruits for a stunning centrepiece on a cake.

Classic Cakes

Classic Cakes includes innovative interpretations and designs for much-loved favourites which are a must for every cake-maker's basic repertoire. From simply decorated sponge cakes, to delicious dessert cakes and sumptuous gâteaux, there are recipes here for every taste and every occasion.

Black Forest Gâteau

A perfect gâteau for a special occasion tea party, or for serving as a sumptuous dessert at a dinner party.

Ingredients

Serves 10–12

5 size 3 eggs
175 g/6 oz/$^{3}/_{4}$ cup caster sugar
50 g/2 oz/$^{1}/_{2}$ cup plain flour, sifted
50 g/2 oz/$^{1}/_{3}$ cup cocoa powder, sifted
75 g/3 oz/6 tbsp butter, melted

For the Filling

5–6 tbsp Kirsch
575 ml/1 pint/2$^{1}/_{2}$ cups double cream
1 x 425 g/15 oz can black cherries, drained, stoned and chopped

To Decorate

225 g/8 oz plain chocolate
15–20 fresh cherries, preferably with stems
sifted icing sugar (optional)

STORING

This cake is not suitable for storing.

1 Preheat the oven to 180°C/350°F/Gas 4. Grease two deep 20 cm/8 inch round cake tins, line the bases with greaseproof paper and grease the paper.

2 ▲ Place the eggs and sugar in a large mixing bowl and beat with an electric mixer for about 10 minutes or until the mixture is thick and pale.

3 Sift together the flour and cocoa powder, then sift again into the whisked mixture. Fold in very gently, then slowly trickle in the melted butter and continue to fold in gently.

4 Divide the mixture between the tins and smooth the surfaces. Bake in the centre of the oven for about 30 minutes, or until springy to the touch. Leave in the tin for about 5 minutes, then turn out on to a wire rack, peel off the lining paper and leave to cool.

5 ▲ Cut each cake in half horizontally and lay on a work surface. Sprinkle the four layers with the Kirsch.

6 ▲ In a large bowl, whip the cream until it holds soft peaks. Transfer two-thirds of the cream to another bowl and stir in the chopped cherries. Place a layer of cake on a serving plate or cake board and spread over one-third of the filling. Top with another layer of cake and continue layering, finishing with a layer of cake.

7 Use the remaining whipped cream to cover the top and sides of the gâteau, spreading it evenly with a knife.

8 To decorate the gâteau, melt the chocolate in a bowl over a pan of hot water, or in a double boiler. Spread the chocolate out on to a plastic chopping board and allow to set.

9 ▲ Using a long sharp knife, scrape along the surface of the melted chocolate to make thin shavings and use these to cover the sides of the cake and to decorate the top. Finish by arranging the cherries on top of the gâteau. Dust with sifted icing sugar, if wished.

Tip

If liked, the cherries can be coated or half-coated in chocolate before arranging on the cake. To do this, reserve 2–3 tbsp of the melted chocolate and dip the cherries into it. Allow the dipped cherries to set on greaseproof paper.

Crunchy-topped Madeira Cake

Traditionally served with a glass of Madeira wine in Victorian England, this light sponge still makes a perfect tea-time treat.

INGREDIENTS

Serves 8–10

200 g/7 oz/14 tbsp butter, softened
finely grated zest of 1 lemon
150 g/5 oz/3/4 cup caster sugar
3 size 3 eggs
75 g/3 oz/3/4 cup plain flour, sifted
150 g/5 oz/1 1/4 cups self-raising flour, sifted

For the Topping

3 tbsp clear honey
115 g/4 oz/3/4 cup plus 2 tbsp chopped mixed peel
50 g/2 oz/1/2 cup flaked almonds

STORING

This cake can be kept for up to three days in an airtight container.

1 Preheat the oven to 180°C/350°F/Gas 4. Grease a 450 g/1 lb loaf tin, line the base and sides with greaseproof paper and grease the paper.

2 ▲ Place the butter, lemon zest and sugar in a mixing bowl and beat until light and fluffy. Beat in the eggs, one at a time, until evenly blended.

3 ▲ Sift together the flours, then stir into the egg mixture. Transfer the cake mixture to the prepared tin and smooth the surface.

4 ▲ Bake in the centre of the oven for 45–50 minutes or until a skewer inserted into the centre of the cake comes out clean. Leave the cake in the tin for about 5 minutes. Turn out on to a wire rack, peel off the lining paper and leave to cool completely.

5 ▲ To make the topping, place the honey, chopped mixed peel and almonds in a small saucepan and heat gently until the honey melts. Remove from the heat and stir briefly to coat the peel and almonds, then spread over the top of the cake. Allow to cool completely before serving.

Cherry Batter Cake

This colourful tray bake looks pretty cut into neat squares or fingers.

INGREDIENTS
Serves 8–10
225 g/8 oz/2 cups self-raising flour
1 tsp baking powder
75 g/3 oz/6 tbsp butter, softened
150 g/5 oz/⅔ cup soft light brown sugar
1 size 3 egg, lightly beaten
150 ml/¼ pint/⅔ cup milk

For the Topping
1 x 680 g/1½ lb jar black cherries or blackcurrants, drained
175 g/6 oz/¾ cup soft light brown sugar
50 g/2 oz/½ cup self-raising flour
50 g/2 oz/4 tbsp butter, melted
sifted icing sugar, to decorate
whipped cream, to serve (optional)

STORING
This cake can be kept for up to two days in an airtight container.

1 Preheat the oven to 190°C/375°F/ Gas 5. Grease a 33 x 23 cm/13 x 9 inch Swiss roll tin, line the base and sides with greaseproof paper and grease the paper.

2 To make the base, sift the flour and baking powder into a mixing bowl. Add the butter, sugar, egg and milk. Beat the mixture until the batter becomes smooth, then turn into the prepared tin and smooth the surface.

3 ▲ Scatter the drained fruit evenly over the batter mixture.

4 ▲ Mix together the remaining topping ingredients and spoon evenly over the fruit. Bake in the centre of the oven for about 40 minutes, or until golden brown and the centre is firm to the touch.

5 Leave to cool, then dredge with icing sugar. Serve with whipped cream, if wished.

Chestnut Cake

An Italian speciality, this is definitely a cake to mark an occasion. Rich, moist and heavy, it can be made up to a week in advance and kept, undecorated, wrapped and stored in an airtight container. Allow the cake to come to room temperature before serving.

INGREDIENTS

Serves 8–10

150 g/5 oz/1¼ cups plain flour
pinch of salt
225 g/8 oz/1 cup butter, softened
150 g/5 oz/¾ cup caster sugar
439 g/15½ oz can chestnut purée
9 size 3 eggs, separated
7 tbsp dark rum
300 ml/½ pint/1¼ cups double cream

To Decorate

marrons glacés, chopped
icing sugar, sifted

STORING

Once decorated do not store.

1 Preheat the oven to 180°C/350°F/Gas 4. Grease a 21 cm/8½ inch springform cake tin, line the base with greaseproof paper and grease the paper.

2 Sift together the flour and salt, and set aside. Place the butter and three-quarters of the sugar in a bowl and beat until fluffy.

3 ▲ Fold in two-thirds of the chestnut purée, alternating with the egg yolks, and beat. Fold in the flour and salt.

4 ▲ Whisk the egg whites in a clean, dry bowl until stiff. Beat a little of the egg whites into the chestnut mixture, until evenly blended, then fold in the remainder.

5 ▲ Transfer the cake mixture to the prepared tin and smooth the surface. Bake in the centre of the oven for about 1¼ hours, or until a skewer inserted into the centre of the cake comes out clean.

6 Place the cake, still in the tin, on a wire rack. Using a skewer, pierce holes evenly all over the cake. Sprinkle 4 tbsp of the rum over the top, then allow the cake to cool completely.

7 ▲ Remove the cake from the tin, peel off the lining paper and cut horizontally into two layers. Place the bottom layer on a serving plate. Whisk the cream in a mixing bowl with the remaining rum, sugar and chestnut purée until thick and smooth.

8 To assemble the cake, spread two-thirds of the chestnut cream mixture over the bottom layer and place the other layer on top. Spread some of the remaining chestnut cream over the top and sides of the cake, then fill a greaseproof paper piping bag, fitted with a star nozzle, with the rest of the chestnut mixture. Pipe big swirls around the outside edge of the cake. Decorate with the marrons glacés and sifted icing sugar.

Tip

In order to have the most control over a piping bag, it is important to hold it in a relaxed position. You may find it easier to hold it with one or both hands.

Banana Coconut Cake

Slightly over-ripe bananas are best for this perfect coffee morning cake.

INGREDIENTS
Serves 8–10
75 g/3 oz/1½ cups desiccated coconut
115 g/4 oz/½ cup butter, softened
115 g/4 oz/½ cup caster sugar
2 size 3 eggs
115 g/4 oz/1 cup self-raising flour
50 g/2 oz/½ cup plain flour
1 tsp bicarbonate of soda
100 ml/4 fl oz/½ cup milk
2 large bananas, peeled and mashed

For the Topping
25 g/1 oz/2 tbsp butter
2 tbsp clear honey
115 g/4 oz/2 cups shredded coconut

STORING
This cake will keep for up to two days in an airtight container.

1 Preheat the oven to 190°C/375°F/Gas 5. Grease a deep 18 cm/7 inch square cake tin, line the base and sides with greaseproof paper and then grease the paper.

2 ▲ Spread the desiccated coconut out on a baking sheet and place under a hot grill for about 5 minutes, stirring and turning the coconut until evenly toasted.

3 Place the butter and sugar in a mixing bowl and beat until they are smooth and creamy. Beat in the eggs, one at a time.

4 Sift together the flours and bicarbonate of soda, then sift half of this mixture into the butter and egg mixture and stir to mix.

5 Mix together the milk and mashed banana in a small bowl, then add half to the egg mixture. Beat well to combine, then add the remaining flour and toasted coconut together with the remaining banana mixture. Stir to mix, then transfer to the prepared cake tin and smooth the surface.

6 Bake in the centre of the oven for about 1 hour, or until a skewer inserted into the centre of the cake comes out clean. Leave the cake in the tin for about 5 minutes, then turn out on to a wire rack, peel off the lining paper and leave to cool completely.

7 To make the topping, place the butter and honey in a small saucepan and heat gently until melted. Stir in the shredded coconut and cook, stirring constantly, for about 5 minutes or until lightly browned. Remove from the heat and allow to cool slightly.

8 ▲ Spoon the topping over the top of the cake and allow to cool completely before serving.

Almond and Apricot Cake

Although canned apricots can be used in this recipe, nothing quite beats using the fresh fruit in season. Choose sweet-smelling, ripe fruit for this delicious cake.

INGREDIENTS

Serves 6–8

4–5 tbsp fine dry white breadcrumbs
225 g/8 oz/1 cup butter, softened
225 g/8 oz/1 cup caster sugar
4 size 3 eggs
175 g/6 oz/1½ cups self-raising flour
1–2 tbsp milk
115 g/4 oz/1⅓ cups ground almonds
few drops of almond essence
450 g/1 lb fresh apricots, stoned and halved
sifted caster sugar, to decorate

STORING

This cake can be kept for up to three days in an airtight container.

1 Preheat the oven to 180°C/350°F/Gas 4. Grease a 23 cm/9 inch round cake tin, line the base with greaseproof paper and grease the paper.

2 ▲ Sprinkle the breadcrumbs into the prepared cake tin and tap them around the tin to coat the base and sides evenly.

3 ▲ Place the butter and sugar in a mixing bowl and beat with an electric mixer until light and fluffy. Beat in the eggs, one at a time, then fold in the flour, milk, ground almonds and almond essence.

4 ▲ Spoon half of the cake mixture into the prepared tin and smooth the surface. Arrange half of the apricots over the top, then spoon over the remaining cake mixture. Finish with the other half of the apricots. Bake the cake in the centre of the oven for 30–35 minutes, or until a skewer inserted into the centre of the cake comes out clean.

5 Turn the cake out on to a wire rack, peel off the lining paper and sprinkle over the sifted caster sugar. Serve warm or leave to cool.

Chocolate Chestnut Roulade

A traditional version of the classic Bûche de Nöel, the famous and delicious French Christmas gâteau.

INGREDIENTS
Serves 6–8
225 g/8 oz plain chocolate
50 g/2 oz white chocolate
4 size 3 eggs, separated
114 g/4 oz/½ cup caster sugar, plus extra for dredging

For the Chestnut Filling
150 ml/¼ pint/⅔ cup double cream
1 x 225 g/8 oz can chestnut purée
4–5 tbsp icing sugar, plus extra for dredging
1–2 tbsp brandy

STORING
This cake can be kept for up to two days in the refrigerator.

1 Preheat the oven to 180°C/350°F/ Gas 4. Grease a 23 x 33 cm/9 x 13 inch Swiss roll tin, line with greaseproof paper and grease the paper.

2 Place 50 g/2 oz of the plain chocolate and the white chocolate in two bowls and set over saucepans of hot water. Stir until melted.

3 ▲ Pour the plain chocolate on to a plastic chopping board and spread out evenly. When just set, do the same with the white chocolate. Leave to set.

4 To make the chocolate curls, hold a long, sharp knife at a 45° angle to the chocolate and push it along the chocolate, turning the knife in a circular motion. Carefully place the plain and white chocolate curls on a baking sheet lined with greaseproof paper and set aside until needed.

5 ▲ Place the remaining plain chocolate in another bowl set over a saucepan of hot water and stir until melted. Set aside. Place the egg yolks and caster sugar in a mixing bowl and beat with an electric mixer until thick and pale. Stir in the chocolate.

6 Whisk the egg whites in a clean dry bowl, until they hold stiff peaks. Fold into the chocolate mixture and then turn into the prepared tin. Bake in the centre of the oven for 15–20 minutes, or until risen and firm. Place on a wire rack, cover with a just-damp cloth and leave to cool completely.

7 Place a sheet of greaseproof paper on the work surface and sprinkle with a little caster sugar. Turn the roulade out on to the greaseproof paper. Peel away the lining paper and trim the edges of the roulade. Cover again with a just-damp cloth.

8 To make the filling, whip the double cream in a mixing bowl, until it holds soft peaks.

9 ▲ Place the chestnut purée and icing sugar in a clean bowl. Add the brandy and beat until smooth and evenly combined, then fold in the whipped cream.

10 ▲ Spread the mixture over the roulade, leaving a little border at the top edge. Roll up the roulade, using the greaseproof paper to help and transfer it to a serving plate. Top with the chocolate curls and sprinkle with sifted icing sugar, to serve.

Strawberry Cream Gâteau

Fresh raspberries also work well for this recipe.

INGREDIENTS
Serves 8–10
2 egg yolks
4 size 3 eggs
finely grated zest of 1 lemon
115 g/4 oz/½ cup caster sugar
115 g/4 oz/1 cup plain flour, sifted
115 g/4 oz/½ cup butter, melted

For the Strawberry Cream
225 g/8 oz/1½ cups fresh strawberries, washed, dried and hulled
275 ml/½ pint/1¼ cups double cream
50 g/2 oz/½ cup icing sugar
1 tbsp strawberry liqueur or Kirsch

STORING
This cake can be kept for up to two days in the refrigerator.

1 Preheat the oven to 150°C/300°F/ Gas 2. Grease a 20 cm/8 inch round cake tin, line the base with greaseproof paper and grease the paper.

2 Place the eggs yolks, egg, lemon zest and sugar in a mixing bowl and beat with an electric mixer for about 10 minutes or until thick and pale. Add the flour and melted butter. Whisk for a further minute, then transfer to the prepared cake tin.

3 ▲ Bake in the centre of the oven for 30–35 minutes or until a skewer inserted into the centre of the cake comes out clean. Turn out on to a wire rack, peel off the lining paper and leave to cool completely.

4 ▲ To make the strawberry cream, place all but one of the strawberries in a food processor or blender and purée until smooth. Place the double cream in a mixing bowl and whisk until it holds peaks. Fold the purée into the cream with the icing sugar and liqueur.

5 ▲ Place the cooled cake on a plate and spread the strawberry cream evenly over the top and sides, making swirls for an attractive finish. Decorate with the sliced reserved strawberry.

Upside-down Pear & Ginger Cake

A light spicy sponge topped with glossy baked fruit and ginger. This is also good served warm for pudding.

INGREDIENTS
Serves 6–8
1 x 900 g/2 lb can pear halves, drained
8 tbsp finely chopped stem ginger
8 tbsp ginger syrup from the jar
175 g/6 oz/1½ cups self-raising flour
½ tsp baking powder
1 tsp ground ginger
175 g/6 oz/¾ cup soft light brown sugar
175 g/6 oz/¾ cup butter, softened
3 size 3 eggs, lightly beaten

STORING
This cake is not suitable for storing.

1 Preheat the oven to 180°C/350°F/Gas 4. Grease a deep 20 cm/8 inch round cake tin, line the base with greaseproof paper and grease the paper.

2 ▲ Fill the hollow in each pear with half the chopped ginger. Arrange the pear halves, flat sides down, over the base of the cake tin, then spoon half the ginger syrup over the top.

3 Sift the flour, baking powder and ground ginger into a mixing bowl. Stir in the soft brown sugar and butter, then add the eggs and beat together for 1–2 minutes until level and creamy.

4 ▲ Carefully spoon the mixture into the tin and smooth the surface.

5 ▲ Bake in the centre of the oven for about 50 minutes, or until a skewer inserted in the centre of the cake comes out clean. Leave the cake to cool in the tin for about 5 minutes. Turn out on to a wire rack, peel off the lining paper and leave to cool completely. Add the reserved chopped ginger to the pear halves and drizzle over the remaining ginger syrup.

One-stage Victoria Sandwich

Originally made in an oblong shape, today's Victoria sandwich is made using a variety of different flavourings and decorations, and is baked and cut into all sorts of shapes and sizes. Use this basic recipe to suit the occasion.

INGREDIENTS
Serves 6–8
175 g/6 oz/1½ cups self-raising flour
pinch of salt
175 g/6 oz/¾ cup butter, softened
175 g/6 oz/¾ cup caster sugar
3 size 3 eggs

To Finish
4–6 tbsp raspberry jam
caster sugar or icing sugar

STORING
This cake can be stored for up to three days in an airtight container.

1 Preheat the oven to 180°C/375°F/Gas 4. Grease two deep 18 cm/7 inch round cake tins, line the bases with greaseproof paper and grease the paper.

2 ▲ Place all the ingredients in a mixing bowl and whisk together using an electric hand whisk. Divide the mixture between the prepared tins and smooth the surfaces. Bake in the centre of the oven for 25–30 minutes, or until a skewer inserted into the centre of the cakes comes out clean. Turn out on to a wire rack, peel off the lining paper and leave to cool completely.

3 ▲ Place one of the cakes on a serving plate and spread with the raspberry jam. Place the other cake on top, then dredge with caster or icing sugar, to serve.

Variation

Makes 8–10 iced fancies

1 ▲ Place the cake mixture in a greased and lined 23 x 33 cm/9 x 13 inch Swiss roll tin and smooth the surface. Bake in the centre of the oven for 25–30 minutes, or until a skewer inserted into the centre of the cake comes out clean. Turn out on to a wire rack, peel off the lining paper and leave to cool completely.

2 ▲ Cut the cake into individual sized shapes, such as fingers, diamonds, squares or small rounds, using a knife or biscuit cutters. Using one quantity of Butter Icing, cover with decorative piping. You can flavour or colour the butter icing by substituting orange or lemon juice for the milk and/or adding a few drops of food colouring.

3 For alternative decorations, you could try a selection of the following: glacé cherries, angelica, jellied fruits, grated chocolate, chopped or whole nuts, or choose one of your own ideas.

Tip

To make the decorative stencilled pattern with icing sugar shown here, cut out star shapes from paper. Lay the paper stars over the top of the cake and then dredge with icing sugar. Remove the paper shapes carefully to reveal the stencilled pattern. You could also use a paper doiley as a stencil.

Flourless Fruit Cake

A really easy recipe which everyone will enjoy. Children can have fun crushing the cornflakes and helping you to beat the ingredients together.

INGREDIENTS

Serves 12–15

1 x 450 g/1 lb jar mincemeat
350 g/12 oz/2 cups dried mixed fruit
115 g/4 oz/1 cup no-soak dried apricots, chopped
115 g/4 oz/1 cup no-soak dried figs, chopped
115 g/4 oz/½ cup glacé cherries, halved
115 g/4 oz/1 cup walnut pieces
225 g/8 oz/8–10 cups cornflakes, crushed
4 size 3 eggs, lightly beaten
1 x 410 g/14½ oz can evaporated milk
1 tsp ground mixed spice
1 tsp baking powder
mixed glacé fruits, chopped, to decorate

STORING

This cake can be kept for up to a week in an airtight container.

1 Preheat the oven to 150°C/300°F/Gas 2. Grease a 25 cm/10 inch round cake tin, line the base and sides with a double thickness of greaseproof paper and grease the paper.

2 Put all the ingredients into a large mixing bowl. Beat together well.

3 ▲ Turn into the prepared tin and smooth the surface with the back of a spoon.

4 ▲ Bake in the centre of the oven for about 1¾ hours, or until a skewer inserted in the centre of the cake comes out clean. Allow the cake to cool in the tin for 10 minutes, then turn out on to a wire rack, peel off the lining paper and leave to cool completely. Decorate with the chopped glacé fruits.

Tip

This cake may be iced and marzipanned to make a Christmas or birthday cake. A useful recipe for anyone who needs to avoid eating wheat flour.

Exotic Celebration Gâteau

Use any tropical fruits you can find to make a spectacular display of colours and tastes.

INGREDIENTS

Serves 8–10

175 g/6 oz/¾ cup butter, softened
175 g/6 oz/¾ cup caster sugar
3 size 3 eggs, beaten
250 g/9 oz/2¼ cups self-raising flour
2–3 tbsp milk
6–8 tbsp light rum
425 ml/¾ pt/scant 2 cups double cream
25 g/1 oz/¼ cup icing sugar, sifted

To Decorate

450 g/1 lb mixed fresh exotic and soft fruits, such as figs, redcurrants, star fruit, kiwi fruit, etc.
6 tbsp apricot jam, warmed and sieved
2 tbsp warm water
sifted icing sugar

STORING

This cake will keep for up to two days in the refrigerator

1 Preheat the oven to 190°C/375°F/Gas 5. Grease and flour a deep 20 cm/8 inch ring mould.

2 ▲ Place the butter and sugar in a mixing bowl and beat until light and fluffy. Gradually beat in the eggs, then fold in the flour with the milk.

3 Spoon the cake mixture into the prepared tin and smooth the surface. Bake in the centre of the oven for about 45 minutes, or until a skewer inserted into the centre of the cake comes out clean. Turn out on to a wire rack and leave to cool completely.

4 ▲ Place the cake on a serving plate, then use a thin skewer to make holes randomly over the cake. Drizzle over the rum and allow to soak in.

5 ▲ Place the cream and icing sugar in a mixing bowl and beat with an electric mixer until the mixture holds soft peaks. Spread all over the top and sides of the cake.

6 Arrange the fruits attractively in the hollow centre of the cake, allowing the fruits to overhang the edges a little. Mix together the apricot jam and water, then use to brush evenly over the fruit. Sift over a little icing sugar, to decorate.

Carrot and Almond Cake

Made with grated carrots and ground almonds, this unusual fat-free sponge makes a delicious afternoon treat.

INGREDIENTS
Serves 8–10
5 size 3 eggs, separated
finely grated zest of 1 lemon
300 g/10 oz/1⅓ cups caster sugar
350 g/12 oz/5–6 carrots, peeled and finely grated
225 g/8 oz/1¼ cups ground almonds
115 g/4 oz/1 cup self-raising flour, sifted
sifted icing sugar, to decorate
marzipan carrots, to decorate (optional)

STORING
This cake can be kept for up to two days in an airtight container.

Tip

To make the marzipan carrots, knead a little orange food colouring into 115 g/4 oz marzipan until evenly blended. On a work surface lightly dusted with icing sugar, divide the marzipan into even-sized pieces, about the size of small walnuts. Mould into carrot shapes and press horizontal lines along each carrot with a knife blade. Press a tiny stick of angelica into the end of each piece to resemble the carrot top. Position the marzipan carrots on the cake, to decorate.

1 Preheat the oven to 190°C/375°F/Gas 5. Grease a deep 20 cm/8 inch round cake tin, line the base with greaseproof paper and grease the paper.

2 ▲ Place the egg yolks, lemon zest and sugar in a bowl. Beat with an electric mixer for about 5 minutes, until the mixture is thick and pale.

3 ▲ Mix in the grated carrot, ground almonds and flour and stir until evenly combined.

4 In a clean, dry bowl, whisk the egg whites until stiff. Using a large metal spoon or rubber spatula, mix a little of the whisked egg whites into the carrot mixture, then fold in the rest.

5 ▲ Spoon the mixture into the prepared cake tin and bake in the centre of the oven for about 1¼ hours, or until a skewer inserted into the centre of the cake comes out clean. Leave the cake in the tin for about 5 minutes, then turn out on to a wire rack, peel off the lining paper and leave to cool completely.

6 ▲ Decorate with sifted icing sugar and marzipan carrots.

Vegan Chocolate Gâteau

It isn't often that vegans can indulge in a slice of chocolate cake and this one tastes so delicious, they'll all be back for more!

Ingredients

Serves 8–10

300 g/10 oz/2½ cups self-raising wholemeal flour
50 g/2 oz/⅓ cup cocoa powder
3 tsp baking powder
250 g/9 oz/1¼ cups caster sugar
few drops of vanilla essence
9 tbsp sunflower oil
350 ml/12 fl oz/1½ cups water
sifted cocoa powder, to decorate
25 g/1 oz/¼ cup chopped nuts, to decorate

For the Chocolate Fudge

50 g/2 oz/¼ cup vegan (soya) margarine
3 tbsp water
250 g/9 oz/2⅓ cups icing sugar
2 tbsp cocoa powder
1–2 tbsp hot water

STORING

This cake can be kept for up to two days in the refrigerator.

1 Preheat the oven to 170°C/325°F/Gas 3. Grease a deep 20 cm/8 inch round cake tin, line the base and sides with greaseproof paper and grease the paper.

2 Sift the flour, cocoa powder and baking powder into a large mixing bowl. Add the caster sugar and vanilla essence, then gradually beat in the sunflower oil and water to make a smooth batter.

3 Pour the cake mixture into the prepared tin and smooth the surface with the back of a spoon.

4 ▲ Bake in the centre of the oven for about 45 minutes or until a skewer inserted into the centre of the cake comes out clean. Leave in the tin for about 5 minutes, then turn out on to a wire rack, peel off the lining paper and leave to cool. Cut the cake in half.

5 ▲ To make the chocolate fudge, place the margarine and water in a pan and heat gently until the margarine has melted. Remove from the heat and add the sifted icing sugar and cocoa powder, beating until smooth and shiny. Allow to cool until firm enough to spread and pipe.

6 ▲ Place the bottom layer of cake on a serving plate and spread over two-thirds of the chocolate fudge mixture. Top with the other layer of cake. Fit a piping bag with a star nozzle, fill with the remaining chocolate fudge and pipe stars over the cake. Sprinkle with cocoa powder and chopped nuts.

Gorgeous Chocolate Cake

This recipe will definitely make you famous. Make sure you serve it with paper and pens, as everyone will want to take down the recipe.

4 ▲ Place the remaining butter and remaining melted plain chocolate in a saucepan. Heat very gently, stirring constantly, until melted. Pour over the cake, allowing the topping to coat the sides too. Leave to set for at least an hour. To decorate, fill a piping bag with the melted white chocolate and snip the end. Drizzle all around the edges to make a double border. Use any remaining chocolate to make leaves (see Trailing Orchid Wedding cake, steps 2 and 3).

INGREDIENTS

Serves 8–10

175 g/6 oz/3/4 cup butter, softened
115 g/4 oz/1/2 cup caster sugar
250 g/9 oz/9 squares plain chocolate, melted
200 g/7 oz/2 1/3 cups ground almonds
4 size 3 eggs, separated
115 g/4 oz/4 squares white chocolate, melted, to decorate

STORING

This cake can be kept for up to four days in an airtight container.

1 Preheat the oven to 180°C/350°F/Gas 4. Grease a deep 21 cm/8 1/2 inch springform cake tin, then line the base with greaseproof paper and grease the paper.

2 ▲ Place 115 g/4 oz/1/2 cup of the butter and all the sugar in a mixing bowl and beat until light and fluffy. Add two thirds of the plain chocolate, the ground almonds and the egg yolks and beat until evenly blended.

3 ▲ Whisk the egg whites in another clean, dry bowl until stiff. Fold them into the chocolate mixture, then transfer to the prepared tin and smooth the surface. Bake for 50–55 minutes or until a skewer inserted into the centre of the cake comes out clean. Leave the cake in the tin for about 5 minutes, then turn out on to a wire rack, peel off the lining paper and leave to cool completely.

Tip

Place a large sheet of greaseproof paper or a baking sheet under the wire rack before pouring the chocolate topping over the cake. This will catch all the drips and keep the work surface clean.

Mocha-hazelnut Battenberg

The traditional Battenberg cake originated in Germany when the Prince of Battenberg married Queen Victoria's daughter, Beatrice. This recipe is a variation of the original theme.

Ingredients

Serves 6–8

115 g/4 oz/½ cup butter, softened
115 g/4 oz/½ cup caster sugar
2 size 3 eggs
115 g/4 oz/1 cup self-raising flour, sifted
50 g/2 oz/⅔ cup ground hazelnuts
2 tsp coffee essence
1 tbsp cocoa powder

To Finish

7 tbsp apricot jam, warmed and sieved
225 g/8 oz yellow marzipan
50 g/2 oz/⅔ cup ground hazelnuts
sifted icing sugar, for rolling out
ground hazelnuts, to decorate

STORING

This cake can be kept for up to three days in an airtight container.

1 Preheat the oven to 180°C/350°F/Gas 4. Grease an 18 cm/7 inch square cake tin, line the base with greaseproof paper and grease the paper.

2 ▲ Place the butter and sugar in a bowl and beat until fluffy. Gradually beat in the eggs, then fold in the flour. Transfer half the mixture to another bowl.

3 ▲ Stir the ground hazelnuts into one half of the cake mixture and the coffee essence and cocoa powder into the other half.

4 ▲ Prepare a strip of foil to fit the width and height of the cake tin, then place the mocha-flavoured cake mixture in one half of the tin. Position the strip of foil down the centre, then spoon the hazelnut-flavoured cake mixture into the other half of the tin. Smooth the surface of both mixtures.

5 Bake for 30–35 minutes or until a skewer inserted into the centre of both halves comes out clean. Leave the cakes to cool in the tin for about 5 minutes, then turn out on to a wire rack, peel off the lining paper and leave to cool completely.

6 ▲ Separate the cakes and cut each one in half lengthways. Take one portion of the mocha-flavoured cake and brush along one long side with a little apricot jam. Sandwich this surface with a portion of the hazelnut-flavoured cake. Brush the top of the cakes with apricot jam and position the other portion of mocha-flavoured cake on top of the hazelnut base. Brush along the inner long side with apricot jam and sandwich with the final portion of hazelnut-flavoured cake. Set aside.

7 Knead the marzipan on the work surface to soften, then knead in the ground hazelnuts until evenly blended. On the work surface lightly dusted with icing sugar, roll out the marzipan into a rectangle large enough to wrap around the cake, excluding the ends.

8 Brush the long sides of the cake with apricot jam, then lay the cake on top of the marzipan. Wrap the marzipan around the cake, sealing the edge neatly. Place the cake on a serving plate, seal-side down, and pinch the edges of the marzipan to give an attractive finish. Score the top surface with a knife and sprinkle with ground hazelnuts.

Greek New Year Cake

A gold coin wrapped in foil is baked into this cake and tradition holds that good luck will come to the person who finds it.

INGREDIENTS

Serves 8–10

275 g/10 oz/2½ cups plain flour
2 tsp baking powder
50 g/2 oz/⅔ cup ground almonds
225 g/8 oz/1 cup butter, softened
175 g/6 oz/¾ cup plus 2 tbsp caster sugar, plus a little extra
4 size 3 eggs
150 ml/¼ pint/⅔ cup fresh orange juice
50 g/2 oz/½ cup blanched almonds
1 tbsp sesame seeds

STORING

This cake can be kept for up to four days in an airtight container.

1 ▲ Preheat the oven to 180°C/350°F/Gas 4. Grease a 23 cm/9 inch square cake tin, line the base and sides with greaseproof paper and grease the paper.

2 ▲ Sift the flour and baking powder into a mixing bowl and stir in the ground almonds.

3 ▲ In another mixing bowl, cream together the butter and sugar until light and fluffy. Beat in the eggs, one at a time, using an electric mixer. Fold in the flour mixture, alternating with the orange juice, until evenly combined.

4 ▲ Add a coin wrapped in foil if you wish to make the cake in the traditional manner, then spoon the cake mixture into the prepared tin and smooth the surface. Arrange the almonds on top, then sprinkle over the sesame seeds. Bake in the centre of the oven for 50–55 minutes or until a skewer inserted into the centre of the cake comes out clean. Leave to cool in the tin for about 5 minutes, then turn out on to a wire rack, peel off the lining paper and leave to cool completely. Serve cut into diamond shapes.

Simnel Cake

A traditional cake for Easter.

Ingredients

Serves 10–12

225 g/8 oz/1 cup butter, softened
225 g/8 oz/1 cup caster sugar
4 size 3 eggs, beaten
550 g/1¼ lb/3 cups mixed dried fruit
115 g/4 oz/½ cup glacé cherries
3 tbsp sherry (optional)
275 g/10 oz/2½ cups plain flour, sifted
3 tsp ground mixed spice
1 tsp baking powder
675 g/1½ lb yellow marzipan
1 egg yolk, beaten
ribbons and sugared eggs, to decorate

STORING

This cake can be kept for up to two weeks in an airtight container.

1 Preheat the oven to 160°C/325°F/ Gas 3. Grease a deep 20 cm/8 in round cake tin, line with a double thickness of greaseproof paper and grease the paper.

2 Place the butter and sugar in a large mixing bowl and beat until light and fluffy. Gradually beat in the eggs. Stir in the dried fruit, glacé cherries and sherry, if using.

3 ▲ Sift together the flour, mixed spice and baking powder, then fold into the cake mixture. Set aside.

4 ▲ Cut off half of the marzipan and roll out on a work surface lightly dusted with icing sugar to a 20 cm/8 inch round. Spoon half of the cake mixture into the prepared tin and smooth the surface with the back of a spoon. Place the marzipan round on top, then add the other half of the cake mixture and smooth the surface.

5 Bake in the centre of the oven for about 2½ hours or until golden and springy to the touch. Leave the cake in the tin for about 15 minutes, then turn out on to a wire rack, peel off the lining paper and leave to cool completely.

6 ▲ Roll out the other half of the marzipan to a round to fit on top of the cooled cake. Brush the top of the cake with a little of the egg yolk and position the marzipan round on top. Flute the edges of the marzipan and, if liked, make a decorative pattern on top with a fork. Brush with more egg yolk.

7 Put the cake on a baking sheet and place under a grill for 5 minutes or until the top is lightly browned. Leave to cool completely before decorating with ribbons and sugared eggs.

Chocolate Gâteau Terrine

A spectacular finale to a special-occasion meal. You'll find this is well worth the time and effort to make.

INGREDIENTS
Serves 10–12
115 g/4 oz/½ cup butter, softened
few drops of vanilla essence
115 g/4 oz/½ cup caster sugar
2 size 3 eggs
115 g/4 oz/1 cup self-raising flour, sifted
50 ml/2 fl oz/¼ cup milk
25 g/1 oz/½ cup desiccated coconut, to decorate
fresh bud roses, or other flowers, to decorate

For the Light Chocolate Filling
115 g/4 oz/½ cup butter, softened
2 tbsp icing sugar, sifted
75 g/3 oz/3 squares plain chocolate, melted
225 ml/8 fl oz/1 cup double cream, lightly whipped

For the Dark Chocolate Filling
115 g/4 oz/4 squares plain chocolate, chopped
115 g/4 oz/½ cup butter
2 size 3 eggs
2 tbsp caster sugar
225 ml/8 fl oz/1 cup double cream, lightly whipped
50 g/2 oz/½ cup cocoa powder
1 tbsp dark rum (optional)
2 tbsp gelatine powder dissolved in 2 tbsp hot water

For the White Chocolate Topping
225 g/8 oz/8 squares white chocolate
115 g/4 oz/½ cup butter

STORING
This cake is not suitable for storing.

1 Preheat the oven to 180°C/350°F/Gas 4. Grease a 900 g/2 lb loaf tin, line the base and sides with greaseproof paper and grease the paper.

2 To make the cake, place the butter, vanilla essence and sugar in a mixing bowl and beat until light and fluffy. Add the eggs, one at a time, beating well after each addition. Sift the flour again and fold it and the milk into the cake mixture.

3 Transfer the cake mixture to the prepared tin and bake in the centre of the oven for 25–30 minutes or until a skewer inserted into the centre of the cake comes out clean. Leave the cake in the tin for about 5 minutes, then turn out on to a wire rack, peel off the lining paper and leave to cool completely.

4 ▲ To make the light chocolate filling, place the butter and icing sugar in a mixing bowl and beat until creamy. Add the chocolate and cream until evenly blended. Cover and set aside in the refrigerator, until required.

5 To make the dark chocolate filling, place the chocolate and butter in a small saucepan and heat very gently, stirring frequently, until melted. Set aside to cool. Place the eggs and sugar in a bowl and beat with an electric mixer until thick and frothy. Fold in the cream, cocoa, rum and dissolved gelatine until evenly blended.

6 ▲ To assemble the terrine, wash and dry the loaf tin, then line with clear film, allowing plenty of film to hang over the edges. Using a long serrated knife, cut the cake horizontally into three even layers.

7 ▲ Spread two of the layers with the light chocolate filling, then place one of these layers, filling side up, in the base of the tin.

8 Cover with half of the dark chocolate filling, then chill for about 10 minutes. Place the second light chocolate-topped layer in the terrine, filling side up. Spread over the remaining dark chocolate filling, then chill for another 10 minutes. Top with the remaining layer of cake and chill the terrine again for about 10 minutes.

9 To make the white chocolate topping, place the chocolate and butter in a small saucepan and heat very gently, stirring frequently, until melted and well blended. Allow to cool slightly.

10 To finish the terrine, turn it out on to a wire rack, removing the clear film. Trim the edges with a long, sharp knife, then pour over the white chocolate topping, spreading it evenly over the sides. Sprinkle the coconut over the top and sides. Allow to set before transferring the terrine to a serving plate and decorating with fresh bud roses.

Lemon and Apricot Cake

This more-ish cake is topped with a crunchy layer of flaked almonds and pistachio nuts, and is soaked in a tangy lemon syrup after baking to keep it really moist.

INGREDIENTS

Serves 10–12

175 g/6 oz/¾ cup butter, softened
175 g/6 oz/1½ cups self-raising flour, sifted
½ tsp baking powder
175 g/6 oz/¾ cup caster sugar
3 size 3 eggs, lightly beaten
finely grated zest of 1 lemon
175 g/6 oz/1½ cups no-soak dried apricots, finely chopped
75 g/3 oz/1 cup ground almonds
40 g/1½ oz/⅓ cup pistachio nuts, chopped
50 g/2 oz/⅓ cup flaked almonds
15 g/½ oz/2 tbsp whole pistachio nuts

For the Syrup

freshly squeezed juice of 1 lemon
3 tbsp caster sugar

STORING

This cake can be kept for up to three days in an airtight container.

1 Preheat the oven to 180°C/350°F/Mark 4. Grease a 900 g/2 lb loaf tin, line the base and sides with greaseproof paper and grease the paper.

2 Place the butter together with the sifted flour and baking powder into a mixing bowl, then add the sugar, eggs and lemon zest. Beat for 1–2 minutes until smooth and glossy, and then stir in the apricots, ground almonds and the chopped pistachio nuts.

3 ▲ Spoon the mixture into the prepared tin and smooth the surface. Sprinkle with the flaked almonds and the whole pistachio nuts. Bake in the centre of the oven for about 1¼ hours, or until a skewer inserted into the centre of the cake comes out clean. Check the cake after about 45 minutes and cover with a piece of foil when the top is nicely brown. Leave the cake to cool in the tin.

4 ▲ To make the lemon syrup, put the lemon juice and caster sugar into a small saucepan and heat gently, stirring until the sugar has dissolved.

5 ▲ Spoon the syrup over the cake. When the cake is completely cooled, turn it carefully out of the tin and peel off the lining paper.

Gooseberry Cake

This cake is delicious served warm with fresh whipped cream.

INGREDIENTS

Serves 6–8

115 g/4 oz/½ cup butter
165 g/5½ oz/1⅓ cups self-raising flour
1 tsp baking powder
2 size 3 eggs, beaten
115 g/4 oz/½ cup caster sugar
1–2 tsp rose water
pinch of freshly grated nutmeg
1 x 115 g/4 oz jar gooseberries in syrup, drained, juice reserved
caster sugar, to decorate
whipped cream, to serve

STORING

This cake can be kept for up to three days in an airtight container.

1 Preheat the oven to 180°C/350°F/Gas 4. Grease an 18 cm/7 inch square cake tin, line the base and sides with greaseproof paper and then grease the paper.

2 Place the butter in a medium saucepan and melt over a gentle heat. Remove the pan from the heat, transfer the melted butter to a mixing bowl and allow to cool.

3 ▲ Sift together the flour and baking powder and add to the melted butter. Beat in the eggs, one at a time, the sugar, rose water and grated nutmeg, to make a smooth batter.

4 ▲ Mix in 1–2 tbsp of the reserved gooseberry juice, then pour half of the batter mixture into the prepared tin. Scatter over the gooseberries. Pour over the remaining batter mixture, evenly covering the gooseberries.

5 Bake in the centre of the oven for about 45 minutes, or until a skewer inserted into the centre of the cake comes out clean.

6 ▲ Leave in the cake tin for about 5 minutes, then turn out on to a wire rack, remove the lining paper and allow to cool for a further 5 minutes. Dredge with caster sugar and serve immediately with whipped cream, or leave the cake to cool completely before decorating and serving.

Jewel Cake

This pretty tea-time cake is excellent served as an afternoon treat with tea or coffee.

Ingredients

Serves 10–15

115 g/4 oz/½ cup mixed coloured glacé cherries, halved, washed and dried
50 g/2 oz/¼ cup stem ginger in syrup, chopped, washed and dried
50 g/2 oz/⅓ cup chopped mixed peel
115 g/4 oz/1 cup self-raising flour
75 g/3 oz/¾ cup plain flour
25 g/1 oz/3 tbsp cornflour
175 g/6 oz/¾ cup butter
175g/6 oz/¾ cup caster sugar
3 size 3 eggs
finely grated zest of 1 orange

To Decorate

175 g/6 oz/1½ cups icing sugar, sifted
2–3 tbsp freshly squeezed orange juice
50 g/2 oz/¼ cup mixed coloured glacé cherries, chopped
25 g/1 oz/2½ tbsp mixed peel, chopped

STORING

This cake can be kept for up to two days in an airtight container.

Tip

To ring the changes, bake the cake in a 18 cm/7 inch round cake tin, if wished. Use the same quantities of ingredients and follow the method as described here. Decorate with crystallized citrus fruits instead of the glacé cherries and mixed peel.

1 Preheat the oven to 180°C/350°F/ Gas 4. Grease a 900 g/2 lb loaf tin, line the base and sides with greaseproof paper and grease the paper.

2 ▲ Place the cherries, stem ginger and mixed peel in a plastic bag with 25 g/1 oz/1 tbsp of the self-raising flour and shake to coat evenly. Sift the remaining flours and cornflour into a small bowl.

3 ▲ Place the butter and sugar in a mixing bowl and beat until light and fluffy. Beat in the eggs, one at a time, until evenly blended. Fold in the sifted flours with the orange zest, then stir in the dried fruit.

4 ▲ Transfer the cake mixture to the prepared tin and bake in the centre of the oven for about 1¼ hours, or until a skewer inserted into the centre of the cake comes out clean. Leave the cake in the tin for about 5 minutes, then turn out on to a wire rack, peel off the lining paper and leave to cool completely.

5 ▲ To decorate the cake, place the icing sugar in a mixing bowl. Stir in the orange juice and mix until smooth. Drizzle the icing over the cake. Mix together the chopped glacé cherries and mixed peel in a small bowl, then use to decorate the cake. Allow the icing to set before serving.

Vegan Dundee Cake

Containing no eggs or other dairy products, this cake is a rare treat for vegans. There are several different types of dairy-free margarines on the market, many of which are suitable for baking.

INGREDIENTS

Serves 8–10

350 g/12 oz/3 cups plain wholemeal flour
1 tsp ground mixed spice
175 g/6 oz/¾ cup vegan (soya) margarine
175 g/6 oz/¾ cup plus 2 tbsp dark muscavado sugar
175 g/6 oz/1 cup sultanas
175 g/6 oz/1 cup currants
175 g/6 oz/1 cup raisins
75 g/3 oz/⅔ cup chopped mixed peel
150 g/5 oz/⅔ glacé cherries, halved
finely grated zest of 1 orange
2 tbsp ground almonds
25 g/1 oz/¼ cup blanched almonds, chopped
125 ml/4 fl oz/½ cup soya milk
75 ml/3 fl oz/6 tbsp sunflower oil
2 tbsp malt vinegar
1 tsp bicarbonate of soda

To Decorate

mixed nuts, such as pistachios, pecans and macadamia, glacé cherries and angelica
4 tbsp clear honey, warmed

STORING

This cake can be kept for up to one week in an airtight container.

1 Preheat the oven to 150°C/300°F/Gas 2. Grease a deep 20 cm/8 inch square loose-bottom cake tin, line with a double thickness of greaseproof paper and grease the paper.

2 ▲ Sift the flour and mixed spice into a large mixing bowl, adding the bran left in the sieve. Rub the margarine into the flour until it resembles fine breadcrumbs. Stir in the sugar, dried fruits, mixed peel, cherries, orange zest and ground and blanched almonds.

3 ▲ Warm 50 ml/2 fl oz/¼ cup of the soya milk in a saucepan, then add the sunflower oil and vinegar. Dissolve the bicarbonate of soda in the rest of the milk, then combine the two mixtures and stir into the dry ingredients.

4 ▲ Spoon the cake mixture into the prepared tin and smooth the surface. Bake in the centre of the oven for about 2½ hours or until a skewer inserted into the centre of the cake comes out clean. Leave the cake in the tin for about 5 minutes, then turn out on to a wire rack, peel off the lining paper and leave to cool completely.

5 Place the mixed nuts, glacé cherries and angelica on top of the cake, then brush with the warmed honey.

Autumn Cake

Greengages, plums or stoned semi-dried prunes are delicious in this recipe.

Ingredients

Serves 6–8

115 g/4 oz/½ cup butter, softened
150 g/5 oz/¾ cup caster sugar
3 size 3 eggs, beaten
75 g/3 oz/1 cup ground hazelnuts
150 g/5 oz/1¼ cup shelled pecan nuts, chopped
50 g/2 oz/½ cup plain flour
1 tsp baking powder
½ tsp salt
675 g/1½ lb stoned plums, greengages or semi-dried prunes
4 tbsp lime marmalade
1 tbsp lime juice
2 tbsp blanched almonds, chopped, to decorate

STORING

This cake is not suitable for storing.

1 Preheat the oven to 180°C/350°F/Gas 4. Grease a 23 cm/9 inch round, fluted tart tin.

2 ▲ Place the butter and sugar in a mixing bowl and beat with an electric mixer until light and fluffy. Gradually beat in the eggs, alternating with the ground hazelnuts, until evenly combined.

3 Stir in the pecan nuts, then sift in the flour, baking powder and salt. Fold in until evenly combined, then transfer the mixture to the prepared tin.

4 ▲ Bake in the centre of the oven for 45–50 minutes or until a skewer inserted into the centre of the cake comes out clean.

5 ▲ Remove from the oven and carefully arrange the fruit on top. Return to the oven and bake for a further 10–15 minutes until the fruit has softened. Transfer to a wire rack to cool completely then remove the cake from the tin.

6 Place the marmalade and lime juice in a small saucepan and warm gently. Brush over the fruit, then sprinkle with the almonds. Allow to set, then chill before serving.

Autumn Passionettes

Perfect for a tea party or packed lunch, this passion cake mixture can also be made as one big cake to serve for a celebration or as a dessert.

INGREDIENTS

Makes 24

150 g/5 oz/¾ cup butter, melted
200 g/7 oz/⅞ cup soft light brown sugar
115 g/4 oz/1 cup carrots, peeled and finely grated
50 g/2 oz/1 cup dessert apples, peeled and finely grated
pinch of salt
1–2 tsp ground mixed spice
2 size 3 eggs
200 g/7 oz/1¾ cups self-raising flour
2 tsp baking powder
115 g/4 oz/1 cup shelled walnuts, finely chopped

For the Topping

175 g/6 oz/¾ cup full-fat soft cheese
4–5 tbsp single cream
50 g/2 oz/½ cup icing sugar, sifted
25 g/1 oz/¼ cup shelled walnuts, halved
2 tsp cocoa powder, sifted

STORING

Both the large and small cakes can be kept for up to four days in an airtight container.

1 Preheat the oven to 180°C/350°F/Gas 4. Arrange 24 fairy cake paper cases in bun tins and put to one side.

2 ▲ Place the butter, sugar, carrots, apples, salt, mixed spice and eggs in a mixing bowl and beat well to combine.

3 ▲ Sift together the flour and baking powder into a small bowl, then sift again into the mixing bowl. Add the chopped walnuts and fold in until evenly blended.

4 ▲ Fill the paper cases half-full with the cake mixture, then bake for 20–25 minutes, or until a skewer inserted into the centres of the cakes comes out clean.

5 Leave the cakes in the tins for about 5 minutes, before transferring them to a wire rack to cool completely.

6 ▲ To make the topping, place the full-fat soft cheese in a mixing bowl and beat in the cream and icing sugar until smooth. Put a dollop of the topping in the centre of each cake, then decorate with the walnuts. Dust with sifted cocoa powder and allow the icing to set before serving.

Tip

To make one big cake, which will serve 6–8, grease a 20 cm/8 inch fluted American bundt cake tin and line the base with greaseproof paper. Grease the paper. Place all of the cake mixture in the tin and bake for about 1¼ hours, or until a skewer inserted into the centre of the cake comes out clean. Leave the cake in the tin for about 5 minutes. Turn out on to a wire rack, peel off the lining paper and leave to cool completely. Decorate with the topping mixture, walnuts and sifted cocoa powder.

Apple Crumble Cake

In the autumn use windfall apples. Served warm with thick cream or custard this cake doubles as a dessert.

Ingredients

Serves 8-10

For the Topping

75 g/3 oz/¾ cup self-raising flour
½ tsp ground cinnamon
40 g/1½ oz/3 tbsp butter
25 g/1 oz/2 tbsp caster sugar

For the Base

50 g/2 oz/4 tbsp butter, softened
75 g/3 oz/6 tbsp caster sugar
1 size 3 egg, beaten
115 g/4 oz/1 cup self-raising flour, sifted
2 cooking apples, peeled, cored and sliced
50 g/2 oz/⅓ cup sultanas

To Decorate

1 red dessert apple, cored, thinly sliced and tossed in lemon juice
2 tbsp caster sugar, sifted
pinch of ground cinnamon

STORING

This cake can be kept for up to two days in an airtight container.

1 Preheat the oven 180°C/350°F/ Gas 4. Grease a deep 18 cm/7 inch springform tin, line the base with greaseproof paper and grease the paper.

2 ▲ To make the topping, sift the flour and cinnamon into a mixing bowl. Rub the butter into the flour until it resembles breadcrumbs, then stir in the sugar. Set aside.

3 ▲ To make the base, put the butter, sugar, egg and flour into a bowl and beat for 1–2 minutes until smooth . Spoon into the prepared tin.

4 ▲ Mix together the apple slices and sultanas and spread them evenly over the top. Sprinkle with the topping.

5 Bake in the centre of the oven for about 1 hour. Cool in the tin for 10 minutes before turning out on to a wire rack and peeling off the lining paper. Serve warm or cool, decorated with slices of red dessert apple and caster sugar and cinnamon sprinkled over.

Summer Strawberry Shortcake

A summer-time treat. Serve with a cool glass of pink sparkling wine for a truly refreshing dessert.

Ingredients

Serves 6–8

225 g/8 oz/2 cups plain flour
1 tbsp baking powder
½ tsp salt
50 g/2 oz/4 tbsp caster sugar
50 g/2 oz/4 tbsp butter, softened
150 ml/¼ pint/⅔ cup milk
300 ml/½ pint/1¼ cups double cream
450 g/1 lb fresh strawberries, halved and hulled

STORING

This cake is not suitable for storing.

1 Preheat the oven to 220°C/425°F/Gas 7. Grease a baking sheet, line the base with greaseproof paper and grease the paper.

2 ▲ Sift the flour, baking powder and salt together into a large mixing bowl. Stir in the sugar, cut in the butter and toss into the flour mixture until it resembles coarse breadcrumbs. Stir in just enough milk to make a soft dough.

3 ▲ Turn out the dough on to a lightly floured work surface and pat, using your fingers, into a 30 x 15 cm/12 x 6 inch rectangle. Using a template, cut out two 15 cm/6 inch rounds, indent one of the rounds dividing it into eight equal portions, and place them on the baking sheet.

4 ▲ Bake in the centre of the oven for 10–15 minutes or until slightly risen and golden. Leave the shortcake on the baking sheet for about 5 minutes, then transfer to a wire rack, peel off the lining paper and leave to cool completely.

5 Place the cream in a mixing bowl and whip with an electric mixer until it holds soft peaks. Place the unmarked shortcake on a serving plate and spread or pipe with half of the cream. Top with two-thirds of the strawberries, then the other shortcake. Use the remaining cream and strawberries to decorate the top layer. Chill for at least 30 minutes before serving.

Fresh Fruit Genoese

This Italian classic, 'Genovese con Panne e Frutta', can be made with any type of soft fresh fruit.

INGREDIENTS

Serves 8–10

For the Sponge

175 g/6 oz/1½ cups plain flour, sifted
pinch of salt
4 size 3 eggs
115 g/4 oz/½ cup caster sugar
6 tbsp orange-flavoured liqueur

For the Filling and Topping

600 ml/1 pint/2½ cups double cream
4 tbsp vanilla sugar
450 g/1 lb fresh soft fruit, such as raspberries, blueberries, cherries, etc.
150 g/5 oz/1¼ cups shelled pistachio nuts, finely chopped
4 tbsp apricot jam, warmed and sieved, to glaze

STORING

This cake is not suitable for storing.

Tip

To save time and money, use shop-bought chopped mixed nuts to coat the sides of the gâteau instead of pistachios.

1 Preheat the oven to 180°C/350°F/Gas 4. Grease a 21 cm/8½ inch round springform cake tin, line the base with greaseproof paper and grease the paper.

2 ▲ Sift the flour and salt together three times, then set aside.

3 Place the eggs and sugar in a mixing bowl and beat with an electric mixer for about 10 minutes or until thick and pale.

4 ▲ Sift the reserved flour mixture into the mixing bowl, then fold in very gently. Transfer the cake mixture to the prepared tin. Bake in the centre of the oven for 30–35 minutes or until a skewer inserted into the centre of the cake comes out clean. Leave the cake in the tin for about 5 minutes, then turn out on to a wire rack, peel off the lining paper and leave to cool completely.

5 Cut the cake horizontally into two layers, and place the bottom layer on a serving plate. Sprinkle the orange-flavoured liqueur over both layers.

6 ▲ Place the double cream and vanilla sugar in a mixing bowl and beat with an electric mixer until it holds peaks.

7 ▲ Spread two-thirds of the cream mixture over the bottom layer of cake and top with half the fruit. Place the second layer of the cake on top and spread the remaining cream over the top and sides.

8 Using a knife, lightly press the chopped nuts evenly around the sides. Arrange the remaining fresh fruit on top and brush over a light glaze using the apricot jam.

Marbled Spice Cake

This cake is baked in a fluted ring-shaped tin called a kugelhupf, or gugelhupf, mould from Germany and Austria to give it a pretty shape.

INGREDIENTS
Serves 8–10
75 g/3 oz/6 tbsp butter, softened
115 g/4 oz/½ cup caster sugar
2 size 3 eggs, lightly beaten
few drops of vanilla essence
130 g/4½ oz plain flour
1½ tsp baking powder
3 tbsp milk
3 tbsp black treacle
1 tsp ground mixed spice
½ tsp ground ginger
175 g/6 oz/1⅛ cups icing sugar, sifted, to decorate

STORING
This cake can be kept for up to two days in an airtight container.

1 Preheat the oven to 180°C/350°F/ Gas 4. Grease and flour a 900 g/2 lb kugelhupf mould or ring-shaped cake tin.

2 Cream the butter and sugar together in a bowl until light and fluffy. Beat in the egg and vanilla essence.

3 ▲ Sift together the flour and baking powder, then fold into the mixture, alternating with the milk, until evenly combined.

4 Spoon about one-third of the mixture into a small bowl and stir in the treacle and spices.

5 ▲ Drop alternating spoonfuls of the light and dark mixtures into the tin. Run a knife or skewer through them to give a marbled effect.

6 ▲ Bake in the centre of the oven for about 50 minutes or until a skewer inserted into the centre comes out clean. Leave in the tin for 10 minutes before turning out on to a wire rack to cool.

7 ▲ To decorate, stir enough warm water into the icing sugar to make a smooth icing. Spoon quickly over the cake. Allow to set before serving.

Tip

If you do not have a kugelhupf mould or a ring-shaped cake tin, use a 20 cm/8 inch round cake tin.

Apricot Brandy-snap Roulade

A magnificent combination of soft and crisp textures, this cake looks impressive and is easy to prepare.

INGREDIENTS
Serves 6–8
4 size 3 eggs, separated
½ tbsp fresh orange juice
115 g/4 oz/½ cup caster sugar
175 g/6 oz/2 cups ground almonds
4 brandy-snap biscuits, crushed, to decorate

For the Filling
150 g/5 oz canned apricots, drained
300 ml/½ pint/1¼ cups double cream
25 g/1 oz/4 tbsp icing sugar

STORING
This cake is not suitable for storing.

1 ▲ Preheat the oven to 190°C/375°F/Gas 5. Grease a 33 x 23 cm/13 x 9 inch Swiss roll tin, line the base with greaseproof paper and grease the paper.

2 Place the egg yolks, orange juice and sugar in a mixing bowl and beat with an electric mixer for about 10 minutes until thick and pale. Fold in the ground almonds.

3 ▲ Whisk the egg whites until they hold stiff peaks. Fold the egg whites into the almond mixture, then transfer to the Swiss roll tin and smooth the surface. Bake in the centre of the oven for about 20 minutes or until a skewer inserted into the centre comes out clean. Leave to cool in the tin, covered with a clean, just-damp cloth.

4 ▲ To make the filling, place the apricots in a blender or food processor and purée until smooth. Place the cream and icing sugar in a mixing bowl and whip until the cream holds soft peaks. Fold in the apricot purée.

5 Spread out the crushed brandy-snaps, on a sheet of greaseproof paper. Spread about one-third of the cream mixture over the cake, then invert it on to the crushed brandy-snaps. Peel away the lining paper.

6 Use the remaining cream mixture to cover the cake, then, using the greaseproof paper as a guide, tightly and neatly roll up the roulade from a short end. Transfer to a serving dish, sticking on any extra pieces of crushed brandy-snaps.

Special Occasion Cakes

Here you will find inspired ideas for christenings, Christmas, Hallowe'en, Easter, birthdays and Valentine's day. Employing an imaginative variety of decorating techniques, the recipes range from a sumptuous chocolate-iced anniversary cake to a wonderful royal-iced wedding extravaganza.

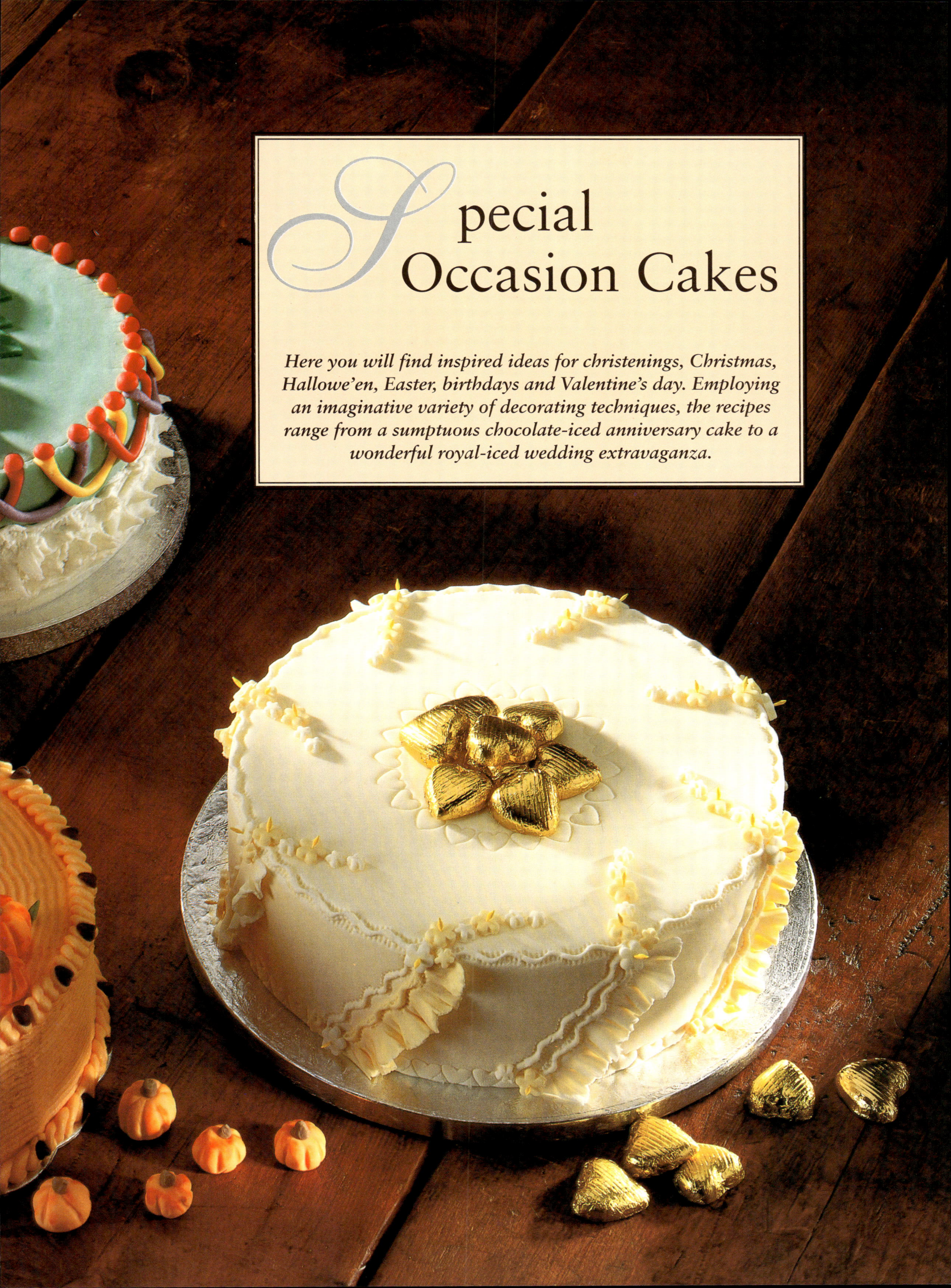

Teddy Bear Christening Cake

To personalise the cake, make a simple plaque for the top and pipe or write the name of the new baby with a food colouring pen.

Ingredients

Serves 30

20 cm/8 inch square Light Fruit Cake
3 tbsp apricot jam, warmed and sieved
900 g/2 lb marzipan
800 g/1¾ lb/2⅓ x quantity Sugarpaste Icing
peach, yellow, blue and brown food colourings
115 g/4oz/⅙ quantity Royal Icing

MATERIALS AND EQUIPMENT

25 cm/10 inch square cake board
crimping tool
blossom cutter or plunger
foam pad
7.5 cm/3 inch round cutter
frill cutter
wooden cocktail stick
peach ribbon
small blue ribbon bow

STORING

The finished cake can be stored for up to four weeks in an airtight container.

1 Brush the cake with the apricot jam. Roll out the marzipan on a work surface lightly dusted with icing sugar, then use to cover the cake. Leave to dry for 12 hours.

2 Colour 500 g/1¼ lb of the sugarpaste icing peach. Roll out the icing. Brush the marzipan with a little water and cover the cake with the icing.

3 ▲ Position the cake on the cake board. Using a crimping tool dipped in cornflour, crimp the top and bottom edges of the cake.

4 Divide the remaining sugarpaste into three portions. Leave one-third white and colour one-third yellow. Cut the remaining third in half and colour one portion peach and the other blue.

5 ▲ To make the flowers, roll out the peach and blue sugarpaste thinly on a work surface lightly dusted with icing sugar. Dip the end of the blossom cutter or a plunger in cornflour and cut out small and larger flowers. Place a small ball of peach icing in the centre of the blue flowers; and a small ball of blue icing in the centre of the peach flowers. Secure with water, if necessary. Leave the flowers to dry on a foam pad for several hours or overnight. Gather together the blue icing trimmings and set aside, wrapped in clear film.

6 ▲ Make the teddy bear with the yellow icing. Shape the head, body, arms and ears of the bear and press together with a little water to secure. Make the button for the chest out of a little blue icing. Paint on highlights, such as eyes, nose and mouth, with brown food colouring. Leave the bear to dry on a piece of greaseproof paper for several hours or overnight.

7 To make the blanket, roll out the blue icing and cut out a circle with the 7.5 cm/3 inch round cutter. Slice off a small piece, about 1 cm/½ inch, to give a straight line for the top. Set aside. Roll out the white icing thinly and, using the frill cutter, cut out a ring. Put the end of the wooden cocktail stick over about 5 mm/¼ inch of the outer edge of the ring. Roll the stick around the edge firmly back and forth with your finger so the edge becomes thinner and begins to frill. Continue until the ring is completely frilled. Using a sharp knife, cut through the ring once to open it up. Gently ease it open.

8 ▲ Brush the edge of the blue blanket with water and secure the white frill on to the edge.

9 Decorate the cake with the ribbon. Position the bear on top and lay the blanket over it, securing with a little water or royal icing. Secure the flowers with a little royal icing and then the bow to the bear's neck in the same way.

Rose Blossom Wedding Cake

The traditional white wedding cake, with its classic lines and elegant piping, is still a favourite choice for many brides and grooms.

INGREDIENTS

Serves 80
23 cm/9 inch square Rich Fruit Cake
15 cm/6 inch square Rich Fruit Cake
75 ml/7 tbsp apricot jam, warmed and sieved
1.5 kg/3½ lb marzipan
1.5 kg/3½ lb/2⅓ x quantity Royal Icing, to coat
675 g/1½ lb/1 quantity Royal Icing, to pipe
pink and green food colourings

MATERIALS AND EQUIPMENT

28 cm/11 inch square cake board
20 cm/8 inch square cake board
No 1 writing and No 42 nozzles
several greaseproof paper piping bags
thin pink ribbon
8 pink bows
3–4 cake pillars
about 12 miniature roses
few fern sprigs

STORING

The finished cake can be kept for up to three months in an airtight container.

1 Brush the cakes with the apricot jam and cover with marzipan, allowing 450 g/l lb marzipan for the 15 cm/6 inch cake and the remainder for the 23 cm/ 9 inch cake. Place the cakes on the cake boards and leave to dry for 12 hours.

2 Make the royal icing for coating the cake. Secure the cakes to the cake boards with a little of the icing. Flat ice the cakes with three or four layers of smooth icing, allowing each layer to dry overnight before applying the next. The royal icing should be very dry before assembling the cake, so it can be made to this stage and stored in cardboard cake boxes for several days.

3 Make the royal icing for piping, and colour a small amount pale pink and another small portion pale green. To make the piped sugar pieces, draw the double-triangle design on a piece of greaseproof paper several times. You will need 40 pieces, but make extra in case of breakages. Tape the paper to a baking sheet or flat board and secure a piece of baking parchment over the top. Tape it down at the corners.

4 ▲ Fit a piping bag with a No 1 writing nozzle. Half-fill with white royal icing and fold over the top to seal. Pipe over each design, carefully following the outlines with a continuous thread of icing. Spoon a little of the pink icing and a little of the green icing into separate paper piping bags fitted with No 1 writing nozzles. Pipe pink dots on the corners of the top triangle in each design and green on the corners of the bottom triangle in each design. Leave to dry for at least two hours.

5 Mark four triangles on the top and side of each cake with a pin. Work from the centre of each side, so each triangle is 6 cm/2½ inches wide at the base and 4 cm/1½ inches high on the smaller cake, and 7.5 cm/3 inches wide at the base and 5 cm/2 inches high on the larger cake. Fit a paper piping bag with a clean No 1 writing nozzle and half-fill with some of the white icing. Using the pin marks as a guide, pipe double lines to outline the triangles.

6 ▲ Using the same nozzle, pipe cornelli inside all the triangles.

7 ▲ Fit a piping bag with a No 42 nozzle and half-fill with white icing. Pipe shells around the top and bottom edges of each cake, but not within the triangles.

8 Using the piping bags fitted with No 1 writing nozzles and filled with pink and green icing, pipe dots on the corners of each cake.

9 ▲ Remove the piped sugar pieces from the paper by carefully turning it back and lifting off each piece with a palette knife. Secure them to the cake and cake board with a little icing.

10 Decorate the cake with the ribbon and bows. Just before serving, assemble the cake with the cake pillars and decorate with the roses and fern sprigs.

Flickering Birthday Candle Cake

Stripy icing candles are flickering and ready to blow out on this birthday celebration cake for all ages.

Ingredients

Serves 15–20

20 cm/8 inch square Madeira Cake
1 quantity Butter Icing
3 tbsp apricot jam, warmed and sieved
800 g/1$^{3}/_{4}$ lb/2$^{1}/_{3}$ x quantity Sugarpaste Icing
pink, yellow, purple and jade food colourings
edible silver balls, to decorate

MATERIALS AND EQUIPMENT

23 cm/9 inch square cake board
leaf cutter
small round cutter
pink and purple food colouring pens
5 mm/$^{1}/_{4}$ inch wide jade-coloured ribbon

STORING

The finished cake can be kept for up to one week in an airtight container.

1 Cut the cake horizontally into three layers, using a long serrated knife. Sandwich the layers together with the butter icing and brush the cake with the apricot jam. Roll out 500 g/1$^{1}/_{4}$ lb of the sugarpaste icing on a work surface lightly dusted with icing sugar and use to cover the cake. Position on the cake board.

2 Divide the remaining sugarpaste into four portions and colour one portion pink, one portion yellow, one portion pale purple and one portion jade. Roll out the jade icing and cut into six 1 cm/$^{1}/_{2}$ inch wide strips of slightly different lengths, but each long enough to go over the side and on to the top of the cake. Make a diagonal cut at one end of each strip.

3 ▲ Roll out the yellow icing and cut out six candle flames with the leaf cutter. Place a silver ball in each flame. Set aside the remaining yellow icing, wrapped in clear film. Arrange the candles on top of the cake, securing with a little water. Mould small strips, fractionally longer than the width of each candle, from the yellow and purple icings. Arrange alternate colours on the candles at a slight angle, securing with water. Position the flames at the end of each jade strip, also securing with water.

4 ▲ Roll out the pink and remaining purple icings, then cut out wavy pieces with a sharp knife. Attach to the cake, above the candles, with a little water. Gather together the pink icing trimmings and roll into a ball.

5 ▲ Using the leftover yellow and pink icings, make the decorations for the sides of the cake. Roll out the yellow icing and cut out circles with the small round cutter or the end of a piping nozzle. Make small balls from the pink icing and attach to the yellow circles with a little water. Press a silver ball in the centre of each pink ball.

6 Arrange the decorations around the bottom edge of the cake, securing with water.

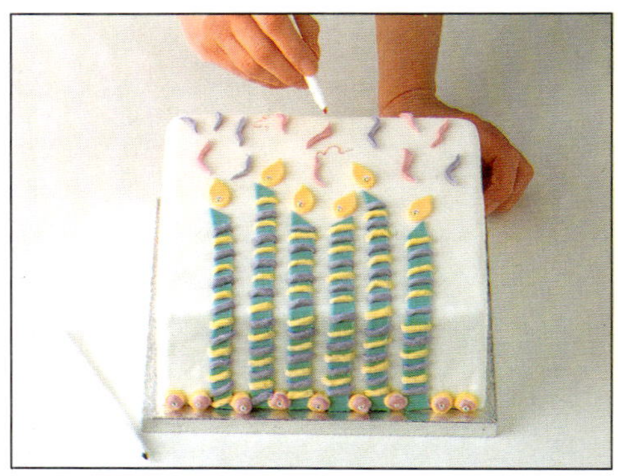

7 ▲ Using food colouring pens, draw wavy lines and dots coming from the purple and pink wavy icings. Decorate the sides of the cake board with the ribbon, securing at the back with a little softened sugarpaste.

Jazzy Chocolate Gâteau

This cake is made with Father's Day in mind, though really it can be made for anyone who loves chocolate.

Ingredients

Serves 12–15

2 x quantity chocolate-flavour Quick-Mix Sponge Cake mix
75 g/3 oz/3 squares plain chocolate
75 g/3 oz/3 squares white chocolate
½ quantity Fudge Frosting
½ quantity Glacé Icing
1 tsp weak coffee
8 tbsp chocolate hazelnut spread

MATERIALS AND EQUIPMENT

2 x 20 cm/8 inch round cake tins
greaseproof paper piping bag
No 1 writing nozzle

STORING

The finished cake can be kept for up to three days in the fridge.

1 Preheat the oven to 160°C/325°F/Gas 3. Grease the cake tins, line the bases with greaseproof paper and grease the paper. Divide the cake mixture evenly between the tins and smooth the surfaces. Bake in the centre of the oven for 20–30 minutes, or until firm to the touch. Turn out on to a wire rack, peel off the lining paper and leave to cool completely.

2 Meanwhile, cover a large baking sheet or board (or two smaller ones) with baking parchment and tape it down at each corner. Melt each chocolate in separate bowls over pans of hot water, stirring until smooth, then pour on to the baking parchment. Spread out the chocolates evenly with a palette knife. Allow to cool until the surfaces are firm enough to cut, but not so hard that they will break. The chocolate should no longer feel sticky when touched with your finger.

3 ▲ Cut out haphazard shapes of chocolate and set aside.

4 ▲ Make the fudge frosting and, when cool enough to spread, use to sandwich the two cakes together. Place the cake on a stand or plate.

5 Make the glacé icing, using 1 tsp weak coffee (to colour it very slightly) along with enough water to form a spreading consistency, and spread on top of the cake almost to the edges. Spread the side of the cake with enough chocolate hazelnut spread to cover.

6 ▲ Arrange the chocolate pieces around the side of the cake, pressing into the hazelnut spread to secure.

7 To decorate, spoon about 3 tbsp of the chocolate hazelnut spread into a piping bag fitted with a No 1 nozzle and pipe 'jazzy' lines over the glacé icing.

Mother's Day Bouquet

A piped bouquet of flowers can bring as much pleasure as a fresh one for a Mother's Day treat.

INGREDIENTS
Serves 8–10
1 quantity Quick-Mix Sponge Cake mix
2 x quantity Butter Icing
green, blue, yellow and pink food colourings

MATERIALS AND EQUIPMENT
2 x 18 cm/7 inch round cake tins
serrated scraper
5 greaseproof paper piping bags
No 3 writing and petal nozzles

STORING
The finished cake can be kept for up to three days in an airtight container in the fridge.

1 Preheat the oven to 160°C/325°F/ Gas 3. Grease the cake tins, line the bases with greaseproof paper and grease the paper. Divide the cake mixture evenly between the tins and smooth the surfaces. Bake in the centre of the oven for about 20 minutes or until firm to the touch. Turn out on to a wire rack, peel off the lining paper and leave to cool.

2 ▲ Place one of the cakes on paper on a turntable. Use half to two-thirds of the butter icing to sandwich the cakes together and to coat the top and sides. Coat the top using a palette knife and the sides using the scraper.

3 Transfer the cake to a serving plate, then divide the remaining butter icing into four bowls and colour one portion green, one portion blue, one portion yellow and one portion pink. Spoon the blue icing into a greaseproof paper piping bag fitted with the No 3 writing nozzle. Pipe the vase on top of the cake in lines and beads.

4 ▲ Spoon the green icing into a fresh piping bag fitted with a clean No 3 writing nozzle. Pipe the flower stems coming out of the vase.

5 Spoon the pink icing into a fresh piping bag fitted with the petal nozzle. Pipe pink petals on the ends of some of the stems. Pipe beads of blue icing in the centres.

6 Spoon most of the yellow icing into a fresh piping bag fitted with a clean petal nozzle and pipe yellow flowers on the remaining stems. Pipe beads of blue icing in the centres.

7 ▲ Decorate the side of the cake. Pipe stems with leaves evenly spaced all around the side with the green icing, and pipe beads of the blue icing to make flowers at the end of each stem. Spoon the reserved yellow icing into a fresh piping bag fitted with a clean No 3 writing nozzle and pipe small beads in the centre of the blue flowers.

8 Pipe beads of green icing round the top and bottom edges of the cake.

Valentine's Heart Cake

Cakes decorated with hearts can be very adaptable. Although this one was designed with Valentine's Day in mind, it could also be used to celebrate a birthday for someone special, an anniversary, or be made as two tiers for a wedding cake.

Ingredients

Serves 30

20 cm/8 inch square Light Fruit Cake
3 tbsp apricot jam, warmed and sieved
900 g/2 lb marzipan
1.5 kg/3 lb/2 x quantity Royal Icing
115 g/4 oz/1/3 quantity Sugarpaste Icing
red food colouring

Materials and Equipment

1 x 25 cm/10 inch square cake board
5 cm/2 inch heart-shaped cutter
2.5 cm/1 inch heart-shaped cutter
4 greaseproof paper piping bags
No 1 and No 2 writing and No 42 star nozzles
heart-patterned ribbon

Storing

The finished cake can be kept for up to four weeks in an airtight container.

1 Brush the cake with the apricot jam. Roll out the marzipan on a surface lightly dusted with icing sugar and cover the cake. Leave to dry for 12 hours.

2 Secure the cake to the cake board with a little of the royal icing. Flat ice the cake with three or four layers of smooth icing, allowing each layer to dry overnight before applying the next. Set aside a little of the royal icing in an airtight container for piping.

3 ▲ To make the heart decorations, colour the sugarpaste icing red. Roll out the red icing on a work surface lightly dusted with icing sugar and cut out 12 hearts with the 5 cm/2 inch heart-shaped cutter. Place the 2.5 cm/1 inch heart-shaped cutter in the centre of each larger heart and cut out a smaller heart, so you have 12 small hearts and 12 larger hollow hearts. Cut out four more smaller hearts from the red icing so you have 16 total. Place the hearts on a board covered with greaseproof paper.

4 ▲ Spoon a little of the reserved royal icing into a greaseproof paper piping bag fitted with a No 1 writing nozzle. Pipe wavy lines around the edges of four of the small hearts. Leave all the hearts to dry for several hours or overnight.

5 ▲ Spoon some more royal icing into a fresh piping bag fitted with a No 42 nozzle. Pipe swirls around the top and bottom edges of the cake with some of the royal icing.

6 ▲ Colour a heaped tablespoon of the remaining royal icing red and spoon into a fresh piping bag fitted with a clean No 1 writing nozzle. Pipe red dots on top of each white swirl of icing.

7 ▲ Arrange four of the large hearts on top of the cake, securing with a little royal icing.

8 Decorate with the ribbon. Spoon the remaining white royal icing into a fresh piping bag fitted with a No 2 writing nozzle. Pipe beads of icing down each side of the cake, above and below the ribbon. Allow all the piping to dry for several hours.

9 Arrange the remaining large hearts on top of the cake, securing with a little royal icing. Arrange the remaining small hearts on the sides.

Harvest Blackberry Ring

Gracious blackberry branches twisting their way over the cake, and leaves tinged with reddish-brown, create an autumnal theme.

Ingredients

Serves 20

1 quantity 18 cm/7 inch round Light Fruit Cake mix
3 tbsp apricot jam, warmed and sieved
450 g/1 lb marzipan
900 g/2 lb/2⅔ x quantity Sugarpaste Icing
tangerine, purple, green and paprika food colourings

MATERIALS AND EQUIPMENT

20 cm/8 inch ring mould
25 cm/10 inch round cake board

STORING

The finished cake can be kept for up to four weeks in an airtight container.

1 Preheat the oven to 150°C/300°f/ Gas 2. Grease the cake tin, line with greaseproof paper and grease the paper. Spoon in the cake mixture and smooth the surface with the back of a wet metal spoon. Bake in the centre of the oven for 1½–2 hours or until a skewer inserted in the centre of the cake comes out clean. Leave the cake to cool in the mould on a wire rack. When completely cool, turn out.

2 Brush the cake with the apricot jam. Measure half the circumference of the cake with a piece of string. Measure the height to include the top as well as the sides of the cake (see step 4 for guidance). Take three-quarters of the marzipan and cut in half. Cover the cake in two halves as follows. Roll out each piece of marzipan on a work surface lightly dusted with icing sugar and trim each using the string measurements as a guide. Trim and press the joins together to secure.

3 Measure the height and circumference of the inside of the ring with string. Cover the inside by rolling out the remaining one-quarter of marzipan. Trim to fit and press the joins together to secure. Position the cake on the board. Leave to dry for 12 hours.

4 ▲ Measure half the circumference of the cake with a piece of string. Measure the height to include the top as well as the sides of the cake.

5 ▲ Colour 675 g/1½ lb of the sugarpaste icing pale tangerine. Cut off three-quarters of this and cut in half. Keep the remaining icing well wrapped. Brush the marzipan lightly with water. Cover the top and sides of the cake in two pieces by rolling out each piece of icing. Trim and press the joins together.

6 Measure the height and circumference of the inside of the ring with string. Cover the inside of the ring by rolling out the remaining one-quarter of sugarpaste icing, using the string measurement as a guide. Trim to fit and press the joins together to secure.

7 ▲ Colour one-quarter of the white sugarpaste icing purple. To mould the blackberries, take a little of the purple icing and form into balls of different sizes for the bases. Make a number of smaller balls and stick them on the outside of the larger ones, securing with water. Place on a piece of greaseproof paper and leave to dry while making the leaves and branches.

8 ▲ Colour two-thirds of the remaining white sugarpaste icing green and the rest paprika. Reserve half of the green icing for the stems, and knead the remaining green and the paprika icing lightly together until marbled. Roll out and cut out leaf shapes. Make the branches by rolling the green icing into long thin strands.

9 To assemble, arrange the branches on the cake, securing them with a little water and twisting them as necessary, covering any joins in the icing where possible. Attach the leaves, bending them into shape, then arrange the blackberries on the cake attaching all with a little water.

Pansy Retirement Cake

Sugar-frosted edible flowers make a very effective cake decoration. If pansies are not in season, use other edible flowers such as nasturtiums, roses or tiny daffodils to wish someone a happy retirement. Just co-ordinate the colour of the icing, piping and ribbon with the colour of the flowers.

INGREDIENTS

Serves 20–25

20 cm/8 inch round Light Fruit Cake
3 tbsp apricot jam, warmed and sieved
675 g/1½ lb marzipan
1.1 kg/2½ lb/1⅔ x quantity Royal Icing
orange food colouring
1 size 3 egg white, lightly beaten
caster sugar, for frosting
about 7 pansies (orange and purple)

MATERIALS AND EQUIPMENT

25 cm/10 inch round cake board
2 greaseproof paper piping bags
No 19 star and No 1 writing nozzles
2 cm/¾ inch wide purple ribbon
3 mm/⅛ inch wide dark purple ribbon

STORING

The finished cake can be kept for up to four weeks in an airtight container.

1 Brush the cake with the apricot jam. Roll out the marzipan on a work surface lightly dusted with icing sugar and cover the cake. Leave to dry for 12 hours.

2 Secure the cake to the cake board with a little of the royal icing. Colour one-quarter of the royal icing pale orange. Flat ice the cake with three or four layers of smooth icing, allowing each layer to dry overnight before applying the next, using the orange icing for the top and the white for the sides. Set aside a little of both icings in airtight containers, to decorate the cake.

3 ▲ To sugar-frost the pansies, have ready a small bowl with the egg white and a plate with caster sugar. Dry the pansies on kitchen paper. If possible, leave some stem attached. Evenly brush the pansies all over on both sides of the petals with the egg white. Holding the flowers by their stems, sprinkle them evenly with the sugar, then shake off any excess. Place the frosted flowers on a flat board or wire rack covered with greaseproof or kitchen paper and leave to dry in a warm place overnight.

4 ▲ Spoon the reserved white royal icing into a greaseproof paper piping bag fitted with a No 19 star nozzle. Pipe a row of scrolls around the top of the cake.

5 ▲ Reverse the direction of the scrolls and pipe another row directly underneath the first row.

6 ▲ Pipe another row of scrolls around the bottom of the cake. Spoon the reserved orange icing into a fresh piping bag fitted with a No 1 writing nozzle. Pipe around the outline of the top of each scroll.

7 Using the same piping bag, pipe a row of single dots underneath the top row of reverse scrolls and a double row of dots above the bottom row of scrolls. Arrange the sugar-frosted pansies on top of the cake. Decorate with the ribbons, centring the narrow, darker ribbon on top of the wider one.

Birthday Parcel

Here is a birthday cake that is all wrapped up and ready to eat. The pattern on the iced parcel can be changed by using different shaped cutters.

INGREDIENTS

Serves 10

15 cm/6 in square Madeira Cake
¾ quantity orange-flavour Butter Icing
3 tbsp apricot jam, warmed and sieved
450 g/1 lb/1⅓ x quantity Sugarpaste Icing
blue, orange and green food colourings

MATERIALS AND EQUIPMENT

15–18 cm/7–8 inch square cake board
small round and triangular cocktail cutters

STORING

The finished cake can be kept for up to one week in an airtight container.

1 Cut the cake in half horizontally and sandwich together with the butter icing. Brush the cake with apricot jam. Colour three-quarters of the sugarpaste icing blue. Divide the remaining sugarpaste icing in half and colour one-half orange and the other half green. Wrap the orange and green sugarpaste separately in clear film and set aside. Roll out the blue icing on a work surface lightly dusted with icing sugar and use it to cover the cake. Position on the cake board.

2 While the sugarpaste covering is still soft, cut out circles and triangles from the blue icing with the cocktail cutters, lifting out the shapes to expose the cake.

3 ▲ Roll out the orange and green icings and use the same cutters to cut out circles and triangles. Replace the exposed holes in the blue icing with the orange and green shapes, easing in to fit. Gather together the orange and green trimmings.

4 ▲ Roll out the orange trimmings and cut three strips about 2 cm/¾ inch wide and long enough to go over each corner of the cake. Roll out the green trimmings and cut three very thin strips the same length as the orange ones. Place the orange and green strips next to each other to give three striped ribbons, and secure the pieces together with a little water.

5 Place one striped ribbon over one corner of the cake, securing with a little water. Place a second strip over the opposite corner.

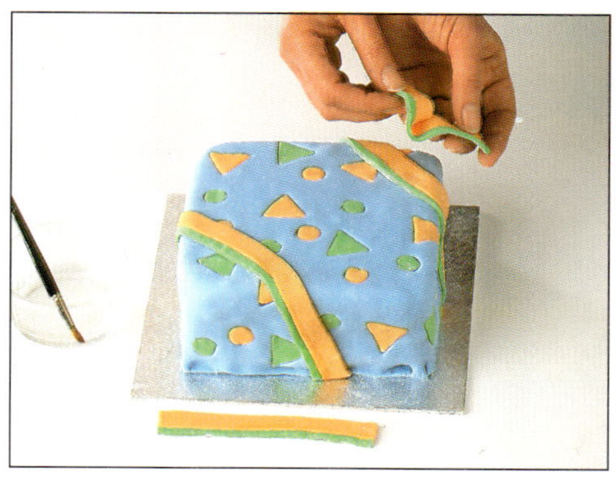

6 ▲ Cut the remaining ribbon in half. Bend each half to make loops and attach both to one corner of the cake with water to form a loose bow.

Easter Egg Nest Cake

Celebrate Easter with a fresh-tasting lemon sponge, colourfully adorned with marzipan nests and chocolate eggs.

INGREDIENTS

Serves 10

1 quantity lemon-flavour Quick-Mix Sponge Cake mix
350 g/12 oz/1 quantity lemon-flavour Butter Icing
225 g/8 oz marzipan
pink, green and purple food colourings
foil-wrapped chocolate eggs

MATERIALS AND EQUIPMENT

20 cm/8 inch ring mould
25 cm/10 inch cake board

STORING

This cake can be kept for up to three days in an airtight container, stored in the refrigerator.

1 Preheat the oven to 160°C/325°F/Gas 3. Grease and flour the ring mould. Spoon the cake mixture into the mould and smooth the surface. Bake in the centre of the oven for about 25 minutes, or until firm to the touch. Turn out on to a wire rack and leave to cool completely.

2 ▲ Cut the cake in half horizontally and sandwich together with about one-third of the butter icing. Position the cake on the cake board. Spread the remaining icing over the outside of the cake to cover completely.

3 Smooth the top of the cake with a palette knife and swirl the icing around the side of the cake.

4 ▲ To make the marzipan plaits, divide the marzipan into three portions and colour it pink, green and purple. Cut each portion in half. Using one-half of each of the colours, roll each one out with your fingers on a work surface lightly dusted with icing sugar to make a thin sausage shape long enough to go around the bottom edge of the cake. Pinch the ends together at the top, then twist the individual strands into a rope. Pinch the other ends to seal neatly.

5 ▲ Place the rope on the cake board around the bottom edge of the cake.

6 To make the nests, take the remaining portions of coloured marzipan and divide each colour into five. Roll each piece into a rope about 16 cm/6 ½ inches long. Take a rope of each colour, pinch the ends together, twist to form a multi-coloured rope and pinch the other ends. Form the rope into a circle and repeat to make the remaining four nests.

7 ▲ Arrange the nests so they are evenly spaced on the top of the cake and place several chocolate eggs in the middle of each.

Bluebird Bon Voyage Cake

This cake is sure to see someone off on an exciting journey in a very special way.

INGREDIENTS
Serves 12–15
450 g/1 lb/⅔ quantity Royal Icing
blue food colouring
800 g/1¾ lb/2⅓ x quantity Sugarpaste Icing
20 cm/8 inch round Madeira Cake
1 quantity Butter Icing
3 tbsp apricot jam, warmed and sieved
silver balls

MATERIALS AND EQUIPMENT
25 cm/10 inch round cake board
greaseproof paper piping bags
No 1 writing nozzle
thin pale blue ribbon

STORING
The finished cake can be kept for up to one week in an airtight container.

1 Make up the royal icing, keeping about two-thirds softer for filling in, and the rest stiffer for the outlines and further piping. Colour the softer icing blue. Cover the icings and leave overnight. Stir before using.

2 ▲ On greaseproof paper, draw the birds several times in two sizes. Tape the paper to a baking sheet, then secure a piece of baking parchment over the top.

3 ▲ Fit a paper piping bag with a No 1 writing nozzle and spoon in some of the stiffer icing for piping the outlines. Pipe over the outlines of the birds with a continuous thread of icing.

4 ▲ Half-fill a fresh paper piping bag with the blue icing. Cut the pointed end off the bag in a straight line. Do not make the opening too large or the icing will flow too quickly. Pipe the icing into the outlines to fill, working from the outlines into the centre. Do not touch the outlines or they may break. To prevent air bubbles, keep the end of the bag in the icing. The icing should look overfilled and rounded, as it will shrink slightly as it dries.

5 Working quickly, brush through the icing to fill in any gaps and to ensure it goes right to the outlines. If any air bubbles appear, smooth them out or burst with a pin. Leave the run-outs on the paper for two days to dry.

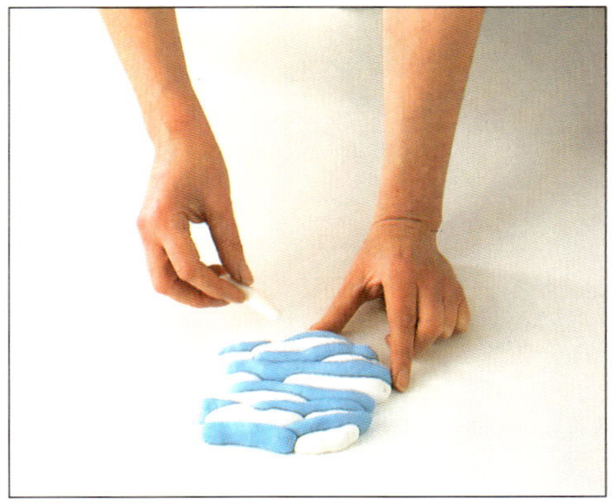

6 ▲ Colour two-thirds of the sugar-paste icing blue and leave the rest white. Form the icing into small rolls and place them together on a work surface lightly dusted with icing sugar, alternating the colours. Form into a round and lightly knead together until the icing is marbled. Do not over-knead or you will lose the effect. Cut off about one-quarter of the sugarpaste icing, wrap in clear film and set aside.

7 Cut the cake horizontally into three even layers and sandwich together with the butter icing. Brush with the apricot jam. Roll out the marbled sugarpaste icing and use it to cover the cake. Roll out the reserved sugarpaste icing to a 25 cm/10 inch circle and use it to cover the cake board.

8 ▲ Position the cake to one edge of the board. Fit a piping bag with the writing nozzle and half-fill with the remaining stiffer royal icing. Pipe a wavy line all around the edge of the cake board. Working quickly before the icing dries, position the silver balls so they are evenly spaced in the icing.

9 Remove the birds from the greaseproof paper using a palette knife and secure them to the cake with a little royal icing. Pipe a bead of white icing on each for the eye and place a silver ball in the centre. Drape the ribbon between the birds' beaks, securing with icing.

Fudge-frosted Starry Roll

Whether it's a birthday or another occasion you are wanting to celebrate, this sumptuous looking cake is sure to please.

Ingredients

Serves 8

1 quantity Swiss Roll mix
$\frac{1}{2}$ quantity chocolate-flavour Butter Icing
50 g/2 oz white chocolate
50 g/2 oz plain chocolate
$1\frac{1}{2}$ x quantity Fudge Frosting

Materials and Equipment

23 x 33 cm/9 x 13 inch Swiss roll tin
small star cutter
several greaseproof paper piping bags
No 19 star nozzle

Storing

This cake can be kept for up to two days in an airtight container, stored in the refrigerator.

1 Preheat the oven to 180°C/350°F/ Gas 4. Grease the tin, line the base with greaseproof paper and grease the paper. Spoon in the cake mixture and gently smooth the surface. Bake for 12–15 minutes, or until springy to the touch.

2 Turn out on to a sheet of greaseproof paper lightly sprinkled with caster sugar, peel off the lining paper and roll up the Swiss roll, leaving the lining paper inside. When cold, unroll carefully, remove the paper and spread the cake with the butter icing. Re-roll and set aside on a sheet of greaseproof paper on a wire rack.

3 ▲ To make the chocolate decorations, cover a board with baking parchment and tape down at each corner. Melt the white chocolate, then pour on to the baking parchment. Spread the chocolate evenly with a palette knife and allow to stand until the surface is firm enough to cut, but not so hard that it will break. It should no longer feel sticky when touched with your finger. Press a small star cutter firmly through the chocolate and lift off the paper with a palette knife. Set aside.

4 ▲ Melt the plain chocolate and allow to cool slightly. Cover a rolling pin with baking parchment and attach it with tape. Fill a paper piping bag with the chocolate and cut a small piece off the pointed end in a straight line. Pipe lines of chocolate backwards and forwards over the baking parchment, to the size you choose. Make at least nine curls so you have extra in case of breakages. Leave the chocolate lace curls to set in a cool place, then carefully peel off the paper.

5 ▲ Make the fudge frosting. When cool enough to spread, cover the Swiss roll with about two-thirds of it, making swirls with a palette knife.

6 ▲ Fit a fresh paper piping bag with the No 19 star nozzle and spoon in the remaining frosting. Pipe diagonal lines, like a twisted rope, on either side of the roll and across both ends.

7 ▲ Position the lace curls in the icing, and arrange the stars. Transfer the cake to a serving plate and decorate with more stars.

Marbled Cracker Cake

Here is a Christmas cake decorated in an untraditional way. The cake can be made well ahead of Christmas and then decorated nearer the time.

INGREDIENTS

Serves 20–25

20 cm/8 inch round Rich Fruit Cake
3 tbsp apricot jam, warmed and sieved
675 g/1½ lb marzipan
800 g/1¾ lb/2⅓ x quantity Sugarpaste Icing
red and green food colourings
edible gold balls

MATERIALS AND EQUIPMENT

wooden cocktail sticks
25 cm/10 inch round cake board
red, green and gold thin gift wrapping ribbon
3 red and 3 green ribbon bows

STORING

The finished cake can be kept for up to three months in an airtight container.

1 Brush the cake with the jam. Roll out the marzipan on a work surface lightly dusted with icing sugar and cover the cake. Leave to dry for 12 hours.

2 ▲ Take 500 g/1¼ lb of the sugarpaste icing and form a smooth roll. Put some red food colouring on the end of a cocktail stick and dab a few drops on to the icing. Repeat with the green. Knead just a few times. Roll out the sugarpaste, on a work surface lightly dusted with icing sugar, until marbled.

3 Brush the marzipan with a little water and cover with the icing. Position the cake on the cake board.

4 ▲ Colour half of the remaining sugarpaste icing red and the rest green. Roll about half of the red icing into five 5 x 1 cm/2 x ½ inch rectangles for the crackers. Roll half of the green icing into a 13 x 1 cm/5 x ½ inch roll and cut off ten 1 cm/½ inch lengths. These are the ends of the crackers. Attach two green ends to each red cracker with a little water. Gather together any icing trimmings. Roll out a small piece of green icing thinly and cut into two 13 x 1 cm/5 x ½ inch strips. Cut each strip into five diamonds. Attach two green diamonds to each cracker, then press a gold ball in the centre. Leave to dry on greaseproof paper for several hours or overnight.

5 ▲ Meanwhile, roll out the remaining red and green icings, including any trimmings, into 1 cm/½ inch wide strips. Cut each strip into diamonds – you will need about 24 diamonds in each colour.

6 ▲ Attach alternate red and green diamonds around the top and base of the cake, securing with water.

7 ▲ Cut the ribbons into about 10 cm/4 inch lengths. Run the blade of a pair of scissors or a sharp knife down the length of them to curl.

8 Arrange the crackers in a pile on top of the cake and decorate with the curled ribbons. Attach the bows in alternate colours with a little softened sugarpaste icing, evenly spaced between the diamonds around the top edge of the cake.

Tip

Add the colour to the icing sparingly at first because the colour becomes more intense as the icing stands. It is advisable to leave the icing for about 10 minutes to see if it is the shade you need.

Double Heart Engagement Cake

For a celebratory engagement party, these sumptuous cakes make the perfect centrepiece.

INGREDIENTS
Serves 20
2 x quantity chocolate-flavour Quick-Mix Sponge Cake mix
350 g/12 oz/12 squares plain chocolate
2 x quantity coffee-flavour Butter Icing
icing sugar, for sifting
fresh raspberries, to decorate

MATERIALS AND EQUIPMENT
2 x 20 cm/8 inch heart-shaped cake tins
2 x 23 cm/9 inch heart-shaped cake boards

STORING
The finished cakes can be kept for up to three days in an airtight container in the fridge.

1 Preheat the oven to 160°C/325°F/Gas 3. Grease the tins, line the bases with greaseproof paper and grease the paper. Divide the cake mixture evenly between the tins and smooth the surfaces. Bake in the centre of the oven for 25–30 minutes or until firm to the touch. Turn out on to a wire rack, peel off the lining paper and leave to cool completely.

2 Meanwhile, melt the chocolate in a heatproof bowl over a saucepan of hot water (you may find it easier to work with half the chocolate at a time). Pour the melted chocolate on to a firm, smooth surface such as a marble or plastic laminate set on a slightly damp cloth to prevent slipping. Spread the chocolate out evenly with a large palette knife. Leave the chocolate to cool slightly. It should feel just set, but not hard.

3 ▲ To make the chocolate curls, hold a large sharp knife at a 45° angle to the chocolate and push it along the chocolate in short sawing movements from right to left and left to right. Remove the curls by sliding the point of the knife underneath each one and lifting off. Leave to firm on baking parchment. Repeat with remaining chocolate.

4 ▲ Cut each cake in half horizontally. Use about one-third of the butter icing to fill both cakes, then sandwich them together.

5 Use the remaining icing to coat the tops and sides of the cakes.

6 ▲ Place the cakes on the cake boards. Generously cover the tops and sides of the cakes with the chocolate curls, pressing them gently into the butter icing.

7 Sift a little icing sugar over the top of each cake and decorate with raspberries. Chill until ready to serve.

Chocolate-iced Anniversary Cake

This cake is special enough to celebrate any wedding anniversary. Tropical fruits and a glossy chocolate icing make it very appealing for all ages.

Ingredients
Serves 12–15
20 cm/8 inch round Madeira Cake
$1^1/_2$ x quantity chocolate-flavour Butter Icing
1 quantity Satin Chocolate Icing
chocolate buttons
selection of fresh fruits, such as kiwi, nectarine or peach, apricot, Cape gooseberries

MATERIALS AND EQUIPMENT
greaseproof paper piping bag
No 22 star nozzle
thin gold ribbon, about 5 mm/$^1/_4$ in wide
florist's wire

STORING
This cake can be kept for up to five days in the refrigerator.

1 Cut the cake into three horizontal layers and sandwich together with about three-quarters of the chocolate butter icing. Place the cake on a wire rack with a baking sheet underneath.

2 ▲ Make the satin chocolate icing and immediately pour over the cake to coat completely. Working quickly, ease the icing gently over the surface of the cake, using a palette knife if necessary. Allow to set.

3 ▲ Transfer the cake to a serving plate. Fit a paper piping bag with the star nozzle and spoon in the remaining chocolate butter icing. Pipe scrolls around the top edge of the cake.

4 Cut several chocolate buttons into quarters and use to decorate the butter icing.

5 ▲ Prepare the fruit for the top of the cake. Peel and slice the kiwi and cut into quarters, and slice the nectarine or peach, apricot and gooseberries.

6 Arrange the fruit on top of the cake. For each ribbon decoration, make two small loops using the thin gold ribbon. Twist a piece of florist's wire around the ends of the ribbon to secure the loops. Trim the ends of the ribbon. Cut the wire to the length you want and use it to put the loops in position on the cake. Make about seven ribbon decorations. Remove the ribbons and wire before serving.

Lucky Horseshoe

This horseshoe-shaped cake, made to wish 'good luck', is made from a round cake and the horseshoe shape is then cut out.

INGREDIENTS
Serves 30–35
25 cm/10 inch Rich Fruit Cake
4 tbsp apricot jam, warmed and sieved
800 g/1¾ lb marzipan
1 kg/2¼ lb/3 x quantity Sugarpaste Icing
peach and blue food colourings
silver balls
115 g/4 oz/⅙ quantity Royal Icing

MATERIALS AND EQUIPMENT
28–30 cm/11–12 inch round cake board
crimping tool
large blossom cutter
small blossom cutter
pale blue ribbon, 3 mm/⅛ in wide

STORING
The cake can be kept for up to three months in an airtight container.

1 Draw a horseshoe shape on a sheet of greaseproof paper. Cut this shape out of the cake, using the template as a guide. Brush the cake with the apricot jam. Roll out 350 g/12 oz of the marzipan to a 25 cm/10 inch circle on a work surface lightly dusted with icing sugar. Using the template as a guide, cut out the shape and cover the top of the cake with the marzipan. Reserve the trimmings for the inside of the ring.

2 Measure the circumference of the cake as far as the openings of the horseshoe and the height of the side with string. Take the remaining marzipan and roll out for the side, using the string measurement as a guide. Use to cover the side. Using the same method and the reserved trimmings, cover the inside of the horseshoe. Position the cake on the board and leave to dry for 12 hours.

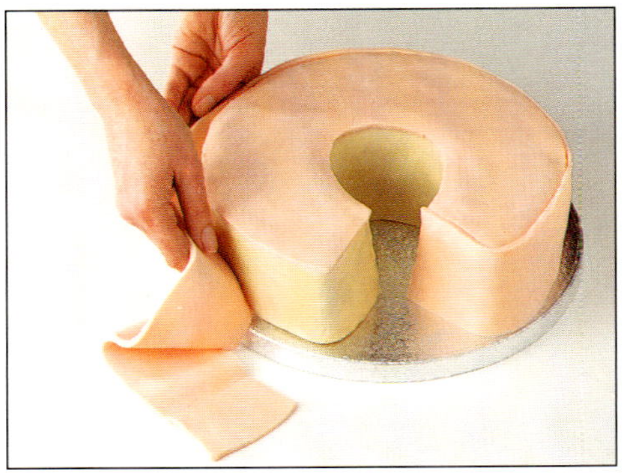

3 ▲ Colour 800 g/1¾ lb of the sugarpaste icing peach. Brush the marzipan lightly with water and cover the cake with the sugarpaste icing in the same way as described for the marzipan, covering first the top, then the side, then the inside of the horseshoe.

4 Using a crimping tool dipped in cornflour, carefully crimp the top edge of the cake.

5 Draw and measure the design for the ribbon insertion on the horseshoe template. Cut 13 pieces of pale blue ribbon fractionally longer than the size of each slit.

6 ▲ Place the template on the cake, securing with pins if necessary, and cut through the drawn lines into the icing with a scalpel to make slits for the ribbon. Remove the template.

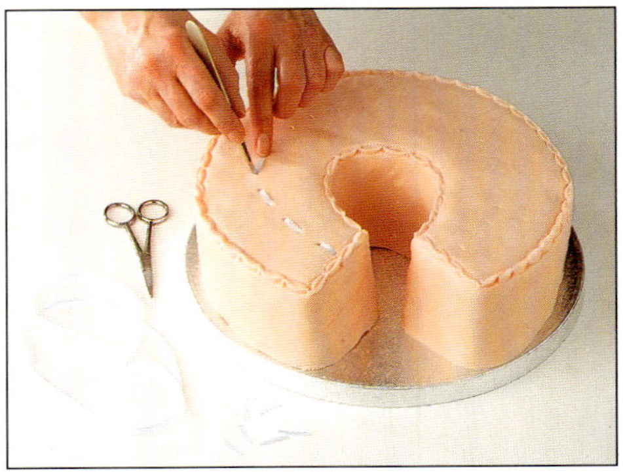

7 ▲ With the aid of a pointed tool, insert one end of the ribbon into the first slit and the other end into the second slit. Leave a space and repeat, filling all the slits with the pieces of ribbon. Leave to dry for 12 hours.

8 ▲ Draw a small horseshoe shape on a piece of card and cut out. Take the remaining sugarpaste icing and colour one-half pale blue and leave the other half white. Roll out the blue icing on a work surface lightly dusted with icing sugar. Using the card template as a guide, cut out nine shapes with a sharp knife. Mark small lines around the centre of each horseshoe with the knife. Cut out 12 large and 15 small blossoms with the blossom cutters, then press a silver ball into the centres of the larger blossoms. Leave to dry on greaseproof paper. Repeat with the white icing.

9 Decorate the cake with the ribbon. Arrange the horseshoes and blossoms on the cake and board, securing with a little royal icing.

Tip

Save the discarded section of the round cake to use in the Truffle Mix, if wished. Horseshoe-shaped tins can be purchased or hired from cake decorating specialists.

Golden Wedding Heart Cake

Creamy gold colours, delicate frills and dainty iced blossoms give this cake a special celebratory appeal.

INGREDIENTS

Serves 30

23 cm/9 inch round Rich Fruit Cake
4 tbsp apricot jam, warmed and sieved
900 g/2 lb marzipan
900 g/2 lb/2⅔ x quantity Sugarpaste Icing
cream food colouring
115 g/4 oz/⅙ quantity Royal Icing

MATERIALS AND EQUIPMENT

28 cm/11 inch round cake board
crimping tool
small heart-shaped plunger tool
7.5 cm/3 inch plain cutter
dual large and small blossom cutter
stamens
frill cutter
foil-wrapped chocolate hearts

STORING

The finished cake can be kept for up to three months in an airtight container.

1 Brush the cake with apricot jam. Roll out the marzipan on a work surface lightly dusted with icing sugar and use it to cover the cake. Leave to dry for 12 hours.

2 Colour 675 g/1½ lb of the sugarpaste icing very pale cream. Roll out the icing on a work surface lightly dusted with icing sugar. Brush the marzipan with a little water and cover the cake with the sugarpaste icing. Position the cake on the cake board. Using a crimping tool dipped in cornflour, carefully crimp the top edge of the cake.

3 ▲ Divide the circumference of the top of the cake into eight equal sections, and stick pins in as markers. Use these as a guide to crimp evenly spaced slanting lines going from the top to the bottom edges of the cake. Using the plunger tool, emboss the bottom edge of the cake. Place the plain cutter lightly in the centre of the cake and use as a guide to emboss more hearts in a circle around the cutter. Leave the cake to dry for several hours.

4 ▲ Take the remaining sugarpaste icing and colour one-half cream and the other half pale cream. Retain half of each colour, and wrap the remainder in clear film. Roll out each colour evenly and thinly. Dip the end of the blossom cutter in cornflour and cut out the flower shapes. Make a pin hole in the centre of each larger flower as you make it. Leave to dry on a foam pad. When dry, pipe a little royal icing on to a stamen and thread it through the hole of each larger flower. This will hold it in position. Allow to dry.

5 ▲ To make the frills, roll out the two shades of reserved sugarpaste icing thinly. Using the frill cutter, cut out two rings from each colour.

6 ▲ Position the end of a wooden cocktail stick over 5 mm/¼ inch of the outer edge of the ring. Roll the stick firmly back and forth around the edge with your finger until the edge becomes thinner and begins to frill. Continue until the ring is completely frilled. Repeat with remaining rings. Using a sharp knife, cut each ring in half to make two frills. You should have four frills in each shade.

7 ▲ Using a little water, attach the frills in alternate shades next to the crimped lines running down the side of the cake. Crimp the edges of the deeper coloured frills.

8 Arrange the blossom flowers on the top and side of the cake, securing with a little royal icing. Before serving, place the chocolate hearts in the centre of the cake.

Christmas Tree Cake

No piping is involved in this bright and colourful Christmas tree cake, making it a good choice for all the family to help decorate.

INGREDIENTS
Serves 20 – 25
20 cm/8 inch round Rich Fruit Cake
3 tbsp apricot jam, warmed and sieved
900 g/2 lb marzipan
green, red, yellow and purple food colourings
225 g/8 oz/⅓ quantity Royal Icing
silver balls

MATERIALS AND EQUIPMENT
25 cm/10 inch round cake board

STORING
The finished cake can be kept for up to three months in an airtight container.

1 Brush the cake with the apricot jam. Colour 675 g/1½ lb of the marzipan green. Roll out the green marzipan on a work surface lightly dusted with icing sugar and use it to cover the cake. Leave to dry for 12 hours.

2 ▲ Make the royal icing. Secure the cake to the cake board with a little of the icing. Spread the icing evenly on the side of the cake to cover just half way up. Starting at the bottom of the cake, press the flat side of a palette knife into the icing, then pull away sharply to form a peak. Repeat until the iced area is covered with peaks.

3 ▲ Draw three Christmas tree shapes in different sizes on to a piece of card and cut out. Take half of the remaining marzipan and colour it a slightly deeper shade of green than the top. Using the card templates as a guide, cut out three Christmas tree shapes. Arrange the trees on top of the cake.

4 ▲ Divide the remaining marzipan into three portions and colour it red, yellow and purple. Use a little of the marzipan to make five 9 cm/3 inch rolls from each colour. Loop the coloured lengths alternately around the top edge of the cake, pressing on to the top to secure firmly.

5 ▲ Make small balls from red marzipan and press on to the end of each loop.

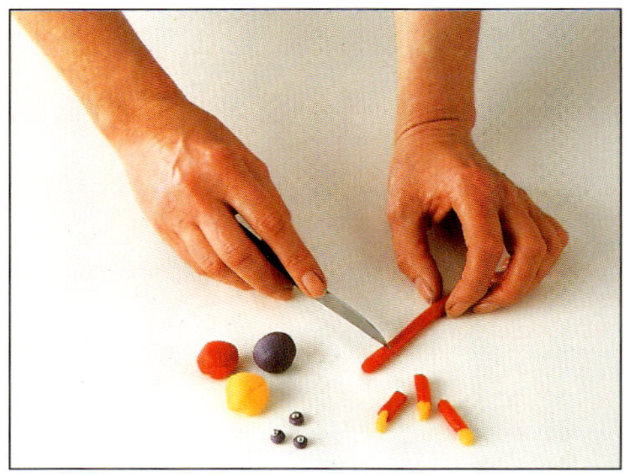

6 ▲ Use the remaining marzipan to make the tree decorations. Roll the red marzipan into a thin rope and cut into eight 2.5 cm/1 inch lengths for the candles. Shape eight flames from the yellow icing and stick on the end of each candle. Mould 11 small balls from the purple icing and press a silver ball into the centre of each.

7 Arrange the candles and balls on the trees, securing them with a little water if necessary.

Hallowe'en Pumpkin Patch

Pumpkins have sprung up all over this orange and chocolate cake, making it the ideal design to celebrate Hallowe'en.

INGREDIENTS
Serves 12–15
2 x quantity chocolate-flavour Quick-Mix Sponge Cake mix
175 g/6 oz/2 x quantity Sugarpaste Icing
orange and brown food colourings
2 x quantity orange-flavour Butter Icing
chocolate chips
angelica

MATERIALS AND EQUIPMENT
2 x 20 cm/8 inch round cake tins
23 cm/9 inch round cake board
serrated scraper
greaseproof paper piping bag
No 7 writing nozzle

STORING
This cake can be kept for up to three days in the refrigerator.

1 Preheat the oven to 160°C/325°F/Gas 3. Grease the cake tins, line the bases with greaseproof paper and grease the paper.

2 Divide the mixture between the tins and smooth the surfaces. Bake for 20–30 minutes or until firm to the touch. Turn out on to a wire rack, peel off the lining paper and leave to cool.

3 ▲ To make the pumpkins, colour a very small piece of the sugarpaste icing brown, and the rest orange. Dust your fingers with a little cornflour. Shape small balls of the orange icing the size of walnuts and some a bit smaller. Make the ridges with a wooden cocktail stick. Make the stems from the brown icing and press into the top of each pumpkin, securing with a little water. Paint highlights on each pumpkin with orange food colouring. Leave to dry on greaseproof paper.

4 Cut each cake in half horizontally. Use one-quarter of the butter icing to sandwich the cakes together. Place the cake on the cake board. Use about two-thirds of the remaining icing to coat the top and sides of the cake.

5 Texture the cake sides with a serrated scraper. Decorate the top with the same scraper, moving the scraper sideways to make undulations and a ridged spiral pattern in a slight fan shape. The texturing should resemble a ploughed field.

6 ▲ Fit a paper piping bag with the writing nozzle and spoon in the remaining butter icing. Pipe a twisted rope pattern around the top and bottom edges of the cake.

7 Decorate the piping with chocolate chips.

8 ▲ Cut the angelica into diamond shapes and arrange on the cake with the pumpkins.

Coffee Almond Flower Gâteau

There are all kinds of reasons for making a cake for someone - sometimes it may be simply to say 'thank you'.

INGREDIENTS
Serves 8–10
1 quantity Quick-Mix Sponge Cake mix
25 g/1 oz/¼ cup nuts, such as almonds or walnuts, finely chopped
1½ x quantity coffee-flavour Butter Icing
75 g/3oz/3 squares plain chocolate
20 blanched almonds
4 chocolate-coated espresso beans

MATERIALS AND EQUIPMENT
2 x 18 cm/7 inch round cake tins
serrated scraper
2 greaseproof paper piping bags
No 2 writing nozzle

STORING
The finished cake can be kept for up to three days in an airtight container in the fridge.

1 Preheat the oven to 160°C/325°F/Gas 3. Grease the cake tins, line the bases with greaseproof paper and grease the paper. Fold the nuts into the cake mixture. Divide the mixture evenly between the tins and smooth the surfaces. Bake in the centre of the oven for about 20 minutes or until firm to the touch. Turn out on to a wire rack, peel off the lining paper and leave to cool completely.

2 Place one of the cakes on a piece of greaseproof paper on a turntable. Use the butter icing to sandwich the cakes together and to ice the top and side. Coat the top by spreading the icing smoothly with a palette knife. Coat the side with a serrated scraper. Reserve two spoonfuls of icing for piping.

3 ▲ Melt the chocolate in a heatproof bowl over a pan of hot water. Remove from the heat, then dip half of each almond into the chocolate at a slight angle. Shake off any excess chocolate and leave the almonds to dry on baking parchment. Return the chocolate to the pan of hot water (off the heat) so it does not set. Remove and allow to cool slightly before using for piping.

4 Arrange the almonds on top of the cake to represent flowers.

5 ▲ Place a chocolate-coated espresso bean in the centre of each almond flower. Spoon the remaining melted chocolate into a greaseproof paper piping bag. Cut a small piece off the end in a straight line. Pipe the chocolate in wavy lines over the top of the cake and in small beads around the top edge.

6 Transfer the cake to a cake stand or serving plate. Work quickly so the chocolate in the piping bag does not become too firm to pipe. Place the reserved butter icing in a fresh piping bag fitted with the No 2 writing nozzle. Pipe beads of icing all around the bottom of the cake, then top with small beads of chocolate, allowing the chocolate to drizzle on to the stand.

Cloth of Roses Cake

This cake says 'congratulations' for whatever reason - passing an exam, getting a new job, getting engaged, or for just achieving a life long ambition.

INGREDIENTS

Serves 20–25

20 cm/8 inch round Light Fruit Cake

3 tbsp apricot jam, warmed and sieved

675 g/1½ lb marzipan

900 g/2 lb/2⅔ x quantity Sugarpaste Icing

yellow, orange and green food colourings

115 g/4oz/⅙ quantity Royal Icing

MATERIALS AND EQUIPMENT

25 cm/10 inch cake board

7 cm/2¾ inch plain cutter

petal cutter

thin yellow ribbon

STORING

The finished cake can be kept for up to four weeks in an airtight container.

1 Brush the cake with apricot jam. Roll out the marzipan on a work surface lightly dusted with icing sugar and cover the cake. Leave for 12 hours.

2 Cut off 675 g/1½ lb of the sugarpaste icing and divide in half. Colour one-half very pale yellow and the other very pale orange. Wrap separately in clear film and set aside.

3 Cut out a template for the orange icing from greaseproof paper, as follows. Draw a 25 cm/10 inch circle using the cake board as a guide. Using the plain cutter, draw half circles 2.5 cm/1 inch wide all around the outside of the large circle. Cut out the template.

4 Roll out the yellow sugarpaste icing on a work surface lightly dusted with icing sugar to the same length and height as the side of the cake. Brush the side of the cake with a little water and cover with the sugarpaste icing. Position the cake on the cake board.

5 ▲ Roll out the orange sugarpaste icing to about a 30 cm/12 inch circle. Place the template on the icing and cut out the scalloped shape.

6 ▲ Brush the top of the cake with water and cover with the orange icing so the scallops fall just over the edge. Bend them slightly to look like a cloth. Leave to dry overnight.

7 Meanwhile make the roses and leaves. Cut off about three-quarters of the remaining sugarpaste icing and divide into four portions. (Wrap the other piece in clear film and reserve for the leaves.) Colour the four portions pale yellow, deep yellow, orange, and marbled yellow and orange.

8 ▲ For each rose, dust your fingers with cornflour, take a small ball of coloured icing and form into a cone shape. For each petal, take a small piece of icing and work it with your fingers into a petal shape which is slightly thicker at the base. Wrap the petal around the cone so it sits above the top of it, pressing together to stick. Curl the ends of the petal back. Mould the next petal and attach so it just overlaps the first one. Curl the ends back. Repeat with several more petals, making them slightly larger each time. Cut off the base so the rose will stand on the cake. Make about 18 roses. Leave to dry on greaseproof paper.

9 ▲ Colour the reserved piece of sugarpaste icing green for the leaves. Roll out thinly and cut out leaves with a petal cutter. Make about 24 leaves. Leave to dry on greaseproof paper.

10 Arrange the leaves and roses, securing with a little royal icing. Decorate the cake with the ribbon.

Daisy Christening Cake

A ring of moulded daisies sets off this pretty pink christening cake. It can be made in easy stages, giving time for the various icings to dry before adding the next layer.

INGREDIENTS
Serves 20–25
20 cm/8 inch round Rich Fruit Cake
3 tbsp apricot jam, warmed and sieved
675 g/1½ lb marzipan
900 g/2 lb/1⅓ x quantity Royal Icing
115 g/4 oz/⅓ quantity Sugarpaste Icing
pink and yellow food colourings

MATERIALS AND EQUIPMENT
25 cm/10 inch round cake board
5 cm/2 inch fluted cutter
wooden cocktail stick
2 greaseproof paper piping bags
No 42 nozzle
pink and white ribbon

STORING
This cake can be kept for up to three months in an airtight container.

1 Brush the cake with the apricot jam. Roll out the marzipan on a work surface lightly dusted with icing sugar and use to cover the cake. Leave to dry for 12 hours.

2 Secure the cake to the cake board with a little of the icing. Colour three-quarters of the icing pink. Flat ice the cake with three or four layers of smooth icing, using the white icing for the top and the pink for the sides. Allow each layer to dry overnight before applying the next. Set aside a little of both icings in airtight containers, to decorate the cake.

3 Meanwhile, make the daisies. You will need about 28. For each daisy cut off a small piece of sugarpaste icing. Dust your fingers with a little cornflour to prevent sticking.

4 ▲ Shape the icing with your fingers to look like a golf tee, with a stem and a thin, flat, round top.

5 ▲ Using scissors, make small cuts all the way around the edge of the daisy. Carefully curl the cut edges slightly in different directions. Place the daisies on a sheet of greaseproof paper to dry.

6 ▲ When dry, trim the stems and paint the edges with pink and the centres with yellow food colouring.

7 ▲ To make the plaque, roll out the remaining sugarpaste icing on a work surface lightly dusted with icing sugar and cut out a circle with the fluted cutter. Position the end of a wooden cocktail stick over 5 mm/¼ inch of the outer edge of the circle. Roll the stick firmly back and forth around the edge with your finger until the edge becomes thinner and begins to frill. Continue until the edge of the plaque is completely frilled. Place on a sheet of greaseproof paper to dry, then paint the name in the centre of the plaque and the edges with pink food colouring.

8 ▲ Fit a paper piping bag with the nozzle and pipe a twisted rope around the top and bottom edges of the cake with the remaining white royal icing. Wash the nozzle, fit it in a fresh paper piping bag and pipe a row of stars around the top of the cake with the remaining pink icing.

9 Secure the plaque to the centre of the cake with a little royal icing. Arrange the daisies on the cake, also securing with the icing, and decorate with the ribbons.

Anna

Birthday Bowl of Strawberries

All kinds of fun designs can be painted on cakes with edible food colourings. With this one the strawberry theme is carried on into the moulded decorations too, providing a fresh, summery birthday cake.

INGREDIENTS

Serves 20

1 quantity Butter Icing

20 cm/8 inch petal-shaped Madeira Cake (make using quantities for a 20 cm/8 inch round cake)

3 tbsp apricot jam, warmed and sieved

675 g/1½ lb/2 x quantity Sugarpaste Icing

pink, red, yellow, green and claret food colourings

yellow powdered food colouring

MATERIALS AND EQUIPMENT

25 cm/10 inch petal-shaped cake board

paint palette or small saucers

thin red and green ribbons

STORING

The finished cake can be kept for up to one week in an airtight container.

1 Colour the butter icing pink. Cut the cake into three horizontal layers and sandwich together with the butter icing. Brush the cake with apricot jam. Roll out 500 g/1¼ lb of the sugarpaste icing on a work surface lightly dusted with icing sugar and use to cover the cake. Position on the cake board and leave to dry for 12 hours.

2 ▲ To make the strawberries, colour three-quarters of the remaining sugarpaste icing red, and equal portions of the rest yellow and green. Dust your fingers with cornflour to prevent sticking, and mould the red icing into strawberry shapes. Make tiny oval shapes from the yellow icing to represent seeds and lightly press on to the strawberries. Secure with water if necessary. Shape the green icing into small flat circles slightly bigger than the tops of the strawberries. Using scissors, make small cuts all the way round the circles and carefully curl the cut edges slightly. Attach to the tops of the strawberries, securing with a little water. Leave to dry on greaseproof paper.

3 ▲ Put the red, green, yellow and claret food colourings in a palette and water them down slightly. Draw or paint on an outline of the vase with the claret colour, then fill in the pattern.

4 ▲ Use a little powdered yellow food colouring to add highlights.

5 ▲ Finish painting the design, filling in the strawberries in the bowl and around the edge of the cake.

6 ▲ Decorate the cake with the ribbons. Secure two strawberries to the top of the cake, and arrange the others around the bottom edge.

Holly Leaf Log

Christmas cakes can be made in all shapes and sizes. This log-shaped cake is for chocolate and coffee lovers.

INGREDIENTS

Serves 8

1 quantity Swiss Roll mix

½ quantity coffee-flavour Butter Icing

75 g/3 oz/3 squares plain chocolate

1½ x quantity Fudge Frosting

MATERIALS AND EQUIPMENT

Swiss roll tin

holly leaf cutter

2 greaseproof paper piping bags

No 1 writing and No 30 star nozzles

STORING

This cake can be kept for two days in the fridge in an airtight container.

1 Make and bake the Swiss roll. Turn out on to a sheet of greaseproof paper lightly sprinkled with caster sugar and roll up leaving the lining paper inside. Leave to cool completely on a wire rack.

2 ▲ Unroll the cake carefully and remove the paper. Reserve a spoonful of the butter icing for piping on the holly leaves, and spread the remainder over the cake. Re-roll the cake, place on a sheet of greaseproof paper on a wire rack and set aside.

3 To make the chocolate decorations, cover a baking sheet with baking parchment and tape it down at each corner. Melt the chocolate in a heatproof bowl over a pan of hot water, then pour on to the baking parchment.

4 Spread out the chocolate evenly with a palette knife, and allow to cool until the surface is firm enough to cut, but not so hard that it will break. The chocolate should no longer feel sticky when touched with your finger.

5 ▲ Press a holly leaf cutter firmly through the chocolate and lift off the leaves with a small palette knife. Spoon the reserved butter icing into a greaseproof paper piping bag fitted with the No 1 writing nozzle. Use to pipe decorations on the chocolate leaves.

6 ▲ Make the fudge frosting and, when cool enough to spread, quickly cover the Swiss roll with about two-thirds of the frosting. Working quickly before the frosting becomes too stiff, make swirls over the surface with a palette knife.

7 ▲ Spoon the remaining frosting into a fresh piping bag fitted with the No 30 star nozzle. Pipe several lines of scrolls down the length of the cake.

8 Transfer to a serving plate and arrange the chocolate leaves on the cake, pressing lightly to secure.

Starry New Year Cake

Although it is not so traditional to welcome in the New Year with a cake as it is at Christmas, why not start a new tradition?

INGREDIENTS
Serves 15–20
23 cm/9 inch round Madeira Cake
2 x quantity Butter Icing
800 g/1¾ lb/2⅓ x quantity Sugarpaste Icing
grape violet and mulberry food colourings
gold, lilac shimmer and primrose sparkle powdered food colourings

MATERIALS AND EQUIPMENT
star-shaped cutter
florist's wire
28 cm/11 inch round cake board
purple ribbon with gold stars

STORING
The finished cake can be kept for up to one week in an airtight container.

1 Cut the cake horizontally into three layers. Sandwich the layers together with three-quarters of the butter icing. Spread the remaining butter icing in a thin layer over the top and sides.

2 Colour 500 g/1¼ lb of the sugarpaste icing purple with the grape violet and a touch of the mulberry food colourings. Roll out on a work surface lightly dusted with icing sugar and cover the cake. Leave to dry overnight.

3 ▲ Place the cake on a sheet of greaseproof paper to protect the work surface. Water down a little of the gold and lilac shimmer powdered food colourings, then load up the end of a paintbrush with one of the colours. Position the brush over the area you want to colour, then flick your wrist in the direction of the cake, so the colour falls on to it in small beads. Repeat with the other colour until the whole cake is covered. Leave to dry.

4 To make the stars, divide the remaining sugarpaste icing into three portions. Colour one portion purple, the same as the coated cake, one portion with the lilac shimmer and one portion with the primrose sparkle. Roll out each colour separately to about 3 mm/⅛ inch thick. Cut out stars with the star-shaped cutter and place on a piece of greaseproof paper. You will need 30 stars total. Highlight the stars with the dry powdered colours, brushing gold on the purple stars, primrose on the yellow and lilac on the lilac stars. Using the watered-down gold and lilac colours, flick them on to each star as before.

5 ▲ While the icing is still soft, cut short lengths of florist's wire and carefully push them through the middle of 15 of the stars, but not all the way through. Leave to dry overnight.

6 ▲ Position the cake on the cake board or plate. Arrange three unwired stars in each colour in a diagonal line on the top edge of the cake, securing with a little water. Repeat to make four more groupings of the stars. Stick the wired stars at angles all over the top of the cake as you arrange the flat ones.

7 Decorate the base of the cake with the ribbon.

Trailing Orchid Wedding Cake

A special celebration such as a wedding deserves a very special cake.

INGREDIENTS
Serves 100
30 cm/12 inch round Madeira Cake mix
25 cm/10 inch round Madeira Cake mix
50 g/2 oz/2 squares plain chocolate
50 g/2 oz/2 squares white chocolate
7½ x quantity Butter Icing
1½ x quantity chocolate-flavour Butter Icing

MATERIALS AND EQUIPMENT
30 cm/12 inch oval cake tin
25 cm/10 inch oval cake tin
about 22 rose leaves
plain scraper
several greaseproof paper piping bags
No 4 writing and basket-weave nozzles
35 cm/14 inch oval thick cake board
25 cm/10 inch oval thin cake board
orchids

STORING
Decorate the cake the day before the wedding, adding the leaves and flowers on the day.

1 Grease the oval cake tins, line with a double thickness of greaseproof paper and grease the paper. Make the cakes one at a time and bake, following the baking times for the 30 cm/12 inch and 25 cm/10 inch round Madeira cakes. Leave to cool slightly in the tin, then turn out on to a wire rack, peel off the lining paper and leave to cool.

2 To make the chocolate leaves, wash and dry the rose leaves well on kitchen paper. Melt the chocolates in two separate heatproof bowls over pans of hot water.

3 ▲ Brush the underside of each leaf, some with plain, some with the white chocolate. Do not go over to the other side of the leaf. Place the leaves chocolate-side up on baking parchment, and leave to set in a cool place. Peel the leaf from the chocolate. Handle the chocolate as little as possible as the warmth of your hands will melt it. If the chocolate seems too thin, re-coat.

4 Make the butter icings in batches, whisking until smooth. Level off the tops of the cakes if they have domed. Cut each cake in half horizontally, then sandwich each one back together with some of the plain butter icing.

5 Invert each cake on to a board covered with greaseproof paper. Spread some of the plain butter icing over the sides and smooth with the scraper.

6 ▲ Spread the icing over the top of each cake. To make the surface really smooth, spread with a long metal palette knife which has been dipped into hot water.

7 ▲ To pipe the basket-weave design on each cake, spoon some of the chocolate-flavour butter icing into a greaseproof paper piping bag fitted with a No 4 writing nozzle. (You will need to work in batches with several piping bags.) Pipe a vertical line on the side of the cake from the base to the top of the cake. Pipe several more lines.

8 Spoon some of the plain butter icing into a fresh piping bag fitted with a basket-weave nozzle. (You will need to work in batches with several piping bags.) Across the second vertical line of chocolate icing, pipe 2 cm/¾ inch horizontal lines of basic butter icing, going across the vertical line at 1 cm/½ inch intervals. You will need about three horizontal lines across each vertical for the smaller cake and three to four for the larger one. Fill in the spaces between the horizontal lines with an alternating row of horizontal lines over the third chocolate vertical. Repeat until the sides of each cake have been covered with the design.

9 ▲ Transfer the larger cake to the thick cake board and the smaller cake to the thin one (you should not be able to see the thin board). Keeping the smaller cake on the thin board, position it on top of the larger cake, to one end. Using a piping bag fitted with a No 4 writing nozzle, pipe beads of chocolate butter icing round the top and bottom edges of each cake. Keep in a cool place overnight. On the day, arrange the chocolate leaves and orchids on the tops of each cake. Keep in a cool place until required.

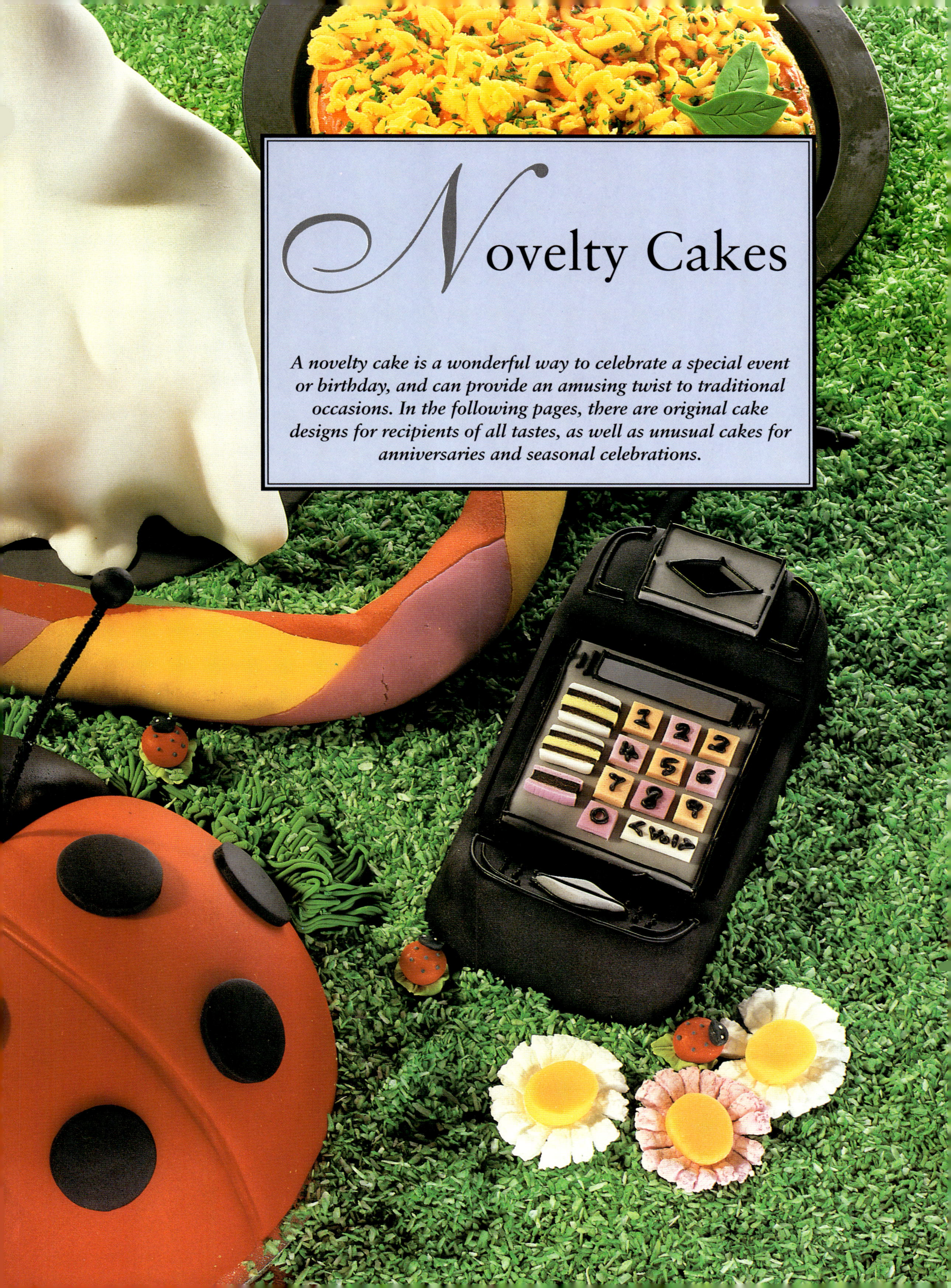

Novelty Cakes

A novelty cake is a wonderful way to celebrate a special event or birthday, and can provide an amusing twist to traditional occasions. In the following pages, there are original cake designs for recipients of all tastes, as well as unusual cakes for anniversaries and seasonal celebrations.

Mobile Phone Cake

For the upwardly mobile man, this novel cake is the business!

INGREDIENTS
Serves 8–10
1 quantity Quick-Mix Sponge Cake mix
2 tbsp apricot jam, warmed and sieved
350 g/12 oz/1 quantity Sugarpaste Icing
black food colouring
10 small square sweets
1–2 striped liquorice sweets
2–3 tbsp icing sugar
½–1 tsp water

MATERIALS AND EQUIPMENT
900 g/2 lb loaf tin
23 x 18 cm/9 x 7 in cake board
diamond-shaped biscuit cutter
piping bag fitted with a small plain nozzle

STORING
The finished cake can be kept in a cool, dry place for three to four days.

Tip

The dial pad is made from small sweets. However, you could increase the quantity of sugarpaste icing slightly, colour it as wished, then cut it to shape.

1 Preheat the oven to 180°C/350°F/ Gas 4. Grease the tin, line with greaseproof paper and grease the paper. Spoon the cake mixture into the prepared tin and smooth the surface. Bake in the centre of the oven for 40–50 minutes, or until a skewer inserted into the centre of the cake comes out clean. Leave the cake in the tin for 5 minutes, then turn out on to a wire rack, peel off the lining paper and leave to cool.

2 ▲ Turn the cake upside-down and starting about 2.5 cm/1 in along the cake, slice into it, across and at an angle, about 1 cm/½ in deep. Cut out this wedge, then slice horizontally along the length of the cake, stopping about 2.5 cm/1 in away from the end. Withdraw the knife and re-insert it at the end of the cake and slice vertically into the cake to meet up with the horizontal cut. Remove the inner piece of cake and discard.

3 ▲ Place the cake on the cake board and brush the cake evenly with the apricot jam. Colour three-quarters of the sugarpaste icing black. On a work surface lightly dusted with icing sugar, roll out to a 5 mm/¼ in thickness and use to cover the cake. Trim away any excess sugarpaste and reserve, wrapped in clear film.

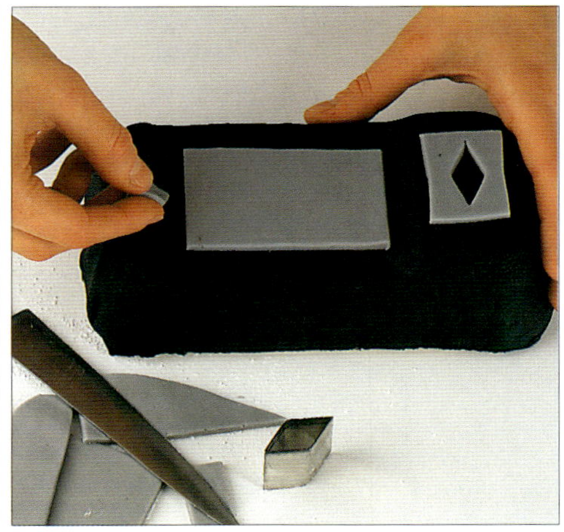

4 ▲ Colour the remaining sugarpaste icing grey with a little black food colouring. On a work surface lightly dusted with icing sugar, roll out to a 5 mm/¼ in thickness. Cut out an oblong to fit the centre of the cake, leaving a 1 cm/½ in border. Cut out another piece about 2.5 cm/1 in square and stamp out the centre of the square using the diamond-shaped biscuit cutter. Stick all the pieces on the phone with a little water, placing the diamond at the bottom of the phone and the square at the top.

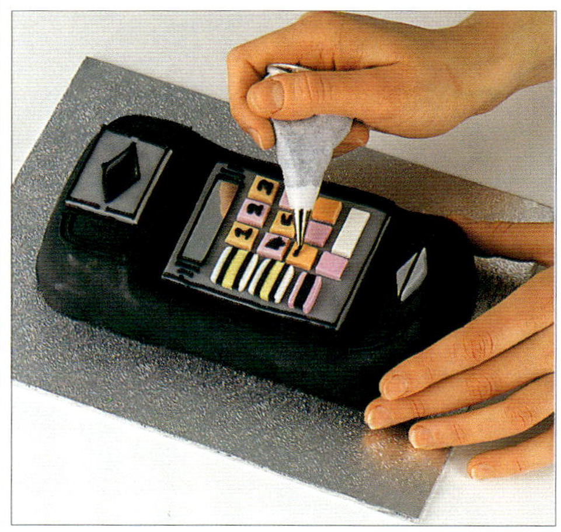

5 ▲ Position the sweets and a strip of kitchen foil for the dial pad. To make the glacé icing, mix the icing sugar with the water and black food colouring to a piping consistency. Fill the piping bag and pipe border lines around the edges of the phone and the grey pieces. Pipe the numbers on the keys.

6 Knead the reserved black sugarpaste icing and, with your hands, roll into a sausage shape for the aerial. Indent the top with a knife and position at the top of the phone to one side. Secure with a little water.

1
2
3
4
5
6
7
8
9
0
<Vol>

Terracotta Flowerpot

Ideal for celebrating a gardener's birthday or Mother's Day, this cake is baked in a pudding basin for the flowerpot shape and filled with a colourful arrangement of icing flowers and foliage.

INGREDIENTS

Serves 15

3-egg quantity Madeira Cake mix
175 g/6 oz jam
175 g/6 oz/½ quantity Butter Icing
2 tbsp apricot jam, warmed and sieved
550 g/1¼ lb/1⅔ x quantity Sugarpaste Icing
125 g/4 oz/⅙ quantity Royal Icing
dark orange, black, red, silver, green, purple and yellow food colourings
2 chocolate-flake bars, coarsely crushed

MATERIALS AND EQUIPMENT

1.1 L/2 pt pudding basin
string
paintbrush
thin green wire
23 cm/9 in round cake board

STORING

The finished cake can be kept in an airtight container for up to three days.

1 Preheat the oven to 160°C/325°F/Gas 3. Grease the basin, line the base with greaseproof paper and grease the paper. Spoon the cake mixture into the prepared basin and smooth the surface. Bake in the centre of the oven for 1¼ hours, or until a skewer inserted into the centre of the cake comes out clean. Cover with kitchen foil for the last 10 minutes if the top begins to brown. Turn the cake out on to a wire rack, peel off the lining paper and leave to cool.

2 Trim the top of the cake flat if it has domed. Cut the cake horizontally into three and fill with the jam and butter icing.

3 Cut out a shallow circle from the top of the cake, leaving a 1 cm/½ in rim around the edge.

4 ▲ Brush the outside of the cake and the rim with the apricot jam. Colour two-thirds of the sugarpaste icing dark orange. Measure the circumference of the cake at its widest part and the height, including a turnover for the rim, with string. On a work surface lightly dusted with icing sugar, roll out the icing to these measurements and use to cover the cake. Reserve any trimmings, wrapped in clear film. Leave the cake to dry for 12 hours.

5 ▲ Using the reserved trimmings, shape the decorations and handles for the flowerpot. Leave to dry on greaseproof paper. Sprinkle the crushed chocolate into the top of the flowerpot for soil.

6 Colour a small piece of the remaining sugarpaste icing a very pale orange, roll out into an oblong and fold over to make a seed bag. Colour a little of the icing black and make the seeds. Colour two more small pieces of icing red and silver and shape the trowel. Leave to dry on greaseproof paper.

7 ▲ Colour the remaining sugarpaste icing green, purple and a very small amount yellow. Mould individual flower petals with the purple icing and stick them together in flower shapes with royal icing. Roll out the yellow icing and cut out the flower centres with a small knife. Position in the centre of each flower with a small ball of yellow icing, securing with royal icing. Leave to dry on greaseproof paper.

8 ▲ Shape the leaves with the green icing using your fingers and mark the veins with a knife. Insert short pieces of wire up some of the stems so you can arrange them in the flowerpot. Leave to dry over the handle of a wooden spoon. Roll out any remaining green icing and snip to represent grass. Paint a design on the seed packet with food colourings.

9 Attach the dark-orange decorations to the flowerpot with royal icing. Arrange the leaves and flowers in the pot. Place the cake on the cake board and position the trowel, seed packet and grass around the outside. Remove the wire from the leaves before serving.

Ladybird Cake

Create a little animal magic and make this cake for a nature lover or gardener.

Ingredients

Serves 10–12

1½ x quantity lemon-flavoured Quick-Mix Sponge Cake mix
175 g/6 oz/½ quantity lemon-flavoured Butter Icing
2 tbsp apricot jam, warmed and sieved
4 tbsp lemon curd, warmed
1 kg/2¼ lb/3 x quantity Sugarpaste Icing
red, black and green food colourings
5 marshmallows
50 g/2 oz yellow marzipan
edible ladybird icing decorations (optional)

MATERIALS AND EQUIPMENT

1.1 L/2 pt ovenproof mixing bowl
28 cm/11 in round cake board
4 cm/1½ in and 5 cm/2 in plain round biscuit cutters
garlic press
2 pipe cleaners

STORING

The finished cake can be kept in a cool, dry place for three to four days.

1 Preheat the oven to 180°C/350°F/Gas 4. Grease the bowl, line the base with greaseproof paper and grease the paper. Spoon the cake mixture into the prepared bowl and smooth the surface. Bake in the centre of the oven for 55–60 minutes, or until a skewer inserted into the centre of the cake comes out clean. Leave the cake in the basin for 5 minutes, then turn out on to a wire rack, peel off the lining paper and leave to cool.

2 ▲ Cut the cake in half horizontally and sandwich together with the butter icing. Cut off about one-third of the cake and brush both pieces of cake with the lemon curd.

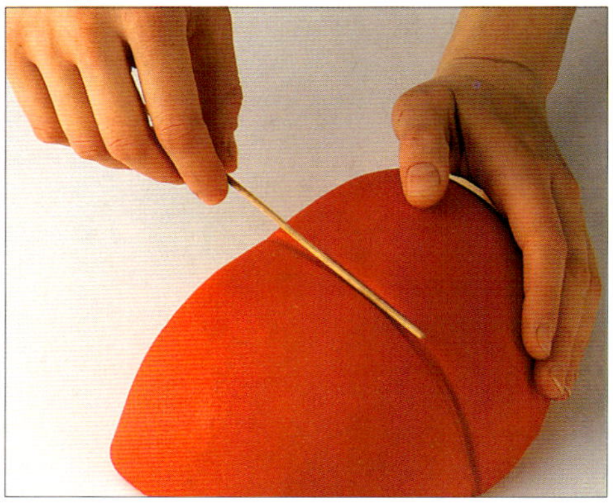

3 ▲ Colour a little less than half of the sugarpaste icing red. On a work surface lightly dusted with icing sugar, roll out to about a 5 mm/¼ in thickness and use to cover the large piece of cake. Using a wooden skewer or the back of a knife, make an indentation down the centre of the cake for the wing casings.

4 Colour just over half of the remaining sugarpaste icing black. Roll out three-quarters of the icing and use to cover the small piece of cake. Place the cakes on the cake board and assemble the ladybird's head and body, gently pressing them together to secure.

5 Roll out a little of the white sugarpaste icing and cut out two circles for the eyes, using the 5 cm/2 in round biscuit cutter. Stick in position with a little water.

6 ▲ Roll out the reserved black sugarpaste icing and cut out eight circles, using the 4 cm/1½ in round biscuit cutter. Stick one on each eye and stick the rest on to the body with a little water. Reserve the trimmings.

7 Colour the remaining sugarpaste icing green. To make the grass, break off small pieces and squeeze through the garlic press. Trim off with a knife. Brush the cake board with a little water and position the grass.

8 ▲ To make the marshmallow flowers, roll the marzipan into a 2 cm/¾ in long sausage shape and cut into slices. Set aside. On a work surface lightly dusted with icing sugar, flatten each marshmallow with a rolling pin. Snip around the marshmallows to make petals. Press a marzipan circle into the centre of each flower.

9 To make the antennae, paint the pipe cleaners with black food colouring and press a small ball of the reserved black sugarpaste icing on to the end of each one. Bend each pipe cleaner slightly and insert into the cake between the head and the body. Arrange the ladybird decorations around the cake, if using.

Easter Cake

This delicious, spicy Easter fruit cake is covered with ribbons and miniature eggs made from chocolate modelling paste.

INGREDIENTS
Serves 16
125 g/4 oz/½ cup soft margarine
125 g/4 oz/½ cup light brown sugar
3 eggs
175 g/6 oz/1½ cups plain flour
2 tsp ground mixed spice
400 g/14 oz/3½ cups mixed dried fruit
50 g/2 oz/¼ cup glacé cherries, chopped
50 g/2 oz/¼ cup hazelnuts
3 tbsp apricot jam, warmed and sieved
450 g/1 lb marzipan
brown food colouring

For the Chocolate Moulding Icing
125 g/4 oz plain or milk chocolate
2 tbsp liquid glucose
1 egg white
450 g/1 lb/3½ cups icing sugar

For the Chocolate Modelling Paste
50 g/2 oz plain chocolate
50 g/2 oz white chocolate
2 tbsp liquid glucose
pink food colouring

MATERIALS AND EQUIPMENT
1.5 L/2½ pt pudding basin
25 cm/10 in round gold cake board
clean piece of sponge
several squares of gold foil

STORING
The finished cake can be kept for up to four weeks.

1 Preheat the oven to 150°C/300°F/Gas 2. Grease the basin, line the base with greaseproof paper and grease the paper. Cream together the margarine and brown sugar and gradually add the eggs. Sift the remaining flour and the spice into the bowl and stir in the fruit and nuts.

2 Spoon the cake mixture into the prepared basin and smooth the surface. Bake in the centre of the oven for 1½ hours, or until a skewer inserted into the centre of the cake comes out clean. Turn the cake out on to a wire rack, peel off the lining paper and then leave to cool.

3 To make the chocolate moulding icing, break up the chocolate and place in a bowl with the glucose over a pan of hot water. Leave until melted, cool slightly then add the egg white. Gradually add the icing sugar, beating well after each addition, until too stiff to stir. Turn out on to a work surface lightly dusted with icing sugar and knead in the remaining sugar until stiff.

4 To make the modelling paste, melt the plain and white chocolate in separate bowls. Add half the glucose to the plain chocolate and mix to a stiff paste. Add some pink food colouring and the remaining glucose to the white chocolate and mix to a stiff paste. Wrap the pastes separately in clear film and chill until firm.

5 ▲ Cut a triangular wedge out of the cake. Place the cake on the board and brush with the apricot jam. On a work surface lightly dusted with icing sugar, roll out the marzipan and use to cover the cake, tucking the marzipan into the cut front section. Reserve the trimmings, wrapped in clear film.

6 On a work surface lightly dusted with cornflour, roll out the chocolate moulding icing and use to cover the cake. Cut two thin strips from the marzipan trimmings and stick on the inside edges of the cut-out wedge with a little water.

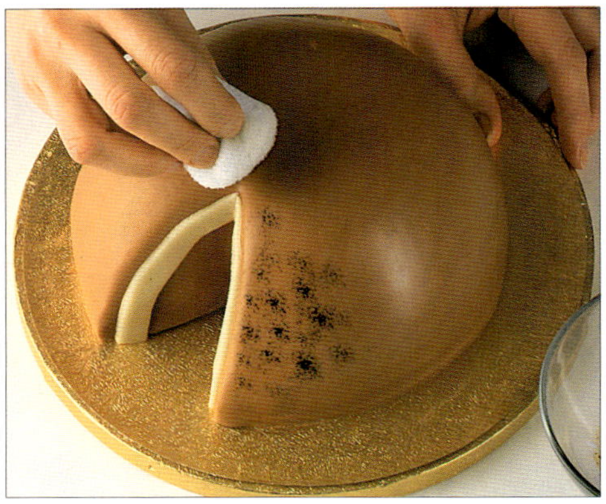

7 ▲ Thin the brown food colouring with water. Dip the sponge in the colour and pat over the surface of the icing. Leave to dry.

8 ▲ Lightly knead two-thirds of each of the modelling pastes and shape into 18 small eggs. Cover some of the eggs with gold foil and position them all inside the cut-out wedge. To make the bow, roll out the remaining modelling paste and cut two strips 2 cm/¾ in wide and 25 cm/10 in long from the dark paste and two strips 5 mm/¼ in wide and 20 cm/8 in long from the pink paste. Stick the pink strips to the dark ones with a little water. From these strips, cut two 13 cm/ 5 in lengths, press the ends together to form loops and secure to the cake. Secure two 8 cm/3 in lengths for ribbons ends and cover the centre of the bow with another small strip. Place a piece of crumpled kitchen foil under each strip until hardened.

Pizza Cake

Quick, easy and impressive – this deliciously sweet cake is a definite winner for pizza fanatics everywhere. Serve in small wedges.

Ingredients
Serves 8–10
1 quantity Quick-Mix Sponge Cake mix
350 g/12 oz/1 quantity Butter Icing
175 g/6 oz yellow marzipan
1 tbsp desiccated coconut
red and green food colouring
icing sugar
25 g/1 oz sugarpaste icing

MATERIALS AND EQUIPMENT
23 cm/9 in shallow round cake tin
25 cm/10 in pizza plate
cheese grater

STORING
The finished cake can be kept in the refrigerator for up to one week.

Tip

This recipe can be adapted easily for peperoni pizza fanatics. You will need an extra 175 g/6 oz/½ quantity of sugarpaste icing. Colour with brown food colouring, then roll out to a thick sausage shape with your hands. Slice thinly and add to the pizza cake as an extra topping ingredient.

1 Preheat the oven to 180°C/350°F/Gas 4. Grease the tin, line the base with greaseproof paper and grease the paper. Spoon the cake mixture into the prepared tin and smooth the surface. Bake in the centre of the oven for 40–50 minutes, or until a skewer inserted into the centre of the cake comes out clean. Leave the cake in the tin for 5 minutes, then turn out on to a wire rack, peel off the lining paper and leave to cool.

2 ▲ Colour the butter icing red. Place the cake on the pizza plate and spread evenly with the butter icing to represent the tomato topping. Leave a 1 cm/½ in border around the edge of the cake.

3 ▲ Knead the marzipan for a few minutes to soften it slightly, then grate it. Sprinkle over the red butter icing to represent cheese.

4 ▲ Colour the sugarpaste icing green. On a work surface lightly dusted with icing sugar, roll out to about a 5 mm/¼ in thickness. Cut out two leaf shapes freehand or cut around a real leaf. Mark the veins with a knife and add to the pizza cake for the garnish.

5 ▲ Place the desiccated coconut in a small bowl and colour with green food colouring. Scatter over the pizza cake to represent chopped herbs.

Christening Sampler

Instead of embroidering a sampler to welcome a new-born baby, why not make a sampler cake to celebrate?

Ingredients

Serves 30

20 cm/8 in square Rich Fruit Cake
3 tbsp apricot jam, warmed and sieved
450 g/1 lb marzipan
675 g/1½ lb/2 x quantity Sugarpaste Icing
brown, blue, pink, yellow, orange, green, cream and purple food colourings

MATERIALS AND EQUIPMENT

25 cm/10 in square cake board
paintbrush
small heart-shaped biscuit cutter

STORING

The finished cake can be kept in an airtight container for up to three weeks.

Tip

Using the same techniques described here, you can change the overall design by modelling different figures and choosing different colours. You could also make a larger name plaque and pipe the baby's christian name on to it.

1 Brush the cake with the apricot jam. On a work surface lightly dusted with icing sugar, roll out the marzipan and use to cover the cake. Leave to dry for 12 hours.

2 Take two-thirds of the sugarpaste icing and cut off one-third of this. Roll out the smaller portion to the size of the top of the cake. Brush the top of the cake with a little water and cover with the icing.

3 ▲ Colour the larger portion of sugarpaste icing brown and divide into four equal amounts. Roll out each to the width of the cake side and about 1 cm/½ in longer than the height. Brush each cake side with a little water, than press the brown icing into place, folding over the extra at the top to represent a picture frame. Cut off each corner at an angle to make a mitred join. Reserve any trimmings. Place the cake on the cake board.

4 ▲ Paint the sides with brown food colouring thinned with a little water to represent wood grain.

5 ▲ Take the remaining sugarpaste icing and colour small amounts yellow, orange, brown, purple, cream, and two shades each of blue, green and pink. Leave a little white. Use these colours to shape the ducks, teddy bear, bulrushes, water, apple-blossom branch and leaves. Roll out a small piece of pink icing and cut out a heart with the small heart-shaped biscuit cutter. Roll out a small piece of white icing and cut out the baby's initial. For the border, roll out strips of light blue and yellow icing and cut into oblongs and squares. Make small balls and squares from the purple icing.

For the apple blossom, gently work together the two pinks and the white sugarpaste to give a marbled effect. Shape the flowers and add a small white ball in the centre of each. Leave all the shapes to dry on greaseproof paper. Then stick all the decorations on to the cake with a little water.

6 ▲ With any leftover coloured icing, roll out long strips of icing with your hands to make the embroidery threads. Form them into loops and use small strips of brown icing to hold the threads together. Arrange around the base of the cake.

E

Rainbow Snake Cake

This wild cake doesn't need any cooking and its heavy texture and sweet flavour make it an excellent party cake. For a large party, double the ingredients to make an extra big snake.

INGREDIENTS

Serves 10–15

675 g/1½ lb white marzipan
red, yellow, orange, purple and green food colouring
1 quantity Truffle Cake mix
2 round red sweets
125 g/4 oz/2 cups desiccated coconut
jelly snake sweets (optional)

MATERIALS AND EQUIPMENT

5 cocktail sticks
25 cm/10 in round cake board
small piece of thin red card, cut into a tongue shape
small star-shaped biscuit cutter

STORING

The finished cake can be kept in an airtight container for up to four days.

1 ▲ Divide the marzipan into five equal portions and colour one portion red, one portion yellow, one orange, one purple and one green. Remove a tiny ball of icing from the green portion and reserve, wrapped in clear film.

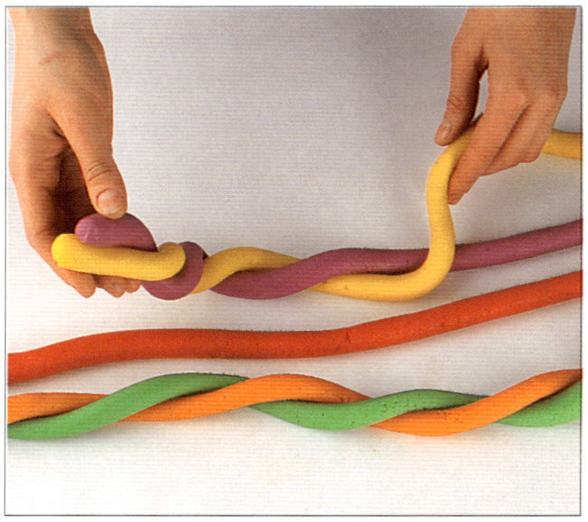

2 ▲ On a work surface lightly dusted with icing sugar, roll out each piece of marzipan into a sausage shape with your hands. They should be about 1 cm/½ in in diameter. Line up the sausage shapes next to one another and twist together the two outside sausages on either side. Firmly push the twists up against the middle sausage.

3 ▲ Roll out the marzipan, making short, sharp downward movements with the rolling pin. Starting at one end, roll out the marzipan a little at a time until about 15 cm/6 in wide. Keep the width even all along the snake. Carefully slide a heavy, sharp knife underneath the marzipan and flip the marzipan over.

4 ▲ Spoon the truffle mix evenly down the centre of the marzipan and mould into a sausage shape. Starting at one end, gather up the sides of the marzipan around the cake mixture and pinch the sides together firmly to seal. Shape the head and the tail.

5 ▲ Carefully coil the snake on to the cake board. Make a small incision for the mouth and insert the red card tongue. Roll out the reserved green marzipan and cut out two eyes using the small star biscuit cutter. Stick the eyes to the head with a little water and press the red sweets on top.

6 Place the desiccated coconut in a bowl and add a few drops of green food colouring and a little water. Stir until the coconut is flecked with green. Scatter around the snake on the cake board for grass.

Market Stall

An open-air market stall is the theme for this cake, bursting with colourful produce. Vary this design if you like, adding as wide a variety of fruit and vegetables as you can think of.

INGREDIENTS
Serves 30
30 cm/8 in square Rich Fruit Cake
3 tbsp apricot jam, warmed and sieved
900 g/2 lb marzipan
450 g/1 lb/1⅓ x quantity Sugarpaste Icing
125 g/4 oz/⅙ quantity Royal Icing
brown, green, red, orange, yellow, peach, purple, pink and black food colourings

MATERIALS AND EQUIPMENT
25 cm/10 in square cake board
piping bag fitted with a small plain nozzle
paintbrush

STORING
The finished cake can be kept in an airtight container for up to three weeks.

1 Slice 4 cm/1½ in off one side of the cake. Brush the cake pieces with the apricot jam. Take half of the marzipan and cut off one-quarter. On a work surface lightly dusted with icing sugar, roll out the small piece of marzipan and use to cover one long side, the top and the two short sides of the cake slice. Roll out the larger piece of marzipan and use to cover the large piece of cake. Leave to dry for 12 hours.

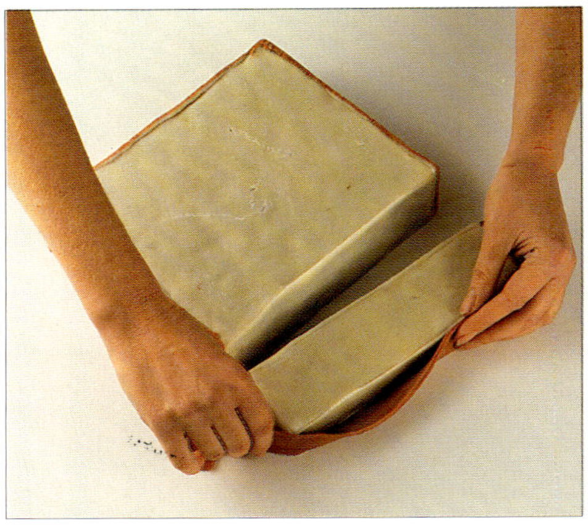

2 ▲ Colour half of the sugarpaste icing brown and other half green. Using three-quarters of the brown icing, cover three sides of the large cake (not the cut side), brushing the marzipan first with a little water. With the remaining brown icing, cover the marzipanned sides of the cake slice in the same way. With the brown trimmings, roll out and cut narrow dividers to fit the top of the cake. Leave to dry on greaseproof paper for several hours.

3 ▲ Place the large piece of cake on the cake board, with the cake slice in front to form a step. Stick the cakes together and to the cake board with a little royal icing.

4 ▲ Measure the length and width of the cake, including the step. Roll out the green sugarpaste icing to about 4 cm/1½ in wider and longer than the measured length. Brush the marzipan tops with a little water and cover the cakes loosely with the green icing. Allow the icing to fall naturally into folds over the edges of the cake. Leave to dry for several hours.

5 ▲ Take the remaining marzipan, reserve a little for the stall-holder, and colour the rest red, orange, yellow, green, brown, peach and purple. Use these colours to shape the fruits and vegetables. Add markings with a paintbrush and food colouring to the melons, peaches and potatoes. For the front of the stall, shape baskets and a potato sack out of different shades of brown. For the stall-holder, colour the reserved marzipan pink, purple, black and flesh-coloured and shape the head, body and arms separately. Stick the figure together with a little royal icing. Make the hands, the facial features and hair, and press on with a little water. Place a melon in the stall-holder's arms. Leave all the marzipan shapes to dry on greaseproof paper for several hours. Assemble on the cake just before serving, attaching the dividers, baskets and the stall-holder to the cake with royal icing.

Ghostly Spectre

This fun Hallowe'en cake is really simple to make, yet very effective. Use an 18 cm/7 in square cake of your choice, such as a citrus or chocolate-flavoured Madeira or a light fruit cake.

Ingredients

Serves 14

2 x quantity orange-flavoured Quick-Mix Sponge Cake mix
900 g/2 lb/2⅔ x quantity Sugarpaste Icing
black food colouring
350 g/12 oz/1 quantity Butter Icing

MATERIALS AND EQUIPMENT

18 cm/7 in square cake tin
300 ml/½ pt pudding basin
23 cm/9 in round cake board
paintbrush

STORING

The finished cake can be kept in a cool, dry place for up to four days.

1 Preheat the oven to 150°C/300°F/Gas 2. Grease the tin and the pudding basin, line the bases with greaseproof paper and grease the paper. Half-fill the basin with the cake mixture and turn the remainder into the tin. Smooth the surfaces and bake in the centre of the oven for 25 minutes for the basin and 1½ hours for the tin, or until a skewer inserted into the centre of the cakes comes out clean. Leave to cool for 5 minutes, then turn out on to a wire rack, peel off the lining paper and leave to cool.

2 Knead a little black food colouring into about one-eighth of the sugarpaste icing. On a work surface lightly dusted with icing sugar, roll out and use to cover the cake board.

3 ▲ Cut two small corners off the large cake and two larger wedges off the other two corners. Stand the large cake on the cake board and secure with a little butter icing. Halve the large cake trimmings and wedge around the base of the cake.

4 ▲ Secure the small cake to the top of the large cake with a little of the butter icing for the head. Secure the small cake trimmings on either side of the head with butter icing for the shoulders. Use the remaining butter icing to cover the cake completely.

5 ▲ On a work surface lightly dusted with icing sugar, roll out the remaining sugarpaste icing to an oval shape about 51 cm/20 in long and 30 cm/12 in wide. Position over the cake, letting the icing fall into folds around the sides. Gently smooth the icing over the top half of the cake.

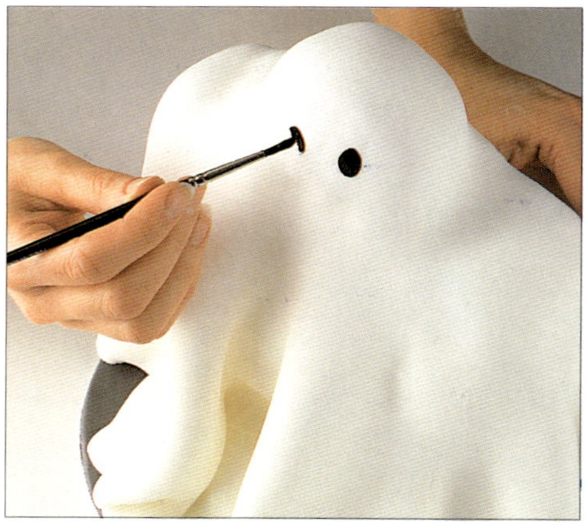

6 ▲ Using black food colouring, paint two oval eyes on to the head.

Artist's Box and Palette

Making cakes is an art in itself, and this cake proves it. It is the perfect celebration cake for artists of all ages.

INGREDIENTS

Serves 30

20 cm/8 in square Rich Fruit Cake
3 tbsp apricot jam, warmed and sieved
450 g/1 lb marzipan
800 g/$1\frac{3}{4}$ lb/$2\frac{1}{3}$ x quantity Sugarpaste Icing
125 g/4 oz/$\frac{1}{6}$ quantity Royal Icing
brown, yellow, blue, black, silver, orange, green and purple food colourings

MATERIALS AND EQUIPMENT

stiff paper for template
25 cm/10 in square cake board
paintbrush

STORING

The finished cake can be kept in an airtight container for up to three weeks.

1 Brush the cake with the apricot jam. On a work surface lightly dusted with icing sugar, roll out the marzipan and use to cover the cake. Leave to dry for 12 hours.

2 Make a template out of stiff paper in the shape of an artist's palette that will fit the top of the cake. Colour just less than one-quarter of the sugarpaste icing a pale brown. On a work surface lightly dusted with icing sugar, roll out to the size of the template and cut out the palette shape.

3 Colour about two-thirds of the remaining sugarpaste icing brown. Roll out, brush the marzipanned cake with a little water and cover the cake with the icing. Place the cake on the cake board and leave to dry for several hours.

4 ▲ With the remaining sugarpaste icing, leave half white and divide the remainder into seven equal portions. Colour these yellow, blue, black, silver, orange, green and purple. Shape the box handle with black icing and the box clips and paintbrush ferrules with silver icing. Shape the paintbrush bristles with orange icing and mark the hairs of the bristles with a knife. Shape the paintbrush handles in various colours and attach the handles, ferrules and bristles with a little royal icing. Leave all the pieces to dry on greaseproof paper for several hours.

5 ▲ Make two paint tubes from some of the white icing. Roll out an oblong shape for each one and then wrap these around 'sausages' of icing, sealing the edges with a little water. Paint lettering and coloured bands on the tubes with food colouring.

6 ▲ Shape the squeezed-out paint in various colours and attach one to each of the paint tubes with a little royal icing. Leave all the pieces to dry on greaseproof paper for several hours.

7 Using the remaining white icing, roll out two small rectangles for sheets of paper and brush on patterns with watered-down food colouring. Leave the sheets to dry on greaseproof paper for several hours.

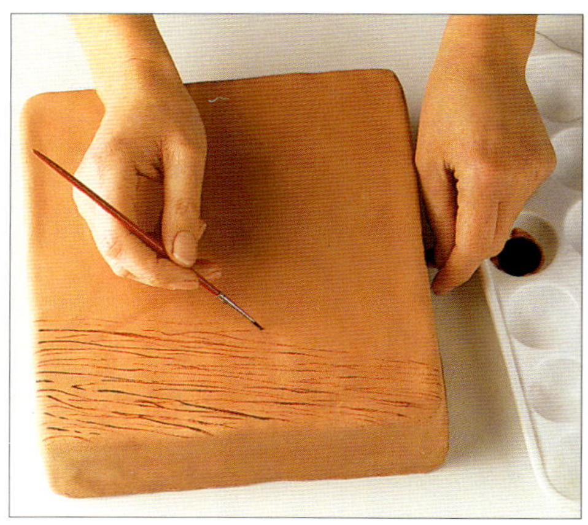

8 ▲ Paint wood markings on to the cake box with watered-down brown food colouring and leave to dry. To assemble the cake, attach the handles and clips to the front side of the box and the palette to the top of the cake with a little royal icing. Position the paintbrushes, tubes, squeezed-out paint and the sheets of paper on the cake and around the cake board.

Indian Elephant

Make this cake to celebrate a birthday, to wish someone 'Bon Voyage' or for a festive occasion. Be as colourful as you like with the decorations.

Ingredients

Serves 30

30 cm/12 in square Madeira Cake
675 g/1½ lb/2 x quantity Butter Icing
225 g/8 oz marzipan
black, green, yellow and pink food colourings
chocolate coins, silver balls, coloured and white chocolate buttons and two sweets
125 g/4 oz/2 cups desiccated coconut
2 tbsp apricot jam, warmed and sieved

MATERIALS AND EQUIPMENT

stiff paper for template
36 cm/14 in square cake board

STORING

The finished cake can be kept in an airtight container for up to three days.

1 ▲ Make a template from stiff paper in the shape of an elephant. Trace off the design from the photograph of the finished cake and enlarge by 150%, if wished. Place the template on top of the cake and cut out the shape with a sharp knife. Position the cake on the cake board.

2 ▲ Colour the butter icing pale grey using the black food colouring. Cover the top and sides of the cake with the icing and swirl with a palette knife.

3 ▲ Using a cocktail stick and black food colouring, swirl black highlights into the icing.

4 ▲ On a work surface lightly dusted with icing sugar, roll out half of the marzipan and cut out shapes for the elephant's tusk, headpiece and blanket. Place them in position on the cake. Colour the remaining marzipan green, yellow and pink. Roll out thinly and cut out patterns for the blanket, headpiece, trunk and tail. Roll small balls of yellow and pink marzipan to make the ankle bracelets.

5 ▲ Place all the decorations, including the silver balls, chocolate coins and coloured chocolate buttons, in position. Cut the white chocolate buttons in half and use for the toenails and the sweets for the eye.

6 Mix a little green food colouring into the coconut. Brush the cake board with a little apricot jam and sprinkle with the coconut for grass.

The Beautiful Present Cake

For a best friend, mother, grandmother, aunt or sister, this beautiful cake can mark any special occasion.

INGREDIENTS

Serves 15–20

2 x quantity Quick-Mix Sponge Cake mix

350 g/12 oz/1 quantity Butter Icing

4 tbsp apricot jam, warmed and sieved

575 g/1¼ lb marzipan

900 g/2 lb/2⅔ x quantity Sugarpaste Icing

purple and pink food colourings

MATERIALS AND EQUIPMENT

23 cm/9 in square cake tin

25 cm/10 in square cake board

heart-shaped biscuit cutter

small round fluted cutter

pink food-colouring pen

STORING

The finished cake can be kept in a cool, dry place for up to three or four days.

1 Preheat the oven to 180°C/350°F/Gas 4. Grease the tin, line the base and sides with greaseproof paper and grease the paper. Spoon the cake mixture into the prepared tin and smooth the surface. Bake in the centre of the oven for 1¼–1½ hours, or until a skewer inserted into the centre of the cake comes out clean. Leave the cake in the tin for 5 minutes, then turn out on to a wire rack, peel off the lining paper and leave to cool.

2 Cut the cake in half horizontally and spread with the butter icing. Sandwich the cake together and place in the centre of the cake board. Brush the cake with the apricot jam. On a work surface lightly dusted with icing sugar, roll out the marzipan to about a 5 mm/¼ in thickness and use to cover the cake.

3 Colour about five-eighths of the sugarpaste icing purple. On a work surface lightly dusted with icing sugar, roll out and use to cover the cake.

4 ▲ Using the heart-shaped cutter, stamp out hearts from the sugarpaste icing to make an even pattern. Remove the hearts with a small, sharp knife, taking care not to damage the surrounding sugarpaste. Knead the hearts together and reserve, wrapped in clear film.

5 ▲ Colour the remaining sugarpaste icing pink and roll out to a 5 mm/¼ in thickness. Using the heart-shaped cutter, cut out as many hearts as you need to fill the spaces left by the purple ones, re-rolling the pink sugarpaste as necessary. Reserve the trimmings, wrapped in clear film. Carefully insert the pink hearts into the spaces.

6 Roll out the reserved pink sugarpaste and cut into three strips about 2 cm/¾ in wide and 30 cm/12 in long. Lay one strip across the centre of the cake and another at right angles across the centre, brushing the strips with a little water to secure. Reserve the trimmings.

7 ▲ Divide the remaining strip of pink sugarpaste into quarters and arrange in the centre of the cake to make a bow. Secure with a little water and reserve the trimmings.

8 ▲ Roll out the remaining purple and pink sugarpaste and cut out two rounds from each colour using the small round fluted cutter. With a cocktail stick, carefully roll out the edges of the rounds to make frilled petals. Use a little of the purple sugarpaste to make two tiny balls for the flower centres. Assemble the flowers, securing with a little water and position on the cake. Knead the pink and purple trimmings together, roll out and cut out a name tag. Write a message or a name using the food-colouring pen and position on the cake.

JANE

Valentine's Box of Chocolates

This special cake would also make a wonderful gift for Mother's Day. Choose your favourite chocolates to go inside.

INGREDIENTS

Serves 10–12

$1\frac{1}{2}$ x quantity chocolate-flavour Quick-Mix Sponge Cake mix
275 g/10 oz yellow marzipan
8 tbsp apricot jam, warmed and sieved
900 g/2 lb/$2\frac{2}{3}$ x quantity Sugarpaste Icing
red food colouring
225 g/8 oz/about 16–20 hand-made chocolates

MATERIALS AND EQUIPMENT

heart-shaped cake tin
23 cm/9 inch square piece of stiff card
23 cm/9 inch square cake board
piece of string
small heart-shaped cutter
length of ribbon and a pin
petits fours *cases*

STORING

The finished cake can be kept in a cool, dry place for up to three days.

1 Preheat the oven to 180°C/350°F/Gas 4. Grease the tin, line the base with greaseproof paper and grease the paper. Spoon the cake mixture into the tin and smooth the surface. Bake in the centre of the oven for 45–50 minutes, or until a skewer inserted into the centre of the cake comes out clean. Leave the cake in the tin for about 5 minutes, then turn out on to a wire rack, peel off the lining paper and leave to cool completely.

2 ▲ Place the cake on the piece of card and draw around it with a sharp pencil. Cut the heart shape out of the card and set aside. This will be used as the support for the box lid.

3 ▲ Using a large, sharp knife, cut through the cake horizontally just below where the cake starts to dome. Carefully lift the top section on to the heart-shaped card and place the bottom section on the cake board.

4 Use the piece of string to measure around the outside of the bottom section of cake.

5 ▲ On a work surface lightly dusted with icing sugar, roll out the marzipan into a long sausage shape to the same length as the string. Place the marzipan sausage on the cake around the outside edge. Brush both sections of the cake evenly with apricot jam.

6 Colour the sugarpaste icing red and cut off about one-third. Cut another portion from the larger piece, about 50 g/2 oz in weight. Wrap these two portions separately in clear film and set aside. On a work surface lightly dusted with icing sugar, roll out the icing to a 35 cm/14 inch square and use it to cover the bottom section of cake.

7 ▲ Stand the lid on a raised surface, such as a glass or bowl. Roll out the reserved one-third of sugarpaste icing to a 30 cm/12 inch square and cover the lid section of the cake. Roll out the remaining piece of icing and stamp out small hearts with the cutter. Stick them around the edge of the lid with a little water. Tie the ribbon in a bow and secure on top of the lid with the pin. Carefully lift the top section on to the heart-shaped card and place the bottom section on the cake board.

8 Place the chocolates in the *petits fours* cases and arrange in the bottom section of the cake. Position the lid, placing it slightly off centre, to reveal the chocolates inside. Remove the ribbon and pin before serving.

The Beehive

The perfect cake for an outdoors spring or summer party. Take the bees along separately on their wires and insert them into the cake at the picnic.

INGREDIENTS

Serves 8–10

1 quantity Quick-Mix Sponge Cake mix
900 g/2 lb yellow marzipan
5 tbsp apricot jam, warmed and sieved
black food colouring
25 g/1 oz sugarpaste icing

MATERIALS AND EQUIPMENT

900 g/2 lb pudding basin
23 cm/9 inch fluted or round cake board
20 cm/8 inch square of rice paper
florist's wire covered in florist's tape

STORING

The finished cake can be kept in a cool, dry place for up to two days.

1 Preheat the oven to 180°C/350°F/Gas 4. Grease and flour the pudding basin. Spoon in the cake mixture and smooth the surface. Bake in the centre of the oven for 40–45 minutes or until a skewer inserted into the centre of the cake comes out clean. Leave the cake in the basin for about 5 minutes, then turn out on to a wire rack and leave to cool completely.

2 Cut off about 175 g/6 oz of marzipan and set aside, wrapped in clear film. Knead the remainder on a work surface lightly dusted with icing sugar, then roll it out into a long, thin sausage shape. If it breaks when it gets too long, make more than one sausage. Place the cake, dome side up, on the cake board and brush evenly with apricot jam.

3 ▲ Starting at the back of the base, coil the marzipan sausage around the cake, keeping it neat and tight all the way to the top. Any joins that have to be made should be placed at the back of the cake.

4 ▲ Using a small, sharp knife, cut an arched doorway at the front of the cake. Remove the cut-out section and cut away some of the inside cake to make a hollow. Brush the crumbs away from the doorway.

5 ▲ To make six bees, divide the reserved marzipan in half and colour one portion black. Set aside a cherry-sized ball of black marzipan, and wrap in clear film. Divide both the black and the yellow marzipan into 12 small balls. To make a bee, pinch together two balls of each colour, alternately placed. Stick them together with a little water, if necessary. Cut the rice paper into six pairs of rounded wings, then stick them to the bees with a tiny drop of water.

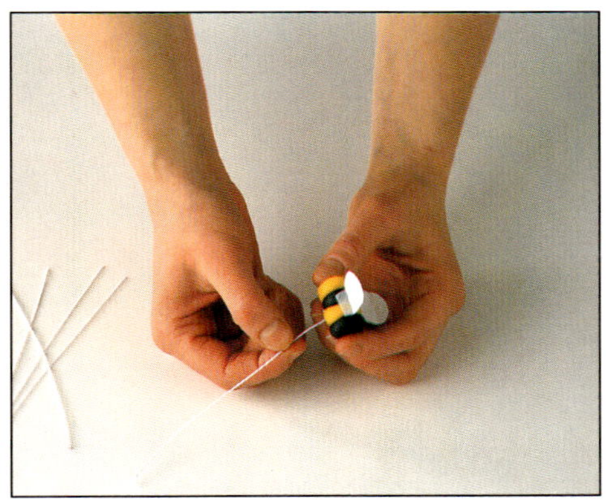

6 ▲ Use the reserved black marzipan and sugarpaste icing to make the facial features. Then cut the florist's wire into various lengths and then use it to pierce the bees from underneath. Once secure, press the other end of the wire into the cake in various places. The wires must be removed before serving.

Strawberry Cake

A summer-time cake or for someone who's simply mad about strawberries!

Ingredients
Serves 10–12
1 quantity Quick-Mix Sponge Cake mix
650 g/1 lb 7oz marzipan
green, red and yellow food colourings
caster sugar, to dredge

MATERIALS AND EQUIPMENT
900 g/2 lb heart-shaped tin
30 cm/12 inch round cake board
icing smoother

STORING
The finished cake can be kept in a cool, dry place for up to two days.

Tip

You can also sandwich the cake with a half quantity of strawberry-flavour Butter Icing before brushing it with apricot jam for extra flavour! Use a long, serrated knife and cut the cake horizontally into two layers.

1 Preheat the oven to 180°C/350°F/ Gas 4. Grease the heart-shaped tin, line the base with greaseproof paper and grease the paper. Spoon in the cake mixture and smooth the surface. Bake in the centre of the oven for 35–40 minutes or until a skewer inserted into the centre of the cake comes out clean.

2 Leave in the tin for about 5 minutes, then turn out on to a wire rack, peel off the lining paper and leave to cool completely.

3 ▲ Cut off about 175 g/6 oz of the marzipan and colour it green. Brush the cake board with a little apricot jam, then roll out the green marzipan on the work surface lightly dusted with icing sugar and use to cover the cake board. Trim the edges. Use an icing smoother to make the marzipan as flat and as smooth as possible.

4 ▲ Evenly brush the remaining apricot jam over the top and sides of the cake. Position the cake on the cake board. Cut off about 275 g/10 oz of the remaining marzipan and colour it red. Roll it out to about 5 mm/¼ inch thick and use to cover the cake, smoothing down the sides and edges. Trim the edges. Use the handle of a teaspoon to indent the strawberry evenly and lightly all over.

5 To make the stalk, cut off another 175 g/6 oz of marzipan and colour it bright green. Cut it in half and roll out one portion into a 10 x 15 cm/4 x 6 inch rectangle. Use a sharp knife to cut 'V' shapes out of the rectangle, leaving a 2.5 cm/1 inch border across the top, to form the calyx. Position this on the cake, curling and moving the sections to make them look more realistic.

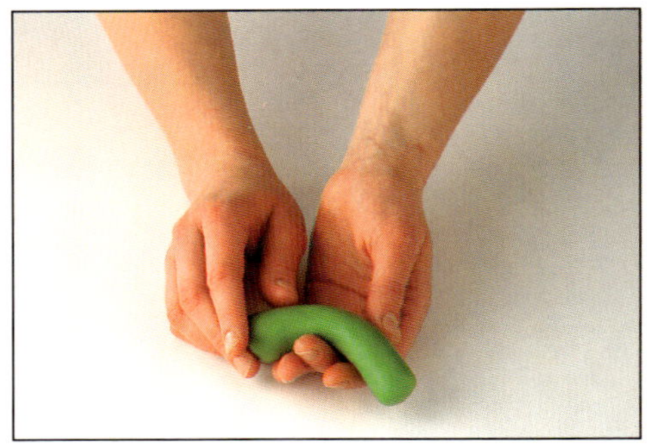

6 ▲ Roll the other half of the green marzipan in your hands into a sausage shape about 13 cm/5 inches long. Bend it slightly, then position it on the cake to form the stalk.

7 ▲ To make the strawberry seeds, colour the remaining marzipan yellow. Pull off tiny pieces about the size of an apple pip and roll them into little tear-shaped seeds. Place them in the indentations all over the strawberry. Dust the cake and board with sifted caster sugar.

An Apple Tree

For this unusual centrepiece, choose whichever fruit you prefer. You could make the apples green instead of red, or have a mixture of red and green apples or golden pears.

Ingredients

Serves 10–12

1 quantity chocolate-flavour Quick-Mix Sponge Cake mix
1 quantity chocolate-flavour Swiss Roll, baked and rolled with ¼ quantity chocolate-flavour Butter Icing
¼ quantity chocolate-flavour Butter Icing
½ quantity Butter Icing, coloured green with food colouring
225 g/8 oz marzipan
red and green food colouring
green-coloured desiccated coconut (see Puppies in Love, step 4)
tiny fresh flowers, to decorate (optional)

Materials and Equipment

450 g/1 lb fluted round cake tin or pudding basin
15cm/6 inch round cake board
wooden cocktail stick
2 x 30 cm/12 inch lengths of florist's wire
florist's tape
greaseproof paper piping bag
leaf nozzle

Storing

The finished cake can be kept in a cool, dry place for up to a day.

Tip

To stand the tree up at a slight angle, you can cut out a template of thick card from around the un-iced cake. Then decorate the cake on the card and prop it up on a small block of wood. Alternatively, decorate the cake flat on a cake board.

1 Preheat the oven to 180°F/350°C/Gas 4. Grease and flour the tin or pudding basin. Spoon in the cake mixture and smooth the surface. Bake in the centre of the oven for 35–40 minutes or until a skewer inserted into the centre of the cake comes out clean. Leave in the tin for about 5 minutes, then turn out on to a wire rack and leave to cool.

2 ▲ Arrange the Swiss roll on the card template or cake board (see Tip), trimming it, if necessary. Spread the chocolate butter icing over the tree trunk, making swirls. Use about three-quarters of the green butter icing for the top of the tree, making it peak and swirl. Position on top of the tree trunk.

3 ▲ Colour about 25 g/1 oz of the marzipan green. Colour the remainder red, then roll it into cherry-size balls. Roll the green marzipan into tiny sausage shapes to make the stalks and leaves. Use the cocktail stick to make tiny holes in the tops of the apples, then insert the stalks and leaves.

4 ▲ Twist the florist's tape around the florist's wire, then cut it into 7.5 cm/3 inch lengths. Press the lengths of wire through the apples, bending the ends so the apples cannot fall off when hanging. Press the hanging apples into the tree, reserving the extra apples to scatter around the bottom.

5 ▲ Use the remaining green butter icing to fill the piping bag. Practise piping the leaves on a piece of greaseproof paper before piping leaves all over the tree top. Scatter the green desiccated coconut around the base of the tree and pipe a few extra leaves. Add a few tiny fresh flowers for effect, if liked. The wires must be removed from the cake before serving.

Banjo Cake

The perfect cake for the musician in the family. It can be set on a large tray or you could cut out card for a template to support it.

Ingredients

Serves 15–20

2 x quantity Quick-Mix Sponge Cake mix
115 g/4 oz/6 tbsp seedless raspberry jam, warmed
900 g/2 lb/2⅔ x quantity Sugarpaste Icing
lime green food colouring
2 coloured sticks of liquorice
4 round lollipops
4 tbsp coloured vermicelli
piece of flat green liquorice
2 long red liquorice bootlaces
4 long green liquorice bootlaces
sugarpaste stars, or other decoration

MATERIALS AND EQUIPMENT

20 cm/8 inch round cake tin
18 cm/7 inch square cake tin
54 cm/21 inch stiff card
5 cm/2 inch round cutter
ribbon and 2 pins, for the strap

STORING

The finished cake can be made up to two days in advance and kept in a cool, dry place.

1 Preheat the oven to 180°C/350°F/Gas 4. Grease the tins, line the bases with greaseproof paper and grease the paper. Divide the cake mixture between the two tins and smooth the surfaces. Bake for 35–40 minutes, or until firm to the touch. Turn out on to a wire rack, peel off the lining paper and leave to cool completely.

2 ▲ Cut off the dome from the round cake and place bottom side up on the work surface. Cut the dome off the square cake, then cut in half down the middle. Place the cakes together to form the banjo shape, then draw around them on to stiff card. Cut out the shape to make the reinforcing template.

3 ▲ Use the cutter to stamp out a shallow hollow from the centre of the round cake. Place both cakes on the card base and brush with the raspberry jam. Colour the sugarpaste icing with the lime green food colouring and roll out on a work surface lightly dusted with icing sugar to about a 62 x 25 cm/25 x 10 inch rectangle. Use to cover the banjo in one piece, easing the icing into the hollow and down the sides. Make finger indentations along the length of the neck of the banjo.

4 Cut off four 1 cm/½ inch pieces from one of the sticks of liquorice and press into the cake at the top end of the neck to resemble stays for the strings. Place the remains of the liquorice stick with the other one at the base of the banjo, next to the hollow. Dip the lollipops in water, then in the coloured vermicelli to coat. Press the lollipops into the sides of the neck end so that they line up with the pieces of liquorice stick forming the stays.

5 Place the two flat pieces of liquorice side by side at the base, securing with a little water. Cut the red liquorice bootlace into about 5 cm/2 inch lengths and position them along the length of the banjo neck, in the indentations. Use a little water to stick them in place, if necessary.

6 ▲ Dip the green liquorice bootlaces in hot water, then stretch and smooth each one until perfectly straight. Wrap one end of the banjo strings around the liquorice sticks at the top of the neck end and bring the other ends down so they meet together on the flat liquorice at the rounded end. Secure the ribbon strap with pins pushed through each end and into the cake. Decorate the banjo with sugarpaste stars and more coloured vermicelli, if wished. The pins *must* be removed from the cake before serving.

A Basket of Flowers

This attractive arrangement of flowers looks very impressive, yet none of the stages are very difficult to do.

INGREDIENTS
Serves 10–12
1½ x quantity orange-flavour Quick-Mix Sponge Cake mix
2 x quantity orange-flavour Butter Icing
orange, yellow, pink, red, black and green food colourings
900 g/2 lb/2⅔ x quantity Sugarpaste Icing

MATERIALS AND EQUIPMENT
deep 20 cm/8 inch round cake tin
20 cm/8 inch oval cake board
3 greaseproof paper piping bags
small round nozzle
small straight serrated nozzle
selection of small flower and leaf cutters
30 cm/12 inch piece of strong wire, bent to a curve with the two ends about 20 cm/8 inch apart
plasticine

STORING
The finished cake can be kept in a cool, dry place for up to three days.

1 Preheat the oven to 180°C/350°F/Gas 4. Grease the cake tin, line the base with greaseproof paper and grease the paper. Spoon the cake mixture into the prepared tin and smooth the surface. Bake in the centre of the oven for 45–50 minutes or until a skewer inserted into the centre of the cake comes out clean. Turn out on to a wire rack, peel off the lining paper and leave the cake to cool completely.

2 Place the butter icing in a bowl and beat in a few drops of orange food colouring. Cut the cake in half down the middle and spread the bottom of one half with a little of the butter icing. Sandwich with the other half of the cake, base to base.

3 Cut a thin slice from the bottom of the sandwiched cake. Place a little butter icing on the cake board and position the cake on top, with the large flat surface facing upwards.

4 ▲ Spread more of the butter icing over the cut surface of the cake, covering right up to the edges.

5 Place about 4 tbsp of the butter icing in a small bowl and colour it with a little more orange food colouring to make it a slightly deeper colour. Fit a paper piping bag with the small round nozzle and fill with the deeper orange butter icing. Pipe a decorative border around the top edge of the basket.

6 Fit the clean round nozzle into a fresh paper piping bag and fill with the lighter orange butter icing. Pipe vertical lines about 2.5 cm/1 inch apart all around the sides of the cake. Fit a fresh paper piping bag with the serrated nozzle and fill with more orange butter icing. Starting at the top of the cake pipe short lines alternately crossing over, then stopping at the vertical lines to give a basket-weave effect.

7 Divide the sugarpaste icing into two. Cut one of the portions in half and colour one half pale orange and the other half darker orange. Wrap these separately in clear film and set aside. Divide the other portion of sugarpaste icing into five equal amounts. Colour these yellow, pink, red, black and green.

8 ▲ Roll out the yellow, pink and red portions on a work surface lightly dusted with icing sugar and use the flower cutters to stamp out the flower shapes. Place some of the flowers in an egg carton so they dry curved and place others on a baking sheet so they dry flat. Leave the flowers for at least 2 hours to dry out.

9 Use a little of the orange, yellow and black sugarpaste icings to roll into tiny balls to make the centres of the flowers, sticking them in place with a little water.

10 Roll out the green icing and use a leaf-shaped cutter to stamp out leaves, indenting them with a small sharp knife and curling them slightly to give them more interest. Place them on the baking sheet to dry out.

11 When dry, arrange the flowers and leaves attractively on top of the basket and the cake board.

12 ▲ To make the handle for the basket, roll the two shades of orange sugarpaste icing into balls about the size of small marbles. Thread these alternately on to the curved piece of wire, leaving about 2.5 cm/1 inch of wire exposed at each end. Stand the handle in two pieces of plasticine stuck to the work surface or a baking sheet, supported by a tea towel pushed under the handle to stop it falling over. Leave to dry for at least 2 hours. To finish, gently press the handle into the cake, pushing it in until secure.

Children's Party Cakes

A special cake is the perfect way to celebrate a child's birthday or other important event. Filled with novelty and fun cake ideas for children of all ages – dinosaurs, monsters, clowns, caterpillars, puppies and many, many more – the cakes in this chapter will make every kid's party an instant success.

Elephant Cake

Any medium-sized roasting tin will work for this cake, but one with rounded edges is preferable as this improves the finished result.

INGREDIENTS

Serves 10–12

1½ x quantity lemon-flavour Quick-Mix Sponge Cake mix
1 quantity lemon-flavour Butter Icing (optional)
8 tbsp apricot jam, warmed and sieved
900 g/2 lb/2⅔ x quantity Sugarpaste Icing
pink, blue and grey food colourings

MATERIALS AND EQUIPMENT

30 x 23 cm/12 x 9 inch roasting tin
18 cm/7 inch round cake tin, or card, to use as a template
40 cm/16 inch round cake board, with a support for the trunk, or 40 x 25 cm/16 x 10 inch square cake board (optional)
wooden cocktail stick
medium-size round cutter (optional)
bow made from pretty ribbon
pin

STORING

The finished cake can be kept in a cool, dry place for up to two days.

1 Preheat the oven to 180°C/350°F/ Gas 4. Grease the roasting tin, line the base and sides with greaseproof paper and grease the paper. Spoon in the cake mixture and smooth the surface. Bake in the centre of the oven for 45–50 minutes or until a skewer inserted into the centre of the cake comes out clean. Leave in the tin for about 5 minutes, then turn out on to a wire rack, peel off the lining paper and leave to cool completely.

2 ▲ Place the cake, dome side down, on the work surface and position the template in the centre on the flat surface. Use a sharp knife to cut around the template, holding it steady and firm as you cut. Lift out the cut-out circle, keeping the outside piece intact.

3 ▲ Use the template to cut out the elephant's trunk. Place the template close to one edge of the short side of the remaining cake and cut out a crescent shape. Cut off one end of the crescent to make the elephant's mouth. Cut off the other end of the cake, just past the rounded corners, to make the ear. Discard the two small, middle sections of cake. Cut horizontally through the face, ear, trunk and mouth sections of the cake, then sandwich them back together with lemon butter icing, if you are using it.

4 ▲ Assemble the cake on a board or directly on the table. Place the ear piece on one side of the round face, then place the flat edge of the trunk section up against the face, opposite the ear. Place the mouth section in the space between the trunk and the face. Brush the whole surface with jam.

5 Cut off about 50 g/2 oz of sugarpaste icing and set aside, wrapped in clear film. Cut off another 175 g/6 oz of sugarpaste icing and colour it pink, and 15 g/½ oz and colour it blue. Set aside, wrapped in clear film. Colour the remaining icing grey, cut off about 75 g/3 oz and set aside. Dust the work surface with icing sugar then roll out the larger portion of grey icing into a 50 x 25 cm/20 x 10 inch rectangle. Use this to cover the entire cake. Smooth down the sides and edges, snipping with scissors or cutting the icing in the places where it overlaps. Trim the edges.

6 To make the ear piece, roll out the reserved portion of grey icing into a 20 x 10 cm/8 x 4 inch rectangle, then roll it in small sections with the cocktail stick, to give a ruffled effect (see Teddy Bear Christening cake, step 7). Lay this section on top of the ear, slightly off centre. Cut off about 150 g/5 oz of the pink icing and roll it out to a slightly smaller rectangle, then repeat the ruffling process with the cocktail stick. Lay this piece on top of the grey ruffle.

7 Roll out the reserved blue and white icings and cut out the eye parts, using the round cutter, if preferred. Stick in place with a little water, placing a small round ball of the remaining pink icing in the centre. Roll out the remaining pink icing and cut out a triangular piece for the mouth. Shape the remaining white icing into a tusk and then stick them both in place with a little water. Finally, position the bow, securing in place with the pin, which must be removed before serving the cake.

Clown Cake

Made from a clown-shaped tin, this is a quick and easy cake to make and decorate. Choose your own nozzle shapes for the designs, following the contours of the cake.

INGREDIENTS

Serves 10–15

1½ x quantity Quick-Mix Sponge Cake mix
115 g/4 oz/⅓ quantity Sugarpaste Icing
2 x quantity Butter Icing
yellow, red, pink and blue food colourings
small coloured sweets, for the features

MATERIALS AND EQUIPMENT

900 g/2 lb clown-shaped cake tin
25 x 30 cm/10 x 12 inch cake board
greaseproof paper piping bags
small star, small plain and large star nozzles
small party hat

STORING

The finished cake can be stored in an airtight container in a cool, dry place for up to two days.

1 ▲ Preheat the oven to 180°C/350°F/Gas 4. Grease the cake tin generously. Spoon in the cake mixture and smooth the surface. Bake in the centre of the oven for 45–50 minutes or until a skewer inserted into the centre of the cake comes out clean. Leave for 5 minutes before turning out on to a wire rack to cool.

2 ▲ To make a template for the clown's face, hold a piece of greaseproof paper firmly over the face on the cooled tin. Draw around the outline using a pencil and cut around the shape.

3 ▲ On a work surface lightly dusted with icing sugar, roll out the sugarpaste icing to about 5 mm/¼ inch thick, then place the greaseproof paper template on top. Use a small sharp knife to cut around the outline of the template. Place the cut-out sugarpaste on a baking sheet and cover with clear film.

4 To colour the butter icing, place about one-third of the icing in a small mixing bowl and colour it yellow. Place another third in another mixing bowl and colour it red. Divide the remaining butter icing between two small bowls and colour one pink and the other blue.

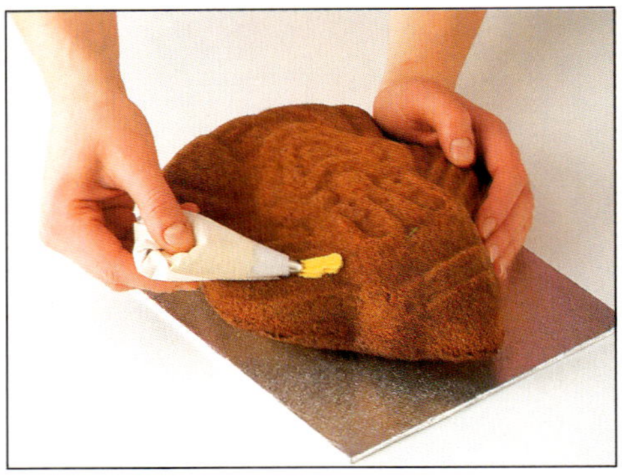

5 ▲ Place the cake on the cake board. Fit a small star nozzle in a paper piping bag and fill it with the yellow butter icing. Use to pipe along the contours of the hair on the clown's head. Place the cut-out sugarpaste template in position on the cake, then place a small plain nozzle in another piping bag and fill with the red butter icing. Use it to pipe decoratively around the neck and torso area of the clown. Pipe around the mouth, then change the nozzle to a large star shape and pipe in the nose.

6 Place a small star nozzle in another small piping bag and fill with the pink icing. Use to pipe a star border around the edges of the sugarpaste template. Place a large star nozzle in another piping bag and fill with the blue icing. Use to pipe in the buttons and the clown's eyes. Place the sweets in the centres of the eyes, nose and buttons. Position the hat.

Spiders' Web Cake

A spooky cake for any occasion, fancy dress or otherwise. Put as many spiders as you like on the cake, but any leftover ones can be put on the children's plates or arranged to look like they're crawling all over the table.

INGREDIENTS

Serves 6–8

1 quantity lemon-flavour Quick-Mix Sponge Cake mix
1 quantity lemon-flavour Glacé Icing
yellow and black food colourings

For the Spiders

115 g/4 oz/4 squares plain chocolate, broken into pieces
150 ml/¼ pint/⅔ cup double cream
3 tbsp ground almonds
cocoa powder, for dusting
chocolate vermicelli
2-3 liquorice wheels, sweet centres removed
15 g/½ oz Sugarpaste Icing

MATERIALS AND EQUIPMENT

900 g/2 lb fluted dome-shaped tin or pudding basin
20 cm/8 inch cake board
small greaseproof paper piping bag
wooden skewer

STORING

The finished cake can be kept in a cool, dry place for up to two days.

1 Preheat the oven to 180°C/350°F/Gas 4. Grease and flour the fluted dome-shaped tin or pudding basin. Spoon in the cake mixture and smooth the surface. Bake in the centre of the oven for 35–40 minutes or until a skewer inserted into the centre of the cake comes out clean.

2 ▲ Leave the cake in the tin for about 5 minutes, then turn out on to a wire rack and leave to cool completely.

3 Place about 3 tbsp of the glacé icing in a small bowl. Stir a few drops of yellow food colouring into the larger quantity of icing and colour the small quantity black. Place the cake on the cake board, dome side up, and pour over the yellow icing, allowing it to run, unevenly, down the sides. Fill the piping bag with the black icing. Seal the bag and snip the end, making a small hole for the nozzle.

4 ▲ Starting on the top of the cake, in the centre, drizzle the black icing round the cake in a spiral, keeping the line as continuous and as evenly spaced as possible. Use the wooden skewer to draw through the icing, downwards from the centre at the top of the cake, to make a web effect. Wipe away the excess icing with a damp cloth, then allow the icing to set at room temperature.

5 To make the spiders, place the chocolate and cream in a small, heavy-based saucepan and heat gently, stirring frequently, until the chocolate melts. Transfer the mixture to a small mixing bowl and allow to cool.

6 ▲ When cool, beat the mixture for about 10 minutes or until thick and pale. Stir in the ground almonds, then chill until firm enough to handle. Dust your hands with a little cocoa, then make a ball the size of a large walnut out of the chocolate mixture. Roll each ball in chocolate vermicelli until evenly coated. Repeat this process until all the mixture is used.

7 ▲ To make the spiders' legs, cut the liquorice into 4 cm/1½ inch lengths. Make small cuts into the sides of each spider, then insert the legs. To make the spiders' eyes, pull off a piece of sugarpaste icing about the size of a hazelnut and colour it with black food colouring. Use the white icing to make tiny balls and the black icing to make even smaller ones. Use a little water to stick the eyes in place. Arrange the spiders on and around the cake.

Daisy Cow

A really fun cake to make for a child who loves animals or the countryside.

INGREDIENTS

Serves 10–12

1½ x quantity Quick-Mix Sponge Cake mix

9 tbsp apricot jam, warmed and sieved

1.67 kg/3 lb 12 oz/5 x quantity Sugarpaste Icing

black, brown, blue, yellow and red food colourings

MATERIALS AND EQUIPMENT

2 x deep 18 cm/7 inch round cake tins

25 x 33 cm/10 x 13 inch cake board

4 cm/1½ inch and 2.5 cm/1 inch plain round pastry cutters

6 cm/2½ inch fluted round pastry cutter

wooden cocktail stick

25 cm/10 inch florist's wire covered in florist's tape

STORING

The finished cake can be kept in a cool, dry place for up to three days.

1 Preheat the oven to 180°C/350°F/ Gas 4. Grease the tins, line the bases with greaseproof paper and grease the paper. Divide the cake mixture equally between the two tins and smooth the surfaces. Bake in the centre of the oven for 30–35 minutes or until a skewer inserted into the centre of each cake comes out clean. Turn out on to wire racks, peel off the lining paper and leave to cool completely.

2 ▲ Using a sharp, pointed knife, cut a crescent-shaped piece from the side of one cake, then cut it in half to make the cow's ears.

3 ▲ This is how the cake should be assembled. On the work surface, brush the cake with apricot jam and push the two rounds together to make the face.

4 Colour 950 g/2 lb 2 oz of the sugarpaste icing with black food colouring. Cut off 500 g/1 lb 2 oz and set aside, wrapped in clear film. Roll out the remainder on a work surface dusted with icing sugar into a rectangle about 5 mm/¼ inch thick. Roll out two-thirds of the white icing, then cut into rounds using plain round cutters. Place some of the rounds of white icing in a random pattern on the rolled-out black icing and roll again lightly with the rolling pin to flatten them into the surface. Cover the cow's face with the black and white icing, trimming it neatly around the bottom edge. Brush the cake board evenly with apricot jam. Roll out 275 g/10 oz of the reserved black icing into an oblong large enough to cover the cake board.

5 Arrange the circles of white icing on top of the black icing and roll lightly into the surface. Lay over the cake board and trim the edges. Set aside 50 g/2 oz of the black icing, break off two marble-size pieces and set aside from the rest for the cow's eyes. Roll out the icing that is left and use to cover the ear shapes.

6 Carefully lift the cow's head on to the cake board, set aside 90 g/3½ oz of the white icing then roll out the rest thinly. Cut out a pear shape for the cow's nose. Brush the back with a little water and stick on to the cake. Roll two small pieces of white icing into walnut-size balls, then flatten with a rolling pin and reserve for the eyes.

7 To make the cow's eyes, colour 40 g/1½ oz sugarpaste icing brown, then cut out two rounds with the 4 cm/1½ inch round pastry cutter. Colour 25 g/1 oz icing blue, then cut out two rounds with the 2.5 cm/1 inch round cutter. Assemble the cow's eyes from the brown and blue rounds and the reserved white and black icings. Stick them in place with a little water.

8 Divide the reserved 50 g/2 oz of the black sugarpaste icing in half, and roll out one half thinly into a rectangle of about 15 x 10 cm/6 x 4 inches. Cut along the icing at intervals, leaving a 1 cm /½ inch border along the top, to create the fringe. Position between the ears. Divide the remaining sugarpaste icing in half and use for the nose.

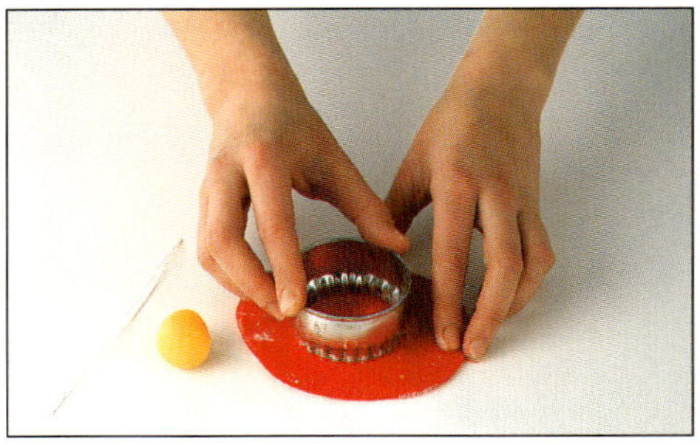

9 ▲ Colour 25 g/1 oz of the remaining icing bright yellow and the rest red. Roll two-thirds of the red icing into a sausage shape, to make a mouth. To make the flower, roll out the remaining red icing and cut out a 6 cm/2½ inch round, using the fluted cutter.

10 Roll the edge of the red icing using a cocktail stick to make it frilly (see Teddy Bear Christening Cake, step 7). Roll the yellow icing into a ball to finish off the flower. Push the florist's wire through the cake. Remove before serving.

Monsters on the Moon

A great cake for little monsters!
This cake is best eaten on the day of making.

INGREDIENTS

Serves 12–15
1 quantity Quick-Mix Sponge Cake mix
115 g/4 oz/$^{1}/_{3}$ quantity Sugarpaste Icing
edible silver glitter powder (optional)

For the Icing
375 g/12 oz/$1^{3}/_{4}$ cups plus 2 tbsp caster sugar
2 size 3 egg whites
4 tbsp water

MATERIALS AND EQUIPMENT
ovenproof wok
various sizes of plain round cutters
30 cm/12 inch round cake board
several small monster toys

1 ▲ Preheat the oven to 180°C/350°F/ Gas 4. Grease the wok, line the base with greaseproof paper and grease the paper. Spoon in the cake mixture and smooth the surface. Bake in the centre of the oven for 35–40 minutes or until a skewer inserted into the centre of the cake comes out clean. Leave the cake in the wok for about 5 minutes, then turn out on to a wire rack, peel off the lining paper and leave to cool completely.

2 ▲ With the cake dome side up, use the round cutters to cut out craters. Press in a cutter about 2.5 cm/1 inch deep, then remove and use a knife to cut out the cake to make a crater.

3 ▲ Pull off small pieces of the sugarpaste icing and press them into uneven strips which can be moulded around the edges of the craters. Make one of the craters especially deep by adding an extra-wide sugarpaste strip to make the edges higher.

4 Place the cake on the cake board. To make the icing, place all the ingredients in a heatproof bowl, then sit the bowl over a saucepan of simmering water. Beat until thick and peaky. Spoon the icing over the cake, swirling it into the craters and peaking it unevenly. Sprinkle over the silver glitter powder, if using, then position the monsters on the cake.

Tip

To cover the cake board, roll out 450 g/1 lb of black sugarpaste icing. Trim the edges. Using various sizes of star-shaped cutters, stamp out stars from the black icing. Roll out 285 g/8 oz of yellow marzipan thinly and use the star-shaped cutters to stamp out replacement stars. Dust with a little extra silver powder.

Ice-cream Cornets

Individual cakes make a change for a party, the idea being that each guest has one to themselves. You could even put a candle in the special person's one.

INGREDIENTS

Makes 9

1 quantity Quick-Mix Sponge Cake mix
9 ice-cream cornets
1 quantity Butter Icing
red, green and brown food colourings
selection of coloured vermicelli, wafers, chocolate sticks, etc.

MATERIALS AND EQUIPMENT

9 fairy cake paper cases
bun tin

STORING

The finished cakes can be kept in a cool, dry place for up to a day.

Tip

To have 3 sets of 3 ice cream cakes placed on the table, you will need 3 egg boxes, which hold 12 eggs each. Place a ball of marzipan in 3 evenly spaced holes in the upturned egg box. Cover the box in foil, then pierce the foil and make a small hole with your finger where the marzipan balls are. Insert the iced ice cream cornets, pressing them in gently, so they stand securely.

1 Preheat the oven to 180°C/350°F/Gas 4. Place the paper cases in the bun tin, then spoon in the cake mixture until they are all at least half full. Bake in the centre of the oven for about 20 minutes or until the cakes have risen and are golden. Transfer the cakes to a wire rack to cool completely. Remove the cases.

2 ▲ Gently press a fairy cake into a cornet, taking care not to damage the cornet. If the bases of the cakes are a little large to insert into the cornets, trim them down with a small, sharp knife. The cakes should feel quite secure once inserted into the cornets.

3 Divide the butter icing into three small bowls and colour one portion pale red, one portion green and one portion brown.

4 ▲ Using a small palette knife, spread each cake with some of one of the icings. Place in the ice-cream stand (see Tip). Continue coating the cornets, making sure the icing isn't too smooth so it looks like ice cream.

5 ▲ To insert a wafer or chocolate stick into an ice cream, use a small, sharp knife to make a hole or incision through the icing and into the cake, then insert the wafer or stick. Add the finishing touches by sprinkling over some coloured vermicelli.

Magic Carpet Cake

The Master of the Lamp can also be made out of coloured sugarpaste icing, instead of marzipan, if you prefer.

INGREDIENTS
Serves 8–10
1 quantity Quick-Mix Sponge Cake mix
675 g/1½ lb/2 x quantity Sugarpaste Icing
blue, brown, red, orange, yellow, purple and black food colourings
115 g/4 oz/4 squares milk or plain chocolate, melted
350 g/12 oz white marzipan
small sweet or diamond-shaped cake decoration
small brightly coloured feather

MATERIALS AND EQUIPMENT
23 x 15 cm/6 x 9 inch cake tin
33 cm/13 inch round cake board
2.5 cm/1 inch and 6 cm/2½ inch round fluted pastry cutters
small piece of yellow crepe paper

STORING
The finished cake can be kept in a cool, dry place for up to three days.

1 Preheat the oven to 180°C/350°F/Gas 4. Grease the cake tin, line the base and sides with greaseproof paper and grease the paper. Spoon in the cake mixture and smooth the surface. Bake in the centre of the oven for 30–35 minutes or until a skewer inserted into the centre of the cake comes out clean. Turn out on to a wire rack, peel off the lining paper and leave to cool completely.

2 Colour 275 g/10 oz sugarpaste icing with blue food colouring. Remove a piece about the size of a walnut and set aside, wrapped in clear film. Roll out the rest of the blue icing thinly on a surface dusted with icing sugar into a round about the same size as the cake board.

3 ▲ Roll out about 150 g/5 oz of white icing and cut out rounds using the pastry cutters. Arrange these on the blue icing to resemble clouds, then roll lightly into the icing. Brush the cake board lightly with water and cover with the blue and white icing, smoothing it with your hands to exclude air bubbles. Leave the icing draped over the edge of the board, if liked, or trim level with the edge of the board.

4 ▲ Colour 175 g/6 oz sugarpaste icing dark brown, then roll it out thinly into an oblong large enough to cover the top and sides of the cake generously. Trim the edges. Knead the trimmings into a ball and set aside, wrapped in clear film. Brush the cake with melted chocolate, then place on the cake board. Drape the brown icing over the top of the cake, being careful not to flatten it at the sides too much.

5 Divide 75 g/3 oz sugarpaste icing into two equal pieces. Colour one piece red and the other orange. Then unwrap the reserved pieces of blue and brown icing.

6 Divide each of the four colours into three or four smaller pieces, then knead them together to make a marbled ball of icing. Roll it out into a rectangle slightly larger than the top of the cake. Trim the edges, then lay over the brown icing and stick into place with water.

7 ▲ Colour 75 g/3 oz marzipan yellow, then roll most of it into a long, thin sausage shape. Press it around the edge of the carpet to make a trim. Decorate with small balls of yellow marzipan. Snip pieces of yellow crepe paper with scissors to make tassels. Push into the small balls of icing.

8 ▲ To make the figure, roll about 75 g/3 oz of white marzipan into a pear shape, then cut in half to make two legs. Bend the legs into a sitting position. Colour 65 g/2½ oz marzipan dark brown and shape into a head, body and arms. Make the eyes and mouth from tiny pieces of coloured icing or marzipan and press on to the face. Press the head and body on to the legs. Colour 25 g/1 oz of marzipan purple and use it to make the jacket. Press the arms on to the figure.

9 Colour small pieces of marzipan black and deep red or purple and use to make hair and a hat respectively. Colour the remaining marzipan bright orange. Roll a tiny piece into a ball and press on to the hat. Decorate with a tiny diamond-shaped sweet or cake decoration and coloured feather. Use the rest of the orange marzipan to make slippers and a lamp. Position the figure and the lamp on the carpet.

Crazy Caterpillar

A no-bake cake made from sponge cake crumbs, home-made or bought. You can double the quantity for an extra-large party, but remember the cake is rich and heavy in texture so you only serve a small amount. One ball per person is more than enough!

Ingredients

Serves 11

1 quantity Truffle Cake mix
675 g/1½ lb yellow marzipan
green, brown and orange food colourings
selection of coloured liquorice sticks, or sweets, for the feet
green-coloured desiccated coconut (see Puppies in Love, step 4), for the grass
small flowers, to decorate (optional)

MATERIALS AND EQUIPMENT

40 x 20 cm/16 x 8 inch cake board (optional)
small round fluted cutter
round fluted aspic cutter

STORING

The finished cake can be wrapped in clear film and kept in a cool, dry place for up to four days.

1 ▲ Using slightly damp hands, roll the truffle cake mixture into balls about the size of a large walnut. Place them on a baking sheet as you make them, then cover with clear film and set to one side.

2 ▲ Divide the marzipan into three equal portions, then colour one portion green, one portion brown and the other portion orange. Remove a small amount of orange and green marzipan, to make the face features, and set aside, covered with clear film.

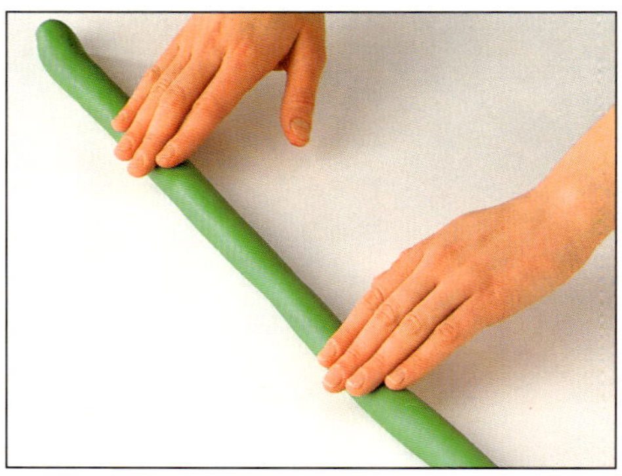

3 ▲ Roll each colour of marzipan into a sausage shape about 45 cm/18 inches long on a work surface lightly dusted with icing sugar. Make sure the sausage shape is even all the way along; if it breaks, compress the marzipan into a ball and start again.

4 ▲ Place the three long sausages side-by-side on the work surface. Starting at one end, hold them together firmly and start to turn them in a twisting motion — do not squeeze. Place the twist back on the work surface, then use a rolling pin to push and roll the twist gently until it is flat and the colours merge. It should be about 50 cm/20 inches long.

5 Lay the truffle balls all along the length of the marzipan strip, then wrap the marzipan evenly around the balls, sealing the join by pinching the marzipan together. (An extra pair of hands is useful for this stage.) Turn the caterpillar over so the join is underneath, tucking in and cutting off any excess marzipan from the ends. Lift the caterpillar on to the cake board, if using, otherwise position it on the table, curving it slightly.

6 Roll out the reserved orange and green marzipan thinly and use the fluted cutters to stamp out rounds for the eyes. Use a little water to stick the smaller green rounds on the orange rounds, then stick them on to one end of the caterpillar to make the face. Roll a tiny piece of orange marzipan into a little sausage, shape and stick it on to make the mouth. Cut the liquorice sticks into small pieces and position them along either side, to make the feet. Scatter the green-coloured coconut all around. Add a few flowers, if you like.

Dinosaur Cake

For a dino-crazy kid, this cake is just the ticket. Put it on a cake board or build a little scene using bits and pieces from around the house and garden.

Ingredients

Serves 8–10

1 quantity Quick-Mix Sponge Cake mix
½ quantity Butter Icing
1 quantity Truffle Cake mix
900 g/2 lb/2⅔ x quantity Sugarpaste Icing
pink, yellow, green and black food colourings
4 tbsp apricot jam, warmed and sieved

MATERIALS AND EQUIPMENT

900 g/2 lb heart-shaped tin
5 x 25 cm/2 x 10 inch piece of card
small block of wood, for raising the cake

STORING

The finished cake can be kept in a cool, dry place for up to two days.

1 Preheat the oven to 180°C/350°F/Gas 4. Grease the heart-shaped tin, line the base with greaseproof paper and grease the paper. Spoon in the cake mixture and smooth the surface. Bake in the centre of the oven for 35–40 minutes or until a skewer inserted into the centre of the cake comes out clean. Turn out on to a wire rack, peel off the lining paper and leave to cool completely.

2 ▲ Cut the heart-shaped cake in half vertically, then sandwich the halves together with the butter icing so they form a half heart shape. Place the cake in the centre of the strip of card, positioned on the long, straight side. Stand the cake on the small block of wood to raise it up slightly.

3 ▲ Divide the truffle mixture in half. Shape one portion into the tail, making it thicker and flattened at one end and more pointed at the other. This will fit on the pointed end of the cake. Mould the other half of the truffle cake mix into the head shape, starting with a ball and then flattening one side, so the diameter matches the width of the head end of the cake. Mould the other end of the head into a pointed shape for the nose.

4 Place the head and tail in position at either end of the cake, moulding the truffle cake mix on to the cake a little. Cut off about 500 g/1¼ lb of the sugarpaste icing and colour it pink. Lightly dust the work surface with icing sugar and roll out the icing to a long, thin, rectangular shape. Brush the cake evenly with jam and cover the dinosaur with the icing in one piece from head to toe. Smooth down the sides and edges with your hands, then trim.

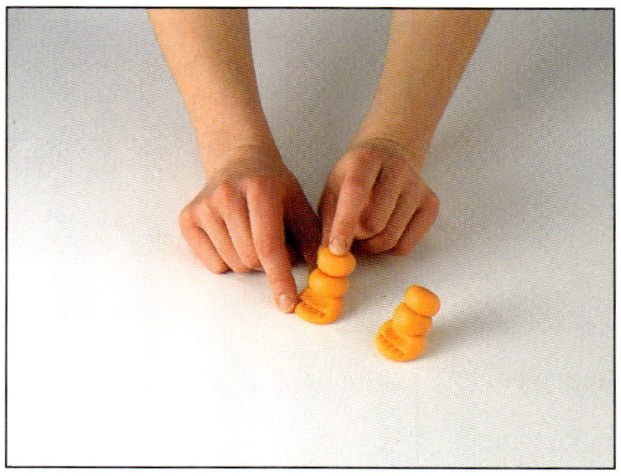

5 ▲ To make the dinosaur's legs, cut off about 115 g/4 oz of the remaining sugarpaste icing and colour it yellow. Remove about 25 g/1 oz and set aside, wrapped in clear film. Use the remainder to roll out 10 evenly sized balls, each about the size of a small walnut. Squeeze together two balls for each of the back legs and three for each of the front ones. Indent the toes with a fork, then using a little water stick the legs on the dinosaur.

6 ▲ Use the reserved yellow sugarpaste icing to make one small and three large horns, then stick these in place with a little water. Cut off about 75 g/3 oz of the remaining icing and colour it green. Divide it into about 11 evenly sized pieces and shape each into a cone. Stick these on to the dinosaur with a little water. Divide the remaining icing in half and colour one portion black. Use the white and black icings to make the mouth, eyes and eyebrows for the dinosaur. Stick on with a little water.

Personal Stereo

This loud cake in noisy colours will be a smash hit! The cake board is optional.

INGREDIENTS
Serves 4–6
1 quantity chocolate-flavour Quick-Mix Sponge Cake mix
¼ quantity chocolate-flavour Butter Icing
4 tbsp apricot jam, warmed and sieved
350 g/12 oz/1 quantity Sugarpaste Icing
orange, green, purple and black food colourings
3 sweets, for the buttons
2 liquorice sweets, for the cassette holes
2 long liquorice bootlaces
2 liquorice wheels

EQUIPMENT AND MATERIALS
20 x13 cm/8 x 5 inch shallow cake tin
edible black ink pen

STORING
The finished cake can be kept in a cool, dry place for up to two days.

1 Preheat the oven to 180°C/350°F/ Gas 4. Grease the cake tin, line the base and sides with greaseproof paper and grease the paper. Spoon in the cake mixture and smooth the surface. Bake in the centre of the oven for 35–40 minutes or until a skewer inserted into the centre of the cake comes out clean. Turn out on to a wire rack, peel off the lining paper and leave to cool completely. Trim the top of the cake to make it perfectly flat, then cut horizontally in half.

2 ▲ Spread the chocolate butter icing over one half, then top with the other half. Brush the cake evenly with the apricot jam. Colour about 250 g/ 9 oz of the sugarpaste icing orange. Lightly dust the work surface with icing sugar and roll out the icing until it is large enough to cover the cake. Smooth and ease it over the sides and edges. Trim the edges.

3 ▲ Colour about 50 g/2 oz of the remaining sugarpaste icing green. Colour all but a small ball of the remaining icing purple, then colour the small ball black. Roll out the green and purple icings thinly. Cut the green icing into a rectangle about 1 cm/½ inch smaller than the top surface of the cake. Stick it in place with a little water. Cut the purple icing into a 2.5 x 10 cm/1 x 4 inch strip and stick in place on top of the green rectangle with a little water.

4 Press the sweets for the buttons into one side of the cake through the orange icing, then position the liquorice sweets for the cassette holes, sticking them in place with a little water. Use the edible ink pen to draw tiny lines around the sweets.

5 Cut a few short pieces off the bootlace liquorice and stick on the personal stereo with a little water. Stick the reserved piece of black icing in place at the side of the cake with a little water.

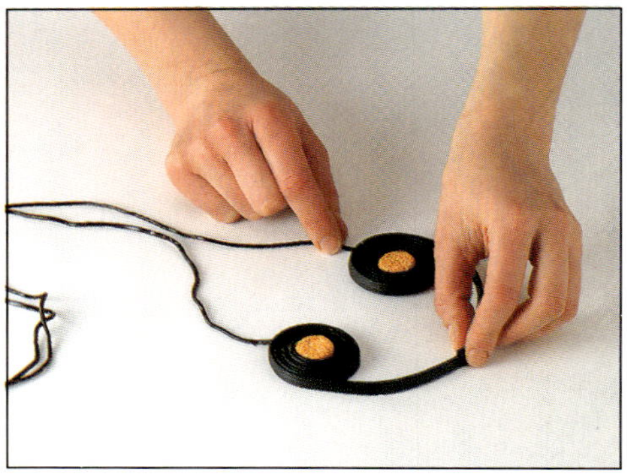

6 ▲ To make the headphones, unravel a little of each of the liquorice wheels and place in position on the table or board, if you are using. Overlap the unravelled ends of the liquorice wheels, sticking them together with a little water. Use a pin or thin metal skewer to make a small hole in the bottoms of the liquorice wheels, then press a liquorice bootlaces into each one. Brush three-quarters of the liquorice bootlace with a little water and stick them together with your fingers, removing the excess water. Press the joined end into the black icing on the cake.

MADE IN GERMANY
RT-60MC
Panasonic
MC-60

Ducks on a Pond

A real treat at a children's party. A scrumptious combination of coconut cake, jelly and cream.

INGREDIENTS

Serves 8–10

1 quantity Quick-Mix Sponge Cake mix
575 ml/1 pint/2½ cups double cream
green, yellow and red food colourings
225 g/8 oz/4 cups desiccated coconut
1 x 135 g/4½ oz packet of green jelly, made up to the manufacturer's instructions
200 g/7 oz/½ quantity Sugarpaste Icing
a few tiny sweets
75 g/3 oz marzipan
5 pink marshmallows

MATERIALS AND EQUIPMENT

18 cm/7 inch flan tin
23 cm/9 inch round cake board
duck-shaped cutter
cocktail sticks
garlic press

STORING

The finished cake can be refrigerated for up to three days.

1 Preheat the oven to 180°C/350°F/Gas 4. Grease the flan tin, line the base with greaseproof paper and grease the paper. Spoon the cake mixture into the prepared tin and smooth the surface. Bake in the centre of the oven for 35–40 minutes or until firm to the touch. Leave the cake in the tin for about 3 minutes, then turn out on to a wire rack, peel off the lining paper and leave to cool completely.

2 ▲ Add a few drops of green food colouring to the double cream, and beat until it holds soft peaks. Place the cake on the cake board and spread the cream evenly over the cake.

3 ▲ To make the grassy bank, place the coconut in a bowl and add a few drops of green food colouring diluted with a dash of water. Stir until the coconut is speckled green and white.

4 ▲ Cut up the set jelly into 1 cm/½ inch pieces. Carefully place the jelly pieces in the centre of the cake.

5 To make the ducks, take 75 g/3 oz of the sugarpaste icing and colour it yellow. Roll out on a work surface lightly dusted with icing sugar until about 5 mm/¼ inch thick.

6 ▲ Using a duck-shaped cutter, stamp out the ducks, then skewer the bottom of each one with a cocktail stick. Lay the ducks on a baking sheet and leave them in a warm, dry place to harden.

7 Use the tiny sweets, or sugarpaste icing, for the ducks' eyes, securing with a drop of water. Take off a small piece of marzipan, about the size of a hazelnut, then colour the remainder green and shape into a frog, using a small, sharp knife to open the mouth and make the feet. Colour the reserved piece of marzipan red, shape into the frog's tongue and secure in position with a little water. Use sweets or blue and white sugarpaste icing for the eyes. Place the frog on the cake board.

8 To make the grass, colour the remaining sugarpaste icing green and push through a garlic press, cutting it off with a small, sharp knife. Place the grass around the pond. To make the flowers, flatten the marshmallows with a rolling pin, then snip the edges with scissors to make the petals. Place the flowers around the pond and put a coloured sweet in the centre of each. The wooden cocktail sticks must be removed from the ducks before serving.

Dumper Truck

Any large, round biscuits will work well for the wheels, and all sorts of coloured sweets can go in the truck.

INGREDIENTS
Serves 8–10
$1^1/_2$ x quantity Quick-Mix Sponge Cake mix
6 tbsp apricot jam, warmed and sieved
900 g/2 lb/$2^2/_3$ x quantity Sugarpaste Icing
yellow, red and blue food colouring
icing sugar, to dredge
sandwich wafer biscuits
4 coconut swirl biscuits
115 g/4 oz coloured sweets
5 cm/2 inch piece blue liquorice stick
demerara sugar, for the sand

MATERIALS AND EQUIPMENT
900 g/2 lb loaf tin
30 x 18 cm/12 x 7 inch cake board
18 x 7.5 cm/7 x 3 inch piece of cake card, brushed with apricot jam
small crescent-shaped cutter

STORING
The cake can be completed up to three days in advance and kept in a cool, dry place.

1 Preheat the oven to 180°C/350°F/Gas 4. Grease the tin, line the base and sides with greaseproof paper and grease the paper. Spoon the cake mixture into the tin and smooth the surface. Bake in the centre of the oven for 40 – 45 minutes or until a skewer inserted into the centre of the cake comes out clean. Turn out on to a wire rack, peel off the lining paper and leave to cool completely.

2 Using a large, sharp knife, cut off the top of the cake to make a flat surface. Then cut off one-third of the cake to make the cabin of the truck.

3 ▲ Take the larger piece of cake, and, with the cut side up, cut a hollow in the centre, leaving a 1 cm/½ inch border. Brush the hollowed cake evenly with apricot jam.

4 ▲ Colour 350 g/12 oz of the sugarpaste icing yellow and remove a piece about the size of a walnut. Set aside, wrapped in clear film. Roll out the remainder on a work surface lightly dusted with icing sugar until about 5mm/¼ inch thick. Use to cover the hollowed out piece of cake, carefully pressing it into the hollow. Trim the bottom edges and set aside.

5 Colour 350 g/12 oz of the sugarpaste icing red. Cut off one-third of this and set aside, wrapped in clear film. Roll out the rest on a work surface until about 5mm/¼ inch thick. Use to cover the remaining piece of cake and trim the edges.

6 Take the reserved red icing, break off a piece the size of a walnut and wrap in clear film. Roll out the rest and use to cover the cake card.

7 ▲ Brush the wafers with a little apricot jam and stick them together in two equal piles. Place the piles on the cake board, about 7.5 cm/3 inches apart. Place the red-covered cake card on top of the wafers. Place a little of the remaining white sugarpaste icing about halfway along the covered card in order to tip the dumper part of the truck slightly. Place the dumper on top, with the cabin in front. Stand the coconut biscuits in position for the wheels.

8 ▲ Roll out the reserved piece of yellow sugarpaste icing to make a 5 x 2.5 cm/2 x 1 inch rectangle. Colour the remaining white sugarpaste icing with blue food colouring and roll out thinly. Use the crescent-shaped cutter to stamp out the eyes. Make simple ones, or overlay with white crescent shapes for detail.

9 Roll out the reserved red sugarpaste icing thinly and stamp out a mouth shape with an appropriate cutter. Use a little water to stick the yellow panel on to the front of the truck, then stick on the features in the same way.

10 To finish, fill the dumper part of the truck with brightly coloured sweets and push a piece of coloured liquorice into the top of the cabin. Scatter the sugar around the base of the dumper truck to resemble sand.

Train Cake

This quick-and-easy train cake is made from a shaped tin, so all you need to do is decorate it!

Ingredients

Serves 8–10

1½ x quantity Quick-Mix Sponge Cake mix
yellow food colouring
2 x quantity Butter Icing
red liquorice bootlaces
6–8 tbsp coloured vermicelli
4 liquorice wheels

MATERIALS AND EQUIPMENT

train-shaped cake tin
25 x 38 cm/10 x 15 inch cake board
2 fabric piping bags
small round and small star nozzles
pink and white cotton wool balls

STORING

The decorated cake should be made and served on the same day.

Tip

When applying butter icing to a cake, it is a good idea to have a small bowl of very hot water at the ready to dip your palette knife into. This will ensure you get a really smooth finish on the cake.

1 Preheat the oven to 180°C/350°F/Gas 4. Grease and flour the cake tin and stand firmly on a greased baking sheet. Grease some strips of foil and press along the edges of the cake tin to prevent the cake mixture escaping. Spoon the cake mixture into the prepared tin and smooth the surface. Bake in the centre of the oven for 40–45 minutes or until a skewer inserted into the centre of the cake comes out clean. Leave the cake to cool in the tin.

2 ▲ Slice off the top surface of the cake to make it perfectly flat. Run a knife around the edges of the cake to release it from the tin, then turn out the cake and place on the cake board.

3 ▲ Add a few drops of yellow food colouring to the butter icing and beat well until evenly blended.

4 ▲ Using a palette knife, cover the cake smoothly with about half the butter icing.

5 ▲ Fit a piping bag with a round nozzle and fill with about one-quarter of the remaining butter icing. Pipe a straight border around the edges of the cake. Repeat the process to make a double-edged border.

6 ▲ Position the red liquorice bootlaces around the edge of the cake, on top of the piped border. Snip the bootlaces with scissors as you bend them around the curves on the train.

7 Fit a piping bag with a small star nozzle and fill with the remaining butter icing. Pipe small stars evenly over the top of the cake. Add extra details to the train with the liquorice, or by piping, if you like. Use a palette knife to press on the coloured vermicelli all around the sides of the cake.

8 Pull a few balls of cotton wool apart for the steam and stick in position with a little butter icing. Press the liquorice wheels in place.

Telephone Cake

A great idea for a first or second birthday, as the telephone is an endless source of amusement for many toddlers.

INGREDIENTS

Serves 8–10

1 quantity chocolate-flavour Quick-Mix Sponge Cake mix
6 tbsp apricot jam, warmed and sieved
550 g/1$\frac{1}{4}$ lb/1$\frac{2}{3}$ x quantity Sugarpaste Icing
1 quantity Butter Icing
red, blue, yellow and green food colourings
black liquorice ribbon

MATERIALS AND EQUIPMENT

18 cm/7 inch square cake tin
20 cm/8 inch square cake board
3 greaseproof paper piping bags
small round cutter

STORING

The iced cake can be kept in a cool, dry place for up to three days.

1 Preheat the oven to 180°C/350°F/Gas 4. Grease the tin, line with greaseproof paper and grease the paper. Spoon the mixture into the tin and smooth the surface. Bake in the centre of the oven for 35–40 minutes or until firm. Turn out and leave to cool.

2 ▲ Cut off a 4 cm/1½ inch strip for the receiver. Cut the main body of the telephone in half. Cut about one-quarter off the top half of the main body of the telephone for the receiver rest.

3 ▲ Brush the centre of the main cake with apricot jam and reposition the top of the cake, leaving space to replace the receiver rest.

4 ▲ To shape the receiver rest, cut a 1 cm/½ inch cross out of the centre of this portion, then cut away the four end corners. Brush the base with apricot jam and position on the cake.

5 ▲ Brush the top surface of the cake evenly with apricot jam. On a work surface lightly dusted with icing sugar, roll out 350 g/12 oz of the sugarpaste icing to a 30 cm/12 inch square and use to cover the telephone cake. Place the cake on the cake board.

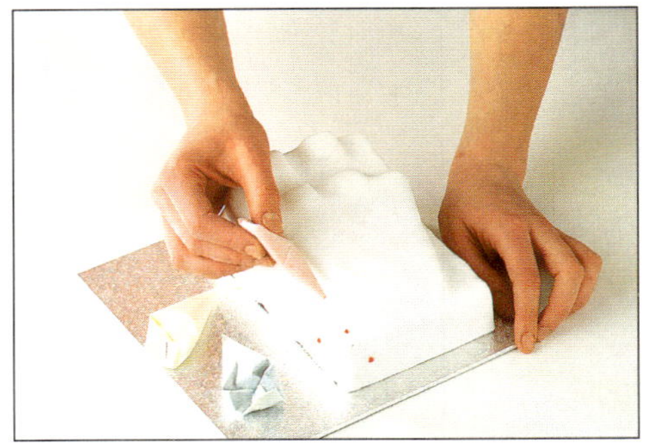

6 ▲ Divide the butter icing into three separate bowls, colouring one red, one blue and one yellow. Fill the piping bags with the coloured butter icings and snip the end off each one to make a small hole. Pipe spots in all three colours evenly over the cake.

7 Colour 175 g/6 oz of the remaining sugarpaste icing green. Cut off about 25 g/1 oz and set aside, wrapped in clear film. Brush the receiver piece of cake with a little apricot jam, then roll out the larger piece of green sugarpaste icing and use to cover the receiver. Position the receiver on the cake.

8 Take a small piece of the remaining green sugarpaste icing and roll it into a ball. Stick it on to the side of the receiver with a little water.

9 Roll out the remaining green sugarpaste icing and cut out a flower pot shape, measuring approximately 7.5 cm/3 inches across the top. Place on the front of the telephone, sticking it down with a little water. For the dial, colour the remaining sugarpaste icing red and roll out to a 7.5 cm/3 inch round, or stamp it out using a cutter. Use a tiny round cutter to stamp out the finger holes, then position the dial on the cake. Use any remaining butter cream to pipe in the numbers.

10 To make the telephone cord, twist the piece of liquorice around a pencil until tightly coiled and leave it for about 10 minutes. Carefully remove the pencil, and press one end of the liquorice into the ball of green sugarpaste icing on the receiver and the other end into the back of the cake.

NON-TOXIC
MADE IN CHINA

Number 7 Cake

Any combination of colours works well for this marbled cake.

INGREDIENTS

Serves 8–10
1½ x quantity Quick-Mix Sponge Cake mix
1 quantity orange-flavour Butter Icing
4 tbsp apricot jam, warmed and sieved
675 g/1½ lb/2 x quantity Sugarpaste Icing
green and blue food colourings

MATERIALS AND EQUIPMENT

23 x 30 cm/9 x 12 inch roasting tin
25 x 33 cm/10 x 13 inch cake board
small No 7 cutter

STORING

The finished cake can be kept in a cool, dry place for up to three days.

Tip

If you feel unsure about shaping the number seven cake freehand, you can purchase or hire shaped cake tins from specialist cake decorating shops.

1 Preheat the oven to 180°C/350°F/Gas 4. Grease the roasting tin, line the base and sides with greaseproof paper and grease the paper. Spoon the cake mixture into the prepared tin and smooth the surface. Bake in the centre of the oven for 45–50 minutes, or until a skewer inserted into the centre of the cake comes out clean. Leave the cake in the tin for about 5 minutes, then turn out on to a wire rack, peel off the lining paper and leave to cool completely.

2 ▲ Working with the cake flat side up, lightly mark out the shape of the number seven on the cake. Cut through the cake, starting at the bottom end and working up.

3 ▲ Slice through the cake horizontally, then carefully lift off the top layer and place on the work surface. Place the bottom layer of cake on the cake board and spread with the butter icing. Reassemble the cake.

4 Brush the cake evenly with apricot jam. Divide the sugarpaste icing into three equal portions. Leave one portion white, colour one blue and the last green. Cut off about 50 g/2 oz from each of the blue and green icings, wrap each separately in clear film and set aside. Marble the remaining blue and green with the white portion of sugarpaste icing.

5 ▲ Roll out the marbled icing on a work surface lightly dusted with icing sugar to a rectangle 35 x 28 cm/14 x 11 inches and use to cover the number seven. Smooth the icing with a cake smoother or with your hands.

6 ▲ Use the cutter to cut random shapes out of the covered cake. Press the cutter into the icing carefully, but firmly. Remove the cutter and the shape should be wedged in the cutter. Poke out the shape with a cocktail stick and discard. This stage needs to be done immediately after the cake has been covered, or the sugarpaste icing will start drying out.

7 ▲ Roll out the reserved blue and green coloured sugarpaste icing and use the cutter to stamp out a combination of blue and green shapes. Use these to replace the stamped out shapes from the cake, pressing them in gently to fill the holes.

PARTY TIME!
I am 7

Puppies in Love

Out of one Swiss roll come two gorgeous puppy dogs. This cake looks extremely impressive, without being too difficult to prepare.

INGREDIENTS
Serves 8–10
1 quantity chocolate-flavour Swiss Roll mix
¼ quantity chocolate-flavour Butter Icing
115 g/4 oz yellow marzipan
green, brown, pink and red food colourings
75 g/3 oz/1½ cups desiccated coconut
450 g/1 lb/1⅓ x quantity Sugarpaste Icing
4 tbsp apricot jam, warmed and sieved

MATERIALS AND EQUIPMENT
33 x 23 cm/13 x 9 inch Swiss roll tin
25 cm/10 inch square cake board
small round cutter
10 cm/4 inch piece of thin ribbon

STORING
The finished cake can be kept in a cool, dry place for up to two days.

1 Preheat the oven to 180°C/350°F/Gas 4. Grease the Swiss roll tin, line with greaseproof paper and grease the paper. Spoon in the cake mixture and smooth the surface. Bake in the centre of the oven for about 12 minutes or until springy when touched in the centre. Leave to cool in the tin, on a wire rack, covered with a clean, just-damp cloth. Then invert the cake on to a sheet of greaseproof paper, dredged with icing sugar.

2 Trim the edges of the cake, then spread with the chocolate butter icing, reserving a tiny amount. Roll up the Swiss roll, using the greaseproof paper as a guide, then cut in half widthways.

3 ▲ To make the faces, cut the marzipan in half and roll each portion into a ball, then into a squat cone shape. Use a little of the reserved butter icing to stick the faces on to the bodies.

4 Place a few drops of green food colouring in a bowl with the desiccated coconut. Add a few drops of water and stir until the coconut is flecked with green and white. Scatter it over the cake board then position the two puppies a little apart on the board.

5 Cut off about 25 g/1 oz of the sugarpaste icing and set aside, wrapped in clear film. Colour half the remaining icing brown and half pink. Cut off about 50 g/2 oz from each colour and wrap in clear film.

6 ▲ Lightly dust the work surface with icing sugar and roll out the larger portions of brown and pink icings into 11 x 35 cm/4½ x 14 inch rectangles. Cut in half widthways and trim the edges. Cover all four sections with clear film and set aside.

7 ▲ Roll out the reserved pieces of brown and white icings, then use the small round cutter to stamp out several shapes. Gather up the icing trimmings and set aside, wrapped in clear film. Stick the white rounds on to one of the brown rectangles, then the brown rounds on to one of the pink rectangles, using a little water. Use a rolling pin to press them in slightly.

8 Use a sharp knife to slash all four icing rectangles along the two short edges. Brush the body of each puppy with jam, then lay the brown icing without spots over one body, and the pink icing without spots over the other. Place a little water on the back of each, then put the brown spotty icing over the brown dog and the pink spotty icing over the pink dog.

9 ▲ Roll half of the reserved icings in your hands to make little tails. Stick them in place with a little reserved butter icing. Make a little fringe from the brown icing for the brown puppy, and tie a few strands of pink icing together with the ribbon to make a fringe for the pink puppy. Stick them in place with a little water.

10 Use the remaining pieces of sugarpaste icing to make the facial features for each puppy, choosing your own expressions, then stick them in place with some water. The little heart-shaped food bowl is an optional extra, or you can make a small bone, if you prefer.

Lion Cake

For an animal lover or a celebration cake for a Leo, this cake is quick and surprisingly easy to make.

INGREDIENTS

Serves 10–15

1½ x quantity Quick-Mix Sponge Cake mix
1 quantity orange-flavour Butter Icing
orange and red food colourings
675 g/1½ lb yellow marzipan
50 g/2 oz/⅙ quantity Sugarpaste Icing
red or orange liquorice bootlaces
long and round marshmallows

MATERIALS AND EQUIPMENT

25 x 30 cm/10 x 12 inch roasting tin
30 cm/12 inch square cake board
cheese grater
small heart-shaped cutter

STORING

The finished cake can be kept in a cool, dry place for up to four days.

1 Preheat the oven to 180°C/350°F/Gas 4. Grease the roasting tin, line the base and sides with greaseproof paper and grease the paper. Spoon the cake mixture into the prepared tin and smooth the surface. Bake in the centre of the oven for 45–50 minutes, or until a skewer inserted into the centre of the cake comes out clean. Leave the cake in the tin for about 5 minutes, then turn out on to a wire rack, peel off the lining paper and leave to cool completely.

2 ▲ Place the cake, base side up, on the work surface. Use a small, sharp knife to cut around the edge of the cake in an uneven scallop design. You may need to do this several times in order to cut through to the bottom. Discard the excess cake from the edges. Turn the cake over and trim the top so that it sits squarely.

3 ▲ Place the cake on the cake board. Mix the orange-flavour butter icing in a bowl together with the orange food colouring. Spoon the butter icing on top of the cake and spread evenly over the surface and down the sides, using a small palette knife.

4 On a work surface lightly dusted with icing sugar, roll out about 115 g/4 oz of marzipan to a 15 cm/6 inch square. Place the marzipan square in the centre of the cake, gently pressing down to secure.

5 ▲ Grate the remaining marzipan on to a sheet of greaseproof paper. Use a palette knife to lift the grated marzipan carefully on to the cake, evenly covering the sides and top up to the edges of the face panel.

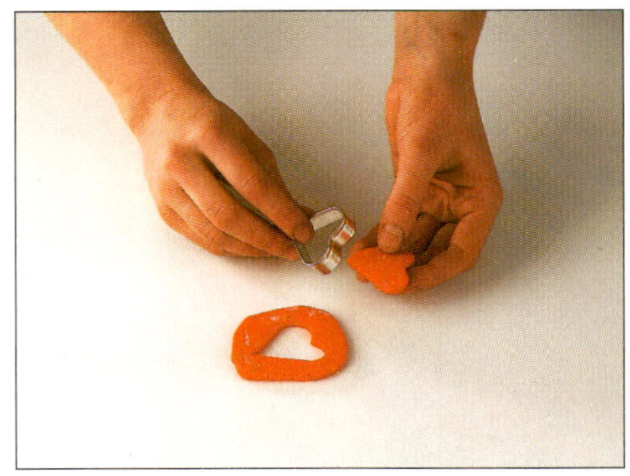

6 ▲ Colour the sugarpaste icing red, then roll out on a work surface lightly dusted with icing sugar. Use the heart-shaped cutter to stamp out the lion's nose and position on the cake, securing it with a little water. Take a little of the excess sugarpaste icing and use your fingers to roll out two thin, short strands for the mouth. Position on the cake, securing with water.

7 Cut the liquorice sticks into graduated lengths, and place on the cake for the whiskers. For the eyes, flatten two round marshmallows and place on the cake, securing with water.

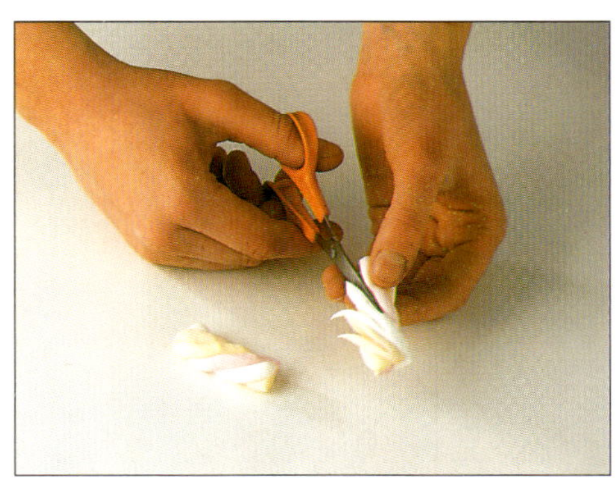

8 ▲ To make the eyebrows, cut the long marshmallows into 5 cm/2 in lengths, and snip along one side. Place them on the cake, securing with water.

Jack-in-the-Box Cake

An impressive, colourful cake which will delight a small party of young children. This cake does require a little extra time and patience, so be sure to start the cake well in advance and not on the morning of the party!

INGREDIENTS

Serves 6–8

1 quantity chocolate-flavour Quick-Mix Sponge Cake Mix
6 tbsp apricot jam, warmed and sieved
1 kg/2¼ lb/3 x quantity Sugarpaste Icing
purple, yellow, orange and green food colourings
1 large round doughnut
1 small round doughnut
2 marshmallow sweets, for the eyes
2 coloured sweets, for the buttons

MATERIALS AND EQUIPMENT

deep 10 cm/4 inch square cake tin
18 cm/7 inch cake board
9 cm/3½ inch square piece of stiff card
3 cocktail sticks
garlic press
ice-cream cornet
balloon
small star cutter
butterfly cutter
wooden skewer

STORING

The finished cake can be kept for up to four days.

1 Preheat the oven to 180°C/350°F/ Gas 4. Grease the cake tin, line the base and sides with greaseproof paper and grease the paper. Spoon the cake mixture into the prepared tin and smooth the surface. Bake in the centre of the oven for 35–40 minutes, or until a skewer inserted into the centre of the cake comes out clean. Leave the cake in the tin for about 5 minutes, then turn out on to a wire rack, peel off the lining paper and leave to cool completely.

2 ▲ Place the cake on the work surface and cut a 2.5 cm/1 inch slice off the top for the lid. Use a small, sharp knife to hollow out the centre of the box section of cake, leaving a 1 cm/½ inch border. Spread a little apricot jam in the centre of the cake board and some on the square piece of card. Place the bottom section of cake on the cake board and position the lid on the card. Brush the box and lid with apricot jam.

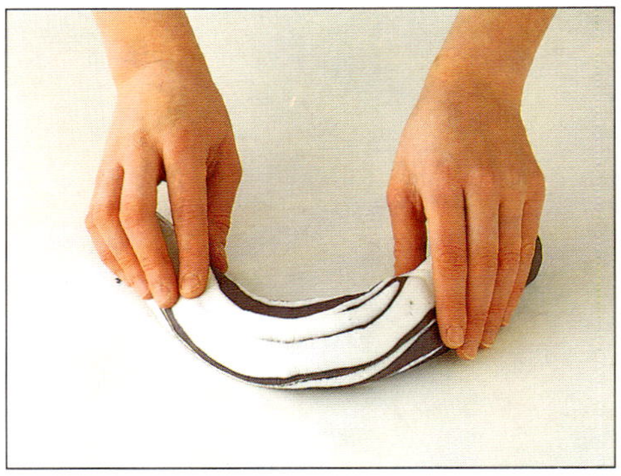

3 ▲ Pull off a walnut-sized piece of sugarpaste icing, wrap in clear film and set aside. Then take about half of the remaining sugarpaste icing and marble in the purple food colouring. Cut off about one-quarter of the marbled icing and roll out on a surface lightly dusted with icing sugar to about a 15 cm/6 inch square. Use to cover the lid section of the cake, wrapping the icing around the card. Set aside, card side down. Reserve the trimmings.

4 Roll out the remaining marbled icing and use to cover the box section of cake, lightly pressing the icing into the hollow. Reserve the trimmings.

5 Colour about half of the remaining sugarpaste icing yellow and pull off two pieces, each the size of a cherry. Wrap these in clear film and set aside. Cut a thin slice off the side of the large doughnut for the body to give it a flat base. Lay it down on the work surface and place the small doughnut above it for the head. Brush the head and body with jam. Roll out the large portion of yellow sugarpaste icing until about 5mm/¼ inch thick and use to cover the head and body of the clown. Wrap the icing around the back and pinch it together to seal.

6 ▲ Pierce a cocktail stick into the base of the body, leaving about half of it exposed. Place the body in position on the box section of the cake, pressing the exposed cocktail stick into the cake for extra stability.

7 ▲ Cut off about half of the remaining sugarpaste icing and colour it orange. Push about one-quarter of this through a garlic press on to a sheet of greaseproof paper for the hair. Stick it on to the clown's head with a little water. Use the remaining orange icing to make one hand, the nose, mouth and a few spots for the bow tie. Allow the hand to dry out on a baking sheet, but cover the other features with clear film and set aside.

8 ▲ Colour the remaining sugarpaste icing green. To make the hat, cut off about 15 g/½ oz of the green icing and roll out into a thin strip. Brush the pointed end of the ice-cream cornet with a little apricot jam, then roll the strip of green sugarpaste icing around it, starting at the pointed end and working downwards. Use scissors to cut off the excess cornet. Stick the hat in position on the clown's head with a little water. Reserve any trimmings.

9 Use the reserved piece of yellow sugarpaste icing to make two small ovals for the arms. Thread each one on to a cocktail stick and carefully press the hand on to one of them. Press the cocktail sticks into the body of the clown. Tie a slightly blown up balloon on to the arm without the hand.

10 Roll out the remaining piece of white sugarpaste icing and stamp out two small stars with the star cutter. Use a little water to stick them in place for the eyes. Stick the marshmallow sweets on top.

11 Position the orange nose and mouth, sticking them in place with a little water. Roll out the remaining green icing to about 5mm/¼ inch thick and stamp out a butterfly and six small stars with the cutters. Stick the reserved red spots on to the butterfly bow tie, using a little water, then place the bow tie on the clown in the same way. Place the green stars around the edges of the cake board. Stick the two coloured sweets in place for the clown's buttons, using a little more water.

12 To position the lid, carefully sit it, card side out, on the back edge of the box section of the cake. Use the wooden skewer and the reserved icing trimmings to support the lid and hold it in place. This stage is best completed when the cake is in position on the table and unlikely to be moved again.

Peepo Rabbits

An easy cake to make for a chocoholic who loves rabbits. All the fun is in the decorating.

INGREDIENTS
Serves 6–8
For the Toadstools
2 size 3 egg whites
25 g/1 oz/2 tbsp caster sugar

For the Cake
1 quantity Swiss Roll cake mix
1 quantity chocolate-flavour Butter Icing
150 g/5 oz/2½ cups desiccated coconut
25 g/1 oz/3 tbsp cocoa powder, plus a little extra for dusting
225 g/8 oz/⅔ quantity Sugarpaste Icing
pink, yellow, green and brown food colourings

MATERIALS AND EQUIPMENT
piping bag fitted with a small round nozzle
23 x 33 cm/9 x 13 inch Swiss roll tin
23 cm/9 inch square cake board
small rabbit cutter
small butterfly cutter
1 cocktail stick
small leaf cutter

STORING
The finished cake can be refrigerated for up to two days.

1 Preheat the oven to 135°C/275°F/Gas 1. To make the meringue toadstools, place a sheet of baking parchment on a baking sheet. Place the egg whites in a clean, dry mixing bowl and whisk until they hold soft peaks. Whisk in half of the sugar, then add the rest. Whisk until the mixture holds stiff peaks. Fill the piping bag with the meringue mixture and pipe several small rounds and several 2.5 cm/1 inch stalks. Bake for about 1 hour, or until dry. Leave to cool completely.

2 ▲ To assemble the toadstools, gently press a stalk into a small meringue round. Set aside. Increase the oven temperature to 180°C/350°F/Gas 4.

3 Grease the tin, line the base and sides with greaseproof paper and grease the paper. Spoon the cake mixture into the tin and smooth the surface. Bake in the centre of the oven for about 12 minutes, or until firm to the touch. Leave the cake in the tin, covered, to cool completely.

4 Lay a sheet of greaseproof paper on the work surface and sprinkle with icing sugar. Tip the cake on to the greaseproof paper and remove the lining paper. Spread with about one-third of the butter icing and roll up. Cut off one-third of the roll and stand the larger section on the cake board, sticking it in place with a little butter icing.

5 ▲ Position the smaller log next to the larger one, then cover both in the remaining butter icing. Peak and swirl the icing quite unevenly to make it look like bark.

6 Place the coconut in a bowl and sift in the cocoa powder. Stir well until evenly blended. Spoon the coconut all around the cake.

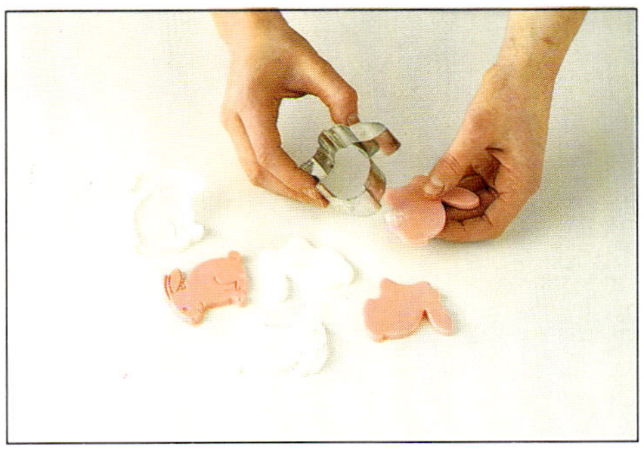

7 ▲ Take half of the sugarpaste icing and divide into two portions. Colour one portion pink. Roll out each piece on a work surface lightly dusted with icing sugar until about 5 mm/¼ inch thick. Stamp out two rabbits in each colour. Use the pink and white trimmings to make tiny balls for the eyes, securing them in place with a little water. Place the rabbits on a baking sheet and leave until dried out.

8 Cut off about one-quarter of the remaining sugarpaste icing and colour it yellow. Roll out until about 5 mm/¼ inch thick and stamp out a butterfly. Use the cocktail stick to indent the centre of the butterfly gently and fold it a little. Press half of the cocktail stick through the base of the butterfly. Place the butterfly on the baking sheet with the rabbits, resting one wing on the edge of the baking sheet so that it dries in that position.

9 Cut off one-third of the remaining sugarpaste icing and colour it green. Roll it out thinly, then cut it into strips using scissors and snip the strips into pointed sections to make the grass. Position the pieces of grass randomly in the coconut around the cake.

10 Colour the remaining icing brown and roll out thinly. Cut out several leaf shapes, and then use a small, sharp knife to make the leaf indentations. Gently twist and bend the leaves a little, then place them in the coconut. Reserve the trimmings.

11 To assemble the rabbits, use a little of the reserved brown icing to stick them securely in place around the cake. Press the butterfly's cocktail stick into the back of the cake. Finally, position the meringue toadstools and dust them with a little cocoa powder.

Nurse's Set

This is a simple cake to make. Any toy medical equipment is suitable to use, but make sure it doesn't get confused with the edible bits!

INGREDIENTS
Serves 12–15
1½ x quantity chocolate-flavour Quick-Mix Sponge Cake mix
8 tbsp apricot jam, warmed and sieved
675 g/1½ lb/2 x quantity Sugarpaste Icing
pink and red food colourings

MATERIALS AND EQUIPMENT
35 x 20 cm/14 x 8 inch roasting tin
25 cm/10 inch square cake board
selection of toy medical equipment

STORING
The finished cake can be kept in a cool, dry place for up to two days.

1 Preheat the oven to 180°C/350°F/Gas 4. Grease the roasting tin, line the base and sides with greaseproof paper and grease the paper. Spoon in the cake mixture and smooth the surface. Bake in the centre of the oven for 45–50 minutes or until a skewer inserted into the centre of the cake comes out clean. Leave the cake in the tin for about 5 minutes, then turn out on to a wire rack, peel off the lining paper and leave to cool completely.

2 ▲ Place the cake, dome side down, and cut in half widthways.

3 ▲ Turn one half of the cake dome side up, then use a small, sharp knife to indent a border about 1 cm/½ inch in from the edge and about the same measurement deep, around the three uncut edges. Cut out the centre in strips, keeping the edges neat. Brush the tops and sides of both halves of the cake with the apricot jam.

4 Cut off about 150 g/5 oz of the sugarpaste icing and colour it deep pink. Cut off about 15 g/½ oz from this and shape into a small handle for the box. Carefully wrap in clear film and set aside. Lightly dust the work surface with icing sugar and roll out the remaining pink icing and use to cover the cake board. Trim the edges. Cut off about 15 g/½ oz from the remaining white icing and colour it red. Cover with clear film and set aside. Colour the remaining icing light pink and divide into two portions, one slightly bigger than the other.

5 Roll out the slightly bigger portion of light pink icing and use to cover the base of the nurse's box, gently easing it into the hollow and along the edges. Trim the edges, then position the covered cake on the cake board.

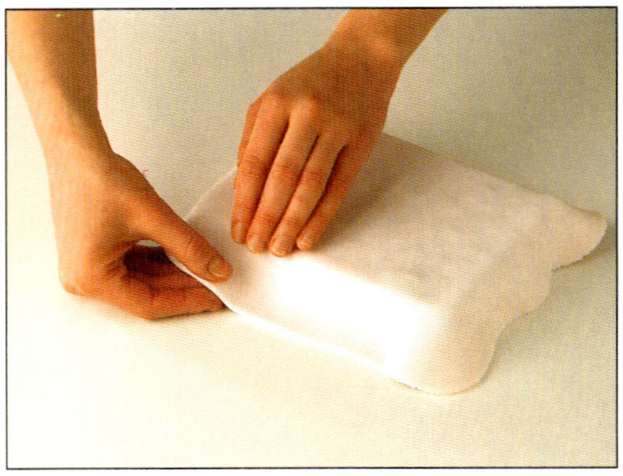

6 ▲ Roll out the other portion of light pink icing and use to cover the lid of the box, using your hands to ease it over the edges. Trim the edges. Place on top of the other cake, back a little and slightly turned to an angle.

7 ▲ Stick the handle on to the bottom section of the box, using a little water. Roll out the red icing and cut out a small cross. Use a little water to stick the cross on the lid of the box. Carefully insert a few toy items into the box, allowing them to hang over the edges a little. Arrange any other items of toy medical equipment around the board and cake when it is positioned on the table.

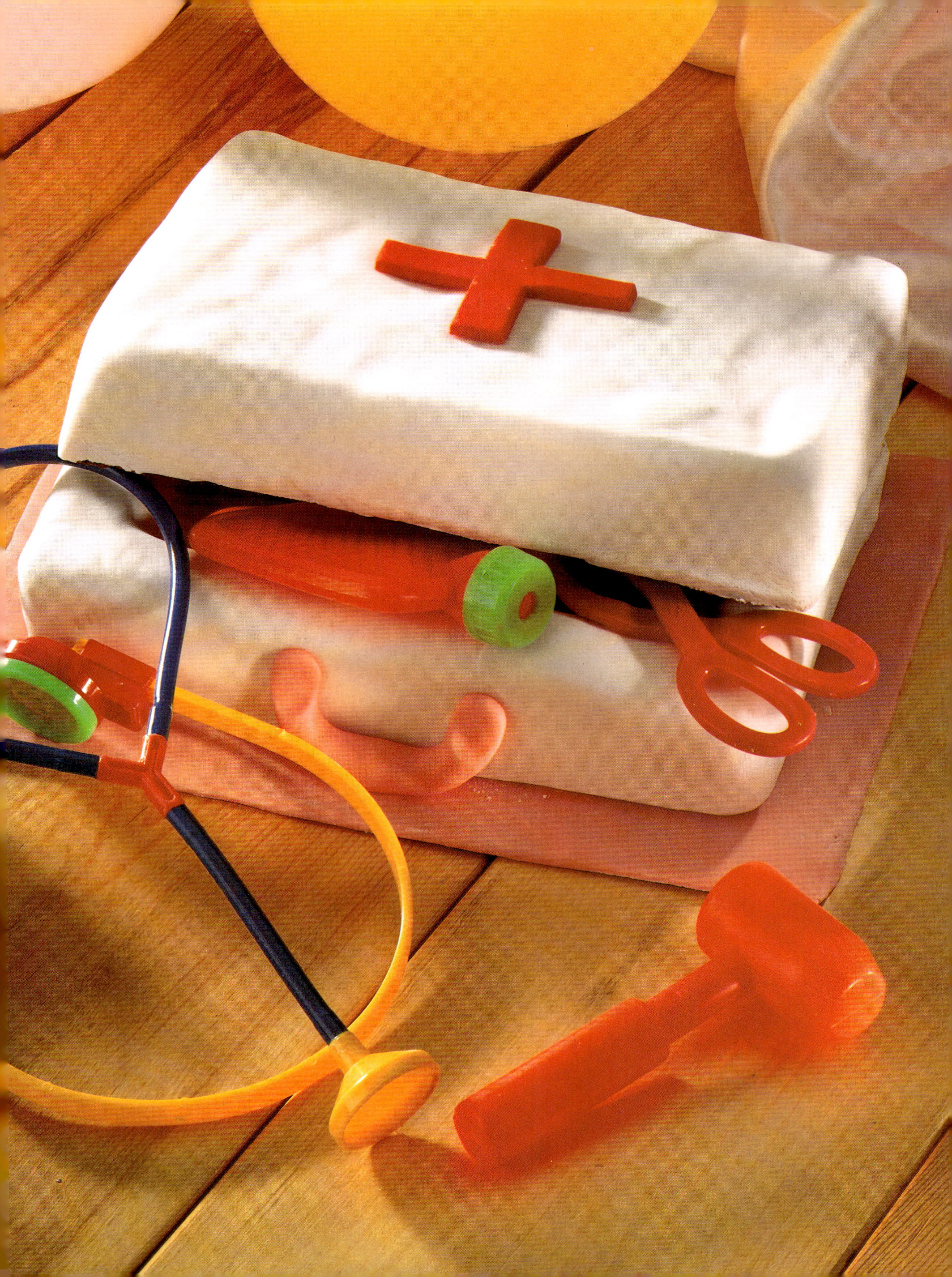

Hot Dog Cake

Make a meal of a cake! This hot dog tastes nothing like the real thing - it is much more delicious and looks very attractive when cut into slices.

INGREDIENTS

Serves 6–8

1 quantity Swiss Roll mix
icing sugar, to dredge
½ quantity coffee-flavour Butter Icing
⅓ quantity Truffle Cake Mix
6 tbsp apricot jam, warmed and sieved
450 g/1 lb/1⅓ x quantity Sugarpaste Icing
brown and red food colouring
1–2 tbsp toasted sesame seeds
¼ quantity Glacé Icing

MATERIALS AND EQUIPMENT

23 x 33 cm/9 x 13 inch Swiss roll tin
2 small greaseproof paper piping bags

STORING

The decorated cake should be made and served on the day.

1 Preheat the oven to 180°C/350°F/Gas 4. Grease the tin, line the base and sides with greaseproof paper and grease the paper. Spoon the cake mixture into the tin and smooth the surface. Bake in the centre of the oven for about 12 minutes or until springy to the touch. Cover and leave to cool.

2 Turn the cake out on to greaseproof paper dusted with icing sugar and remove the lining paper. Spread over the butter icing, then roll the cake up using the greaseproof paper.

3 ▲ Shape the truffle cake mix into a sausage about 23 cm/9 inches long.

4 Place the Swiss roll on the work surface and slice along the middle lengthways, almost through to the bottom. Ease the two halves apart to resemble a partially opened bun.

5 Colour the sugarpaste icing brown, then cut off about 50 g/2 oz and set aside, wrapped in clear film. Roll out the rest on a work surface lightly dusted with icing sugar until about 5mm/¼ inch thick and use to cover the bun. Ease the icing into the centre and down the sides of the cake.

6 ▲ Dilute a few drops of brown food colouring in a little water and paint the top of the bun very lightly to give a toasted effect. Dab on a little colour, then rub it around gently with a finger until blended in. Carefully place the truffle cake sausage in position.

7 ▲ Divide the glacé icing between two small bowls. Colour one half brown and the other red. Fill the piping bags with the icings and snip off the ends with scissors. Pipe red icing along the sausage for the ketchup, then overlay with brown icing for the mustard. Sprinkle the sesame seeds over the bun.

8 Roll out the reserved brown sugarpaste icing and cut thin strips to resemble onion rings. Place on the cake so that the joins lie under the sausage. Carefully place the cake on a napkin and serving plate, with a knife and fork.

Hallowe'en Coffin

A simple, spooky cake for the centrepiece of a Hallowe'en party.

INGREDIENTS
Serves 4–6
1 quantity Quick-Mix Sponge Cake mix
5 tbsp apricot jam, warmed and sieved
350 g/12 oz/1 quantity Sugarpaste Icing
black food colouring
75 g/3 oz yellow marzipan
$^1/_4$ quantity Butter Icing
golden caster sugar, for dusting

MATERIALS AND EQUIPMENT
900 g/2 lb loaf tin
23 cm/9 inch square piece of thick card
small fluted oval cutter
small plastic skeleton and other Hallowe'en toys
piping bag fitted with a small star nozzle

STORING
The finished cake can be made up to two days in advance and kept in a cool, dry place.

1 Preheat the oven to 180°C/350°F/Gas 4. Grease the tin, line the base and sides with greaseproof paper and grease the paper. Spoon the mixture into the tin and smooth the surface. Bake in the centre of the oven for 35–40 minutes, or until a skewer inserted into the cake comes out clean. Leave the cake in the tin for 5 minutes, then turn out on to a rack, peel off the lining paper and leave to cool.

2 To shape the cake, use a large, sharp knife to slice off the risen surface to make it completely flat. Turn the cake upside-down and score the shape of the coffin in the cake. Cut off the two top corners at an angle, then cut diagonally down from the corners to the base of the coffin.

3 ▲ To make the lid of the coffin, slice about 1 cm/$^1/_2$ inch off the top of the cake. To make a base to reinforce the coffin and lid, place both pieces of cake on the card and draw around them with a pencil. Remove the cakes and cut out the shapes on the card. Brush the cakes with apricot jam.

4 Use a small, sharp knife to hollow out the base of the coffin, leaving about a 1 cm/$^1/_2$ inch border. Place the coffin and lid on the cards. Brush the cakes with apricot jam.

5 Colour the sugarpaste icing black, then cut off about one-third and set aside, wrapped in clear film. Roll out the larger portion of sugarpaste icing on a work surface lightly dusted with icing sugar and use to cover the base of the coffin, easing it into the hollow and down the sides. Trim the edges. Roll out the remaining black icing and use to cover the lid. Trim the edges.

6 ▲ To make the coffin handles, pull off six small pieces of the marzipan and shape into sausages with rounded ends. To make the plaque on the lid, roll out the kneaded trimmings of marzipan thinly and stamp out a fluted oval with the cutter. Stick the handles and plaque in position with a little butter icing.

7 Lay the skeleton in the coffin. Colour the remaining butter icing black and use to pipe a small star border around the coffin and down the sides. Sprinkle with sifted caster sugar and decorate with the Hallowe'en toys.

Mermaid Cake

Pretty, elegant and chocolatey! Every little girl's dream.

INGREDIENTS
Serves 6–8
1 quantity chocolate-flavour Quick-Mix Sponge Cake mix
450 g/1 lb plain chocolate
25 g/1 oz/3 cups unflavoured popcorn
450 g/1 lb/1⅓ x quantity Sugarpaste Icing
lilac and pink food colouring
3 tbsp apricot jam, warmed and sieved
1 egg white, lightly beaten
demerara sugar

MATERIALS AND EQUIPMENT
900 g/2 lb loaf tin
30 x 15 cm/12 x 6 inch cake board
doll, similar in dimensions to a 'Barbie' or 'Sindy' doll
small crescent-shaped cutter
small fluted round cutter
15 cm/6 inch piece of thin lilac ribbon

STORING
The finished cake can be made up to three days in advance and kept in a cool, dry place.

Tip

For an even more chocolatey version of this cake, cut the sponge into three horizontally and use 1 quantity chocolate-flavour Butter Icing to spread between the layers. Reassemble the cake and then cover with chocolate popcorn.

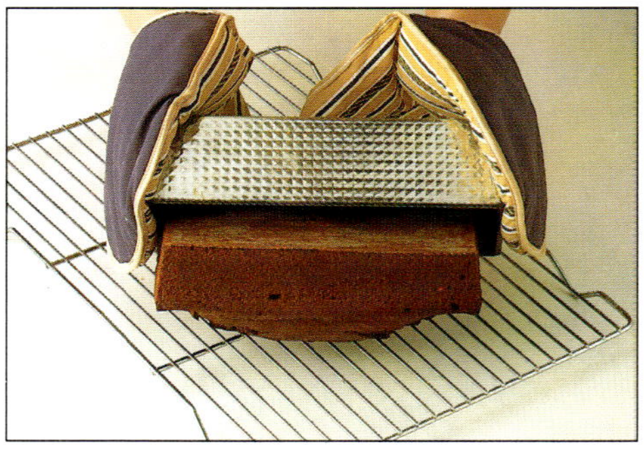

1 ▲ Preheat the oven to 180°C/350°F/Gas 4. Grease the tin, line the base and sides with greaseproof paper and grease the paper. Spoon the cake mixture into the prepared tin and smooth the surface. Bake in the centre of the oven for 35–40 minutes, or until a skewer inserted into the centre of the cake comes out clean. Leave the cake in the tin for about 5 minutes, then turn out on to a wire rack, peel off the lining paper and leave to cool.

2 ▲ Turn the cake dome side up and place on the cake board. Melt the chocolate in a bowl placed over hot water. Add the popcorn and stir until evenly coated. Spoon the popcorn around the sides of the cake and on the cake board. Spread any remaining melted chocolate over the top of the cake until evenly covered. Set aside at room temperature.

3 Cut off about one-quarter of the sugarpaste icing. Colour the larger piece lilac and the smaller piece pink. Cut off about one-third of the lilac icing, wrap this and the pink icing separately in clear film and set aside.

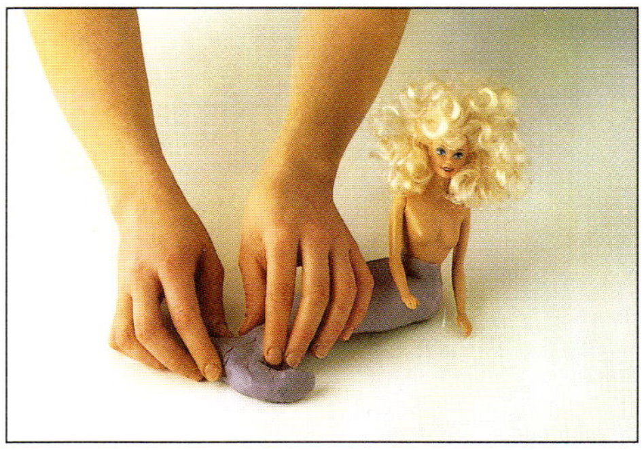

4 ▲ On a work surface lightly dusted with icing sugar, roll out the larger portion of lilac sugarpaste icing to an oblong shape wide enough to wrap around the doll's legs and about 5 cm/2 inches longer. Brush the doll from the waist down with the apricot jam, then wrap her in the rolled out sugarpaste icing, lightly pinching and squeezing it around her legs to make it stick. Working downwards towards her feet, pinch the end of the tail to form a fin shape, curling the ends slightly.

5 ▲ Position the mermaid on the cake, moving her slightly until she feels secure and then pressing down firmly. Roll out the reserved lilac and pink sugarpaste icing and use the crescent-shaped cutter to stamp out the scales. Cover the scales and the reserved trimmings with clear film to prevent them drying out. Starting at the fin end of the tail, brush the scales with a tiny amount of egg white and stick on to the tail, overlapping all the time, until the tail is completely covered.

6 Re-roll the reserved icing trimmings and use the small fluted cutter to stamp out a shell-shaped bra top for the mermaid. Make indentations on the top with the back of a knife, then stick in place with a little extra apricot jam. Use the ribbon to tie up the mermaid's hair.

7 Position the cake on the serving table or large board, then scatter the demerara sugar around the base of the cake for the sand and add a few real shells, if you like. Remove the doll before serving the cake.

Helicopter Cake

Perfect for a party of boys or girls who are partial to helicopters. The cake involves a little creative use of non-edible items which must be removed before eating.

INGREDIENTS

Serves 6–8

1 quantity Quick-Mix Sponge Cake mix
2 fan wafers
6–8 tbsp apricot jam, warmed and sieved
450 g/12 oz/1 quantity Sugarpaste Icing
red, blue and black food colourings
small round sweet
¼ quantity Butter Icing
2 sweets, for the headlights
2 x 15 cm/6 inch pieces of flat liquorice
4 x 2.5 cm/1 inch pieces of liquorice sticks
50 g/2 oz/1 cup toasted desiccated coconut

MATERIALS AND EQUIPMENT

900 g/2 lb loaf tin
small round cutter
2 wooden skewers
wood glue
small wooden block, to raise helicopter
18 cm/7 inch square cake board
13 cm/5 inch piece of white ribbon
piping bag fitted with a small plain nozzle

STORING

The finished cake can be kept in a cool, dry place for up to two days.

1 Preheat the oven to 180°C/350°F/ Gas 4. Grease the tin, line with greaseproof paper and grease the paper. Spoon the cake mixture into the prepared tin and smooth the surface. Bake in the centre of the oven for 35–40 minutes, or until a skewer inserted into the centre of the cake comes out clean. Turn out on to a wire rack, peel off the lining paper and leave to cool.

2 ▲ To shape the cake, stand it flat side down and use a large, sharp knife to cut it into the shape of a teardrop. Trim the sides from top to bottom so that the top is wider than the bottom. Turn the cake on its side, and cut a wedge shape out of the back part.

3 ▲ Invert the cake so the flat side is uppermost. Use the cutter to stamp out a hole for the cockpit, indenting about 2.5 cm/1 inch. Remove the round piece and reserve.

4 Cut a thin slice from each of the wafers, reserve one for the tail fin and discard the other slice. Cut each wafer in half lengthways. Measure the long side of one of the wafers and then cut the wooden skewers double that length. Glue the skewers together in the centre to form a cross and set aside.

5 Remove a small piece of sugarpaste icing. Take another piece of icing about the size of an egg and colour it deep blue. Wrap these pieces in clear film and set aside.

6 Colour the remaining sugarpaste icing pale blue. Remove an egg-sized piece, wrap in clear film and set aside. Brush the cake with apricot jam. Roll out the pale blue sugarpaste on a work surface lightly dusted with icing sugar and use to cover the helicopter. Position the covered cake on the small block of wood on the cake board.

7 To make the propeller support, brush the reserved piece of round cake cut out for the pilot's cockpit with apricot jam. Roll out the reserved pale blue sugarpaste icing and cover the round cake. Reserve the trimmings. Position the propeller support on the helicopter, halfway between the cockpit and the tail, sticking it in place with a spot of jam. Place the crossed skewers on top of the propeller support and secure them in place with a little of the pale blue icing. Place the wafers over the skewers, securing them underneath with more icing. Place the small round sweet on top.

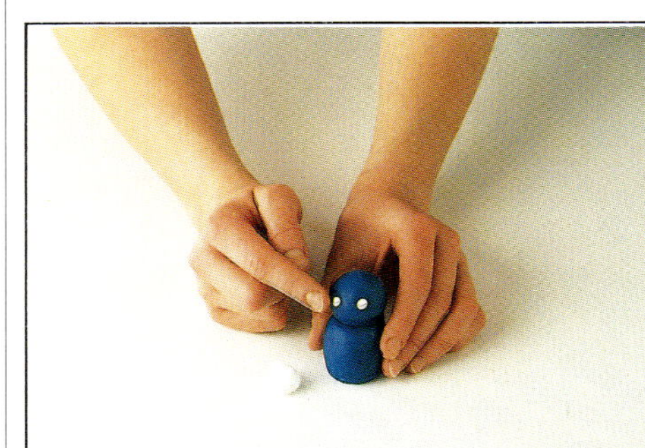

8 ▲ To make the pilot, shape the dark blue sugarpaste icing into a small head and body to fit into the cockpit. Colour a little of the reserved white icing red for the nose and mouth and use white icing for the buttons. Stick the details in place with a little water. Shape some of the reserved pale blue icing into the pilot's hat and place on his head, securing with a little water if necessary. Sit the pilot in his seat and tie the ribbon scarf around his neck.

9 Colour the butter icing black and fill the piping bag. First pipe in the pilot's eyes, then pipe the zigzag and straight borders around the helicopter. Stick the headlight sweets in position with a little of the remaining butter icing and stick the tail fin on in the same way. To make the landing feet, smooth out the flat pieces of liquorice and fold in half lengthways. Position on the cake board, wedged in with the liquorice sticks. Scatter the desiccated coconut around the cake board.

Index

A

B

C

I

J

L

M

N

O

P

Q

R

S

Acknowledgements

The publisher and authors would like to thank Scenics Cakes Boards, Colours Direct (0181–441 3082) and the Cloth Store (01293 560943) for supplying props and materials, Braun and Kenwood for the use of their equipment, Stork Cookery Service for the Rich Fruit Cake chart and Jackie Mason for her help.